The Art of the Critic

The Art of the Critic
Literary Theory and Criticism from the Greeks to the Present

Volume 11
Contemporary (conclusion)
Glossary and Index

EDITED WITH AN INTRODUCTION BY
HAROLD BLOOM
Sterling Professor of the Humanities, Yale University

1990
CHELSEA HOUSE PUBLISHERS
NEW YORK   PHILADELPHIA

Project Editor: S. T. Joshi
Assistant Editor: Neal Dolan
Editorial Coordinator: Karyn Gullen Browne
Copy Chief: Richard Fumosa
Editorial Staff: Leslie D'Acri, Anne Knepler, Katherine Theodore
Design: Susan Lusk

Copyright © 1990 by Chelsea House Publishers, a division of Main Line Book Co. Introduction copyright © 1990 by Harold Bloom.

All rights reserved. No part of this publication may be reproduced or transmitted in any form or by any means, without the written permission of the publisher.

Printed and bound in the United States of America.

Library of Congress Cataloging in Publication Data
Main entry under title:

The Art of the Critic.

    Includes bibliographies and Index.
    Contents: v. 1. Classical and medieval— —v. 11. Contemporary (conclusion), glossary, and index.
    1. Criticism—Collected works. 2. Literature—Philosophy—Collected works. I. Bloom, Harold.
PN86.A77   1985   809   84–15547
ISBN 0-87754-493-X (set)
    0-87754-504-9 (v. 11)

Contents

Introduction · vii ·
Raymond Williams · 3 ·
    From *The Long Revolution* · 5 ·
Jacques Derrida · 33 ·
    From *Writing and Difference* · 37 ·
Angus Fletcher · 71 ·
    From *Allegory* · 73 ·
Leo Bersani · 91 ·
    From *A Future for Astyanax* · 93 ·
Susan Sontag · 105 ·
    The Pornographic Imagination · 107 ·
Fredric Jameson · 121 ·
    From *The Political Unconscious* · 123 ·
Edward W. Said · 139 ·
    From *The World, the Text, and the Critic* · 141 ·
Sandra M. Gilbert and Susan Gubar · 167 ·
    From *The Madwoman in the Attic* · 171 ·
Stanley E. Fish · 197 ·
    Interpreting the Variorum · 199 ·
Tzvetan Todorov · 219 ·
    From *Literature and Its Theorists* · 221 ·
Frank Lentricchia · 233 ·
    From *Criticism and Social Change* · 235 ·
Julia Kristeva · 251 ·
    Word, Dialogue and Novel · 253 ·
Elaine Showalter · 275 ·
    Women's Time, Women's Space: Writing the History of Feminist Criticism · 277 ·
Shoshana Felman · 291 ·
    From *Writing and Madness* · 293 ·
Nina Auerbach · 309 ·
    Women on Women's Destiny: Maturity as Penance · 311 ·
Terry Eagleton · 319 ·
    From *Literary Theory* · 321 ·
Leslie Brisman · 339 ·
    From *Milton's Poetry of Choice and Its Romantic Heirs* · 341 ·

Alice Walker   · 347 ·
    The Black Writer and the Southern Experience   · 349 ·
Barbara Johnson   · 353 ·
    From *A World of Difference*   · 355 ·
Henry Louis Gates, Jr.   · 365 ·
    From *Figures in Black*   · 367 ·
Bibliography   · 393 ·

Editor's Note to Glossary and Index   · 405 ·
Glossary of Critical Terms   · 407 ·
Index to Critics   · 433 ·
Index to Works   · 437 ·
Index of Names and Titles   · 445 ·
Acknowledgments   · 501 ·

The Future of Literary Criticism as an Art

Harold Bloom

Western literary criticism, as Bruno Snell first emphasized, originated in the context of satiric comedy. Aristophanes fathered criticism as a literary art essential to every other mode of literature, whether dramatic, epic, lyric, or narrative. Plato and Aristotle, in very different ways, sought to make criticism a part of philosophy, which was still the enterprise of such recent and current Gallic mystagogues as Foucault, de Man, and Derrida, all of them heirs of Nietzsche. Longinus, when he subtly renewed the contest between Plato and Homer, returned criticism to its agonistic origins in Aristophanes' vision of the strife between his admired Aeschylus and his despised Euripides. As a disciple of Longinus, I prophesy that the future of criticism will see its return from philosophy and social science and politics, its current morasses, to its ancient function as the branch of the literary art that judges and enables the rest of literature.

The art of criticism in English, which reached a first culmination in the Christian neoclassicism of Dr. Samuel Johnson, achieved a second height in such Romantic readers as William Hazlitt and John Ruskin, and Ralph Waldo Emerson in America. Romantic criticism exalted the Imagination, an apotheosis that could survive only through transformation in what remains the Age of Freud, half a century after the death of the founder of psychoanalysis. Freud affirmed the pragmatic primacy of fantasy over biology, even while extending an almost transcendental fealty to reality testing, or the equation of the biological necessity of dying with the Reality Principle. Kenneth Burke, still foremost among living critics, keeps his central position because he has been able to reaffirm imaginative values even in a Freudian context.

The art of criticism, to survive, will escape the nets of Marx and Heiddeger, Foucault and Derrida, but still must accommodate itself to the prophecies of Nietzsche and of Freud. Nietzsche's ultimate teaching may be the paradox that human existence can be justified only as an aesthetic phenomenon, even though the aesthetic always depends upon our capacity to believe our own lies to ourselves. Truth would destroy us; art protects us. This Nietzschean formulation cannot, I think, be reconciled with Freud's worship of the Reality Principle, but that may mean that Freud retained, despite himself, a vestige of Platonism, while Nietzsche indeed had rejected the last transcendentalism.

The function of criticism, in any age, is to protect art against belief, whether that belief be societal or transcendental, or something in between. The literary critic, qua critic, is not primarily an agent of social change. Her work fundamentally is to build a hedge about the aesthetic, and to raise up disciples to it, because the social vision of any single generation cannot legislate human possibilities for the generations to come. Feminist literary criticism will remain in its infancy until it can become a lens for a new aesthetic perceptiveness rather than a mirror for protest and for social progress, however admirable. Until then, feminist criticism will suffer all the disabilities of every moral mode of literary criticism, be it Christian, Marxist, African-American, or most of what passes for Freudian criticism. Perhaps the only Western belief that escapes the stifling consequences of belief is a faith in the aesthetic, since the believer in imaginative literature, like Nietzsche and Pater, Emerson and Wallace Stevens, believes as William James the Pragmatist believed, knowing that what one believes in is a fiction, true only insofar as it is memorable, and as it enhances the possibilities of human surmise or human existence.

Criticism is necessarily a mixed mode, since it is both a branch of literature and an overt instrument of education. Homer was the schoolbook for the Greeks, despite Plato's opposition, but the allegorists of Homer, his critics, ultimately made Dante possible even though Dante never read Homer. Is that not a paradigm for all criticism? Doing its job, it will prepare the way for an art it cannot necessarily anticipate. Perhaps the only art it must be able to prophesy is its own future, which returns me to the burden of this introduction. How can literary criticism continue to be a central component in Western education, in an age that incessantly becomes ever more ideological? What is the role of the aesthetic in an era that seems to compel flight from, or repression of, the aesthetic? My own students of a previous generation, who once seemed to me as possessed by aesthetic fervor as I remain, all too often march now under the banners of what Nietzsche might have called the School of Resentment. This parade away from aesthetic values is a sixfold movement: Marxists, feminists, semioticians, deconstructors, Lacanians, and Foucault-inspired, self-dubbed New Historicists. But ultimately all these mix together as moral historicisms or philosophical reductions, while literary fictions continue to take place *between* philosophy and history. If literature is, as the late Paul de Man insisted it must be, identical with rhetoric, then this rhetoric cannot be conceived of as synchronic, which means that what our age considers to be irony is not likely to be the literary irony of any other era. Another way of saying this is that our criticism can legislate neither its own past nor its own future, which returns me to all the paradoxes of the educational function of criticism, particularly at the present time.

Ultimately the critic can only teach herself when she teaches, because critical experience invariably will show her, given enough time, that there is no method except herself. In an ideological age, the self always is put into question, with method embraced instead, and such flight from the self inevitably becomes also a flight from the aesthetic. The growth of Western literature, whether you take it as progressive or regressive, is the story of the ever-expanding inner self, until this expansion touches its limits in Freud's speculations. An inner self that will not cease in its extensions had to seek representation in order to survive, and, whether that representation was Shakespeare's Hamlet, Milton's Satan, Wordsworth's own individual mind, or Freud's narcissistic and largely unconscious ego, the function of such mimesis was to ally inextricably the self and the pleasures of imaging the self. Criticism can turn Sublime, as it did in Longinus or Shelley or Emerson or Pater, and so can urge us to surrender pleasure, but only in order to open us to more difficult

INTRODUCTION

pleasures, to chronicles of even more inward selves. What criticism cannot do is to urge us to yield up aesthetic pleasures in order to hasten or to guarantee social change, however admirable such change might prove to be.

Method in literature is always a trope, and changes in method, in criticism, always reveal themselves to be changes in critical vocabulary. I wish to worry once more the educational dilemma of criticism: how can the aesthetic itself be saved from becoming an ideology? Those contemporaries against whom I write would insist that it cannot, so that my own defense of literary originality, of critical authority, of the authorial self, of literary character, is to be regarded as patriarchal, elitist, socially exploitative and so only as another mask for Western capitalism, with all of its notorious record that tropes greed as self-reliance, solipsism as imagination. Against this one must observe, in all mildness, that a poem or a story, a drama or a novel, must establish its own identity within a tradition of utterance before it is able to please us, and to instruct us by and through pleasing. The most exemplary and politically correct ideas of social redemption, as outlined by such current sages as Doris Lessing and Alice Walker, will fail their ideological purpose precisely to the extent that they manifestly lack art, or substitute moral virtue for the aesthetic experience. The disorders of society, like the disorders of the human, are proper candidates for the role of *materia poetica*, but so is very nearly everything else. Eloquence depends upon the hard work that is art, and not upon moral indignation, however sincere. Daily I receive in the mail volumes of the most sincere verse, and novels of admirable social sincerity. More than ever, all our bad verse and weak fiction is passionately sincere, encouraged by sincere Professors of Resentment. A part, at least, of the educational function of criticism at this time is to remind us that sincerity cannot substitute itself for the labor of representation. The sins of the ages may be a proper subject for a great Bard of Resentment to come, but alas she is not yet with us. And when she arrives, she will be recognized only because her usurpation of the aesthetic itself will be a major manifestation of aesthetic values.

But what *are* aesthetic values? The question is hardly to be asked, let alone answered, by any critic who possesses a depth of aesthetic awareness, but I learn daily to come to terms with it, since my students will not stop asking it. The aesthetic is now what always it has been, a mode of cognitive perception, and of cognitive sensation, rather than a pathway to supposed cognitive truth. Parmenides first attacked the aesthetic, on behalf of thought, and we can recall that Heraclitus, with his fabled darkness, asserted that the only reality to be found in the aesthetic is change as such, an assertion developed rather negatively by Plato. Aristotle tried for a more balanced view, but his balance seems to me more medical than anything else. Epicurus, ultimate ancestor of Pater, Wilde, and Wallace Stevens, seems to have been the first Western speculator who would acknowledge perception and sensation as valid quests for truth. The art of literary criticism must follow Epicurus in defending perception and sensation (hardly societal modes) as endeavors that rival cognition, because perception and sensation together constitute the essence of the aesthetic. To educate in perception and sensation is to follow Epicurus, and so to advocate no ideology except the Epicurean, which in the context of our moment is not an ideology at all. A literary critic qua critic, in my judgment, cannot be a Christian or a normative Jew, cannot be a Marxist or a feminist or any other apostle of an extra-aesthetic light. But she can be, indeed should be, an Epicurean before she is anything else. Her function is to compare and judge perceptions and sensations, the perceptions and sensations not only represented by imaginative literature, but themselves the product of poetry and prose fictions. Resentment will not take one far into the realms of perception and of sensation.

What is now called "theory" in literary criticism is not what I could accept as literary theory because it is anything but literary. Most of it is a reworking of a handful of tropes that ensue from French misreadings of German texts during the last quarter century. Literary theory, to be literary, will have to speculate upon the perceptions and sensations we have of poems, and also experiences through poems. There is no common denominator of poetic perception or of poetic sensation. We scarcely have begun to study perception and sensation in Shakespeare, even now. Literary criticism will not be adequate to Shakespeare's originality until it becomes aesthetic again, for the aesthetic founds itself upon originality of perception and origination of sensation. Criticism educates when it defines poetry against ideology, which means against what is sanctimonious in the reader. Perhaps there is the center that I seek. The function of criticism (and its future) is to purge us not of selfhood but of self-righteousness, of moral virtue, of what Blake referred to as "the selfish virtues of the natural heart."

The Art of the Critic

Raymond Williams
1921–1988

Raymond Henry Williams was born on August 31, 1921, in Monmouthshire, Wales, and was educated at Trinity College, Cambridge. After service in the British army during World War II, he began a forty-year teaching career, first at Oxford as staff tutor in literature from 1946 to 1961, then as a member of the faculty of Jesus College, Cambridge, with which he remained associated until his death on January 26, 1988, in London.

As a sociological critic of literature, Williams is recognized as a significant figure in postwar English letters. Long interested in the relationship between literature and society, influenced by both Marxism and the cultural radicalism of F. R. Leavis, Williams's first publishing venture was the short-lived journal of opinion *Politics and Letters* (1946–47), which he launched with two associates about the time he joined the Oxford faculty. His first book, *Reading and Criticism*, was published in 1950, and over the next four decades he wrote thirteen additional critical works, including *Drama from Ibsen to Eliot* (1952; rev. 1968); *Culture and Society 1780–1950* (1958); *The English Novel from Dickens to Lawrence* (1970); *The Country and the City* (1973); and *Marxism and Literature* (1977).

Perhaps his best-known book, *Culture and Society* examines the relationship between artistic and social development in nineteenth- and early twentieth-century England, and offers a sympathetic appraisal of the work and thought of Coleridge, Mill, Ruskin, and Lawrence. Inherent in Williams's presentation is a plea for the working-class notion of a collective society and a rejection of the bourgeois concept of an individualistic society. He argues that the major elements of the national culture should not remain the province a select few, but should be disseminated throughout society.

The Country and the City, perhaps equally well-known among Williams's *oeuvre*, surveys English literature in terms of changing attitudes toward both the countryside and the developing urban landscape throughout much of English history, as in *Culture and Society* relating literary works to the societal conditions that engendered them, and again emphasizing the idea of community, expressing hope for "new forms of cooperative effort."

Williams was also the author of a critical biography of George Orwell, and wrote four novels which explore the ideas of community discussed in his criticism. His fiction, Williams always maintained, was just as important as his criticism, and in the following passage from the essay "Realism and the Contemporary Novel" (published in the collection *The Long Revolution*, 1961) he seems to have brought together his ideas on literature and community: "The experience of isolation, of alienation, and of self-exile is an important part of the contemporary structure of feeling, and any contemporary realist novel would have come to real terms with it. . . . The truly creative effort of our time is the struggle for relationships, of a whole kind, and it is possible to see this as both personal and social: the practical learning of *extending* relationships."

FROM

THE LONG REVOLUTION

THE CREATIVE MIND

No word in English carries a more consistently positive reference than 'creative', and obviously we should be glad of this, when we think of the values it seeks to express and the activities it offers to describe. Yet, clearly, the very width of the reference involves not only difficulties of meaning, but also, through habit, a kind of unthinking repetition which at times makes the word seem useless. I propose to examine the significance of the 'creative' idea: first, by reviewing its history; second, by comparing its development as a term in the arts with some important recent scientific work on perception and communication; third, by looking at it as a possible key term in our contemporary discussion of culture—a discussion which centres on the relations between art and learning and the whole complex of our activities that we call our society.

I

The history of the 'creative' idea is in many ways difficult to trace. It seems to me to begin, essentially, in the thought of the Renaissance, but, when we look at these sources, we find its originators referring the idea to classical thought, as if unaware of the new emphasis they seem to be making. In any past writing, only part of the original meaning is recoverable, for the meaning as a whole has come to us through many minds, and even when we have distinguished their influence we find that the original significance is, with its context, still partly withheld. Yet as I read the authors, in particular Aristotle and Plato, on whom these Renaissance thinkers relied, I see a distinction, an altered significance, which seems of fundamental importance. The activity being described is a common activity, but its description, essentially, has altered.

We speak now of the artist's activity as 'creation', but the word used by Plato and Aristotle is the very different 'imitation'. The general meaning of the Greek word *mimesis* is either 'doing what another has done', or 'making something like something else'. In actual use it included the activities of the dancer, the singer, the musician, the painter, the sculptor, the actor, the dramatist, and the common quality in these activities was seen as 'the representation of something else': 'imitation'. Aristotle wrote:

> The general origin of poetry was due to two causes, each of them part of human nature. Imitation is natural to man from childhood, one of his advantages over the lower animals being this, that he is the most imitative creature in the world, and learns at first by imitation. And it is also natural for all to delight in works of imitation. The truth of this second point is shown by experience: though the objects themselves

may be painful to see, we delight to view the most realistic representations of them in art, the forms for example of the lowest animals and of dead bodies. The explanation is to be found in a further fact: to be learning something is the greatest of pleasures not only to the philosopher but also to the rest of mankind, however small their capacity for it; the reason of the delight in seeing the picture is that one is at the same time learning—gathering the meaning of things.

It seems clear from this, as from the whole of his main argument, that Aristotle considers art primarily as a representation of some hitherto-existing reality. The artist imitates this, and by his imitation, which is akin to our first process of learning, we gather the meaning of the thing that is imitated.

Plato, similarly, described the artist as an 'imitator' of a pre-existing reality. God was the creator of things; workmen the artificers of things; artists the imitators of things. Thus, Plato and Aristotle agree on the fact of imitation, but go on to draw different conclusions from it. For Plato, although in the *Ion* he describes the poet as divinely inspired, the act of imitation is at two removes from reality (the Idea, then the material thing, then the imitation) and the famous discussion in the *Republic*, proposing the censorship of poets, emphasizes the dangers of the influence of these 'mere imitators' on the weaker parts of the mind.

> The art of imitation is the worthless mistress of a worthless friend, and the parent of a worthless progeny. . . . The imitative poet . . . resembles the painter in producing things that are worthless when tried by the standard of truth, and he resembles him also in this, that he holds intercourse with a part of the soul which is like himself, and not with the best part. . . . He excites and feeds this worthless part of the soul, and thus destroys the rational part.

Aristotle, on the other hand, not only emphasizes imitation as part of the normal learning process, but introduces a new principle, that of 'the universal':

> The poet's function is to describe, not the thing that has happened, but a kind of thing that might happen, i.e. what is possible as being probable or necessary. . . . Hence poetry is something more philosophic and of graver import than history, since its statements are of the nature rather of universals, whereas those of history are singulars. By a universal statement I mean one as to what such or such a kind of man will probably or necessarily say or do—which is the aim of poetry though it affixes proper names to the characters; by a singular statement, one as to what, say, Alcibiades did or had done to him.

Thus while Plato emphasizes the dangers of fiction, as the imitation not even of ultimate reality but of mere appearances, Aristotle develops his concept of imitation as a form of learning towards its definition as the highest form of learning, in that it shows, through its universal statements, the permanent and the necessary.

The immense intellectual tradition which flowed from Plato and Aristotle came to include not only these two opposing valuations, but an extraordinary series of modifications, transvaluations, developments, and interpretations. Thus Platonism came to include a theory of art directly opposed to that of the *Republic,* arguing that the divinely inspired poet was able to teach the highest reality because he penetrated mere appearance, and embodied in his work the divine Idea. Aristotle's idea of universals, which in context reads primarily as the embodiment of general truths about human nature, became identified, in many minds, as the same doctrine: the universals were the divine Ideas, and the poet embodied them. Still, however, even after these developments, the process of art was 'imitation' and not 'creation'.

From the excitement and confusion of Renaissance theory four doctrines of art emerged. The first defined art as an imitation of the hidden reality, thus making it a form of revelation; this was particularly useful to some Christian thinkers, who could then see art as an allegory of the mind of God. This developed into the idea of art as an esoteric activity, and a high valuation of works of an allegorical or symbolic kind. The second doctrine, from much the same source but less affected by Christian thinking, saw art as a perpetual imitation and embodiment of the 'Idea of Beauty'. This came to include, in practice, the idea of imitating, not slavishly yet seriously, earlier works of art in which this Idea of Beauty was embodied (this is the major tradition which became known as classicism). The third doctrine, developing some of the emphases of Aristotle, saw art as the 'idealization of nature'; that is to say, showing things not as they are but as they ought to be. This, while based on the same source as allegiance to the 'Idea of Beauty', moved not towards classicism, but towards an important tradition of exemplary, moralizing and didactic works. The fourth doctrine, from which the 'creative' emphasis primarily springs, saw nature as God's art (Tasso) and saw art as a form of energy which vies with nature. As Castelvetro put it:

> Art is not a thing different from nature, nor can it pass beyond the limits of nature; it sets out with the same purpose as that of nature.

This purpose is a distinct form of creation. Nature is God's creation; art is man's creation. 'There are two creators', Tasso wrote, 'God and the poet.'

In any particular Renaissance work one is likely to find the four doctrines that I have here distinguished, not as alternatives, but frequently involved with each other, as the extreme ambiguity and vagueness of the terms make easily possible. But in the more important writers the tendency towards a distinctly humanist theory of art is quite marked. For some centuries yet, the idea of art as creation, in a kind of rivalry with God, would seem blasphemous. Yet, entangled as it was with both actual and false reliance on Plato and Aristotle, complicated as it was by different kinds of Christian tradition, the emergence of this idea can be seen as part of the new thinking of the Renaissance, and at the head of a line which leads down to our day. In the English tradition, its classical statement is that of Sidney. All other 'arts' and 'sciences' (astronomy, mathematics, music, philosophy, law, history, grammar, rhetoric, medicine, metaphysics) are, Sidney argues, tied to nature.

> Onely the Poet, disdayning to be tied to any such subjection, lifted up with the vigor of his owne invention, dooth growe in effect another nature, in making things either better then Nature bringeth forth, or, quite a newe, formes such as never were in Nature, as the Heroes, Demigods, Cyclops, Chimeras, Furies, and such like: so as hee goeth hand in hand with Nature, not inclosed within the narrow warrant of her guifts, but freely ranging onely within the Zodiack of his owne wit.
>
> Nature never set forth the earth in so rich a tapistry as divers poets have done, neither with plesant rivers, fruitful trees, sweet smelling flowers, nor whatsoever els may make the too much loved earth more lovely. Her world is brasen, the Poets only deliver a golden. But let those things alone and goe to man, for whom as the other things are, so it seemeth in him her uttermost cunning is imployed, and knowe whether shee have brought foorth so true a lover as Theagenes, so constant a friend as Pylades, so valiant a man as Orlando, so right a Prince as Xenophon's Cyrus, so excellent a man every way as Virgils Aeneas. Neither let this be jestingly conceived, because the works of the one be essentiall, the other, in imitation or fiction; for any understanding knoweth the skil of the Artificer standeth in that Idea or foreconceite of the work, and not in the work it selfe. And that the Poet hath that Idea is manifest, by delivering them forth in such excellencie as hee hath imagined them. Which delivering forth also is not wholie imaginative, as we are wont to say by them that build Castles in the ayre; but so farre substantially it worketh, not onely to make a Cyrus, which had been but a particular excellencie, as Nature might have done, but to bestow a Cyrus upon the worlde, to make many Cyrus's, if they wil learne aright why and how that Maker made him.
>
> Neyther let it be deemed too sawcie a comparison to ballance the highest poynt of mans wit with the efficacie of Nature: but rather give right honour to the heavenly Maker of that maker, who, having made man to his owne likenes, set him beyond and over all the works of that second nature, which in nothing hee sheweth so much as in Poetrie, when with the force of a divine breath he bringeth things forth far surpassing her doings, with no small argument to the incredulous of that first accursed fall of Adam, sith our erected wit maketh us know what perfection is, and yet our infected will keepeth us from reaching it.

The strands of many traditions can be seen in this, but the decisive novelty (it is not Sidney's, but of his period) is clear. This is the doctrine of man the creator, who 'with the force of a divine breath' brings forth 'things far surpassing' nature. Sidney glances back at one part of Plato's teaching, to find this force given by God to one kind of man, the poet. But the claim occurs within a larger movement of thought, in which man is asserting his right to break out of the order of nature: to see the rest of nature as subordinate to his creative will. For Sidney, poetry can be supernatural because it is an energy of the soul which in discovering God is able to create beyond natural limits. But another way of making the same claim is to assert a purely human creativity, the powers of the emergent mind. When imitation, the learning of reality, becomes creation, man making new reality, a critical stage in art and thought has been reached.

II

As we follow the historical argument, we find a growing complexity, as the implications of this claim are realized. In Marvell's famous verse in 'The Garden', we are still with Sidney, but the point is interestingly put:

> The mind, that ocean where each kind
> Does straight its own resemblance find;
> Yet it creates, transcending these,
> Far other worlds, and other seas,
> Annihilating all that's made
> To a green thought in a green shade.

This 'creation' is still, as the whole poem makes clear, an energy of the soul which is an approach to God. But it assumes, as a contrast with this, an order of natural seeing, 'where each kind does straight its own resemblance find'. Sidney also had assumed this, but had claimed that only the poet could go beyond it. In Marvell this is a creative activity of the human mind as such. It is this emphasis that we must bear in mind as we watch the extraordinary flowering of the creative idea in the development of what we now call Romantic thought. The attachment of 'creative' to the work of the artist remains the easiest to trace. Donne spoke of poetry as 'a counterfeit Creation'. Mallet, in 1728, spoke of the 'companion of the Muse, Creative Power, Imagination'. By the end of the eighteenth century, this emphasis, with its key-word, 'imagination', was becoming paramount. The main line runs as an emphasis on 'creative imagination' as a general human faculty, which is seen at its highest in the poet. This is the basis of Shelley's *Defence of Poetry,* which like Sidney's *Apologie* contains many strands of traditional thought, but is most significant in relation to developing ideas of perception and imagination:

> Man is an instrument over which a series of external and internal impressions are driven, like the alternations of an ever-changing wind over an Aeolian lyre, which move it by their motion to ever-changing melody. But there is a principle within the human being, and perhaps within all sentient beings, which acts otherwise than in the lyre, and produces not melody, alone, but harmony, by an internal adjustment of the sounds or motions thus excited to the impressions which excite

them. It is as if the lyre could accommodate its chords to the motions of that which strikes them, in a determined proportion of sound.

This, of course, is still 'imitation', with the addition of the organizing principle—what Shelley calls 'synthesis'—as the creative human act. The child and the savage imitate external objects, and

> language and gesture, together with plastic or pictorial imitation, become the image of the combined effect of those objects, and of his apprehension of them.

To be a poet is to carry to its highest form this general activity:

> to apprehend . . . the good which exists . . . in the relation subsisting first between existence and perception, and secondly between perception and expression.

The poet does this through the use of a language which is

> vitally metaphorical; that is, it marks the before unapprehended relations of things and perpetuates their apprehension.

The 'authors of revolutions in opinion' act similarly, for

> their words unveil the permanent analogy of things by images which participate in the life of truth.

A poem is

> the creation of actions according to the unchangeable forms of human nature, as existing in the mind of the creator, which is itself the image of all other minds.

Here Shelley returns to the emphasis of Sidney, which in other parts of his argument he had perhaps been moving beyond. He returns again, but with altered emphasis, in his most famous definition:

> All things exist as they are perceived; at least in relation to the percipient. 'The mind is its own place, and of itself can make a Heaven of Hell, a Hell of Heaven.' But poetry defeats the curse which binds us to be subjected to the accident of surrounding impressions. And whether it spreads its own figured curtain, or withdraws life's dark veil from before the scene of things, it equally creates for us a being within our being. It makes us the inhabitants of a world to which the familiar world is chaos. It reproduces the common Universe of which we are portions or percipients, and it purges from our inward sight the film of familiarity which obscures from us the wonder of our being. It compels us to feel that which we perceive, and to imagine that which we know. It creates anew the universe, after it has been annihilated in our minds by the recurrence of impressions blunted by reiteration. It justifies that bold and true word of Tasso: Non Merita nome di creatore, se non

Iddio ed il Poeta (none merits the name of creator, except God and the poet).

It is an eloquent argument, and remains important, but it fluctuates between *imitative and creative ideas of perception,* seeming to reserve real creation to secondary association, and it tends towards a denial of general human creativity, and its special reservation to the poet. It was, typically, Coleridge, in one of those extraordinary flashes of intelligence, who extended the idea of creation to all perception:

The primary IMAGINATION I hold to be the living Power and prime Agent of all human perception, and as a repetition in the finite mind of the eternal act of creation.

With this startling hypothesis, of which only later shall we see the full significance, the transformation of 'imitative' into 'creative' theories reaches its next critical stage.

III

We must now turn aside to notice an effect of the 'creative' theory, as it existed before Coleridge. The claim that art represented a 'superior reality', essentially higher than that accessible to other human faculties, was, naturally enough, contested. The basis of the opposition goes back to Plato. What the new thinkers called creation Plato had called falsehood. Art was fiction, and as such inferior to reality. The persistence of this attitude needs no emphasis. It is a commonplace of modern thought, as anyone who says he prefers biographies to novels 'because at least they are true' will affirm. What I want to observe is that the claim of art to 'superior reality' and its contemptuous description as 'inferior fiction' have been, in modern thought, counterparts. If you rely on the theory of art as imitation, this is inevitable, at a certain stage. Even in a culture in which it is deeply accepted that there is a 'reality' beyond 'appearances', it is by no means certain that the artist's singular ability to reach and depict this will be accepted. If a religion is the medium of belief in a 'higher reality', the artist's singularity will certainly not be conceded, although his role in depicting such a reality, in the accepted terms of the religion, will often be stressed. In such a case, however, this will not be a special kind of 'creative' act. The belief in artistic creation as the medium of a superior reality seems most likely to be held in a period of transition from a primarily religious to a primarily humanist culture, for it embodies elements of both ways of thinking: that there is a reality beyond ordinary human vision, and yet that man has supreme creative powers. But, in such a transition, the latter claim will be made on general grounds, thus tending to challenge the artist's singularity. Moreover, there will be elements in the assertion of human powers which will tend to devalue 'imagination', or at least to make it ambiguous. The growth of scepticism, which will be part of the movement from a primarily religious culture, will extend into this province, putting increasing emphasis upon the possibility of delusion or the idle construction of 'mere romance'. Historically, this has been the general development, for the artist's claim that he is a creator of superior reality has been counterpointed, from the beginning, by a stress on the possible delusions of imagination and the misleading elements of fiction and romance.

From the hundreds of possible examples, a famous passage from Shakespeare may be taken, for its ambiguity:

> T: More strange than true. I never may believe
> These antique fables, nor these fairy toys.
> Lovers and madmen have such seething brains,
> Such shaping fantasies, that apprehend
> More than cool reason ever comprehends.
> The lunatic, the lover and the poet
> Are of imagination all compact.
> One sees more devils than vast hell can hold;
> That is the madman. The lover, all as frantic,
> Sees Helen's beauty in a brow of Egypt.
> The poet's eye, in a fine frenzy rolling,
> Doth glance from heaven to earth, from earth to heaven,
> And as imagination bodies forth
> The forms of things unknown, the poet's pen
> Turns them to shapes, and gives to airy nothing
> A local habitation, and a name.
> Such tricks hath strong imagination
> That if it would but apprehend some joy
> It comprehends some bringer of that joy.
> Or in the night, imagining some fear,
> How easy is a bush supposed a bear.
> H: But all the story of the night told over,
> And all their minds transfigured so together,
> More witnesseth than fancy's images,
> And grows to something of great constancy.

The lines about the poet are frequently quoted, in the 'creative' tradition to which they obviously belong, but it is less often observed that the context of the description is a general description of delusion. The valuation seems to veer, even in the writing, and perhaps fairly represents a continuing line of belief: that delusion, or illusion, is common, but that there is a special category of illusion, used by artists, which is valuable.

Almost every possible variation of position, in this confused debate, has in fact been taken up. In practice, since the beginning of the eighteenth century, we have seen an alternation, but only of emphasis, between a naïve realism—'describing things as they really are', and the varying kinds of romanticism, from 'describing things as they ought to be, as they ideally are' to the simple 'superior reality' claim, as here in Shelley:

> He will watch from dawn to gloom
> The lake-reflected sun illume
> The yellow bees in the ivy bloom,
> Nor heed nor see, what things they be;
> But from these create he can
> Forms more real than living man,
> Nurslings of immortality.

Two strong emphases, nearer our own time, have been widely made. The growing belief in a simple kind of materialism, usually accompanied by an explicit denial of any kind of supernatural reality, any reality beyond man's reach, has made room for art in terms of its 'reflection of reality' (imitation) or, more subtly, its 'organization of reality'—the artist selects, organizes (Shelley's 'synthesis') and thus gives meaning and value. The new psychology, on the other hand, particularly in Freud and Jung, has repeated, in a different form, the claim that there is a reality beyond man's reach: the 'unconscious'. Or rather, beyond man's ordinary reach, and here might be the entry, either for a new science or for a new definition of art. For Freud, the material of art was 'phantasy', which he contrasted with 'reality'. The artist is one who from a certain psychological disposition

> turns away from reality and transfers all his interest, and all his libido too, on to the creation of his wishes in the life of phantasy. . . . But the way back to reality is found by the artist thus: he is not the only one who has a life of phantasy; the intermediate world of phantasy is sanctioned by general human consent. . . . But to those who are not artists the gratification that can be drawn from the springs of phantasy is very limited. . . . A true artist has more at his disposal. First of all he understands how to elaborate his daydreams, so that they lose that personal note which grates upon strange ears. . . . He knows too how to modify them sufficiently so that their origin in prohibited sources is not easily detected. Further, he possesses the mysterious ability to mould his particular material until it expresses the ideas of his phantasy faithfully, and then he knows how to attach to this reflection of his phantasy-life so strong a stream of pleasure that, for a time at least, the repressions are outbalanced and dispelled by it. When he can do all this he opens out to others the way back to the comfort and consolation of their own unconscious sources of pleasure, and so reaps their gratitude and admiration. . . .

The 'gratitude and admiration', it will be noted, are the 'reality' to which the artist finds his way back.

A development of this position is found in Herbert Read, who starts from Freud's account of the mind:

> If we picture the regions of the mind as three superimposed strata (we have already noted how inadequate such a picture must be), then

> continuing our metaphor we can imagine in certain rare cases a phenomenon comparable to a 'fault' in geology, as a result of which in one part of the mind the layers become discontinuous, and exposed to each other at unusual levels. . . . Some such hypothesis is necessary to explain that access, that lyrical intuition, which is known as inspiration and which in all ages has been the rare possession of those few individuals we recognize as artists of genius.

In Jung, on the other hand, there is a distinction between two kinds of artistic creation, one 'psychological', drawn from the materials of consciousness raised to intensity, the other 'visionary', drawn from 'timeless depths . . . the hinterland of man's mind'. He further distinguishes the private personality of the artist and the nature of his activity as an artist, which latter he sees as 'an impersonal creative process'. The creative activity is a general human process, of which the artist is, in his art, the impersonal embodiment, taking us back to

> that level of experience at which it is man who lives, and not the individual.

Thus, the 'creative' idea has undergone a further development, the ordinarily inaccessible reality being placed within man himself, with the artist as a specially gifted person who is able to penetrate to this region. But the association with 'phantasy', especially in Freud, links with the ordinary realist position, in which it is assumed that the material of art is different from and inferior to 'reality'. This has been countered, from the realist side in art, either with the reassertion that the material of art is ordinary reality, but that the artist, in imitating it, is doing something valuable—imitating, recording, and teaching; or with the claim that art is a special kind of exploration and organization of reality, the artist being primarily an 'emotional' explorer, whereas the scientist, by contrast, is a 'rational' explorer. The extreme positions have emerged as, on the one hand, that the material of art is a special kind of abnormal experience, devalued as 'phantasy' or valued as 'inspiration'; on the other hand, that the material is 'ordinary everyday reality', which the artist imitates or organizes. The linguistic curiosity, in this often angry debate, is that by all schools and from all assumptions, art and the artist are referred to as 'creative'. It would be a brave man who would say, after even the briefest review of the long inquiry into the nature of art, that he is sure, once the habit is checked, what 'creative' quite means. It is at this point that we can turn to recent work on perception, as a process of the brain and the nervous system. It seems to me, certainly, that it enables us to take a decisive step forward, in the necessary clarification.

IV

> The brain of each one of us does literally create his or her own world.

This startling sentence, from Professor J. Z. Young's *Doubt and Certainty in Science—A Biologist's Reflections on the Brain,* introduces clearly enough a new stage in the discussion. In the traditional discussion, the 'creative' emphasis had rested clearly enough on an implied opposite, which was natural seeing. A Platonist would express this as:

> Man—natural seeing—Appearances.
> Artist—exceptional seeing—Reality.

A Romantic would express it as:

> Man—natural seeing—Reality.
> Artist—exceptional seeing—Superior Reality.

A typical modern account would be:

> Man—natural seeing—Reality.
> Artist—exceptional seeing—Art.

There are indeed almost innumerable variations of expression of this relationship, for the word 'reality' can be used in so many ways, but at the centre of all of them is the common assumption: that there is an ordinary everyday kind of perception, and that this can exceptionally be transcended by a certain kind of man or a certain kind of activity. Most versions, furthermore, would describe the product of the everyday perception as 'reality'—the things in themselves as they really are—so that the product of the artist's perception must be seen as in any of a number of ways an alteration (organization, idealization, transcendence) of this 'reality' that is shared by all other men. This way of thinking is so deeply built into our language and intellectual tradition that the necessary revaluation, in terms of what we now know about perception, is exceptionally difficult. The challenge in Young's sentence is the use of the word 'create' to describe not merely the artist's activity, but the activity of every human mind.

The central fact of this new account of the activity of our brains is that each one of us *has to learn to see*. The growth of every human being is a slow process of learning what Young calls 'the rules of seeing', without which we could not in any ordinary sense see the world around us. There is no reality of familiar shapes, colours, and sounds, to which we merely open our eyes. The information that we receive through our senses from the material world around us has to be interpreted, according to certain human rules, before what we ordinarily call 'reality' forms. The human brain has to perform this 'creative' activity before we can, as normal human beings, see at all:

> The visual receiving system in its untrained state has only very limited powers. We are perhaps deceived by the fact that the eye is a sort of camera. Contrary to what we might suppose, the eyes and brain do not simply record in a sort of photographic manner the pictures that pass in front of us. The brain is not by any means a simple recording system like a film. . . . Many of our affairs are conducted on the assumption that our sense organs provide us with an accurate record, independent of ourselves. What we are now beginning to realize is that much of this is an illusion, that we have to learn to see the world as we do.

That is Young's account, and he goes on:

> In some sense we literally create the world we speak about. . . . The point to grasp is that we cannot speak simply as if there is a world around us of which our senses give true information. In trying to speak about what the world is like we must remember all the time that what we see and what we say depends on what we have learned; we ourselves come into the process.

Or, as Sir Russell Brain puts it:

> The sensory qualities of normal perception, such as colours, sounds, smells and touches are generated by the brain of the percipient and are unlike those external events which constitute the states of objects by which they are caused.

The philosophical implications of this view are both far-reaching and difficult, but there can be little doubt that henceforth we must start from the position that reality *as we experience it* is in this sense a human creation; that all our experience is a human version of the world we inhabit. This version has two main sources: the human brain as it has evolved, and the interpretations carried by our cultures. Man's version of the world he inhabits has a central biological function: it is a form of interaction with his environment which allows him to maintain his life and to achieve greater control over the environment in which this must be done. We 'see' in certain ways—that is, we interpret sensory information according to certain rules—as a way of living. But these ways—these rules and interpretations—are, as a whole, neither fixed nor constant. We can learn new rules and new interpretations, as a result of which we shall literally see in new ways. There are thus two senses in which we can speak of this activity as 'creative'. The evolution of the human brain, and then the particular interpretations carried by particular cultures, give us certain 'rules' or 'models', without which no human being can 'see' in the ordinary sense, at all. In each individual, the learning of these rules, through inheritance and culture, is a kind of creation, in that the distinctively human world, the ordinary 'reality' that his culture defines, forms only as the rules are learned. Particular cultures carry particular versions of reality, which they can be said to create, in the sense that cultures carrying different rules (though on a common basis of the evolved human brain) create their own worlds which their bearers ordinarily experience. But, further, there is not only variation between cultures, but the individuals who bear these particular cultural rules are capable of altering and extending them, bringing in new or modified rules by which an extended or different reality can be experienced. Thus, new areas of reality can be 'revealed' or 'created', and these need not be limited to any one individual, but can, in certain interesting ways, be communicated, thus adding to the set of rules carried by the particular culture.

The effect of this new knowledge seems to me to be of the greatest importance, but I know from my own attempts to absorb it that it is so difficult to grasp, in any substantial sense, that its application must meet with all kinds of resistance and confusion. The formulation of the knowledge (for any detailed account of which the original accounts must be turned to) is in itself an effort towards a new interpretation, a new rule, which is very difficult either to learn or to communicate. Yet, if we have followed the 'creative' idea thus far, we are perhaps in an exceptionally favourable position to understand the nature of this effort, and to clarify it.

V

The theories of 'imitation' and of 'creation' can best be seen as attempts to define the relationship between two named areas of fact—'reality' and 'art'. We have seen how various these definitions can be, but nevertheless we must observe, finally, that virtually the whole body of the theory of art contains, and starts from, this assumed opposition between two distinct kinds of thing. Art is the imitation of reality, and this may be valued as a form of learning or record, or dismissed as mere fiction—second-hand reproduction—or falsehood. Art is creation, and this may be valued as revelation or transcendence, or dismissed as mere fancy or phantasy. In all of these positions, the assumption of a fundamental duality is clear. High theory and low prejudice share this position equally. Plato or a Puritan or a modern Practical Man can dismiss art as inferior. Aristotle or a Renaissance theorist or a modern Romantic or aesthete can praise art as superior. Yet the long and often bitter dialogue between these contrasted positions leads now, not to a taking of sides, but to a rejection of the premises which both parties share. The contrast between art and reality can be seen, finally, as a false meaning.

Sophisticated modern thinking about art, in a century which has seen a great variety and confusion of styles, has evolved a position which can be stated as follows. One kind of art, which we call representational or realistic or naturalistic, offers an ordinary description or reproduction of reality, in the most common and objective terms. Another kind, less easily labelled but sometimes called romantic, offers not merely a representation of reality, but this representation modified by the artist's subjective emotional reactions to it—reality has been organized, selected, idealized, caricatured, by the artist's personal vision. A third kind, most commonly called abstract, is neither the reproduction of reality nor the subjective modification of reality, but the direct expression of purely 'aesthetic' experience, the representation in art, not of reality, but of the artist's vision. Some such classification as this was obviously necessary, as an attempt to come to terms with the observable difference in modern artistic methods. But again we can now see that it is basically inadequate, because again it is based on the assumed duality: the separation of art and reality, or of man and the world he observes.

The crucial importance of what we now know about perception is that it opens the way to ending this duality, and thus transforming our thinking about art. The new facts about perception make it impossible for us to assume that there is any reality experienced by man into which man's own observations and interpretations do not enter. Thus the assumptions of naïve realism—seeing the things as they really are, quite apart from our reactions to them—become impossible. Yet equally, the facts of perception in no way lead us to a late form of idealism; they do not require us to suppose that there is no kind of reality outside the human mind; they point rather to the insistence that all human experience is an interpretation of the non-human reality. But this, again, is not the duality of subject and object—the assumption on which almost all theories of art are based. We have to think, rather, of human experience as both objective and subjective, in one inseparable process. As Caudwell put it:

> Body and environment are in constant determining relations. Perception is not the decoding of tappings on the skin. It is a determining relation between neural and environmental electrons. Every part of the body not only affects the other parts but is also in determining relations with the rest of reality. It is determined by it and determines it, this interchange producing development—the constantly changing series of interlocking events. . . . Of this multitude of relations . . . we distinguish a certain group, changing as the world changes, not with it or separately from it but in mutually determining interaction with it. This selection, rich, highly organized and recent, we call the consciousness, or our ego. We do not select it out. In the process of development it separates out, as life separated out, as suns and planets and the elements separated out from the process of becoming. Separated out, and still changing, it is consciousness, it is *us* in so far as we regard ourselves as conscious egos. But in separating out, it does not completely separate out, any more than any element did. It remains like them, in determining relation with the rest of the Universe, and the study of the organization of this developed structure, of its inner relations and the relations of the system with all other systems in the Universe, is psychology.

The difficulty of this conception hardly needs stressing, and to grasp it in any substantial way needs long effort. Yet it is interesting to see that we have approached this conception, not only through the science of perception, but also through some of our traditional thinking about art as 'creation'. Coleridge, as I have noted earlier, was very near to it, when he wrote of 'the primary imagination' as

> the living Power and prime Agent of all human perception . . . a repetition in the finite mind of the eternal act of creation.

Yet the pull of earlier thinking limited even this, in the movement towards personifying this process (a Power, an Agent), and in the implied opposition of the 'finite mind' and a personified 'Creation'. We can look at this again in Young's conclusion, as a biologist:

> Our short experience of time and existence does not warrant us in postulating any creation or beginning at all. To do so is our crude way of talking about things, in terms of the model that speaks of the basic reality of life as an I, with a beginning and an end. Biological discovery has shown that this assumption of a sudden beginning for each of us is not true. Our organization, the most essential and enduring thing about us, does not begin from nothing, but is passed on continually. . . . Perhaps instead of focusing on beginning as the act of creation we should do exactly the opposite and centre our speech on continuity. The sense in which we do see creation is in the building of organization that goes on in the life of each individual, especially, in the case of men, in our brains. . . . There appear to be two general laws of the universe: first, that of association, of binding, the tendency for randomly distributed processes to become linked together to form larger units; second is the law that such unity is not permanent, but sooner or later dissolves, providing fresh randomness. This certainly seems to be a general principle in biology and we have seen how it usefully describes the progress of the growth of our brains and of the whole organization of our species, by alternation of aggregation and disaggregation. Each species remains in balance with its surroundings by alternate periods of development and death, followed by replacement by a new version of the organization. This is the means by which life maintains, as it were, communication with the non-living world. . . . There is a rhythmic building by alternation of organization and disorder, a continuous process of 'creation'.

Thus man shares with all living creatures this fundamental process, but in fact has evolved in such a way that his 'building of organization' is a continual process of learning and relearning, as compared with the relatively fixed instinct-mechanisms of animals. It is man's nature, and the history of his evolution, to be continually learning by the processes described. Since this continuing organization and reorganization of consciousness is, for man, the organization and reorganization of reality—the consciousness a way of learning to control his environment—it is clear that there is a real sense in which man can be called a creator.

All living forms have communication systems of a kind, but again, in man, the process of learning and relearning, which is made possible by social organization and tradition, has led to a number of communication-systems of great complexity and power. Gesture, language, music, mathematics are all systems of this kind. We can think of them as separate systems, yet to understand their nature, in any depth, we must see them in their context of the whole process of social learning. At one level we can oppose art to science, or emotion to reason, yet the activities described by these names are in fact deeply related parts of the whole human process. We cannot refer science to the object, and art to the subject, for the view of human activity we are seeking to grasp rejects this duality of subject and object: the consciousness is part of the reality, and the reality is part of the consciousness, in the whole process of our living organization. Coleridge spoke of 'substantial knowledge' as

> that intuition of things which arises when we possess ourselves as one with the whole.

This realization, the capacity for 'substantial knowledge', is the highest form of human organization, though the process it succeeds in grasping is the common form of our ordinary living. At a less organized level, we fall back on what Coleridge called 'abstract knowledge', when we

> think of ourselves as separated beings, and place nature in antithesis to the mind, as object to subject, thing to thought, death to life.

The antithesis of nature to the mind, 'as object to subject', we now know to be false, yet so much of our thinking is based on it that to grasp the substantial unity, the sense of a whole process, is to begin a long and difficult revolution in the mind. Yet it is certain that theories of art which begin from the separated categories of 'artist' and 'reality' are, from now on, irrelevant. We have to retrace our steps and look for new definitions.

VI

We learn to see a thing by learning to describe it; this is the normal process of perception, which can only be seen as complete when we have interpreted the incoming sensory information either by a known configuration or rule, or by some new configuration which we can try to learn as a new rule. The process of interpretation is neither arbitrary nor abstract; it is a central and necessary vital function, by which we seek so to understand our environment that we can live more successfully in it. But to say that we see by learning to describe is in fact to relate seeing to communication in a fundamental way. We have many ways of describing, both by learned rules—conventional descriptions—and by certain kinds of response, in gesture, language, image, which we often literally feel ourselves creating as we struggle to describe certain new information for which the conventional descriptions are inadequate. This vital descriptive effort—which is not merely a subsequent effort to describe something known, but literally a way of seeing new things and new relationships—has often been observed, by artists, yet it is not the activity of artists alone. The same effort is made, not only by scientists and thinkers, but also, and necessarily, by everyone. The history of a language is a very good example of this, for the ways in which a language changes, to amend old descriptions or accommodate new ones, are truly social, in the most ordinary business of living. It is not in this activity that the special function of the arts, or the special nature of the artist, can be discerned. A vital imaginative life, and the deep effort to describe new experience, are found in many others besides artists, and the communication of new descriptions and new meanings is carried out in many ways—in art, thought, science, and in the ordinary social process. What we call an art is one of a number of ways of describing and communicating, and most arts, quite clearly, are developments of ways commonly used—as dance from gesture, poetry from speech. Yet description is a function of communication, and we can best understand the arts if we look at this vital relationship, in which experience has to be described to be realized (this description being, in fact, putting the experience into a communicable form) and has then, because this is the biological purpose of the description, to be shared with another organism. The distinction of the arts is that in different ways they command very powerful means of this sharing; although again, in most arts, these means are developments from general communication.

Rhythm, as the most obvious of these means, may be taken as an example. We are only beginning to investigate this on any scientific basis, but it seems clear from what we already know that rhythm is a way of transmitting a description of experience, in such a way that the experience is re-created in the person receiving it, not merely as an 'abstraction' or an 'emotion' but as a physical effect on the organism—on the blood, on the breathing, on the physical patterns of the brain. We use rhythm for many ordinary purposes, but the arts (I would say all the arts, though in the visual arts this would be more difficult to prove) comprise highly developed and exceptionally powerful rhythmic means, by which the communication of experience is actually achieved. Man has made and is making these rhythms, as he has also 'made' colours. The dance of the body, the movement of the voice, the sounds of instruments are, like colours, forms, patterns, means of transmitting his experience in so powerful a way that the experience can be literally lived by others. This has been felt, again and again, in actual experience of the arts, and we are now beginning to see how and why it is more than a 'way of speaking'; it is a physical experience as real as any other.

Thus the arts are certain intense forms of general communication, but at this stage we encounter a further difficulty. For, of course, the speaking voice, the dancing body, the sculpture, the picture are, in their turn, 'objects' which have to be interpreted and received. The sensory information which comes to us from a painting is no more 'like' that painting than the sensory information which comes to us from a stone or a tree. The painting, like other visual 'objects', has itself to be interpreted and described before, in any normal sense, it is seen. We realize, from this, the necessary social basis of any art, for nobody can see (not understand, but *see*) the artist's actual work unless he and the artist can come to share the complex details and means of a learned communication system. But of course there are many possible levels of communication, from absolute failure (which within a given culture would hardly ever occur) through partial failure and misinterpretation to something like full reception. We may, as we put it, see the painting but not feel it. Something is coming through, but not at a significant level. This may be anybody's fault (the artist's as often as the spectator's) but to stray into the usual recriminations is less useful than to realize the nature and difficulty of what is being attempted: the substantial communication of experience from one organism to another. Art cannot exist unless a working communication can be reached, and this communication is an activity in which both artist and spectator participate.

When art communicates, a human experience is actively offered and actively received. Below this activity threshold there can be no art.

The nature of the artist's activity, in this process, may be further defined. The artist shares with other men what is usually called the 'creative imagination': that is to say, the capacity to find and organize new descriptions of experience. Other men share with the artist the capacity to transmit these descriptions, which are only in the full sense descriptions when they are in a communicable form. The special nature of the artist's work is his use of a learned skill in a particular kind of transmission of experience. His command of this skill is his art (we remember that the traditional meaning of 'art' was, precisely, 'skill'). But the purpose of the skill is similar to the purpose of all general human skills of communication: the transmission of valued experience. Thus the artist's impulse, like every human impulse to communicate, is the felt importance of his experience; but the artist's activity is the actual work of transmission. There can be no separation, in this view, between 'content' and 'form', because finding the form is literally finding the content—this is what is meant by the activity we have called "describing'. It is, in the first instance, to every man, a matter of urgent personal importance to 'describe' his experience, because this is literally a remaking of himself, a creative change in his personal organization, to include and control the experience. This struggle to remake ourselves—to change our personal organization so that we may live in a proper relation to our environment—is in fact often painful. Many neurologists would now say that the stage before description is achieved, the state of our actual organization before new sensory experience is comprehended, the effort to respond adequately while the new experience is still disorganized and disturbing, is biologically identical with what we call 'physical pain'. The creative agony, sometimes thought of as hyperbole, is literally true. Further, the impulse to communicate is a learned human response to disturbance of any kind. For the individual, of course, the struggle is to communicate successfully by describing adequately. The state often noticed in artists, when the struggle for adequate description—an actual manipulation of words or paint— seems primarily of personal importance, without regard to its effect on others, is to be understood in this sense. For unless the description is adequate, there can be no relevant communication. To think merely of making contact with others, rather than of making contact with this precise experience, is irrelevant and distracting. Genuine communication depends on this absorbed attention to precise description, but of course it does not follow that the description is for its own sake; the attention, rather, is a condition of relevant communication.

We respond to the disturbance not only by remaking ourselves, but, if we can, by changing the environment. Indeed these are parts of a single process, as consciousness and reality interpenetrate. The artist's way of remaking himself is, as in man generally, by work, which is remaking the environment and, in learning to work, remaking himself. This is so in the arts of language, sound, and movement, where the artist's transmission of experience is intended to alter existing real relationships. It can be seen more simply in an art like that of the sculptor, where an object is worked on, in what seems a whole process of modelling experience and yet discovering the experience by the act of modelling. The artist works on the material until it is 'right', but when the material is right he also is right: the art-work has been made and the artist has remade himself, in a continuous process. In abstraction we can say that he has worked on the material until it retransmits, to himself, his experience; or that he has discovered, by working on the material, a new kind of experience, which he has in effect learned from it. But, difficult though it may be to hold in the mind, the actual process is neither of these. It is neither subject working on object, nor object on subject: it is, rather, a dynamic interaction, which in fact is a whole and continuous process. The man makes the shape, and the shape remakes the man, but these are merely alternative descriptions of one process, well known by artists and in fact central to man himself. The excitement and pain of the effort are followed by the delight and rest of completion, and this is not only how the artist lives and works, but how men live and work, in a long process, ending and beginning again.

VII

The true importance of our new understanding of perception and communication is that it verifies the creative activity of art in terms of a general human creativity. The word 'creative' was turned to because of the tradition, yet the forces which made the tradition led also to use of the 'creative' idea in other fields. We must now note one effect of this on the definition of art.

J. Z. Young writes:

> The creative artist is an observer whose brain works in new ways, making it possible for him to convey information to others about matters that were not a subject for communication before. It is by search for means of communication that we sharpen our powers of observation. The discoveries of the artist and scientist are exactly alike in this respect.

And again:

> The painter has his own way of communicating his observations. Original painters find new ways of doing this, new art-forms. These literally enlarge the vision both of the artist himself and of those who look at his paintings. Artists have discovered new aspects of space with one symbolism, just as physicists have with another.

Now this is a very useful and acceptable argument, so far as it goes, but there is a problem in the description of valuable art as 'new', once we stop thinking about art in general and turn to actual works. It is quite common for philosophers and scientists to restrict their discussion of art, perhaps unconsciously, to great and original works: a restriction that can hardly be observed by the critic, who has to live with art of all kinds. The best aesthetic definitions can seem quite unreal as we turn back to the latest novel, the new book of poems, the current play or film, the ordinary exhibition. And if this is true of the usual run of art, it is even more true of the really bad art, of which we all see sufficient examples. The makers of all kinds of art claim the 'creative' description, quite reasonably, though it is obvious that only a few of them 'convey information . . . about matters that were not a subject for communication before'. It is customary to evade this difficulty by saying that works which do not fit the definition are 'not art', 'not really art', or 'the products of poetasters'. But will this do? Almost all art works are the result of the same general activity, the same *kinds* of skill, as produced *Lear,* Blake's 'Sunflower' or van der Weyden's *Pieta*. The disparity in value is not evidence of a fundamentally different practice and intention, especially since we find not only great art and bad art, but a range of infinite gradations between these, with no obvious line where a difference in kind can be drawn. The fact is, I think, that aesthetic theory, even when profoundly enriched by new knowledge about perception and communication, has normally retained two traditional ideas of what it is to be 'creative'. It has retained, in a curious way, the idea that the artist is specially inspired, which offers an easy but false solution to the problem of quality in art: 'we mean by art the work of those who are artists, that is specially inspired, and not the work of those who though they write, paint and compose are not artists, in that they are not inspired'. This sounds very silly, spelled out, but we have all learned it, in effect. Secondly, the idea of 'revelation', the discovery of a 'superior reality', has been similarly retained, and of course leads us to believe that the work of the artist is to make new discoveries about the world ('creative' equals 'new'). Yet this is a really disabling idea, in that it forces the exclusion of a large amount of art, which it is clearly our business to understand. By returning the ideas to their place in the tradition, we can become conscious enough of them to reject them, and when we have done so, we shall find that it is possible, as a part of our ordinary account of perception and communication, to describe all art, and not merely selected examples.

It is characteristic of aesthetic theory that it tacitly excludes communication, as a social fact. Yet communication is the crux of art, for any adequate description of experience must be more than simple transmission; it must also include reception and response. However successfully an artist may have embodied his experience in a form capable of transmission, it can be received by no other person without the further 'creative activity' of all perception: the information transmitted by the work has to be interpreted, described, and taken into the organization of the spectator. It is not a question of 'inspired' or 'uninspired' transmission to a passive audience. It is, at every level, an offering of experience, which may then be accepted, rejected, or ignored. Any art-work that we are conscious of having seen at all we have in the simple sense received, but in every spectator's mind there is a further and crucial stage. The experience reaches the spectator in some sense, but exactly how, and with what effects?

In certain cases, the artist's experience, described by his work in a given medium, will be accepted by the spectator in the sense that the means will be interpreted in the spectator's mind, in the artist's terms, in such a way that the experience literally becomes part of him. Such experience, accessible through these means, is what Young refers to as the 'literal enlargement' of vision, but 'enlargement' is not perhaps the best word. Sometimes indeed it is a kind of extension, a new way of seeing. But some experience of art, including great art, is not 'new' in this sense. Our experience includes the apparently different quality of 'recognition': that this, literally, is what we have always known. Now there need be no difficulty in this, if we look at the history of art. In many societies it has been the function of art to embody what we can call the common meanings of the society. The artist is not describing new experiences, but embodying known experiences. There is great danger in the assumption that art serves only on the frontiers of knowledge. It serves on these frontiers, particularly in disturbed and rapidly changing societies. Yet it serves, also, at the very centre of societies. It is often through the art that the society expresses its sense of being a society. The artist, in this case, is not the lonely explorer, but the voice of his community. Even in our own complex society, certain artists seem near the centre of common experience while others seem out on the frontiers, and it would be wrong to assume that this difference is the difference between 'mediocre art' and 'great art'. Not all 'strange' art, by any means, is found valuable, nor is all 'familiar' art found valueless.

It seems better to speak of art in terms of the organization of experience, especially in its effect on a spectator or an audience. If people have lived together, and come to share a certain kind of organization by which their minds have been trained to activity, we shall find that the processes of organization are in fact institutions, of which art is usually one. Young points out how the central building of a community, from mound to cathedral, is in fact a means of communication: it both organizes and *continues to express* a common meaning by which its people live. The discovery of a means of communication is the discovery of a common meaning, and the artist's function, in many societies, is to be skilled in the means by which this meaning can continue to be experienced and activated. The human bodies which carry the meanings die, but either the lasting monument, or the inherited and traditional artistic skills, embodied in the making of certain images, patterns, rhythms, survive to continue the process of organization. It has to be a continual re-creation of meaning, by the society as a whole and by every individual in it. Even the skills themselves are not commodities to be passively inherited, but processes that have to be learned, as part of any individual artist's growth: the means and the meaning, in a whole process, have to find this personal verification. Yet, the common experience which the meanings interpret will itself be changing, either slowly and hardly noticeably or at a variety of rates to one so rapid that the fact of change is a matter of general consciousness. The relationships between men and their environment change, yet consciousness of these relationships has to be achieved by descriptions capable of being communicated. The organization of received meanings has to be made compatible with possible new meanings that are emerging, and this is a process of great complexity. It is not just a matter of 'a society' changing, but of real changes in the personal organization of all its members. Moreover, though the members share an area of common meaning, the actual process of organization, in each individual, is necessarily personal. According to his position within the complex of real relationships in the society, and according to an important degree of inherited individuality (the result of a particular selection from the great complex of variable factors in human inheritance) the individual will learn in his own way by interaction with the changing organization of his society. Thus we see a series of unique individuals, in real relationships, learning and contributing to a changing pattern. It is in this context that we must understand both change and failure in art.

The individual artist may either re-create common meanings, in the quite literal sense that he builds his personal organization in their terms, or he may create new meanings, in the sense that to organize his actual experience he has to find new descriptions. For the individual artist, in his actual work, these processes will be similar, for in either case he is engaged in a substantial effort to make a particular form of experience so active in himself that he can communicate it to others. Yet, in the process of communication, the exact degree of relation between his personal meanings and the common meanings will be of vital importance. Where the relation is very close, he will be able to draw in a direct way on practised means of communication, with which his audience will be familiar. So far from this being simply 'conventional' art, with the implication that it is less likely to be valuable, it is probable that most great art has been made in these conditions. For the artist, in such a case, is not simply 'copying' the common meanings; the meanings are his own, in a deep realization, and yet the conditions for their communication are powerfully available. At the opposite extreme, where the relation between common and personal meanings is distant, the struggle to find means of communication will obviously be long and hard.

In practice, the process of change in art is normally one of extension of meanings, or modification of means. Beyond a certain point, a new meaning could hardly be communicated at all, or perhaps even described; the pressure would simply break up the artist's organization. The 'creative' act, of any artist, is in any case the process of making a meaning active, by communicating an organized experience to others. We have to see the process as one of many meanings being offered, by particular means, and only some of these meanings being received. Often, the art of a society changes without awareness of discontinuity: an effective number of individual offerings are taken up and composed into new common meanings, and there is no effective residue of rejected meanings to constitute challenge and tension. In our own time, clearly, we have change of such complexity, due not only to the rapidity of change in common experience but to the great extension and diversification of communities, that for a time at least discontinuity seems central, and we are primarily aware of art as the series of individual offerings, the making of common meanings being almost lost. It is in such a period that we develop theories of art which while rightly stressing the individual offering neglect the reality of communication. A tension between artist and audience is assumed as inevitable, and one form of this tension is described in terms of the artist's function to describe 'new' experience. In fact, however, even in this complex situation, a substantial number of the offered meanings are composed into new common meanings, though after initial disturbance and with a time-lag that again makes us conscious of the fact of change. This is an ordinary process of growth, and of course, whether the meaning is new or not (in the sense of having never been previously described) it can be felt as new (in the sense of being freshly and personally experienced). But to maintain growth, a significant area of common description and response must be maintained, and one of the functions of art, like other communication systems, is to recharge this area, with our own living energy. Much new art does this, and also the art of earlier periods and of other places, which we have preserved for just this reason, as a means of re-creation of a sense of common experience. (How we use this older art we shall see later, in discussing the nature of tradition.) At the same time, other new art succeeds in describing and communicating new experience, and in doing so may lead us to new kinds of response and activity. Here also, art from earlier periods and other places may succeed in communicating descriptions and responses that are new to us. Yet, whether it is communicating known forms of organization or moving us to new forms, art comes to us as part of our actual growth, not entering a 'special area' of the mind, but acting on and interacting with our whole personal and social organization. The distinction of value, in actual works of art, is always in the first instance, in the actual power to communicate. Since the meaning and the means cannot be separated, it is on the artist's actual ability to live the experience that successful communication depends. By living the experience we mean that, whether or not it has been previously recorded, the artist has literally made it part of himself, so deeply that his whole energy is available to describe it and transmit it to others. Bad art is then the failure or relative failure of this kind of personal organization, which we know now to be more than a figure of speech but an actual process by which we live. Our actual human organization is for the purpose of communicating, and in art as in other kinds of communication—most notably sexual relationship, which is our fundamental communicating process, in which life is offered and accepted—the ability to communicate is not a matter of abstract qualities, such as feeling, intelligence, or will, but is rooted in certain whole patterns of organization: success or failure is a matter of the whole self. The various communication systems which human beings have developed make personal organization ever more varied and complex. The special attachments of particular individuals to certain kinds of communication, the selection of certain classes of means which they value highly and in which they are capable of becoming highly skilled, are forms of growth within the great range of genetic variety and social inheritance and experience. We cannot say that art is a substitute for other kinds of communication, since when successful it evidently communicates experience which is not apparently communicable in other ways. We must see art, rather, as an extension of our capacity for organization: a vital faculty which allows particular areas of reality to be described and communicated.

To succeed in art is to convey an experience to others in such a form that the experience is actively re-created—not 'contemplated', not 'examined', not passively received, but by response to the means, actually lived through, by those to whom it is offered. At this stage, a number of art-works already fail, fundamentally because the artist's experience is insufficiently organized and in consequence he cannot discover the means by which the experience could be shared. There are absolute failures, in this sense, but there are also many partial failures or partial successes, in which certain parts of the experience come through, and can be shared as a lived reality, while other parts reach us with diminished or insignificant strength. We can often see, in the cases of failure, how the process of organization, which is also description, breaks down. We see the relapse to mere imitation of other works, in general pattern or in details of the pattern, and the failure is not that the methods of the other works are intrinsically inadequate, but that they are incongruous with this particular experience; active description has become mechanical repetition. Such failure is common, but hardly less so than a kind less often noticed theoretically, where the effort towards new descriptions is obvious, yet communication fails. It has often been said that audiences must be patient, if they are to learn an artist's 'new language', but this, while true, must not carry the implication that every new language can be learned, given time. To suppose this is to forget that for members of the audience, as for artists, communication is a way of living: to receive and live an artist's experience is no casual activity, but an actual living change. We depend for our growth on new descriptions being offered, but whether we accept them depends on our capacity to grow in such ways, and it is clear that some offered ways will be impossible to us, others actively rejected. Successful communication depends on the organization of audiences as well as artists, and while it is right that we should hold ourselves open to learn, it is necessary to remember that any response is part of a way of living, and that the selection of responses is a condition of any organization. In some cases we will be literally unable to receive what is offered; we simply cannot see the world, cannot respond to experience, in that way. Often, again, the power of the work will move us, yet still, later, we will reject it. For the experience has to be fitted into our whole organization, and in some cases, after a process of comparison that may be prolonged over years, acceptance will not be possible. Again, an apparent failure may eventually succeed, or will be valued by some while rejected by others. If we think of the real process of communication, we can find something better than the popular (and sentimental) formula: artist's new language, initial resistance, eventual acceptance. For the history of art shows not only this sequence, but three other sequences: artist's new language, initial acceptance, continued acceptance; artist's new language, initial acceptance, eventual rejection; artist's new language, initial resistance, eventual rejection. And indeed this range is what we should expect, for communication is a process between real individuals, who are all learning. Because of the range of these individuals, communication will always be uneven, and when it is a matter of new descriptions this unevenness will be very marked. Whether the new descriptions will become a new general way of seeing will depend on the direction of the common experience. In favourable cases, a work that virtually failed initially may become very successful, as the movement of common experience finds its terms valuable. In unfavourable cases, the work will simply be forgotten, however new and valuable it seemed to some people at the time. It is the same with the art of common meanings, for here again, while the meanings still satisfy the art will be preserved to recharge them, but when the meanings really fail the art loses its power to move us, unless, as quite often happens, we take it and reinterpret it according to meanings of our own.

We must remember, finally, that our increasing consciousness of the importance of art has led us to a complicated process of recording and preserving, which has in effect changed its status. By recording and preserving, in our many techniques, we gain control over some of the inherent problems of communication, in particular that of unevenness. Communication is no longer, in most cases, a single act. The transmission is recorded or stored, and we value certain communication-systems precisely because they are capable of this kind of permanence. The offering of experience is preserved, for long consideration, and communication can take place over a gap of a hundred generations. Because of the complexity of growth, it is obviously wise to keep alive as many offerings as possible, for we can never be sure in advance what may eventually be taken up, and this habit of storing experience has been central in man's whole organization. However, we only use such stores, as we use new art, by the active process already described. Like new ways of seeing, old ways must be actively learned.

VIII

To see art as a particular process in the general human process of creative discovery and communication is at once a redefinition of the status of art and the finding of means to link it with our ordinary social life. The traditional definition of art as 'creative' was profoundly important, as an emphasis, but when this was extended to a contrast between art and ordinary experience the consequences were very damaging. In modern industrial societies, particularly, it came to be felt that art would be lost unless it was given this special status, but the height of the claim ran parallel with a widespread practical rejection and exclusion. So powerful has been the tendency to exclude art from serious practical concerns, that, in a natural mood of defence, the claim that art is special and extraordinary has been urgent and even desperate; even to question this produces reactions of extreme violence, from those who are convinced that they are the sole defenders of art in a hostile world. The suggestion that art and culture are ordinary provokes quite hysterical denials, although, with every claim that they are essentially extraordinary, the exclusion and hostility that are complained of are in practice reinforced. The solution is not to pull art down to the level of other social activity as this is habitually conceived. The emphasis that matters is that there are, essentially, no 'ordinary' activities, if by 'ordinary' we mean the absence of creative interpretation and effort. Art is ratified, in the end, by the fact of creativity in all our living. Everything we see and do, the whole structure of our relationships and institutions, depends, finally, on an effort of learning, description and communication. We create our human world as we have thought of art being created. Art is a major means of precisely this creation. Thus the distinction of art from ordinary living, and the dismissal of art as unpractical or secondary (a 'leisure-time activity'), are alternative formulations of the same error. If all reality must be learned by the effort to describe successfully, we cannot isolate 'reality' and set art in opposition to it, for dignity or indignity. If all activity depends on responses learned by the sharing of descriptions, we cannot set 'art' on one side of a line and 'work' on the other; we cannot submit to be divided into 'Aesthetic Man' and 'Economic Man'.

The arts, like other ways of describing and communicating, are learned human skills, which must be known and practised in a community before their great power in conveying experience can be used and developed. Human community grows by the discovery of common meanings and common means of communication. Over an active range, the patterns created by the brain and the patterns materialized by a community continually interact. The individual creative description is part of the general process which creates conventions and institutions, through which the meanings that are valued by the community are shared and made active. This is the true significance of our modern definition of culture, which insists on this community of process.

Communication is the process of making unique experience into common experience, and it is, above all, the claim to live; for what we basically say, in any kind of communication, is: 'I am living in this way because this is my experience'. The ability to live in a particular way depends, ultimately, on acceptance of this experience by others, in successful communication. Thus our descriptions of our experience come to compose a network of relationships, and all our communication systems, including the arts, are literally parts of our social organization. The selection and interpretation involved in our descriptions embody our attitudes, needs and interests, which we seek to validate by making them clear to others. At the same time the descriptions we receive from others embody their attitudes, needs and interests, and the long process of comparison and interaction is our vital associative life. Since our way of seeing things is literally our way of living, the process of communication is in fact the process of community: the sharing of common meanings, and thence common activities and purposes; the offering, reception and comparison of new meanings, leading to the tensions and achievements of growth and change.

It is of the utmost importance to realize this sense of communication as a whole social process. If we have done so, we can then usefully look at particular kinds and means of communication, which have, as it were, separated out, but not separated out altogether. The fatally wrong approach, to any such study, is from the assumption of separate orders, as when we ordinarily assume that political institutions and conventions are of a different and separate order from artistic institutions and conventions. Politics and art, together with science, religion, family life and the other categories we speak of as absolutes, belong in a whole world of active and interacting relationships, which is our common associative life. If we begin from the whole texture, we can go on to study particular activities and their bearings on other kinds. Yet we begin, normally, from the categories themselves, and this has led again and again to a very damaging suppression of relationships. Each kind of activity in fact suffers, if it is wholly abstracted and separated. Politics, for example, has gravely suffered by its separation from ordinary relationships, and we have seen the same process in economics, science, religion, and education. The abstraction of art has been its promotion or relegation to an area of special experience (emotion, beauty, phantasy, the imagination, the unconscious), which art in practice has never confined itself to, ranging in fact from the most ordinary daily activities to exceptional crises and intensities, and using a range of means from the words of the street and common popular stories to strange systems and images which it has yet been able to make common property. It has been the purpose of this review of creative activity to allow us to acknowledge this, which is the real history of art and yet which we are kept from by definitions and formulas that were stages in its interpretation but that we must now move beyond. A further consequence of this sense of creative activity is that we are helped, by what it shows of communication and community, to review the nature of our whole common life: the terms of this review are the terms of the definition of culture. When we have grasped the fundamental relation between meanings arrived at by creative interpretation and description, and meanings embodied by conventions and institutions, we are in a position to reconcile the meanings of culture as 'creative activity' and 'a whole way of life', and this reconciliation is then a real extension of our powers to understand ourselves and our societies.

Jacques Derrida
1930–

Jacques Derrida was born in El Biar, Algeria, to Sephardic Jewish parents, in 1930. He moved to France in 1949 to continue his education, studying philosophy and publishing essays in academic publications—in particular the influential journal *Tel Quel.* Since 1965 he has taught the history of philosophy at the Ecole Normale Supérieure in Paris.

Derrida is most commonly recognized as the founding theoretician of a type of criticism known as "deconstruction." Although it has been brought to the attention of American students and scholars by literary critics—J. Hillis Miller, Paul de Man, and Geoffrey H. Hartman from Yale—deconstruction for Derrida is primarily a philosophical enterprise. Most generally, it is a critique of a metaphysical conception of language and meaning—that attitude toward language typical of philosophy and science which attempts to reduce words to transparent and univocal signifiers of fixed meanings which lie somewhere beyond or before the words themselves. This conception of the sign has traditionally been theological, Derrida claims, because it must posit a nonlinguistic source of meaning in some transcendental end or origin or essence, such as Platonic ideas, the Aristotelian telos, the Judeo-Christian God, or even the more conventional Freudian notion of the "self." "The sign and divinity," he writes in *Of Grammatology,* "have the same place and time of birth. The age of the sign is essentially theological." This theological sign has structured all Western discourse from Plato through Descartes to the most ordinary of contemporary language. Even the most rigorous would-be critics of metaphysics such as Husserl and Heidegger and the recent French structuralists fall back uncritically upon a metaphysical use of language when they privilege the "signified"—the structure or the essence or the "meaning"—over the signifier—the words themselves. Thus, as Nietzsche observed, language in Western philosophy has come to resemble a coin whose image has been worn down and erased; it is valued only as a cipher for a certain amount of value/meaning, not as a sensible and aesthetic being of its own. Derrida attempts to subvert this metaphysical tendency of philosophy by calling attention to the rhetorical status of its language. He attempts to make philosophy aware of its assumptions and blindnesses by calling attention to how it uses words—to the metaphorical, textual, and figurative dimensions of philosophical discourse.

In pursuit of this critique, Derrida has developed several innovative strategies for approaching texts, which have been adopted by questioning scholars in virtually every discipline that concerns itself with the reading of texts. Primary among these is to ask the previously unconsidered question of writing itself: what does it mean for a text to be *written* rather than *spoken,* and is it enough to understand writing simply as a deferred or displaced form of speech? Is there not a legitimate type of meaning which is uniquely textual and independent of any analogy with speaking? This question is typical of another Derridean tactic which insists upon the "thematic scrutiny" of concepts. In Derrida's work no concept is appropriated naively or uncritically; he attempts to make himself and his reader rigorously aware of the historical and metaphorical valences of every important term he uses. It is this examination of concepts that has led him to point out how most Western discourses are structured along the axes of one or more of several fundamental rhetorical oppositions—good vs. evil, positive vs. negative, inside vs. outside, light vs. dark, being vs. nothingness, truth vs. error, identity vs. difference, to name just a few. Another characteristically Derridean strategy is to analyze textual language in a manner analagous to the way Freud analyzed the language of his patients—attending to the significance of prefaces, footnotes, and ellipses just as Freud attended to casual remarks, asides, slips of the tongue, or what was left unsaid. Indeed, Derrida's project might be well characterized as an inquiry into what was left unsaid by Western philosophy—the repressed and excluded material which usually has to do with the second of the oppositional terms listed above—evil, negativity, absence, darkness, nothingness, etc.

Like Nietzsche and Heidegger, who must be seen as his primary precursors, Derrida has recognized that the work of modern philosophy is "always already" hermeneutic—bound up in the act of interpretation of prior texts. For this task Derrida has taken on as essential to his style what Nietzsche said he himself hoped to teach above everything else—"the art of slow reading." Although he has unfortunately become notorious for sponsoring a kind of "free play" attitude toward signification which has been taken as an excuse to attribute any meaning whatsoever to a given sign, Derrida's own readings only come to a conception of play by first laboriously distinguishing the ambiguities and alternative possibilities for interpretation that a given text suggests. He then typically questions the claim of any authority to privilege one interpretation over another, finding meaning himself in the play of their differences. Thus in "Force and Signification" he takes issue with the tendency of structuralist literary critics to reduce the meaning of a work to the structure that the critic has devised as a means for explaining it. This reduces the dynamic "force" of the work to a static and idealized "form." The work would be better served by a vigilant sensitivity to the endless play of difference between form and force, the Apollonian and Dionysian.

Derrida's first widely read works were published in 1967: *La Voix et le phénomène* (translated in 1973 as *Speech and Phenomena*), an introduction to the problem of the sign in Husserl's phenomenology; *L'Écriture et la différence* (translated in 1978 as *Writing and Difference*), which extends his critique of metaphysical signification to several of the major structuralists then working in Paris, including Claude Lévi-Strauss, Michel Foucault, and Emile Benveniste, and analyzes the works of figures sympathetic to Derrida like Artaud and the philosopher Levinas; and *De la grammatologie* (translated in 1976 as *Of Grammatology*), an effort to shift theoretical attention away from the concept of "language" to the concept of "writing." In 1972 he published another series of works: *Positions* (translated in 1981), a collection of interviews; *Marges de la philosophie* (translated in 1982 as *Margins of Philosophy*), in which he advances his critiques of Heidegger, Saussure, Hegel, and Husserl among others; and *La Dissémination* (translated in 1981 as *Dissemination*), which is principally devoted to an exhaustive analysis of the concept of the Pharmacy and the "Pharmakon" in Plato's *Phaedrus*. In 1974 he published *Glas* (translated in 1986), a huge and bewildering montage of texts from Hegel and Genet informed by Derrida's own conceptual and linguistic puns and personal commentary. Since *La Vérité en peinture* (1978), Derrida has turned his attention increasingly toward Freud and the possibility and forms of autobiography—especially in *La Carte postale: De Socrate à Freud et au-delà* (1980) and *Otobiographies: L'Enseignement de Nietzsche et le politique du nom propre* (1984). Among his works that address questions specific to literary criticism are *Signéponge* (1984), *Mémoires: For Paul de Man* (1986), *Schibboleth pour Paul Célan* (1986), and *Ulysse gramophone: Deux Mots pour Joyce* (1987).

FROM
WRITING AND DIFFERENCE

FORCE AND SIGNIFICATION

> It might be that we are all tattooed savages since Sophocles. But there is more to Art than the straightness of lines and the perfection of surfaces. Plasticity of style is not as large as the entire idea. . . . We have too many things and not enough forms.
> (Flaubert, *Préface à la vie d'écrivain*)

If it recedes one day, leaving behind its works and signs on the shores of our civilization, the structuralist invasion might become a question for the historian of ideas, or perhaps even an object. But the historian would be deceived if he came to this pass: by the very act of considering the structuralist invasion as an object he would forget its meaning and would forget that what is at stake, first of all, is an adventure of vision, a conversion of the way of putting questions to any object posed before us, to historical objects—his own—in particular. And, unexpectedly among these, the literary object.

By way of analogy: the fact that universal thought, in all its domains, by all its pathways and despite all differences, should be receiving a formidable impulse from an anxiety about language—which can only be an anxiety of language, within language itself—is a strangely concerted development; and it is the nature of this development not to be able to display itself in its entirety as a spectacle for the historian, if, by chance, he were to attempt to recognize in it the sign of an epoch, the fashion of a season, or the symptom of a crisis. Whatever the poverty of our knowledge in this respect, it is certain that the question of the sign is itself more or less, or in any event something other, than a sign of the times. To dream of reducing it to a sign of the times is to dream of violence. Especially when this question, an unexpectedly historical one, approaches the point at which the simple significative nature of language appears rather uncertain, partial, or inessential. It will be granted readily that the analogy between the structuralist obsession and the anxiety of language is not a chance one. Therefore, it will never be possible, through some second- or third-hand reflection, to make the structuralism of the twentieth century (and particularly the structuralism of literary criticism, which has eagerly joined the trend) undertake the mission that a structuralist critic has assigned to himself for the nineteenth century: to contribute to a "future history of imagination and affectivity."[1] Nor will it be possible to reduce the fascination inherent in the notion of structure to a phenomenon of fashion,[2] except by reconsidering and taking seriously the meanings of imagination, affectivity, and fashion—doubtless the more urgent task. In any event, if some aspect of structuralism belongs to the domains of imagination, affectivity, or fashion, in the popular sense of these words, this aspect will never be the essential one. The structuralist stance, as well as our own attitudes assumed before or within language, are not only moments of history. They are an astonishment rather, by language as the origin of history. By historicity itself. And also, when confronted by the possibility of speech and always ready within it, the finally acknowledged repetition of a surprise finally extended to the dimensions of world culture—a surprise incomparable to any other, a surprise responsible for the activation of what is called Western thought, the thought whose destiny is to extend its domains while the boundaries of the West are drawn back. By virtue of its innermost intention, and like all questions about language, structuralism escapes the classical history of ideas which already supposes structuralism's possibility, for the latter naively belongs to the province of language and propounds itself within it.

Nevertheless, by virtue of an irreducible region of irreflection and spontaneity within it, by virtue of the essential shadow of the undeclared, the structuralist phenomenon will deserve examination by the historian of ideas. For better or for worse. Everything within this phenomenon that does not in itself transparently belong to the question of the sign will merit this scrutiny; as will everything within it that is methodologically effective, thereby possessing the kind of infallibility now ascribed to sleepwalkers and formerly attributed to instinct, which was said to be as certain as it was blind. It is not a lesser province of the social science called history to have a privileged concern, in the acts and institutions of man, with the immense region of somnambulism, the *almost-everything* which is not the pure waking state, the sterile and silent acidity of the question itself, the *almost-nothing*.[3]

Since we take nourishment from the fecundity of structuralism, it is too soon to dispel our dream. We must muse upon what it *might* signify from within it. In the future it will be interpreted, perhaps, as a relaxation, if not a lapse, of the attention given to *force,* which is the tension of force itself. *Form* fascinates when one no longer has the force to understand force from within itself. That is, to create. This is why literary criticism is structuralist in every age, in its essence and destiny. Criticism has not always known this, but understands it now, and thus is in the process of thinking itself in its own concept, system and method. Criticism henceforth knows itself separated from force, occasionally avenging itself on force by gravely and profoundly proving that separation is the condition of the work, and not only of the discourse on the work.[4] Thus is explained the low note, the melancholy pathos that can be perceived behind the triumphant cries of technical ingenuity or mathematical subtlety that sometimes accompany certain so-called "structural" analyses. Like melancholy for Gide, these analyses are possible only after a certain defeat of force and within the movement of diminished ardor. Which makes the structural consciousness consciousness in general, as a conceptualization of the past, I mean of facts in general. A reflection of the accomplished, the constituted, the *constructed*. Historical, eschatalogical, and crepuscular by its very situation.

But within structure there is not only form, relation, and configuration. There is also interdependency and a totality which is always concrete. In literary criticism, the structural "perspective" is, according to Jean-Pierre Richard's expression, "interrogative and totalitarian."[5] The force of our weakness is that impotence separates, disengages, and emancipates. Henceforth, the totality is more clearly perceived, the panorama and the panoramagram are possible. The panoramagram, the very image of the structuralist instrument, was invented in 1824, as Littré states, in order "to obtain immediately, on a flat surface, the development of depth vision of objects on the horizon." Thanks to a more or less openly acknowledged schematization and spatialization, one can glance over the field divested of its forces more freely or diagrammatically. Or one can glance over the totality divested of its forces, even if it is the totality of form and meaning, for what is in question, in this case, is meaning rethought as form; and structure is the *formal* unity of form and meaning. It will be said that this neutralization of meaning by form is the author's responsibility before being the critic's, and to a certain extent— but it is just this extent which is in question—this is correct. In any event, the project of a conceptualization of totality is more easily stated today, and such a project in and of itself escapes the *determined* totalities of classical history. For it is the project of exceeding them. Thus, the relief and design of structures appear more clearly when content, which is the living energy of meaning, is neutralized. Somewhat like the architecture of an uninhabited or deserted city, reduced to its skeleton by some catastrophe of nature or art. A city no longer inhabited, not simply left behind, but haunted by meaning and culture. This state of being haunted, which keeps the city from returning to nature, is perhaps the general mode of the presence or absence of the thing itself in pure language. The pure language that would be housed in pure literature, the object of pure literary criticism. Thus it is in no way paradoxical that the structuralist consciousness is a catastrophic consciousness, simultaneously destroyed and destructive, *destructuring,* as is all consciousness, or at least the moment of decadence, which is the period proper to all movement of consciousness. Structure is perceived through the incidence of menace, at the moment when imminent danger concentrates our vision on the keystone of an institution, the stone which encapsulates both the possibility and the fragility of its existence. Structure then can be *methodically* threatened in order to be comprehended more clearly and to reveal not only its supports but also that secret place in which it is neither construction nor ruin but lability. This operation is called (from the Latin) *soliciting.* In other words, *shaking* in a way related to the *whole* (from *sollus,* in archaic Latin "the whole," and from *citare,* "to put in motion"). The structuralist solicitude and solicitation give themselves only the illusion of technical liberty when they become methodical. In truth, they reproduce, in the register of method, a solicitude and solicitation of Being, a historico-metaphysical threatening of foundations. It is during the epochs of historical dislocation, when we are expelled from the *site,* that this structuralist passion, which is simultaneously a frenzy of experimentation and a proliferation of schematizations, develops for itself. The baroque would only be one example of it. Has not a "structural poetics" "founded on a rhetoric"[6] been mentioned in relation to the baroque? But has not a "burst structure" also been spoken of, a "rent poem whose structure appears as it bursts apart"?[7]

The liberty that this critical (in all the senses of this word)[8] disengagement assures us of, therefore, is a solicitude for and an opening into totality. But what does this opening hide? And hide, not by virtue of what it leaves aside and out of sight, but by virtue of its very power to illuminate. One continually asks oneself this question in reading Jean Rousset's fine book: *Forme et signification: Essais sur les structures littéraires de Corneille à Claudel*.[9] Our question is not a reaction against what others have called "ingenuity" and what seems to us, except in a few instances, to be something more and something better. Confronted by this series of brilliant and penetrating exercises intended to illustrate a method, it is rather a question of unburdening ourselves of a mute anxiety, and of doing so at the point at which this anxiety is not only ours, the reader's, but also seems to conform, beneath the language, operations, and greatest achievements of this book, to the anxiety of the author himself.

Rousset certainly acknowledges kinships and affiliations: Bachelard, Poulet, Raymond, Picon, Starobinski, Richard, etc. However, despite the familial air, the many borrowings and numerous respectful acknowledgments, *Forme et signification* seems to us, in many respects, a solitary attempt.

In the first place, this is due to a *deliberate* difference. Rousset does not isolate himself within this difference, keeping his distance; rather, he scrupulously examines a community of intentions by bringing to the surface enigmas hidden beneath values that are today accepted and respected—modern values they may be, but values already traditional enough to have become the commonplaces of criticism, making them, therefore, open to reflection and suspicion. Rousset presents his theses in a remarkable methodological introduction that, along with the introduction to *L'Univers imaginaire de Mallarmé*, should become an important part of the discourse on method in literary criticism. In multiplying his introductory references Rousset does not muddle his discourse but, on the contrary, weaves a net that tightens its originality.

For example: that in the literary fact language is one with meaning, that form belongs to the content of the work; that, according to the expression of Gaeton Picon, "for modern art, the work is not expression but creation"[10]—these are propositions that gain unanimous acceptance only by means of a highly equivocal notion of form or expression. The same goes for the notion of *imagination*, the power of mediation or synthesis between meaning and literality, the common root of the universal and the particular—as of all other similarly dissociated couples—the obscure origin of these structural frameworks and of the empathy between "form and content" which makes possible both the work and the access to its unity. For Kant, the imagination was already in itself an "art," was art itself, which originally did not distinguish between truth and beauty; and despite all the differences, Kant speaks of the same imagination in the *Critique of Pure Reason* and the *Critique of Judgment* as does Rousset. It is art, certainly, but a "hidden art"[11] that cannot be "revealed to the eyes."[12] "Now since the reduction of a representation of the imagination to concepts is equivalent to giving its exponents, the aesthetic idea may be called an *inexponible* representation of the imagination (in its free play)."[13] Imagination is the freedom that reveals itself only in its works. These works do not exist *within* nature, but neither do they inhabit a world *other* than ours. "The imagination (as a productive faculty of cognition) is a powerful agent for creating, as it were, a second nature out of the material supplied to it by actual nature."[14] This is why intelligence is not necessarily the essential faculty of the critic when he sets out to encounter imagination and beauty; "in what we call beautiful, intelligence is at the service of the imagination, and the latter is not at the service of intelligence."[15] For "the freedom of the imagination consists precisely in the fact that it schematizes without a concept."[16] This enigmatic origin of the work as a structure and indissociable unity—and as an object for structuralist criticism—is, according to Kant, "the first thing to which we must pay attention."[17] According to Rousset also. From his first page on, he links "the nature of the literary fact," always insufficiently examined, to the "role in art of imagination, that fundamental activity" about which "uncertainties and oppositions abound." This notion of an imagination that produces metaphor—that is, everything in language except the verb *to be*—remains for critics what certain philosophers today call a naively utilized *operative concept*. To surmount this technical ingenuousness is to reflect the operative concept as a *thematic concept*. This seems to be one of Rousset's projects.

To grasp the operation of creative imagination at the greatest possible proximity to it, one must turn oneself toward the invisible interior of poetic freedom. One must be separated from oneself in order to be reunited with the blind origin of the work in its darkness. This experience of conversion, which founds the literary act (writing or reading), is such that the very words "separation" and "exile," which always designate the interiority of a breaking-off with the world and a making of one's way within it, cannot directly manifest the experience; they can only indicate it through a metaphor whose genealogy itself would deserve all of our efforts.[18] For in question here is a departure from the world toward a place which is neither a *non-place* nor an *other* world, neither a utopia nor an alibi, the creation of "a universe to be added to the universe," according to an expression of Focillon's cited by Rousset (*Forme et signification*, p. 11). This universe articulates only that which is in excess of everything, the essential nothing on whose basis everything can appear and be produced within language; and the voice of Maurice Blanchot reminds us, with the *insistence* of profundity, that this excess is the very possibility of writing and of literary *inspiration* in general. Only *pure absence* not the absence of this or that, but the absence of everything in which all presence is announced—can *inspire*, in other words, can *work,* and then make one work. The pure book naturally turns toward the eastern edge of this absence which, beyond or within the prodigiousness of all wealth, is its first and proper content. The pure book, the book itself, by virtue of what is most irreplaceable within it, must be the "book about nothing" that Flaubert dreamed of—a gray, negative dream, the origin of the total Book that haunted other imaginations. This emptiness as the situation of literature must be acknowledged by the critic as that which constitutes the specificity of his object, as that *around which* he always speaks. Or rather, his proper object—since nothing is not an object—is the way in which this nothing *itself* is determined by disappearing. It is the transition to the determination of the work as the disguising of its origin. But the origin is possible and conceivable only in disguise. Rousset shows us the extent to which spirits as diverse as Delacroix, Balzac, Flaubert, Valéry, Proust, T. S. Eliot, Virginia Woolf, and many others had a sure consciousness of this. A sure and certain consciousness, although in principle not a clear and distinct one, as there is not intuition of a thing involved.[19] To these voices should be added that of Antonin Artaud, who was less roundabout: "I made my debut in literature by writing books in order to say that I could write nothing at all. My thoughts, when I had something to say or write, were that which was furthest from me. I never had any ideas, and two short books, each seventy pages long, are about this profound, inveterate, endemic absence of any idea. These books are *L'Ombilic des limbes* and *Le Pèse-nerfs*."[20] The consciousness of having something to say as the consciousness of nothing: this is not the poorest, but the most oppressed of consciousnesses. It is the consciousness of nothing, upon which all consciousness of something enriches itself, takes on meaning and shape. And upon whose basis all speech can be brought forth. For the thought of the thing as *what* it *is* has already been confused with the experience of pure speech; and this experience has been confused with experience *itself*. Now, does not pure speech require inscription[21] somewhat in the manner that the Leibnizian essence requires existence and pushes on toward the world, like power toward the act? If the anguish of writing is not and must not be a *determined* pathos, it is because this anguish is not an empirical modification or state of the writer, but is the responsibility of *angustia*:[22] the necessarily restricted passageway of speech against which all possible meanings push each other, preventing each other's emergence. Preventing, but calling upon each other, provoking each other too, unforeseeably and as if despite oneself, in a kind of autonomous overassemblage of meanings, a power of pure equivocality that makes the creativity of the classical God appear all too poor. Speaking frightens me because, by never saying enough, I also say too much. And if the necessity of becoming breath or speech restricts meaning—and our responsibility for it—writing restricts and constrains speech further still.[23] Writing is the anguish of the Hebraic *ruah*,[24] experienced in solitude by human responsibility; experienced by Jeremiah subjected to God's dictation ("Take thee a roll of a book, and write therein all the words that I have spoken unto thee"), or by Baruch transcribing Jeremiah's dictation (Jeremiah 36:2,4); or further, within the properly human moment of *pneumatology*, the science of *pneuma, spiritus,* or *logos* which was divided into three parts: the divine, the angelical and the human. It is the moment at which we must *decide* whether we will engrave what we hear. And whether engraving preserves or betrays speech. God, the God of Leibniz, since we have just spoken of him, did not know the anguish of the choice between various possibilities: he conceived possible choices in action and disposed of them as such in his Understanding or Logos; and, in any event, the narrowness of a passageway that is *Will* favors the "best" choice. And each existence continues to "express" the totality of the Universe. There is, therefore, no tragedy of the book. There is only one Book, and this same Book is distributed throughout all books. In the *Theodicy,* Theodorus, who "had become able to confront the divine radiancy of the daughter of Jupiter," is led by her to the "palace of the fates;" in this palace "Jupiter, having surveyed them before the beginning of the existing world, classified the possibilities into worlds, and chose the best of all. He comes sometimes to visit these places, to enjoy the pleasure of recapitulating things and of renewing his own choice, which cannot fail to please him." After being told all this by Pallas, Theodorus is led into a hall which "was a world." "There was a great volume of writings in this hall: Theodorus could not refrain from asking what that meant. It is the history of this world which we are now visiting, the Goddess told him; it is the book of its fates. You have seen a number on the forehead of Sextus. Look in this book for the place which it indicates. Theodorus looked for it, and found there the history of Sextus in a form more ample than the outline he had seen. Put your finger on any line you please, Pallas said to him, and you will see represented actually in all its detail that which the line broadly indicates. He obeyed, and he saw coming into view all the characteristics of a portion of the life of that Sextus."[25]

To write is not only to conceive the Leibnizian book as an impossible possibility. Impossible possibility, the limit explicitly named by Mallarmé. To Verlaine: "I will go even further and say: the Book, for I am convinced that there is only One, and that it has [unwittingly] been attempted by every writer, even by Geniuses."[26] ". . . revealing that, in general, all books contain the amalgamation of a certain number of age-old truths; that actually there is only one book on earth, that it is the law of the earth, the earth's true Bible. The difference between individual works is simply the difference between individual interpretations of one true and established text, which are proposed in a mighty gathering of those ages we call civilized or literary."[27] To write is not only to know that the Book does not exist and that forever there are books, against which the meaning of a world not conceived by an absolute subject is shattered, before it has even become a unique meaning; nor is it only to know that the non-written and the non-read cannot be relegated to the status of having no basis by the obliging negativity of some dialectic, making us deplore the absence of the Book from under the burden of "too many texts!" It is not only to have lost the theological certainty of seeing every page bind itself into the unique text of the truth, the "book of reason" as the journal in which accounts *(rationes)* and experiences consigned for Memory was formerly called,[28] the genealogical anthology, the Book of Reason this time, the infinite manuscript read by a God who, in a more or less deferred way, is said to have given us use of his pen. This lost certainty, this absence of divine writing, that is to say, first of all, the absence of the Jewish God (who himself writes, when necessary), does not solely and vaguely define something like "modernity." As the absence and haunting of the divine sign, it regulates all modern criticism and aesthetics. There is nothing astonishing about this. "Consciously or not," says Georges Canguilhem, "the idea that man has of his poetic power corresponds to the idea he has about the creation of the world, and to the solution he gives to the problem of the radical origin of things. If the notion of creation is equivocal, ontological and aesthetic, it is not so by chance or confusion."[29] To write is not only to know that through writing, through the extremities of style, the best will not necessarily transpire, as Leibniz thought it did in divine creation, nor will the transition to what transpires always be *willful,* nor will that which is noted down always infinitely *express* the universe, resembling and reassembling it.[30] It is also to be incapable of making meaning absolutely precede writing: it is thus to lower meaning while simultaneously elevating inscription. The eternal fraternity of theological optimism and of pessimism: nothing is more reassuring, but nothing is more despairing, more destructive of our books than the Leibnizian Book. On what could books in general live, what would they be if they were not alone, so alone, infinite, isolated worlds? To write is to know that what has not yet been produced within literality has no other dwelling place, does not await us as prescription in some *topos ouranios,* or some divine understanding. Meaning must await being said or written in order to inhabit itself, and in order to become, by differing from itself, what it is: meaning. This is what Husserl teaches us to think in *The Origin of Geometry.* The literary act thus recovers its true power at its source. In a fragment of a book he intended to devote to *The Origin of Truth,* Merleau-Ponty wrote: "Communication in literature is not the simple appeal on the part of the writer to meanings which would be part of an a priori of the mind; rather, communication arouses these meanings in the mind through enticement and a kind of oblique action. The writer's thought does not control his language from without; the writer is himself a kind of new idiom, constructing itself."[31] "My own words take me by surprise and teach me what I think,"[32] he said elsewhere.

It is because writing is *inaugural,* in the fresh sense of the word, that it is dangerous and anguishing. It does not know where it is going, no knowledge can keep it from the essential precipitation toward the meaning that it constitutes and that is, primarily, its future. However, it is capricious only through cowardice. There is thus no insurance against the risk of writing. Writing is an initial and graceless recourse for the writer, even if he is not an atheist but, rather, a writer. Did Saint John Chrysostom speak of the writer? "It were indeed meet for us not at all to require the aid of the written Word, but to exhibit a life so pure, that the grace of the spirit should be instead of books to our souls, and that as these are inscribed with ink, even so should our hearts be with the Spirit. But, since we have utterly put away from us this grace, come let us at any rate embrace the second best course."[33] But, all faith or theological assurance aside, is not the experience of *secondarity* tied to the strange redoubling by means of which constituted—written—meaning presents itself as prerequisitely and simultaneously *read:* and does not meaning present itself as such at the point at which the other is found, the other who maintains both the vigil and the back-and-forth motion, the work, that comes between writing and reading, making this work irreducible? Meaning is neither before nor after the act. Is not that which is called God, that which imprints every human course and recourse with its secondarity, the passageway of deferred reciprocity between reading and writing? or the absolute witness to the dialogue in which what one sets out to write has already been read, and what one sets out to say is already a response, the third party as the transparency of meaning? Simultaneously part of creation and the Father of Logos. The circularity and traditionality of Logos. The strange labor of conversion and adventure in which grace can only be that which is missing.

Thus, the notion of an Idea or "interior design" as simply anterior to a work which would supposedly be the expression of it, is a prejudice: a prejudice of the traditional criticism called *idealist*. It is not by chance that this theory—or, one could now say, this theology—flowered during the Renaissance. Rousset, like so many others past or present, certainly speaks out against this "Platonism" or "Neo-Platonism." But he does not forget that if creation by means of "the form rich in ideas" (Valéry) is not the purely transparent expression of this form, it is nevertheless, simultaneously, revelation. If creation were not revelation, what would happen to the finitude of the writer and to the solitude of his hand abandoned by God? Divine creativity, in this case, would be reappropriated by a hypocritical humanism. If writing is *inaugural* it is not so because it creates, but because of a certain absolute freedom of speech, because of the freedom to bring forth the already-there as a sign of the freedom to augur. A freedom of response which acknowledges as its only horizon the world as history and the speech which can only say: Being has always already begun. To create is to reveal, says Rousset, who does not turn his back on classical criticism. He comprehends it, rather, and enters into dialogue with it: "Prerequisite secret and unmasking of this secret by the work: a reconciliation of ancient and modern aesthetics can be observed, in a certain way, in the possible correspondence of the preexisting secret to the Idea of the Renaissance thinkers stripped of all Neo-Platonism."

This revelatory power of true literary language as poetry is indeed the access to free speech, speech unburdened of its signalizing functions by the word "Being" (and this, perhaps, is what is aimed at beneath the notion of the "primitive word" or the "theme-word," *Leitwort,* of Buber).[34] It is when that which is written is *deceased* as a sign-signal that it is born as language; for then it says what is, thereby referring only to itself, a sign without signification, a game or pure functioning, since it ceased to be *utilized* as natural, biological, or technical information, or as the transition from one existent to another, from a signifier to a signified. And, paradoxically, inscription alone—although it is far from always doing so—has the power of poetry, in other words has the power to arouse speech from its slumber as sign. By enregistering speech, inscription has as its essential objective, and indeed takes this fatal risk, the emancipation of meaning—as concerns any actual field of perception—from the natural predicament in which everything refers to the disposition of a contingent situation. This is why writing will never be simple "voice-painting" (Voltaire). It creates meaning by enregistering it, by entrusting it to an engraving, a groove, a relief, to a surface whose essential characteristic is to be infinitely transmissible. Not that this characteristic is always desired, nor has it always been; and writing as the origin of pure historicity, pure traditionality, is only the *telos* of a history of writing whose philosophy is always to come. Whether this project of an infinite tradition is realized or not, it must be acknowledged and respected in its sense as a project. That it can always fail is the mark of its pure finitude and its pure historicity. If the play of meaning can overflow signification (signalization), which is always enveloped within the regional limits of nature, life and the soul, this overflow is the moment of the attempt-to-write. The attempt-to-write cannot be understood on the basis of voluntarism. The will to write is not an ulterior determination of a primal will. On the contrary, the will to write reawakens the willful sense of the will: freedom, break with the domain of empirical history, a break whose aim is reconciliation with the hidden essence of the empirical, with pure historicity. The will and the attempt to write are not the desire to write, for it is a question here not of affectivity but of freedom and duty. In its relationship to Being, the attempt-to-write poses itself as the only way out of affectivity. A way out that can only be aimed at, and without the certainty that deliverance is possible or that it is outside affectivity. To be affected is to be finite: to write could still be to deceive finitude, and to reach Being—a kind of Being which could neither be, nor affect me by *itself*—from without existence. To write would be to attempt to forget difference: to forget writing in the presence of so-called living and pure speech.[35]

In the extent to which the literary act proceeds from this attempt-to-write, it is indeed the acknowledgment of pure language, the responsibility confronting the vocation of "pure" speech which, once understood, constitutes the writer as such. Heidegger says of pure speech that it cannot "be conceived in the rigor of its essence" on the basis of its "character-as-sign" (*Zeichencharakter*), "nor even perhaps of its character-as-signification" (*Bedeutungscharakter*).[36]

Does not one thus run the risk of identifying the work with original writing in general? Of dissolving the notion of art and the value of "beauty" by which literature is currently distinguished from the letter in general? But perhaps by removing the specificity of beauty from aesthetic values, beauty is, on the contrary, liberated? Is there a specificity of beauty, and would beauty gain from this effort?

Rousset believes so. And the structuralism proper to Jean Rousset is defined, at least theoretically, against the temptation to overlook this specificity (the temptation that would be Poulet's, for example, since he "has little interest in art"),[37] putting Rousset close to Leo Spitzer and Marcel Raymond in his scrupulousness about the formal autonomy of the work—an "independent, absolute organism that is self-sufficient" (*Forme et signification,* p. xx). "The work is a totality and always gains from being experienced as such" (p. xxi). But here again, Rousset's position depends upon a delicate balance. Always attentive to the unified foundations of dissociation, he circumvents the "objectivist" danger denounced by Poulet by giving a definition of structure that is not purely objective or formal; or circumvents it by at least not in principle dissociating form from intention, or from the very act of the writer: "I will call 'structures' these formal constants, these liaisons that betray a mental universe reinvented by each artist according to his needs" (p. xii). Structure is then the unity of a form and a meaning. It is true that in some places the form of the work, or the form as the work, is treated *as if* it had no origin, as if, again, in the masterpiece—and Rousset is interested only in masterpieces—the wellbeing of the work was without history. Without an intrinsic history. It is here that structuralism seems quite vulnerable, and it is here that, by virtue of one whole aspect of his attempt—which is far from covering it entirely—Rousset too runs the risk of conventional Platonism. By keeping to the legitimate intention of protecting the *internal* truth and meaning of the work from historicism, biographism or psychologism (which, moreover, always lurk near the expression "mental universe"), one risks losing any attentiveness to the internal historicity of the work itself, in its relationship to a subjective origin that is not simply psychological or mental. If one takes care to confine classical literary history to its role as an "indispensable" "auxiliary," as "prologomenon and restraint" (p. xii, n. 16), one risks overlooking another history, more difficult to conceive: the history of the meaning of the work itself, of its *operation*. This history of the work is not only its *past*, the eve or the sleep in which it precedes itself in an author's intentions, but is also the impossibility of its ever being *present,* of its ever being summarized by some absolute simultaneity or instantaneousness. This is why, as we will verify, there is no *space* of the work, if by space we mean *presence* and *synopsis*. And, further on, we will see what the consequences of this can be for the tasks of criticism. It seems, for the moment, that if "literary history" (even when its techniques and its "philosophy" are renewed by "Marxism," "Freudianism," etc.) is only a restraint on the internal criticism of the work, then the structuralist moment of this criticism has the counterpart role of being the restraint on an internal geneticism, in which value and meaning are reconstituted and reawakened in their proper historicity and temporality. These latter can no longer be *objects* without becoming absurdities, and the structure proper to them must escape all classical categories.

Certainly, Rousset's avowed plan is to avoid this stasis of form, the stasis of a form whose completion appears to liberate it from work, from imagination and from the origin through which alone it can continue to signify. Thus, when he distinguishes his task from that of Jean-Pierre Richard,[38] Rousset aims directly at this totality of thing and act, form and intention, entelechy and becoming, the totality that is the literary fact as a concrete form: "Is it possible to embrace simultaneously imagination and morphology, to experience and to comprehend them in a simultaneous act? This is what I would like to attempt, although well persuaded that this undertaking, before being unitary, will often have to make itself *alternative* [my italics]. But the end in sight is indeed the simultaneous comprehension of a homogenous reality in a unifying operation" (p. xxii).

But condemned or resigned to alternation, the critic, in acknowledging it, is also liberated and acquitted by it. And it is here that Rousset's difference is no longer *deliberate*. His personality, his *style* will affirm themselves not through a methodological decision but through the play of the critic's spontaneity within the freedom of the "alternative." This spontaneity will, in fact, unbalance an alternation construed by Rousset as a theoretical norm. A practiced inflection that also provides the style of criticism—here Rousset's—with its structural form. This latter, Claude Lévi-Strauss remarks about social models and Rousset about structural motifs in a literary work, "escapes creative will and clear consciousness" (p. xv). What then is the imbalance of this preference? What is the preponderance that is more actualized than acknowledged? It seems to be *double*.

II

There are lines which are monsters. . . . A line by itself has no meaning; a second one is necessary to give expression to meaning. Important law. (Delacroix)

Valley is a common female dream symbol. (Freud)

On the one hand, structure becomes the object itself, the literary thing itself. It is no longer what it almost universally was before: either a heuristic instrument, a method of reading, a characteristic particularly revelatory of content, or a system of objective relations, independent of content and terminology; or, most often, both at once, for the fecundity of structure did not exclude, but, on the contrary, rather implied that relational configuration exists within the literary object. A structural realism has always been practiced, more or less explicitly. But never has structure been the exclusive *term*—in the double sense of the word—of critical description. It was always a *means* or relationship for reading or writing, for assembling significations, recognizing themes, ordering constants and correspondences.

Here, structure, the framework of construction, morphological correlation, becomes *in fact and despite his theoretical intention* the critic's sole preoccupation. His sole or almost sole preoccupation. No longer a method within the *ordo cognescendi*, no longer a relationship in the *ordo essendi*, but the very being of the work. We are concerned with an ultrastructuralism.

On the other hand (and consequently), structure as the literary thing is this time taken, or at least practiced, *literally*. Now, stricto sensu, the notion of structure refers only to space, geometric or morphological space, the order of forms and sites. Structure is first the structure of an organic or artificial work, the internal unity of an assemblage, a *construction*; a work is governed by a unifying principle, the *architecture* that is built and made visible in a location. "Superbes monuments de l'orgueil des humains, / Pyramides, tombeaux, dont la noble structure / a temoigné que l'art, par l'adresse des mains / Et l'assidu travail peut vaincre la nature" ("Splendid monuments of human pride, pyramids, tombs, whose noble structure Bears witness that art, through the skill of hands and hard work, can vanquish nature"—Scarron). Only metaphorically was this *topographical* literality displaced in the direction of its Aristotelean and *topical* signification (the theory of commonplaces in language and the manipulation of motifs or arguments). In the seventeenth century they spoke of "the choice and arrangement of words, the *structure* and harmony of the composition, the modest grandeur of the thoughts."[39] Or further: "In bad *structure* there is always something to be added, or diminished, or changed, not simply as concerns the topic, but also the words."[40]

How is this history of metaphor possible? Does the fact that language can determine things only by spatializing them suffice to explain that, in return, language must spatialize itself as soon as it designates and reflects upon itself? This question can be asked in general about all language and all metaphors. But here it takes on a particular urgency.

Hence, for as long as the metaphorical sense of the notion of structure is not acknowledged *as such*, that is to say interrogated and even destroyed as concerns its figurative quality so that the nonspatiality or original spatiality designated by it may be revived, one runs the risk, through a kind of sliding as unnoticed as it is *efficacious*, of confusing meaning with its geometric, morphological, or, in the best of cases, cinematic model. One risks being interested in the figure itself to the detriment of the play going on within it metaphorically. (Here, we are taking the word "figure" in its geometric as well as rhetorical sense. In Rousset's style, figures of rhetoric are always the figures of a geometry distinguished by its suppleness.)

Now, despite his stated propositions, and although he calls structure the union of formal structure and intention, Rousset, in his analyses, grants an absolute privilege to spatial models, mathematical functions, lines, and forms. Many examples could be cited in which the essence of his descriptions is reduced to this. Doubtless, he acknowledges the interdependency of space and time (*Forme et signification*, p. xiv). But, in fact, time itself is always reduced. To a *dimension* in the best of cases. It is only the element in which a form or a curve can be displayed. It is always in league with a line or design, always extended in space, level. It calls for measurement. Now, even if one does not follow Claude Lévi-Strauss when he asserts that there "is no necessary connection between measure and *structure*,"[41] one must acknowledge that for certain kinds of structures—those of literary ideality in particular—this connection is excluded in principle.

The geometric or morphological elements of *Forme et signification* are corrected only by a kind of mechanism, never by energetics. Mutatis mutandis, one might be tempted to make the same reproach to Rousset, and through him to the best literary formalism, as Leibniz made to Descartes: that of having explained everything in nature with figures and movements, and of ignoring force by confusing it with the quantity of movement. Now, in the sphere of language and writing, which, more than the body, "corresponds to the soul," "the ideas of size, figure and motion are not so distinctive as is imagined, and . . . stand for something imaginary relative to our perceptions."[42]

This geometry is only metaphorical, it will be said. Certainly. But metaphor is never innocent. It orients research and fixes results. When the spatial model is hit upon, when it functions, critical reflection rests within it. In fact, and even if criticism does not admit this to be so.

One example among many others.

At the beginning of the essay entitled "*Polyeucte,* or the Ring and the Helix," the author prudently warns us that if he insists upon "schemas that might appear excessively geometrical, it is because Corneille, more than any other, practiced symmetry." Moreover, "this geometry is not cultivated for itself," for "in the great plays it is a means subordinated to the ends of passion" (p. 7).

But what, in fact, does this essay yield? Only the geometry of a theater which is, however, one of "mad passion, heroic enthusiasm" (p. 7). Not only does the geometric structure of *Polyeucte* mobilize all the resources and attention of the author, but an entire teleology of Corneille's progress is coordinated to it. Everything transpires as if, until 1643, Corneille had only gotten a glimpse of, or anticipated the design of, *Polyeucte,* which was still in the shadows and which would eventually coincide with the Corneillean design itself, thereby taking on the dignity of an entelechy toward which everything would be in motion. Corneille's work and development are put into perspective and interpreted teleologically on the basis of what is considered its destination, its final structure. *Before Polyeucte,* everything is but a sketch in which only what is missing is due consideration, those elements which are still shapeless and lacking as concerns the perfection to come, or which only foretell this perfection. "There were several years between *La Galerie du palais* and *Polyeucte.* Corneille looks for and finds himself. I will not here trace the details of his progress, in which *Le Cid* and *Cinna* show him inventing his own structure" (p. 9). After *Polyeucte*? It is never mentioned. Similarly, among the works prior to it, only *La Galerie du palais* and *Le Cid* are taken into account, and these plays are examined, in the style of preformationism, only as structural prefigurations of *Polyeucte.*

Thus, in *La Galerie du palais* the inconstancy of Célidée separates her from her lover. Tired of her inconstancy (but why?), she draws near him again, while he, in turn, feigns inconstancy. They thus separate, to be united at the end of the play, which is outlined as follows: "Initial accord, separation, median reunification that fails, second separation symmetrical to the first, final conjunction. The destination is a return to the point of departure after a circuit in the form of a crossed ring" (p. 8). What is singular is the crossed ring, for the destination as return to the point of departure is of the commonest devices. Proust himself . . . (cf. p. 144).

The framework is analogous in *Le Cid:* "The ring-like movement with a median crossing is maintained" (p. 9). But here a new signification intervenes, one that panorography immediately transcribes in a new dimension. In effect, "at each step along the way, the lovers develop and grow, not only each one for himself, but through the other and for the other, according to a *very Corneillean* [my italics] law of progressively discovered interdependence; their union is made stronger and deeper by the very ruptures that should have destroyed it. Here, the phases of distanciation are no longer phases of separation and inconstancy, but tests of fidelity" (p. 9). The difference between *La Galerie du palais* and *Le Cid,* one could be led to believe, is no longer in the design and movement of presences (distance-proximity), but in the *quality* and inner intensity of the experiences (tests of fidelity, manner of being for the other, force of rupture, etc.). And it could be thought that by virtue of the very enrichment of the play, the structural metaphor will now be incapable of grasping the play's quality and intensity, and that the work of forces will no longer be translated into a difference of form.

In believing so one would underestimate the resources of the critic. The dimension of *height* will now complete the analogical equipment. What is gained in the tension of sentiments (quality of fidelity, way of being-for-the-other, etc.) is gained in terms of *elevation;* for values, as we know, mount scalewise, and the Good is most high. The union of the lovers is deepened by an "aspiration toward the highest" (p. 9). *Altus:* the deep is the high. The ring, which remains, has become an "ascending spiral" and "helical ascent." And the horizontal flatness of *La Galerie* was only an appearance still hiding the essential: the ascending movement. *Le Cid* only begins to reveal it: "Also the destination (in *Le Cid*), even if it apparently leads back to the initial conjunction, is not at all a return to the point of departure; the situation has changed, for the characters have been elevated. *This is the essential* [my italics]: the *Corneillean movement* is a movement of violent elevation . . ." (but where has this violence and the force of movement, which is more than its quantity or direction, been spoken of?) ". . . of aspiration toward the highest; joined to the crossing of two rings, it now traces an ascending spiral, helical ascent. This formal combination will receive all the richness of its signification in *Polyeucte*" (p. 9). The structure thus was a receptive one, waiting, like a girl in love, ready for its future meaning to marry and fecundate it.

We would be convinced if beauty, which is value and force, were subject to regulation and schematization. Must it be shown once more that this is without sense? Thus, if *Le Cid* is beautiful, it is so by virtue of that within it which surpasses schemes and understanding. Thus, one does not speak of *Le Cid* itself, if it is beautiful, in terms of rings, spirals, and helices. If the movement of these lines is not *Le Cid*, neither will it become *Polyeucte* as it perfects itself still further. It is not the *truth of Le Cid* or *of Polyeucte*. Nor is it the psychological truth of passion, faith, duty, etc., but, it will be said, it is this truth according to Corneille; not according to Pierre Corneille, whose biography and psychology do not interest us here: the "movement toward the highest," the greatest specificity of the schema, is none other than the *Corneillean movement* (p. 1). The progress indicated by *Le Cid*, which also aspires to the heights of *Polyeucte* is a "progress in the Corneillean meaning" (ibid.). It would be helpful here to reproduce the analysis of *Polyeucte*,[43] in which the schema reaches its greatest perfection and greatest internal complication; and does so with a mastery such that one wonders whether the credit is due Corneille or Rousset. We said above that the latter was too Cartesian and not Leibnizian enough. Let us be more precise. He is also Leibnizian: he seems to think that, confronted with a literary work, one should always be able to find a line, no matter how complex, that accounts for the unity, the totality of its movement, and all the points it must traverse.

In the *Discourse on Metaphysics,* Leibniz writes, in effect: "Because, let us suppose for example that someone jots down a quantity of points upon a sheet of paper helter skelter, as do those who exercise the ridiculous art of Geomancy; now I say that it is possible to find a geometrical line whose concept shall be uniform and constant, that is, in accordance with a certain formula, and which line at the same time shall pass through all of those points, and in the same order in which the hand jotted them down; also if a continuous line be traced, which is now straight, now circular, and now of any other description, it is possible to find a mental equivalent, a formula or an equation common to all the points of this line by virtue of which formula the changes in the direction of the line must occur. There is no instance of a fact whose contour does not form part of a geometric line and which can not be traced entire by a certain mathematical motion."[44]

But Leibniz was speaking of divine creation and intelligence: "I use these comparisons to picture a certain imperfect resemblance to the divine wisdom. . . . I do not pretend at all to explain thus the great mystery upon which depends the whole universe."[45] As concerns qualities, forces and values, and also as concerns nondivine works read by finite minds, this confidence in mathematical-spatial *representation* seems to be (on the scale of an entire civilization, for we are no longer dealing with the question of Rousset's language, but with the totality of our language and its credence) *analogous* to the confidence placed by Canaque artists[46] in the level representation of depth. A confidence that the structural ethnographer analyzes, moreover, with more prudence and less abandon than formerly.

Our intention here is not, through the simple motions of balancing, equilibration or overturning, to oppose duration to space, quality to quantity, force to form, the depth of meaning or value to the surface of figures. Quite to the contrary. To counter this simple alternative, to counter the simple choice of one of the terms or one of the series against the other, we maintain that it is necessary to seek new concepts and new models, an *economy* escaping this system of metaphysical oppositions. This economy would not be an energetics of pure, shapeless force. The differences examined *simultaneously* would be differences of site[47] and differences of force. If we appear to oppose one series to the other, it is because from within the classical system we wish to make apparent the noncritical privilege naively granted to the other series by a certain structuralism. Our discourse irreducibly belongs to the system of metaphysical oppositions. The break with this structure of belonging can be announced only through a *certain* organization, a certain *strategic* arrangement which, within the field of metaphysical opposition, uses the strengths of the field to turn its own stratagems against it, producing a force of dislocation that spreads itself throughout the entire system, fissuring it in every direction and thoroughly *delimiting* it.[48]

Assuming that, in order to avoid "abstractionism," one fixes upon—as Rousset does at least theoretically—the union of form and meaning, one then would have to say that the aspiration toward the highest, in the "final leap which will unite them . . . in God," etc., the passionate, qualitative, intensive, etc., aspiration, finds *its* form in the spiraling movement. But to say further that this union—which, moreover authorizes *every* metaphor of elevation—is *difference itself,* Corneille's own idiom—is this to say much? And if this were the essential aspect of "Corneillean movement," where would Corneille be? Why is there more beauty in *Polyeucte* than in "an ascending movement of two rings"? The force of the work, the force of genius, the force, too, of that which engenders in general is precisely that which resists geometrical metaphorization and is the proper object of literary criticism. In another sense than Poulet's, Rousset sometimes seems to have "little interest in art."

Unless Rousset considers every line, every spatial form (but every form is spatial) beautiful a priori, unless he deems, as did a certain medieval theology (Considérans in particular), that form is transcendentally beautiful, since it is and makes things be, and that Being is Beautiful; these were truths for this theology to the extent that monsters themselves, as it was said, were beautiful, in that they exist through line or form, which bear witness to the order of the created universe and reflect divine light. *Formosus* means beautiful.

Will Buffon not say too, in his *Supplement to Natural History* (vol. XI, p. 417): "Most monsters are such with symmetry, the disarray of the parts seeming to have been arranged in orderly fashion?"

Now, Rousset does not seem to posit, in his theoretical Introduction, that every form is beautiful, but only the form that is aligned with meaning, the form that can be understood because it is, above all, in league with meaning. Why then, once more, this geometer's privilege? Assuming, in the last analysis, that beauty lets itself be espoused or exhausted by the geometer, is he not, in the case of the sublime—and Corneille is said to be sublime—forced to commit an act of violence?

Further, for the sake of determining an essential "Corneillean movement," does one not lose what counts? Everything that defies a geometrical-mechanical framework—and not only the pieces which cannot be constrained by curves and helices, not only force and quality, which are meaning itself, but also *duration,* that which is pure qualitative heterogeneity within movement—is reduced to the appearance of the inessential for the sake of this essentialism or teleological structuralism. Rousset understands theatrical or novelistic movement as Aristotle understood movement in general: transition to the act, which itself is the repose of the desired form. Everything transpires as if everything within the dynamics of Corneillean meaning, and within each of Corneille's plays, came to life with the aim of final peace, the peace of the structural *energeia: Polyeucte.* Outside this peace, before and after it, movement, in its pure duration, in the labor of its organization, can itself be only sketch or debris. Or even debauch, a fault or sin as compared to *Polyeucte,* the "first impeccable success." Under the word "impeccable," Rousset notes: "*Cinna* still sins in this respect" (p. 12).

Preformationism, teleologism, reduction of force, value and duration—these are as one with geometrism, creating structure. This is the *actual* structure which governs, to one degree or another, all the essays in this book. Everything which, in the first Marivaux, does not announce the schema of the "double register" (narration and look at the narration) is "a series of youthful novelistic exercises" by which "he prepares not only the novels of maturity, but also his dramatic works" (p. 47). "The *true* Marivaux is still *almost* absent from it" (my italics). "From our perspective, there is only one fact to retain . . ." (ibid.). There follows an analysis and a citation upon which is concluded: "This outline of a dialogue above the heads of the characters, through a broken-off narration in which the presence and the absence of the author alternate, is the outline of the veritable Marivaux. . . . Thus is sketched, in a first and rudimentary form, the properly Marivauldian combination of spectacle and spectator, perceived and perceiver. We will see it perfect itself" (p. 48).

The difficulties accumulate, as do our reservations, when Rousset specifies that this "permanent structure of Marivaux's,"[49] although invisible or latent in the works of his youth, "belongs," as the "willful dissolution of novelistic illusion," to the "burlesque tradition" (p. 50; cf. also p. 60). Marivaux's originality, which "retains" from this tradition only "the free construction of a narration which simultaneously shows the work of the author and the author's reflection on his work," is then "critical consciousness" (p. 51). Marivaux's idiom is not to be found in the structure described but in the intention that animates a traditional form and creates a new structure. The truth of the general structure thus restored does not *describe* the Marivauldian organism along its own lines. And less so its force.

Yet: "The structural fact thus described—the double register—appears as a constant. . . . *At the same time* [my italics] it corresponds to the knowledge that Marivauldian man has of himself: a 'heart' without vision, caught in the field of a consciousness which itself is only vision" (p. 64). But how can a "structural fact," traditional during this era (assuming that as it is defined, it is determined and original enough to belong to an era) "correspond" to the consciousness of "Marivauldian man"? Does the structure correspond to Marivaux's most singular intention? Is Marivaux not, rather, a *good example*—and it would have to be demonstrated why he is a *good* example—of a literary structure of the times and, through it, an example of a structure of the era itself? Are there not here a thousand unresolved methodological problems that are the prerequisites for a *single* structural study, a monograph on an author or a work?

If *geometrism* is especially apparent in the essays on Corneille and Marivaux, preformationism triumphs à propos of Proust and Claudel. And this time in a form that is more organicist than topographical. It is here too, that preformationism is most fruitful and convincing. First, because it permits the mastering of a richer subject matter, penetrated more from within. (May we be permitted to remark that we feel that what is best about this book is not due to its method, but to the quality of the attention given to its objects?) Further, because Proust's and Claudel's aesthetics are profoundly aligned with Rousset's.

For Proust himself—and the demonstration given leaves no doubt on this subject, if one still had any—the demands of structure were constant and conscious, manifesting themselves through marvels of (neither true nor false) symmetry, recurrence, circularity, light thrown backward, superimposition (without adequation) of the first and last, etc. Teleology here is not a product of the critic's projection, but is the author's own theme. The implication of the end in the beginning, the strange relationships between the subject who writes the book and the subject of this book, between the consciousness of the narrator and that of the hero—all this recalls the style of becoming and the dialectic of the "we" in the *Phenomenology of the Mind*.[50] We are indeed concerned with the phenomenology of a mind here: "One can discern still more reasons for the importance attached by Proust to this circular form of a novel whose end returns to its beginning. In the final pages one sees the hero and the narrator unite too, after a long march during which each sought after the other, sometimes very close to each other, sometimes very far apart; they coincide at the moment of resolution, which is the instant when the hero becomes the narrator, that is, the author of his own history. The narrator is the hero revealed to himself, is the person that the hero, throughout his history, desires to be but never can be; he now takes the place of this hero and will be able to set himself to the task of edifying the work which has ended, and first to the task of writing *Combray*, which is the origin of the narrator as well as of the hero. The end of the book makes its existence possible and comprehensible. The novel is conceived such that its end engenders its beginning" (p. 144). Proust's aesthetics and critical method are, ultimately, not outside his work but are the very heart of his creation: "Proust will make this aesthetic into the real subject of his work" (p. 135). As in Hegel, the philosophical, critical, reflective consciousness is not only contained in the scrutiny given to the operations and works of history. What is first in question is the history of this consciousness *itself*. It would not be deceptive to say that this aesthetic, as a concept of the work in general, exactly overlaps Rousset's. And this aesthetic is indeed, if I may say so, a practiced preformationism: "The *last chapter* of the last volume," Proust notes, "was written immediately after the *first chapter* of the first volume. Everything in between was written afterward."

By preformationism we indeed mean preformationism: the well-known biological doctrine, opposed to epigenesis, according to which the totality of hereditary characteristics is enveloped in the germ, and is already in action in reduced dimensions that nevertheless respect the forms and proportions of the future adult. A theory of *encasement* was at the center of preformationism which today makes us smile. But what are we smiling at? At the adult in miniature, doubtless, but also at the attributing of something more than finality to natural life—providence in action and art conscious of its works. But when one is concerned with an art that does not imitate nature, when the artist is a man, and when it is consciousness that engenders, preformationism no longer makes us smile. *Logos spermatikos* is in its proper element, is no longer an export, for it is an anthropomorphic concept. For example: after having brought to light the necessity of *repetition* in Proustian composition, Rousset writes: "Whatever one thinks of the device which introduces *Un Amour de*

Swann, it is quickly forgotten, so tight and organic is the liaison that connects the part to the whole. Once one has finished reading the *Recherche,* one perceives that the episode is not at all isolable; without it, the ensemble would be unintelligible. *Un Amour de Swann* is a novel within a novel, a painting within a painting . . . , it brings to mind, not the stories within stories that so many seventeenth- or eighteenth-century novelists encase in their narratives, but rather the inner stories that can be read in the *Vie de Marianne,* in Balzac or Gide. At one of the entryways to his novel, Proust places a small convex mirror which reflects the novel in abbreviated form" (p. 146). The metaphor and operation of encasement impose themselves, even if they are finally replaced by a finer, more adequate image which, at bottom, signifies the same relationship of implication. A reflecting and representative kind of implication, this time.

It is for these same reasons that Rousset's aesthetic is aligned with Claudel's. Moreover, Proust's aesthetic is defined at the beginning of the essay on Claudel. And the affinities are evident, above and beyond all the differences. These affinities are assembled in the theme of "structural monotony": "'And thinking once more about the monotony of Vinteuil's works, I explained to Albertine that great writers have created only a single work, or rather have refracted the same beauty that they bring to the world through diverse elements'" (p. 171). Claudel: "'*Le Soulier de satin* is *Tête d'or* in another form. It summarizes both *Tête d'or* and *Partage de midi.* It is even the conclusion of *Partage de midi* . . .'" "'A poet does hardly anything but develop a preestablished plan'" (p. 172).

This aesthetic which neutralizes duration and force as the *difference* between the acorn and the oak, is not autonomously Proust's or Claudel's. It translates a metaphysics. Proust also calls "time in its pure state" the "atemporal" or the "eternal." The truth of time is not temporal. Analogously (analogously only), time as irreversible succession, is, according to Claudel, only the phenomenon, the epidermis, the surface image of the essential truth of the universe as it is conceived and created by God. This truth is absolutely *simultaneity.* Like God, Claudel, the creator and composer, "has a taste for things that exist together" (*Art poétique*).[51]

This metaphysical intention, in the last resort, validates, through a series of mediations, the entire essay on Proust and all the analyses devoted to the "fundamental scene of Claudel's theater" (p. 183), the "pure state of the Claudelian structure" (p. 177) found in *Partage de midi,* and to the totality of this theater in which, as Claudel himself says, "time is manipulated like an accordion, for our pleasure" such that "hours last and days are passed over" (p. 181).

We will not, of course, examine in and of themselves this metaphysics or theology of temporality. That the aesthetics they govern can be legitimately and fruitfully applied to the reading of Proust or Claudel is evident, for these are *their* aesthetics, daughter (or mother) of *their* metaphysics. It is also readily demonstrable that what is in question is the metaphysics implicit in all structuralism, or in every structuralist proposition. In particular, a structuralist reading, by its own activity, always presupposes and appeals to the theological simultaneity of the book, and considers itself deprived of the essential when this simultaneity is not accessible. Rousset: "In any event, reading, which is developed in duration, will have to make the work simultaneously present in all its parts in order to be global. . . . Similar to a 'painting in movement,' the book is revealed only in successive fragments. The task of the demanding reader consists in overturning this natural tendency of the book, so that it may present itself in its entirety to the mind's scrutiny. The only complete reading is the one which transforms the book into a simultaneous network of reciprocal relationships: it is then that surprises emerge" (p. xiii). (What surprises? How can simultaneity hold surprises in store? Rather, it neutralizes the surprises of nonsimultaneity. Surprises emerge from the dialogue between the simultaneous and the nonsimultaneous. Which suffices to say that structural simultaneity *itself* serves to reassure.) Jean-Pierre Richard: "The difficulty of every structural account resides in that it must describe sequentially, successively, that which in fact exists all at once, simultaneously" (*L'Univers imaginaire de Mallarmé*, p. 28). Thus, Rousset invokes the difficulty of gaining access to the simultaneity which is truth within reading, and Richard the difficulty of accounting for it within writing. In both cases, simultaneity is the myth of a total reading or description, promoted to the status of a regulatory ideal. The search for the simultaneous explains the capacity to be fascinated by the spatial image: is space not "the order of coexistences" (Leibniz)? But by saying "simultaneity" instead of space, one attempts to *concentrate* time instead of *forgetting* it. "Duration thus takes on the illusory form of a homogenous milieu, and the union between these two terms, space and duration, is simultaneity, which could be defined as the intersection of time with space."[52] In this demand for the flat and the horizontal, what is intolerable for structuralism is indeed the richness implied by the volume, every element of signification that cannot be spread out into the simultaneity of a form. But is it by chance that the book is, first and foremost, volume?[53] And that the meaning of meaning (in the general sense of meaning and not in the sense of signalization) is infinite implication, the indefinite referral of signifier to signifier? And that its force is a certain pure and infinite equivocality which gives signified meaning no respite, no rest, but engages it in its own *economy* so that it always signifies again and differs? Except in the *Livre irréalisé* by Mallarmé, that which is written is never identical to itself.

Unrealized: this does not mean that Mallarmé did not succeed in realizing a Book which would be at one with itself—he simply did not want to. He unrealized the unity of the Book by making the categories in which it was supposed to be securely conceptualized tremble: while speaking of an "identification with itself" of the Book, he underlines that the Book is at once "the same and other," as it is "made up of itself." It lends itself not only to a "double interpretation," but through it, says Mallarmé, "I sow, so to speak, this entire double volume here and there ten times."[54]

Does one have the right to constitute this metaphysics or aesthetics so well adapted to Proust and Claudel as the general method of structuralism?[55] This, however, is precisely what Rousset does, in the extent to which, as we have at least tried to demonstrate, he decides that everything not intelligible in the light of a "preestablished" teleological framework, and not visible in its simultaneity, is reducible to the inconsequentiality of accident or dross. Even in the essays devoted to Proust and Claudel, the essays guided by the most comprehensive structure, Rousset must decide to consider as "genetic accidents" "each episode, each character" whose "eventual independence" from the "central theme" or "general organization of the work" is noticeable (p. 164); he must accept the confrontation of the "true Proust" with the "Novelist" to whom, moreover, he can sometimes "do wrong," just as the true Proust, according to Rousset, is also capable of missing the "truth" of love, etc. (p. 166). In the same way that "the true Baudelaire is perhaps only in the *Balcon,* and all of Flaubert is in *Madame Bovary*" (p. xix), the true Proust is not simultaneously everywhere. Rousset must also conclude that the characters of *L'Otage* are severed not by "circumstance," but, "to express it better," by the "demands of the Claudelian framework" (p. 179); he must deploy marvels of subtlety to demonstrate that in *Le Soulier de satin* Claudel does not "repudiate himself" and does not "renounce" his "constant framework" (p. 183).

What is most serious is that this "ultrastructuralist" method, as we have called it, seems to contradict, in certain respects, the most precious and original intention of structuralism. In the biological and linguistic fields where it first appeared, structuralism above all insists upon preserving the coherence and completion of each totality at its own level. In a given configuration, it first prohibits the consideration of that which is incomplete or missing, everything that would make the configuration appear to be a blind anticipation of, or mysterious deviation from, an orthogenesis whose own conceptual basis would have to be a *telos* or an ideal norm. To be a structuralist is first to concentrate on the organization of meaning, on the autonomy and idiosyncratic balance, the completion of each moment, each form; and it is to refuse to relegate everything that is not comprehensible as an ideal type to the status of aberrational accident. The pathological itself is not the simple absence of structure. It is organized. It cannot be understood as the deficiency, defect, or decomposition of a beautiful, ideal totality. It is not the simple undoing of *telos*.

It is true that the rejection of finalism is a rule, a methodological norm, that structuralism can apply only with difficulty. The rejection of finalism is a vow of infidelity to *telos* which the actual effort can never adhere to. Structuralism lives within and on the difference between its promise and its practice. Whether biology, linguistics, or literature is in question, how can an organized totality be perceived without reference to its end, or without presuming to know its end, at least? And if meaning is meaningful only within a totality, could it come forth if the totality were not animated by the anticipation of an end, or by an intentionality which, moreover, does not necessarily and primarily belong to a consciousness? If there are structures, they are possible only on the basis of the fundamental structure which permits totality to open and overflow itself such that it *takes on meaning* by anticipating a *telos* which here must be understood in its most indeterminate form. This opening is certainly that which liberates time and genesis (even coincides with them), but it is also that which risks enclosing progression toward the future—becoming—by giving it form. That which risks stifling force under form.

It may be acknowledged, then, that in the rereading to which we are invited by Rousset, light is menaced from within by that which also metaphysically menaces every structuralism: the possibility of concealing meaning through the very act of uncovering it. *To comprehend* the structure of a becoming, the form of a force, is to lose meaning by finding it. The meaning of becoming and of force, by virtue of their pure, intrinsic characteristics, is the repose of the beginning and the end, the peacefulness of a spectacle, horizon or face.[56] Within this peace and repose the character of becoming and of force is disturbed by meaning itself. The meaning of meaning is Apollonian by virtue of everything within it that can be seen.[57]

To say that force is the origin of the phenomenon is to say nothing. By its very articulation force becomes a phenomenon. Hegel demonstrated convincingly that the explication of a phenomenon by a force is a tautology.[58] But in saying this, one must refer to language's peculiar inability to emerge from itself in order to articulate its origin, and not to the *thought* of force. Force is the other of language without which language would not be what it is.

In order to respect this strange movement within language, in order not to reduce it in turn, we would have to attempt a return to the metaphor of darkness and light (of self-revelation and self-concealment), the founding metaphor of Western philosophy as metaphysics. The founding metaphor not only because it is a photological one—and in this respect the entire history of our philosophy is a photology, the name given to a history of, or treatise on, light—but because it is a metaphor. Metaphor in general, the passage from one existent to another, or from one signified meaning to another, authorized by the initial *submission* of Being to the existent, the *analogical* displacement of Being, is the essential weight which anchors discourse in metaphysics, irremediably repressing discourse into its metaphysical state.[59] This is a fate which it would be foolish to term a regrettable and provisional accident of "history"—a slip, a mistake of thought occurring *within* history (*in historia*). *In historiam,* it is the fall of thought into philosophy which gets history under way. Which suffices to say that the metaphor of the "fall" deserves its quotation marks. In this heliocentric metaphysics, force, ceding its place to *eidos* (i.e., the form which is visible for the metaphorical eye), has already been separated from itself in acoustics.[60] How can force or weakness be understood in terms of light and dark?

That modern structuralism has grown and developed within a more or less direct and avowed dependence upon phenomenology suffices to make it a tributary of the most purely traditional stream of Western philosophy, which, above and beyond its anti-Platonism, leads Husserl back to Plato. Now, one would seek in vain a concept in phenomenology which would permit the conceptualization of intensity or force. The conceptualization not only of direction but of power, not only the *in* but the *tension* of intentionality. All value is first constituted by a theoretical subject. Nothing is gained or lost except in terms of clarity and nonclarity, obviousness, presence or absence for a consciousness, coming to awareness or loss of consciousness. Diaphanousness is the supreme value; as is univocity. Hence the difficulties in thinking the genesis and pure temporality of the transcendental ego, of accounting for the successful or unsuccessful incarnation of *telos*, and the mysterious failures called crises. And when, in certain places, Husserl ceases to consider the phenomena of crisis and the failure of *telos* as "accidents of genesis," or as the *inessential (Unwesen)*, it is in order to demonstrate that forgetting is eidetically dictated, and is necessary, under the rubric of "sedimentation," for the development of truth. For the revealing and illumination of truth. But why these forces and failures of consciousness? And why the force of weakness which dissimulates in the very act by which it reveals? If this "dialectic" of force and weakness is the finitude of thought itself in its relationship to Being, it can only be articulated in the language of form, through images of shadow and light. For force is not darkness, and it is not hidden under a form for which it would serve as substance, matter, or crypt. Force cannot be conceived on the basis of an oppositional couple, that is, on the basis of the complicity between phenomenology and occultism. Nor can it be conceived, from within phenomenology, as the *fact* opposed to *meaning*.

Emancipation from this language must be attempted. But not as an *attempt* at emancipation from it, for this is impossible unless we forget *our* history. Rather, as the dream of emancipation. Nor as emancipation from it, which would be meaningless and would deprive us of the light of meaning. Rather, as resistance to it, as far as is possible. In any event, we must not abandon ourselves to this language with the abandon which today characterizes the worst exhilaration of the most nuanced structural formalism.

Criticism, if it is called upon to enter into explication and exchange with literary writing, some day will not have to wait for this resistance first to be organized into a "philosophy" which would govern some methodology of aesthetics whose principles criticism would receive. For philosophy, during its history, has been determined as the reflection of poetic inauguration. Conceived apart, it is the twilight of forces, that is, the sun-splashed morning in which images, forms, and phenomena speak; it is the morning of ideas and idols in which the relief of forces becomes repose, its depth flattened in the light as it stretches itself into horizontality. But the enterprise is hopeless if one muses on the fact that literary criticism has already been determined, knowingly or not, voluntarily or not, as the philosophy of literature. As such—that is to say, until it has purposely opened the strategic operation we spoke of above, which cannot simply be conceived under the authority of structuralism— criticism will have neither the means nor, more particularly, the motive for renouncing eurythmics, geometry, the privilege given to vision, the Apollonian ecstasy which "acts above all as a force stimulating the eye, so that it acquires the power of vision."[61] It will not be able to exceed itself to the point of embracing both force and the movement which displaces lines, nor to the point of embracing force as movement, as desire, for itself, and not as the accident or epiphany of lines. To the point of embracing it as writing.

Hence the nostalgia, the melancholy, the fallen Dionysianism of which we spoke at the outset. Are we mistaken in perceiving it beneath the praise of structural and Claudelian "monotony" which closes *Forme et signification?*

We should conclude, but the debate is interminable. The divergence, the *difference* between Dionysus and Apollo, between ardor and structure, cannot be erased in history, for it is not *in* history. It too, in an unexpected sense, is an original structure: the opening of history, historicity itself. *Difference* does not simply belong either to history or to structure. If we must say, along with Schelling, that "all is but Dionysus," we must know—and this is to write—that, like pure force, Dionysus is worked by difference. He sees and lets himself be seen. And tears out (his) eyes. For all eternity, he has had a relationship to his exterior, to visible form, to structure, as he does to his death. This is how he appears (to himself).

"Not enough forms . . . ," said Flaubert. How is he to be understood? Does he wish to celebrate the other of form? the "too many things" which exceed and resist form? In praise of Dionysus? One is certain that this is not so. Flaubert, on the contrary, is sighing, "Alas! not enough forms." A religion of the work as form. Moreover, the things for which we do not have enough forms are already phantoms of energy, "ideas" "larger than the plasticity of style." In question is a point against Leconte de Lisle, an affectionate point, for Flaubert "likes that fellow a lot."[62]

Nietzsche was not fooled: "Flaubert, a new edition of Pascal, but as an artist with this instinctive belief at heart: 'Flaubert est toujours haïssable, l'homme n'est rien, l'oeuvre est tout.'"[63]

We would have to choose then, between writing and dance.

Nietzsche recommends a dance of the pen in vain: ". . . dancing with the feet, with ideas, with words, and need I add that one must also be able to dance with the pen—that one must learn how to write?"[64] Flaubert was aware, and he was right, that writing cannot be thoroughly Dionysiac. "One can only think and write sitting down," he said. Joyous anger of Nietzsche: "Here I have got you, you nihilist! A sedentary life is the real sin against the Holy Spirit. Only those thoughts that come when you are walking have any value."[65]

But Nietzsche was certain that the writer would never be upright; that writing is first and always something over which one bends. Better still when letters are no longer figures of fire in the heavens.

Nietzsche was certain, but Zarathustra was positive: "Here do I sit and wait, old broken tables around me and also new half tables. When cometh mine hour?—The hour of my descent, of my down-going."[66] "Die Stunde meines Niederganges, Unterganges." It will be necessary to descend, to work, to bend in order to engrave and carry the new Tables to the valleys, in order to read them and have them read. Writing is the outlet as the descent of meaning outside itself within itself: metaphor-for-others-aimed-at-others-here-and-now, metaphor as the possibility of others here-and-now, metaphor as metaphysics in which Being must hide itself if the other is to appear. Excavation within the other toward the other in which the same seeks its vein and the true gold of its phenomenon. Submission in which the same can always lose (itself). *Nieder-*

gang, Untergang. But the same is nothing, is not (it)self before taking the risk of losing (itself). For the fraternal other is not first in the peace of what is called intersubjectivity, but in the work and the peril of inter-rogation; the other is not certain within the peace of the *response* in which two affirmations *espouse each other,* but is called up in the night by the excavating work of interrogation. Writing is the moment of this original Valley of the other within Being. The moment of depth as decay. Incidence and insistence of inscription.

"Behold, here is a new table; but where are my brethren who will carry it with me to the valley and into hearts of flesh?"[67]

NOTES

Translator's interpolations in author's notes are enclosed in brackets.

1. In *L'Univers imaginaire de Mallarmé* (Paris: Editions du Seuil, 1961, p. 30, n. 27), Jean-Pierre Richard writes: "We would be content if our work could provide some new materials for a future history of imagination and affectivity; this history, not yet written for the nineteenth century, would probably be an extension of the works of Jean Rousset on the baroque, Paul Hazard on the eighteenth century, André Monglond on preromanticism."

2. In his *Anthropology* (New York: Harcourt, Brace and World, 1948, p. 325) A. L. Kroeber notes: "'Structure' appears to be just a yielding to a word that has a perfectly good meaning but suddenly becomes fashionably attractive for a decade or so—like 'streamlining'—and during its vogue tends to be applied indiscriminately because of the pleasurable connotations of its sound."

To grasp the profound necessity hidden beneath the incontestable phenomenon of fashion, it is first necessary to operate negatively: the choice of a word is first an ensemble—a structural ensemble, of course—of exclusions. To know why one says "structure" is to know why one no longer wishes to say *eidos,* "essence," form, *Gestalt,* "ensemble," "composition," "complex," "construction," "correlation," "totality," "Idea," "organism," "state," "system," etc. One must understand not only why each of these words showed itself to be insufficient but also why the notion of structure continues to borrow some implicit signification from them and to be inhabited by them.

3. TN. The most consistently difficult sections of Derrida's texts are his "prefatory" remarks, for reasons that he has explained in "Hors-livre," the preface to *La Dissémination* (Paris: Seuil, 1972). The question hinges upon the classical difference between a philosophical text and its preface, the preface usually being a recapitulation of the truth presented by the text. Since Derrida challenges the notion that a *text* can *present* a *truth,* his prefaces—in which this challenge is anticipated—must especially mark that which makes a text explode the classical ideas of truth and presence. And they must do so without letting the preface anticipate this "conclusion" as a single, clear, luminous truth. Thus the *complication* of these prefaces. One way of complicating a preface is to leave as a knot that which will later become several strands. Here, the relationship between history, somnambulism, the "question" and the difference between almost-everything and almost-nothing is not explained, for the unraveling of this question touches at least on the topics of the relationship between history and philosophy (cf. below, "Violence and Metaphysics"), and the relation of both of these, as

writing or texts, to Freud's analysis of the "text of somnambulism," i.e., *The Interpretation of Dreams* (cf. below, "Freud and the Scene of Writing").

4. On the theme of the *separation* of the writer, cf. particularly chapter 3 of Jean Rousset's introduction of his *Forme et signification*. Delacroix, Diderot, Balzac, Baudelaire, Mallarmé, Proust, Valéry, Henry James, T. S. Eliot, Virginia Woolf are called upon to bear witness to the fact that separation is diametrically opposed to critical impotency. By insisting upon this separation between the critical act and creative force, we are only designating the most banally essential—others might say, structural—necessity attached to these two actions and moments. Impotence, here, is a property not of the critic but of criticism. The two are sometimes confused. Flaubert does not deny himself this confusion. This is brought to light in the admirable collection of letters edited by Geneviève Bollème and entitled *Préface à la vie d'écrivain* (Paris: Seuil, 1963). Attentive to the fact that the critic takes his material from the work rather than bringing anything to it, Flaubert writes: "One writes criticism when one cannot create art, just as one becomes a spy when one cannot be a soldier. . . . Plautus would have laughed at Aristotle had he known him! Corneille resisted him all he could! Voltaire himself was belittled by Boileau! We would have been spared much evil in modern drama without Schlegel. And when the translation of Hegel is finished, Lord knows where we will end up!" (Bollème, p. 42). The translation of Hegel hasn't been finished, thank the Lord, thus explaining Proust, Joyce, Faulkner and several others. The difference between Mallarmé and these authors is perhaps the reading of Hegel. Or that Mallarmé chose, at least, to approach Hegel. In any event, genius still has some respite, and translations can be left unread. But Flaubert was right to fear Hegel: "One may well hope that art will continue to advance and perfect itself, but its form has ceased to be the highest need of the spirit. In all these relationships art is and remains for us, on the side of its highest vocation, something past" ("Vorlesungen über die Aesthetik," in Martin Heidegger: *Poetry, Language, Thought,* trans. Albert Hofstadter [New York: Harper and Row, 1971]). The citation continues: "It [art] has lost, for us, its truth and its life. It invites us to a philosophical reflection which does not insure it any renewal, but rigorously recognizes its essence."

5. Richard, *L'Univers imaginaire de Mallarmé*, p. 14.

6. Cf. Gérard Genette, "Une Poétique structurale," *Tel Quel,* no. 7, Autumn 1961, p. 13.

7. Cf. Jean Rousset, *La Littérature de l'âge baroque en France,* vol. 1: *Circe et le paon* (Paris: José Corti, 1954). In particular, the following passage à propos of a German example, can be read: "Hell is a world in pieces, a pillage that the poem imitates closely through its disordered shouts, bristling with scattered tortures in a torrent of exclamations. The sentence is reduced to its disordered elements, the framework of the sonnet is broken: the lines are too short or too long, the quatrains unbalanced; the poem bursts" (ibid., p. 194).

8. TN. The play is on the etymology of the word *critic,* which comes from the Greek verb *krinein,* meaning both "to separate, to cut into" and "to discern, to judge."

9. Jean Rousset, *Forme et signification: Essais sur les structures littéraires de Corneille à Claudel* (Paris: José Corti, 1962).

10. After citing (ibid., p. vii) this passage of Picon: "Before modern art, the work seems to be the expression of a previous experience . . . , the work says what has been conceived or seen; so much so that from the experience to the work there is only the transition to the techniques of execution. For modern art the work is not expression but creation: it makes visible what was not visible before it, it forms instead of reflecting." Rousset makes this idea more specific with this distinction: "An important difference

and, in our eyes, an important conquest of modern art, *or rather of the consciousness of the creative process achieved by this art . . .* " (my italics; according to Rousset, we are becoming conscious *today* of the *creative process in general*). For Picon, the mutation affects art and not only the modern consciousness of art. He wrote elsewhere: "The history of modern poetry is entirely that of the substitution of a language of creation for a language of expression. . . . Language must now produce the world that it can no longer express" (*Introduction à une esthétique de la littérature,* vol. 1: *L'Écrivain et son ombre* [Paris: Gallimard, 1953], p. 195).

11. *Critique of Pure Reason,* translated by Norman Kemp Smith (London: Macmillan and Co., 1929). The texts of Kant to which we will refer—and numerous other texts which we will call upon later—are not utilized by Rousset. It will be our rule to refer directly to the page numbers of *Forme et signification* each time that a citation presented by Rousset is in question.

12. Ibid.

13. *The Critique of Judgment,* trans. James Creed Meridith (London: Oxford University Press, 1952), p. 212.

14. Ibid., p. 176.

15. Ibid., p. 88.

16. Ibid., p. 43.

17. *Critique of Pure Reason.*

18. TN. On the nonmetaphoricity of the verb *to be* and the philosophical implications of tracing a word's genealogy through its etymology, cf. "Violence and Metaphysics," III, 1, B, and "Of Ontological Violence." In question is the notion of metaphor, which implies the transfer of the name of a thing to another thing with a different name. In a sense, any application of a name to a thing is always metaphorical, and for many philosophies (e.g., those of Rousseau and Condillac) metaphor is the origin of language. The question, then, is whether there is an *origin* of metaphor, an absolutely nonmetaphorical concept, as, for example, the verb *to be,* or the notion of breathing, for which Nietzsche says the notion of Being is a metaphor (in *Greek Philosophy during the Tragic Age*). If it could be shown that there is no absolute origin of metaphor, the separation or space implied in metaphor as transfer would become problematical, as it would then be nonreducible.

19. TN. The reference is to Descartes, for whom everything perceived clearly and distinctly had to be something understandable, could not be nothing. Cf. *Meditations.*

20. Cited by Maurice Blanchot in *L'Arche,* nos. 27–28 (August–September, 1948), p. 133. Is not the same situation described in *L'Introduction à la méthode de Léonard de Vinci?*

21. Is it not constituted by this requirement? Is it not a kind of privileged representation of inscription?

22. TN. The play is on the etymology of *anguish,* from the Latin *angustia,* meaning narrowness or distress.

23. Also, the anguish of a breath that cuts itself off in order to reenter itself, to aspirate itself and return to its original source. Because to speak is to know that thought *must* become alien to itself in order to be pronounced and to appear. It wishes, then, to take itself back by offering itself. This is why one senses the gesture of withdrawal, of retaking possession of the exhaled word, beneath the language of the authentic writer, the writer who wishes to maintain the greatest proximity to the origin of his act. This too is inspiration. One can say of original language what Feuerbach says of philosophical language: "Philosophy emerges from mouth or pen only in order to return immediately to its proper *source;* it does not speak for the pleasure of speaking—whence its

antipathy for fine phrases—but in order not to speak, in order *to think*. . . . To demonstrate is simply to show that what I *say* is *true;* simply to grasp once more the alienation (*Entäusserung*) of thought at the *original source* of thought. Thus the signification of the demonstration cannot be conceived without reference to the signification of language. Language is nothing other than the *realization of the species,* the mediation between the I and the thou which is to represent the unity of the species by means of the suppression *(Aufhebung)* of their individual isolation. This is why the element of speech is air, the most spiritual and most universal vital medium" (*Zur Kritik der Hegelschen Philosophie*, 1839, in L. Feuerbach, *Sämtliche Werke*, vol. 2 [Stuttgart–Bad Canstatt, 1959], pp. 169–70).

But did Feuerbach muse upon the fact that *vaporized* language forgets itself? That air is not the element in which history develops if it does not rest (itself) on earth? Heavy, serious, solid earth. The earth that is worked upon, scratched, written upon. The no less universal element in which meaning is engraved so that it will last.

Hegel would be of more assistance here. For even though he too, in a spiritual metaphorization of natural elements, thinks that "air is the unchanging factor, purely universal and transparent; water, the reality that is forever being resolved and given up; fire, their animating unity," he nevertheless posits that "earth is the tightly compact knot of this articulated whole, the subject in which these realities *are*, where their processes take effect, that which they start from and to which they return" (*Phenomenology of the Mind,* trans. J. B. Baillie [London: George Allen & Unwin, 1931], p. 518).

The problem of the relation between writing and the earth is also that of the possibility of such a metaphorization of the elements. Of its origin and meaning.

24. TN. The Hebrew *ruah*, like the Greek *pneuma*, means both wind or breath and soul or spirit. Only in God are breath and spirit, speech and thought, absolutely identical; man can always be duplicitous, his speech can be other than his thought.

25. G. W. Leibniz, *Theodicy: Essays on the Goodness of God, the Freedom of Man, and the Origin of Evil,* trans. E. M. Huggard (New Haven: Yale University Press, 1952), pp. 370–72. [At issue again is the distinction between the divine and the human, the Book and books. For Leibniz, God's thought is his action and he is not in the world; but for man, whose action is limited but whose thoughts are not, being in the world means that he must always choose between alternatives. Man's will, the power to choose between alternatives as a function of their merits, implies that he is finite, that his actions do not always equal his thought. God is infinite *because* his thought and his action are coextensive, because he is extraworldly, transcendent.—Trans.]

26. Stéphane Mallarmé, *Selected Poems, Essays and Letters,* trans. Bradford Cook (Baltimore: Johns Hopkins University Press, 1956), p. 15.

27. ". . . à illuminer ceci—que, plus ou moins, tous les livres contiennent la fusion des quelques redites complètes: même il n'en serait qu'un—au monde sa loi—bible comme la simulent les nations. La différence, d'un ouvrage à l'autre, offrant autant de leçons proposées dans un immense councours pour le texte véridique, entre les âges dits civilisés—ou lettrés." Ibid., pp. 41–42.

28. TN. The *Livre de raison* was the journal kept by the head of a family during the Middle Ages.

29. "Réflexions sur la création artistique selon Alain," *Revue de Métaphysique et de Morale,* April–June 1952, p. 171. This analysis makes evident that the *Système des beaux-arts,* written during the First World War, does more than foretell the most apparently original themes of "modern" aesthetics. Particularly through a certain anti-Platonism which does not exclude, as Canguilhem demonstrates, a profound alliance with Plato, beyond Platonism "understood without malice."

30. TN. According to Leibniz, each monad—the spiritual (nonmaterial) building blocks of the universe—is the representation of the entire universe as preordained by God. Cf. *Monadology.*

31. Maurice Merleau-Ponty, "An Unpublished Text," trans. Arleen B. Ballery, in *The Primacy of Perception,* ed. James M. Edie (Evanston: Northwestern University Press, 1964), pp. 8–9. The text was first published in the *Revue de Metaphysique et de Morale,* October–December, 1962.

32. "Problèmes actuels de la phénoménologie," in *Actes du colloque internationale de phénoménologie* (Paris, 1952), p. 97.

33. Saint John Chrysostom, *Homilies on the Gospel of Saint Matthew,* vol. 10 of the *Select Library of the Nicene and Post-Nicene Fathers of the Christian Church,* ed. Philip Schaff (Grand Rapids: William B. Eerdman, 1956), p. 1.

34. TN. In his translation of the Old Testament, Buber attempted to restore as much as possible the polysemantic structure of certain key words upon which he based his interpretations. Derrida here is attempting to examine the presuppositions of construing certain words or ideas as the source of the play of difference implied in linguistic multivalence. The idea that seems to support the next few sentences (in the text) is that if there is no source of "Being," "Being" must then be understood like a game, that is, only in function of itself. Language would then most accurately "approximate" Being when it, too, functions only in relation to itself—"poetry"—without attempting to adequate itself to any particular existent. One could then be led to speak of language as having no reference to signified meanings but rather as creating these meanings through the play of signifiers. The signifier is always that which is inscribed or written.

35. TN. Finitude: empiricity and historicity. Derrida's vocabulary here is Heideggerean—which is not to say that he is simply adopting Heidegger's ideas, but is rather gradually putting Heidegger into question. To suggest that the hidden essence of the empirical is historicity, to deal with affectivity as the index of finitude—these are all Heideggerean themes related to the problem of transcendence as discussed at length, and unreproduceably, in Heidegger's *Kant and the Question of Metaphysics,* trans. James S. Churchill (Bloomington: Indiana University Press, 1962).

36. "Brief über den 'Humanismus,'" in *Wegmarken* (Frankfurt, 1967), p. 158.

37. Rousset, *Forme et signification,* p. xviii, "For this very reason, Georges Poulet has little interest in *art,* in the work as a reality incarnated in a language and in formal structures; he suspects them of 'objectivity': the critic runs the risk of grasping them from without."

38. "Jean-Pierre Richard's analyses are so intelligent, his results so new and so convincing that one must agree with him, regarding his own questions. But in conformity with his own perspectives, he is primarily interested in the imaginary world of the poet, in the latent work, rather than in the work's morphology and style."

39. Guez de Balzac, book 8, letter 15.

40. Vaugelas, *Rem.,* vol. 2, p. 101.

41. Claude Lévi-Strauss, *Structural Anthropology,* trans. C. Jacobson and B. G. Schoepf (New York: Basic Books, 1963), p. 283.

42. G. W. Leibniz, *Discourse on Metaphysics, Correspondence with Arnauld and Monadology,* trans. George R. Montgomery (LaSalle, Ill.: Open Court Publishing Co., 1968), pp. 18–19.

43. Let us at least reproduce the synthesizing conclusion, the résumé of the essay: "An itinerary and a metamorphosis, we said after the analysis of the first and fifth acts, as concerns their symmetry and variants. We must now affix to this another essential characteristic of Corneillean drama: the movement it describes is an ascending move-

ment toward a center situated in infinity." (In this spatial schema, what happens to infinity, which is here the essential, that is, is not only the irreducible *specificity* of the "movement," but also its *qualitative* specificity?) "Its nature can be further specified. An upward movement of two rings is a helical ascent; two ascending lines separate, cross, move away from and rejoin each other in a common profile beyond the play itself . . ." (the structural meaning of the expression "beyond the play itself?") ". . . Pauline and Polyeucte meet and separate in the first act; they meet again, closer to each other and on a higher plane, in the third act, only to separate again; they climb up another level and reunite in the fifth act, the culminating phase of the ascension, from whence they jump forth in a final leap which will unite them definitively, at the supreme point of freedom and triumph, in God" (Rousset, *Forme et signification,* p. 6).

44. Leibniz, *Discourse on Metaphysics,* p. 10.

45. Ibid.

46. Cf., for example, Maurice Leenhardt, *L'Art océanien: Gens de la grande terre,* p. 99; *Do kamo,* pp. 19–21.

47. TN. I.e., of structure as a metaphor for locality, site.

48. TN. This is the question of the closure of metaphysics, for metaphysics contains every discourse that attempts to emerge from it. According to Derrida, metaphysics can only be destroyed from within, by making its own language—which is the only language we have—work against it.

49. Here are several formulations of this "permanent structure": "where is the true play? It is in the superimposing and interweaving of the two levels, in the separations and exchanges established between them, offering us the subtle pleasure of binocular viewing and double reading" (Rousset, *Forme et signification,* p. 56). "From this point of view, all of Marivaux's plays could be defined as an organism existing on two levels whose designs gradually approach until they are completely joined. The play is over when the two levels are indistinguishable, that is, when the group of heroes watched by the spectators sees itself as the spectator-characters saw them. The real resolution is not the marriage promised to us at the fall of the curtain but the encounter of heart and vision" (ibid., p. 58). "We are invited to follow the development of the play in two registers, which offer us two parallel curves that are separated, however, different in their importance, their language, and their function: the one rapidly sketched, the other fully drawn in all its complexity, the first letting us guess the direction that the second will take, the second deeply echoing the first, providing its definitive meaning. This play of interior reflections contributes to the imparting of a rigorous and supple geometry to Marivaux's play, while at the same time closely linking the two registers, even up to the movements of love" (ibid., p. 59).

50. TN. In the *Phenomenology* Hegel takes the reader on a "voyage of discovery" that Hegel himself has already made. The dialectical turning points of the *Phenomenology* are always marked by the reader's being brought to a point where he can grasp what Hegel has already grasped, the concept in question becoming true "for us," the distance between subject and object having been annihilated. Hegel defines the structure of the *Phenomenology* as circular, a return to its point of departure.

51. Cited in *Forme et signification,* p. 189. And Rousset, in fact, comments: "Not isolated, such a declaration is valid for all orders of reality. Everything obeys the law of *composition,* which is the law of the artist as it is of the Creator. For the universe is a simultaneity, by virtue of which things at a remove from each other lead a concerted existence and form a harmonic solidarity; to the metaphor that unites them corresponds, in the relations between beings, love, the link between separated souls. It is thus natural for Claudel's thought to admit that two beings severed from each other by

distance can be conjoined in their simultaneity, henceforth resonating like two notes of a chord, like Prouhèze and Rodrigue in their inextinguishable relationship."

52. Bergson, *Essai sur les données immédiates de la conscience.*

53. For the man of literary structuralism (and perhaps of structuralism in general), the letter of books—movement, infinity, lability, and instability of meaning rolled up in itself in the wrapping, the volume—has not yet replaced (but can it ever?) the letter of the flattened, established Law: the commandment on the Tables.

54. On this "identification with itself" of the Mallarméan book, cf. Jacques Scherer, *Le 'Livre' de Mallarmé,* p. 95 and leaf 94, and p. 77 and leaves 129–30.

55. We will not insist upon this type of question, banal but difficult to get around, and posing itself, moreover, at each step of Rousset's work, whether he is concerned with an author taken by himself or with an isolated work. Is there only one fundamental structure each time? How is it to be recognized and given its privilege? The criterion can be neither an empirical-statistical accumulation, nor an intuition of an essence. It is the problem of induction which presents itself to a structuralist science concerned with works, that is to say, with things whose structure is not apriorical. Is there a material a priori of the work? But the intuition of a material a priori poses formidable preliminary problems.

56. TN. This is a reference to Levinas and his attempted pacification of philosophy through the notion of the Other as face. For Derrida, philosophy, metaphysics, is irreducibly violent, practices an economy of violence. Cf. "Violence and Metaphysics."

57. TN. The reference is to Nietzsche's opposition of the Apollonian and the Dionysian (sculpture/music, individuation/unification of the many with the one, tranquility/bacchanal) in *The Birth of Tragedy*.

58. TN. This explication is to be found in the chapter of the *Phenomenology* entitled "Force and Understanding." The title of that chapter alone demonstrates its relationship to this essay.

59. TN. Cf. above, note 18.

60. TN. Derrida here is specifying several characteristics of metaphysics without demonstrating their interrelatedness. 1. "Heliocentric metaphysics" refers to the philosophical language founded on metaphors of light and dark, e.g., truth as light, error as dark, etc. 2. This language always implies a privileged position of "acoustics," i.e., a privilege accorded to a phonological, spoken model of the *presence* of truth in living, spoken discourse, and a concomitant abasement of the silent work of the "force" of differentiation. This abasement is typically revealed in the philosophical treatment of writing. 3. This system is set in motion by Platonism, whose doctrine of the *eidos* implies both points just mentioned.

61. Friedrich Nietzsche, *The Twilight of the Idols,* translated by Anthony M. Ludovici (New York: Russell and Russell, 1964), p. 67.

62. Flaubert, *Préface à la vie d'écrivain,* p. 111.

63. Friedrich Nietzsche, "Nietzsche contra Wagner," in *The Case of Wagner,* trans. Anthony M. Ludovici (New York: Russell and Russell, 1964), p. 116. [In Nietzsche's text the French is left untranslated: "Flaubert is always despicable, the man is nothing, the work everything."] It is not without interest, perhaps, to juxtapose this barb of Nietzsche's with the following passage from *Forme et signification:* "Flaubert's correspondence is precious, but in Flaubert the letter writer I cannot find Flaubert the novelist; when Gide states that he prefers the former I have the feeling that he chooses the lesser Flaubert or, at least, the Flaubert that the novelist did everything to eliminate" (Rousset, p. xx).

64. Nietzsche, *The Twilight of the Idols*, p. 59.
65. Ibid., p. 6.
66. Friedrich Nietzsche, *Thus Spake Zarathrustra,* trans. Thomas Common (New York: Russell and Russell, 1964), p. 239.
67. Ibid., p. 242, slightly modified.

Angus Fletcher
1930–

Angus Fletcher was born on June 23, 1930, in New York City. He graduated from Yale University in 1950 and then studied at the University of Grenoble for one year before returning to Yale for a master's degree (1952). He received his Ph.D. in English from Harvard in 1958.

Fletcher began his teaching career at Cornell in 1958 as an instructor in English; four years later he joined the faculty of Columbia University (1962–68), eventually becoming an associate professor. From 1968 to 1974 Fletcher was a professor of English at the State University of New York–Buffalo. Since 1974 he has been Distinguished Professor of English and Comparative Literature at Lehman College of the City University of New York.

Fletcher's first book, *Allegory: The Theory of a Symbolic Mode*, was published in 1964. *The Transcendental Masque: An Essay on Milton's* Comus appeared in 1971, and in that same year he published *The Prophetic Moment: An Essay on Spenser*. Fletcher's other books include *Positive Negation: Threshold, Sequence, and Personification in Coleridge* (1972) and *I. A. Richards and the Art of Critical Balance* (1973). Fletcher also edited and wrote the foreword to *The Literature of Fact: Selected Papers from the English Institute* (1976).

In *Allegory* Fletcher seeks to revive critical consideration of a literary mode thought to be outdated. He develops a Freudian theory of allegory as that form of symbolic action which corresponds to the psychological structures of compulsion and ambivalence. All obsessional neurotic forms of thought characterized by a daemonic need to impose rigid and exhaustive hierarchies find symbolic expression in allegories—the virtues and vices of medieval morality plays, for example, or the obsessive repetitions of religious rituals. He acknowledges that allegories often seem wooden and mechanical to modern readers, but he draws attention to their rich and subtle differentiations and rigorous organization. He argues that poetic allegory must be viewed as a species of the literature of the sublime—that mode of literature which takes as its purpose not a pleasing effect of any conventional kind, but rather a raising up of the mind to an apprehension of difficulty and strangeness beyond the merely pleasurable.

FROM

ALLEGORY

PSYCHOANALYTIC ANALOGUES: OBSESSION AND COMPULSION

Over half a century has passed since Freud laid the groundwork for a psychoanalytic theory of symbolism in his *Interpretation of Dreams*,[1] and in the meantime his methods and his orientation toward the dynamic character of symbolic behavior have radically altered our ideas about language,[2] whether in everyday life or in specialized uses such as religion or literature. There is no need to justify a tempered employment of Freudian concepts, despite the technical objections that have been raised against them by psychologists and philosophers. For whereas Freud and his successors may have failed to construct an adequate behavioral theory that can be experimentally tested, and may have failed to meet epistemological criticism from philosophy, they have not failed in their description of symbolic action. The naïve assumption would be to see in psychoanalysis a reductive sort of methodology; rather it is almost too willing to see in the dream, in the neuroses, and in the "psychopathology of everyday life" a wide range of cultural contents.[3] There is no strait-jacketing in this methodology; if anything, its fault is an opposite tendency to overcomplicate the processes by which feeling is expressed symbolically. Of the particular syndrome which I wish to emphasize, Freud said: "The wildest psychiatric fantasy could not have invented such an illness, so different, so striking, and so individual is the symptomatology."[4] He was willing to admit that in spite of the techniques of interpretation he advocated, many dreams would finally resist full interpretation, would remain too enigmatic to be understood analytically, while on the other side it might happen that an overly ingenious interpreter would read too much into a dream. Freud, and the shrewdest of his successors, were well aware of the complications of symbolic behavior. We need have no fear, either, that he was unaware of the conventional tricks and skills of literary artists; his awe of these skills knew no bounds, and was equaled only by his own skill in the art of exposition.[5]

Applications of psychoanalysis. Psychoanalytic concepts need therefore no general justification. But there is a difficulty about their use which is specific to literary criticism. They have been far too much used in a genetic way, that is, as a way of ascertaining why a given author wrote as he did, or why a given character in a fiction acts as he does. These two kinds of genetic criticism need a word of comment.

The first is a psychobiographical approach to literary history. To explain the literary behavior of a given author, the critic plays the part of a diagnostician relating literary symptoms to biographically known causes, which will usually be traumatic events of the author's childhood and adolescence. The critic may read Franz Kafka's "Letter to My Father," and from this and other such personal documents he constructs an etiology of Kafka's writing behavior. Or, by an analysis of Swift's letters and his *Journal to Stella,* the critic accounts for the obsessional scatology that pervades Swift's fictional works. Or, by a similar analysis of Ezra Pound's letters, he attempts to determine where the line of sanity is to be drawn in the *Cantos.* Freud's essays on artists are mainly of this sort, and in "The Relation of the Poet and Day-dreaming" (1908) he argued that by technical devices the poet is able to make his fantasies and daydreams public,[6] to make them pleasing for an audience to share in, to make them into adequate substitutes for real satisfactions—chiefly sexual—that would otherwise be lacking in the artist's life. Such arguments are bound to be concerned in large part with the poet's life and character and environment—a concern which we as critics may wish to reserve for the literary historian, on the ground that psychobiography is strictly speaking a nonformal, nonaesthetic concern.

The second familiar genetic criticism stemming from Freudian theory is very like the first, but is focused on the fictional worlds thus created. Ernest Jones's study of the motivations in *Hamlet* uses the theory of the Oedipus complex to account for the seeming contradictions in Hamlet's behavior.[7] Henry Murray has similarly treated Melville's *Pierre.*[8] Freud again sets the pattern for this in his essay on Dostoyevski,[9] and in essays on "The Theme of the Three Caskets,"[10] on "Those Wrecked by Success,"[11] which dealt with the revelation of character in *The Merchant of Venice* and *Macbeth.* In this as in the other case the critic attempts to find out the sources, the origins, the causes of behavior; he is only secondarily concerned with literary form, although character analysis may well move over into analysis of reversals and discoveries, and thence of dramatic form.

If, however, we are to find adequate formal criteria in psychoanalysis, we shall need especially to examine the neuroses as *patterns* of behavior. The neuroses are typical shapings of unbalanced behavior for which it is in fact possible to find cultural analogues, since each neurosis is very like a creative, positive, civilizing "symbolic action."

Psychological analogues. In *Totem and Taboo* Freud drew analogies between three kinds of neurosis and three kinds of nonneurotic activity, namely between obsessions and religious ritual, between paranoia and philosophy, between hysteria and mimetic art.[12] In the last of these—the analogue that would appear to concern us, since we are talking about art—the fundamental point of similarity was the mimetic, miming, identifying, gesturing process that was found common to both art and hysteria. The hysteric acts out his fears and desires for sexual contact, by what is called "conversion," that is, by a kind of mimetic gesturing. Other points of similarity existed, but were subordinate to this primary mimetic function. We know, however, that not all art is mimetic, and the question is therefore left open as to what may be, if any, the correct analogy to the nonmimetic arts of myth and allegory.

Psychoanalytic evidence suggested plentifully that myth had a correlate in the dream, with its extreme degrees of "condensation,"[13] "displacement,"[14] "negation,"[15] "timelessness,"[16] and character of "wish fulfillment,"[17] and psychoanalysts like Karl Abraham, Géza Róheim, and Otto Rank were quick to collect from folklore the necessary materials to bear out this analogy between dream and myth. The so-called "true symbols" of the dream (what we would call "Freudian symbols") were indeed found to be present in a wide variety of mythological vocabularies.[18] So far so good—myth has its correlate in dream. But we still have the other type of literature, the allegorical, for which to find an exploratory analogue. It will be apparent that if we hit upon the correct formula, we shall be saying something new about the form of allegories, in the broadest sense of their inner dynamics.

The analogue to allegory. Let us suppose then that the proper analogue to allegory is the *compulsive syndrome,* which Freud himself had made parallel to religious behavior.[19] One condition must be laid down: that we are not talking about the compulsive behavior of authors as men; we are talking about literary products which have this form, a form we can discern regardless of its causes, a form which for our purposes exists as a thing in itself. In each of the five areas we have mapped out—agency, imagery, action, causality, and theme—there should be some psychoanalytic clarification of the true nature of allegory.

Agency: obsessional anxiety. The typical agent in an allegorical fiction has been seen as a daemon, for whom freedom of active choice hardly exists. This appears to have a major correlate in the theory of compulsive behavior, where it is observed that the mind is suddenly obsessed by an idea over which it has no control, which as it were "possesses" the mind. The commonest experience of the compulsive neurotic is that he is suddenly disturbed by impulses that have no apparent rational meaning, and thence are seen as arbitrary and external "commands." It is this foreignness that is emphasized by psychoanalysts.

> An obsession is an idea or desire which forces itself persistently into the patient's mind in what he experiences as an irrational fashion. A compulsion is an act actually carried out, which similarly forces itself upon the patient. Obsessive ideas and compulsive acts are often closely linked: for instance, the obsession that there may be dangerous germs on one's hands leads to the compulsion of handwashing. Minor obsessions and compulsions are familiar in everyone's experience. We keep wondering whether we turned off the gas burner, or we knock on wood after mentioning our good fortune. These everyday phenomena resemble neurotic obsessions and compulsions to the extent that they are sensed as irrational. We know they are foolish, but they seem to have a little push of their own and it is easier to let them have their way. In neurotic obsessions and compulsions, this quality is greatly magnified. The ideas and acts are like foreign bodies, forcing themselves upon the patient yet experienced as no part of the self. Moreover . . . if the patient tries to stop his obsessive ruminations or his compulsive rituals, he is plunged into an attack of anxiety.[20]

This anxiety is precisely the quality of the actions performed by the daemonic character, since he is always determined to get to some goal, to reach home, to reach the Celestial City. Fear of not reaching that goal is even greater than fear of the particular terrors along the way. On the other hand, it is characteristic of allegorical plots that they preserve, on some level of literal meaning, a highly ordered sequence of events, which suggests that the anxiety does not usually break through the unbroken *surface* of compulsive fictions. The anxiety is kept in bounds by the rigid sequence of events leading to the winning of the quest.[21] The well-known stubbornness, conscientiousness, and idealism of the compulsive neurotic come through in fictional works as the undeviating, totally committed, absolutist ethics of characters like the creative thinkers in Hawthorne, the Christians of Bunyan, the Knights and Ladies of Spenser, the eternally fixed immortal souls of *The Divine Comedy*. The perfect instance of a compulsive character working in the pursuit of high cultural aims, and therefore transcending the bounds of neurosis, while still retaining the formative character type implied by the neurosis, would be Aeneas. Virgil's hero does not deviate from the destined path, and it is only natural that during the middle ages the *Aeneid* be given an allegorical reading. Aeneas is the original "Displaced person," as Eliot has said, implying his alienation from a home toward which he always gravitates, and for which he is compelled to create a substitute. As our theory will show, Aeneas also manages to avoid an accusation of hostility to his fellow man, under the guise of his preordained "destiny." The characteristic aggressions of the compulsive are here serving the "higher" ends of a cultural dream, as with later Christian heroes they serve the Christian concept of a fated Providential destiny, but this should not deter us from perceiving the latent hostility, which is only covered up by a surface appearance of gentlemanly calm, or calm gentleness of bearing. This so-called "withdrawal of affect" is a main characteristic of the neurosis, and in literature it clearly sets the systematic, unfeeling tone of allegories, where real violence is inherent in the well-ordered meaning.[22] Sometimes, to be sure, open violence appears in allegory, as in the struggles of the early *psychomachia*. The excessive violence in Spenser would be a good case, because Spenser's poem fully accepts the fact that violence, aggression, and hate are primary problems even in the Faery world.[23]

Above all, the agency suggested by the analogue with compulsion neurosis will be an agency of psychic *possession*. As if he became a daemon, the compulsive character (it is apparent we are not talking about the author here) becomes singled down to a narrow one-track function—a kind of narrowing that is both the strength and the weakness of the compulsive, since on the one hand it enables him to work hard and long at single, difficult tasks, but on the other may prevent him from discovering flexible paths, new short cuts.

Image: the idée fixe. With imagery our parallel implies much the same sort of narrowing process. It is found with obsessional behavior that the daemonic impulse to perform some irrational act is very soon displaced onto some associatively remote item of imagery. The impulse to kill a loved one is accepted into consciousness by the neurotic mind, because this irrational impulse is attached to some object which is only indirectly associated with that loved person. The typical impulse of this sort becomes frozen into an *idée fixe,* it becomes a compulsion, that is to say, we have the same process in compulsive behaviors that we have already noticed in the case of allegorical imagery: it is often a kind of frozen agency. The tendency of agents to become images, which allowed agents to represent the "cosmic" order of allegories, has in psychoanalysis an equivalent in the process of "encapsulation," or "isolation," as it is called.[24]

The antisocial impulse that plagues the patient at the same time cries out for an antidote, which it finds in a mental process by which the patient denies his own connection with that impulse. He surrounds it with symbolic barriers. If it were an impulse to dirty himself, he would set aside just one particular moment of the day when it would be all right *(noa)* to do so, and at all other times would steadfastly resist any such temptation.[25] The impulse becomes a little island of desire to which certain recurrent images will be attached, and in time those images will be an adequate substitute (by metonymy) for the impulse. This means that the compulsive syndrome employs ornament in the sense of *kosmos*, partly because the fetishistic detail that fascinates the compulsive is a gemlike talisman, bounded by very strict lines, and partly because each detail is integrated into a highly systematic order of acts, known as the "compulsive ritual."[26]

Action: compulsive rituals. Compulsive behavior is highly orderly; it is supersystematic; it is excessively scrupulous, even when no particularly unusual "ritual" is performed. Of the compulsive neurotic White says: "Orderliness may become the demon in his life, committing him to an endless task of straightening, arranging, recording, and filing."[27] The form in which this cleaning-up goes on is twofold: it can either involve *symmetrical* grouping of items or *ritualistic* grouping of items. There is likely to be one part of the day in which the neurotic expresses a whole series of aggressive, hostile acts; he may do this symbolically and not overtly. Then, in exact opposition to these aggressions, he will pass the rest of the day in "undoing" the antisocial impulses, by accumulating a series of exactly parallel equal-and-opposite "good deeds."[28] "Orderliness, rituals, cleanliness, propitiatory acts, self-imposed duties, and punishments all testify to the patient's need to counteract and set right his antisocial tendencies."[29] This psychomachia naturally displays a seesaw motion and its form is highly symmetrical.

At the same time the patient acts according to the classical symptomatic pattern of the compulsion neurosis, namely the ritual. Such a ritual would, for example, be a series of rearrangements of some precise number of objects in a room: the objects would first be given one order, then given a second order, then a third, then a fourth, and so on, until the patient felt he had gone through a ritual that was long enough, precise enough, and rigid enough to be a proper expiation for some kind of impurity. Compulsive rituals have an infinite number of kinds of materials. Almost any object, any image, any word or words, any icon will do for this purpose, since what makes something a ritual is not a particular substance, but a particular order and repetition of parts. The compulsive performs his rituals in order to allay anxiety; he counts sheep, or counts the squares on the ceiling or the posts in a fence—not once, but several times, and with each new count of the total he becomes less sure than before, because while statistically he might be said to be approaching certainty, the very fact that he has found himself recounting the total suggests *to him* that there may have been an error. Thus in these rituals there is an element of rumination, and if the form of allegories is reduced finally to a "progress" form, we must keep in mind that this progress does not truly advance. Allegory progresses with an "apparent motion," making the circular movements of the Wheel of Fortune. *Plus ça change, plus c'est la même chose.*

It follows from the ruminant character of such ritual behavior that there will always be new rituals added onto the existing sequences. This proliferation of ritual suggests what actually occurs all the time in allegory, where either the progress is turned aside in a "digression," or else there are double, triple, and quadruple plots all going at once with Gothic exuberance. The encyclopedic allegory like the *Confessio Amantis* or the *Passetyme of Pleasure*[30] has a certain economy, it is true, but it is an economy of riches, where no limit beyond sheer endurance is ever invoked by the poet. The classic criterion of brevity has no place here, except as an arbitrary imposition as in a poem like "The Phoenix and the Turtle," or "The Dialogue of Self and Soul" of Marvell, where one feels a definite constraint and a search for the most desiccated form possible. This form is a naming of parts, since compulsive rumination seeks the stability of feeling that is conferred by the verbal spell itself.

Causality: magical practices. In *Totem* and *Taboo* Freud pointed out that obsessional behavior required the use of contagious magic, since it is by a contagion from one sign to the next that the ritual acquires its efficacy. The *magic of names*,[31] which more than any other linguistic phenomenon dominates the allegorical work, is likewise an essential ingredient in the neurosis. Names are felt to be adequate substitutes for things, even better than adequate since it is easier to manipulate names than things. Rather than accumulate a large number of objects associated with the person one wished to curse or bless, one could more readily find names that might be applied to him—the Catholic custom of giving a number of Christian names to the child is a nonprimitive instance of "verbal icons." In allegory we have numerous instances of "number symbolism,"[32] which is perhaps the purest form ever taken by the magic of names, but the belief that icons of any kind can have the "power of the word" is no doubt at the base of the naturalistic type of allegorical fiction. Such fiction builds a whole world out of documentary detail, which at first appears intended solely to inform the reader, but which on second view appears intended to control the reader.

> The creation of this replica of the real world makes it possible to calculate and act out in advance in this "model world" before real action is taken.... Words and worded concepts are shadows of things, constructed for the purpose of bringing order through trial action into the chaos of real things. The macrocosm of real things outside is reflected in the microcosm of thing-representatives inside. The thing-representatives have the characteristics of the things, but lack the

character of "seriousness" which the things have; and they are "possessions"; that is, they are mastered by the ego; they are an attempt to endow the things with "ego quality" for the purpose of achieving mastery over them. He who knows a word for a thing, masters the thing. This is the core of the "magic of names," which plays such an important part in magic in general. It is represented in the old fairy tale of Rumpelstilzchen, in which the demon loses his power once his name is known.[33]

I have insisted that virtue, the positive ideal of moral allegory, needs to be given its original sense of "power," and moral fables need then to be reinterpreted as having chiefly to do with polarities of strength and weakness, confidence and fear, certainty and doubt, rather than with some ideal constellation of Christian graces and fallen states.

The highly ordered sequence of events in the typical fable likewise has at first a deceptive, seemingly scientific order. Yet, as Fenichel observes, "Compulsive systematizing, performed not for the purpose of mastering reality, but rather in order to deny certain aspects of it, falsifying reality, is a caricature of science." This is precisely the caricature that Swift deliberately employed in the third book of *Gulliver's Travels,* and which occurs with somewhat less irony in some of the less sophisticated science fiction of today, where an elaborate jargon of technical performance lards the text of otherwise bald romances. This presumably might be the pseudo science of Fletcher's *The Purple Island,* where quaint learning takes the place of the kind of speculation and real anatomical work being in fact done in the very same period by William Harvey. Harvey, like Phineas Fletcher, somehow believes in the old imagery likening the state to a human body, but he keeps this belief for his dedication to the king, and thus keeps his text free for science and empirical observation, for "the purpose of mastering reality." On the contrary a Phineas Fletcher is not so much trying to pass on sound knowledge as to fix knowledge in compartments that will not change, that will become fixed images instead of testable hypothetical constructs. It is natural for such a poet to flee "from the macrocosm of things to the microcosm of words." Nothing is more remarkable than the iconographic complexity of some allegorical systems, yet this ingenuity can be accounted for in terms of a belief that runs concurrent with the magic of names, the so-called "omnipotence of words," which is explained as a sort of superabstract withdrawal into a verbal universe.

> Compulsive thinking is not only abstract, it is also *general,* directed toward systematization and categorization; it is theoretical instead of real. The patients are interested in maps and illustrations rather than in countries and things. . . . The overvaluation of intellect often makes compulsion neurotics develop their intellect very highly. However, the high intelligence shows archaic features and is full of magic and superstition. Their ego shows a cleavage, one part being logical, another magical. The defensive mechanism of isolation makes the maintenance of such a cleavage possible.[34]

Nowhere is this mixture of logic and superstition clearer than in the allegorical use of oracles, which is often accompanied by the creation of a "double" who can foresee the future (thus the magical mirror of a Merlin). And this oracular mentality also characterizes the compulsive.

> Patients consult oracles, make bets with God, fear the magical effect of the words of others, act as if they believe in ghosts, demons, and especially in a very malicious sage, and yet otherwise are intelligent persons, completely aware of the absurdity of these ideas.[35]

Psychoanalysis takes a skeptical attitude toward this absurdity, but it must be understood that the main stream of religious allegory is, from the analyst's point of view, closely akin to a mentally dangerous belief in oracles. The main stream is prophetic. Scriptural exegesis interprets Holy Writ in historical terms, as being capable of foretelling the future and explaining the past and present, by assuming that the prophets were divinely inspired through voices from God or his angels. The method absolutely requires a belief in daemonic agency and inspiration. The psychoanalyst therefore differs from the exegete in the values he places upon the truth of oracular messages and occult signs. The findings of the psychoanalyst are borne out further by the uses to which oracles are put in the poetry of the ancient world, where they authorize given lines of conduct.

> Consulting an oracle, in principle, means either forcing permission or forgiveness for something ordinarily prohibited or an attempt to shift the responsibility for the things about which one feels guilty onto God. The oracle is asked for a divine permission, which may act as a counterweight against conscience.[36]

This counterweighting of conscience implies the strong temptations that characterize the compulsive moral life. The compulsive personality is both attracted and repelled at once by the objects of desire.

Theme: ambivalence in "antithetical primal words." Psychoanalysts seem to agree that at the heart of the compulsion neurosis there is a high degree of ambivalence, which in turn is bound to accompany any extreme development of the superego, or conscience. The ritual of atonement arises out of the need to break the bonds of the ambivalence. Stekel's "bipolarity of thinking," which would in older parlance have been called "moral dualism," though the latter implies too conscious a process, is of course endlessly complicated by the merging of the polar opposites. This merging would appear to be a logical impossibility. But psychologically it is quite possible, and proceeds by the means of displacement and "negation," by which is meant that in the unconscious and generally in neurotic behavior anything can come to mean its opposite. As with "antithetical primal words" like the Latin *altus,* which means both *high* and *deep,* an image in a compulsive ritual can hold two contrary significances.[37]

Such double meanings are essential to any tabooed object, which will always mean both the most desirable (holy) and repulsive (dreadful) thing the mind can conceive. The best case of this in psychoanalytic findings will be probably the ambivalent valuation of *money*. It is found that money is both the finest and richest object on the one hand, and the dirtiest, lowest object on the other. (This is institutionalized in Christian teachings about the virtue of poverty, teachings which are couched in ambiguous language, since the good Christian is exhorted to lay up "riches" in heaven, if not on earth.) This kind of ambivalence appears clearly in Orwell's novel, *Keep the Aspidistra Flying*.

> The money-stink, everywhere the money-stink. He stole a glance at the Nancy [*sic*]. . . . The skin at the back of his neck was as silky-smooth as the inside of a shell. You can't have a skin like that under five hundred a year. A sort of charm he had, a glamour, like all moneyed people. Money and charm; who shall separate them?[38]

The money is contaminated, as befits a tabooed object, and while it is richly desirable, it is also deadly to the touch, with a sort of poisonous magical "charm."

This double cathexis has been reduced at times to its better-known form, moral dualism, and there it seems easier to relate to the traditions of allegorical literature. In treating compulsive neurotics, the psychoanalyst is concerned chiefly with the therapeutic transference of a dangerous authoritarianism.[39] The therapy must destroy the hold of some authoritarian figure, since this particular neurosis has its source in the period of strictest parental disciplining, the toilet-training period, when the child is first learning to control his own excretory processes, and thence (by generalization) to control himself in all areas where parental authority has set a standard of behavior.[40] The "authoritarian personality," so-called, which closely parallels the compulsive personality, has simply (or not so simply) achieved an "automatization of conscience." When trying to account for the large number of automatized, robotlike characters of moral fable we should examine the degree to which, therefore, there is inherent in their actions some fixed image of conflicting emotions, since the parental figure and the parental command are bound to elicit such emotions. Part II of *Faust* is a major allegorical expression of the mixed attitude toward the Mother.[41] The noticeably less mimetic quality of this second part seems to result from the need to give a more rigid organization to the analysis of the problem of authority; whereas the first part in fact could concern itself with the power of love, Goethe's sequel is concerned with the love of power.

We can finally ascribe the analytic character of major allegory to the generalized effects of ambivalence of emotion.

> Moral conflict, if radical and stubborn, results in a division, an inflexible dualism, in all branches of feeling and thought, which so influences the sufferer's apperceptions, that every significant object becomes ambivalent to him, that is, it both attracts and repels him, being composed, as he sees it, of two contrary elements, one good and one evil, which cannot be reconciled or blended. He discovers in due

time a radical defect in every person who has appealed to him and begins hating what he has loved, though unconsciously he continues loving the object of his hate. Thus no whole-hearted embracement of anyone is possible, and the constructive tendency toward synthesis and integration is perpetually obstructed.[42]

In conclusion, it is apparent that psychoanalytic theory has brought us to our final point about *theme*, that allegory always demonstrates a degree of inner conflict, which we call "ambivalence." Psychoanalysis has also described the other major characteristics already stressed: the daemonic agency (the compulsive believes in daemonic possession); the cosmic imagery (he believes that metonymic signs "contain" or "encapsulate" his large-scale problems); the magical causality (he believes in contagious magic, in the "magic of names," and in oracular destiny); the ritualized action (he performs compulsive rituals, in either arcane or mundane forms); and finally the ambivalent thematic structure (he is constantly ruminating about his own desires, suffering extreme temptation). When we say that the compulsive "believes" in these various illusions, we are implying that he *acts* according to his beliefs, so that his behavior can be studied as a pattern in itself. No biographical information is required to see that a man is a cripple, if you watch him walk; similarly, no such information is required to show that a given action is compulsively ordered. The analyst simply has to inspect the rhythm of the action. Thus it is with literary criticism. No psychobiography of authors is required, though it can become a useful control, when the works they create correspond to known patterns. Only the pattern itself needs to be considered in this rather idealized criticism. If one wanted to go further and write psychobiography, one could, but the personal history of the author's life and character is not a requisite of a psychoanalytic criticism, however interesting it may be on its own merits, as long as that criticism remains focused on the formal properties of works.

The use of the analogy. Looking back over the points of analogy between the compulsive syndrome and allegorical literature, we discern a number of similarities, of both form and content. But it may be asked, what is the use of the analogy? We can answer that such comparisons refer allegory, as a mode of communication, back to some kind of essential behavior, which we find in the skeletal structure of the compulsive ritual. Further, while compulsive behavior is often a form of physical human action (the rite consists of actual body movements, for example), it is even more profoundly a form of "symbolic action," and therefore can be properly compared to the "symbolic action" known as allegory. It becomes possible to predict what is going to happen in allegories. With our analogy in hand we learn to look afresh at the mode. In both cases, therefore, we find an authoritarian sort of behavior, rigid, anxious, fatalistic; the hero of an allegorical epic will be presented to us doing things the way a compulsive person does things, regularly, meticulously, blindly. In both cases there is great play for magical influence, psychic possession, taboo restrictions. In both cases we shall expect events to be isolated from each other into highly episodic forms, thereby "encapsulating" particular moments of contagion and beatitude. The compulsive pattern of behavior often shows a use of oracular omens, which are felt to be binding, and this provides the overall sublime pattern for a prophetic literature, where the hero is compelled ever onward and is held on his path by these predestinating omens and oracles. In both cases we meet a language of taboo, of "antithetical primal words," in which the single term contains diametrically opposed meanings, allowing for paradoxes and ironies at the heart of allegories. The presence of paradox is not always apparent, and inexpert authors may be unaware of its availability. But the great allegories show no lack of irony. The paradoxes of taboo combine with the other major traits of compulsive behavior to give allegory a function in the rendering of a large part of our psychic life. As such it is bound to have widespread interest, and partly conscious understanding, even among readers who are not schooled in the particular niceties of iconography. We are, after all, all of us compulsive in some way or other.

NOTES

1. Sigmund Freud, *The Interpretation of Dreams*, tr. James Strachey (2d print., New York, 1956). This supplants the old Brill edition (Modern Library ed.). On allegorical interpretation of dreams see 96–100, and 524 on Silberer's notion of "anagogic interpretation."

2. On the notion of a "dynamic" psychology, see Freud, *Interpretation,* chs. vi and vii; "Formulations regarding the Two Principles in Mental Functioning," *Collected Papers*, IV, ed. Joan Riviere (London, 1950); also the article "Repression" in the same volume. A review article by Sandor Rado, "Psychodynamics as a Basic Science," is in his *Psychoanalysis of Behavior: Collected Papers* (New York, 1956). The most illuminating collection of essays in this field is, I believe, David Rapaport's *Organization and Pathology of Thought* (New York, 1951). Rapaport includes two selections of papers on "Symbolism" and "Fantasy-thinking."

3. Freud, *The Psychopathology of Everyday Life* (1901) (Standard ed., London, 1953–1962), VI, or in *Basic Writings of Sigmund Freud,* ed. A. A. Brill (New York, 1938).

4. Quoted by Wilhelm Stekel, *Compulsion and Doubt,* tr. Emil A. Gutheil (New York, 1949), Introduction, I.

5. See Ernest Jones, *The Life and Work of Sigmund Freud* (New York, 1957), III, ch. xv, "Art," ch. xvi, "Literature." Also, Ludwig Marcuse, "Freuds Aesthetik," *PMLA*, LXXII (June 1957), 446–463. Relevant essays by Freud have been collected in *On Creativity and the Unconscious,* ed. Benjamin Nelson (New York, 1958).

6. *Collected Papers,* IV, 182–192.

7. Ernest Jones, *Hamlet and Oedipus* (Anchor ed., New York, 1955).

8. See the Introduction to Melville's *Pierre* (New York, 1949).

9. Freud, "Dostoevsky and Parricide" (1928), *Collected Papers,* V, 222–242.

10. Freud, "The Theme of the Three Caskets" (1913), *Collected Papers,* IV, 244–256. This essay observes and analyzes the parallel between the choice of caskets and the choice Lear makes between his three daughters.

11. Freud, "Those Wrecked by Success," *Collected Papers,* IV, 323–341. This forms part of a longer essay entitled "Some Character-Types Met with in Psychoanalytic Work" (1915). The earlier part of this essay deals with Shakespeare's *Richard III*.

12. "In one way the neuroses show a striking and far-reaching correspondence with the great social productions of art, religion and philosophy, while again they seem like distortions of them. We may say that hysteria is a caricature of an artistic creation, a compulsion neurosis, a caricature of a religion, and a paranoiac delusion, a caricature of a philosophic system. In the last analysis this deviation goes back to the fact that the neuroses are asocial formations; they seek to accomplish by private means what arose in society through collective labour. . . . Genetically the asocial nature of the neurosis springs from its original tendency to flee from a dissatisfying reality to a more pleasureable world of phantasy. This real world which neurotics shun is dominated by the society of human beings and by the institutions created by them; the estrangement from reality is at the same time a withdrawal from human companionship" (Freud, *Totem and Taboo,* in *Basic Writings,* 863–864).

The collocation of art and hysteria will be less surprising if one makes one or two prior conditions: (1) Freud was aware of the fact that "psychological" novels split up their characters into separate daemons, but he did not pursue this line of thought ("Relation of the Poet to Day-dreaming," in *Collected Papers,* IV). Instead Freud saw art clustered around the mimetic center, a center to which our art traditionally comes back, after flights into mannerism of either the mythopoeic or the allegorical kind. (2) Hysteria must be understood in its *outgoing,* extroverted character: the hysteric, in normal conditions, is a markedly outgoing person, who seeks intimate contact—one might say, erotic contact—with others. It is this impulse to come into intimate knowledge and contact which characterizes the mimetic mode also, the mode which Freud equated with "art." The chief ground for making art the analogue of hysteria is therefore the common fact of *identification*. To make his dramas and fictions the poet "identifies" with other real or imaginary people, imitating their actions and passions. In hysteria identification "enables patients to express in their symptoms not only their own experiences but those of a large number of other people; it enables them, as it were, to suffer on behalf of a whole crowd of people and to act all the parts in a play single-handed. I shall be told that this is not more than the familiar hysterical imitation, the capacity of hysterics to imitate any symptoms in other people that have struck their attention—sympathy, as it were, intensified to the point of reproduction. . . . Identification is not simple imitation but *assimilation* on the basis of a similar aetiological pretension; it expresses a resemblance and is derived from a common element which remains in the unconscious" (*The Interpretation of Dreams,* 149–150).

As to Freud's equation (through parody) of compulsion and religion, there is nothing to prevent us from saying that allegory is the most religious of the modes, obeying, as it does, the commands of the Superego, believing in Sin, portraying atonements through ritual. That it can also be philosophical only speaks for the proximity of paranoia and compulsion.

13. Cf. Freud, *Interpretation,* 279–305.

14. Cf. Freud, *Interpretation,* 305–310. Northrop Frye, *Anatomy of Criticism* (Princeton, 1957), 188: "In literary criticism the myth is normally the metaphorical key to the displacement of romance." "The central principle of displacement is that what can be metaphorically identified in a myth can only be linked in romance by some form of simile: analogy, significant association, incidental accompanying imagery, and the like. In a myth we can have a sun-god or a tree-god; in a romance we may have a person

who is significantly associated with the sun or trees. In more realistic modes the association becomes less significant and more a matter of incidental, even coincidental or accidental, imagery" (*Anatomy*, 137). This notion of displacement follows from the original Freudian idea that by symbolic changes of referent one makes a dangerous, antisocial, or vicious thought acceptable.

15. Cf. Freud, *Interpretation*, 310–339. Also Freud, *Collected Papers*, IV, 184–191. See also, Freud's article, "Negation" (1925), in the *Collected Papers*, V, 181–183. "Affirmation, as being a substitute for union, belongs to Eros; while negation, the derivative of expulsion, belongs to the instinct of destruction" (185). Frye calls *negation* "demonic modulation" (*Anatomy*, 156–157). Its clearest examples are to be found in Gnosticism, on which see, specifically, Hans Jonas, *The Gnostic Religion* (Boston, 1958), ch. iii, "Gnostic Imagery and Symbolic Language," 48–100.

Denis de Rougemont, in *Love in the Western World*, tr. Montgomery Belgion (New York, 1957), 162, gives a list of negations current in the rhetoric of courtly love, where the ambivalence of feeling issues in the classic formulations: "To die of not being able to die," "The struggle of love in which it is needful to be defeated," "Love's dart that wounds but does not kill," "The sweet cautery," etc. In a way Freud's term "negation" names the process by which, unconsciously, the mind selects terms to express its ambivalence. Extreme dualism must cause symbolic antiphrases. One gets the impression sometimes that the most powerful satirists are dualists, users of "negation," to the point that they become naïve gnostics. They, like Gnostics, hover on an edge of extreme asceticism which can drop off absolutely into an extreme libertinism. See Jonas, also Johan Huizinga, *The Waning of the Middle Ages*, tr. F. Hopman (New York, 1954), 109. Huizinga's conception of the waning is that it mingled the extremes of brutality and moral chaos on the one hand, and ornamental refinement and rigid cosmology on the other.

16. Freud, "The Unconscious," in *Collected Papers*, IV, 119. See also, on the timelessness of mythical thought, Mircea Eliade, *The Myth of the Eternal Return*, tr. W. R. Trask (New York, 1954). Eliade studies in detail the way in which "archaic man tolerates 'history' with difficulty, and attempts periodically to abolish it." That would be, in Freud's terms, a regression to the time scheme of the dream. Eliade maintains that in order for primitive man to remain in this "paradise of archetypes" (his timeless world), he must periodically get rid of his sense of "sin," and thus he creates rituals of exorcism. These rituals are the compulsive technique by which the sense of guilt is kept out of consciousness, or else reduced in psychic intensity. Cf. Benjamin Lee Whorf, "Time, Space and Language," in *Culture in Crisis: A Study of the Hopi Indians*, ed. Laura Thompson (New York, 1950), 152 ff.

17. Cf. Freud, *Interpretation*, ch. iii, and ch. vii, sec. C, for a more technical account of wish fulfillment. Also, "Formulations regarding the Two Principles," *Collected Papers*, IV.

18. See Géza Róheim, *The Eternal Ones of the Dream* (New York, 1945), 248: "The laws that govern the use of symbols for the purpose of allegory are one of the future tasks of psychoanalytic anthropology. Perhaps my meaning is not quite clear. When I say a symbol, I mean a symbol with an unconscious content (a 'mythical' symbol); in this case, the water-rainbow-snake as representing the combined parent concept. *By allegory I mean something the natives have no reason to repress*, such as the snake representing rain, clouds, water. The use of symbols as allegories is thus an indicator of man's unconscious in relation to environment. The first aim attained is therefore to project an internal strain, but the second function is to minimize environmental dangers by equating them with infantile situations, with dangers that were

dangers only in the past." See also Otto Rank, *Art and Artist* (New York, 1932), "Myth and Metaphor," 207–235; *The Myth of the Birth of the Hero and Other Writings*, ed. Philip Freund (New York, 1959) (this edition includes chapters from *Art and Artist*).

Ernest Jones, for example, in his essay, "The Theory of Symbolism" (1916), *British Journal of Psychology*, IX (1918), 181. (Cassirer resisted the cross-over between psychoanalysis and the theory of myth.) See Karl Abraham, *Traum und Mythus* (Vienna, 1909). Jung and his followers have inspired innumerable mythic interpretations of literary works, e.g., Maud Bodkin's *Archetypal Patterns in Poetry*, not to mention some of Frye's most important work. For a general, and typical, account of myth, see Austin Warren and René Wellek, *Theory of Literature* (New York, 1949), 195 ff. "Myth" has come to mean many things, sometimes implying fixed rituals, sometimes fluid dream images, sometimes implying a story, sometimes implying the breakdown of story. Its classic, and primary Greek sense is "a fable," "a story," "a legend." Frye uses it in a somewhat special way in his article, "Myth as Information," *Hudson Review*, Summer, 1954: "The formal principle is a conceptual myth, a structure of ambiguous and emotionally charged ideas or sense data. Myths in this sense are readily translatable. They are, in fact, the communicable ideogrammatic structures of literature" (234–235). Here "myth" equals Aristotle's *dianoia* and strongly suggests an allegorical framework or, better, a *cosmic* framework. The term is protean, whatever else we say of it.

19. The major Freudian document on obsession-compulsion is the "Notes on a Case of Obsessional Neurosis," *Collected Papers*, III. See his later *The Problem of Anxiety* (1926) (Standard ed., XX). The work of Karl Abraham is important for the relation between melancholia and obsessive behavior. Stekel's two-volume *Compulsion and Doubt* contains a wide variety of case studies, reported in detail. From it one can gain a picture of the breadth of the problem of compulsion. For a general treatment in summary form, see Bertram D. Lewin, "Obsessional Neuroses," in *Psychoanalysis Today*, ed. Sandor Lorand (London, 1948). Professor J. W. Beach's *Obsessive Images*, published posthumously, is a discerning account of a number of key images that recur in modern literature, Beach argued, with the frequency of obsessions.

20. R. W. White, *The Abnormal Personality* (New York, 1948), 291. White gives a good summary of the syndrome. For an extended account see Otto Fenichel, *The Psychoanalytic Theory of the Neuroses* (New York, 1945), ch. xiv, "Obsession and Compulsion."

21. Cf. Fenichel, *Psychoanalytic Theory*, 284.

22. Ibid., 304. This defensive behavior has been characterized as an "armoring" of the body, when it makes the muscles tense and rigid. See Wilhelm Reich, *Character Analysis* (New York, 1961), 39–77, 158–179.

23. See White, *Abnormal Personality*, 293: "The patient knows that his obsessions and compulsions are inside him; he does not use projection and attribute them to external forces. Yet they feel to him like foreign bodies, not part of the tissue of the self. They intrude themselves from unknown parts of his mind."

24. See Freud, "A Case of Obsessional Neurosis," 377–378. Fenichel, *Psychoanalytic Theory*, 288: "Thinking in compulsive categories represents a caricature of logical thinking: logical thinking too, is based on a kind of isolation. But the logical isolation serves the purpose of objectivity, the compulsive isolation that of defense. . . . Isolation, it has been mentioned, is related to the ancient taboo of touching. Numerous compulsive systems regulate the modes in which objects should be or must not be touched. . . . 'Clean' things must not communicate with 'dirty' ones . . . Isolation frequently separates constituents of a whole from one another, where the noncompulsive person would only be aware of the whole and not of the constituents. Compulsion

neurotics, therefore, frequently experience sums instead of unities, and many compulsive character traits are best designated as 'inhibition in the experiencing of *gestalten*.'"

25. Sometimes the ritual is represented by what Fenichel discovered in one of his patients, a compulsive disorder, a rigid avoidance of any order in any form—the effect Sterne was trying to convey in *Tristram Shandy;* this is a main aim of the literature of "stream of consciousness," where the paradoxical order-disorder relationship makes for a crucial problem as to *intention*. Frequently the compulsive neurotic displays a division of his world into an ordered and a disordered half; in the one all is neatness, in the other all chaos. A classic instance would be the dress and manners of Erik Satie, divided into public and private appearance. "It is the paragon of punctuality who in many instances is surprisingly unpunctual, the cleanest person who is in some curious respect astonishingly dirty" (Fenichel, *Psychoanalytic Theory,* 280).

26. See F. W. J. Hemmings' *Emile Zola* (Oxford, 1953), ch. iii, "Blueprint for a Life's Work," a discussion of Zola's *manie de perfection,* and his indebtedness to the *Traité de l'hérédité naturelle* of Prosper Lucas, a convenient, powerful pseudoscientific system of "election"; Zola's concept of heredity, derived from Lucas, became a magical one; Zola was not fooled into considering himself a true scientist (41). Instead he created characters who "all suffer from being too completely at the mercy of the fatality that overwhelms them, too passive in the current of physiological necessity that sweeps them along. . . . *Thérèse Raquin* and *Madeleine Férat* are just fate-tragedies in which the mysterious 'laws of physiology' take the place of the ancestral curse that powers certain dramas of the German Romantics, or of the Erinyes that hunt the protagonist of a Greek tragedy. The two novels have many of the incidental characteristics of such productions" (30).

On the side of the creator, we have evidence of Zola's quite consciously exercised "encyclopedic instinct": he himself admitted "I always try, as we say, to bite off more than I can chew. When I attack a subject, *I would like to force the whole universe into it. Hence my torments, in this desire for the enormous and for totality which is never satisfied*" (my italics). These constitute a perfect criterion for the sublime, and therefore, to my mind, of what is essentially allegorical during the period following the post-Renaissance weakening of Christian scriptural norms. There is a nice corroboration of the idea that in Zola a compulsive "collector's mania" found its perfect literary exponent, in that he was himself, as Hemmings put it, "the junk-shop dealer's natural victim"—"There was that in Zola which made hugeness and comprehensiveness come more naturally than daintiness and selection. He had the collector's instinct and the architect's brain.

"The two things were symbolized in his house at Médan. . . . Inside, the visitor was bewildered by an indescribable medley of miscellaneous pieces of furniture and *objets d'art,* for Zola was the junk-shop dealer's natural victim; contemporary prints of the interior of the house show well this concentration of bric-a-brac. Outside the house the builders were seldom idle, adding and elaborating under Zola's personal direction. Médan was *Les Rougon-Macquart* edited in bricks and mortar and upholstery" (36). In terms of the "collector's mania" Rabelais had earlier made a cosmic satire on scholasticism.

27. White, *Abnormal Personality,* 292. E. M. W. Tillyard makes this a crucial point, on which he must defend allegory. "Indeed what appears to aim at a very hampering rigidity may actually result in the elusive and ambiguous and iridescent. If all three or four senses are not maintained throughout but come and go, there must be a transfer from complex to simpler scales of allegory and back again; and such acts of transfer will themselves become the habit of mind, the contrary of the ancient Greek,

that refuses to stick to one fixed humanistic centre of reference and varies its abode from earth to heaven. This habit of mind lasted, though in less spiritual form, to Spenser, whose *Faerie Queene* constantly varies in the amount of attention the allegorical meaning required" (*Poetry Direct and Oblique* [London, 1945], 144).

28. See Fenichel, *Psychoanalytic Theory*, 288 ff., and White, *Abnormal Personality*, 294.

29. White, *Abnormal Personality*, 292.

30. C. S. Lewis, *The Allegory of Love* (Oxford, 1936), 280–281: "Perhaps Hawes himself would have been neither able nor willing to throw much light on the deeper obscurities of his poem. He loves darkness and strangeness, 'fatall fictions,' as he says, and 'clowdy figures' for their own sake; he is a dreamer and a mutterer, dazed by the unruly content of his own imagination, a poet (in his way) as possessed as Blake. It is at once his strength and his weakness that he writes under a kind of compulsion. Hence the prolixity and frequent *longueurs* of his narrative, but hence also the memorable pictures, whether homely or fantastic, which sometimes start up and render this dreariness almost a 'visionary dreariness.'" If one had to find a parallel, in psychoanalytic theory, for the sudden visions of Hawes, it would surely be those strange outbursts which Freud calls "deliria"—a hybrid symptom in this case. See "Notes on a Case of Obsessional Neurosis," *Collected Papers*, III, 358. "Delirium" here has the original meaning of the plough jumping out of the furrow.

31. Cf. Fenichel, *Psychoanalytic Theory*, 295–296, and 300 ff. Also Freud, *Totem and Taboo*, in *Basic Writings*, 849–851. Otto Jespersen, in *Mankind, Nation and Individual* (London, 1946), 169, says: "We shall never thoroughly understand the nature of language, if we take as our starting point the sober attitude of the scientifically trained man of today, who regards the words he uses as a means for communication, or further developing thought. To children and savages a word is something very different. To them there is something magical or mystical in a name."

32. See Vincent F. Hopper, *Medieval Number Symbolism: Its Sources, Meaning and Influence on Thought and Expression* (New York, 1938), especially 90 ff., on the relation between number symbolism and astrology, with its implied control over human action; on the connection between this symbolism and the body-image, see n. 30, page 17: Francesco Sizzi, arguing against Galileo's discovery of more than 7 planets: "There are 7 windows in the head, 2 nostrils, 2 eyes, 2 ears, and a mouth; so in the heavens there are 2 favorable stars, 2 unpropitious, 2 luminaries, and Mercury alone undecided and indifferent." Curtius' Excurses XV and XVI in *European Literature and the Latin Middle Ages*, "Numerical Composition," and "Numerical Apothegms," were written independently of Hopper's work. Recently A. Kent Hieatt has performed a remarkable numerological exegesis: *Short Time's Endless Monument: the Symbolism of the Numbers in Edmund Spenser's* Epithalamion (New York, 1960); see also the amplifying essay, Hieatt, "The Daughters of Horus: Order in the Stanzas of *Epithalamion*," in *Form and Convention in the Poetry of Edmund Spenser*, ed. William Nelson (English Institute Essays; New York and London, 1961), 103–121. Our problem with such exegesis, insofar as we are twentieth-century readers, lies in the difficulty of taking numbers magically.

33. Fenichel, *Psychoanalytic Theory*, 295.

34. Ibid., 296–297.

35. Ibid., 302.

36. Ibid., 270. Also, the classic statement of ambivalence, Freud, "Notes on a Case of Obsessional Neurosis," *Collected Papers*, III, 374: "The other conflict, that between love and hatred, strikes us more strangely. We know that incipient love is often per-

ceived as hatred, and that love, if it is denied satisfaction, may easily be partly converted into hatred, and poets tell us that in the more tempestuous stages of love the two opposed feelings may subsist side by side for a while as though in rivalry with each other. But the chronic co-existence of love and hatred, both directed towards the same person and both of the highest degree of intensity, cannot fail to astonish us. We should have expected that the passionate love would have long ago conquered the hatred or been devoured by it. And in fact such a protracted survival of two opposites is only possible under quite peculiar psychological conditions and with the co-operation of the state of affairs in the unconscious. The love has not succeeded in extinguishing the hatred but only in driving it down into the unconscious; and in the unconscious the hatred, safe from the danger of being destroyed by the operations of consciousness, is able to persist and even to grow. In such circumstances the conscious love attains as a rule, by way of reaction, an especially high degree of intensity, so as to be strong enough for the perpetual task of keeping its opponent under repression."

37. Stekel, *Compulsion and Doubt,* translator's Introduction, sec. iii, 10–23, on "mechanisms." Cf. Freud, "Antithetical Sense of Primal Words" (1910).

38. See the commentary on this passage in Anthony West, *Principles and Persuasions* (New York, 1957). The chapter on Orwell appeared originally in *The New Yorker*. On mixed attitudes toward money and property, see J. C. Flugel, *Man, Morals and Society* (New York, 1961), 295–297. This work is of considerable importance to the study of conscience, since it analyzes the "projections of the super-ego." Flugel, furthermore, has written another work relevant to the study of *kosmos* and allegory, *The Psychology of Clothes* (London, 1930), in which see especially ch. ii, "Decoration—Purposive Aspects." Cf. Baudelaire, "The Painter of Modern Life," especially sec. ii, "In Praise of Cosmetics."

39. See Adorno, Frenkel-Brunswik, Levinson, and Sanford, *The Authoritarian Personality* (New York, 1950), where Elsa Frenkel-Brunswik develops her notion of "intolerance of ambiguity." See also Abraham and Edith Luchins, *Rigidity of Behavior* (Eugene, Ore., 1959), for a complete review of the literature on "einstellung" (set), including summaries of various psychoanalytic positions (ch. i). Two figures, it seems to me, emerge as having primary importance in this field, Wilhelm Reich, author of *Character Analysis,* and Heinz Werner, author of *Comparative Psychology.* Their approaches to the problem of rigid behavior are obviously quite different.

40. Cf. Fenichel, *Psychoanalytic Theory,* 278–284.

41. *Faust:* Then, quick, let these be told!
Mephistopheles:
   Loth am I now high mystery to unfold:
   Goddesses dwell, in solitude, sublime,
   Enthroned beyond the world of place or time;
   Even to speak of them dismays the bold.
   These are the Mothers.
Faust: Mothers?
Mephistopheles: Stand you daunted?
Faust: The Mothers! The Mothers—sound with wonder haunted.
Mephistopheles:
   True, goddesses unknown to mortal mind,
   And named indeed with dread among our kind.

The second part of *Faust* ends with a double image of the Woman, first, that of the burial scene in Act V, where the jaws of Hell appear to be identified with the "terrible mother," and, second, in the final scene of redemption, where Woman becomes a virgin goddess, represented by the penitents, including the penitent Gretchen, and by the Mater Gloriosa. The attitude toward Woman is then highly ambivalent, as in Part I, where there is a constant suggestion that Gretchen is both Faust's lover and his "mother." (I have used Philip Wayne's translation, Penguin ed., Baltimore, 1959.)

42. Henry Murray, ed., Introduction to Melville's *Pierre*, xv.

Leo Bersani
1931–

Leo Bersani was born in New York City on April 16, 1931. He graduated cum laude from Harvard University in 1952, and six years later received a Ph.D. in comparative literature from the same institution. From 1957 to 1967 he taught at Wellesley College, then was on the faculty at Rutgers University for six years before becoming professor of French and department chairman at the University of California–Berkeley in 1973, a position he currently holds.

Bersani's first book, *Marcel Proust: The Fictions of Life and Art*, was published in 1965. *Balzac to Beckett: Center and Circumference in French Fiction* appeared in 1970. Devoting individual chapters to Balzac, Stendhal, Flaubert, Proust, Camus, Robbe-Grillet, and Beckett, Bersani examines the writings of each author as attempts at self-identity. His next book, *A Future for Astyanax: Character and Desire in Literature* (1976), discusses nineteenth- and twentieth-century French writers as well as George Eliot, Austen, Hawthorne, Henry James, Lawrence, and Emily Brontë, examining and analyzing the sexual desires and fantasies of their literary characters. Again critics noted the "extraordinary difficulty" that Bersani's prose style posed to the common reader, but the work received generally positive, even enthusiastic attention.

Baudelaire and Freud, (1977) Bersani's fourth book, juxtaposes passages from Freud's essays with Baudelaire's poems in a study of Baudelaire's erotic fantasies and their psychoanalytic implications, drawing as well upon the insights of the structuralist Jacques Lacan. A fifth book-length work by Bersani, *The Death of Stéphane Mallarmé*, appeared in 1982.

Bersani is a frequent contributor to such periodicals as *Partisan Review*, the *Yale Review*, and the *New Republic*, and has been the recipient of fellowships from the Guggenheim Foundation and the National Endowment for the Humanities.

FROM
A FUTURE FOR ASTYANAX

MURDEROUS LOVERS

In Racine's *Andromaque,* Ménélas has sent Oreste into the province of Epire in order to demand that Pyrrhus surrender Hector's son Astyanax to the Greeks. Fearful lest Astyanax one day attempt to avenge the massacre of his family and the defeat of his people at Troy, the Greeks insist that the child must die. For Pyrrhus, Oreste's mission is, in part, an opportunity for sexual blackmail. He is in love with Astyanax' mother, Andromaque, and in Scene Seven of Act Three Pyrrhus' threats to Hector's widow become brutally explicit. Marry me, he tells her, or watch me condemn your son to death by handing him over to the Greeks. When Andromaque's confidante urges her, in the following scene, to marry Pyrrhus in order to save Astyanax, Andromaque, in a famous passage, evokes her first vision of Pyrrhus on that "cruel night" at Troy when he led the Greeks in the slaughter of her countrymen:

> Songe, songe, Céphise, à cette nuit cruelle
> Qui fut pour tout un peuple une nuit éternelle;
> Figure-toi Pyrrhus, les yeux étincelants,
> Entrant à la lueur de nos palais brûlants,
> Sur tous mes frères morts se faisant un passage,
> Et, de sang tout couvert, échauffant le carnage;
> Songe aux cris des vainqueurs, songe aux cris des mourants
> Dans la flamme étouffés, sous le fer expirants;
> Peins-toi dans ces horreurs Andromaque éperdue:
> Voilà comme Pyrrhus vint s'offrir à ma vue;
> Voilà par quels exploits il sut se couronner;
> Enfin, voilà l'époux que tu me veux donner.[1]

Luridly illuminated nights of violence (or of potential violence) are not uncommon in Racine. They indicate a traumatic break in the time and in the meanings of Racinian tragedy. Under the fitful light of torches and in the midst of a crowd's confused shouting, the hero's life is fragmented; its continuity is broken, something abruptly ends and something else abruptly begins. Titus the lover dies and Titus the emperor is born on the "nuit enflammée" when the people of Rome and the royal ambassadors from abroad acclaim him as their leader in *Bérénice*. In *Bajazet*, the chaotic spectacle of terrified soldiers, slaves and women wandering in the seraglio marks the end of Roxane's reign, and Mithridate's career as leader of the world's resistance to Roman tyranny comes to a close in the "désordre partout" and the "horreur d'un combat ténébreux" in which Pompée defeats an army of half-naked soldiers hiding in the night's shadows. In *Andromaque,* the nocturnal scene described in the passage I quoted a moment ago is catastrophic, but, as in the scene of carnage evoked by Josabet early in *Athalie,* a child is saved.

These traumatizing nocturnal tableaux indicate the death of the old and the birth of the new, a violent passage from one psychological and social order to another. I think that they are also dramatic metaphors for a fragmentation of meaning which is the Racinian hero's only hope of escape from the continuities and the coherent patterns of desire which condemn him to a life of repetition. Of course, what is repeated in Racine is a certain scheme of sexual passion, and it's true that Pyrrhus' spectacularly dramatic encounter with Andromaque imprisons him within the structures of Racinian passion. But his relation to Andromaque includes the possibility of feelings mostly undefined in the play but which are, I think, alien to those structures. In Racine's claustrophobic theater there are the outlines, however blurred, of a theater of freedom. And by that I mean a theater in which the self would be liberated from the unhappy and limiting coherence in which a psychology of sexual passion entraps it. Even when the consequences of those nocturnal traumatic scenes monotonously repeat a mode of feeling or of desiring which preceded them, the scenes themselves suggest an intention more radical than anything Racine imagines for his characters' sustained relations with one another. Only violence, in any case, could destroy the structure of those relations; and for Racine the question seems to be whether anything at all would survive what is fundamentally an explosion of being.

For criticism, literary scenes such as the one from Racine which we have been looking at have a dangerously elusive density. They seem to be charged with meaning, and yet they resist interpretation with the interrogative stillness of nondiscursive art. With our speculations, we wander around their enigmatic shapes, in the same way as the characters in James's *The Golden Bowl* helplessly wander, with their endless critical appreciations, around Maggie Verver's enigmatic, sculptural and silent presence. These scenes, which appear to condense passionate intentions into coercive images, can (and probably should) be the object of the critic's fascination; they can't, however, be taken as substitutes for his arguments. Even within these introductory remarks, we should perhaps put some distance between the two scenes being evoked, unfold their meanings, in our first interval of critical argument and reasoned interpretation.

This book will be a study of the correlations between different ways of conceiving desire and different ways of conceiving character in literature. From Racine to contemporary theater and some recent erotic fiction, I will be following stages in the *deconstruction of the self* in modern literature. My general organization will be in terms of a polarity between structured desires and fragmented desires. By structured desires I mean desiring impulses sublimated into emotional "faculties" or passions and thereby providing the basis for the notion of a distinct and coherently unified personality. We probably first experience desire in our lives as a naïve confusion of the self with the world. In the scenic (and hallucinatory) mode of desire which will be most effectively represented for us in Rimbaud's *Illuminations*, the theatricalized self *is* a series of pictures of the world. But our desires are of course also—and perhaps primarily—repressed. A sense both of the forbidden nature of certain desires and of the incompatibility of reality with our desiring imagination makes the negation of desire inevitable. But to deny desire is not to eliminate it; in fact, such denials multiply the appearances of each desire in the self's history. In denying a desire, we condemn ourselves to finding it everywhere. Repressed desire is repeated, disguised and sublimated. Its reappearances in various forms at different levels of mental life create the intelligible structures, the psychic continuities which can be formulated as an individual's personality or character. The disguised repetitions of inhibited desires constitute the coherent self.

But, as we shall see principally in the discussions of Racine and of realistic fiction in the first half of our study, this psychic coherence involves a serious crippling of desire. The viability of the structured self depends on an impoverishment of desire. The desiring imagination's contacts with the world are limited by the need for preserving the intelligibility of a psychic structure. Even more dangerously, the renunciation of desire, as Freud suggested, may increase our sense of guilt instead of assuaging it. And heightened guilt welcomes the potentially ferocious punishments of conscience and of external moral authority. An important psychological consequence of sublimated (civilized) desire may be a suicidal melancholy. In our sublimations, our desires never die. But the endless repetition of desires suppressed by guilt and angry frustration ultimately leads to the fantasy of death as the absolute pleasure. (D. H. Lawrence's *Women in Love* will provide us with a novelistic version of this equivalence between death and unending repetition.) The repeated refusal to confess our desires gives them a kind of criminally immortal activity from which only the definitive immobility of death might rescue us.

The political implications of suicidal melancholy in a culture of repression and sublimation would in themselves adequately justify our asking about the possibility of reversing the process which I've just outlined—that is, the possibility of desublimating desire (and, correlatively, of deconstructing the self). Can a psychology of fragmentary and *dis*continuous desires be reinstated? What are the strategies by which the self might be once again theatricalized? How might desire recover its original capacity for projecting nonstructurable *scenes*? Questions similar to these have been asked by other writers. Freud's remarkable disciple Sándor Ferenczi spoke of human character as an abnormality, as a mechanization of a particular mode of reaction. Post-Oedipal character-formations would involve the centralizing (and the spiritualizing) of pre-Oedipal fetishistic attachments. More recently, critiques of Freudianism have enjoyed a certain notoriety in our culture. I'm of course thinking of Norman O. Brown, Herbert Marcuse, R. D. Laing and the "anti-psychiatry" movement, and in France, Gilles Deleuze and Félix Guattari's impressive and intensely polemical *L'Anti-Oedipe*.[2] In different ways, all these writers are interested in helping us to reinstate a heterogeneity of our desiring impulses;

and this project involves—especially in Brown and Deleuze—a militant intellectual campaign against the sublimating processes of mental life and a hyperbolic defense of the desublimated desire. With only a modest injustice to both works, *Life against Death* and *L'Anti-Oedipe* could be read as philosophical pastorals of pre-Oedipal desire; they sketch the outlines of an Arcadia of polymorphous perversity. More interestingly, they suggest that a new emphasis on the *peripheries* of our desiring attention would not only diversify desire but would also keep it mobile. Peripheral seductions would no longer be discarded because they can't be related to a dominant interest; even our dominant interest—our "centers" of desire—would have merely a provisional, peripheral appeal. *The* desiring self might even disappear as we learn to multiply our discontinuous and partial desiring selves.

I want to raise these issues again for three reasons. First of all, I think that the thought of the men I've just mentioned is weakened by their tendency to politicize psychology somewhat glibly. Obviously, no psychology is apolitical;[3] every theory of the mind has a *strategic* value for the culture in which it is developed. But the implication of many recent critiques of Freudian thought is that an analysis of the social orders which psychological theory serves makes unnecessary any further argument about the epistemological validity of the theory. Unfortunately, however, even the most abhorrent system of thought is never adequately refuted by an exposure of the political manipulations which it either inspires or rationalizes; it must also be approached as an argument about "truth." This double approach would, ideally, make for a continuous moving back and forth between an analysis of certain logical weaknesses or contradictions in a psychological theory (for example, the attempt to repress the discovery of repression in Freud himself and especially in post-Freudian ego psychologists), and a study of the hidden political assumptions which may explain the need or the convenience of such contradictions.

Political action alone will never invalidate a philosophical argument about truth. It may make the argument seem superfluous, and it may almost fully discredit the historical use to which that argument has been put. But even in a society which realizes our brightest, most exaltingly generous dreams of the human community, we may find ourselves haunted by the impulses of a self which we had too easily dismissed as an outmoded superstructure of a rejected form of social organization. The history of a human being's desiring impulses includes modes of exchange between the self and the world, or between consciousness and the unconscious, which would probably reappear and would therefore have to be taken into account in *any* society. If, for instance, we were violently to break free from the forms of social organization which institutionalize the Oedipal structure and its conflicts, would this free us from the necessity of passing through the complexities of Oedipal love, hate, guilt and renunciation in the history of individual desires? The mere fact that every living organism has to accommodate itself to a field of reality in which its needs can never be entirely fulfilled suggests that the self, far from being only an ideological construct, would always have to go through a difficult negotiating process between its own appetitive energies and both a world *and* an internal economy which limit the possibilities of performing our energies and satisfying our appetites.⟨. . .⟩

The Freud of the Oedipus complex is of course the best-known Freud. There is, however, another Freud, a much more difficult and ambiguous thinker who has been brought to our attention by contemporary French psychoanalytic theory.[4] My second major reason for reopening the discussion of sublimation and desublimation in this book is that this other Freud—the Freud of *Beyond the Pleasure Principle,* or of the essays "Instincts and Their Vicissitudes," "A Child Is Being Beaten" and "From the History of an Infantile Neurosis" (the "Wolf Man" case), should help us to reformulate the terms of that discussion and to make our arguments more sophisticated. The contrasts which I've been proposing—between sublimated and desublimated desires, between the structured self and the fragmented self—are, I think, valid, but they are nonetheless rather crudely schematic. The deconstruction of the self involves much more than a happy return to the polymorphous pleasures of sensual intensities not yet petrified (as a result of being denied) into fixed and partial character structures. Our thought about this process of deconstruction should engage us in a problematic reflection about different forms of psychic mobility. In Lautréamont and Emily Brontë, for instance, we will find the phenomenon of a mysterious scattering of the self (a phenomenon far more subversive of stable psychic identities than the diffusions of the self along the narrative surfaces of Proust's *A la recherche du temps perdu*). With *Les Chants de Maldoror* and *Wuthering Heights,* we will be confronting metamorphoses of the self, as well as the possibility of an almost unthinkable and yet compelling identity between the self and the other. And, inspired by a particularly dense and rich passage of Freud's "Instincts and Their Vicissitudes," I will be considering, at the end of this study, both the menace and the strangely humanizing potential of a sado-masochistic sexuality which shatters the self out of a dangerous security about its own sexual identity. There is a post-Oedipal security which, as we shall see in *Histoire d'O,* may divide the world into two hostile camps and condemn each sex to a panicky wish to annihilate the irreducible difference of the other sex.

Finally, I think that there is a special profit to be gained from a study of character and desire *in literature*. First of all, literature is a privileged area for a study of an oscillation between thought and sensation. By virtue of its purely verbal mode of existence, literature inevitably defends the abstract and the highly structured. Because language is a system, and because words may be, as Freud argued, compromise-formations for nonverbal scenes and satisfactions, literature is, in part, always a sublimating activity. It gives structure and continuity to what may be fragmented and discontinuous in the history of our desires. On the other side, there is a strong desublimating tendency in literature, an attempt perhaps to revive, through verbal stimulation, memories of intense bodily pleasures. As in other modes of fantasy, the writer, in the privacy and leisure of composition, may be engaged in inventing repetitions of sensual intensities. Furthermore, in the act of writing, the word itself seems to be experienced partly as an insubstantial sign referring to meanings beyond itself, and partly as a sensuous object referring to nothing but its own shape, sound and position in a design of numerous word-objects. The profound connection between literature and sensation is suggested in testimony as diverse as Proust's use of his body's involuntary memories as a principle of narrative organization in the novel, Nietzsche's suggestion that in the "esthetic state" sensuality doesn't disappear but is simply transfigured and no longer enters consciousness as sexual excitement, and Flaubert's demonstration in *Madame Bovary* of literature's paradoxical (and treacherous) status as an abstract guarantee of sensual ecstasy.

Literature has an even more profound relevance to the subject of these essays. It is not merely instructive *about* desire; in a sense, desire *is* a phenomenon of the literary imagination. Desire is an activity within a lack; it is an appetite stimulated by an absence. But it is never only a lack. Desire is a hallucinated satisfaction in the absence of the source of satisfaction. In other words, it is an appetite of the imagination. Indeed, the infant is already an artist of sorts in the sense that he invents and is excited by imaginary equivalents of remembered satisfactions. The activity of desiring is inseparable from the activity of fantasizing. There is no scene of desire which is not an elaboration, a kind of visual interpretation, of other scenes. In the same way that literary works are always critical revisions of other literary works, our desires reformulate both other desires and the pleasures which are at the source of all desire. ⟨. . .⟩

It is perhaps the role of sublimation, conscience and character-formation to modify the potentially limitless aggressiveness of desire. In pornographic literature, the characters use one another's bodies with the same freedom from any constraining resistances or consequences as the fantasies of desire naturally tend to use the world. A more realistic sense of the extent to which reality can accommodate our desires produces a literature which, on the one hand, too frequently argues for a petrification of our desires within the character structures least threatening to established psychological and social orders. But what we call realism in art can also be an exercise in the beneficently unsettling interpretation of desire. Much of the *art* of realistic fiction consists of critical arguments, demonstrations and interpretations. And the discursively problematic chatter of criticism breaks up the sculptural finality of scenic desire and invites us to a certain skepticism about *any* fixed forms of desire or of the self. Criticism is a type of agitated thought; at best it can dislocate the obsessive desire and promote mobility in our self-definitions.

Strangely enough, we can find the promise of a similar mobility in the violence of desire itself. Pyrrhus—"les yeux étincelants" and "de sang tout couvert, échauffant le carnage"— is *carried away* by sadistic excitement on the night of Troy's destruction. It is this image of shaken cruelty that he presents to Andromaque as a possible source of erotic stimulation. Pyrrhus "outside of himself" is Andromaque's first image of the man who, later on, will threaten her in a far more calculated—and sinister—fashion. Nothing is more curious than this suggestion (which *L'Image* and *Histoire d'O* will document for us) that the activity of desiring may include a pleasure intense enough to shatter the desiring self. If this is the case, then the fantasies of both criticism *and* art could take place in those oddly mobile intervals of mental life which, at the beginning of these remarks, I had mistakenly reserved for the touchingly insecure (if proud) procedures of rational critical thought.

PERSONS IN PIECES

The penetration of art by criticism already exists within art, for the latter is always a kind of interpretive discourse. All languages construct fictions—that is, interpretations of reality—and the difference between art and criticism is one of interpretive modes rather than one of ontological status. Art does not tell us the "truth" about the real any more than criticism tells us the "truth" about art. The interpretive activity naturally associated with criticism is intrinsic to all our mental operations. Desire is inseparable from fantasy—which is to say that the longing to repeat a remembered satisfaction includes a revised version of the satisfaction, an interpretive re-creation of an original (if unlocatable) pleasure. The differences among mental activities are differences of interpretive procedures. And once criticism stops fishing for the truth in art, it can engage in the only activity which demonstrates both its own specificity and its affinities with art. That is, criticism can openly assume its status as an interpretive fiction, and yet demonstrate that its particular brand of interpretation consists in the elucidation of the sense-making procedures in art. Criticism is an interpretive reflection on the modes of interpretation in art. And in assuming what I take to be its only essential difference from art, criticism can help us to see the problematic nature of its relation to art. For the very nature of the difference between the two designates the profound similarity between the two. The identity of art is in part *to be* criticism, just as the very identity of criticism subverts any secure identifications of criticism and allows for the unpredictable "sliding" of critical discourse into the grooves or modes of artistic discourse.

Indeed, some of the most interesting modern criticism—especially in France since Gaston Bachelard—has demonstrated that the more seriously criticism takes its official function of remaining faithful to the text, the more it resembles art. The most profound fidelity to the work of art is to imitate it: the critic follows his writer so closely that he begins to duplicate the latter's achievement. Or, to put it in another way, critical discourse begins to resemble the literature which is its object by drawing attention to itself. While criticism continues to lean on other texts, it also now seems to be making a claim for the esthetic appeal of its own procedures; the myth of criticism as a transparent explication of literature is abandoned. The critic may not only borrow some of the sense-making procedures which he rightly attributes to art (for example, the use of a metaphor to convey an interpretive judgment, or—in the case of Blanchot—an indulgence in paradoxical "argument"). He may also draw attention to the seductiveness of the most discursive or even rationalistic aspects of critical argument. The *play* of criticism becomes visible. And we discover that the pleasures of conceptual experimentation, of dismissible speculation, are the specific pleasures of critical form. Thus the critical text comes to have an opacity not unlike that which the poet's fascination with the materiality of words gives to poetic language. Critical argument has "shapes" or "gestures" perhaps as seductive as those of sculpture or dance. . . . We have moved toward a community of writers, and away from hierarchical distinctions among poets, novelists and critics.[5]

But however problematic the separate identities of criticism and art may become, to a certain extent the former will always undermine an art of the fragmentary and the discontinuous. Significantly, the criticism which, until now, has most successfully sought to duplicate the intimate "movements" in art is also committed to making visible the individualizing coherence of a writer's work. The studies of Georges Poulet and of Jean-Pierre Richard, for example, are subversive of traditional criticism in the sense that they ignore the latter's insistence on analytical detachment and certain kinds of judgment. But thematic criticism also reinforces the traditional esthetic criterion of an artistic unity based on a coherent "vision of the world." Nothing could be more alien to this "artistic" criticism than a fragmentary or a collective art—or, at the extreme, an art without authorship.[6]

But such art is probably alien to any effort at critical interpretation. What differentiates criticism from art is precisely an interpretive mode intent on sorting out persistent meanings or intentions, and on elucidating the structural sense of art. Criticism strains toward continuity, unity and centrality of argument. Confronted with the anonymous particularity of scenes from Rimbaud's *Illuminations* or Robert Wilson's theater, the critic perhaps can't help but seek out—or invent—a "self" whose unifying designs he finds, if not in the content of those scenes, then in the very enterprise of doing away with structurable content, of eliminating repetition. The theatricalized self brings us back to the scenic mode of desire, and therefore to a kind of art much more remote from criticism than, say, the comparatively discursive art of realistic fiction. Criticism reformulates scenic desire in terms of persistent intentions and unifying structures. However profound the critic's sympathy may be with the discontinuous, the fragmentary and the peripheral, his own enterprise is always an argument for the inescapable presence, and even the irresistible appeal, of the general design.

Nonetheless, art and criticism take place within a single field of interpretation, and consequently every critical act and every artistic performance are, potentially, reminders of the problematic nature of the critic's and the artist's identities. The potential for criticism in art and for art in criticism, can, I think, be a major force in the promotion of psychic mobility. And psychic mobility can rescue us from the tyrannical rigidities of both sublimated desire (petrified and disguised in character structures) and scenic desire. If I have, on the whole, been arguing for an art which mocks our faith in psychological coherence and in the civilizing value of sublimation, it is because I think that an imagination of the deconstructed, perhaps even demolished, self is the necessary point of departure for an authentically civilizing skepticism about the nature of our desires and the nature of our being. Scenic desire, as we have had ample occasion to see, lends itself all too easily to devastations of being. But in the literary universe of partial selves—inhabited by such different works as Rimbaud's *Illuminations* and "Jean de Berg's" *L'Image*—there is nonetheless a greater likelihood of movements *among* different forms of desire and of being than in a world of fixed character structures. For what we call character is also a partial self. Its appearance of completeness, of wholeness, may be nothing more than the illusion created by the *centralizing* of a partial self. Such centralization involves both the organization of our desires into psychic structures and the expulsion of nonstructurable desires. Character, in short, is also a piece of a person; it has the factitious coherence of all obsessions. Only the mobility of desublimated desires preserves the mobility of being itself. An exuberant indefiniteness about our own identity can both preserve the heterogeneity of our desires and rescue us from the totalitarian insistence natural to all desire.

It would, however, be impossible to eliminate all fixed character structures. The theatrical self of the *Illuminations* or of a Robert Wilson extravaganza is a triumph for desublimated desire which can be sustained only in literature, and even then only momentarily. To live entirely without sublimation and psychic continuities is unthinkable. And even in the imaginary, "irresponsible" spaces of literature, psychic coherence, as we have seen most dramatically in Rimbaud, inevitably reappears. But we might argue that even the structured self can enter that play of mobile desire without which any project of radical self-revision runs the risk of merely changing the mode in which the self seeks terroristically to impose its desires on the world. I have spoken of a problematic reflectiveness about our identity. There is the nonreflective psychic mobility of the scenic self; but a certain mobility of being can also be achieved by the sort of multiplicity of *verbal* self-interpretations which we find in Proust. For such reflectiveness to take place, the repression, repetition and sublimation of desire must have proceeded to a point at which the very notion of the self has become a coherent and rather elaborate fiction. It's true that such fictions tend to immobilize us in a single identity. But they must also be sustained in time, and the accidents of history happily subvert those sense-making impulses which would reduce history to the persistence of orders and systems.

To live in time is an apprenticeship in techniques for deflecting desire into activities and a personality which are socially viable. Literature is instructive in this respect: scenes of desire in literary works are surrounded by and submitted to *developments* which compromise but which also humanize desire. On the one hand, literature hallucinates the world in order to accommodate desire. On the other hand, it illustrates the ways in which we learn, in time, to make what Melanie Klein called reparations to the world for our imaginary devastations of it. Literature thus makes a double argument. It invites us to return to that variety of scenes of desire which is stifled by the interpretive tracing back of all desires to a single, continuous design in a supposed maturing of desire. The literary imagination reinstates the world of desiring fantasies as a world of reinvented, richly fragmented and diversified body-memories. But, at the same time, it also gives ample space to those processes by which we make a continuous *story* of our desires, processes which also teach us to give up the intensities of an infinitely desirable hallucinated world for the somewhat disappointing enjoyments of fulfilled desires.

NOTES

1.   Think, think, Cephissa, of that cruel night
     which fell eternally for a whole people;
     see Pyrrhus, his eyes flashing in the glare
     of our burning palaces, who trampled his way
     across my murdered brothers; see him enter,
     well-smeared with blood, cheering the carnage on;
     recall the victors' cries, recall the cries
     of the dying, choked in fire, put to the sword;
     and, crazed among those horrors, Andromache:
     that is how Pyrrhus came into my view;
     those are the glories with which he crowned himself;
     there, indeed, is the husband you offer.

This is George Dillon's translation in the University of Chicago Press edition of *Three Plays of Racine: Phèdre, Britannicus, Andromaque* (1961).

2. *L'Anti-Oedipe* (1972) was announced as the first volume of *Capitalisme et schizophrénie*. In 1975, Deleuze and Guattari published *Kafka/Pour une littérature mineure*.

3. Michel Foucault's forthcoming study of sexuality in Western civilization includes a persuasive consideration of both the epistemology and the therapeutic techniques of psychoanalysis as political strategies designed to reinforce social control of the individual's desires.

4. I'm thinking especially of the work of Jacques Lacan, Jean Laplanche, J.-B. Pontalis and Serge Leclair. The best English introduction to these important thinkers is the issue of *Yale French Studies* entitled *French Freud*, ed. Jeffrey Mehlman (No. 48).

5. In one of the most stimulating passages of S/Z, Roland Barthes suggests that we stop considering literature and painting from within "une réflexion hiérarchique." Barthes asks: "Why not renounce the plurality of 'arts,' in order to affirm more effectively the plurality of 'texts'?" (p. 62). The best example of seductively artistic criticism I know is Lawrence's *Studies in Classic American Literature*.

6. When Deleuze and Derrida talk about literary works, they are (unlike Poulet, Richard and Starobinski) interested in "partial selves," self-fragmentations and more or less successful enterprises in the subversion of a cult of psychic totality and full psychic presence. But the critical essays in which this interest is expressed are themselves closer to a traditionally discursive, analytically detached criticism which the now rather old-fashioned work of Richard and of Poulet had in fact moved beyond. The mode of critical writing was more radically new in critics who sought out traditional values in literature (a coherent intentionality) than in the writers who have most effectively contested those values (in a discursive mode derived from them . . .). But Derrida's

latest work—*Glas*—is a fascinating attempt to move toward authentically new shapes of "critical" discourse.

I should also add that there is an extremity of critical discourse which is also depersonalized, inexpressive of any self at all. But we must distinguish between the anonymous *particularities* of the *Illuminations* and the anonymity occasionally reached by criticism: the latter is the result of verbal speculation, of a surrender to the appeals of abstract design in language.

Susan Sontag
1933–

In the sixties and seventies no American critic better defined or represented what was avant-garde and modernist than Susan Sontag. While certain ideas will for a long time remain associated with her work, even by those who have not read it, it is now clear, after years of criticism erected by the rhetoric of theoretical argument and polemics, that she has not yet presented a system. In the introduction to *A Sontag Reader* (1981) Elizabeth Hardwick wrote of Sontag that "her theme is the wide, elusive, variegated sensibility of modernism." A question for the present might be: do we diminish her reputation as a critical thinker by suggesting that her many essays constitute "a kind of autobiography of sensibility"?

Susan Sontag was born on January 16, 1933, in New York City, grew up in Tucson and Los Angeles, and, at the age of fifteen, entered the University of California–Berkeley. After a year she transferred to the University of Chicago, where she received a B.A. in philosophy in 1951. At Harvard University she earned master's degrees in English (1954) and philosophy (1955). She continued her graduate studies abroad at St. Anne's College, Oxford, and at the Sorbonne. She has taught at Harvard, the University of Connecticut–Storrs, the City College of New York, Sarah Lawrence College, and Columbia University.

Sontag's work has taken many directions. She was one of the first critics to introduce American audiences to Nathalie Sarraute, Antonin Artaud, Walter Benjamin, Maurice Blanchot, Simone Weil, Claude Lévi-Strauss, and others. She has written novels, screenplays, book reviews, and essays on culture, photography, theatre, and film. *Against Interpretation and Other Essays* (1966) is a collection of previously published pieces unified by a theme that had already been expressed in her first novel, *The Benefactor* (1963), in which the central character Hippolyte asks, "Why not take dreams at face value? Perhaps I did not need to 'interpret' my dreams at all. . . . I wanted to enact my dreams, not simply observe them." The essays in *Against Interpretation* provide the foundation and models for criticism that would encounter art as concrete, sensory experience, "not just a text or commentary on the world."

Sontag's second collection of critical essays, *Styles of Radical Will* (1969), extends some of the ideas of *Against Interpretation* by demonstrating in studies of Emil M. Cioran, Ingmar Bergman, Jean-Luc Godard, and other contemporary artists how "art is the objectifying of the will in a thing or performance, and the provoking or arousing of the will." Two influential essays, "The Aesthetics of Silence" and "The Pornographic Imagination," explain how normative societal standards and definitions of art suppress unrest and sustain in America the "national psychosis, founded, as are all psychoses, on the efficacious denial of reality."

In *On Photography* (1977) Sontag takes a somewhat ambivalent attitude towards her subject. While photographs challenge interpretation by setting up "a chronic voyeuristic relation to the world which levels the meaning of all events," their proliferation "contributes to the erosion of the very notions of meaning." In the long run, she says, photography "clears our eyes." *Illness as Metaphor* (1978) grew out of Sontag's discovery in 1976 that she had breast cancer. Like many who have survived serious illnesses, she felt an intensified interest in living; but the experience led her to expose the contaminating effect of the language with which we talk about disease. Her most recent book, *AIDS and Its Metaphors* (1988), extends this argument to the way in which we speak about this disease.

THE PORNOGRAPHIC IMAGINATION

No one should undertake a discussion of pornography before acknowledging the pornograph*ies*—there are at least three—and before pledging to take them on one at a time. There is a considerable gain in truth if pornography as an item in social history is treated quite separately from pornography as a psychological phenomenon (according to the usual view, symptomatic of sexual deficiency or deformity in both the producers and the consumers), and if one further distinguishes from both of these another pornography: a minor but interesting modality or convention within the arts.

It's the last of the three pornographies that I want to focus upon. More narrowly, upon the literary genre for which, lacking a better name, I'm willing to accept (in the privacy of serious intellectual debate, not in the courts) the dubious label of pornography. By literary genre I mean a body of work belonging to literature considered as an art, and to which inherent standards of artistic excellence pertain. From the standpoint of social and psychological phenomena, all pornographic texts have the same status; they are documents. But from the standpoint of art, some of these texts may well become something else. Not only do Pierre Louÿs' *Trois Filles de leur mère*, Georges Bataille's *Histoire de l'oeil* and *Madame Edwarda*, the pseudonymous *Story of O* and *The Image* belong to literature, but it can be made clear why these books, all five of them, occupy a much higher rank as literature than *Candy* or Oscar Wilde's *Teleny* or the Earl of Rochester's *Sodom* or Apollinaire's *The Debauched Hospodar* or Cleland's *Fanny Hill*. The avalanche of pornographic potboilers marketed for two centuries under and now, increasingly, over the counter no more impugns the status as literature of the first group of pornographic books than the proliferation of books of the caliber of *The Carpetbaggers* and *Valley of the Dolls* throws into question the credentials of *Anna Karenina* and *The Great Gatsby* and *The Man Who Loved Children*. The ratio of authentic literature to trash in pornography may be somewhat lower than the ratio of novels of genuine literary merit to the entire volume of sub-literary fiction produced for mass taste. But it is probably no lower than, for instance, that of another somewhat shady sub-genre with a few first-rate books to its credit, science fiction. (As literary forms, pornography and science fiction resemble each other in several interesting ways.) Anyway, the quantitative measure supplies a trivial standard. Relatively uncommon as they may be, there are writings which it seems reasonable to call pornographic—assuming that the stale label has any use at all—which, at the same time, cannot be refused accreditation as serious literature.

The point would seem to be obvious. Yet, apparently, that's far from being the case. At least in England and America, the reasoned scrutiny and assessment of pornography is held firmly within the limits of the discourse employed by psychologists, sociologists, historians, jurists, professional moralists, and social critics. Pornography is a malady to be diagnosed and an occasion for judgment. It's something one is for or against. And taking sides about pornography is hardly like being for or against aleatoric music or Pop Art, but quite a bit like being for or against legalized abortion or federal aid to parochial schools. In fact, the same fundamental approach to the subject is shared by recent eloquent defenders of society's right and obligation to censor dirty books, like George P. Elliott and George Steiner, and those like Paul Goodman, who foresee pernicious consequences of a policy of censorship far worse than any harm done by the books themselves. Both the libertarians and the would-be censors agree in reducing pornography to pathological symptom and problematic social commodity. A near unanimous consensus exists as to what pornography is—this being identified with notions about the *sources* of the impulse to produce and consume these curious goods. When viewed as a theme for psychological analysis, pornography is rarely seen as anything more interesting than texts which illustrate a deplorable arrest in normal adult sexual development. In this view, all pornography amounts to is the representation of the fantasies of infantile sexual life, these fantasies having been edited by the more skilled, less innocent consciousness of the masturbatory adolescent, for purchase by so-called adults. As a social phenomenon—for instance, the boom in the production of pornography in the societies of Western Europe and America since the eighteenth century—the approach is no less unequivocally clinical. Pornography becomes a group pathology, the disease of a whole culture, about whose cause everyone is pretty well agreed. The mounting output of dirty books is attributed to a festering legacy of Christian sexual repression and to sheer physiological ignorance, these ancient disabilities being now compounded by more proximate historical events, the impact of drastic dislocations in traditional modes of family and political order and unsettling change in the roles of the sexes. (The problem of pornography is one of "the dilemmas of a society in transition," Goodman said in an essay several years ago.) Thus, there is a fairly complete consensus about the *diagnosis* of pornography itself. The disagreements arise only in the estimate of the psychological and social *consequences* of its dissemination, and therefore in the formulating of tactics and policy.

The more enlightened architects of moral policy are undoubtedly prepared to admit that there is something like a "pornographic imagination," although only in the sense that pornographic works are tokens of a radical failure or deformation of the imagination. And they may grant, as Goodman, Wayland Young, and others have suggested, that there also exists a "pornographic society": that, indeed, ours is a flourishing example of one, a society so hypocritically and repressively constructed that it must inevitably produce an effusion of pornography as both its logical expression and its subversive, demotic antidote. But nowhere in the Anglo-American community of letters have I seen it argued that some pornographic books are interesting and important works of art. So long as pornography is treated as only a social and psychological phenomenon and a locus for moral concern, how could such an argument ever be made?

II

There's another reason, apart from this categorizing of pornography as a topic of analysis, why the question whether or not works of pornography can be literature has never been genuinely debated. I mean the view of literature itself maintained by most English and American critics—a view which in excluding pornographic writings *by definition* from the precincts of literature excludes much else besides.

Of course, no one denies that pornography constitutes a branch of literature in the sense that it appears in the form of printed books of fiction. But beyond that trivial connection, no more is allowed. The fashion in which most critics construe the nature of prose literature, no less than their view of the nature of pornography, inevitably puts pornography in an adverse relation to literature. It is an airtight case, for if a pornographic book is defined as one not belonging to literature (and vice versa), there is no need to examine individual books.

Most mutually exclusive definitions of pornography and literature rest on four separate arguments. One is that the utterly singleminded way in which works of pornography address the reader, proposing to arouse him sexually, is antithetical to the complex function of literature. It may then be argued that pornography's aim, inducing sexual excitement, is at odds with the tranquil, detached involvement evoked by genuine art. But this turn of the argument seems particularly unconvincing, considering the respected appeal to the reader's moral feelings intended by "realistic" writing, not to mention the fact that some certified masterpieces (from Chaucer to Lawrence) contain passages that do properly excite readers sexually. It is more plausible just to emphasize that pornography still possesses only one "intention," while any genuinely valuable work of literature has many.

Another argument, made by Adorno among others, is that works of pornography lack the beginning-middle-and-end form characteristic of literature. A piece of pornographic fiction concocts no better than a crude excuse for a beginning; and once having begun, it goes on and on and ends nowhere.

Another argument: pornographic writing can't evidence any care for its means of expression as such (the concern of literature), since the aim of pornography is to inspire a set of nonverbal fantasies in which language plays a debased, merely instrumental role.

Last and most weighty is the argument that the subject of literature is the relation of human beings to each other, their complex feelings and emotions; pornography, in contrast, disdains fully formed persons (psychology and social portraiture), is oblivious to the question of motives and their credibility and reports only the motiveless tireless transactions of depersonalized organs.

Simply extrapolating from the conception of literature maintained by most English and American critics today, it would follow that the literary value of pornography has to be nil. But these paradigms don't stand up to close analysis in themselves, nor do they even fit their subject. Take, for instance, *Story of O*. Though the novel is clearly obscene by the usual standards, and more effective than many in arousing a reader sexually, sexual arousal doesn't appear to be the sole function of the situations portrayed. The narrative does have a definite beginning, middle, and end. The elegance of the writing hardly gives the impression that its author considered language a bothersome necessity. Further, the characters do possess emotions of a very intense kind, although obsessional and indeed wholly asocial ones; characters do have motives, though they are not psychiatrically or socially "normal" motives. The characters in *Story of O* are endowed with a "psychology" of a sort, one derived from the psychology of lust. And while what can be learned of the characters within the situations in which they are placed is severely restricted—to modes of sexual concentration and explicitly rendered sexual behavior—O and her partners are no more reduced or foreshortened than the characters in many non-pornographic works of contemporary fiction.

Only when English and American critics evolve a more sophisticated view of literature will an interesting debate get underway. (In the end, this debate would be not only about pornography but about the whole body of contemporary literature insistently focused on extreme situations and behavior.) The difficulty arises because so many critics continue to identify with prose literature itself the particular literary conventions of "realism" (what might be crudely associated with the major tradition of the nineteenth-century novel). For examples of alternative literary modes, one is not confined only to much of the greatest twentieth-century writing—to *Ulysses,* a book not about characters but about media of transpersonal exchange, about all that lies outside individual psychology and personal need; to French Surrealism and its most recent offspring, the New Novel; to German "expressionist" fiction; to the Russian post-novel represented by Biely's *St. Petersburg* and by Nabokov; or to the nonlinear, tenseless narratives of Stein and Burroughs. A definition of literature that faults a work for being rooted in "fantasy" rather than in the realistic rendering of how lifelike persons in familiar situations live with each other couldn't even handle such venerable conventions as the pastoral, which depicts relations between people that are certainly reductive, vapid, and unconvincing.

An uprooting of some of these tenacious clichés is long overdue: it will promote a sounder reading of the literature of the past as well as put critics and ordinary readers better in touch with contemporary literature, which includes zones of writing that structurally resemble pornography. It is facile, virtually meaningless, to demand that literature stick with the "human." For the matter at stake is not "human" versus "inhuman" (in which choosing the "human" guarantees instant moral self-congratulation for both author and reader) but an infinitely varied register of forms and tonalities for transposing *the human voice* into prose narrative. For the critic, the proper question is not the relationship between the book and "the world" or "reality" (in which each novel is judged as if it were a unique item, and in which the world is regarded as a far less complex place than it is) but the complexities of consciousness itself, as the medium through which a world exists at all and is constituted, and an approach to single books of fiction which doesn't slight the fact that they exist in dialogue with each other. From this point of view, the decision of the old novelists to depict the unfolding of the destinies of sharply individualized "characters" in familiar, socially dense situations within the conventional notation of chronological sequence is only one of many possible decisions, possessing no inherently superior claim to the allegiance of serious readers. There is nothing innately more "human" about these procedures. The presence of realistic characters is not, in itself, something wholesome, a more nourishing staple for the moral sensibility.

The only sure truth about characters in prose fiction is that they are, in Henry James' phrase, "a compositional resource." The presence of human figures in literary art can serve many purposes. Dramatic tension or three-dimensionality in the rendering of personal and social relations is often *not* a writer's aim, in which case it doesn't help to insist on that as a generic standard. Exploring ideas is as authentic an aim of prose fiction, although by the standards of novelistic realism this aim severely limits the presentation of lifelike persons. The constructing or imaging of something inanimate, or of a portion of the world of nature, is also a valid enterprise, and entails an appropriate rescaling of the human figure. (The form of the pastoral involves both these aims: the depiction of ideas and of nature. Persons are used only to the extent that they constitute a certain kind of landscape, which is partly a stylization of "real" nature and partly a neo-Platonic landscape of ideas.) And equally valid as a subject for prose narrative are the extreme states of human feeling and consciousness, those so peremptory that they exclude the mundane flux of feelings and are only contingently linked with concrete persons—which is the case with pornography.

One would never guess from the confident pronouncements on the nature of literature by most American and English critics that a vivid debate on this issue had been proceeding for several generations. "It seems to me," Jacques Rivière wrote in the *Nouvelle Revue Française* in 1924, "that we are witnessing a very serious crisis in the concept of what literature is." One of several responses to "the problem of the possibility and the limits of literature," Rivière noted, is the marked tendency for "art (if even the word can still be kept) to become a completely nonhuman activity, a supersensory function, if I may use that term, a sort of creative astronomy." I cite Rivière not because his essay, "Questioning the Concept of Literature," is particularly original or definitive or subtly argued, but simply to recall an ensemble of radical notions about literature which were almost critical commonplaces forty years ago in European literary magazines.

To this day, though, that ferment remains alien, unassimilated, and persistently misunderstood in the English and American world of letters: suspected as issuing from a collective cultural failure of nerve, frequently dismissed as outright perversity or obscurantism or creative sterility. The better English-speaking critics, however, could hardly fail to notice how much great twentieth-century literature subverts those ideas received from certain of the great nineteenth-century novelists on the nature of literature which they continue to echo in 1967. But the critics' awareness of genuinely new literature was usually tendered in a spirit much like that of the rabbis a century before the beginning of the Christian era who, humbly acknowledging the spiritual inferiority of their own age to the age of the great prophets, nevertheless firmly closed the canon of prophetic books and declared—with more relief, one suspects, than regret—the era of prophecy ended. So has the age of what in Anglo-American criticism is still called, astonishingly enough, "experimental" or "avant-garde" writing been repeatedly declared closed. The ritual celebration of each contemporary genius's undermining of the older notions of literature was often accompanied by the nervous insistence that the writing brought forth was, alas, the last of its noble, sterile line. Now, the results of this intricate, one-eyed way of looking at modern literature have been several decades of unparalleled interest and brilliance in English and American—particularly American—criticism. But it is an interest and brilliance reared on bankruptcy of taste and something approaching a fundamental dishonesty of method. The critics' retrograde awareness of the impressive new claims staked out by modern literature, linked with their chagrin over what was usually designated as "the rejection of reality" and "the failure of the self" endemic in that literature, indicates the precise point at which most talented Anglo-American literary criticism leaves off considering structures of literature and transposes itself into criticism of culture.

I don't wish to repeat here the arguments that I have advanced elsewhere on behalf of a different critical approach. Still, some allusion to that approach needs to be made. To discuss even a single work of the radical nature of *Histoire de l'oeil* raises the question of literature itself, of prose narrative considered as an art form. And books like those of Bataille could not have been written except for that agonized reappraisal of the nature of literature which has been preoccupying literary Europe for more than half a century; but lacking that context, they must prove almost unassimilable for English and American readers—except as "mere" pornography, inexplicably fancy trash. If it is even necessary to take up the issue of whether or not pornography and literature are antithetical, if it is at all necessary to assert that works of pornography *can* belong to literature, then the assertion must imply an overall view of what art is.

To put it very generally: art (and art-making) is a form of consciousness; the materials of art are the variety of forms of consciousness. By no *aesthetic* principle can this notion of the materials of art be construed as excluding even the extreme forms of consciousness that transcend social personality or psychological individuality.

In daily life, to be sure, we may acknowledge a moral obligation to inhibit such states of consciousness in ourselves. The obligation seems pragmatically sound, not only to maintain social order in the widest sense but to allow the individual to establish and maintain a humane contact with other persons (though that contact can be renounced, for shorter or longer periods). It's well known that when people venture into the far reaches of consciousness, they do so at the peril of their sanity, that is, of their humanity. But the "human scale" or humanistic standard proper to ordinary life and conduct seems misplaced when applied to art. It oversimplifies. If within the last century art conceived as an autonomous activity has come to be invested with an unprecedented stature—the nearest thing to a sacramental human activity acknowledged by secular society—it is because one of the tasks art has assumed is making forays into and taking up positions on the frontiers of consciousness (often very dangerous to the artist as a person) and reporting back what's there. Being a freelance explorer of spiritual dangers, the artist gains a certain license to behave differently from other people; matching the singularity of his vocation, he may be decked out with a suitably eccentric life style, or he may not. His job is inventing trophies of his experiences—objects and gestures that fascinate and enthrall, not merely (as prescribed by older notions of the artist) edify or entertain. His principal means of fascinating is to advance one step further in the dialectic of outrage. He seeks to make his work repulsive, obscure, inaccessible; in short, to give what is, or seems to be, *not* wanted. But however fierce may be the outrages the artist perpetrates upon his audience, his credentials and spiritual authority ultimately depend on the audience's sense (whether something known or inferred) of the outrages he commits upon himself. The exemplary modern artist is a broker in madness.

The notion of art as the dearly purchased outcome of an immense spiritual risk, one whose cost goes up with the entry and participation of each new player in the game, invites a revised set of critical standards. Art produced under the aegis of this conception certainly is not, cannot be, "realistic." But words like "fantasy" or "surrealism," that only invert the guidelines of realism, clarify little. Fantasy too easily declines into "mere" fantasy; the clincher is the adjective "infantile." Where does fantasy, condemned by psychiatric rather than artistic standards, end and imagination begin?

Since it's hardly likely that contemporary critics seriously mean to bar prose narratives that are unrealistic from the domain of literature, one suspects that a special standard is being applied to sexual themes. This becomes clearer if one thinks of another kind of book, another kind of "fantasy." The ahistorical dreamlike landscape where action is situated, the peculiarly congealed time in which acts are performed—these occur almost as often in science fiction as they do in pornography. There is nothing conclusive in the well-known fact that most men and women fall short of the sexual prowess that people in pornography are represented as enjoying; that the size of organs, number and duration of orgasms, variety and feasibility of sexual powers, and amount of sexual energy all seem grossly exaggerated. Yes, and the spaceships and the teeming planets depicted in science-fiction novels don't exist either. The fact that the site of narrative is an ideal *topos* disqualifies neither pornography nor science fiction from being literature. Such negations of real, concrete, three-dimensional social time, space, and personality—and such "fantastic" enlargements of human energy—are rather the ingredients of another kind of literature, founded on another mode of consciousness.

The materials of the pornographic books that count as literature are, precisely, one of the extreme forms of human consciousness. Undoubtedly, many people would agree that the sexually obsessed consciousness can, in principle, enter into literature as an art form. Literature about lust? Why not? But then they usually add a rider to the agreement which effectually nullifies it. They require that the author have the proper "distance" from his obsessions for their rendering to count as literature. Such a standard is sheer hypocrisy, revealing once again that the values commonly applied to pornography are, in the end, those belonging to psychiatry and social affairs rather than to art. (Since Christianity upped the ante and concentrated on sexual behavior as the root of virtue, everything pertaining to sex has been a "special case" in our culture, evoking peculiarly inconsistent attitudes.) Van Gogh's paintings retain their status as art even if it seems his manner of painting owed less to a conscious choice of representational means than to his being deranged and actually seeing reality the way he painted it. Similarly, *Histoire de l'oeil* does not become case history rather than art because, as Bataille reveals in the extraordinary autobiographical essay appended to the narrative, the book's obsessions are indeed his own.

What makes a work of pornography part of the history of art rather than of trash is not distance, the superimposition of a consciousness more conformable to that of ordinary reality upon the "deranged consciousness" of the erotically obsessed. Rather, it is the originality, thoroughness, authenticity, and power of that deranged consciousness itself, as incarnated in a work. From the point of view of art, the exclusivity of the consciousness embodied in pornographic books is in itself neither anomalous nor anti-literary.

Nor is the purported aim or effect, whether it is intentional or not, of such books—to excite the reader sexually—a defect. Only a degraded and mechanistic idea of sex could mislead someone into thinking that being sexually stirred by a book like *Madame Edwarda* is a simple matter. The singleness of intention often condemned by critics is, when the work merits treatment as art, compounded of many resonances. The physical sensations involuntarily produced in someone reading the book carry with them something that touches upon the reader's whole experience of his humanity—and his limits as a personality and as a body. Actually, the singleness of pornography's intention is spurious. But the aggressiveness of the intention is not. What seems like an end is as much a means, startlingly and oppressively concrete. The end, however, is less concrete. Pornography is one of the branches of literature—science fiction is another—aiming at disorientation, at psychic dislocation.

In some respects, the use of sexual obsessions as a subject for literature resembles the use of a literary subject whose validity far fewer people would contest: religious obsessions. So compared, the familiar fact of pornography's definite, aggressive impact upon its readers looks somewhat different. Its celebrated intention of sexually stimulating readers is really a species of proselytizing. Pornography that is serious literature aims to "excite" in the same way that books which render an extreme form of religious experience aim to "convert." ⟨. . .⟩

V

The prominent characteristics of all products of the pornographic imagination are their energy and their absolutism.

The books generally called pornographic are those whose primary, exclusive, and overriding preoccupation is with the depiction of sexual "intentions" and "activities." One could also say sexual "feelings," except that the word seems redundant. The feelings of the personages deployed by the pornographic imagination are, at any given moment, either identical with their "behavior" or else a preparatory phase, that of "intention," on the verge of breaking into "behavior" unless physically thwarted. Pornography uses a small crude vocabulary of feeling, all relating to the prospects of action: feeling one would like to act (lust); feeling one would not like to act (shame, fear, aversion). There are no gratuitous or nonfunctioning feelings; no musings, whether speculative or imagistic, which are irrelevant to the business at hand. Thus, the pornographic imagination inhabits a universe that is, however repetitive the incidents occurring within it, incomparably economical. The strictest possible criterion of relevance applies: everything must bear upon the erotic situation.

The universe proposed by the pornographic imagination is a total universe. It has the power to ingest and metamorphose and translate all concerns that are fed into it, reducing everything into the one negotiable currency of the erotic imperative. All action is conceived of as a set of sexual *exchanges*. Thus, the reason why pornography refuses to make fixed distinctions between the sexes or allow any kind of sexual preference or sexual taboo to endure can be explained "structurally." The bisexuality, the disregard for the incest taboo, and other similar features common to pornographic narratives function to multiply the possibilities of exchange. Ideally, it should be possible for everyone to have a sexual connection with everyone else.

Of course the pornographic imagination is hardly the only form of consciousness that proposes a total universe. Another is the type of imagination that has generated modern symbolic logic. In the total universe proposed by the logician's imagination, all statements can be broken down or chewed up to make it possible to rerender them in the form of the logical language; those parts of ordinary language that don't fit are simply lopped off. Certain of the well-known states of the religious imagination, to take another example, operate in the same cannibalistic way, engorging all materials made available to them for retranslation into phenomena saturated with the religious polarities (sacred and profane, etc.).

The latter example, for obvious reasons, touches closely on the present subject. Religious metaphors abound in a good deal of modern erotic literature—notably in Genet—and in some works of pornographic literature, too. *Story of O* makes heavy use of religious metaphors for the ordeal that O undergoes. O "wanted to believe." Her drastic condition of total personal servitude to those who use her sexually is repeatedly described as a mode of salvation. With anguish and anxiety, she surrenders herself; and "henceforth there were no more hiatuses, no dead time, no remission." While she has, to be sure, entirely lost her freedom, O has gained the right to participate in what is described as virtually a sacramental rite.

> The word "open" and the expression "opening her legs" were, on her lover's lips, charged with such uneasiness and power that she could never hear them without experiencing a kind of internal prostration, a sacred submission, as though a god, and not he, had spoken to her.

Though she fears the whip and other cruel mistreatments before they are inflicted on her, "yet when it was over she was happy to have gone through it, happier still if it had been especially cruel and prolonged." The whipping, branding, and mutilating are described (from the point of view of *her* consciousness) as ritual ordeals which test the faith of someone being initiated into an ascetic spiritual discipline. The "perfect submissiveness" that her original lover and then Sir Stephen demand of her echoes the extinction of the self explicitly required of a Jesuit novice or Zen pupil. O is "that absentminded person who has yielded up her will in order to be totally remade," to be made fit to serve a will far more powerful and authoritative than her own.

As might be expected, the straightforwardness of the religious metaphors in *Story of O* has evoked some correspondingly straight readings of the book. The novelist Mandiargues, whose preface precedes Paulhan's in the American translation, doesn't hesitate to describe *Story of O* as "a mystic work," and therefore "not, strictly speaking, an erotic book." What *Story of O* depicts "is a complete spiritual transformation, what others would call an *ascesis*." But the matter is not so simple. Mandiargues is correct in dismissing a psychiatric analysis of O's state of mind that would reduce the book's subject to, say, "masochism." As Paulhan says, "the heroine's ardor" is totally inexplicable in terms of the conventional psychiatric vocabulary. The fact that the novel employs some of the conventional motifs and trappings of the theatre of sado-masochism has itself to be explained. But Mandiargues has fallen into an error almost as reductive and only slightly less vulgar. Surely, the only alternative to the psychiatric reductions is not the religious vocabulary. But that only these two foreshortened alternatives exist testifies once again to the bone-deep denigration of the range and seriousness of sexual experience that still rules this culture, for all its much-advertised new permissiveness.

My own view is that "Pauline Réage" wrote an erotic book. The notion implicit in *Story of O* that eros is a sacrament is not the "truth" behind the literal (erotic) sense of the book—the lascivious rites of enslavement and degradation performed upon O—but, exactly, a metaphor for it. Why say something stronger, when the statement can't really *mean* anything stronger? But despite the virtual incomprehensibility to most educated people today of the substantive experience behind religious vocabulary, there is a continuing piety toward the grandeur of emotions that went into that vocabulary. The religious imagination survives for most people as not just the primary but virtually the only credible instance of an imagination working in a total way.

No wonder, then, that the new or radically revamped forms of the total imagination which have arisen in the past century—notably, those of the artist, the erotomane, the left revolutionary, and the madman—have chronically borrowed the prestige of the religious vocabulary. And total experiences, of which there are many kinds, tend again and again to be apprehended only as revivals or translations of the religious imagination. To try to make a fresh way of talking at the most serious, ardent, and enthusiastic level, heading off the religious encapsulation, is one of the primary intellectual tasks of future thought. As matters stand, with everything from *Story of O* to Mao reabsorbed into the incorrigible survival of the religious impulse, all thinking and feeling gets devalued. (Hegel made perhaps the grandest attempt to create a post-religious vocabulary, out of philosophy, that would command the treasures of passion and credibility and emotive appropriateness that were gathered into the religious vocabulary. But his most interesting followers steadily undermined the abstract meta-religious language in which he had bequeathed his thought, and concentrated instead on the specific social and practical applications of his revolutionary form of process-thinking, historicism. Hegel's failure lies like a gigantic disturbing hulk across the intellectual landscape. And no one has been big enough, pompous enough, or energetic enough since Hegel to attempt the task again.)

And so we remain, careening among our overvaried choices of kinds of total imagination, of species of total seriousness. Perhaps the deepest spiritual resonance of the career of pornography in its "modern" Western phase under consideration here (pornography in the Orient or the Moslem world being something very different) is this vast frustration of human passion and seriousness since the old religious imagination, with its secure monopoly on the total imagination, began in the late eighteenth century to crumble. The ludicrousness and lack of skill of most pornographic writing, films, and painting is obvious to everyone who has been exposed to them. What is less often remarked about the typical products of the pornographic imagination is their pathos. Most pornography—the books discussed here cannot be excepted—points to something more general than even sexual damage. I mean the traumatic failure of modern capitalist society to provide authentic outlets for the perennial human flair for high-temperature visionary obsessions, to satisfy the appetite for exalted self-transcending modes of concentration and seriousness. The need of human beings to transcend "the personal" is no less profound than the need to be a person, an individual. But this society serves that need poorly. It provides mainly demonic vocabularies in which to situate that need and from which to initiate action and construct rites of behavior. One is offered a choice among vocabularies of thought and action which are not merely self-transcending but self-destructive.

VI

But the pornographic imagination is not just to be understood as a form of psychic absolutism—some of whose products we might be able to regard (in the role of connoisseur, rather than client) with more sympathy or intellectual curiosity or aesthetic sophistication.

Several times before in this essay I have alluded to the possibility that the pornographic imagination says something worth listening to, albeit in a degraded and often unrecognizable form. I've urged that this spectacularly cramped form of the human imagination has, nevertheless, its peculiar access to some truth. This truth—about sensibility, about sex, about individual personality, about despair, about limits—can be shared when it projects itself into art. (Everyone, at least in dreams, has inhabited the world of the pornographic imagination for some hours or days or even longer periods of his life; but only the full-time residents make the fetishes, the trophies, the art.) That discourse one might call the poetry of transgression is also knowledge. He who transgresses not only breaks a rule. He goes somewhere that the others are not; and he knows something the others don't know.

Pornography, considered as an artistic or art-producing form of the human imagination, is an expression of what William James called "morbid-mindedness." But James was surely right when he gave as part of the definition of morbid-mindedness that it ranged over "a wider scale of experience" than healthy-mindedness.

What can be said, though, to the many sensible and sensitive people who find depressing the fact that a whole library of pornographic reading material has been made, within the last few years, so easily available in paperback form to the very young? Probably one thing: that their apprehension is justified, but may not be in scale. I am not addressing the usual complainers, those who feel that since sex after all *is* dirty, so are books reveling in sex (dirty in a way that a genocide screened nightly on TV, apparently, is not). There still remains a sizeable minority of people who object to or are repelled by pornography not because they think it's dirty but because they know that pornography can be a crutch for the psychologically deformed and a brutalization of the morally innocent. I feel an aversion to pornography for those reasons, too, and am uncomfortable about the consequences of its increasing availability. But isn't the worry somewhat misplaced? What's really at stake? A concern about the uses of knowledge itself. There's a sense in which *all* knowledge is dangerous, the reason being that not everyone is in the same condition as knowers or potential knowers. Perhaps most people don't need "a wider scale of experience." It may be that, without subtle and extensive psychic preparation, any widening of experience and consciousness is destructive for most people. Then we must ask what justifies the reckless unlimited confidence we have in the present mass availability of other kinds of knowledge, in our optimistic acquiescence in the transformation of and extension of human capacities by machines. Pornography is only one item among the many dangerous commodities being circulated in this society and, unattractive as it may be, one of the less lethal, the less costly to the community in terms of human suffering. Except perhaps in a small circle of writer-intellectuals in France, pornography is an inglorious and mostly despised department of the imagination. Its mean status is the very antithesis of the considerable spiritual prestige enjoyed by many items which are far more noxious.

In the last analysis, the place we assign to pornography depends on the goals we set for our own consciousness, our own experience. But the goal A espouses for his consciousness may *not* be one he's pleased to see B adopt, because he judges that B isn't qualified or experienced or subtle enough. And B may be dismayed and even indignant at A's adopting goals that he himself professes; when A holds them, they become presumptuous or shallow. Probably this chronic mutual suspicion of our neighbor's capacities—suggesting, in effect, a hierarchy of competence with respect to human consciousness—will never be settled to everyone's satisfaction. As long as the quality of people's consciousness varies so greatly, how could it be?

In an essay on the subject some years ago, Paul Goodman wrote: "The question is not *whether* pornography, but the quality of the pornography." That's exactly right. One could extend the thought a good deal further. The question is not *whether* consciousness or *whether* knowledge, but the quality of the consciousness and of the knowledge. And that invites consideration of the quality or fineness of the human subject—the most problematic standard of all. It doesn't seem inaccurate to say most people in this society who aren't actively mad are, at best, reformed or potential lunatics. But is anyone supposed to act on this knowledge, even genuinely live with it? If so many are teetering on the verge of murder, dehumanization, sexual deformity and despair, and we were to act on that thought, then censorship much more radical than the indignant foes of pornography ever envisage seems in order. For if that's the case, not only pornography but all forms of serious art and knowledge—in other words, all forms of truth—are suspect and dangerous.

Fredric Jameson
1934–

Fredric Jameson was born on April 14, 1934, in Cleveland. He attended Haverford College (B.A., 1954) and Yale University (M.A., 1956; Ph.D., 1960). Jameson taught at Harvard (1959–67), the University of California–San Diego (1967–76), Yale (1976–83), and the University of California–Santa Cruz (1983–85) before going to Duke University in 1986 as the William A. Lane Professor of Comparative Literature.

Jameson is considered the preeminent Marxist critic in America. In the course of his academic career he has introduced both structuralist and Marxist critical theory from Europe to the United States and has strengthened his Marxist approach over the years in response to challenges from other critical theorists. As a Hegelian dialectician Jameson has brought into his discourse the ideas of such Continental philosophers as Theodor W. Adorno, Walter Benjamin, Ernst Bloch, Georg Lukács, and Jean-Paul Sartre, establishing himself as a critic not only of literature but of twentieth-century culture.

In his first book, *Sartre: The Origins of a Style* (1961), an outgrowth of his Ph.D. dissertation, Jameson establishes the concern for problems of narrative that runs throughout his work. Narrative forms for Jameson cannot be interpreted as reflections; they express an underlying mode of production, lending them to an allegorical interpretation rooted in Marxist hermeneutics.

Jameson again considers Sartre in his second book, *Marxism and Form: Twentieth-Century Dialectical Theories of Literature* (1972), and also instructs the reader in the thought of Bloch, Adorno, Benjamin, Herbert Marcuse, and Lukács, stressing the wider social implications of literature beyond its "literariness"; one commentator has termed the book "a hermeneutics of structuralism." Jameson's interest in structuralist theory is further amplified in *The Prison-House of Language: A Critical Account of Structuralism and Russian Formalism* (1972), published shortly after *Marxism and Form*. To some extent a companion to the earlier book, *Prison-House* offers an introductory examination and critique of Continental literary theory and formalism, then not widely known in the United States.

Jameson takes on modernism in his next book, *Fables of Aggression: Wyndham Lewis, the Modernist as Fascist* (1979), in which he examines the relationship between Lewis's art and the sociopolitical underpinnings of Lewis's life and thought. This work was followed two years later by *The Political Unconscious: Narrative as a Socially Symbolic Act*.

In addition to his books, Jameson has published numerous essays of equal significance. These include "Metacommentary" (*PMLA*, January 1971; winner of the MLA's William Riley Parker Prize); "Imaginary and Symbolic in Lacan:

Marxism, Psychoanalytic Criticism, and the Problem of the Subject" (*Yale French Studies*, 1977); "Science versus Ideology" (*Humanities in Society*, 1983); and "Postmodernism, or the Cultural Logic of Late Capitalism" (*New Left Review*, July–August 1984). Many of Jameson's essays have now been collected in *The Ideologies of Theory: Essays 1971–1986* (1988; 2 vols.).

Jameson has been a guest lecturer and visiting professor at universities here and abroad, and has received Rotary, Woodrow Wilson, Fulbright, and Guggenheim fellowships. Cofounder of the Marxist Literary Group, he is coeditor of *Social Text* and a contributing editor of the *Minnesota Review*.

FROM

The Political Unconscious

CONCLUSION: THE DIALECTIC OF UTOPIA AND IDEOLOGY

> As in all previous history, whoever emerges as victor still participates in that triumph in which today's rulers march over the prostate bodies of their victims. As is customary, the spoils are borne aloft in that triumphal parade. These are generally called the cultural heritage. The latter finds a rather distanced observer in the historical materialist. For such cultural riches, as he surveys them, everywhere betray an origin which he cannot but contemplate with horror. They owe their existence, not merely to the toil of the great creators who have produced them, but equally to the anonymous forced labor of the latters' contemporaries. There has never been a document of culture which was not at one and the same time a document of barbarism.
> —Walter Benjamin,
> "Theses on the Philosophy of History," VII

The conception of the political unconscious developed in the preceding pages has tended to distance itself, at certain strategic moments, from those implacably polemic and demystifying procedures traditionally associated with the Marxist practice of ideological analysis. It is now time to confront the latter directly and to spell out such modifications in more detail. The most influential lesson of Marx—the one which ranges him alongside Freud and Nietzsche as one of the great negative diagnosticians of contemporary culture and social life—has, of course, rightly been taken to be the lesson of false consciousness, of class bias and ideological programming, the lesson of the structural limits of the values and attitudes of particular social classes, or in other words of the constitutive relationship between the praxis of such groups and what they conceptualize as value or desire and project in the form of culture.

In a splendidly argued confrontation with Marxism, the anthropologist Marshall Sahlins has attempted to demonstrate that it is by its very philosophical structure locked into an approach to culture which must thus remain functional or instrumental in the broadest sense.[1] Given the Marxian orientation toward the reading or demystification of superstructures in terms of their base, or relations of production, even the most sophisticated Marxian analyses of cultural texts must, according to Sahlins, necessarily always presuppose a certain structural functionality about culture: the latter will always "ultimately" (if not far more immediately) be grasped as the instrument, witting or unwitting, of class domination, legitimation, and social mystification. Sahlins is untroubled by the paradox that Marx himself reserved his most brilliant polemic onslaughts for the classical form taken by an instrumental theory of culture in his own time, namely utilitarianism; nor does Sahlins seem aware that his own targets—economism, technological determinism, the primacy of the forces of production—are also those that have been subjected to powerful critiques by a range of contemporary Marxisms which regard them as deviations from the authentic Marxist spirit. It may, however, readily be admitted that what he calls the instrumentalization of culture is a temptation or tendency within all Marxisms, without, for all that, being a necessary and fatal consequence.

Before offering a perspective in which this particular problem becomes a false one, we must clarify the troubled position of the individual subject within it. We suggested in our opening chapter that most forms of contemporary criticism tend, as toward their ideal, toward a model of immanence: on the theoretical level that concerns us here, this is to say that the phenomenological ideal—that of some ideal unity of consciousness or thinking and experience or the "objective" fact—continues to dominate modern thought even where phenomenology as such is explicitly repudiated.[2] Even the Freudian model of the unconscious, which has been exemplary in our own proposal of a properly political unconscious here, is everywhere subverted by the neo-Freudian nostalgia for some ultimate moment of *cure,* in which the dynamics of the unconscious proper rise to the light of day and of consciousness and are somehow "integrated" in an active lucidity about ourselves and the determinations of our desires and our behavior. But the cure in that sense is a myth, as is the equivalent mirage within a Marxian ideological analysis: namely, the vision of a moment in which the individual subject would be somehow fully conscious of his or her determination by class and would be able to square the circle of ideological conditioning by sheer lucidity and the taking of thought. But in the Marxian system, only a collective unity—whether that of a particular class, the proletariat, or of its "organ of consciousness," the revolutionary party—can achieve this transparency; the individual subject is always positioned within the social totality (and this is the sense of Althusser's insistence on the *permanence* of ideology).

What this impossibility of immanence means in practice is that the dialectical reversal must always involve a painful "decentering" of the consciousness of the individual subject, whom it confronts with a determination (whether of the Freudian or the political unconscious) that must necessarily be felt as extrinsic or external to conscious experience. It would be a mistake to think that anyone ever really learns to live with this ideological "Copernican revolution," any more than the most lucid subjects of psychoanalysis ever really achieve the habit of lucidity and self-knowledge; the approach to the Real is at best fitful, the retreat from it into this or that form of intellectual comfort perpetual. But if this is so, it follows that we must bracket that whole dimension of the critique of the Marxist doctrine of determination by social being which springs from exasperation with this unpleasant reflexivity. In particular, it should be stressed that the process of totalization outlined in our opening chapter offers no way out of this the "labor and suffering of the negative," but must necessarily be accompanied by it, if the process is to be authentically realized.

Once this unavoidable experiential accompaniment of the dialectic is granted, however, the theoretical problem of interpretive alternatives to an instrumental or functional theory of culture may more adequately be raised. That such alternatives are at least abstractly conceivable may be demonstrated by Paul Ricoeur's seminal reflections on the dual nature of the hermeneutic process:

> At one pole, hermeneutics is understood as the manifestation and restoration of a meaning addressed to me in the manner of a message, a proclamation, or as is sometimes said, a kerygma; according to the other pole, it is understood as a demystification, as a reduction of illusion. . . . The situation in which language finds itself today comprises this double possibility, this double solicitation and urgency: on the one hand, to purify discourse of its excrescences, liquidate the idols, go from drunkenness to sobriety, realize our state of poverty once and for all; on the other hand, to use the most "nihilistic," destructive, iconoclastic movements so as to *let speak* what once, what each time, was *said,* when meaning appeared anew, when meaning was at its fullest. Hermeneutics seems to me to be animated by this double motivation: willingness to suspect, willingness to listen: vow of rigor, vow of obedience. In our time we have not finished doing away with *idols* and we have barely begun to listen to *symbols.*[3]

It is unnecessary to underscore the obvious, namely the origins of Ricoeur's thought and figures in the tradition of religious exegesis and Christian historicism. The limits of Ricoeur's formulation are, however, not specifically theological ones, but are attributable to the persistence of categories of the individual subject: specifically, his conception of "positive" meaning as a kerygma or interpellation (retained in Althusser's theory of ideology[4]) is modeled on the act of communication between individual subjects, and cannot therefore be appropriated as such for any view of meaning as a collective process.

As far as the religious framework of Ricoeur's account is concerned, I have throughout the present work implied what I have suggested explicitly elsewhere, that any comparison of Marxism with religion is a two-way street, in which the former is not necessarily discredited by its association with the latter. On the contrary, such a comparison may also function to rewrite certain religious concepts—most notably Christian historicism and the "concept" of providence, but also the pretheological systems of primitive magic—as anticipatory foreshadowings of historical materialism within precapitalist social formations in which scientific thinking is unavailable as such. Marx's own notion of the so-called Asiatic mode of production (or "Oriental despotism") is the very locus for such reinterpretation of religious categories, as we will see below.

Meanwhile, the historically original form of the negative dialectic in Marxism—whether ideology is in it grasped as mere "false consciousness," or, more comprehensively, as structural limitation—should not be allowed to overshadow the presence in the Marxian tradition of a whole series of equivalents to Ricoeur's doctrine of meaning or positive hermeneutic. Ernst Bloch's ideal of hope or of the Utopian impulse; Mikhail Bakhtin's notion of the dialogical as a rupture of the one-dimensional text of bourgeois narrative, as a carnivalesque dispersal of the hegemonic order of a dominant culture; the Frankfurt School's conception of strong memory as the trace of gratification, of the revolutionary power of that *promesse de bonheur* most immediately inscribed in the aesthetic text: all these formulations hint at a variety of options for articulating a properly Marxian version of meaning beyond the purely ideological.

Yet we have also suggested, in our discussion of Northrop Frye's system in Chapter 1, that even within an ostensibly religious framework such varied options can be measured against the standard of the medieval system of four levels, which helped us to distinguish the resonance of the "moral" level—that of the individual soul, or of the libidinal Utopia of the individual body—from that ultimate and logically prior level traditionally termed the "anagogical," in which even such individual visions of Utopian transfiguration are rewritten in terms of the collective, of the destiny of the human race. Such a distinction allows us to spell out the priority, within the Marxist tradition, of a "positive hermeneutic" based on social class from those still limited by anarchist categories of the individual subject and individual experience. The concept of class is thus the space in which, if anywhere, a Marxian version of the hermeneutics of meaning, of some noninstrumental conception of culture, may be tested, particularly insofar as it is from this same concept of social class that the strongest form of a Marxian "negative hermeneutic"—of the class character and functionality of ideology as such—also derives.

Such a demonstration might be staged under a reversal of Walter Benjamin's great dictum that "there is no document of civilization which is not at one and the same time a document of barbarism," and would seek to argue the proposition that the effectively ideological is also, at the same time, necessarily Utopian. What is logically paradoxical about such a proposition can be understood, if not "resolved," by considering the conceptual limits imposed on our thinking and our language by categories that we have had frequent enough occasion to unmask in the preceding pages, namely those of the ethical code of good and evil, in which even our own terminology of "positive" and "negative" remains unavoidably imprisoned. We have suggested that the vocation of the dialectic lies in the transcendence of this opposition toward some collective logic "beyond good and evil," while noting that the language of the classics of dialectical thought has historically failed to overcome this opposition, which it can only neutralize by reflexive play across these categories. Nor is this particularly surprising, if we take dialectical thought to be the anticipation of the logic of a collectivity which has not yet come into being. In this sense, to project an imperative to thought in which the ideological would be grasped as somehow at one with the Utopian, and the Utopian at one with the ideological, is to formulate a question to which a collective dialectic is the only conceivable answer.

Yet at a lower and more practical level of cultural analysis this proposition is perhaps somewhat less paradoxical in its consequences, and may initially be argued in terms of a manipulatory theory of culture. Such theories, which are strongest in areas like the study of the media and mass culture in contemporary society, must otherwise rest on a peculiarly unconvincing notion of the psychology of the viewer, as some inert and passive material on which the manipulatory operation works. Yet it does not take much reflection to see that a process of compensatory exchange must be involved here, in which the henceforth manipulated viewer is offered specific gratifications in return for his or her consent to passivity. In other words, if the ideological function of mass culture is understood as a process whereby otherwise dangerous and protopolitical impulses are "managed" and defused, rechanneled and offered spurious objects, then some preliminary step must also be theorized in which these same impulses—the raw material upon which the process works—are initially awakened within the very text that seeks to still them. If the function of the mass cultural text is meanwhile seen rather as the production of false consciousness and the symbolic reaffirmation of this or that legitimizing strategy, even this process cannot be grasped as one of sheer violence (the theory of hegemony is explicitly distinguished from control by brute force) nor as one inscribing the appropriate attitudes upon a blank slate, but must necessarily involve a complex strategy of rhetorical persuasion in which substantial incentives are offered for ideological adherence. We will say that such incentives, as well as the impulses to be managed by the mass cultural text, are necessarily Utopian in nature. Ernst Bloch's luminous recovery of the Utopian impulses at work in that most degraded of all mass cultural texts, advertising slogans—visions of external life, of the transfigured body, of preternatural sexual gratification—may serve as the model for an analysis of the dependence of the crudest forms of manipulation on the oldest Utopian longings of humankind.[5] As for the influential Adorno-Horkheimer denunciation of the "culture industry," this same Utopian hermeneutic—implicit in their system as well—is in their *Dialectic of Enlightenment* obscured by an embattled commitment to high culture; yet it has not sufficiently been noticed that it has been displaced to the succeeding chapter of that work,[6] where a similar, yet even more difficult analysis is undertaken, in which one of the ugliest of all human passions, antisemitism, is shown to be profoundly Utopian in character, as a form of cultural envy which is at the same time a repressed recognition of the Utopian impulse.

Still, such analyses, methodologically suggestive though they are, do not go far enough along the lines proposed above. In particular, they depend on an initial separation between means and ends—between Utopian gratification and ideological manipulation—which might well serve as evidence for the opposite of what was to have been demonstrated, and might be invoked to deny the profound identity between these two dimensions of the cultural text. It is possible, indeed, that such a separation springs objectively from the peculiar structure of the mass cultural texts themselves; and that culture proper, by which we may understand the "organic" culture of older societies fully as much as the "high" culture of the present day,[7] may be expected to embody such identity in a rather different form.

We must therefore return to the "strong" form of the problem, and to the class terms in which we began by posing it. Its traditional Marxist formulation would then run as follows: how is it possible for a cultural text which fulfills a demonstrably ideological function, as a hegemonic work whose formal categories as well as its content secure the legitimation of this or that form of class domination—how is it possible for such a text to embody a properly Utopian impulse, or to resonate a universal value inconsistent with the narrower limits of class privilege which inform its more immediate ideological vocation? The dilemma is intensified when we deny ourselves, as we just have, the solution of a coexistence of different functions, as when, for instance, it is suggested that the greatness of a given writer may be separated from his deplorable opinions, and is achieved in spite of them or even against them. Such a separation is possible only for a world-view—liberalism—in which the political and the ideological are mere secondary or "public" adjuncts to the content of a real "private" life, which alone is authentic and genuine. It is not possible for any world-view—whether conservative or radical and revolutionary—that takes politics seriously.

There can, I think, be only one consequent "solution" to the problem thus posed: it is the proposition that *all* class consciousness—or in other words, all ideology in the strongest sense, including the most exclusive forms of ruling-class consciousness just as much as that of oppositional or oppressed classes—is in its very nature Utopian. This proposition rests on a specific analysis of the dynamics of class consciousness which can only briefly be summarized here,[8] and whose informing idea grasps the emergence of class consciousness as such (what in Hegelian language is sometimes called the emergence of a class-for-itself, as opposed to the merely potential class-in-itself of the positioning of a social group within the economic structure) as a result of the struggle between groups or classes. According to this analysis, the prior moment of class consciousness is that of the oppressed classes (whose structural identity—whether a peasantry, slaves, serfs, or a genuine proletariat—evidently derives from the mode of production). On such a view, those who must work and produce surplus value for others will necessarily grasp their own solidarity—initially, in the unarticulated form of rage, helplessness, victimization, oppression by a common enemy—*before* the dominant or ruling class has any particular incentive for doing so. Indeed, it is the glimpse of such sullen resistance, and the sense of the nascent political dangers of such potential unification of the laboring population, which generates the mirror image of class solidarity among the ruling groups (or the possessors of the means of production). This suggests, to use another Hegelian formula, that the *truth* of ruling-class consciousness (that is, of hegemonic ideology and cultural production) is to be found in working-class consciousness. It suggests, even more strongly, that the index of all class consciousness is to be found not in the latter's "contents" or ideological motifs, but first and foremost in the dawning sense of solidarity with other members of a particular group or class, whether the latter happen to be your fellow landowners, those who enjoy structural privileges linked to your own, or, on the contrary, fellow workers and producers, slaves, serfs, or peasants. Only an ethical politics, linked to those ethical categories we have often had occasion to criticize and to deconstruct in the preceding pages, will feel the need to "prove" that one of these forms of class consciousness is good or positive and that other reprehensible or wicked: on the grounds, for example, that working-class consciousness is potentially more universal than ruling-class consciousness, or that the latter is essentially linked to violence and repression. It is unnecessary to argue these quite correct propositions; ideological commitment is not first and foremost a matter of moral choice but of the taking of sides in a struggle between embattled groups. In a fragmented social life—that is, essentially in all class societies—the political thrust of the struggle of all groups against each other can never be immediately universal but must always necessarily be focused on the class enemy. Even in preclass society (what is called tribal or segmentary society, or in the Marxian tradition, primitive communism), collective consciousness is similarly organized around the perception of what threatens the survival of the group: indeed, the most powerful contemporary vision of "primitive communism," Colin Turnbull's description of pygmy society,[9] suggests that the culture of prepolitical society organizes itself around the external threat of the nonhuman or of nature, in the form of the rain forest, conceived as the overarching spirit of the world.

The preceding analysis entitles us to conclude that all class consciousness of whatever type is Utopian insofar as it expresses the unity of a collectivity; yet it must be added that this proposition is an allegorical one. The achieved collectivity or organic group of whatever kind—oppressors fully as much as oppressed—is Utopian not in itself, but only insofar as all such collectivities are themselves *figures* for the ultimate concrete collective life of an achieved Utopian or classless society. Now we are in a better position to understand how even hegemonic or ruling-class culture and ideology are Utopian, not in spite of their instrumental function to secure and perpetuate class privilege and power, but rather precisely because that function is also in and of itself the affirmation of collective solidarity.

Such a view dictates an enlarged perspective for any Marxist analysis of culture, which can no longer be content with its demystifying vocation to unmask and to demonstrate the ways in which a cultural artifact fulfills a specific ideological mission, in legitimating a given power structure, in perpetuating and reproducing the latter, and in generating specific forms of false consciousness (or ideology in the narrower sense). It must not cease to practice this essentially negative hermeneutic function (which Marxism is virtually the only current critical method to assume today) but must also seek, through and beyond this demonstration of the instrumental function of a given cultural object, to project its simultaneously Utopian power as the symbolic affirmation of a specific historical and class form of collective unity.[10] This is a unified perspective and not the juxtaposition of two options or analytic alternatives: neither is satisfactory in itself. The Marxian "negative hermeneutic," indeed, practiced in isolation, fully justifies Sahlins' complaints about the "mechanical" or purely instrumental nature of certain Marxian cultural analyses; while the Utopian or "positive hermeneutic," practiced in similar isolation as it is in Frye's doctrine of the collective origins of art, relaxes into the religious or the theological, the edifying and the moralistic, if it is not informed by a sense of the class dynamics of social life and cultural production.

A number of significant objections can be made to this proposal. It will be observed, for one thing, that it amounts to a generalization of Durkheim's theory of religion to cultural production as a whole; and that, if this observation is correct—and I think it is—serious reservations about the "adaptation" of what is essentially a bourgeois and conservative social philosophy must be raised both from a Marxist position and also, as we shall see shortly, from a post-structuralist one.

Durkheim's system—in which a number of currents, from Rousseau to Hegel and Feuerbach, converge—views religion as the symbolic affirmation of the unity of a given tribe, collectivity, or even social formation;[11] religion is thus in Durkheimian sociology the archaic or Utopian counterpart to the latter's analysis of social dissolution and *anomie* in modern society. Evolved in the emergent years of the Third Republic, then threatened in its secular institutions both by the Right and by working-class agitation, Durkheim's theory is clearly a conservative one; like other forms of positivism, it seeks to project a functional defense of the bourgeois parliamentary state. Indeeed, to theorize religion as an "eternal" drive by which social divisions are suspended or overcome, to propose religious and ritual practices as a symbolic way of affirming social unity in a society which is objectively class divided, is clearly an ideological operation and an attempt to conjure such divisions away by an appeal to some higher (and imaginary) principle of collective and social unity. To stress the purely *symbolic* character of such unification, however, is to place this theory in a perspective in which religious practices and cultural production—the nostalgia for the collective and the Utopian—are harnessed to ideological ends.

We must, however, ask whether even such a theory as Durkheim's can be said to elude Marshall Sahlins' critique of instrumental conceptions of culture as we have outlined it at the beginning of this chapter. There would, in other words, seem to persist an instrumental or functional view of culture and religion even here, since the symbolic affirmation of the unity of society is understood as playing a vital role in the health, survival and reproduction of the social formation in question. In fact, few enough aesthetic systems proper—apart from those of religious inspiration—have been able to dispense with some hypothesis as to the ultimate social functionality of art; only Heidegger's great vision of the work of art as the momentary glimpse of Being itself comes to mind as a purely secular and nonfunctional model of culture; and even in the case of Heidegger, a theological reading of the late texts is certainly possible, as is a political and social one in which the *polis* (the temple) and the peasant community (the pair of peasant shoes, and the "Feldweg") are invoked in the service of an essentially protofascist celebration of the social order.[12]

I would argue that the problem of a functional or instrumental conception of culture is basically transcended and annulled in the Utopian perspective which is ours here. In a classless society, Rousseau's conception of the festival as the moment in which society celebrates itself and its own unity, Durkheim's analogous conception of the unifying "function" of religion, and our own view of culture as the expression of a properly Utopian or collective impulse are no longer basely functional or instrumental in Sahlins' sense. This is to say, if one likes, that Durkheim's view of religion (which we have expanded to include cultural activity generally) as a symbolic affirmation of human relationships, along with Heidegger's conception of the work of art as a symbolic enactment of the relationship of human beings to the nonhuman, to Nature and to Being, are in this society false and ideological; but they will know their truth and come into their own at the end of what Marx calls prehistory. At that moment, then, the problem of the opposition of the ideological to the Utopian, or the functional-instrumental to the collective, will have become a false one.

In the problematic of post-structuralism, however, the Durkheimian formulations must be the object of a rather different critique, in their reliance on categories of the individual subject.[13] It is clear, indeed, that not merely Durkheim's notion of collective "consciousness," but also the notion of "class consciousness," as it is central in a certain Marxist tradition, rests on an unrigorous and figurative assimilation of the consciousness of the individual subject to the dynamics of groups. The Althusserian and post-structuralist critique of these and other versions of the notion of a "subject of history" may readily be admitted. The alternatives presented by the Althusserians, however—the notion of the individual subject or of social class as an "effect of structure," or that of classes as the *Träger* or *bearers* of an ensemble of structures[14] (a conceptual abstraction analogous to Greimas' notion of the *actant* of narrative as opposed to its surface categories of the narrative "character")—have a purely negative or second-degree critical function, and offer no new conceptual categories. What is wanted here—and it is one of the most urgent tasks for Marxist theory today—is a whole new logic of collective dynamics, with categories that escape the taint of some mere application of terms drawn from individual experience (in that sense, even the concept of praxis remains a suspect one). Suggestive work has been done in this area; I think, for example, of the perhaps ultimately unsatisfactory but still largely undiscussed machinery of Sartre's *Critique of Dialectical Reason*.[15] But the problem has rarely been focused in an adequate way. Until this task is completed, it seems possible to continue to use a Durkheimian or Lukácsean vocabulary of collective consciousness or of the subject of history "under erasure," provided we understand that any such discussion refers, not to the concepts designated by such terms, but to the as yet untheorized object—the collective—to which they make imperfect allusion.

As for the idea that the Durkheimian problematic is alien to Marxism, it should be observed that in Marx's own mature work there exists an equivalent to Durkheim's notion of religion, namely the rather Hegelian conception of the Asiatic mode of production formulated in the *Grundrisse:*

> In most of the *Asiatic* land-forms, the *comprehensive unity* standing above all these little communities appears as the higher *proprietor* or as the *sole* proprietor. . . . Because the *unity* is the real proprietor and the real presupposition of communal property . . . the relation of the individual to the *natural* conditions of labor and of reproduction . . . appears mediated for him through a cession by the total unity—a unity realized in the form of the despot, the father of many communities—to the individual, through the mediation of the particular commune.[16]

It is evident that in such a conception of social unity expressed in the "body of the despot," the problem of the ideological function of religion must be raised more urgently than at any other nexus of the Marxian theory of modes of production, and in a far more concrete and historical way than in Durkheim's ahistorical theory of religion. The literature on this much debated but properly Marxian concept is enormous;[17] and the most consequent contemporary critics of Durkheim from a Marxist standpoint have also been among those concerned to expunge the "pseudoconcept" of the Asiatic mode of production from the Marxist problematic and the Marxist tradition.[18] Yet we have perhaps said enough to show that the *problem* of the symbolic enactment of collective unity is inscribed in that problematic by Marx himself at this point, whatever solution may ultimately be devised for it.

Such is then the general theoretical framework in which I would wish to argue the methodological proposition outlined here: that a Marxist negative hermeneutic, a Marxist practice of ideological analysis proper, must in the practical work of reading and interpretation be exercised *simultaneously* with a Marxist positive hermeneutic, or a decipherment of the Utopian impulses of these same still ideological cultural texts. If the Mannheimian overtones of this dual perspective—ideology and Utopia—remain active enough to offer communicational noise and conceptual interference, then alternative formulations may be proposed, in which an *instrumental* analysis is coordinated with a *collective-associational* or *communal* reading of culture, or in which a *functional* method for describing cultural texts is articulated with an *anticipatory* one.

I would not want to conclude, however, without observing that the issues and dilemmas such a proposal seeks to address greatly transcend the limited field of literary or even cultural criticism. One hesitates to defend the privileged position of cultural criticism in a self-serving way. Still, it is a historical fact that the "structuralist" or textual revolution—as, mainly through Althusserianism, it has transformed a whole range of other disciplines, from political science to anthropology, and from economics to legal and juridical studies—takes as its model a kind of decipherment of which literary and textual criticism is in many ways the strong form. This "revolution," essentially antiempiricist, drives the wedge of the concept of a "text" into the traditional disciplines by extrapolating the notion of "discourse" or "writing" onto objects previously thought to be "realities" or objects in the real world, such as the various levels or instances of a social formation: political power, social class, institutions, and events themselves. When properly used, the concept of the "text" does not, as in garden-variety semiotic practice today, "reduce" these realities to small and manageable written documents of one kind or another, but rather liberates us from the empirical object—whether institution, event, or individual work—by displacing our attention to its *constitution* as an object and its *relationship* to the other objects thus constituted.

The specific problems addressed by literary and cultural interpretation today may thus be expected to present suggestive analogies with the methodological problems of the other social sciences (it being understood that for Marxism, literary and cultural analysis *is* a social science). I would go even further and suggest that the solution outlined in this conclusion to those specifically cultural dilemmas has a good deal of relevance for other fields, where indeed analogous solutions are everywhere the order of the day. I will illustrate these analogies with brief reference to three such areas, namely the problem of the state, the constitution of radical legal studies, and the national question. We have already touched earlier on the first, in which a contemporary political science, particularly in the work of Nicos Poulantzas,[19] has sought to free the study of the state and of state power from the older Marxian view in which the state is little more than an instrument or vehicle of class domination. Such traditional reduction of the political corresponds clearly enough to what we have described above as the instrumental-functional view of ideology. As against this tradition, Poulantzas offers a view of the state as a semi-autonomous arena, which is not the vehicle of any one class but rather a space of class struggle generally. Such a view has evident political consequences, and reflects the immense expansion of the public sector in modern societies, as well as the dynamic of nonhegemonic forces such as pressure groups of unemployed or marginalized people and the more militant work of public-sector trade unions. This vision of the state or the public sector as a collectivity in its own right evidently corresponds to what we have called the Utopian reading or decipherment of the "text" of the state.

In radical legal studies, as well as in related areas of the study of public policy such as health care and housing, the problem of the "text" is even more vivid. There is, in the area of the juridical as the Left conceives it today, an open antithesis between a school based on ideological interpretation—which seeks to unmask existing law as the instrument of class domination—and one working in a Utopian perspective—which on the contrary sees its work as the conception and projection of a radically new form of some properly socialist legality that cannot be achieved within the existing institutions, or that is in them merely "emergent." Here too, then, the coordination of the ideological with the Utopian would seem to have a theoretical urgency which is accompanied by very real political and strategic consequences.

Finally, I will take Tom Nairn's pathbreaking book on the national question, *The Break-up of Britain,* as an example of an analogous theoretical solution to that proposed here in an area which remains one of the fundamental ones of contemporary world politics but about which Nairn rightly observes that it stands as "Marxism's great historical failure," blocked precisely by a practice of the traditional Marxian negative hermeneutic for which the national question is a mere ideological epiphenomenon of the economic. "The task of a theory of nationalism . . . must be to embrace both horns of the dilemma. It must be to see the phenomenon as a whole, in a way that rises above these 'positive' and 'negative' sides. . . . [Such] distinctions do not imply the existence of two brands of nationalism, one healthy and one morbid. The point is that, as the most elementary comparative analysis will show, all nationalism is both healthy and morbid. Both progress and regress are inscribed in its genetic code from the start."[20] Nor is this insistence on the simultaneously ideological and Utopian character of the national phenomenon a merely theoretical issue. On the contrary, it is increasingly clear in today's world (if it had ever been in doubt) that a Left which cannot grasp the immense Utopian appeal of nationalism (any more than it can grasp that of religion or of fascism) can scarcely hope to "reappropriate" such collective energies and must effectively doom itself to political impotence.

But at this point, we must restore Benjamin's identification of culture and barbarism to its proper sequence, as the affirmation not merely of the Utopian dimension of ideological texts, but also and above all of the ideological dimension of all high culture. So it is that a Marxist hermeneutic—the decipherment by historical materialism of the cultural monuments and traces of the past—must come to terms with the certainty that all the works of class history as they have survived and been transmitted to people ⟨in⟩ the various museums, canons and "traditions" of our own time, are all in one way or another profoundly ideological, have all had a vested interest in and a functional relationship to social formations based on violence and exploitation; and that, finally, the restoration of the meaning of the greatest cultural monuments cannot be separated from a passionate and partisan assessment of everything that is oppressive in them and that knows complicity with privilege and class domination, stained with the guilt not merely of culture in particular but of History itself as one long nightmare.

Yet Benjamin's slogan is a hard saying, and not only for liberal and apoliticizing critics of art and literature, for whom it spells the return of class realities and the painful recollection of the dark underside of even the most seemingly innocent and "life-enhancing" masterpieces of the canon. For a certain radicalism also, Benjamin's formulation comes as a rebuke and a warning against the facile reappropriation of the classics as humanistic expression of this or that historically "progressive" force. It comes, finally, as an appropriate corrective to the doctrine of the political unconscious which has been developed in these pages, reasserting the undiminished power of ideological distortion that persists even within the restored Utopian meaning of cultural artifacts, and reminding us that within the symbolic power of art and culture the will to domination perseveres intact. It is only at this price—that of the simultaneous recognition of the ideological and Utopian functions of the artistic text—that a Marxist cultural study can hope to play its part in political praxis, which remains, of course, what Marxism is all about.

NOTES

1. Marshall Sahlins, *Culture and Practical Reason* (Chicago: University of Chicago Press, 1976).

2. As far as literary criticism is concerned, it is often easier to denounce this mirage of immanence on the level of theory than to resist its hold on the level of practical exegesis. An instructive and influential example of this contradiction may be found in the contemporary reaction against an "old-fashioned" Lukácsean "content analysis" (as documented in the important Cluny colloquium held by *La Nouvelle Critique* in April, 1970, and published as *Littérature et idéologies*): the codification of a whole new alternate method—which explores the inscription of ideology in an ensemble of purely formal categories, such as representation, narrative closure, the organization around the centered subject, or the illusion of presence—is generally associated with the *Tel quel* and *Screen* groups, and also, in a different way, with the work of Jacques Derrida (see in particular "Hors Livre," in *La Dissémination* [Paris: Seuil, 1972], pp. 9–67). The unmasking of such categories and their ideological consequences is then achieved in the name of newer aesthetic, psychoanalytic, and moral values variously termed heterogeneity, dissemination, discontinuity, schizophrenia, and *écriture,* that is, in the name of explicitly anti-immanent (but also antitranscendent) concepts. Yet the impulse behind the critical practice thereby theorized is often precisely an immanent one, which brackets the historical situations in which texts are effective and insists that ideological positions can be identified by the identification of inner-textual or purely formal features. Such an approach is thereby able to confine its work to individual printed texts, and projects the ahistorical view that the formal features in question always and everywhere bear the same ideological charge. Paradoxically, then, the extrinsic, "contextual" or situational references repudiated by this system turn out to be precisely what is *heterogeneous* to it.

3. Paul Ricoeur, *Freud and Philosophy,* trans. D. Savage (New Haven: Yale, 1970), p. 27.

4. See Louis Althusser, "Ideological State Apparatuses," in *Lenin and Philosophy,* trans. Ben Brewster (New York: Monthly Review, 1971), pp. 170–177.

5. Ernst Bloch, *Das Prinzip Hoffnung* (Frankfurt: Suhrkamp, 1959), pp. 395–409.

6. Max Horkheimer and Theodor W. Adorno, *Dialectic of Enlightenment,* trans. J. Cumming (New York: Herder & Herder, 1972), pp. 168–208.

7. In "Reification and Utopia in Mass Culture" (*Social Text* No. 1, [1979] pp. 130–148), I suggest, however, that it may well be more adequate to study contemporary "high culture" (that is to say, modernism) as part of a larger cultural unity in which mass culture stands as its inseparable dialectical counterpole.

8. See *Marxism and Form*, pp. 376–390; and the related reflections in "Class and Allegory in Contemporary Mass Culture: *Dog Day Afternoon* as a Political Film," *College English,* Vol. 38, No. 7 (March, 1977), reprinted in *Screen Education,* No. 30

(Spring, 1979). These formulations draw on Ralf Dahrendorf, *Class and Class Conflict in Industrial Society* (Palo Alto: Stanford University Press, 1959), pp. 280–289; on E. P. Thompson, *The Making of the English Working Classes* (New York: Vintage, 1966), Preface (but see also his "Eighteenth Century English Society: Class Struggle without Class?" *Social History,* 3 [May, 1978]; and *The Poverty of Theory* [London: Merlin, 1979], pp. 298ff.); and finally on Jean-Paul Sartre, *Critique of Dialectical Reason,* trans. by A. Sheridan-Smith (London: New Left Books, 1976), esp. pp. 363–404, on the "fused group."

9. Colin Turnbull, *The Forest People* (New York: Simon and Schuster, 1962).

10. That this is no mere theoretical or literary-critical issue may be demonstrated by the renewal of interest in the nature and dynamics of fascism, and the urgency of grasping this phenomenon in some more adequate way than as the mere epiphenomenal "false consciousness" of a certain moment of monopoly capitalism. Such attempts, many of them grounded on Reich and seeking to measure the mass "libidinal investment" in fascism constitute the attempt, in our current terminology, to complete an "ideological" analysis of fascism by one which identifies its "Utopian" power and sources. See, for example, Jean-Pierre Faye, *Langages totalitaires* (Paris: Hermann, 1972); Maria Antonietta Macciochi, ed., *Eléments pour une analyse du fascisme,* 2 vols. (Paris: 10/18, 1976); as well as Ernst Bloch's *Erbschaft dieser Zeit* (1935; Frankfurt: Suhrkamp, 1973).

11. Emile Durkheim, *Les Formes élémentaires de la vie religieuse* (Paris: PUF, 1968), pp. 593–638.

12. See, on Heidegger's relationship to Nazism, M. A. Palmier, ed., *Les Ecrits politiques de Heidegger* (Paris: L'Herne, 1968).

13. This is the moment to restore the incriminating sentence strategically omitted from the Durkheim passage which serves as a motto to the present work: "Only a subject which includes all individual subjects would be capable of embracing such an object [society as a totality]" (*Formes élémentaires,* p. 630).

14. See, for example, Nicos Poulantzas, *Political Power and Social Classes,* trans. T. O'Hagan (London: New Left Books, 1973), p. 62.

15. A fuller preliminary discussion of this machinery may be found in *Marxism and Form,* esp. pp. 244–257.

16. Karl Marx, *Grundrisse,* trans. Martin Nicolaus (Harmondsworth: Penguin, 1973), pp. 472–473. A pathbreaking effort to rewrite the concept of "Oriental despotism" in terms of a cultural production that would be specific to it may be found in Gilles Deleuze and Félix Guattari, *Anti-Oedipus,* trans. Robert Hurley, Mark Seem, and Helen R. Lane (New York: Viking, 1977), pp. 192–222 (the "barbarism" section of chap. 3, "Savages, Barbarians, and Civilized"). Maurice Godelier has been the most consistent in extending this concept to the study of primitive society (in *Horizon: Trajets marxistes en anthropologie* [Paris: Maspéro, 1973]), an extension which has drawn a good deal of theoretical criticism of the type to be found in note 17, below. The cultural fantasies which cluster around the notion of "Oriental despotism" in the political unconscious would seem to correspond to that henceforth archaic moment of a "world empire" displaced by the new organization of a properly capitalist world system (see Immanuel Wallerstein, *The Modern World System* [New York: Academic, 1974], esp. pp. 16–18, 32–33, 60–62).

17. See in particular Jean Chesneaux, ed., *Sur le "mode de production asiatique"* (Paris: Editions sociales, 1969); Perry Anderson, "The 'Asiatic Mode of Production,'" in *Lineages of the Absolute State* (London: New Left Books, 1974), pp. 462–549; and Barry Hindess and Paul Hirst, *Pre-Capitalist Modes of Production* (London: Routledge

& Kegan Paul, 1975), chap. 4. (The second and third of these titles develop powerful critiques of the concept.)

18. Speaking of an analogous view of religion in contemporary Marxist anthropology, Hindess and Hirst observe: "Meillassoux clearly interprets the collective hunt as performing the function of a collective ritual serving to reinforce collective sentiments. Such positions may have a place within a Durkheimian problematic of forms of ritual and social cohesion but it has nothing whatever to do with Marxism" (Hindess and Hirst, *Pre-Capitalist Modes*, p. 55). One is tempted to add: in that case, too bad for Marxism!

19. E.g., *Political Power and Social Classes*, chap. 4, "The Relative Autonomy of the Capitalist State."

20. Tom Nairn, *The Break-up of Britain* (London: New Left Books, 1977), pp. 332, 347–348.

Edward W. Said
1935–

Edward W. Said was born on November 1, 1935, in Jerusalem. He was educated in the Middle East and in Massachusetts before attending Princeton University, where he received a B.A. in 1957. Said did graduate work at Harvard (M.A., 1960; Ph.D., 1964) and in 1963 began his teaching career at Columbia, where he is Parr Professor of English and Comparative Literature.

Said's first book, *Joseph Conrad and the Fiction of Autobiography* (1966) examines the influence of Conrad's extensive correspondence on the creation of his short fiction. Said's next book, *Beginnings: Intention and Method* (1975), considers both classic and modernist conceptions of intentionality, discussing Western critical theory from Vico to the French structuralists. In *Orientalism* (1978) Said addresses a central concern that has directed most of his subsequent intellectual inquiry: the "mythical" Western concept of the Orient as an inferior culture that enables the West to assume a posture of world dominance. "Orientalism" as such is a projection of the Western mind and bears little resemblance to the actual East. *The Question of Palestine* (1979), Said's fourth book, is an attempt to expose Western misrepresentation of Palestine and its people, to trace the history of Palestinian self-consciousness, and to affirm the ideals of the Palestinian people, obscured, Said says, by Western Orientalism. *Covering Islam* (1981) is an examination of how Islam is distorted in American news media, which, says Said, focus only on what seems sensationalistic and reprehensible about Islam. Committed to supporting Israel, which itself is strengthened by the myth of Orientalism, Western journalists do not accord Islam the same respect as Judaism and Christianity, resorting to pejorative generalizations and making Islam a scapegoat for present world problems.

Said's other books include *The Palestine Question and the American Context* (1979); *The World, the Text, and the Critic* (1983), a collection of essays written between 1968 and 1983 that address the linkages between criticism and politics; and *After the Last Sky: Palestinian Lives* (1986). Said's uncollected essays include "Opponents, Audiences, Constituencies, and Community" (*Critical Inquiry,* September 1982) and "The Future of Criticism" (*Modern Language Notes,* September 1984).

In addition to his teaching at Columbia, Said has been a visiting professor at a number of leading universities, including Yale, Harvard, and Stanford, and has held Woodrow Wilson, Guggenheim, and NEH fellowships; among his numerous prizes is the René Wellek Award in Literary Theory (1984). *Orientalism* was a runner-up in the criticism category of the National Book Critics Circle Award in 1979.

FROM

THE WORLD, THE TEXT, AND THE CRITIC

INTRODUCTION: SECULAR CRITICISM

Literary criticism is practiced today in four major forms. One is the practical criticism to be found in book reviewing and literary journalism. Second is academic literary history, which is a descendant of such nineteenth-century specialties as classical scholarship, philology, and cultural history. Third is literary appreciation and interpretation, principally academic but, unlike the other two, not confined to professionals and regularly appearing authors. Appreciation is what is taught and performed by teachers of literature in the university and its beneficiaries in a literal sense are all those millions of people who have learned in a classroom how to read a poem, how to enjoy the complexity of a metaphysical conceit, how to think of literature and figurative language as having characteristics that are unique and not reducible to a simple moral or political message. And the fourth form is literary theory, a relatively new subject. It appeared as an eye-catching topic for academic and popular discussion in the United States later than it did in Europe: people like Walter Benjamin and the young Georg Lukács, for instance, did their theoretical work in the early years of this century, and they wrote in a known, if not universally uncontested, idiom. American literary theory, despite the pioneering studies of Kenneth Burke well before World War Two, came of age only in the 1970s, and that because of an observably deliberate attention to prior European models (structuralism, semiotics, deconstruction).

The essays collected in this book derive from all four forms, even if the realms of journalistic book reviewing and classroom literary appreciation are not directly represented. But the fact is that my activities during the twelve years (1969–1981) when these essays were written involved me in all four varieties of literary critical practice. That of course is an ordinary enough thing, and true of most literary critics today. But if what in this volume I call criticism or critical consciousness has any contribution to make, it is in the attempt to go beyond the four forms as defined above. And this effort (if not its success) characterizes the critical work undertaken in these essays over and above the occasions and the conventions to which they are indebted.

Now the prevailing situation of criticism is such that the four forms represent in each instance specialization (although literary theory is a bit eccentric) and a very precise division of intellectual labor. Moreover, it is supposed that literature and the humanities exist generally within the culture ("our" culture, as it is sometimes known), that the culture is ennobled and validated by them, and yet that in the version of culture inculcated by professional humanists and literary critics, the approved practice of high culture is marginal to the serious political concerns of society.

This has given rise to a cult of professional expertise whose effect in general is pernicious. For the intellectual class, expertise has usually been a service rendered, and sold, to the central authority of society. This is the *trahison des clercs* of which Julien Benda spoke in the 1920s. Expertise in foreign affairs, for example, has usually meant legitimization of the conduct of foreign policy and, what is more to the point, a sustained investment in revalidating the role of experts in foreign affairs.[1] The same sort of thing is true of literary critics and professional humanists, except that their expertise is based upon noninterference in what Vico grandly calls the world of nations but which prosaically might just as well be called "the world." We tell our students and our general constituency that we defend the classics, the virtues of a liberal education, and the precious pleasures of literature even as we also show ourselves to be silent (perhaps incompetent) about the historical and social world in which all these things take place.

The degree to which the cultural realm and its expertise are institutionally divorced from their real connections with power was wonderfully illustrated for me by an exchange with an old college friend who worked in the Department of Defense for a period during the Vietnam war. The bombings were in full course then, and I was naively trying to understand the kind of person who could order daily B-52 strikes over a distant Asian country in the name of the American interest in defending freedom and stopping communism. "You know," my friend said, "the Secretary is a complex human being: he doesn't fit the picture you may have formed of the cold-blooded imperialist murderer. The last time I was in his office I noticed Durrell's *Alexandria Quartet* on his desk." He paused meaningfully, as if to let Durrell's presence on that desk work its awful power alone. The further implication of my friend's story was that no one who read and presumably appreciated a novel could be the cold-blooded butcher one might suppose him to have been.[2] Many years later this whole implausible anecdote (I do not remember my response to the complex conjunction of Durrell with the ordering of bombing in the sixties) strikes me as typical of what actually obtains: humanists and intellectuals accept the idea that you can read classy fiction as well as kill and maim because the cultural world is available for that particular sort of camouflaging, and because cultural types are not supposed to interfere in matters for which the social system has not certified them. What the anecdote illustrates is the approved separation of high-level bureaucrat from the reader of novels of questionable worth and definite status.

During the late 1960s, however, literary theory presented itself with new claims. The intellectual origins of literary theory in Europe were, I think it is accurate to say, insurrectionary. The traditional university, the hegemony of determinism and positivism, the reification of ideological bourgeois "humanism," the rigid barriers between academic specialties: it was powerful responses to all these that linked together such influential progenitors of today's literary theorist as Saussure, Lukács, Bataille, Lévi-Strauss, Freud, Nietzsche, and Marx. Theory proposed itself as a synthesis overriding the petty fiefdoms within the world of intellectual production, and it was manifestly to be hoped as a result that all the domains of human activity could be seen, and lived, as a unity.

And yet something happened, perhaps inevitably. From being a bold interventionary movement across lines of specialization, American literary theory of the late seventies had retreated into the labyrinth of "textuality," dragging along with it the most recent apostles of European revolutionary textuality—Derrida and Foucault—whose trans-Atlantic canonization and domestication they themselves seemed sadly enough to be encouraging. It is not too much to say that American or even European literary theory now explicitly accepts the principle of noninterference, and that its peculiar mode of appropriating its subject matter (to use Althusser's formula) is *not* to appropriate anything that is worldly, circumstantial, or socially contaminated. "Textuality" is the somewhat mystical and disinfected subject matter of literary theory.

Textuality has therefore become the exact antithesis and displacement of what might be called history. Textuality is considered to take place, yes, but by the same token it does not take place anywhere or anytime in particular. It is produced, but by no one and at no time. It can be read and interpreted, although reading and interpreting are routinely understood to occur in the form of misreading and misinterpreting. The list of examples could be extended indefinitely, but the point would remain the same. As it is practiced in the American academy today, literary theory has for the most part isolated textuality from the circumstances, the events, the physical senses that made it possible and render it intelligible as the result of human work.

Even if we accept (as in the main I do) the arguments put forward by Hayden White—that there is no way to get past texts in order to apprehend "real" history directly[3]—it is still possible to say that such a claim need not also eliminate interest in the events and the circumstances entailed by and expressed in the texts themselves. Those events and circumstances are textual too (nearly all of Conrad's tales and novels present us with a situation—say a group of friends sitting on a ship's deck listening to a story—giving rise to the narrative that forms the text), and much that goes on in texts alludes to them, *affiliates* itself directly to them. My position is that texts are worldly, to some degree they are events, and, even when they appear to deny it, they are nevertheless a part of the social world, human life, and of course the historical moments in which they are located and interpreted.

Literary theory, whether of the Left or of the Right, has turned its back on these things. This can be considered, I think, the triumph of the ethic of professionalism. But it is no accident that the emergence of so narrowly defined a philosophy of pure textuality and critical noninterference has coincided with the ascendancy of Reaganism, or for that matter with a new cold war, increased militarism and defense spending, and a massive turn to the right on matters touching the economy, social services, and organized labor.[4] In having given up the world entirely for the aporias and unthinkable paradoxes of a text, contemporary criticism has retreated from its constituency, the citizens of modern society, who have been left to the hands of "free" market forces, multinational corporations, the manipulations of consumer appetites. A precious jargon has grown up, and its formidable complexities obscure the social realities that, strange though it may seem, encourage a scholarship of "modes of excellence" very far from daily life in the age of declining American power.

Criticism can no longer cooperate in or pretend to ignore this enterprise. It is not practicing criticism either to validate the status quo or to join up with a priestly caste of acolytes and dogmatic metaphysicians. Each essay in this book affirms the connection between texts and the existential actualities of human life, politics, societies, and events. The realities of power and authority—as well as the resistances offered by men, women, and social movements to institutions, authorities, and orthodoxies—are the realities that make texts possible, that deliver them to their readers, that solicit the attention of critics. I propose that these realities are what should be taken account of by criticism and the critical consciousness.

It should be evident by now that this sort of criticism can only be practiced outside and beyond the consensus ruling the art today in the four accepted forms I mentioned earlier. Yet if this is the function of criticism at the present time, to be between the dominant culture and the totalizing forms of critical systems, then there is some comfort in recalling that this has also been the destiny of critical consciousness in the recent past.

No reader of Erich Auerbach's *Mimesis*, one of the most admired and influential books of literary criticism ever written, has failed to be impressed by the circumstances of the book's actual writing. These are referred to almost casually by Auerbach in the last lines of his epilogue, which stands as a very brief methodological explanation for what is after all a monumental work of literary intelligence. In remarking that for so ambitious a study as "the representation of reality in Western Literature" he could not deal with everything that had been written in and about Western literature, Auerbach then adds:

> I may also mention that the book was written during the war and at Istanbul, where the libraries are not equipped for European studies. International communications were impeded; I had to dispense with almost all periodicals, with almost all the more recent investigations, and in some cases with reliable critical editions of my texts. Hence it is possible and even probable that I overlooked things which I ought to have considered and that I occasionally assert something that modern research has disproved or modified . . . On the other hand, it is quite possible that the book owes its existence to just this lack of a rich and specialized library. If it had been possible for me to acquaint myself with all the work that has been done on so many subjects, I might never have reached the point of writing.[5]

The drama of this little bit of modesty is considerable, in part because Auerbach's quiet tone conceals much of the pain of his exile. He was a Jewish refugee from Nazi Europe, and he was also a European scholar in the old tradition of German Romance scholarship. Yet now in Istanbul he was hopelessly out of touch with the literary, cultural, and political bases of that formidable tradition. In writing *Mimesis,* he implies to us in a later work, he was not merely practicing his profession despite adversity: he was performing an act of cultural, even civilizational, survival of the highest importance. What he had risked was not only the possibility of appearing in his writing to be superficial, out of date, wrong, and ridiculously ambitious (who in his right mind would take on as a project so vast a subject as Western literature in its entirety?). He had also risked, on the other hand, the possibility of *not* writing and thus falling victim to the concrete dangers of exile: the loss of texts, traditions, continuities that make up the very web of a culture. And in so losing the authentic presence of the culture, as symbolized materially by libraries, research institutes, other books and scholars, the exiled European would become an exorbitantly disoriented outcast from sense, nation, and milieu.

That Auerbach should choose to mention Istanbul as the place of his exile adds yet another dose of drama to the actual fact of *Mimesis.* To any European trained principally, as Auerbach was, in medieval and renaissance Roman literatures, Istanbul does not simply connote a place outside Europe. Istanbul represents the terrible Turk, as well as Islam, the scourge of Christendom, the great Oriental apostasy incarnate. Throughout the classical period of European culture Turkey was the Orient, Islam its most redoubtable and aggressive representative.[6] This was not all, though. The Orient and Islam also stood for the ultimate alienation from and opposition to Europe, the European tradition of Christian Latinity, as well as to the putative authority of ecclesia, humanistic learning, and cultural community. For centuries Turkey and Islam hung over Europe like a gigantic composite monster, seeming to threaten Europe with destruction. To have been an exile in Istanbul at that time of fascism in Europe was a deeply resonating and intense form of exile from Europe.

Yet Auerbach explicitly makes the point that it was precisely his distance from home—in all senses of that word—that made possible the superb undertaking of *Mimesis.* How did exile become converted from a challenge or a risk, or even from an active impingement on his European selfhood, into a positive mission, whose success would be a cultural act of great importance?

The answer to this question is to be found in Auerbach's autumnal essay "Philologie der Weltliteratur." The major part of the essay elaborates on the notion first explicitly announced in *Mimesis,* but already recognizable in Auerbach's early interest in Vico, that philological work deals with humanity at large and transcends national boundaries. As he says, "our philological home is the earth: it can no longer be the nation." His essay makes clear, however, that his earthly home is European culture. But then, as if remembering the period of his extra-European exile in the Orient, he adds: "The most priceless and indispensable part of a philologist's heritage is still his own nation's culture and heritage. Only when he is first separated from this heritage, however, and then transcends it does it become truly effective."[7] In order to stress the salutary value of separation from home, Auerbach cites a passage from Hugo of St. Victor's *Didascalicon:*

> It is, therefore, a great source of virtue for the practiced mind to learn, bit by bit, first to change about in visible and transitory things, so that afterwards it may be able to leave them behind altogether. The man who finds his homeland sweet is still a tender beginner; he to whom every soil is as his native one is already strong; but he is perfect to whom the entire world is as a foreign land [the Latin text is more explicit here—*perfectus vero cui mundus totus exilium est*].

This is all that Auerbach quotes from Hugo; the rest of the passage continues along the same lines.

> The tender soul has fixed his love on one spot in the world; the strong man has extended his love to all places; the perfect man has extinguished his. From boyhood I have dwelt on foreign soil, and I know with what grief sometimes the mind takes leave of the narrow hearth of a peasant's hut, and I know, too, how frankly it afterwards disdains marble firesides and panelled halls.[8]

Auerbach associates Hugo's exilic credo with the notions of *paupertas* and *terra aliena,* even though in his essay's final words he maintains that the ascetic code of willed homelessness is "a good way also for one who wishes to earn a proper love for the world." At this point, then, Auerbach's epilogue to *Mimesis* suddenly becomes clear: "it is quite possible that the book owes its existence to just this lack of a rich and specialized library." In other words, the book owed its existence to the very fact of Oriental, non-Occidental exile and homelessness. And if this is so, then *Mimesis* itself is not, as it has so frequently been taken to be, only a massive reaffirmation of the Western cultural tradition, but also a work built upon a critically important alienation from it, a work whose conditions and circumstances of existence are not immediately derived from the culture it describes with such extraordinary insight and brilliance but built rather on an agonizing distance from it. Auerbach says as much when he tells us in an earlier section of *Mimesis* that, had he tried to do a thorough scholarly job in the traditional fashion, he could never have written the book: the culture itself, with its authoritative and authorizing agencies, would have prevented so audacious a one-man task. Hence the executive value of exile, which Auerbach was able to turn into effective use.

Let us look again at the notion of place, the notion by which during a period of displacement someone like Auerbach in Istanbul could feel himself to be out of place, exiled, alienated. The readiest account of place might define it as the nation, and certainly in the exaggerated boundary drawn between Europe and the Orient—a boundary with a long and often unfortunate tradition in European thought[9]—the idea of the nation, of a national-cultural community as a sovereign entity and place set against other places, has its fullest realization. But this idea of place does not cover the nuances, principally of reassurance, fitness, belonging, association, and community, entailed in the phrase *at home* or *in place*. In this book I shall use the word *culture* to suggest an environment, process, and hegemony in which individuals (in their private circumstances) and their works are embedded, as well as overseen at the top by a superstructure and at the base by a whole series of methodological attitudes. It is in culture that we can seek out the range of meanings and ideas conveyed by the phrases *belonging to* or *in a* place, being *at home in a place*.

The idea of culture of course is a vast one. As a systematic body of social and political as well as historical significance, "culture" is similarly vast; one index of it is the Kroeber-Kluckhohn thesaurus on meanings of the word "culture" in social science.[10] I shall avoid the details of these proliferating meanings, however, and go straight to what I think can best serve my purposes here. In the first place, culture is used to designate not merely something to which one belongs but something that one possesses and, along with that proprietary process, culture also designates a boundary by which the concepts of what is extrinsic or intrinsic to the culture come into forceful play. These things are not controversial: most people employing *culture* would assent to them, as Auerbach does in the epilogue when he speaks of being in Istanbul, away from his habitual cultural environment, within its research materials and familiar environment.

But, in the second place, there is a more interesting dimension to this idea of culture as possessing possession. And that is the power of culture by virtue of its elevated or superior position to authorize, to dominate, to legitimate, demote, interdict, and validate: in short, the power of culture to be an agent of, and perhaps the main agency for, powerful differentiation within its domain and beyond it too. It is this idea that is evident in French Orientalism, for example, as distinguished from English Orientalism, and this in turn plays a major role in the work of Ernest Renan, Louis Massignon, and Raymond Schwab, major scholars whose work is assessed in the last part of this book.

When Auerbach speaks of not being able to write such a book as *Mimesis* had he remained in Europe, he refers precisely to that grid of research techniques and ethics by which the prevailing culture imposes on the individual scholar its canons of how literary scholarship is to be conducted. Yet even this sort of imposition is a minor aspect of culture's power to dominate and authorize work. What is more important in culture is that it is a system of values *saturating* downward almost everything within its purview; yet, paradoxically, culture dominates from above without at the same time being available to everything and everyone it dominates. In fact, in our age of media-produced attitudes, the ideological insistence of a culture drawing attention to itself as superior has given way to a culture whose canons and standards are invisible to the degree that they are "natural," "objective," and "real."

Historically one supposes that culture has always involved hierarchies; it has separated the elite from the popular, the best from the less than best, and so forth. It has also made certain styles and modes of thought prevail over others. But its tendency has always been to move downward from the height of power and privilege in order to diffuse, disseminate, and expand itself in the widest possible range. In its beneficent form this is the culture of which Matthew Arnold speaks in *Culture and Anarchy* as stimulating in its adherents a powerful zeal:

> The great men of culture are those who have had a passion for diffusing, for making prevail, for carrying from one end of society to the other, the best knowledge, the best ideas of their time; who have laboured to divest knowledge of all that was harsh, uncouth, difficult, abstract, professional, exclusive; to humanise it, to make it efficient outside the clique of the cultivated and learned, yet still remaining the *best* knowledge and thought of the time [Arnold's definition of culture of course] and a true source, therefore, of sweetness and light.[11]

The question raised by Arnold's passion for culture here is the relationship between culture and society. He argues that society is the actual, material base over which culture tries, through the great men of culture, to extend its sway. The optimum relationship between culture and society then is *correspondence,* the former covering the latter. What is too often overlooked by Arnold's readers is that he views this ambition of culture to reign over society as essentially combative: "the best that is known and thought" must contend with competing ideologies, philosophies, dogmas, notions, and values, and it is Arnold's insight that what is at stake in society is not merely the cultivation of individuals, or the development of a class of finely tuned sensibilities, or the renaissance of interest in the classics, but rather the assertively achieved and *won* hegemony of an identifiable set of ideas, which Arnold honorifically calls culture, over all other ideas in society.

Yet it is still pertinent to ask Arnold where this struggle for hegemony takes place. If we say "in society" we will approach the answer, I think, but we will still have to specify *where* in society. In other words, Arnold's attention is to society defined grossly as, let us say, a nation—England, France, Germany—but more interestingly he seems also to be viewing society as a process and perhaps also an entity capable of being guided, controlled, even taken over. What Arnold always understood is that to be able to set a force or a system of ideas called "culture" over society is to have understood that the stakes played for are an identification of society with culture, and consequently the acquisition of a very formidable power. It is no accident that in his conclusion to *Culture and Anarchy* Arnold resolutely identifies a triumphant culture with the State, insofar as culture is man's best self and the State its realization in material reality. Thus the power of culture is potentially nothing less than the power of the State: Arnold is unambiguous on this point. He tells first of his unqualified opposition to such things as strikes and demonstrations, no matter how noble the cause, and then goes on to prove that such "anarchy" as strikes and demonstrations challenge the authority of the State, which is what morally, politically, and aesthetically they are:

> Because a State in which law is authoritative and sovereign, a firm and settled course of public order, is requisite if man is to bring to maturity anything precious and lasting now, or to found anything precious and lasting for the future.
> Thus in our eyes, the very framework and exterior order of the State,

whoever may administer the State, is sacred; and culture is the most
resolute enemy of anarchy, because of the great hopes and designs for
the State which culture teaches us to nourish.[12]

The interdependence in Arnold's mind between culture, the sustained suzerainty of culture over society (anything precious and lasting), and the framework and quasi-theological exterior order of the State is perfectly clear. And it signifies a coincidence of power, which Arnold's entire rhetoric and thought constantly elaborates. To be for and in culture is to be in and for a State in a compellingly loyal way. With this assimilation of culture to the authority and exterior framework of the State go as well such things as assurance, confidence, the majority sense, the entire matrix of meanings we associate with "home," belonging and community. Outside this range of meanings—for it is the outside that partially defines the inside in this case—stand anarchy, the culturally disfranchised, those elements opposed to culture and State: the homeless, in short.

It is not my intention here to discuss in detail the profoundly important implications of Arnold's concluding remarks on culture. But it is worth insisting on at least a few of those implications in a broader setting than Arnold's. Even as an ideal for Arnold, culture must be seen as much for what it is not and for what it triumphs over when it is consecrated by the State as for what it positively is. This means that culture is a system of discriminations and evaluations—perhaps mainly aesthetic, as Lionel Trilling has said, but no less forceful and tyrannical for that[13]—for a particular class in the State able to identify with it; and it also means that culture is a system of exclusions legislated from above but enacted throughout its polity, by which such things as anarchy, disorder, irrationality, inferiority, bad taste, and immorality are identified, then deposited outside the culture and kept there by the power of the State and its institutions. For if it is true that culture is, on the one hand, a positive doctrine of the best that is thought and known, it is also on the other a differentially negative doctrine of all that is not best. If with Michel Foucault we have learned to see culture as an institutionalized process by which what is considered appropriate to it is kept appropriate, we have also seen Foucault demonstrating how certain alterities, certain Others, have been kept silent, outside or—in the case of his study of penal discipline and sexual repression—domesticated for use inside the culture.

Even if we wish to contest Foucault's findings about the exclusions by classical European culture of what it constituted as insane or irrational, and even if we are not convinced that the culture's paradoxical encouragement and repression of sexuality has been as generalized as he believes, we cannot fail to be convinced that the dialectic of self-fortification and self-confirmation by which culture achieves its hegemony over society and the State is based on a constantly practiced differentiation of itself from what it believes to be not itself. And this differentiation is frequently performed by setting the valorized culture over the Other. This is by no means a metaphysical point, as two nineteenth-century English examples will demonstrate quickly. Both are related to the point I made earlier about Auerbach, that culture often has to do with an aggressive sense of nation, home, community, and belonging. First there is Macaulay's famous Minute of 1835 on Indian education:

> I have no knowledge of either Sanskrit or Arabic. But I have done what I could to form a correct estimate of their value. I have read translations of the most celebrated Arabic and Sanskrit works. I have conversed, both here and at home, with men distinguished by their proficiency in the Eastern tongues. I am quite ready to take the oriental learning at the valuation of the orientalists themselves. I have never found one among them who could deny that a single shelf of a good European library was worth the whole native literature of India and Arabia. The intrinsic superiority of the Western literature is indeed fully admitted by those members of the committee who support the oriental plan of education . . . It is, I believe, no exaggeration to say that all the historical information which has been collected in the Sanscrit language is less valuable than what may be found in the paltry abridgements used at preparatory schools in England. In every branch of physical or moral philosophy, the relative position of the two nations is nearly the same.[14]

This is no mere expression of an opinion. Neither can it be dismissed, as in his *Grammatology* Derrida has dismissed Lévi-Strauss, as a textual instance of ethnocentrism. For it is that and more. Macaulay's was an ethnocentric opinion with ascertainable results. He was speaking from a position of power where he could translate his opinions into the decision to make an entire subcontinent of natives submit to studying in a language not their own. This in fact is what happened. In turn this validated the culture to itself by providing a precedent, and a case, by which superiority and power are lodged both in a rhetoric of belonging, or being "at home," so to speak, and in a rhetoric of administration: the two become interchangeable.

A second instance also concerns India. With admirable perspicacity Eric Stokes has studied the importance of utilitarian philosophy to British rule in India. What is striking in Stokes's *The English Utilitarians and India* is how a relatively small body of thinkers—among them Bentham, of course, and both Mills—were able to argue and implement a philosophic doctrine for India's governance, a doctrine in some respects bearing an unmistakable resemblance to Arnold's and Macaulay's views of European culture as superior to all others. John Stuart Mill among the India House Utilitarians has today a higher cultural status, so much so that his views on liberty and representative government have for generations passed as the advanced liberal cultural statement on these matters. Yet of Mill, Stokes has this to say: "In his essay *On Liberty* John Stuart Mill had carefully stated that its doctrines were only meant to apply to those countries which were sufficiently advanced in civilization to be capable of settling their affairs by rational discussion. He was faithful to his father in holding to the belief that India could still be governed only despotically. But although he himself refused to apply the teachings of *Liberty* or *Representative Government* to India, a few Radical Liberals and a growing body of educated Indians made no such limitations."[15] A quick glance at the last chapter of *Representative Government*—to say nothing of the passage in the third volume of *Dissertations and Discussions* where he speaks of the absence of rights for barbarians—makes absolutely clear Mill's view that what he has to say about the matter cannot really apply to India, mainly because in his culture's judgment India's civilization has not attained the requisite degree of development.

The entire history of nineteenth-century European thought is filled with such discriminations as these, made between what is fitting for us and what is fitting for them, the former designated as inside, in place, common, belonging, in a word *above,* the latter, who are designated as outside, excluded, aberrant, inferior, in a word *below.* From these distinctions, which were given their hegemony by the culture, no one could be free, not even Marx—as a reading of his articles on India and the Orient will immediately reveal.[16] The large cultural-national designation of European culture as the privileged norm carried with it a formidable battery of other distinctions between ours and theirs, between proper and improper, European and non-European, higher and lower: they are to be found everywhere in such subjects and quasi-subjects as linguistics, history, race theory, philosophy, anthropology, and even biology. But my main reason for mentioning them here is to suggest how in the transmission and persistence of a culture there is a continual process of reinforcement, by which the hegemonic culture will add to itself the prerogatives given it by its sense of national identity, its power as an implement, ally, or branch of the state, its rightness, its exterior forms and assertions of itself: and most important, by its vindicated power as a victor over everything not itself.

There is no reason to doubt that all cultures operate in this way or to doubt that on the whole they tend to be successful in enforcing their hegemony. They do this in different ways, obviously, and I think it is true that some tend to be more efficient than others, particularly when it comes to certain kinds of police activities. But this is a topic for comparative anthropologists and not one about which broad generalizations should be risked here. I am interested, however, in noting that if culture exerts the kinds of pressure I have mentioned, and if it creates the environment and the community that allows people to feel they belong, then it must be true that resistance to the culture has always been present. Often that resistance takes the form of outright hostility for religious, social, or political reasons (one aspect of this is well described by Eric Hobsbawm in *Primitive Rebels*). Often it has come from individuals or groups declared out of bounds or inferior by the culture (here of course the range is vast, from the ritual scapegoat to the lonely prophet, from the social pariah to the visionary artist, from the working class to the alienated intellectual). But there is some very compelling truth to Julien Benda's contention that in one way or the other it has often been the intellectual, the *clerc,* who has stood for values, ideas, and activities that transcend and deliberately interfere with the collective weight imposed by the nation-state and the national culture.

Certainly what Benda says about intellectuals (who, in ways specific to the intellectual vocation itself, are responsible for defiance) resonates harmoniously with the personality of Socrates as it emerges in Plato's *Dialogues,* or with Voltaire's opposition to the Church, or more recently with Gramsci's notion of the organic intellectual allied with an emergent class against ruling-class hegemony. Even Arnold speaks of "aliens" in *Culture and Anarchy,* "persons who are mainly led, not by their class spirit, but by a general humane spirit," which he connects directly with ideal culture and not, it would appear, with that culture he was later to identify with the State. Benda is surely wrong, on the other hand, to ascribe so much social power to the solitary intellectual whose authority, according to Benda, comes from his individual voice and from his opposition to organized collective passions. Yet if we allow that it has been the historical fate of such collective sentiments as "my country right or wrong" and "we are whites and therefore belong to a higher race than blacks" and "European or Islamic or Hindu culture is superior to all others" to coarsen and brutalize the individual, then it is probably true that an isolated individual consciousness, going against the surrounding environment as well as allied to contesting classes, movements, and values, is an isolated voice out of place but very much *of* that place, standing consciously against the prevailing orthodoxy and very much for a professedly universal or humane set of values, which has provided significant local resistance to the hegemony of one culture. It is also the case, both Benda and Gramsci agree, that intellectuals are eminently useful in making hegemony work. For Benda this of course is the *trahison des clercs* in its essence; their unseemly participation in the perfection of political passions is what he thinks is dispiritingly the very essence of their contemporary mass sellout. For Gramsci's more complex mind, individual intellectuals like Croce were to be studied (perhaps even envied) for making their ideas seem as if they were expressions of a collective will.

All this, then, shows us the individual consciousness placed at a sensitive nodal point, and it is this consciousness at that critical point which this book attempts to explore in the form of what I call *criticism.* On the one hand, the individual mind registers and is very much aware of the collective whole, context, or situation in which it finds itself. On the other hand, precisely because of this awareness—a worldly self-situating, a sensitive response to the dominant culture—that the individual consciousness is not naturally and easily a mere child of the culture, but a historical and social actor in it. And because of that perspective, which introduces circumstance and distinction where there had only been conformity and belonging, there is distance, or what we might also call criticism. A knowledge of history, a recognition of the importance of social circumstance, an analytical capacity for making distinctions: these trouble the quasi-religious authority of being comfortably at home among one's people, supported by known powers and acceptable values, protected against the outside world.

But to repeat: the critical consciousness is a part of its actual social world and of the literal body that the consciousness inhabits, not by any means an escape from either one or the other. Although as I characterized him, Auerbach was away from Europe, his work is steeped in the reality of Europe, just as the specific circumstances of his exile enabled a concrete critical recovery of Europe. We have in Auerbach an instance both of filiation with his natal culture and, because of exile, *affiliation* with it through critical consciousness and scholarly work. We must look more closely now at the cooperation between filiation and affiliation that is located at the heart of critical consciousness.

Relationships of filiation and affiliation are plentiful in modern cultural history. One very strong three-part pattern, for example, originates in a large group of late nineteenth- and early twentieth-century writers, in which the failure of the generative impulse—the failure of the capacity to produce or generate children—is portrayed in such a way as to stand for a general condition afflicting society and culture together, to say nothing of individual men and women. *Ulysses* and *The Waste Land* are two especially well-known instances, but there is similar evidence to be found in *Death in Venice* or *The Way of All Flesh, Jude the Obscure, À la recherche du temps perdu,* Mallarmé's and Hopkins' poetry, much of Wilde's writing, and *Nostromo*. If we add to this list the immensely authoritative weight of Freud's psychoanalytic theory, a significant and influential aspect of which posits the potentially murderous outcome of bearing children, we will have the unmistakable impression that few things are as problematic and as universally fraught as what we might have supposed to be the mere natural continuity between one generation and the next. Even in a great work that belongs intellectually and politically to another universe of discourse—Lukács' *History and Class Consciousness*—there is much the same thesis being advanced about the difficulties and ultimately the impossibility of natural filiation: for, Lukács says, reification is the alienation of men from what they have produced, and it is the starkly uncompromising severity of his vision that he means by this all the products of human labor, children included, which are so completely separated from each other, atomized, and hence frozen into the category of ontological objects as to make even natural relationships virtually impossible.

Childless couples, orphaned children, aborted childbirths, and unregenerately celibate men and women populate the world of high modernism with remarkable insistence, all of them suggesting the difficulties of filiation.[17] But no less important in my opinion is the second part of the pattern, which is immediately consequent upon the first, the pressure to produce new and different ways of conceiving human relationships. For if biological reproduction is either too difficult or too unpleasant, is there some other way by which men and women can create social bonds between each other that would substitute for those ties that connect members of the same family across generations?

A typical answer is provided by T. S. Eliot during the period right after the appearance of *The Waste Land*. His model now is Lancelot Andrewes, a man whose prose and devotional style seem to Eliot to have transcended the personal manner of even so fervent and effective a Christian preacher as Donne.

In the shift from Donne to Andrewes, which I believe underlies the shift in Eliot's sensibility from the world-view of "Prufrock," *Gerontion,* and *The Waste Land* to the conversion poetry of *Ash-Wednesday* and the *Ariel Poems,* we have Eliot saying something like the following: the aridity, wastefulness, and sterility of modern life make filiation an unreasonable alternative at least, an unattainable one at most. One cannot think about continuity in biological terms, a proposition that may have had urgent corroboration in the recent failure of Eliot's first marriage but to which Eliot's mind gave a far wider application.[18] The only other alternatives seemed to be provided by institutions, associations, and communities whose social existence was not in fact guaranteed by biology, but by affiliation. Thus according to Eliot Lancelot Andrewes conveys in his writing the enfolding presence of the English church, "something representative of the finest spirit of England of the time [and] . . . a masterpiece of ecclesiastical statesmanship." With Hooker, then, Andrewes invoked an authority beyond simple Protestantism. Both men were

> on terms of equality with their Continental antagonists and [were able] to elevate their Church above the position of a local heretical sect. They were fathers of a national Church and they were Europeans. Compare a sermon of Andrewes with a sermon by another earlier master, Latimer. It is not merely that Andrewes knew Greek, or that Latimer was addressing a far less cultivated public, or that the sermons of Andrewes are peppered with allusion and quotation. It is rather that Latimer, the preacher of Henry VIII and Edward VI, is merely a Protestant; but the voice of Andrewes is the voice of a man who has a formed visible Church behind him, who speaks with the old authority and the new culture.[19]

Eliot's reference to Hooker and Andrewes is figurative, but it is meant with a quite literal force, just as that second "merely" (Latimer is merely a Protestant) is an assertion by Eliot of "the old authority and the new culture." If the English church is not in a direct line of filiation stemming from the Roman church, it is nevertheless something more than a mere local heresy, more than a mere protesting orphan. Why? Because Andrewes and others like him to whose antecedent authority Eliot has now subscribed were able to harness the old paternal authority to an insurgent Protestant and national culture, thereby creating a new institution based not on direct genealogical descent but on what we may call, barbarously, *horizontal affiliation.* According to Eliot, Andrewes' language does not simply express the anguished distance from an originating but now unrecoverable father that a protesting orphan might feel; on the contrary, it converts that language into the expression of an emerging affiliative corporation—the English church—which commands the respect and the attention of its adherents.

In Eliot's poetry much the same change occurs. The speakers of "Prufrock" and *Gerontion* as well as the characters of *The Waste Land* directly express the plight of orphanhood and alienation, whereas the personae of *Ash-*

Wednesday and *Four Quartets* speak the common language of other communicants within the English church. For Eliot the church stands in for the lost family mourned throughout his earlier poetry. And of course the shift is publicly completed in *After Strange Gods* whose almost belligerent announcement of a credo of royalism, classicism, and catholicism form a set of affiliations achieved by Eliot outside the filial (republican, romantic, protestant) pattern given him by the facts of his American (and outlandish) birth.

The turn from filiation to affiliation is to be found elsewhere in the culture and embodies what Georg Simmel calls the modern cultural process by which life "incessantly generates forms for itself," forms that, once they appear, "demand a validity which transcends the moment, and is emancipated from the pulse of life. For this reason, life is always in a latent opposition to the form."[20] One thinks of Yeats going from the blandishments of "the honey of generation" to the Presences who are "self-born mockers of man's enterprise," which he set down in *A Vision* according to a spacious affiliative order he invented for himself and his work. Or, as Ian Watt has said about Conrad's contemporaries, writers like Lawrence, Joyce, and Pound, who present us with "the breaking of ties with family, home, class, country, and traditional beliefs as necessary stages in the achievement of spiritual and intellectual freedom": these writers "then invite us to share the larger transcendental [affiliative] or private systems of order and value which they have adopted and invented."[21] In his best work Conrad shows us the futility of such private systems of order and value (say the utopian world created by Charles and Amelia Gould in *Nostromo*), but no less than his contemporaries he too took on in his own life (as did Eliot and Henry James) the adopted identity of an emigré-turned-English-gentleman. On the other side of the spectrum we find Lukács suggesting that only class consciousness, itself an insurrectionary form of an attempt at affiliation, could possibly break through the antinomies and atomizations of reified existence in the modern capitalist world-order.

What I am describing is the transition from a failed idea or possibility of filiation to a kind of compensatory order that, whether it is a party, an institution, a culture, a set of beliefs, or even a world-vision, provides men and women with a new form of relationship, which I have been calling affiliation but which is also a new system. Now whether we look at this new affiliative mode of relationship as it is to be found among conservative writers like Eliot or among progressive writers like Lukács and, in his own special way, Freud, we will find the deliberately explicit goal of using that new order to reinstate vestiges of the kind of authority associated in the past with filiative order. This, finally, is the third part of the pattern. Freud's psychoanalytic guild and Lukács' notion of the vanguard party are no less providers of what we might call a restored authority. The new hierarchy or, if it is less a hierarchy than a community, the new community is greater than the individual adherent or member, just as the father is greater by virtue of seniority than the sons and daughters; the ideas, the values, and the systematic totalizing world-view validated by the new affiliative order are all bearers of authority too, with the result that something resembling a cultural system is established. Thus if a filial relationship was held together by natural bonds and natural forms of authority—involving obedience, fear, love, respect, and instinctual conflict—the new affiliative relationship changes these bonds into what seem to be transpersonal forms—such as guild consciousness, consensus, collegiality, professional respect, class, and the hegemony of a dominant culture. The filiative scheme belongs to the realms of nature and of "life," whereas affiliation belongs exclusively to culture and society.

It is worth saying incidentally that what an estimable group of literary artists have adumbrated in the passage from filiation to affiliation parallels similar observations by sociologists and records corresponding developments in the structure of knowledge. Tönnies' notion of the shift from *Gemeinschaft* to *Gesellschaft* can easily be reconciled with the idea of filiation replaced by affiliation. Similarly, I believe, the increased dependence of the modern scholar upon the small, specialized guild of people in his or her field (as indeed the very idea of a field itself), and the notion within fields that the originating human subject is of less importance than transhuman rules and theories, accompany the transformation of naturally filiative into systematically affiliative relationships. The loss of the subject, as it has commonly been referred to, is in various ways the loss as well of the procreative, generational urge authorizing filiative relationships.

The three-part pattern I have been describing—and with it the processes of filiation and affiliation as they have been depicted—can be considered an instance of the passage from nature to culture, as well as an instance of how affiliation can easily become a system of thought no less orthodox and dominant than culture itself. What I want abruptly to talk about at this juncture are the effects of this pattern as they have affected the study of literature today, at a considerable remove from the early years of our century. The structure of literary knowledge derived from the academy is heavily imprinted with the three-part pattern I have illustrated here. This imprinting has occurred in ways that are impressive so far as critical thought (according to my notion of what it ought to be) is concerned. Let me pass directly now to concrete examples.

Ever since Eliot, and after him Richards and Leavis, there has been an almost unanimously held view that it is the duty of humanistic scholars in our culture to devote themselves to the study of the great monuments of literature. Why? So that they may be passed on to younger students, who in turn become members, by affiliation and formation, of the company of educated individuals. Thus we find the university experience more or less officially consecrating the pact between a canon of works, a band of initiate instructors, a group of younger affiliates; in a socially validated manner all this reproduces the filiative discipline supposedly transcended by the educational process. This has almost always been the case historically within what might be called the cloistral world of the traditional Western, and certainly of the Eastern, university. But we are now, I think, in a period of world history when for the first time the compensatory affiliative relationships interpreted during the academic course of study in the Western university actually exclude more than they include. I mean quite simply that, for the first time in modern history, the whole imposing edifice of humanistic knowledge resting on the classics of European letters, and with it the scholarly discipline inculcated formally into students in Western universities through the forms familiar to us all, represents only a fraction of the real human relationships and interactions now taking place in the world. Certainly Auerbach was among the last great representatives of those who believed that European culture could be viewed coherently and importantly as unquestionably central to human history. There are abundant reasons for Auerbach's view being no longer tenable, not the least of which is the diminishing acquiescence and deference accorded to what has been called the Natopolitan world long dominating peripheral regions like Africa, Asia, and Latin America. New cultures, new societies, and emerging visions of social, political, and aesthetic order now lay claim to the humanist's attention, with an insistence that cannot long be denied.

But for perfectly understandable reasons they are denied. When our students are taught such things as "the humanities" they are almost always taught that these classic texts embody, express, represent what is best in our, that is, the only, tradition. Moreover they are taught that such fields as the humanities and such subfields as "literature" exist in a relatively neutral political element, that they are to be appreciated and venerated, that they define the limits of what is acceptable, appropriate, and legitimate so far as culture is concerned. In other words, the affiliative order so presented surreptitiously duplicates the closed and tightly knit family structure that secures generational hierarchical relationships to one another. Affiliation then becomes in effect a literal form of *re-presentation,* by which what is ours is good, and therefore deserves incorporation and inclusion in our programs of humanistic study, and what is not ours in this ultimately provincial sense is simply left out. And out of this representation come the systems from Northrop Frye's to Foucault's, which claim the power to show how things work, once and for all, totally and predictively. It should go without saying that this new affiliative structure and its systems of thought more or less directly reproduce the skeleton of family authority supposedly left behind when the family was left behind. The curricular structures holding European literature departments make that perfectly obvious: the great texts, as well as the great teachers and the great theories, have an authority that compels respectful attention not so much by virtue of their content but because they are either old or they have power, they have been handed on in time or seem to have no time, and they have traditionally been revered, as priests, scientists, or efficient bureaucrats have taught.

It may seem odd, but it is true, that in such matters as culture and scholarship I am often in reasonable sympathy with conservative attitudes, and what I might object to in what I have been describing does not have much to do with the activity of conserving the past, or with reading great literature, or with doing serious and perhaps even utterly conservative scholarship as such. I have no great problem with those things. What I am criticizing is two particular assumptions. There is first the almost unconsciously held ideological assumption that the Eurocentric model for the humanities actually represents a natural and proper subject matter for the humanistic scholar. Its authority comes not only from the orthodox canon of literary monuments handed down through the generations, but also from the way this continuity reproduces the filial continuity of the chain of biological procreation. What we then have is a substitution of one sort of order for another, in the process of which everything that is nonhumanistic and nonliterary and non-European is deposited outside the structure. If we consider for a minute that most of the world today is non-European, that transactions within what the UNESCO/McBride Report calls the world information order is therefore not literary, and that the social sciences and the media (to name only two modes of cultural production in ascendancy today over the classically defined humanities) dominate the diffusion of knowledge in ways that are scarcely imaginable to the traditional humanistic scholar, then we will have some idea of how ostrichlike and retrograde assertions about Eurocentric humanities really are. The process of representation, by which filiation is reproduced in the affiliative structure and made to stand for what belongs to us (as we in turn belong to the family of our languages and traditions), reinforces the known at the expense of the knowable.

Second is the assumption that the principal relationships in the study of literature—those I have identified as based on representation—ought to obliterate the traces of other relationships within literary structures that are based principally upon acquisition and appropriation. This is the great lesson of Raymond Williams' *The Country and the City*. His extraordinarily illuminating discussion there of the seventeenth-century English country-house poems does not concentrate on what those poems represent, but on what they *are* as the result of contested social and political relationships. Descriptions of the rural manison, for example, do not at bottom entail only what is to be admired by way of harmony, repose, and beauty; they should also entail for the modern reader what in fact has been excluded from the poems, the labor that created the mansions, the social processes of which they are the culmination, the dispossessions and theft they actually signified. Although he does not come out and say it, Williams' book is a remarkable attempt at a dislodgement of the very ethos of system, which has reified relationships and stripped them of their social density. What he tries to put in its place is the great dialectic of acquisition and representation, by which even realism—as it is manifest in Jane Austen's novels—has gained its durable status as the result of contests involving money and power. Williams teaches us to read in a different way and to remember that for every poem or novel in the canon there is a social fact being requisitioned for the page, a human life engaged, a class suppressed or elevated—none of which can be accounted for in the framework rigidly maintained by the processes of representation and affiliation doing above-ground work for the conservation of filiation. And for every critical system grinding on there are events, heterogeneous and unorthodox social configurations, human beings and texts disputing the possibility of a sovereign methodology of system.

Everything I have said is an extrapolation from the verbal echo we hear between the words "filiation" and "affiliation." In a certain sense, what I have been trying to show is that, as it has developed through the art and critical theories produced in complex ways by modernism, filiation gives birth to affiliation. Affiliation becomes a form of representing the filiative processes to be found in nature, although affiliation takes validated nonbiological social and cultural forms. Two alternatives propose themselves for the contemporary critic. One is organic complicity with the pattern I have described. The critic enables, indeed transacts, the transfer of legitimacy from filiation to affiliation; literally a midwife, the critic encourages reverence for the humanities and for the dominant culture served by those humanities. This keeps relationships within the narrow circle of what is natural, appropriate, and valid for "us," and thereafter excludes the nonliterary, the non-European, and above all the political dimension in which all literature, all texts, can be found. It also gives rise to a critical system or theory whose temptation for the critic is that it resolves all the problems that culture gives rise to. As John Fekete has said, this "expresses the modern disaffection for reality, but progressively incorporates and assimilates it within the categories of prevailing social (and cultural) rationality. This endows it with a double appeal, and the expanding scope of the theory, corresponding to the expanding mode of the production and reproduction of social life, gives it authority as a major ideology."[22]

The second alternative is for the critic to recognize the difference between instinctual filiation and social affiliation, and to show how affiliation sometimes reproduces filiation, sometimes makes its own forms. Immediately, then, most of the political and social world becomes available for critical and secular scrutiny, as in *Mimesis* Auerbach does not simply admire the Europe he has lost through exile but sees it anew as a composite social and historical enterprise, made and remade unceasingly by men and women in society. This secular critical consciousness can also examine those forms of writing affiliated with literature but excluded from consideration with literature as a result of the ideological capture of the literary text within the humanistic curriculum as it now stands. My analysis of recent literary theory in this book focuses on these themes in detail, especially in the way critical systems—even of the most sophisticated kind—can succumb to the inherently representative and reproductive relationship between a dominant culture and the domains it rules.

What does it mean to have a critical consciousness if, as I have been trying to suggest, the intellectual's situation is a worldly one and yet, by virtue of that worldliness itself, the intellectual's social identity should involve something more than strengthening those aspects of the culture that require mere affirmation and orthodox compliancy from its members?

The whole of this book is an attempt to answer this question. My position, again, is that the contemporary critical consciousness stands between the temptations represented by two formidable and related powers engaging critical attention. One is the culture to which critics are bound filiatively (by birth, nationality, profession); the other is a method or system acquired affiliatively (by social and political conviction, economic and historical circumstances, voluntary effort and willed deliberation). Both of these powers exert pressures that have been building toward the contemporary situation for long periods of time: my interest in eighteenth-century figures like Vico and Swift, for example, is premised on their knowledge that their era also made claims on them culturally and systematically, and it was their whole enterprise therefore to resist these pressures in everything they did, albeit of course, that they were worldly writers and materially bound to their time.

As it is now practiced and as I treat it, criticism is an academic thing, located for the most part far away from the questions that trouble the reader of a daily newspaper. Up to a certain point this is as it should be. But we have reached the stage at which specialization and professionalization, allied with cultural dogma, barely sublimated ethnocentrism and nationalism, as well as a surprisingly insistent quasi-religious quietism, have transported the professional and academic critic of literature—the most focused and intensely trained interpreter of texts produced by the culture—into another world altogether. In that relatively untroubled and secluded world there seems to be no contact with the world of events and societies, which modern history, intellectuals, and critics have in fact built. Instead, contemporary criticism is an institution for publicly affirming the values of our, that is, European, dominant elite culture, and for privately setting loose the unrestrained interpretation of a universe defined in advance as the endless misreading of a misinterpretation. The result has been the regulated, not to say calculated, irrelevance of criticism, except as an adornment to what the powers of modern industrial society transact: the hegemony of militarism and a new cold war, the depoliticization of the citizenry, the overall compliance of the intellectual class to which critics belong. The situation I attempt to characterize in modern criticism (not excluding "Left" criticism) has occurred in parallel with the ascendancy of Reaganism. The role of the Left, neither repressed nor organized, has been important for its complaisance.

I do not wish to be misunderstood as saying that the flight into method and system on the part of critics who wish to avoid the ideology of humanism is altogether a bad thing. Far from it. Yet the dangers of method and system are worth noting. Insofar as they become sovereign and as their practitioners lose touch with the resistance and the heterogeneity of civil society, they risk becoming wall-to-wall discourses, blithely predetermining what they discuss, heedlessly converting everything into evidence for the efficacy of the method, carelessly ignoring the circumstances out of which all theory, system, and method ultimately derive.

Criticism in short is always situated; it is skeptical, secular, reflectively open to its own failings. This is by no means to say that it is value-free. Quite the contrary, for the inevitable trajectory of critical consciousness is to arrive at some acute sense of what political, social, and human values are entailed in the reading, production, and transmission of every text. To stand between culture and system is therefore to stand *close to*—closeness itself having a particular value for me—a concrete reality about which political, moral, and social judgments have to be made and, if not only made, then exposed and demystified.

If, as we have recently been told by Stanley Fish, every act of interpretation is made possible and given force by an interpretive community, then we must go a great deal further in showing what situation, what historical and social configuration, what political interests are concretely entailed by the very existence of interpretive communities.[23] This is an especially important task when these communities have evolved camouflaging jargons.

I hope it will not seem a self-serving thing to say that all of what I mean by criticism and critical consciousness is directly reflected not only in the subjects of these essays but in the essay form itself. For if I am to be taken seriously as saying that secular criticism deals with local and worldly situations, and that it is constitutively opposed to the production of massive, hermetic systems, then it must follow that the essay—a comparatively short, investigative, radically skeptical form—is the principal way in which to write criticism. Certain themes, naturally enough, recur in the essays that make up this book. Given a relatively wide selection of topics, the book's unity, however, is also a unity of attitude and of concern. With two exceptions, all of the essays collected here were written during the period immediately following the completion of my book *Beginnings: Intention and Method,* which argued the practical and theoretical necessity of a reasoned point of departure for any intellectual and creative job of work, given that we exist in secular history, in the "always-already" begun realm of continuously human effort. Thus each essay presupposes that book. Yet it is more important to point out that (again with two exceptions) all of these essays were written as I was working on three books dealing with the history of relations between East and West: *Orientalism* (1978), *The Question of Palestine* (1979), and *Covering Islam* (1981), books whose historical and social setting is political and cultural in the most urgent way. On matters having to do with the relationship between scholarship and politics, between a specific situation and the interpretation and the production of a text, between textuality itself and social reality, the connection of some essays here to those three books will be evident enough.

The essays collected here are arranged in three interlinked ways. First I look at the worldly and secular world in which texts take place and in which certain writers (Swift, Hopkins, Conrad, Fanon) are exemplary for their attention to the detail of everyday existence defined as situation, event, and the organization of power. For the critic, the challenge of this secular world is that it is not reducible to an explanatory or originating theory, much less to a collection of cultural generalities. There are instead a small number of perhaps unexpected characteristics of worldliness that play a role in making sense of textual experience, among them filiation and affiliation, the body and the senses of sight and hearing, repetition, and the sheer heterogeneity of detail. Next I turn to the peculiar problems of contemporary critical theory as it either confronts or ignores issues raised for the study of texts (and textuality) by the secular world. Finally, I treat the problem of what happens when the culture attempts to understand, dominate, or recapture another, less powerful one.

A word is in order about the special role played by Swift in this book. There are two essays on him, both of them stressing the resistances he offers to the modern critical theorist (resistance being a matter of central relevance to my argument in this book). The reasons for this are not only that Swift cannot easily be assimilated to current ideas about "writers," "the text," or "the heroic author," but that his work is at once occasional, powerful, and—from the point of view of systematic textual practice—incoherent. To read Swift seriously is to try to apprehend a series of events in all their messy force, not to admire and then calmly to decode a string of high monuments. In addition, his own social role was that of the critic involved with, but never possessing, power: alert, forceful, undogmatic, ironic, unafraid of orthodoxies and dogmas, respectful of settled uncoercive community, anarchic in his sense of the range of alternatives to the status quo. Yet he was tragically compromised by his time and his worldly circumstances, a fact alluded to by E. P. Thompson and Perry Anderson in their dispute over his real (progressive or reactionary) political commitments. For me he represents the critical consciousness in a raw form, a large-scale model of the dilemmas facing the contemporary critical consciousness that has tended to be too cloistered and too attracted to easy systematizing. He stands so far outside the world of contemporary critical discourse as to serve as one of its best critics, methodologically unarmed though he may have been. In its energy and unparalleled verbal wit, its restlessness, its agitational and unacademic designs on its political and social context, Swift's writing supplies modern criticism with what it has sorely needed since Arnold covered critical writing with the mantle of cultural authority and reactionary political quietism.

It is an undoubted exaggeration to say, on the other hand, that these essays make absolutely clear what my critical position—only implied by *Orientalism* and my other recent books—really is. To some this may seem like a failing of rigor, honesty, or energy. To others it may imply some radical uncertainty on my part as to what I do stand for, especially given the fact that I have been accused by colleagues of intemperate and even unseemly polemicism. To still others—and this concerns me more—it may seem that I am an undeclared Marxist, afraid of losing respectability and concerned by the contradictions entailed by the label "Marxist."

Without wishing to answer all the questions raised by these matters, I would like my views to be as clear as possible. On the questions of government and foreign policy that particularly involve me, nothing more should be added here than what is said in the last four essays in this book. But on the important matter of a critical position, its relationship to Marxism, liberalism, even anarchism, it needs to be said that criticism modified in advance by labels like "Marxism" or "liberalism" is, in my view, an oxymoron. The history of thought, to say nothing of political movements, is extravagantly illustrative of how the dictum "solidarity before criticism" means the end of criticism. I take criticism so seriously as to believe that, even in the very midst of a battle in which one is unmistakably on one side against another, there should be criticism, because there must be critical consciousness if there are to be issues, problems, values, even lives to be fought for. Right now in American cultural history, "Marxism" is principally an academic, not a political, commitment. It risks becoming an academic subspeciality. As corollaries of this unfortunate truth there are also such things to be mentioned as the absence of an important socialist party (along the lines of the various European parties), the marginalized discourse of "Left" writing, the seeming incapacity of professional groups (scholarly, academic, regional) to organize effective Left coalitions with political-action groups. The net effect of "doing" Marxist criticism or writing at the present time is of course to declare political preference, but it is also to put oneself outside a great deal of things going on in the world, so to speak, and in other kinds of criticism.

Perhaps a simpler way of expressing all this is to say that I have been more influenced by Marxists than by Marxism or any other *ism*. If the arguments going on within twentieth-century Marxism have had any meaning, it is this: as much as any discourse, Marxism is in need of systematic decoding, demystifying, rigorous clarification. Here the work of non-Marxist radicals (Chomsky's, say, or I. F. Stone's) is valuable, especially if the doctrinal walls keeping out non-members have not been put up to begin with. The same is true of criticism deriving from a profoundly conservative outlook, Auerbach's own, for example; at its best, this work also teaches us how to be critical, rather than how to be good members of a school. The positive uses of affiliation are many after all, which is not to say that authoritarianism and orthodoxy are any less dangerous.

Were I to use one word consistently along with *criticism* (not as a modification but as an emphatic) it would be *oppositional*. If criticism is reducible neither to a doctrine nor to a political position on a particular question, and if it is to be in the world and self-aware simultaneously, then its identity is its difference from other cultural activities and from systems of thought or of method. In its suspicion of totalizing concepts, in its discontent with reified objects, in its impatience with guilds, special interests, imperialized fiefdoms, and orthodox habits of mind, criticism is most itself and, if the paradox can be tolerated, most unlike itself at the moment it starts turning into organized dogma. "Ironic" is not a bad word to use along with "oppositional." For in the main—and here I shall be explicit—criticism must think of itself as life-enhancing and constitutively opposed to every form of tyranny, domination, and abuse; its social goals are noncoercive knowledge produced in the interests of human freedom. If we agree with Raymond Williams, "that however dominant a social system may be, the very meaning of its domination involves a limitation or selection of the activities it covers, so that by definition it cannot exhaust all social experience, which therefore always potentially contains space for alternative acts and alternative intentions which are not yet articulated as a social institution or even project,"[24] then criticism belongs in that potential space inside civil society, acting on behalf of those alternative acts and alternative intentions whose advancement is a fundamental human and intellectual obligation.

There is a danger that the fascination of what's difficult—criticism being one of the forms of difficulty—might take the joy out of one's heart. But there is every reason to suppose that the critic who is tired of management and the day's war is, like Yeats's narrator, quite capable at least of finding the stable, pulling out the bolt, and setting creative energies free. Normally, however, the critic can but entertain, without fully expressing, the hope. This is a poignant irony, to be recalled for the benefit of people who maintain that criticism is art, and who forget that, the moment anything acquires the status of a cultural idol or a commodity, it ceases to be interesting. That at bottom is a *critical* attitude, just as doing criticism and maintaining a critical position are critical aspects of the intellectual's life.

NOTES

1. There is a good graphic account of the problem in Noam Chomsky, *Language and Responsibility* (New York: Pantheon, 1977), p. 6. See also Edward W. Said, *Covering Islam* (New York: Pantheon, 1981), pp. 147–164.

2. The example of the Nazi who read Rilke and then wrote out genocidal orders to his concentration-camp underlings had not yet become well known. Perhaps then the Durrell–Secretary of Defense anecdote might not have seemed so useful to my enthusiastic friend.

3. See Hayden White, *Metahistory: The Historical Imagination in Nineteenth Century Europe* (Baltimore: Johns Hopkins University Press, 1973), and his *Tropics of Discourse: Essays in Cultural Criticism* (Baltimore: Johns Hopkins University Press, 1978).

4. See my article "Opponents, Audiences, Constituencies, and Community," *Critical Inquiry* (Fall 1982), for an analysis of the liaison between the cult of textuality and the ascendancy of Reaganism.

5. Erich Auerbach, *Mimesis: The Representation of Reality in Western Literature,* trans. Willard Trask (1953; rprt. Princeton: Princeton University Press, 1968), p. 557.

6. See the evidence in Samuel C. Chew, *The Crescent and the Rose: Islam and England During the Renaissance* (New York: Oxford University Press, 1937).

7. Auerbach, "Philology and *Weltliteratur*," trans. M. and E. W. Said, *Centennial Review*, 13 (Winter 1969), p. 17.

8. Hugo of St. Victor, *Didascalicon,* trans. Jerome Taylor (New York: Columbia University Press, 1961), p. 101.

9. See my *Orientalism* (New York: Pantheon, 1978), esp. chap. 1.

10. A. L. Kroeber and Clyde Kluckhohn, *Culture: A Critical Review of Concepts and Definitions* (1952; rprt. New York: Vintage Books, 1963).

11. Matthew Arnold, *Culture and Anarchy,* ed. J. Dover Wilson (1869; rprt. Cambridge: Cambridge University Press, 1969), p. 70.

12. Ibid., p. 204.

13. Lionel Trilling, *Beyond Culture: Essays on Learning and Literature* (New York: Viking Press, 1965), p. 175.

14. Quoted in Philip D. Curtin, ed., *Imperialism* (New York: Walker and Company, 1971), p. 182.

15. Eric Stokes, *The English Utilitarians and India* (Oxford: Clarendon Press, 1959), p. 298.

16. See *Orientalism,* pp. 153–156; also the important study by Bryan Turner, *Marx and the End of Orientalism* (London: Allen and Unwin, 1978).

17. See my *Beginnings: Intention and Method* (New York: Basic Books, 1975), pp. 81–88 and passim.

18. The information is usefully provided by Lyndall Gordon, *Eliot's Early Years* (Oxford and New York: Oxford University Press, 1977).

19. T. S. Eliot, *Selected Essays* (1932; rprt. London: Faber and Faber, 1953), pp. 343–344.

20. Georg Simmel, *The Conflict in Modern Culture and Other Essays*, trans. and ed. K. Peter Etzkorn (New York: Teachers College Press, 1968), p. 12.

21. Ian Watt, *Conrad in the Nineteenth Century* (Berkeley: University of California Press, 1979), p. 32.

22. John Fekete, *The Critical Twilight: Explorations in the Ideology of Anglo-American Literary Theory from Eliot to McLuhan* (London: Routledge and Kegan Paul, 1977), pp. 193–194.

23. For an extended analysis of the role of interpretive communities, see Stanley Fish, *Is There a Text in This Class?* (Cambridge: Harvard University Press, 1980).

24. Raymond Williams, *Politics and Letters: Interviews with* New Left Review (London: New Left Books, 1979), p. 252.

Sandra M. Gilbert
1936–

Susan Gubar
1944–

Sandra Mortola Gilbert and Susan David Gubar, since the appearance of their first combined publication in 1979, have been figures at the front of feminist revisionist literary criticism. Gilbert was born in New York City on December 27, 1936. She received her B.A. from Cornell University in 1957 and her M.A. from New York University in 1961. She completed her Ph.D. at Columbia University in 1968. Her teaching career began with lecturing at Queens College in the mid-sixties, and from 1967 to 1971 she was at Sacramento State College, where she became an assistant professor of English. In 1972 she was a lecturer at St. Mary's College, Moraga, California, then spent the next two years at Indiana University. During the period 1975–85 she was professor of English at the University of California–Davis. Until recently she was at Princeton University. Gubar was born in 1944 in Brooklyn. She received her B.A. from City College of New York; she did her graduate studies at the University of Michigan and the University of Iowa, completing her Ph.D. at Iowa in 1972. She is a professor of English at Indiana University. For *The Madwoman in the Attic: The Woman Writer and the Nineteenth-Century Literary Imagination* (1979) Gilbert and Gubar won a nomination for the outstanding book of literary criticism in 1979 from the National Book Critics Circle.

In their first book together the authors seek to demonstrate that there is a distinctly female imagination and that despite inimical circumstances for the nineteenth-century woman writer it can nevertheless be detected even if in shapes and forms that are the consequence of suppression. Jane Austen, Charlotte and Emily Brontë, Emily Dickinson, and Mary Shelley had to view themselves as aberrations, and out of this "essentially destructive myth" and their own fears about it they created "their own myths, their own world views." One's estimation of this book's value depends considerably upon one's reaction to its rhetoric, which Rosemary Ashton in the *Times Literary Supplement* found "formidable but unconvincing. It is hard not to suspect that [the authors] found just what they were looking for, and equally hard to give acceptance to their 'findings'." But another reviewer hailed the book as the basis at last for a mature feminist criticism which "by revealing the past, will profoundly alter the present, making it possible . . . for women writers to create their own texts."

Gilbert and Gubar have edited three volumes for which they have written introductions that make gradually more explicit the theme of conflict implicit in difference. *Shakespeare's Sisters: Feminist Essays on Women Poets* (1979) coincided with the publication of *Madwoman in the Attic* and in some ways ran parallel in its preoccupations. *The Norton Anthology of Literature by Women: The Tradition in English* (1985) aims "to recover a long and often neglected literary history," but the very familiarity of most of the authors and works selected suggests that the volume is more of a "no man's land" than a discovering or recovering. They do offer, however, a scholarly apparatus of "headnotes and introductions [that] would not have been available to us were it not for the work that feminist critics and scholars in women's studies have produced over the past fifteen years." With *The Female Imagination and the Modernist Aesthetic* (1986), a collection of critical essays, appear two ideas that are key in the theory of these authors and that are made explicit for the first time. Their introduction finds that "the strategies women writers devised as they confronted a patriarchal tradition [indicate that] women are the major precursors of all twentieth-century modernists, the *avant garde* of the *avant garde,* so to speak." The editors also assert that men and women at the turn of the century were developing "different visions of the world" and that "the female imagination was in fact a central problem for modernist man." Moreover, men's and women's visions "were so different we felt we had to speak not only of male and female modernisms, but of masculinist and feminist modernisms."

No Man's Land: The Place of the Woman Writer in the Twentieth Century (1988) begins a three-volume "sequel" to *Madwoman in the Attic*. It is much larger and seeks to be far more comprehensive and ambitious a project. The authors' range includes culture and history as well as literature. Their effort assumes that "there is a knowable history . . . that texts are written by people whose lives and minds are affected by the material conditions of history." And so, "Once we reimagine the author as a gendered human being whose text reflects key cultural conditions, we can conflate and collate individual literary narratives, so that they constitute one possible metastory, a story of stories about gender strife in this period," beginning, that is, after about 1880. The second volume is *No Man's Land: Sexchanges* (1989). At its heart is the question and fantasy: "What might sex be and what would sex roles be in the midst of, or after, a war between men and women?" As in the first volume, the authors concern themselves most with the period from the *fin de siècle* to the high flowering of modernism in the twenties and thirties, but they also give much attention to later modernist developments. "Our principle focus will be on the changing definition of sex and sex roles as they evolve through three phases: the repudiation or revision of the Victorian ideology of femininity that marked both feminism and fantasy during . . . the overturning of the century; the antiutopian skepticism . . . of such writers as Edith Wharton and Willa Cather, who dramatized their discontent with what they saw as a crippling but inexorable feminization of women; the virtually apocalyptic engendering of the new . . . shaped by an unprecedented confrontation (by both sexes) with the artifice of gender and its consequent discontents." The third volume, not yet published, will bear the title *Letters from the Front.*

Gilbert is a poet and writer of fiction as well as a critic. Her poetry volumes include *The Summer Kitchen* (1983), *Emily's Bread* (1984), and *Blood Pressure* (1988). She is a contributor to *Mademoiselle, Poetry, New Yorker,* and other magazines.

THE MADWOMAN IN THE ATTIC

INFECTION IN THE SENTENCE: THE WOMAN WRITER AND THE ANXIETY OF AUTHORSHIP

The man who does not know sick women does not know women.
—S. Weir Mitchell

I try to describe this long limitation, hoping that with such power as is now mine, and such use of language as is within that power, this will convince any one who cares about it that this "living" of mine had been done under a heavy handicap. . . .
—Charlotte Perkins Gilman

> A Word dropped careless on a Page
> May stimulate an eye
> When folded in perpetual seam
> The Wrinkled Maker lie
>
> Infection in the sentence breeds
> We may inhale Despair
> At distances of Centuries
> From the Malaria—
> —Emily Dickinson

> I stand in the ring
> in the dead city
> and tie on the red shoes
> . . . .
> They are not mine,
> they are my mother's,
> her mother's before,
> handed down like an heirloom
> but hidden like shameful letters.
> —Anne Sexton

What does it mean to be a woman writer in a culture whose fundamental definitions of literary authority are, as we have seen, both overtly and covertly patriarchal? If the vexed and vexing polarities of angel and monster, sweet dumb Snow White and fierce mad Queen, are major images literary tradition offers women, how does such imagery influence the ways in which women attempt the pen? If the Queen's looking glass speaks with the King's voice, how do its perpetual kingly admonitions affect the Queen's own voice? Since his is the chief voice she hears, does the Queen try to sound like the King, imitating his tone, his inflections, his phrasing, his point of view? Or does she "talk back" to him in her own vocabulary, her own timbre, insisting on her own viewpoint? We believe these are basic questions feminist literary criticism—both theoretical and practical—must answer, and consequently they are questions to which we shall turn again and again, not only in this chapter but in all our readings of nineteenth-century literature by women.

That writers assimilate and then consciously or unconsciously affirm or deny the achievements of their predecessors is, of course, a central fact of literary history, a fact whose aesthetic and metaphysical implications have been discussed in detail by theorists as diverse as T. S. Eliot, M. H. Abrams, Erich Auerbach, and Frank Kermode.[1] More recently, some literary theorists have begun to explore what we might call the psychology of literary history—the tensions and anxieties, hostilities and inadequacies writers feel when they confront not only the achievements of their predecessors but the traditions of genre, style, and metaphor that they inherit from such "forefathers." Increasingly, these critics study the ways in which, as J. Hillis Miller has put it, a literary text "is inhabited . . . by a long chain of parasitical presences, echoes, allusions, guests, ghosts of previous texts."[2]

As Miller himself also notes, the first and foremost student of such literary psychohistory has been Harold Bloom. Applying Freudian structures to literary genealogies, Bloom has postulated that the dynamics of literary history arise from the artist's "anxiety of influence," his fear that he is not his own creator and that the works of his predecessors, existing before and beyond him, assume essential priority over his own writings. In fact, as we pointed out in our discussion of the metaphor of literary paternity, Bloom's paradigm of the sequential historical relationship between literary artists is the relationship of father and son, specifically that relationship as it was defined by Freud. Thus Bloom explains that a "strong poet" must engage in heroic warfare with his "precursor," for, involved as he is in a literary Oedipal struggle, a man can only become a poet by somehow invalidating his poetic father.

Bloom's model of literary history is intensely (even exclusively) male, and necessarily patriarchal. For this reason it has seemed, and no doubt will continue to seem, offensively sexist to some feminist critics. Not only, after all, does Bloom describe literary history as the crucial warfare of fathers and sons, he sees Milton's fiercely masculine fallen Satan as *the* type of the poet in our culture, and he metaphorically defines the poetic process as a sexual encounter between a male poet and his female muse. Where, then, does the female poet fit in? Does she want to annihilate a "forefather" or a "foremother"? What if she can find no models, no precursors? Does she have a muse, and what is its sex? Such questions are inevitable in any female consideration of Bloomian poetics.[3] And yet, from a feminist perspective, their inevitability may be just the point; it may, that is, call our attention not to what is wrong about Bloom's conceptualization of the dynamics of Western literary history, but to what is right (or at least suggestive) about his theory.

For Western literary history *is* overwhelmingly male—or, more accurately, patriarchal—and Bloom analyzes and explains this fact, while other theorists have ignored it, precisely, one supposes, because they assumed literature had to be male. Like Freud, whose psychoanalytic postulates permeate Bloom's literary psychoanalyses of the "anxiety of influence," Bloom has defined processes of interaction that his predecessors did not bother to consider because, among other reasons, they were themselves so caught up in such processes. Like Freud, too, Bloom has insisted on bringing to consciousness assumptions readers and writers do not ordinarily examine. In doing so, he has clarified the implications of the psychosexual and sociosexual con-texts by which every literary text is surrounded, and thus the meanings of the "guests" and "ghosts" which inhabit texts themselves. Speaking of Freud, the feminist theorist Juliet Mitchell has remarked that "psychoanalysis is not a recommendation *for* a patriarchal society, but an analysis of one."[4] The same sort of statement could be made about Bloom's model of literary history, which is not a recommendation for but an analysis of the patriarchal poetics (and attendant anxieties) which underlie our culture's chief literary movements.

For our purposes here, however, Bloom's historical construct is useful not only because it helps identify and define the patriarchal psychosexual context in which so much Western literature was authored, but also because it can help us distinguish the anxieties and achievements of female writers from those of male writers. If we return to the question we asked earlier—where does a woman writer "fit in" to the overwhelmingly and essentially male literary history Bloom describes?—we find we have to answer that a woman writer does *not* "fit in." At first glance, indeed, she seems to be anomalous, indefinable, alienated, a freakish outsider. Just as in Freud's theories of male and female psychosexual development there is no symmetry between a boy's growth and a girl's (with, say, the male "Oedipus complex" balanced by a female "Electra complex") so Bloom's male-oriented theory of the "anxiety of influence" cannot be simply reversed or inverted in order to account for the situation of the woman writer.

Certainly if we acquiesce in the patriarchal Bloomian model, we can be sure that the female poet does not experience the "anxiety of influence" in the same way that her male counterpart would, for the simple reason that she must confront precursors who are almost exclusively male, and therefore significantly different from her. Not only do these precursors incarnate patriarchal authority (as our discussion of the metaphor of literary paternity argued), they attempt to enclose her in definitions of her person and her potential which, by reducing her to extreme stereotypes (angel, monster) drastically conflict with her own sense of her self—that is, of her subjectivity, her autonomy, her creativity. On the one hand, therefore, the woman writer's male precursors symbolize authority; on the other hand, despite their authority, they fail to define the ways in which she experiences her own identity as a writer. More, the masculine authority with which they construct their literary personae, as well as the fierce power struggles in which they engage in their efforts of self-creation, seem to the woman writer directly to contradict the terms of her own gender definition. Thus the "anxiety of influence" that a male poet experiences is felt by a female poet as an even more primary "anxiety of authorship"—a radical fear that she cannot create, that because she can never become a "precursor" the act of writing will isolate or destroy her.

This anxiety is, of course, exacerbated by her fear that not only can she not fight a male precursor on "his" terms and win, she cannot "beget" art upon the (female) body of the muse. As Juliet Mitchell notes, in a concise summary of the implications Freud's theory of psychosexual development has for women, both a boy and a girl, "as they learn to speak and live within society, want to take the father's [in Bloom's terminology the precursor's] place, and *only the boy will one day be allowed to do so*. Furthermore both sexes are born into the desire of the mother, and as, through cultural heritage, what the mother desires is the phallus-turned-baby, *both* children desire to be the phallus for the mother. Again, *only the boy can fully recognize himself in his mother's desire*. Thus *both* sexes repudiate the implications of femininity," but the girl learns (in relation to her father) "that her subjugation to the law of the father entails her becoming the representative of 'nature' and 'sexuality,' a chaos of spontaneous, intuitive creativity."[5]

Unlike her male counterpart, then, the female artist must first struggle against the effects of a socialization which makes conflict with the will of her (male) precursors seem inexpressibly absurd, futile, or even—as in the case of the Queen in "Little Snow White"—self-annihilating. And just as the male artist's struggle against his precursor takes the form of what Bloom calls revisionary swerves, flights, misreadings, so the female writer's battle for self-creation involves her in a revisionary process. Her battle, however, is not against her (male) precursor's reading of the world but against his reading of *her*. In order to define herself as an author she must redefine the terms of her socialization. Her revisionary struggle, therefore, often becomes a struggle for what Adrienne Rich has called "Revision—the act of looking back, of seeing with fresh eyes, of entering an old text from a new critical direction . . . an act of survival."[6] Frequently, moreover, she can begin such a struggle only by actively seeking a *female* precursor who, far from representing a threatening force to be denied or killed, proves by example that a revolt against patriarchal literary authority is possible.

For this reason, as well as for the sound psychoanalytic reasons Mitchell and others give, it would be foolish to lock the woman artist into an Electra pattern matching the Oedipal structure Bloom proposes for male writers. The woman writer—and we shall see women doing this over and over again—searches for a female model not because she wants dutifully to comply with male definitions of her "femininity" but because she must legitimize her own rebellious endeavors. At the same time, like most women in patriarchal society, the woman writer does experience her gender as a painful obstacle, or even a debilitating inadequacy; like most patriarchally conditioned women, in other words, she is victimized by what Mitchell calls "the inferiorized and 'alternative' (second sex) psychology of women under patriarchy."[7] Thus the loneliness of the female artist, her feelings of alienation from male predecessors coupled with her need for sisterly precursors and successors, her urgent sense of her need for a female audience together with her fear of the antagonism of male readers, her culturally conditioned timidity about self-dramatization, her dread of the patriarchal authority of art, her anxiety about the impropriety of female invention—all these phenomena of "inferiorization" mark the woman writer's struggle for artistic self-definition and differentiate her efforts at self-creation from those of her male counterpart.

As we shall see, such sociosexual differentiation means that, as Elaine Showalter has suggested, women writers participate in a quite different literary subculture from that inhabited by male writers, a subculture which has its own distinctive literary traditions, even—though it defines itself *in relation to* the "main," male-dominated, literary culture—a distinctive history.[8] At best, the separateness of this female subculture has been exhilarating for women. In recent years, for instance, while male writers seem increasingly to have felt exhausted by the need for revisionism which Bloom's theory of the "anxiety of influence" accurately describes, women writers have seen themselves as pioneers in a creativity so intense that their male counterparts have probably not experienced its analog since the Renaissance, or at least since the Romantic era. The son of many fathers, today's male writer feels hopelessly belated; the daughter of too few mothers, today's female writer feels that she is helping to create a viable tradition which is at last definitively emerging.

There is a darker side of this female literary subculture, however, especially when women's struggles for literary self-creation are seen in the psychosexual context described by Bloom's Freudian theories of patrilineal literary inheritance. As we noted above, for an "anxiety of influence" the woman writer substitutes what we have called an "anxiety of authorship," an anxiety built from complex and often only barely conscious fears of that authority which seems to the female artist to be by definition inappropriate to her sex. Because it is based on the woman's socially determined sense of her own biology, this anxiety of authorship is quite distinct from the anxiety about creativity that could be traced in such male writers as Hawthorne or Dostoevsky. Indeed, to the extent that it forms one of the unique bonds that link women in what we might call the secret sisterhood of their literary subculture, such anxiety in itself constitutes a crucial mark of that subculture.

In comparison to the "male" tradition of strong, father-son combat, however, this female anxiety of authorship is profoundly debilitating. Handed down not from one woman to another but from the stern literary "fathers" of patriarchy to all their "inferiorized" female descendants, it is in many ways the germ of a dis-ease or, at any rate, a disaffection, a disturbance, a distrust, that spreads like a stain throughout the style and structure of much literature by women, especially—as we shall see in this study—throughout literature by women before the twentieth century. For if contemporary women do now attempt the pen with energy and authority, they are able to do so only because their eighteenth- and nineteenth-century foremothers struggled in isolation that felt like illness, alienation that felt like madness, obscurity that felt like paralysis to overcome the anxiety of authorship that was endemic to their literary subculture. Thus, while the recent feminist emphasis on positive role models has undoubtedly helped many women, it should not keep us from realizing the terrible odds against which a creative female subculture was established. Far from reinforcing socially oppressive sexual stereotyping, only a full consideration of such problems can reveal the extraordinary strength of women's literary accomplishments in the eighteenth and nineteenth centuries.

Emily Dickinson's acute observations about "infection in the sentence," quoted in our epigraphs, resonate in a number of different ways, then, for women writers, given the literary woman's special concept of her place in literary psychohistory. To begin with, the words seem to indicate Dickinson's keen consciousness that, in the purest Bloomian or Millerian sense, pernicious "guests" and "ghosts" inhabit all literary texts. For any reader, but especially for a reader who is also a writer, every text can become a "sentence" or weapon in a kind of metaphorical germ warfare. Beyond this, however, the fact that "infection in the sentence *breeds*" suggests Dickinson's recognition that literary texts are coercive, imprisoning, fever-inducing; that, since literature usurps a reader's interiority, it is an invasion of privacy. Moreover, given Dickinson's own gender definition, the sexual ambiguity of her poem's "Wrinkled Maker" is significant. For while, on the one hand, "we" (meaning especially women writers) "may inhale Despair" from all those patriarchal texts which seek to deny female autonomy and authority, on the other hand "we" (meaning especially women writers) "may inhale Despair" from all those "foremothers" who have both overtly and covertly conveyed their traditional authorship anxiety to their bewildered female descendants. Finally, such traditional, metaphorically matrilineal anxiety ensures that even the maker of a text, when she is a woman, may feel imprisoned within texts—folded and "wrinkled" by their pages and thus trapped in their "perpetual seam[s]" which perpetually tell her how she *seems*.

Although contemporary women writers are relatively free of the infection of this "Despair" Dickinson defines (at least in comparison to their nineteenth-century precursors), an anecdote recently related by the American poet and essayist Annie Gottlieb summarizes our point about the ways in which, for all women, "Infection in the sentence breeds":

> When I began to enjoy my powers as a writer, I dreamt that my mother had me sterilized! (Even in dreams we still blame our mothers for the punitive choices our culture forces on us.) I went after the mother-figure in my dream, brandishing a large knife; on its blade was writing. I cried, "Do you know what you are doing? You are destroying my femaleness, my *female power,* which is important to me *because of you!*"[9]

Seeking motherly precursors, says Gottlieb, as if echoing Dickinson, the woman writer may find only infection, debilitation. Yet still she must seek, not seek to subvert, her *"female power,* which is important" to her because of her lost literary matrilineage. In this connection, Dickinson's own words about mothers are revealing, for she alternately claimed that "I never had a mother," that "I always ran Home to Awe as a child. . . . He was an awful Mother but I liked him better than none," and that "a mother [was] a miracle."[10] Yet, as we shall see, her own anxiety of authorship was a "Despair" inhaled not only from the infections suffered by her own ailing physical mother, and her many tormented literary mothers, but from the literary fathers who spoke to her—even "lied" to her—sometimes near at hand, sometimes "at distances of Centuries," from the censorious looking glasses of literary texts.

It is debilitating to be *any* woman in a society where women are warned that if they do not behave like angels they must be monsters. Recently, in fact, social scientists and social historians like Jessie Bernard, Phyllis Chesler, Naomi Weisstein, and Pauline Bart have begun to study the ways in which patriarchal socialization literally makes women sick, both physically and mentally.[11] Hysteria, the disease with which Freud so famously began his investigations into the dynamic connections between *psyche* and *soma*, is by definition a "female disease," not so much because it takes its name from the Greek word for womb, *hyster* (the organ which was in the nineteenth century supposed to "cause" this emotional disturbance), but because hysteria did occur mainly among women in turn-of-the-century Vienna, and because throughout the nineteenth century this mental illness, like many other nervous disorders, was thought to be caused by the female reproductive system, as if to elaborate upon Aristotle's notion that femaleness was in and of itself a deformity.[12] And, indeed, such diseases of maladjustment to the physical and social environment as anorexia and agoraphobia did and do strike a disproportionate number of women. Sufferers from anorexia—loss of appetite, self-starvation—are primarily adolescent girls. Sufferers from agoraphobia—fear of open or "public" places—are usually female, most frequently middle-aged housewives, as are sufferers from crippling rheumatoid arthritis.[13]

Such diseases are caused by patriarchal socialization in several ways. Most obviously, of course, any young girl, but especially a lively or imaginative one, is likely to experience her education in docility, submissiveness, selflessness as in some sense sickening. To be trained in renunciation is almost necessarily to be trained to ill health, since the human animal's first and strongest urge is to his/her *own* survival, pleasure, assertion. In addition, each of the "subjects" in which a young girl is educated may be sickening in a specific way. Learning to become a beautiful object, the girl learns anxiety about—perhaps even loathing of—her own flesh. Peering obsessively into the real as well as metaphoric looking glasses that surround her, she desires literally to "reduce" her own body. In the nineteenth century, as we noted earlier, this desire to be beautiful and "frail" led to tight-lacing and vinegar-drinking. In our own era it has spawned innumerable diets and "controlled" fasts, as well as the extraordinary phenomenon of teenage anorexia.[14] Similarly, it seems inevitable that women reared for, and conditioned to, lives of privacy, reticence, domesticity, might develop pathological fears of public places and unconfined spaces. Like the comb, stay-laces, and apple which the Queen in "Little Snow White" uses as weapons against her hated stepdaughter, such afflictions as anorexia and agoraphobia simply carry patriarchal definitions of "femininity" to absurd extremes, and thus function as essential or at least inescapable parodies of social prescriptions.

In the nineteenth century, however, the complex of social prescriptions these diseases parody did not merely urge women to act in ways which would cause them to become ill; nineteenth-century culture seems to have actually admonished women to *be* ill. In other words, the "female diseases" from which Victorian women suffered were not always byproducts of their training in femininity; they were the goals of such training. As Barbara Ehrenreich and Deirdre English have shown, throughout much of the nineteenth century "Upper- and upper-middle-class women were [defined as] 'sick' [frail, ill]; working-class women were [defined as] 'sickening' [infectious, diseased]." Speaking of the "lady," they go on to point out that "Society agreed that she was frail and sickly," and consequently a "cult of female invalidism" developed in England and America. For the products of such a cult, it was, as Dr. Mary Putnam Jacobi wrote in 1895, "considered natural and almost laudable to break down under all conceivable varieties of strain—a winter dissipation, a houseful of servants, a quarrel with a female friend, not to speak of more legitimate reasons. . . . Constantly considering their nerves, urged to consider them by well-intentioned but short-sighted advisors, [women] pretty soon become nothing but a bundle of nerves."[15]

Given this socially conditioned epidemic of female illness, it is not surprising to find that the angel in the house of literature frequently suffered not just from fear and trembling but from literal and figurative sicknesses unto death. Although her hyperactive stepmother dances herself into the grave, after all, beautiful Snow White has just barely recovered from a catatonic trance in her glass coffin. And if we return to Goethe's Makarie, the "good" woman of *Wilhelm Meister's Travels* whom Hans Eichner has described as incarnating her author's ideal of "contemplative purity," we find that this "model of selflessness and of purity of heart . . . this embodiment of *das Ewig-Weibliche,* suffers from migraine headaches."[16] Implying ruthless self-suppression, does the "eternal feminine" necessarily imply illness? If so, we may have found yet another meaning for Dickinson's assertion that "Infection in the sentence breeds." The despair we "inhale" even "at distances of centuries" may be the despair of a life like Makarie's, a life that *"has no story."*

At the same time, however, the despair of the monster-woman is also real, undeniable, and infectious. The Queen's mad tarantella is plainly unhealthy and metaphorically the result of too much storytelling. As the Romantic poets feared, too much imagination may be dangerous to anyone, male or female, but for women in particular patriarchal culture has always assumed mental exercises would have dire consequences. In 1645 John Winthrop, the governor of the Massachusetts Bay Colony, noted in his journal that Anne Hopkins "has fallen into a sad infirmity, the loss of her understanding and reason, which had been growing upon her divers years, by occasion of her giving herself wholly to reading and writing, and had written many books," adding that "if she had attended her household affairs, and such things as belong to women . . . she had kept her wits."[17] And as Wendy Martin has noted

> in the nineteenth century this fear of the intellectual woman became so intense that the phenomenon . . . was recorded in medical annals. A thinking woman was considered such a breach of nature that a Harvard doctor reported during his autopsy on a Radcliffe graduate he discovered that her uterus had shrivelled to the size of a pea.[18]

If, then, as Anne Sexton suggests (in a poem parts of which we have also used here as an epigraph), the red shoes passed furtively down from woman to woman are the shoes of art, the Queen's dancing shoes, it is as sickening to be a Queen who wears them as it is to be an angelic Makarie who repudiates them. Several passages in Sexton's verse express what we have defined as "anxiety of authorship" in the form of a feverish dread of the suicidal tarantella of female creativity:

> All those girls
> who wore red shoes,
> each boarded a train that would not stop.
> . . . .
> They tore off their ears like safety pins.
> Their arms fell off them and became hats.
> Their heads rolled off and sang down the street.
> And their feet—oh God, their feet in the market place—
> . . . the feet went on.
> The feet could not stop.
> . . . .
> They could not listen.
> They could not stop.
> What they did was the death dance.
>
> What they did would do them in.

Certainly infection breeds in these sentences, and despair; female art, Sexton suggests, has a "hidden" but crucial tradition of uncontrollable madness. Perhaps it was her semi-conscious perception of this tradition that gave Sexton herself "a secret fear" of being "a reincarnation" of Edna Millay, whose reputation seemed based on romance. In a letter to DeWitt Snodgrass she confessed that she had "a fear of writing as a woman writes," adding, "I wish I were a man—I would rather write the way a man writes."[19] After all, dancing the death dance, "all those girls / who wore the red shoes" dismantle their own bodies, like anorexics renouncing the guilty weight of their female flesh. But if their arms, ears, and heads fall off, perhaps their wombs, too, will "shrivel" to "the size of a pea"?

In this connection, a passage from Margaret Atwood's *Lady Oracle* acts almost as a gloss on the conflict between creativity and "femininity" which

Sexton's violent imagery embodies (or dis-embodies). Significantly, the protagonist of Atwood's novel is a writer of the sort of fiction that has recently been called "female gothic," and even more significantly she too projects her anxieties of authorship into the fairy-tale metaphor of the red shoes. Stepping in glass, she sees blood on her feet, and suddenly feels that she has discovered

> The real red shoes, the feet punished for dancing. You could dance, or you could have the love of a good man. But you were afraid to dance, because you had this unnatural fear that if you danced they'd cut your feet off so you wouldn't be able to dance.... Finally you overcame your fear and danced, and they cut your feet off. The good man went away too, because you wanted to dance.[20]

Whether she is a passive angel or an active monster, in other words, the woman writer feels herself to be literally or figuratively crippled by the debilitating alternatives her culture offers her, and the crippling effects of her conditioning sometimes seem to "breed" like sentences of death in the bloody shoes she inherits from her literary foremothers.

Surrounded as she is by images of disease, traditions of disease, and invitations both to disease and to dis-ease, it is no wonder that the woman writer has held many mirrors up to the discomforts of her own nature. As we shall see, the notion that "Infection in the sentence breeds" has been so central a truth for literary women that the great artistic achievements of nineteenth-century novelists and poets from Austen and Shelley to Dickinson and Barrett Browning are often both literally and figuratively concerned with disease, as if to emphasize the effort with which health and wholeness were won from the infectious "vapors" of despair and fragmentation. Rejecting the poisoned apples her culture offers her, the woman writer often becomes in some sense anorexic, resolutely closing her mouth on silence (since—in the words of Jane Austen's Henry Tilney—"a woman's only power is the power of refusal"[21]), even while she complains of starvation. Thus both Charlotte and Emily Brontë depict the travails of starved or starving anorexic heroines, while Emily Dickinson declares in one breath that she "had been hungry, all the Years," and in another opts for "Sumptuous Destitution." Similarly, Christina Rossetti represents her own anxiety of authorship in the split between one heroine who longs to "suck and suck" on goblin fruit and another who locks her lips fiercely together in a gesture of silent and passionate renunciation. In addition, many of these literary women become in one way or another agoraphobic. Trained to reticence, they fear the vertiginous openness of the literary marketplace and rationalize with Emily Dickinson that "Publication—is the Auction / Of the Mind of Man" or, worse, punningly confess that "Creation seemed a mighty Crack— / To make me visible."[22]

As we shall also see, other diseases and dis-eases accompany the two classic symptoms of anorexia and agoraphobia. Claustrophobia, for instance, agoraphobia's parallel and complementary opposite, is a disturbance we shall encounter again and again in women's writing throughout the nineteenth century. Eye "troubles," moreover, seem to abound in the lives and works of literary women, with Dickinson matter-of-factly noting that her eye got "put out," George Eliot describing patriarchal Rome as "a disease of the retina," Jane Eyre and Aurora Leigh marrying blind men, Charlotte Brontë deliberately writing with her eyes closed, and Mary Elizabeth Coleridge writing about "Blindness" that came because "Absolute and bright, / The Sun's rays smote me till they masked the Sun."[23] Finally, aphasia and amnesia—two illnesses which symbolically represent (and parody) the sort of intellectual incapacity patriarchal culture has traditionally required of women—appear and reappear in women's writings in frankly stated or disguised forms. "Foolish" women characters in Jane Austen's novels (Miss Bates in *Emma*, for instance) express Malapropish confusion about language, while Mary Shelley's monster has to learn language from scratch and Emily Dickinson herself childishly questions the meanings of the most basic English words: "Will there really be a 'Morning'? / Is there such a thing as 'Day'?"[24] At the same time, many women writers manage to imply that the reason for such ignorance of language—as well as the reason for their deep sense of alienation and inescapable feeling of anomie—is that they have *forgotten* something. Deprived of the power that even their pens don't seem to confer, these women resemble Doris Lessing's heroines, who have to fight their internalization of patriarchal strictures for even a faint trace memory of what they might have become.

"Where are the songs I used to know, / Where are the notes I used to sing?" writes Christina Rossetti in "The Key-Note," a poem whose title indicates its significance for her. "I have forgotten everything / I used to know so long ago."[25] As if to make the same point, Charlotte Brontë's Lucy Snowe conveniently "forgets" her own history and even, so it seems, the Christian name of one of the central characters in her story, while Brontë's orphaned Jane Eyre seems to have lost (or symbolically "forgotten") her family heritage. Similarly, too, Emily Brontë's Heathcliff "forgets" or is made to forget who and what he was; Mary Shelley's monster is "born" without either a memory or a family history; and Elizabeth Barrett Browning's Aurora Leigh is early separated from—and thus induced to "forget"—her "mother land" of Italy. As this last example suggests, however, what all these characters and their authors really fear they have forgotten is precisely that aspect of their lives which has been kept from them by patriarchal poetics: their matrilineal heritage of literary strength, their "female power" which, as Annie Gottlieb wrote, is important to them *because of* (not in spite of) their mothers. In order, then, not only to understand the ways in which "Infection in the sentence breeds" for women but also to learn how women have won through disease to artistic health we must begin by redefining Bloom's seminal definitions of the revisionary "anxiety of influence." In doing so, we will have to trace the difficult paths by which nineteenth-century women overcame their "anxiety of authorship," repudiated debilitating patriarchal prescriptions, and recovered or remembered the lost foremothers who could help them find their distinctive female power. ⟨. . .⟩

Dis-eased and infected by the sentences of patriarchy, yet unable to deny the urgency of that "poet-fire" she felt within herself, what strategies did the woman writer develop for overcoming her anxiety of authorship? How did she dance out of the looking glass of the male text into a tradition that enabled her to create her own authority? Denied the economic, social, and psychological status ordinarily essential to creativity; denied the right, skill, and education to tell their own stories with confidence, women who did not retreat into angelic silence seem at first to have had very limited options. On the one hand, they could accept the "parsley wreath" of self-denial, writing in "lesser" genres—children's books, letters, diaries—or limiting their readership to "mere" women like themselves and producing what George Eliot called "Silly Novels by Lady Novelists."[26] On the other hand, they could become males *manqués*, mimics who disguised their identities and, denying themselves, produced most frequently a literature of bad faith and inauthenticity. Given such weak solutions to what appears to have been an overwhelming problem, how could there be a great tradition of literature by women? Yet, as we shall show, there is just such a tradition, a tradition especially encompassing the works of nineteenth-century women writers who found viable ways of circumventing the problematic strategies we have just outlined.

Inappropriate as male-devised genres must always have seemed, some women have always managed to work seriously in them. Indeed, when we examine the great works written by nineteenth-century women poets and novelists, we soon notice two striking facts. First, an extraordinary number of literary women either eschewed or grew beyond both female "modesty" and male mimicry. From Austen to Dickinson, these female artists all dealt with central female experiences from a specifically female perspective. But this distinctively feminine aspect of their art has been generally ignored by critics because the most successful women writers often seem to have channeled their female concerns into secret or at least obscure corners. In effect, such women have created submerged meanings, meanings hidden within or behind the more accessible, "public" content of their works, so that their literature could be read and appreciated even when its vital concern with female dispossession and disease was ignored. Second, the writing of these women often seems "odd" in relation to the predominantly male literary history defined by the standards of what we have called patriarchal poetics. Neither Augustans nor Romantics, neither Victorian sages nor pre-Raphaelite sensualists, many of the most distinguished late eighteenth-century and nineteenth-century English and American women writers do not seem to "fit" into any of those categories to which our literary historians have accustomed us. Indeed, to many critics and scholars, some of these literary women look like isolated eccentrics.

We may legitimately wonder, however, if the second striking fact about nineteenth-century literature by women may not in some sense be a function of the first. Could the "oddity" of this work be associated with women's secret but insistent struggle to transcend their anxiety of authorship? Could the "isolation" and apparent "eccentricity" of these women really represent their common female struggle to solve the problem of what Anne Finch called the literary woman's "fall," as well as their common female search for an aesthetic that would yield a healthy space in an overwhelmingly male "Palace of Art"? Certainly when we consider the "oddity" of women's writing in relation to its submerged content, it begins to seem that when women did not turn into male mimics or accept the "parsley wreath" they may have attempted to transcend their anxiety of authorship by *revising* male genres, using them to record their own dreams and their own stories *in disguise*. Such writers, therefore, both participated in and—to use one of Harold Bloom's key terms—"swerved" from the central sequences of male literary history, enacting a uniquely female process of revision and redefinition that necessarily caused them to seem "odd." At the same time, while they achieved essential authority by telling their own stories, these writers allayed their distinctively female anxieties of authorship by following Emily Dickinson's famous (and characteristically female) advice to "Tell all the Truth but tell it slant—."[27] In short, like the twentieth-century American poet H. D., who declared her aesthetic strategy by entitling one of her novels *Palimpsest,* women from Jane Austen and Mary Shelley to Emily Brontë and Emily Dickinson produced literary works that are in some sense palimpsestic, works whose surface designs conceal or obscure deeper, less accessible (and less socially acceptable) levels of meaning. Thus these authors managed the difficult task of achieving true female literary authority by simultaneously conforming to and subverting patriarchal literary standards.

Of course, as the allegorical figure of Duessa suggests, men have always accused women of the duplicity that is essential to the literary strategies we are describing here. In part, at least, such accusations are well founded, both in life and in art. As in the white-black relationship, the dominant group in the male-female relationship rightly fears and suspects that the docility of the subordinate caste masks rebellious passions. Moreover, just as blacks did in the master-slave relationships of the American South, women in patriarchy have traditionally cultivated accents of acquiescence in order to gain freedom to live their lives on their own terms, if only in the privacy of their own thoughts. Interestingly, indeed, several feminist critics have recently used Frantz Fanon's model of colonialism to describe the relationship between male (parent) culture and female (colonized) literature.[28] But with only one language at their disposal, women writers in England and America had to be even more adept at doubletalk than their colonized counterparts. We shall see, therefore, that in publicly presenting acceptable facades for private and dangerous visions women writers have long used a wide range of tactics to obscure but not obliterate their most subversive impulses. Along with the twentieth-century American painter Judy Chicago, any one of these artists might have noted that "formal issues" were often "something that my content had to be hidden behind in order for my work to be taken seriously." And with Judy Chicago, too, any one of these women might have confessed that "Because of this duplicity, there always appeared to be something 'not quite right' about my pieces according to the prevailing aesthetic."[29]

To be sure, male writers also "swerve" from their predecessors, and they too produce literary texts whose revolutionary messages are concealed behind stylized facades. The most original male writers, moreover, sometimes seem "not quite right" to those readers we have recently come to call "establishment" critics. As Bloom's theory of the anxiety of influence implies, however, and as our analysis of the metaphor of literary paternity also suggests, there are powerful paradigms of male intellectual struggle which enable the male writer to explain his rebelliousness, his "swerving," and his "originality" both to himself and to the world, no matter how many readers think him "not quite right." In a sense, therefore, he conceals his revolutionary energies only so that he may more powerfully reveal them, and swerves or rebels so that he may triumph by founding a new order, since his struggle against his precursor is a "battle of strong equals."

For the woman writer, however, concealment is not a military gesture but a strategy born of fear and dis-ease. Similarly, a literary "swerve" is not a motion by which the writer prepares for a victorious accession to power but a necessary evasion. Locked into structures created by and for men, eighteenth- and nineteenth-century women writers did not so much rebel against the prevailing aesthetic as feel guilty about their inability to conform to it. With little sense of a viable female culture, such women were plainly much troubled by the fact that they needed to communicate truths which other (i.e., male) writers apparently never felt or expressed. Conditioned to doubt their own authority anyway, women writers who wanted to describe what, in Dickinson's phrase, is "not brayed of tongue"[30] would find it easier to doubt themselves than the censorious voices of society. The evasions and concealments of their art are therefore far more elaborate than those of most male writers. For, given the patriarchal biases of nineteenth-century literary culture, the literary woman did have something crucial to hide.

Because so many of the lost or concealed truths of female culture have recently been retrieved by feminist scholars, women readers in particular have lately become aware that nineteenth-century literary women felt they had things to hide. Many feminist critics, therefore, have begun to write about these phenomena of evasion and concealment in women's writing. In *The Female Imagination,* for instance, Patricia Meyer Spacks repeatedly describes the ways in which women's novels are marked by "subterranean challenges" to truths that the writers of such works appear on the surface to accept. Similarly, Carolyn Heilbrun and Catharine Stimpson discuss "the presence of absence" in literature by women, the "hollows, centers, caverns within the work—places where activity that one might expect is missing ... or deceptively coded." Perhaps most trenchantly, Elaine Showalter has recently pointed out that feminist criticism, with its emphasis on the woman writer's inevitable consciousness of her own gender, has allowed us to "see meaning in what has previously been empty space. The orthodox plot recedes, and another plot, hitherto submerged in the anonymity of the background, stands out in bold relief like a thumbprint."[31]

But what is this other plot? Is there any *one* other plot? What is the secret message of literature by women, if there is a single secret message? What, in other words, have women got to hide? Most obviously, of course, if we return to the angelic figure of Makarie—that ideal of "contemplative purity" who no doubt had headaches precisely because her author inflicted upon her a life that seemed to have "no story"—what literary women have hidden or disguised is what each writer knows is in some sense her own story. Because, as Simone de Beauvoir puts it, women "still dream through the dreams of men," internalizing the strictures that the Queen's looking glass utters in its kingly voice, the message or story that has been hidden is "merely," in Carolyn Kizer's bitter words, "the private lives of one half of humanity."[32] More specifically, however, the one plot that seems to be concealed in most of the nineteenth-century literature by women which will concern us here is in some sense a story of the woman writer's quest for her own story; it is the story, in other words, of the woman's quest for self-definition. Like the speaker of Mary Elizabeth Coleridge's "The Other Side of a Mirror," the literary woman frequently finds herself staring with horror at a fearful image of herself that has been mysteriously inscribed on the surface of the glass, and she tries to guess the truth that cannot be uttered by the wounded and bleeding mouth, the truth behind the "leaping fire / Of jealousy and fierce revenge," the truth "of hard unsanctified distress." Uneasily aware that, like Sylvia Plath, she is "inhabited by a cry," she secretly seeks to unify herself by coming to terms with her own fragmentation. Yet even though, with Mary Elizabeth Coleridge, she strives to "set the crystal surface" of the mirror free from frightful images, she continually feels, as May Sarton puts it, that she has been "broken in two / By sheer definition."[33] The story "no man may guess," therefore, is the story of her attempt to make herself whole by healing her own infections and diseases.

To heal herself, however, the woman writer must exorcise the sentences which bred her infection in the first place; she must overtly or covertly free herself of the despair she inhaled from some "Wrinkled Maker," and she can only do this by revising the Maker's texts. Or, to put the matter in terms of a different metaphor, to "set the crystal surface free" a literary woman must shatter the mirror that has so long reflected what every woman was supposed to be. For these reasons, then, women writers in England and America, throughout the nineteenth century and on into the twentieth, have been especially concerned with assaulting and revising, deconstructing and reconstructing those images of women inherited from male literature, especially, as we noted in our discussion of the Queen's looking glass, the paradigmatic polarities of angel and monster. Examining and attacking such images, however, literary women have inevitably had consciously or unconsciously to reject the values and assumptions of the society that created these fearsome paradigms. Thus, even when they do not overtly criticize patriarchal institutions or conventions (and most of the nineteenth-century women we shall be studying do *not* overtly do so), these writers almost obsessively create characters who enact their own, covert authorial anger. With Charlotte Brontë, they may feel that there are "evils" of which it is advisable "not too often to think." With George Eliot, they may declare that the "woman question" seems "to overhang abysses, of which even prostitution is not the worst."[34] But over and over again they project what seems to be the energy of their own despair into passionate, even melodramatic characters who act out the subversive impulses every woman inevitably feels when she contemplates the "deep-rooted" evils of patriarchy. ⟨. . .⟩

There is a sense, then, in which the female literary tradition we have been defining participates on all levels in the same duality or duplicity that necessitates the generation of such doubles as monster characters who shadow angelic authors and mad anti-heroines who complicate the lives of sane heroines. Parody, for instance, is another one of the key strategies through which this female duplicity reveals itself. As we have noted, nineteenth-century women writers frequently both use and misuse (or subvert) a common male tradition or genre. Consequently, we shall see over and over again that a "complex vibration" occurs between stylized generic gestures and unexpected deviations from such obvious gestures, a vibration that undercuts and ridicules the genre being employed. Some of the best-known recent poetry by women openly uses such parody in the cause of feminism: traditional figures of patriarchal mythology like Circe, Leda, Cassandra, Medusa, Helen, and Persephone have all lately been reinvented in the images of their female creators, and each poem devoted to one of these figures is a reading that reinvents her original story.[35] But though nineteenth-century women did not employ this kind of parody so openly and angrily, they too deployed it to give contextual force to their revisionary attempts at self-definition. Jane Austen's novels of sense and sensibility, for instance, suggest a revolt against both those standards of female excellence. Similarly, Charlotte Brontë's critical revision of *Pilgrim's Progress* questions the patriarchal ideal of female submissiveness by substituting a questing Everywoman for Bunyan's questing Christian. In addition, as we shall show in detail in later chapters, Mary Shelley, Emily Brontë, and George Eliot covertly reappraise and repudiate the misogyny implicit in Milton's mythology by misreading and revising Milton's story of woman's fall. Parodic, duplicitous, extraordinarily sophisticated, all this female writing is both revisionary and revolutionary, even when it is produced by writers we usually think of as models of angelic resignation.

⟨. . .⟩ the great women writers of the past two centuries are linked by the ingenuity with which all, while no one was really looking, danced out of the debilitating looking glass of the male text into the health of female authority. Tracing subversive pictures behind socially acceptable facades, they managed to appear to dissociate themselves from their own revolutionary impulses even while passionately enacting such impulses. Articulating the "private lives of one half of humanity," their fiction and poetry both records and transcends the struggle of what Marge Piercy has called "Unlearning to not speak."[36]

We must not forget, however, that to hide behind the facade of art, even for so crucial a process as "Unlearning to not speak," is still to be hidden, to be confined: to be secret is to be secreted. In a poignant and perceptive poem to Emily Dickinson, Adrienne Rich has noted that in her "half-cracked way" Dickinson chose "silence for entertainment, / chose to have it out at last / on [her] own premises."[37] This is what Jane Austen, too, chose to do when she ironically defined her work-space as two inches of ivory, what Emily Brontë chose to do when she hid her poems in kitchen cabinets (and perhaps destroyed her Gondal stories), what Christina Rossetti chose when she elected an art that glorified the religious constrictions of the "convent threshold." Rich's crucial pun on the word *premises* returns us, therefore, to the confinement of these women, a confinement that was inescapable for them even at their moments of greatest triumph, a confinement that was implicit in their secretness. This confinement was both literal and figurative. Literally, women like Dickinson, Brontë, and Rossetti were imprisoned in their homes, their father's houses; indeed, almost all nineteenth-century women were in some sense imprisoned in men's houses. Figuratively, such women were, as we have seen, locked into male texts, texts from which they could escape only through ingenuity and indirection. It is not surprising, then, that spatial imagery of enclosure and escape, elaborated with what frequently becomes obsessive intensity, characterizes much of their writing.

In fact, anxieties about space sometimes seem to dominate the literature of both nineteenth-century women and their twentieth-century descendants. In the genre Ellen Moers has recently called "female Gothic,"[38] for instance, heroines who characteristically inhabit mysteriously intricate or uncomfortably stifling houses are often seen as captured, fettered, trapped, even buried alive. But other kinds of works by women—novels of manners, domestic tales, lyric poems—also show the same concern with spatial constrictions. From Ann Radcliffe's melodramatic dungeons to Jane Austen's mirrored parlors, from Charlotte Brontë's haunted garrets to Emily Brontë's coffin-shaped beds, imagery of enclosure reflects the woman writer's own discomfort, her sense of powerlessness, her fear that she inhabits alien and incomprehensible places. Indeed, it reflects her growing suspicion that what the nineteenth century called "woman's place" is itself irrational and strange. Moreover, from Emily Dickinson's haunted chambers to H. D.'s tightly shut sea-shells and Sylvia Plath's grave-caves, imagery of entrapment expresses the woman writer's sense that she has been dispossessed precisely because she is so thoroughly possessed—and possessed in every sense of the word.

The opening stanzas of Charlotte Perkins Gilman's punningly titled "In Duty Bound" show how inevitable it was for a female artist to translate into spatial terms her despair at the spiritual constrictions of what Gilman ironically called "home comfort."

> In duty bound, a life hemmed in,
>   Whichever way the spirit turns to look;
> No chance of breaking out, except by sin;
>   Not even room to shirk—
>   Simply to live, and work.
>
> An obligation preimposed, unsought,
>   Yet binding with the force of natural law;
> The pressure of antagonistic thought;
>   Aching within, each hour,
>   A sense of wasting power.

> A house with roof so darkly low
>   The heavy rafters shut the sunlight out;
> One cannot stand erect without a blow;
>   Until the soul inside
>   Cries for a grave—more wide.[39]

Literally confined to the house, figuratively confined to a single "place," enclosed in parlors and encased in texts, imprisoned in kitchens and enshrined in stanzas, women artists naturally found themselves describing dark interiors and confusing their sense that they were house-bound with their rebellion against being duty bound. The same connections Gilman's poem made in the nineteenth century had after all been made by Anne Finch in the eighteenth, when she complained that women who wanted to write poetry were scornfully told that "the dull mannage of a servile house" was their "outmost art and use." Inevitably, then, since they were trapped in so many ways in the architecture—both the houses and the institutions—of patriarchy, women expressed their anxiety of authorship by comparing their "presumptuous" literary ambitions with the domestic accomplishments that had been prescribed for them. Inevitably, too, they expressed their claustrophobic rage by enacting rebellious escapes.

    Dramatizations of imprisonment and escape are so all-pervasive in nineteenth-century literature by women that we believe they represent a uniquely female tradition in this period. Interestingly, though works in this tradition generally begin by using houses as primary symbols of female imprisonment, they also use much of the other paraphernalia of "woman's place" to enact their central symbolic drama of enclosure and escape. Ladylike veils and costumes, mirrors, paintings, statues, locked cabinets, drawers, trunks, strongboxes, and other domestic furnishing appear and reappear in female novels and poems throughout the nineteenth century and on into the twentieth to signify the woman writer's sense that, as Emily Dickinson put it, her "life" has been "shaven and fitted to a frame," a confinement she can only tolerate by believing that "the soul has moments of escape / When bursting all the doors / She dances like a bomb abroad."[40] Significantly, too, the explosive violence of these "moments of escape" that women writers continually imagine for themselves returns us to the phenomenon of the mad double so many of these women have projected into their works. For it is, after all, through the violence of the double that the female author enacts her own raging desire to escape male houses and male texts, while at the same time it is through the double's violence that this anxious author articulates for herself the costly destructiveness of anger repressed until it can no longer be contained.

    As we shall see, therefore, infection continually breeds in the sentences of women whose writing obsessively enacts this drama of enclosure and escape. Specifically, what we have called the distinctively female diseases of anorexia and agoraphobia are closely associated with this dramatic/thematic pattern. Defining themselves as prisoners of their own gender, for instance, women frequently create characters who attempt to escape, if only into nothingness, through the suicidal self-starvation of anorexia. Similarly, in a metaphorical elaboration of bulimia, the disease of overeating which is anorexia's complement and mirror-image (as Marlene Boskind-Lodahl has recently shown),[41] women writers often envision an "outbreak" that transforms their characters into huge and powerful monsters. More obviously, agoraphobia and its complementary opposite, claustrophobia, are by definition associated with the spatial imagery through which these poets and novelists express their feelings of social confinement and their yearning for spiritual escape. The paradigmatic female story, therefore—the story such angels in the house of literature as Goethe's Makarie and Patmore's Honoria were in effect "forbidden" to tell—is frequently an arrangement of the elements most readers will readily remember from Charlotte Brontë's *Jane Eyre*. Examining the psychosocial implications of a "haunted" ancestral mansion, such a tale explores the tension between parlor and attic, the psychic split between the lady who submits to male dicta and the lunatic who rebels. But in examining these matters the paradigmatic female story inevitably considers also the equally uncomfortable spatial options of expulsion into the cold outside or suffocation in the hot indoors, and in addition it often embodies an obsessive anxiety both about starvation to the point of disappearance and about monstrous inhabitation.

Many nineteenth-century male writers also, of course, used imagery of enclosure and escape to make deeply felt points about the relationship of the individual and society. Dickens and Poe, for instance, on opposite sides of the Atlantic, wrote of prisons, cages, tombs, and cellars in similar ways and for similar reasons. Still, the male writer is so much more comfortable with his literary role that he can usually elaborate upon his visionary theme more consciously and objectively than the female writer can. The distinction between male and female images of imprisonment is—and always has been—a distinction between, on the one hand, that which is both metaphysical and metaphorical, and on the other hand, that which is social and actual. Sleeping in his coffin, the seventeenth-century poet John Donne was piously rehearsing the constraints of the grave in advance, but the nineteenth-century poet Emily Dickinson, in purdah in her white dress, was anxiously living those constraints in the present. Imagining himself buried alive in tombs and cellars, Edgar Allan Poe was letting his mind poetically wander into the deepest recesses of his own psyche, but Dickinson, reporting that "I do not cross my Father's ground to any house in town," was recording a real, self-willed, self-burial. Similarly, when Byron's Prisoner of Chillon notes that "my very chains and I grew friends," the poet himself is making an epistemological point about the nature of the human mind, as well as a political point about the tyranny of the state. But when Rose Yorke in *Shirley* describes Caroline Helstone as living the life of a toad enclosed in a block of marble, Charlotte Brontë is speaking through her about her own deprived and constricted life, and its real conditions.[42]

Thus, though most male metaphors of imprisonment have obvious implications in common (and many can be traced back to traditional images used by, say, Shakespeare and Plato), such metaphors may have very different aesthetic functions and philosophical messages in different male literary works. Wordsworth's prison-house in the "Intimations" ode serves a purpose quite unlike that served by the jails in Dickens's novels. Coleridge's twice-five miles of visionary greenery ought not to be confused with Keats's vale of soul-making, and the escape of Tennyson's Art from her Palace should not be identified with the resurrection of Poe's Ligeia. Women authors, however, reflect the literal reality of their own confinement in the constraints they depict, and so all at least begin with the same unconscious or conscious purpose in employing such spatial imagery. Recording their own distinctively female experience, they are secretly working through and within the conventions of literary texts to define their own lives.

While some male authors also use such imagery for implicitly or explicitly confessional projects, women seem forced to live more intimately with the metaphors they have created to solve the "problem" of their fall. At least one critic does deal not only with such images but with their psychological meaning as they accrue around houses. Noting in *The Poetics of Space* that "the house image would appear to have become the topography of our inmost being," Gaston Bachelard shows the ways in which houses, nests, shells, and wardrobes are in us as much as we are in them.[43] What is significant from our point of view, however, is the extraordinary discrepancy between the almost consistently "felicitous space" he discusses and the negative space we have found. Clearly, for Bachelard the protective asylum of the house is closely associated with its maternal features, and to this extent he is following the work done on dream symbolism by Freud and on female inner space by Erikson. It seems clear too, however, that such symbolism must inevitably have very different implications for male critics and for female authors.

Women themselves have often, of course, been described or imagined as houses. Most recently Erik Erikson advanced his controversial theory of female "inner space" in an effort to account for little girls' interest in domestic enclosures. But in medieval times, as if to anticipate Erikson, statues of the Madonna were made to open up and reveal the holy family hidden in the Virgin's inner space. The female womb has certainly, always and everywhere, been a child's first and most satisfying house, a source of food and dark security, and therefore a mythic paradise imaged over and over again in sacred caves, secret shrines, consecrated huts. Yet for many a woman writer these ancient associations of house and self seem mainly to have strengthened the anxiety about enclosure which she projected into her art. Disturbed by the real physiological prospect of enclosing an unknown part of herself that is somehow also not herself, the female artist may, like Mary Shelley, conflate anxieties about maternity with anxieties about literary creativity. Alternatively, troubled by the anatomical "emptiness" of spinsterhood, she may, like Emily Dickinson, fear the inhabitations of nothingness and death, the transformation of womb into tomb. Moreover, conditioned to believe that as a house she is herself owned (and ought to be inhabited) by a man, she may once again but for yet another reason see herself as inescapably an object. In other words, even if she does not experience her womb as a kind of tomb or perceive her child's occupation of her house/body as depersonalizing, she may recognize that in an essential way she has been defined simply by her purely biological usefulness to her species.

To become literally a house, after all, is to be denied the hope of that spiritual transcendence of the body which, as Simone de Beauvoir has argued, is what makes humanity distinctively human. Thus, to be confined in childbirth (and significantly "confinement" was the key nineteenth-century term for what we would now, just as significantly, call "delivery") is in a way just as problematical as to be confined in a house or prison. Indeed, it might well seem to the literary woman that, just as ontogeny may be said to recapitulate phylogeny, the confinement of pregnancy replicates the confinement of society. For even if she is only metaphorically denied transcendence, the woman writer who perceives the implications of the house/body equation must unconsciously realize that such a trope does not just "place" her in a glass coffin, it transforms her into a version of the glass coffin herself. There is a sense, therefore, in which, confined in such a network of metaphors, what Adrienne Rich has called a "thinking woman" might inevitably feel that now she has been imprisoned within her own alien and loathsome body.[44] Once again, in other words, she has become not only a prisoner but a monster.

As if to comment on the unity of all these points—on, that is, the anxiety-inducing connections between what women writers tend to see as their parallel confinements in texts, houses, and maternal female bodies—Charlotte Perkins Gilman brought them all together in 1890 in a striking story of female confinement and escape, a paradigmatic tale which (like *Jane Eyre*) seems to tell *the* story that all literary women would tell if they could speak their "speechless woe." "The Yellow Wallpaper," which Gilman herself called "a description of a case of nervous breakdown," recounts in the first person the experiences of a woman who is evidently suffering from a severe postpartum psychosis.[45] Her husband, a censorious and paternalistic physician, is treating her according to methods by which S. Weir Mitchell, a famous "nerve specialist," treated Gilman herself for a similar problem. He has confined her to a large garret room in an "ancestral hall" he has rented, and he has forbidden her to touch pen to paper until she is well again, for he feels, says the narrator, "that with my imaginative power and habit of story-making, a nervous weakness like mine is sure to lead to all manner of excited fancies, and that I ought to use my will and good sense to check the tendency" (15–16).

The cure, of course, is worse than the disease, for the sick woman's mental condition deteriorates rapidly. "I think sometimes that if I were only well enough to write a little it would relieve the press of ideas and rest me," she remarks, but literally confined in a room she thinks is a one-time nursery because it has "rings and things" in the walls, she is literally locked away from creativity. The "rings and things," although reminiscent of children's gymnastic equipment, are really the paraphernalia of confinement, like the gate at the head of the stairs, instruments that definitively indicate her imprisonment. Even more tormenting, however, is the room's wallpaper: a sulphurous yellow paper, torn off in spots, and patterned with "lame uncertain curves" that "plunge off at outrageous angles" and "destroy themselves in unheard of contradictions." Ancient, smoldering, "unclean" as the oppressive structures of the society in which she finds herself, this paper surrounds the narrator like an inexplicable text, censorious and overwhelming as her physician husband, haunting as the "hereditary estate" in which she is trying to survive. Inevitably she studies its suicidal implications—and inevitably, because of her "imaginative power and habit of story-making," she revises it, projecting her own passion for escape into its otherwise incomprehensible hieroglyphics. "This wall-paper," she decides, at a key point in her story,

> has a kind of sub-pattern in a different shade, a particularly irritating one, for you can only see it in certain lights, and not clearly then.
> But in the places where it isn't faded and where the sun is just so—I can see a strange, provoking, formless sort of figure, that seems to skulk about behind that silly and conspicuous front design. [18]

As time passes, this figure concealed behind what corresponds (in terms of what we have been discussing) to the facade of the patriarchal text becomes clearer and clearer. By moonlight the pattern of the wallpaper "becomes bars! The outside pattern I mean, and the woman behind it is as plain as can be." And eventually, as the narrator sinks more deeply into what the world calls madness, the terrifying implications of both the paper and the figure imprisoned behind the paper begin to permeate—that is, to *haunt*—the rented ancestral mansion in which she and her husband are immured. The "yellow smell" of the paper "creeps all over the house," drenching every room in its subtle aroma of decay. And the woman creeps too—through the house, in the house, and out of the house, in the garden and "on that long road under the trees." Sometimes, indeed, the narrator confesses, "I think there are a great many women" both behind the paper and creeping in the garden,

> and sometimes only one, and she crawls around fast, and her crawling shakes [the paper] all over. . . . And she is all the time trying to climb through. But nobody could climb through that pattern—it strangles so; I think that is why it has so many heads [30]

Eventually it becomes obvious to both reader and narrator that the figure creeping through and behind the wallpaper is both the narrator and the narrator's double. By the end of the story, moreover, the narrator has enabled this double to escape from her textual/architectural confinement: "I pulled and she shook, I shook and she pulled, and before morning we had peeled off yards of that paper." Is the message of the tale's conclusion mere madness? Certainly the righteous Doctor John—whose name links him to the anti-hero of Charlotte Brontë's *Villette*—has been temporarily defeated, or at least momentarily stunned. "Now why should that man have fainted?" the narrator ironically asks as she creeps around her attic. But John's unmasculine swoon of surprise is the least of the triumphs Gilman imagines for her madwoman. More significant are the madwoman's own imaginings and creations, mirages of health and freedom with which her author endows her like a fairy godmother showering gold on a sleeping heroine. The woman from behind the wallpaper creeps away, for instance, creeps fast and far on the long road, in broad daylight. "I have watched her sometimes away off in the open country," says the narrator, "creeping as fast as a cloud shadow in a high wind."

Indistinct and yet rapid, barely perceptible but inexorable, the progress of that cloud shadow is not unlike the progress of nineteenth-century literary women out of the texts defined by patriarchal poetics into the open spaces of their own authority. That such an escape from the numb world behind the patterned walls of the text was a flight from dis-ease into health was quite clear to Gilman herself. When "The Yellow Wallpaper" was published she sent it to Weir Mitchell, whose strictures had kept her from attempting the pen during her own breakdown, thereby aggravating her illness, and she was delighted to learn, years later, that "he had changed his treatment of nervous prostration since reading" her story. "If that is a fact," she declared, "I have not lived in vain."[46] Because she was a rebellious feminist besides being a medical iconoclast, we can be sure that Gilman did not think of this triumph of hers in narrowly therapeutic terms. Because she knew, with Emily Dickinson, that "Infection in the sentence breeds," she knew that the cure for female despair must be spiritual as well as physical, aesthetic as well as social. What "The Yellow Wallpaper" shows she knew, too, is that even when a supposedly "mad" woman has been sentenced to imprisonment in the "infected" house of her own body, she may discover that, as Sylvia Plath was to put it seventy years later, she has "a self to recover, a queen."[47]

NOTES

Epigraphs: Doctor on Patient (Philadelphia: Lippincott, 1888), quoted in Ilza Veith, *Hysteria: The History of a Disease* (Chicago: University of Chicago Press, 1965), pp. 219–20; *The Living of Charlotte Perkins Gilman* (New York: Harper & Row, 1975; first published 1935), p. 104; J. 1261 in *The Poems of Emily Dickinson*, ed. Thomas Johnson, 3 vols. (Cambridge, Mass.: The Belknap Press of Harvard University Press, 1955: all subsequent references are to this edition); "The Red Shoes," *The Book of Folly* (Boston: Houghton Mifflin, 1972), pp. 28–29.

1. In "Tradition and the Individual Talent," Eliot of course considers these matters; in *Mimesis* Auerbach traces the ways in which the realist includes what has been previously excluded from art; and in *The Sense of an Ending* Frank Kermode shows how poets and novelists lay bare the literariness of their predecessors' forms in order to explore the dissonance between fiction and reality.

2. J. Hillis Miller, "The Limits of Pluralism, III: The Critic as Host," *Critical Inquiry* (Spring 1977):446.

3. For a discussion of the woman writer and her place in Bloomian literary history, see Joanne Feit Diehl, "'Come Slowly—Eden': An Exploration of Women Poets

and Their Muse," *Signs* 3, no. 3 (Spring 1978): 572–87. See also the responses to Diehl in *Signs* 4, no. 1 (Autumn 1978): 188–96.

4. Juliet Mitchell, *Psychoanalysis and Feminism* (New York: Vintage, 1975), p. xiii.

5. Ibid., pp. 404–05.

6. Adrienne Rich, "When We Dead Awaken: Writing as Re-Vision," in *Adrienne Rich's Poetry*, ed. Barbara Charlesworth Gelpi and Albert Gelpi (New York: Norton, 1975), p. 90.

7. Mitchell, *Psychoanalysis and Feminism*, p. 402.

8. See Elaine Showalter, *A Literature of Their Own* (Princeton: Princeton University Press, 1977).

9. Annie Gottlieb, "Feminists Look at Motherhood," *Mother Jones* (November 1976):53.

10. *The Letters of Emily Dickinson*, ed. Thomas Johnson, 3 vols. (Cambridge, Mass.: The Belknap Press of Harvard University Press, 1958), 2:475; 2:518.

11. See Jessie Bernard, "The Paradox of the Happy Marriage," Pauline B. Bart, "Depression in Middle-Aged Women," and Naomi Weisstein, "Psychology Constructs the Female," all in Vivian Gornick and Barbara K. Moran, ed., *Woman in Sexist Society* (New York: Basic Books, 1971). See also Phyllis Chesler, *Women and Madness* (New York: Doubleday, 1972), and—for a summary of all these matters—Barbara Ehrenreich and Deirdre English, *Complaints and Disorders: The Sexual Politics of Sickness* (Old Westbury: The Feminist Press, 1973).

12. In *Hints on Insanity* (1861) John Millar wrote that "Mental derangement frequently occurs in young females from Amenorrhoea, especially in those who have any strong hereditary predisposition to insanity," adding that "an occasional warm hipbath or leeches to the pubis will . . . be followed by complete mental recovery." In 1873, Henry Mauldsey wrote in *Body and Mind* that "the monthly activity of the ovaries . . . has a notable effect upon the mind and body; wherefore it may become an important cause of mental and physical derangement." See especially the medical opinions of John Millar, Henry Maudsley, and Andrew Wynter in *Madness and Morals: Ideas on Insanity in the Nineteenth Century*, ed. Vieda Skultans (London and Boston: Routledge & Kegan Paul, 1975), pp. 230–35.

13. See Marlene Boskind-Lodahl, "Cinderella's Stepsisters: A Feminist Perspective on Anorexia Nervosa and Bulimia," *Signs* 2, no. 2 (Winter 1976): 342–56; Walter Blum, "The Thirteenth Guest" (on agoraphobia), in *California Living, The San Francisco Sunday Examiner and Chronicle* (17 April 1977):8–12; Joan Arehart-Treichel, "Can Your Personality Kill You?" (on female rheumatoid arthritis, among other diseases), *New York* 10, no. 48 (28 November 1977):45: "According to studies conducted in recent years, four out of five rheumatoid victims are women, and for good reason: The disease appears to arise in those unhappy with the traditional female-sex role."

14. More recent discussions of the etiology and treatment of anorexia are offered in Hilde Bruch, M. D., *The Golden Cage: The Enigma of Anorexia Nervosa* (Cambridge, Mass.: Harvard University Press, 1978), and in Salvador Minuchin, Bernice L. Rosman, and Lester Baker, *Psychosomatic Families: Anorexia Nervosa in Context* (Cambridge: Harvard University Press, 1978).

15. Quoted by Ehrenreich and English, *Complaints and Disorders*, p. 19.

16. Eichner, "The Eternal Feminine," Norton Critical Edition of *Faust*, trans. Walter Arndt, ed. Cyrus Hamilton (New York: Norton, 1976), p. 620.

17. John Winthrop, *The History of New England from 1630 to 1649*, ed. James Savage (Boston, 1826), 2:216.

18. Wendy Martin, "Anne Bradstreet's Poetry: A Study of Subversive Piety," *Shakespeare's Sisters,* ed. Gilbert and Gubar (Bloomington: Indiana University Press, 1979), pp. 19–31.

19. "The Uncensored Poet: Letters of Anne Sexton," *Ms.* 6, no. 5 (November 1977):53.

20. Margaret Atwood, *Lady Oracle* (New York: Simon and Schuster, 1976), p. 335.

21. See *Northanger Abbey,* chapter 10: "You will allow, that in both [matrimony and dancing], man has the advantage of choice, woman only the power of refusal."

22. See Dickinson, *Poems,* J. 579 ("I had been hungry, all the Years"), J. 709 ("Publication—is the Auction"), and J. 891 ("To my quick ear the Leaves—conferred"); see also Christina Rossetti, "Goblin Market."

23. See Dickinson, *Poems,* J. 327 ("Before I got my eye put out"), George Eliot, *Middlemarch,* book 2, chapter 20, and M. E. Coleridge, "Doubt," in *Poems by Mary E. Coleridge* (London: Elkin Mathews, 1908), p. 40.

24. See Dickinson, *Poems,* J. 101.

25. *The Poetical Works of Christina G. Rossetti,* 2 vols. (Boston: Little, Brown, 1909), 2:11.

26. See George Eliot, "Silly Novels by Lady Novelists," *Westminster Review* 64 (1856):442–61.

27. Dickinson, *Poems,* J. 1129.

28. See, for instance, Barbara Charlesworth Gelpi, "A Common Language: The American Woman Poet," in *Shakespeare's Sisters,* ed. Gilbert and Gubar, pp. 269–79.

29. Judy Chicago, *Through the Flower: My Struggle as a Woman Artist* (New York: Doubleday, 1977), p. 40.

30. Dickinson, *Poems,* J. 512 ("The Soul has Bandaged moments—").

31. Patricia Meyer Spacks, *The Female Imagination* (New York: Knopf, 1975), p. 317; Carolyn Heilbrun and Catharine Stimpson, "Theories of Feminist Criticism: A Dialogue," in Josephine Donovan, ed., *Feminist Literary Criticism* (Lexington: The University Press of Kentucky, 1975), p. 62; Elaine Showalter, "Review Essay," *Signs* 1, no. 2 (Winter 1975):435. See also Annis V. Pratt, "The New Feminist Criticisms: Exploring the History of the New Space," in *Beyond Intellectual Sexism: A New Woman, a New Reality,* ed. Joan I. Roberts (New York: David McKay, 1976). On p. 183 Pratt describes what she calls her "drowning theory," which "comes from a phenomenon in black culture: You have a little black church back in the marsh and you're going to sing 'Go Down Moses' [but] every now and then the members of the congregation want to break loose and sing 'Oh Freedom' . . . Whenever they sing that, they've got this big old black pot in the vestibule, and as they sing they pound the pot. That way, no white folks are going to hear. The drowning effect, this banging on the pot to drown out what they are actually saying about feminism, came in with the first woman's novel and hasn't gone out yet. Many women novelists have even succeeded in hiding the covert or implicit feminism in their books from themselves. . . . As a result we get explicit cultural norms superimposed upon an authentic creative mind in the form of all kinds of feints, ploys, masks and disguises embedded in the plot structure and characterization."

32. De Beauvoir, *The Second Sex* (New York: Knopf, 1953), p. 132; Kizer, "Three," from "Pro Femina," in *No More Masks!,* ed. Florence Howe and Ellen Bass (New York: Doubleday, 1973), p. 175.

33. Plath, "Elm," *Ariel* (New York: Harper & Row, 1966), p. 16; Sarton, "Birthday on the Acropolis," *A Private Mythology* (New York: Norton, 1966), p. 48.

34. *The George Eliot Letters,* 7 vols., ed. Gordon S. Haight (New Haven: Yale University Press, 1954–55), 5:58.

35. For "complex vibration," see Elaine Showalter, "Review Essay," p. 435. For reinventions of mythology, see Mona Van Duyn, "Leda" and "Leda Reconsidered," in *No More Masks!*, pp. 129–32, and Margaret Atwood, "Circe/Mud Poems," in *You Are Happy* (New York: Harper & Row, 1974), pp. 71–94. A poet like H. D. continually reinvents Persephone, Medusa, and Helen in her uniquely female epics, for example in *Helen in Egypt* (New York: New Directions, 1961).

36. Marge Piercy, "Unlearning to Not Speak," *To Be Of Use* (New York: Doubleday, 1973), p. 38.

37. "I am in danger—sir—," *Adrienne Rich's Poetry*, pp. 30–31.

38. Ellen Moers, *Literary Women* (New York: Doubleday, 1976), pp. 90–112.

39. *The Living of Charlotte Perkins Gilman*, p. 77.

40. Dickinson, *Poems*, J. 512 ("The Soul has Bandaged moments—").

41. Boskind-Lodahl, "Cinderella's Stepsisters."

42. Dickinson, *Letters*, 2:460; Byron, "The Prisoner of Chillon," lines 389–92; Brontë, *Shirley* (New York: Dutton, 1970), p. 316; see also Brontë to W. S. Williams, 26 July 1849.

43. Gaston Bachelard, *The Poetics of Space*, trans. Maria Jolas (Boston: Beacon, 1970), p. xxxii.

44. *Adrienne Rich's Poetry*, p. 12: "A thinking woman sleeps with monsters. / The beak that grips her, she becomes" ("Snapshots of a Daughter-in-Law," #3).

45. Charlotte Perkins Gilman, *The Yellow Wallpaper* (Old Westbury: The Feminist Press, 1973). All references in the text will be to page numbers in this edition.

46. *The Living of Charlotte Perkins Gilman*, p. 121.

47. "Stings," *Ariel*, p. 62.

Stanley E. Fish
1938–

Stanley Eugene Fish was born on April 19, 1938, in Providence, Rhode Island, and grew up in Philadelphia. He received a B.A. in 1959 from the University of Pennsylvania and did graduate work at Yale (Ph.D., 1962). Fish has taught at the University of California–Berkeley and at Johns Hopkins University, and is chairman of the English department at Duke University, where he is also a professor in the law school.

Fish has been deeply influenced by philosophers and historians outside the field of English, including Michel Foucault, John Searle, and Thomas Kuhn. His first book, *John Skelton's Poetry* (1965), reflects to some extent the New Criticism then in vogue at Yale, as well as the influence of Fish's mentor, E. Talbot Donaldson. Two years later Fish attracted wide attention in academia with the publication of *Surprised by Sin: The Reader in* Paradise Lost, in which he demonstrates how Milton manipulates language to involve the reader in a direct experience of the "sin" of Satanic rhetoric. *Self-Consuming Artifacts: The Experience of Seventeenth-Century Literature* (1972) is a further exploration of what one commentator has called the "balance of power between text as catalyst and reader as agent." *The Living Temple: George Herbert and Catechizing* (1978) was followed two years later by *Is There a Text in This Class?: The Authority of Interpretive Communities*. More recent publications by Fish include the essays "Consequences" (in *Against Theory: Literary Studies and the New Pragmatism*, edited by W. J. T. Mitchell, 1985); "Working on the Chain Gang: Interpretation in the Law and Literary Criticism" (*Critical Inquiry,* September 1982); "Profession Despise Thyself: Fear and Self-Loathing in Literary Studies" (*Critical Inquiry*, December 1983); "Anti-Professionalism" (*New Literary History*, Autumn 1985); and, most recently, *Doing What Comes Naturally: Change, Rhetoric and the Practice of Theory in Literary and Legal Studies* (1989).

In "Interpreting the *Variorum*" (*Critical Inquiry,* Spring 1976), Fish rejects all formalist arguments which hold that the aim of interpretation is to arrive at a correct and objectively verifiable conclusion as to the meaning of a given work. The critic's task, Fish argues, is not so much to arrive at a correct conclusion as it is to describe as skillfully and subtly as possible the processes of thought—"the making and revising of assumptions, the rendering and regretting of judgments, the coming to and abandoning of conclusions"— generated by a rigorous engagement with a text. "It is," he argues, "the structure of the reader's experience, rather than any structures available on the page that should be the object of description." Such an approach does not abandon criticism to an anarchy of subjective responses, Fish argues, because in order to make himself understood each new reader will adopt to a certain extent the interpretative strategies by which existing "communities of interpretation" approach their material. Even if a radically new strategy is invented and employed, its use will solicit the attention of established communities and engage them in dialogue the result of which will be the initiation of one side or the other into a newly conceived community.

Interpreting the *Variorum*

I

The first two volumes of the Milton *Variorum Commentary* have now appeared, and I find them endlessly fascinating. My interest, however, is not in the questions they manage to resolve (although these are many) but in the theoretical assumptions which are responsible for their occasional failures. These failures constitute a pattern, one in which a host of commentators—separated by as much as two hundred and seventy years but contemporaries in their shared concerns—are lined up on either side of an interpretive crux. Some of these are famous, even infamous: what is the two-handed engine in "Lycidas"? what is the meaning of Haemony in *Comus*? Others, like the identity of whoever or whatever comes to the window in "L'Allegro," line 46, are only slightly less notorious. Still others are of interest largely to those who make editions: matters of pronoun referents, lexical ambiguities, punctuation. In each instance, however, the pattern is consistent: every position taken is supported by wholly convincing evidence—in the case of "L'Allegro" and the coming to the window there is a persuasive champion for every proper noun within a radius of ten lines—and the editorial procedure always ends either in the graceful throwing up of hands, or in the recording of a disagreement between the two editors themselves. In short, these are problems that apparently cannot be solved, at least not by the methods traditionally brought to bear on them. What I would like to argue is that they are not *meant* to be solved, but to be experienced (they signify), and that consequently any procedure that attempts to determine which of a number of readings is correct will necessarily fail. What this means is that the commentators and editors have been asking the wrong questions and that a new set of questions based on new assumptions must be formulated. I would like at least to make a beginning in that direction by examining some of the points in dispute in Milton's sonnets. I choose the sonnets because they are brief and because one can move easily from them to the theoretical issues with which this paper is finally concerned.

Milton's twentieth sonnet—"Lawrence of virtuous father virtuous son"—has been the subject of relatively little commentary. In it the poet invites a friend to join him in some distinctly Horatian pleasures—a neat repast intermixed with conversation, wine, and song; a respite from labor all the more enjoyable because outside the earth is frozen and the day sullen. The only controversy the sonnet has inspired concerns its final two lines:

> Lawrence of virtuous father virtuous son,
>   Now that the fields are dank, and ways are mire,
>   Where shall we sometimes meet, and by the fire
>   Help waste a sullen day; what may be won

> From the hard season gaining; time will run
>   On smoother, till Favonius reinspire
>   The frozen earth; and clothe in fresh attire
> The lily and rose, that neither sowed nor spun.
> What neat repast shall feast us, light and choice,
>   Of Attic taste, with wine, whence we may rise
>   To hear the lute well touched, or artful voice
> Warble immortal notes and Tuscan air?
>   He who of those delights can judge, and spare
>   To interpose them oft, is not unwise.[1]

The focus of the controversy is the word "spare," for which two readings have been proposed: leave time for and refrain from. Obviously the point is crucial if one is to resolve the sense of the lines. In one reading "those delights" are being recommended—he who can leave time for them is not unwise; in the other, they are the subject of a warning—he who knows when to refrain from them is not unwise. The proponents of the two interpretations cite as evidence both English and Latin syntax, various sources and analogues, Milton's "known attitudes" as they are found in his other writings, and the unambiguously expressed sentiments of the following sonnet on the same question. Surveying these arguments, A. S. P. Woodhouse roundly declares: "It is plain that all the honours rest with" the meaning "refrain from" or "forbear to." This declaration is followed immediately by a bracketed paragraph initialed D. B. for Douglas Bush, who, writing presumably after Woodhouse has died, begins "In spite of the array of scholarly names the case for 'forbear to' may be thought much weaker, and the case for 'spare time for' much stronger, than Woodhouse found them."[2] Bush then proceeds to review much of the evidence marshaled by Woodhouse and to draw from it exactly the opposite conclusion. If it does nothing else, this curious performance anticipates a point I shall make in a few moments: evidence brought to bear in the course of formalist analyses—that is, analyses generated by the assumption that meaning is embedded in the artifact—will always point in as many directions as there are interpreters; that is, not only will it prove something, it will prove anything.

It would appear then that we are back at square one, with a controversy that cannot be settled because the evidence is inconclusive. But what if that controversy is *itself* regarded as evidence, not of an ambiguity that must be removed, but of an ambiguity that readers have always experienced? What, in other words, if for the question "what does 'spare' mean?" we substitute the question "what does the fact that the meaning of 'spare' has always been an issue mean"? The advantage of this question is that it can be answered. Indeed it has already been answered by the readers who are cited in the *Variorum Commentary*. What these readers debate is the judgment the poem makes on the delights of recreation; what their debate indicates is that the judgment is blurred by a verb that can be made to participate in contradictory readings. (Thus the important thing about the evidence surveyed in the *Variorum* is not how it is marshaled, but that it could be marshaled at all, because it then becomes evidence of the equal availability of both interpretations.) In other words, the lines first generate a pressure for judgment—"he who of those delights can judge"—and then decline to deliver it; the pressure, however, still exists, and it is transferred from the words on the page to the reader (the reader is "he who"), who comes away from the poem not with a statement, but with a responsibility, the responsibility of deciding when and how often—if at all—to indulge in "those delights" (they remain delights in either case). This transferring of responsibility from the text to its readers is what the lines ask us to do—it is the essence of their experience—and in my terms it is therefore what the lines *mean*. It is a meaning the *Variorum* critics attest to even as they resist it, for what they are laboring so mightily to do by fixing the sense of the lines is to give the responsibility back. The text, however, will not accept it and remains determinedly evasive, even in its last two words, "not unwise." In their position these words confirm the impossibility of extracting from the poem a moral formula, for the assertion (certainly too strong a word) they complete is of the form, "He who does such and such, of him it cannot be said that he is unwise"; but of course neither can it be said that he is wise. Thus what Bush correctly terms the "defensive" "not unwise" operates to prevent us from attaching the label "wise" to any action, including *either* of the actions—leaving time for or refraining from—represented by the ambiguity of "spare." Not only is the pressure of judgment taken off the poem, it is taken off the activity the poem at first pretended to judge. The issue is finally not the moral status of "those delights"—they become in seventeenth-century terms "things indifferent"—but on the good or bad uses to which they can be put by readers who are left, as Milton always leaves them, to choose and manage by themselves.

Let us step back for a moment and see how far we've come. We began with an apparently insoluble problem and proceeded, not to solve it, but to make it signify; first by regarding it as evidence of an experience and then by specifying for that experience a meaning. Moreover, the configurations of that experience, when they are made available by a reader-oriented analysis, serve as a check against the endlessly inconclusive adducing of evidence which characterizes formalist analysis. That is to say, any determination of what "spare" means (in a positivist or literal sense) is liable to be upset by the bringing forward of another analogue, or by a more complete computation of statistical frequencies, or by the discovery of new biographical information, or by anything else; but if we first determine that everything in the line before "spare" creates the expectation of an imminent judgment, then the ambiguity of "spare" can be assigned a significance in the context of that expectation. (It disappoints it and transfers the pressure of judgment to us.) That context is experiential, and it is within its contours and constraints that significances are established (both in the act of reading and in the analysis of that act). In formalist analyses the only constraints are the notoriously open-ended possibilities and combination of possibilities that emerge when one begins to consult dictionaries and grammars and histories; to consult dictionaries, grammars, and histories is to assume that meanings can be specified independently of the activity of reading; what the example of "spare" shows is that it is in and by that activity that meanings—experiential, not positivist—are created.

In other words, it is the structure of the reader's experience rather than any structures available on the page that should be the object of description. In the case of Sonnet XX, that experiential structure was uncovered when an examination of formal structures led to an impasse; and the pressure to remove that impasse led to the substitution of one set of questions for another. It will more often be the case that the pressure of a spectacular failure will be absent. The sins of formalist-positivist analysis are primarily sins of omission, not an inability to explain phenomena, but an inability to see that they are there because its assumptions make it inevitable that they will be overlooked or suppressed. Consider, for example, the concluding lines of another of Milton's sonnets, "Avenge O Lord thy slaughtered saints."

> Avenge O Lord thy slaughtered saints, whose bones
>   Lie scattered on the Alpine mountains cold,
>   Even them who kept thy truth so pure of old
>   When all our fathers worshipped stocks and stones,
> Forget not: in thy book record their groans
>   Who were thy sheep and in their ancient fold
>   Slain by the bloody Piedmontese that rolled
>   Mother with infant down the rocks. Their moans
> The vales redoubled to the hills, and they
>   To heaven. Their martyred blood and ashes sow
>   O'er all the Italian fields where still doth sway
> The triple Tyrant: that from these may grow
>   A hundredfold, who having learnt thy way
>   Early may fly the Babylonian woe.

In this sonnet, the poet simultaneously petitions God and wonders aloud about the justice of allowing the faithful—"Even them who kept thy truth"—to be so brutally slaughtered. The note struck is alternately one of plea and complaint, and there is more than a hint that God is being called to account for what has happened to the Waldensians. It is generally agreed, however, that the note of complaint is less and less sounded and that the poem ends with an affirmation of faith in the ultimate operation of God's justice. In this reading, the final lines are taken to be saying something like this: From the blood of these martyred, O God, raise up a new and more numerous people, who, by virtue of an early education in thy law, will escape destruction by fleeing the Babylonian woe. Babylonian woe has been variously glossed;[3] but whatever it is taken to mean it is always read as part of a statement that specifies a set of conditions for the escaping of destruction or punishment; it is a warning to the reader as well as a petition to God. As a warning, however, it is oddly situated since the conditions it seems to specify were in fact met by the Waldensians, who of all men most followed God's laws. In other words, the details of their story would seem to undercut the affirmative moral the speaker proposes to draw from it. It is further undercut by a reading that is fleetingly available, although no one has acknowledged it because it is a function, not of the words on the page, but of the experience of the reader. In that experience, line 13 will for a moment be accepted as a complete sense unit and the emphasis of the line will fall on "thy way" (a phrase that has received absolutely no attention in the commentaries). At this point "thy way" can refer only to the way in which God has dealt with the Waldensians. That is, "thy way" seems to pick up the note of outrage with which the poem began, and if we continue to so interpret it, the conclusion of the poem will be a grim one indeed: since by this example it appears that God rains down punishment indiscriminately, it would be best perhaps to withdraw from the arena of his service, and thereby hope at least to be safely out of the line of fire. This is not the conclusion we carry away, because as line 14 unfolds, another reading of "thy way" becomes available, a reading in which "early" qualifies "learnt" and refers to something the faithful should do (learn thy way at an early age) rather than to something God has failed to do (save the Waldensians). These two readings are answerable to the pulls exerted by the beginning and ending of the poem: the outrage expressed in the opening lines generates a pressure for an explanation, and the grimmer reading is answerable to that pressure (even if it is also disturbing); the ending of the poem, the forward and upward movement of lines 10–14, creates the expectation of an affirmation, and the second reading fulfills that expectation. The criticism shows that in the end we settle on the more optimistic reading— it feels better—but even so the other has been a part of our experience, and because it has been a part of our experience, it *means*. What it means is that while we may be able to extract from the poem a statement affirming God's justice, we are not allowed to forget the evidence (of things seen) that makes the extraction so difficult (both for the speaker and for us). It is a difficulty we experience in the act of reading, even though a criticism which takes no account of that act has, as we have seen, suppressed it.

II

In each of the sonnets we have considered, the significant word or phrase occurs at a line break where a reader is invited to place it first in one and then in another structure of syntax and sense. This moment of hesitation, of semantic or syntactic slide, is crucial to the experience the verse provides, but, in a formalist analysis, that moment will disappear, either because it has been flattened out and made into an (insoluble) interpretive crux, or because it has been eliminated in the course of a procedure that is incapable of finding value in temporal phenomena. In the case of "When I consider how my light is spent," these two failures are combined.

> When I consider how my light is spent,
>   Ere half my days, in this dark world and wide,
>   And that one talent which is death to hide,
>   Lodged with me useless, though my soul more bent

> To serve therewith my maker, and present
>   My true account, lest he returning chide,
>   Doth God exact day-labour, light denied,
>   I fondly ask; but Patience to prevent
> That murmur, soon replies, God doth not need
>   Either man's work or his own gifts, who best
>   Bear his mild yoke, they serve him best, his state
> Is kingly. Thousands at his bidding speed
>   And post o'er land and ocean without rest:
>   They also serve who only stand and wait.

The interpretive crux once again concerns the final line: "They also serve who only stand and wait." For some this is an unqualified acceptance of God's will, while for others the note of affirmation is muted or even forced. The usual kinds of evidence are marshaled by the opposing parties, and the usual inconclusiveness is the result. There are some areas of agreement. "All the interpretations," Woodhouse remarks, "recognize that the sonnet commences from a mood of depression, frustration [and] impatience."[4] The object of impatience is a God who would first demand service and then take away the means of serving, and the oft-noted allusion to the parable of the talents lends scriptural support to the accusation the poet is implicitly making: you have cast the wrong servant into unprofitable darkness. It has also been observed that the syntax and rhythm of these early lines, and especially of lines 6–8, are rough and uncertain; the speaker is struggling with his agitated thoughts and he changes directions abruptly, with no regard for the line as a unit of sense. The poem, says one critic, "seems almost out of control."[5]

The question I would ask is "whose control?"; for what these formal descriptions point to (but do not acknowledge) is the extraordinary number of adjustments required of readers who would negotiate these lines. The first adjustment is the result of the expectations created by the second half of line 6—"lest he returning chide." Since there is no full stop after "chide," it is natural to assume that this will be an introduction to reported speech, and to assume further that what will be reported is the poet's anticipation of the voice of God as it calls him, to an unfair accounting. This assumption does not survive line 7—"Doth God exact day-labour, light denied"—which rather than chiding the poet for his inactivity seems to rebuke him for having expected that chiding. The accents are precisely those heard so often in the Old Testament when God answers a reluctant Gideon, or a disputatious Moses, or a self-justifying Job: do you presume to judge my ways or to appoint my motives? Do you think I would exact day-labor, light denied? In other words, the poem seems to turn at this point from a questioning of God to a questioning of that questioning; or, rather, the reader turns from the one to the other in the act of revising his projection of what line 7 will say and do. As it turns out, however, that revision must itself be revised because it had been made within the assumption that what we are hearing is the voice of God. This assumption falls before the very next phrase "I fondly ask," which requires not one, but two adjustments. Since the speaker of line 7 is firmly identified as the poet, the line must be reinterpreted as a continuation of his complaint—Is that the way you operate, God, denying light, but exacting labor?—but even as that interpretation emerges, the poet withdraws from it by inserting the adverb "fondly," and once again the line slips out of the reader's control.

In a matter of seconds, then, line 7 has led four experiential lives, one as we anticipate it, another as that anticipation is revised, a third when we retroactively identify its speaker, and a fourth when that speaker disclaims it. What changes in each of these lives is the status of the poet's murmurings—they are alternately expressed, rejected reinstated, and qualified—and as the sequence ends, the reader is without a firm perspective on the question of record: does God deal justly with his servants?

A firm perspective appears to be provided by Patience, whose entrance into the poem, the critics tell us, gives it both argumentative and metrical stability. But in fact the presence of Patience in the poem finally assures its continuing instability by making it impossible to specify the degree to which the speaker approves, or even participates in, the affirmation of the final line: "They also serve who only stand and wait." We know that Patience to prevent the poet's murmur soon replies (not soon enough however to prevent the murmur from registering), but we do not know when that reply ends. Does Patience fall silent in line 12, after "kingly"? or at the conclusion of line 13? or not at all? Does the poet appropriate these lines or share them or simply listen to them, as we do? These questions are unanswerable, and it is because they remain unanswerable that the poem ends uncertainly. The uncertainty is not in the statement it makes—in isolation line 14 is unequivocal—but in our inability to assign that statement to either the poet or to Patience. Were the final line marked unambiguously for the poet, then we would receive it as a resolution of his earlier doubts; and were it marked for Patience, it would be a sign that those doubts were still very much in force. It is marked for neither, and therefore we are without the satisfaction that a firmly conclusive ending (in *any* direction) would have provided. In short, we leave the poem unsure, and our unsureness is the realization (in our experience) of the unsureness with which the affirmation of the final line is, or is not, made. (This unsureness also operates to actualize the two possible readings of "wait": wait in the sense of expecting, that is waiting for an opportunity to serve actively; or wait in the sense of waiting *in* service, a waiting that is itself fully satisfying because the impulse to self-glorifying action has been stilled.)

The question debated in the *Variorum Commentary* is, how far from the mood of frustration and impatience does the poem finally move? The answer given by an experiential analysis is that you can't tell, and the fact that you can't tell is responsible for the uneasiness the poem has always inspired. It is that uneasiness which the critics inadvertently acknowledge when they argue about the force of the last line, but they are unable to make analytical use of what they acknowledge because they have no way of dealing with or even recognizing experiential (that is, temporal) structures. In fact, more than one editor has eliminated those structures by punctuating them out of existence:

first by putting a full stop at the end of line 6 and thereby making it unlikely that the reader will assign line 7 to God (there will no longer be an expectation of reported speech), and then by supplying quotation marks for the sestet in order to remove any doubts one might have as to who is speaking. There is of course no warrant for these emendations, and in 1791 Thomas Warton had the grace and honesty to admit as much. "I have," he said, "introduced the turned commas both in the question and answer, not from any authority, but because they seem absolutely necessary to the sense."[6]

III

Editorial practices like these are only the most obvious manifestations of the assumptions to which I stand opposed: the assumption that there *is* a sense, that it is embedded or encoded in the text, and that it can be taken in at a single glance. These assumptions are, in order, positivist, holistic, and spatial, and to have them is to be committed both to a goal and to a procedure. The goal is to settle on a meaning, and the procedure involves first stepping back from the text, and then putting together or otherwise calculating the discrete units of significance it contains. My quarrel with this procedure (and with the assumptions that generate it) is that in the course of following it through, the reader's activities are at once ignored and devalued. They are ignored because the text is taken to be self-sufficient—everything is *in* it—and they are devalued because when they are thought of at all, they are thought of as the disposable machinery of extraction. In the procedures I would urge, the reader's activities are at the center of attention, where they are regarded, not as leading to meaning, but as *having* meaning. The meaning they have is a consequence of their not being empty; for they include the making and revising of assumptions, the rendering and regretting of judgments, the coming to and abandoning of conclusions, the giving and withdrawing of approval, the specifying of causes, the asking of questions, the supplying of answers, the solving of puzzles. In a word, these activities are interpretive—rather than being preliminary to questions of value they are at every moment settling and resettling questions of value—and because they are interpretive, a description of them will also be, and without any additional step, an interpretation, not after the fact, but the fact (of experiencing). It will be a description of a moving field of concerns, at once wholly present (not waiting for meaning, but constituting meaning) and continually in the act of reconstituting itself.

As a project such a description presents enormous difficulties, and there is hardly time to consider them here,[7] but it should be obvious from my brief examples how different it is from the positivist-formalist project. Everything depends on the temporal dimension, and as a consequence the notion of a mistake, at least as something to be avoided, disappears. In a sequence where a reader first structures the field he inhabits and then is asked to restructure it (by changing an assignment of speaker or realigning attitudes and positions) there is no question of priority among his structurings; no one of them, even if it is the last, has privilege; each is equally legitimate, each equally the proper object of analysis, because each is equally an event in his experience.

The firm assertiveness of this paragraph only calls attention to the questions it avoids. Who is this reader? How can I presume to describe his experiences, and what do I say to readers who report that they do not have the experiences I describe? Let me answer these questions or rather make a beginning at answering them in the context of another example, this time from Milton's *Comus*. In line 46 of *Comus* we are introduced to the villain by way of a genealogy:

> Bacchus that first from out the purple grape,
> Crushed the sweet poison of misused wine.

In almost any edition of this poem, a footnote will tell you that Bacchus is the god of wine. Of course most readers already know that, and because they know it, they will be anticipating the appearance of "wine" long before they come upon it in the final position. Moreover, they will also be anticipating a negative judgment on it, in part because of the association of Bacchus with revelry and excess, and especially because the phrase "sweet poison" suggests that the judgment has already been made. At an early point then, we will have both filled in the form of the assertion and made a decision about its moral content. That decision is upset by the word "misused"; for what "misused" asks us to do is transfer the pressure of judgment from wine (where we have already placed it) to the abusers of wine, and therefore when "wine" finally appears, we must declare it innocent of the charges we have ourselves made.

This, then, is the structure of the reader's experience—the transferring of a moral label from a thing to those who appropriate it. It is an experience that depends on a reader for whom the name Bacchus has precise and immediate associations; another reader, a reader for whom those associations are less precise will not have that experience because he will not have rushed to a conclusion in relation to which the word "misused" will stand as a challenge. Obviously I am discriminating between these two readers and between the two equally real experiences they will have. It is not a discrimination based simply on information, because what is important is not the information itself, but the action of the mind which its possession makes possible for one reader and impossible for the other. One might discriminate further between them by noting that the point at issue—whether value is a function of objects and actions or of intentions—is at the heart of the seventeenth-century debate over "things indifferent." A reader who is aware of that debate will not only *have* the experience I describe; he will recognize at the end of it that he has been asked to take a position on one side of a continuing controversy; and that recognition (also a part of his experience) will be part of the disposition with which he moves into the lines that follow.

It would be possible to continue with this profile of the optimal reader, but I would not get very far before someone would point out that what I am really describing is the intended reader, the reader whose education, opinions, concerns, linguistic competences, etc. make him capable of having the experience the author wished to provide. I would not resist this characterization because it seems obvious that the efforts of readers are always efforts to discern and therefore to realize (in the sense of becoming) an author's intention. I would only object if that realization were conceived narrowly, as the single act of comprehending an author's purpose, rather than (as I would conceive it) as the succession of acts readers perform in the continuing assumption that they are dealing with intentional beings. In this view discerning an intention is no more or less than understanding, and understanding includes (is constituted by) all the activities which make up what I call the structure of the reader's experience. To describe that experience is therefore to describe the reader's efforts at understanding, and to describe the reader's efforts at understanding is to describe his realization (in two senses) of an author's intention. Or to put it another way, what my analyses amount to are descriptions of a succession of decisions made by readers about an author's intention; decisions that are not limited to the specifying of purpose but include the specifying of every aspect of successively intended worlds; decisions that are precisely the shape, because they are the content, of the reader's activities.

Having said this, however, it would appear that I am open to two objections. The first is that the procedure is a circular one. I describe the experience of a reader who in his strategies is answerable to an author's intention, and I specify the author's intention by pointing to the strategies employed by that same reader. But this objection would have force only if it were possible to specify one independently of the other. What is being specified from either perspective are the conditions of utterance, of what could have been understood to have been meant by what was said. That is, intention and understanding are two ends of a conventional act, each of which necessarily stipulates (includes, defines, specifies) the other. To construct the profile of the informed or at-home reader is at the same time to characterize the author's intention and vice versa, because to do either is to specify the *contemporary* conditions of utterance, to identify, by becoming a member of, a community made up of those who share interpretive strategies.

The second objection is another version of the first: if the content of the reader's experience is the succession of acts he performs in search of an author's intentions, and if he performs those acts at the bidding of the text, does not the text then produce or contain everything—intention *and* experience—and have I not compromised my antiformalist position? This objection will have force only if the formal patterns of the text are assumed to exist independently of the reader's experience, for only then can priority be claimed for them. Indeed, the claims of independence and priority are one and the same; when they are separated it is so that they can give circular and illegitimate support to each other. The question "do formal features exist independently?" is usually answered by pointing to their priority: they are "in" the text before the reader comes to it. The question "are formal features prior?" is usually answered by pointing to their independent status: they are "in" the text before the reader comes to it. What looks like a step in an argument is actually the spectacle of an assertion supporting itself. It follows then that an attack on the independence of formal features will also be an attack on their priority (and vice versa), and I would like to mount such an attack in the context of two short passages from "Lycidas."

The first passage (actually the second in the poem's sequence) begins at line 42:

> The willows and the hazel copses green
> Shall now no more be seen,
> Fanning their joyous leaves to thy soft lays.
> [Ll. 42–44]

It is my thesis that the reader is always making sense (I intend "making" to have its literal force), and in the case of these lines the sense he makes will involve the assumption (and therefore the creation) of a completed assertion after the word "seen," to wit, the death of Lycidas has so affected the willows and the hazel copses green that, in sympathy, they will wither and die (will no more be seen by *anyone*). In other words at the end of line 43 the reader will have hazarded an interpretation, or performed an act of perceptual closure, or made a decision as to what is being asserted. I do not mean that he has done four things, but that he has done one thing the description of which might take any one of four forms—making sense, interpreting, performing perceptual closure, deciding about what is intended. (The importance of this point will become clear later.) Whatever he has done (that is, however we characterize it) he will undo it in the act of reading the next line; for here he discovers that his closure, or making of sense, was premature and that he must make a new one in which the relationship between man and nature is exactly the reverse of what was first assumed. The willows and the hazel copses green will in fact be seen, but they will not be seen by Lycidas. It is he who will be no more, while they go on as before, fanning their joyous leaves to someone else's soft lays (the whole of line 44 is now perceived as modifying and removing the absoluteness of "seen"). Nature is not sympathetic, but indifferent, and the notion of her sympathy is one of those "false surmises" that the poem is continually encouraging and then disallowing.

The previous sentence shows how easy it is to surrender to the bias of our critical language and begin to talk as if poems, not readers or interpreters, did things. Words like "encourage" and "disallow" (and others I have used in this paper) imply agents, and it is only "natural" to assign agency first to an author's intentions and then to the forms that assumedly embody them. What really happens, I think, is something quite different: rather than intention and its formal realization producing interpretation (the "normal" picture), interpretation creates intention and its formal realization by creating the conditions in which it becomes possible to pick them out. In other words, in the analysis of these lines from "Lycidas" I did what critics always do: I "saw" what my interpretive principles permitted or directed me to see, and then I turned around and attributed what I had "seen" to a text and an intention. What my principles direct me to "see" are readers performing acts; the points at which I find (or to be more precise, declare) those acts to have been performed become (by a sleight of hand) demarcations *in* the text; those demarcations are then available for the designation "formal features," and as formal features they can be (illegitimately) assigned the responsibility for producing the interpretation which in fact produced them. In this case, the demarcation my interpretation calls into being is placed at the end of line 42; but of course the end of that (or any other) line is worth noticing or pointing out only because my model *demands* (the word is not too strong) perceptual closures and therefore locations at which they occur; in that model this point will be one of those locations, although (1) it needn't have been (not every line ending occasions a closure) and (2) in another model, one that does not give value to the activities of readers, the possibility of its being one would not have arisen.

What I am suggesting is that formal units are always a function of the interpretative model one brings to bear; they are not "in" the text, and I would make the same argument for intentions. That is, intention is no more embodied "in" the text than are formal units; rather an intention, like a formal unit, is made when perceptual or interpretive closure is hazarded; it is verified by an interpretive act, and I would add, it is not verifiable in any other way. This last assertion is too large to be fully considered here, but I can sketch out the argumentative sequence I would follow were I to consider it: intention is known when and only when it is recognized; it is recognized as soon as you decide about it; you decide about it as soon as you make a sense; and you make a sense (or so my model claims) as soon as you can.

Let me tie up the threads of my argument with a final example from "Lycidas":

> He must not float upon his wat'ry bier
> Unwept . . .
>
> [Ll. 13–14]

Here the reader's experience has much the same career as it does in lines 42–44: at the end of line 13 perceptual closure is hazarded, and a sense is made in which the line is taken to be a resolution bordering on a promise: that is, there is now an expectation that something will be done about this unfortunate situation, and the reader anticipates a call to action, perhaps even a program for the undertaking of a rescue mission. With "Unwept," however, that expectation and anticipation are disappointed, and the realization of that disappointment will be inseparable from the making of a new (and less comforting) sense: nothing will be done; Lycidas will continue to float upon his wat'ry bier, and the only action taken will be the lamenting of the fact that no action will be efficacious, including the actions of speaking and listening to this lament (which in line 15 will receive the meretricious and self-mocking designation "melodious tear"). Three "structures" come into view at precisely the same moment, the moment when the reader having resolved a sense unresolves it and makes a new one; that moment will also be the moment of picking out a formal pattern or unit, end of line/beginning of line, and it will also be the moment at which the reader having decided about the speaker's intention, about what is meant by what has been said, will make the decision again and in so doing will make another intention.

This, then, is my thesis: that the form of the reader's experience, formal units, and the structure of intention are one, that they come into view simultaneously, and that therefore the questions of priority and independence do not arise. What does arise is another question: what produces *them*? That is, if intention, form, and the shape of the reader's experience are simply different ways of referring to (different perspectives on) the same interpretive act, what is that act an interpretation *of*? I cannot answer that question, but neither, I would claim, can anyone else, although formalists try to answer it by pointing to patterns and claiming that they are available independently of (prior to) interpretation. These patterns vary according to the procedures that yield them: they may be statistical (number of two-syllable words per hundred words), grammatical (ratio of passive to active constructions, or of right-branching to left-branching sentences, or of anything else); but whatever they are I would argue that they do not lie innocently in the world but are themselves constituted by an interpretive act, even if, as is often the case, that act is unacknowledged. Of course, this is as true of my analyses as it is of anyone else's. In the examples offered here I appropriate the notion "line ending" and treat it as a fact of nature; and one might conclude that as a fact it is responsible for the reading experience I describe. The truth I think is exactly the reverse: line endings exist by virtue of perceptual strategies rather than the other way around. Historically, the strategy that we know as "reading (or hearing) poetry" has included paying attention to the line as a unit, but it is precisely that attention which has made the line as a unit (either of print or of aural duration) available. A reader so practiced in paying that attention that he regards the line as a brute fact rather than as a convention will have a great deal of difficulty with concrete poetry; if he overcomes that difficulty, it will not be because he has learned to ignore the line as a unit but because he will have acquired a new set of interpretive strategies (the strategies constitutive of "concrete poetry reading") in the context of which the line as a unit no longer exists. In short, what is noticed is what has been *made* noticeable, not by a clear and undistorting glass, but by an interpretive strategy.

This may be hard to see when the strategy has become so habitual that the forms it yields seem part of the world. We find it easy to assume that alliteration as an effect depends on a "fact" that exists independently of any interpretive "use" one might make of it, the fact that words in proximity begin with the same letter. But it takes only a moment's reflection to realize that the sameness, far from being natural, is enforced by an orthographic convention; that is to say, it is the product of an interpretation. Were we to substitute phonetic conventions for orthographic ones (a "reform" traditionally urged by purists), the supposedly "objective" basis for alliteration would disappear because a phonetic transcription would require that we distinguish between the initial sounds of those very words that enter into alliterative relationships; rather than conforming to those relationships the rules of spelling make them. One might reply that, since alliteration is an aural rather than a visual phenomenon when poetry is heard, we have unmediated access to the physical sounds themselves and hear "real" similarities. But phonological "facts" are no more uninterpreted (or less conventional) than the "facts" of orthography; the distinctive features that make articulation and reception possible are the product of a system of differences that must be *imposed* before it can be recognized; the patterns the ear hears (like the patterns the eye sees) are the patterns its perceptual habits make available.

One can extend this analysis forever, even to the "facts" of grammar. The history of linguistics is the history of competing paradigms each of which offers a different account of the constituents of language. Verbs, nouns, cleft sentences, transformations, deep and surface structures, semes, rhemes, tagmemes—now you seem them, now you don't, depending on the descriptive apparatus you employ. The critic who confidently rests his analyses on the bedrock of syntactic descriptions is resting on an interpretation; the facts he points to *are* there, but only as a consequence of the interpretive (man-made) model that has called them into being.

The moral is clear: the choice is never between objectivity and interpretation but between an interpretation that is unacknowledged as such and an interpretation that is at least aware of itself. It is this awareness that I am claiming for myself, although in doing so I must give up the claims implicitly made in the first part of this paper. There I argue that a bad (because spatial) model had suppressed what was really happening, but by my own declared principles the notion "really happening" is just one more interpretation.

IV

It seems then that the price one pays for denying the priority of either forms or intentions is an inability to say how it is that one ever begins. Yet we do begin, and we continue, and because we do there arises an immediate counter-objection to the preceding pages. If interpretive acts are the source of forms rather than the other way around, why isn't it the case that readers are always performing the same acts or a random succession of forms? How, in short, does one explain these two "facts" of reading?: (1) the same reader will perform differently when reading two "different" (the word is in quotation marks because its status is precisely what is at issue) texts; and (2) different readers will perform similarly when reading the "same" (in quotes for the same reason) text. That is to say, both the stability of interpretation among readers and the variety of interpretation in the career of a single reader would seem to argue for the existence of something independent of and prior to interpretive acts, something which produces them. I will answer this challenge by asserting that both the stability and the variety are functions of interpretive strategies rather than of texts.

Let us suppose that I am reading "Lycidas." What is it that I am doing? First of all, what I am not doing is "simply reading," an activity in which I do not believe because it implies the possibility of pure (that is, disinterested) perception. Rather, I am proceeding on the basis of (at least) two interpretive decisions: (1) that "Lycidas" is a pastoral and (2) that it was written by Milton. (I should add that the notions "pastoral" and "Milton" are also interpretations; that is they do not stand for a set of indisputable, objective facts; if they did, a great many books would not now be getting written.) Once these decisions have been made (and if I had not made these I would have made others, and they would be consequential in the same way), I am immediately predisposed to perform certain acts, to "find," by looking for, themes (the relationship between natural processes and the careers of men, the efficacy of poetry or of any other action), to confer significances (on flowers, streams, shepherds, pagan deities), to mark out "formal" units (the lament, the consolation, the turn, the affirmation of faith, etc.). My disposition to perform these acts (and others; the list is not meant to be exhaustive) constitutes a set of interpretive strategies, which, when they are put into execution, become the large act of reading. That is to say, interpretive strategies are not put into execution after reading (the pure act of perception in which I do not believe); they are the shape of reading, and because they are the shape of reading, they give texts their shape, making them rather than, as it is usually assumed, arising from them. Several important things follow from this account:

1. I did not have to execute this particular set of interpretive strategies because I did not have to make those particular interpretive (pre-reading) decisions. I could have decided, for example that "Lycidas" was a text in which a set of fantasies and defenses find expression. These decisions would have entailed the assumption of another set of interpretive strategies (perhaps like that put forward by Norman Holland in *The Dynamics of Literary Response*) and the execution of that set would have made another text.

2. I could execute this same set of strategies when presented with texts that did not bear the title (again a notion which is itself an interpretation) "Lycidas, A Pastoral Monody." . . . I could decide (it is a decision some have made) that *Adam Bede* is a pastoral written by an author who consciously modeled herself on Milton (still remembering that "pastoral" and "Milton" are interpretations, not facts in the public domain); or I could decide, as Empson did, that a great many things not usually considered pastoral were in fact to be so read; and either decision would give rise to a set of interpretive strategies, which, when put into action, would *write* the text I write when reading "Lycidas." (Are you with me?)

3. A reader other than myself who, when presented with "Lycidas," proceeds to put into execution a set of interpretive strategies similar to mine (how he could do so is a question I will take up later), will perform the same (or at least a similar) succession of interpretive acts. He and I then might be tempted to say that we agree about the poem (thereby assuming that the poem exists independently of the acts either of us performs); but what we really would agree about is the way to write it.

4. A reader other than myself who, when presented with "Lycidas" (please keep in mind that the status of "Lycidas" is what is at issue), puts into execution a different set of interpretive strategies will perform a different succession of interpretive acts. (I am assuming, it is the article of my faith, that a

reader will always execute some set of interpretive strategies and therefore perform some succession of interpretive acts.) One of us might then be tempted to complain to the other that we could not possibly be reading the same poem (literary criticism is full of such complaints) and he would be right; for each of us would be reading the poem he had made.

The large conclusion that follows from these four smaller ones is that the notions of the "same" or "different" texts are fictions. If I read "Lycidas" and *The Waste Land* differently (in fact I do not), it will not be because the formal structures of the two poems (to term them such is also an interpretive decision) call forth different interpretive strategies but because my predisposition to execute different interpretive strategies will *produce* different formal structures. That is, the two poems are different because I have decided that they will be. The proof of this is the possibility of doing the reverse (that is why point 2 is so important). That is to say, the answer to the question "why do different texts give rise to different sequences of interpretive acts?" is that *they don't have to*, an answer which implies strongly that "they" don't exist. Indeed it has always been possible to put into action interpretive strategies designed to make all texts one, or to put it more accurately, to be forever making the same text. Augustine urges just such a strategy, for example, in *On Christian Doctrine* where he delivers the "rule of faith" which is of course a rule of interpretation. It is dazzlingly simple: everything in the Scriptures, and indeed in the world when it is properly read, points to (bears the meaning of) God's love for us and our answering responsibility to love our fellow creatures for His sake. If only you should come upon something which does not at first seem to bear this meaning, that "does not literally pertain to virtuous behavior or to the truth of faith," you are then to take it "to be figurative" and proceed to scrutinize it "until an interpretation contributing to the reign of charity is produced." This then is both a stipulation of what meaning there is and a set of directions for finding it, which is of course a set of directions—of interpretive strategies—for making it, that is, for the endless reproduction of the same text. Whatever one may think of this interpretive program, its success and ease of execution are attested to by centuries of Christian exegesis. It is my contention that any interpretive program, any set of interpretive strategies, can have a similar success, although few have been as spectacularly successful as this one. (For some time now, for at least three hundred years, the most successful interpretive program has gone under the name "ordinary language.") In our own discipline programs with the same characteristic of always reproducing one text include psychoanalytic criticism, Robertsonianism (always threatening to extend its sway into later and later periods), numerology (a sameness based on the assumption of innumerable fixed differences).

The other challenging question—"why will different readers execute the same interpretive strategy when faced with the 'same' text?"—can be handled in the same way. The answer is again that *they don't have to*, and my evidence is the entire history of literary criticism. And again this answer implies that the notion "same text" is the product of the possession by two or more readers of similar interpretive strategies.

But why should this ever happen? Why should two or more readers ever agree, and why should regular, that is, habitual, differences in the career of a single reader ever occur? What is the explanation on the one hand of the stability of interpretation (at least among certain groups at certain times) and on the other of the orderly variety of interpretation if it is not the stability and variety of texts? The answer to all of these questions is to be found in a notion that has been implicit in my argument, the notion of *interpretive communities*. Interpretive communities are made up of those who share interpretive strategies not for reading (in the conventional sense) but for writing texts, for constituting their properties and assigning their intentions. In other words these strategies exist prior to the act of reading and therefore determine the shape of what is read rather than, as is usually assumed, the other way around. If it is an article of faith in a particular community that there are a variety of texts, its members will boast a repertoire of strategies for making them. And if a community believes in the existence of only one text, then the single strategy its members employ will be forever writing it. The first community will accuse the members of the second of being reductive, and they in turn will call their accusers superficial. The assumption in each community will be that the other is not correctly perceiving the "true text," but the truth will be that each perceives the text (or texts) its interpretive strategies demand and call into being. This, then, is the explanation both for the stability of interpretation among different readers (they belong to the same community) and for the regularity with which a single reader will employ different interpretive strategies and thus make different texts (he belongs to different communities). It also explains why there are disagreements and why they can be debated in a principled way: not because of a stability in texts, but because of a stability in the makeup of interpretive communities and therefore in the opposing positions they make possible. Of course this stability is always temporary (unlike the longed for and timeless stability of the text). Interpretive communities grow larger and decline, and individuals move from one to another; thus while the alignments are not permanent, they are always there, providing just enough stability for the interpretive battles to go on, and just enough shift and slippage to assure that they will never be settled. The notion of interpretive communities thus stands between an impossible ideal and the fear which leads so many to maintain it. The ideal is of perfect agreement and it would require texts to have a status independent of interpretation. The fear is of interpretive anarchy, but it would only be realized if interpretation (text making) were completely random. It is the fragile but real consolidation of interpretive communities that allows us to talk to one another, but with no hope or fear of ever being able to stop.

In other words interpretive communities are no more stable than texts because interpretive strategies are not natural or universal, but *learned*. This does not mean that there is a point at which an individual has not yet learned any. The ability to interpret is not acquired; it is constitutive of being human. What is acquired are the ways of interpreting and those same ways can also be forgotten or supplanted, or complicated or dropped from favor ("no one reads that way anymore"). When any of these things happens, there is a corresponding change in texts, not because they are being read differently, but because they are being written differently.

The only stability, then, inheres in the fact (at least in my model) that interpretive strategies are always being deployed, and this means that communication is a much more chancy affair than we are accustomed to think it. For if there are no fixed texts, but only interpretive strategies making them; and if interpretive strategies are not natural, but learned (and are therefore unavailable to a finite description), what is it that utterers (speakers, authors, critics, me, you) do? In the old model utterers are in the business of handing over ready made or prefabricated meanings. These meanings are said to be encoded, and the code is assumed to be in the world independently of the individuals who are obliged to attach themselves to it (if they do not they run the danger of being declared deviant). In my model, however, meanings are not extracted but made and made not by encoded forms but by interpretive strategies that call forms into being. It follows then that what utterers do is give hearers and readers the opportunity to make meanings (and texts) by inviting them to put into execution a set of strategies. It is presumed that the invitation will be recognized, and that presumption rests on a projection on the part of a speaker or author of the moves *he* would make if confronted by the sounds or marks he is uttering or setting down.

It would seem at first that this account of things simply reintroduces the old objection; for isn't this an admission that there is after all a formal encoding, not perhaps of meanings, but of the directions for making them, for executing interpretive strategies? The answer is that they will only *be* directions to those who already have the interpretive strategies in the first place. Rather than producing interpretive acts, they are the product of one. An author hazards his projection, not because of something "in" the marks, but because of something he assumes to be in his reader. The very existence of the "marks" is a function of an interpretive community, for they will be recognized (that is, made) only by its members. Those outside that community will be deploying a different set of interpretive strategies (interpretation cannot be withheld) and will therefore be making different marks.

So once again I have made the text disappear, but unfortunately the problems do not disappear with it. If everyone is continually executing interpretive strategies and in that act constituting texts, intentions, speakers, and authors, how can any one of us know whether or not he is a member of the same interpretive community as any other of us? The answer is that he can't, since any evidence brought forward to support the claim would itself be an interpretation (especially if the "other" were an author long dead). The only "proof" of membership is fellowship, the nod of recognition from someone in the same community, someone who says to you what neither of us could ever prove to a third party: "we know." I say it to you now, knowing full well that you will agree with me (that is, understand) only if you already agree with me.

NOTES

1. All references are to *The Poems of John Milton,* ed. John Carey and Alastair Fowler (London: Longmans, 1968).

2. A. S. P. Woodhouse and Douglas Bush, ed., *A Variorum Commentary on the Poems of John Milton,* Vol. 2, p. 2 (New York: Columbia University Press, 1972), p. 475.

3. It is first of all a reference to the city of iniquity from which the Hebrews are urged to flee in Isaiah and Jeremiah. In Protestant polemics Babylon is identified with the Roman Church whose destruction is prophesied in the book of Revelation. And in some Puritan tracts, Babylon is the name for Augustine's earthly city, from which the faithful are to flee inwardly in order to escape the fate awaiting the unregenerate. See Woodhouse and Bush, *Variorum Commentary,* pp. 440–41.

4. Ibid., p. 469.

5. Ibid., p. 457.

6. *Poems upon Several Occasions, English, Italian, and Latin, with Translations, by John Milton,* ed. Thomas Warton (London, 1791), p. 352.

7. See my *Surprised by Sin: The Reader in* Paradise Lost (London and New York: St. Martin's Press, 1967); *Self-Consuming Artifacts: The Experience of Seventeenth-Century Literature* (Berkeley: University of California Press, 1972); "What Is Stylistics and Why Are They Saying Such Terrible Things about It?" in *Approaches to Poetics,* ed. Seymour Chatman (New York: Columbia University Press, 1973), pp. 109–52; "How Ordinary Is Ordinary Language?" in *New Literary History* 5, no. 1 (Autumn 1973): 41–54; "Facts and Fictions: A Reply to Ralph Rader," *Critical Inquiry* 1 (June 1975): 883–91.

Tzvetan Todorov
1939–

Tzvetan Todorov was born on March 1, 1939, in Sofia, Bulgaria. He was educated at the University of Sofia (M.A., 1961) and then at the University of Paris, where he was subsequently awarded two doctoral degrees. Since 1968 Todorov has been the director of research at the Centre National de la Recherche Sciéntifique in Paris and was awarded its bronze medal in 1974.

Regarded as a leading exponent of poststructuralism in France, Todorov has written and edited a number of books in French that have been translated into many languages. His first book to appear in English was *The Fantastic: A Structural Approach to a Literary Genre* (France, 1970; U.S., 1973). Taking as his subject a type of literature that is neither realistic nor "marvelous," Todorov argues that this subgenre is defined by the hesitation and uncertainty of the reader's response.

The Poetics of Prose (France, 1971; U.S., 1977) was Todorov's next book to be translated into English. Here Todorov explores the relationship between poetics and other forms of critical discourse, at the same time offering a useful introduction to structuralism. His brief *Introduction to Poetics* (France, 1973; U.S., 1981) was followed by *Symbolism and Interpretation* (France, 1978; U.S., 1982); *Theories of the Symbol* (France, 1977; U.S., 1982), a discussion of classical, nineteenth-century Romantic, and twentieth-century writers; and *The Conquest of America: The Question of the Other* (1984), an examination of Spain's encounter with New World natives in the sixteenth century. Todorov is the coauthor with Oxwald Ducrot of *The Encyclopedic Dictionary of the Sciences of Language* (France, 1973; U.S., 1979), and has served as an editor of the journal *Poétique*.

Todorov's latest book, *Literature and Its Theorists: A Personal View of Twentieth-Century Criticism* (France, 1984; U.S., 1987), reviews trends in contemporary literary criticism, and in conclusion proposes a "dialogic criticism" that is a departure both from current hermeneutic systems and from Todorov's own previous approach. Dialogic criticism seeks to establish an open dialogue between the critic and the work under discussion, and in so doing raises again issues of the morality and "truth" of literature that have been abolished or ignored by many contemporary theoreticians.

FROM

LITERATURE AND ITS THEORISTS

A Dialogic Criticism?

Everyone knows how hard it is to accept criticism directed at oneself. Either your critics are being aggressive (but that is because they don't know you and aren't trying to understand you; they are upset because you are different from what they would like you to be; they reject you so completely that you no longer feel personally implicated); or else they are (or have been) close to you (but now you are dealing with an emotional rift, and the pain of it outweighs all other considerations: what counts is that you don't love each other any more, not that you yourself may have this quality or that one). Or else the critics continue to love you and thus tell you nothing that you might interpret as a basic challenge: they have accepted you for what you are, whatever their private opinions. It is enough to make one wonder how one ever learns anything at all about oneself on the basis of what others say. But perhaps I am speaking only about myself? And yet, when I take the trouble to think back over my own intellectual itinerary, the memory of two encounters comes to mind, encounters that did bring about change in me, as I have come to realize long after the fact.

At first glance, these two meetings have only superficial features in common. Each took place in the aftermath of one of those occasions that make up an indispensable aspect of my profession: lectures given abroad. Such occasions are part tourism, part spectacle (one is visiting and letting oneself be visited at the same time); personal affinities may arise, and one may also hear acerbic criticism, but generally speaking, nothing that happens has very deep personal impact. The two lectures I am referring to took place in England, a country I rarely visit. And, regrettably, I remember the effect the words spoken had on me much better in each instance than I remember the words themselves.

The first of these encounters occurred in London a little more than ten years ago. I had given a talk on something or other at the French Institute, and during the reception that followed I was introduced to a man older than myself. He had bright blue eyes; the glass of whisky in his hand was drained, I believe, rather quickly. It was Arthur Koestler. I had read *Darkness at Noon* while I was still in Bulgaria; the book had made a strong impression on me. As is the custom, the conversation had nothing to do with my lecture, but rather with the fact that I myself came from an Eastern European country under Communist rule. At the time I professed an attitude toward politics that I had adopted during my adolescence in Bulgaria, one that is shared by many of my generation, I think: an attitude made up of fatalism and indifference. Given that things cannot be other than what they are, this attitude holds, the best approach is one of complete detachment. I was expressing my indifference, then, in conversation with Koestler, presenting it as a position of lucidity and wisdom. I cannot recapture the precise wording of his response, but I know his reaction was made up of politeness, firmness, astonishment, and total disagreement. And upon seeing him I suddenly felt that his very existence was proof that my own words were false. Here was a man who had not adopted a fatalist attitude. He did not challenge or reproach me in the course of the conversation, but he seemed to have a tranquil assurance that he was right because he was who he was.

The second incident took place at Oxford. This time I know that my talk had to do with Henry James and "structural analysis of narrative" (at the time, I knew what that meant). I had been invited by a college whose master was Isaiah Berlin. At that point I had not read anything by that enchanting philosopher and historian, but he was warm and eloquent, and I was seduced at once. He offered me his hospitality (as he must have done other lecturers), and I shall never forget the night we spent in his house, a veritable museum; this time I was the one with a glass of vodka in hand. He refilled it obligingly, all the while telling me anecdotes (they have since been published) drawn from his memories of Pasternak and Akhmatova. He had sat silently through my lecture, and at one point, later in the evening, said something like this: "Henry James, yes; narrative structures, yes, of course. But why don't you look into things like nineteenth-century nihilism and liberalism? All that's quite interesting, you know."

I am well aware that these reminiscences are particularly telling for me alone; the events in question, so insignificant in themselves, take on meaning only in connection with other personal experiences. At the time, moreover, I paid no attention to these two incidents. Only retrospectively, and of course because my memory retained these incidents among countless others, have I discovered that they were important to me; retrospectively, I have begun to look for common features and to muse about what distinguishes these incidents from all the rest. In the two responses addressed to me, I heard something like a reproach and a recommendation. And yet I did not set them aside, as I usually would have, assigning them to the categories of incompetence, ill will, or partisan fervor. No doubt that had something to do with the identity of my interlocutors, who were both well-known and respected individuals; but it also had something to do with their kindness and good will—or perhaps simply their (British) politeness, which I mistook for something else. I tell myself now, too, that both of those men knew what it was to be uprooted, had experienced cultural otherness, as I had, and that because of this they both were better able to live personal otherness, that state in which one acknowledges the other while keeping one's distance.

The fact remains that these two conversations, however trivial, had an unquestionable influence on me. If I were to attempt a rather crude translation of the way I have come to understand them, I would say that in each case I was brought to an awareness of the nonnecessary, or arbitrary, nature of my own position. What I heard Berlin say was that literature is not made up of structures alone but also of ideas and history; Koestler's message as I took it was that there were no "objective" reasons to choose to give up the exercise of freedom. These statements are self-evident, of course; yet they have to be received in a particular way in order to be fully assimilated.

These propositions, along with other factors of which I remain ignorant, led me to revise my ideas about the nature of literature and the role of the critic. As it happened, they fell in fact upon prepared ground. During those same years, curiosity had led me to read a number of ancient works bearing upon my major preoccupations at the time, symbolism and interpretation. I had read these works of rhetoric, hermeneutics, aesthetics, and philosophy of language without any historical project in mind; instead, I was looking for remarks that might have remained "valid," insights into metaphor, allegory, or suggestion. But during my reading I began to realize that it was harder than I had expected to keep the systematic project separate from the historical one. What I had until then viewed as neutral instruments, as purely descriptive concepts (my own), now appeared to me as the consequences of some specific historical choices, which might have been made differently; moreover, these choices had corollaries—"ideological" ones—that I was not always prepared to assume. I have already referred to these articulations in the introduction to this book.

Thus I became aware of two things as I read through those old books: first of all, that my frame of reference was not the truth at last revealed, the tool that makes it possible to measure the degree of error in all earlier views of literature and commentary, but rather it was the result of certain ideological choices; second, that I was not enthusiastic at the idea of being caught up in all the implications of this ideology, whose most familiar faces are individualism and relativism.

But was there any other possibility? To reject these premises would presumably mean an even less tenable return to the earlier form of criticism (though it was not always called "criticism"), which would have to be labeled *dogmatic* to distinguish it from the *immanence* claimed by the moderns: there literature, no longer opposed to other human verbal productions, was to "sign up in the service of the truth," as Augustine said about eloquence. Would commentary in turn have to accept being the servant of a dogma, knowing in advance what meaning had to be found in each text, or at the very least determining the value of that meaning in terms of some preestablished principle?

Having been trained in Bulgaria, I in fact knew that form of criticism very well, even though I had not practiced it except in high school essays. That situation was quite different from the one I found in France when I arrived there in 1963; "theory of literature" ranked among the disciplines that the philology student at Sofia had to master (I still recall how the face of the dean of the faculty of letters at the Sorbonne suddenly froze when I asked him in halting French, in 1963, who taught literary theory there). But the literary theory in question in Bulgaria—which permeated courses in literary history, needless to say—might be boiled down to two basic notions: "the spirit of the people" and "the spirit of the party" (*narodnost and partijnost*). Many writers had the former attribute, but only the best possessed the latter. What writers were supposed to say was known beforehand; all that remained to be determined was the extent to which they would succeed. I think this early training is what awakened, by way of contrast, my initial interest in the Formalists.

Those who hold the "immanentist" position, like those who hold the "dogmatist" one, it seems to me, have always sought to present the adversary's position as the only possible alternative to the one they occupy themselves. The dogmatic conservatives claim that any renunciation of their values is tantamount to giving up all values; the "immanentist" liberals claim that any search for value leads to obscurantism and repression. But do we have to believe them?

The answer to this question came to me, as might be expected, in a roundabout way. After I became a French citizen, I began to feel more acutely than ever the fact that I would never be a Frenchman like any other, because of my simultaneous participation in two cultures. A double belonging, an interiority and an exteriority: it can be experienced as lack or as privilege (I have consistently inclined toward the optimistic view), but in any event it sensitizes one to the problems of cultural alterity and the perception of the "other." I had just conceived of a vast project on that subject when, during another series of lectures, in Mexico this time, quite by chance, I discovered the writings about the conquest of America by the earliest conquistadors. That dazzling example of discovery—and ignorance—of the other preoccupied me deeply for three years. Now as I think back on those topics, I find that I encounter my literary problem once again, although projected on a much larger scale, since here what is in question is the opposition of the universal and the relative in the ethical order. Does obedience to the spirit of tolerance that dominates our mind (even though it may leave our behavior intact) require that we refrain from making any judgment about societies other than our own? And on the other hand, were we to maintain certain values as universal, could we avoid crushing the other in a preestablished mold (our own)? The alternative obviously brings to mind the conflict between "immanentists" and "dogmatists."

What has impelled me to declare that impasse an illusory one is, I think, my more or less fortunate experience as an exile. The choice between possessing the truth and giving up all claim on it does not exhaust all the possibilities that lie before us. Without turning one's back definitively upon universal values, one may posit them as a possible area of agreement with the other rather than as an a priori certainty. We may be aware that we do not possess the truth without giving up our search for it. The truth may be a common horizon, a set of directions for the journey, rather than a point of departure. Instead of abandoning the idea of truth, one may change its status or function, making it into a regulatory principle behind the exchange with the other, rather than the content of the program. In the last analysis, understanding between representatives of different cultures (or between the parts of my own being that stem from one culture or the other) is possible, if the desire for understanding is present: we can go beyond mere "points of view," and it is in human nature to be able to transcend one's own partiality and one's parochialism.

To return to criticism and literature, I must say that this conviction has led me to view them differently. Giving up the search for truth (still in the sense of wisdom and not of correspondence to the facts), the "immanent" critic rules out all possibility of passing judgment; he explains what a work means but does not take that meaning seriously, in a certain sense: he does not respond to it, he acts as if ideas concerning human destiny are not involved. This is because he has transformed the text into an object that it suffices to describe as faithfully as possible; the "immanent" critic contemplates Bossuet and Sade with the same benevolent eye.[1] The "dogmatic" critic, for his part, does not really allow the other to express himself: he swallows the other whole, since the critic himself embodies Providence, or the laws of history, or some other revealed truth; he allows the other to serve only as the illustration (or the counterillustration) of some unshakable doctrine that the reader is expected to share.

Now criticism is dialogue, and its own interest is best served by recognizing this openly; it is a meeting of two voices, author's and critic's, and neither has the advantage over the other. However, critics of various persuasions find common ground in their refusal to recognize this dialogue. Whether consciously or not, the dogmatic critic, followed in this by the "impressionistic" essayist and the partisan of subjectivism, allows a single voice to be heard: his own. On the other side, the ideal of "historical" criticism (a somewhat misleading label, as we saw in connection with Watt) was to allow the authentic voice of the writer to be heard, without anything added by the critic himself. The ideal of identificatory criticism, another variant of "immanent" criticism (as exemplified for instance by Georges Poulet), is to project oneself onto the other to the extent of becoming able to speak in the other's name; while the ideal of structural criticism is to describe the work while completely removing oneself from the picture. But ruling out in this way the possibility of dialogue with literary works and thus the possibility of passing judgment on their truth value is tantamount to amputating one of their essential dimensions, which is precisely that of stating the truth. I recall giving a talk in Brussels on Diderot's aesthetics (these occasions seem to have left their mark to a greater extent than I realized) during which, after presenting Diderot's ideas as best I could, I pronounced them "false" and spoke of his "failure." One member of the audience, a Diderot specialist, intervened: "I agree with your description, but I am surprised by your value judgments. Are you presuming to correct Diderot? Are you not guilty of anachronism?" I think that in his eyes I was lacking in respect for a classical author. But upon reflection (with the advantage of hindsight), I find that he was the one lacking in respect for Diderot, since he refused to discuss Diderot's ideas, and settled for reconstructing them, as if he were putting together a puzzle. Diderot wrote in order to discover the truth; was it an offense to him to recognize this, while continuing the search, with him and against him?

Dialogic criticism speaks not about literary works but to them, or rather with them; it refuses to eliminate either of the two voices involved. The text under study is not an object that must be taken in hand by a "metalanguage," but rather a discourse that is met by the critic's own; the author is a "thou" and not a "he," an interlocutor with whom one discusses human values. But the dialogue is asymmetrical, since the writer's text is closed, whereas the critic's text can go on indefinitely. In order not to load the dice, the critic must allow his interlocutor's voice to be heard with fidelity. The various forms of immanent criticism find their justification here (though along different lines); what better way to contribute to the clarification of the meaning of a passage than to integrate it into broader and broader contexts—first of all that of the work, next that of the writer, then the epoch, finally the entire literary tradition? As it happens, this is precisely what any given "specialist" does. The various integrations are not mutually exclusive, but are either sequentially embedded, or overlapping, or mutually complementary, as Spinoza well knew when he used them as the subdivisions of his new interpretive method. As a critic, I am indeed obliged to choose between one orientation and another (although there are exceptions): not because of any fundamental incompatibilities among them, but because life is short and there is too much else to do. As a reader, however, I have no reason to make an exclusive choice: why should I deprive myself of *either* the competence of a Northrop Frye, who shows me to what literary tradition the image I am looking at belongs (its diachronic context), *or* that of a Paul Bénichou, who reveals to me the ideological ambiance in which that same image was formulated (its synchronic context)?

At this level, then, what the "structuralist" lacks can be made up for by what the specialist in ideologies has to offer, and vice versa. But both of them (I am no longer speaking now of Bénichou or Frye) also lack something else, which is perhaps more important: what we need is not more facts, but more thought. We can deplore the critic's refusal to posit himself as a thinking subject (rather than hiding behind the accumulation of objective facts) and to pass judgments. Taking the opposite course from Spinoza's, or at least from the one indicated by his expressed intentions, we shall not stop, then, with this search for meaning, we shall pursue it through a discussion about truth; not only "what did he say?" but also "is he right?" (Which does not, we can hope, simply amount to saying "I am right.") Although we agree with Spinoza that we must not subject the search for meaning to a truth that would be held in advance, we have no reason to refrain from searching, at the same time, for truth, and from confronting the meaning of the text with it.

That is why I call this kind of criticism "dialogical." The type of truth to which I aspire can be approached only through dialogue: conversely, as we saw with Bakhtin, if dialogue is to be possible, truth has to be posited as a horizon and as a regulatory principle. Dogmatism leads to monologue on the critic's part; immanentism (and thus relativism) leads to monologue on the part of the author being studied; pure pluralism, which is only the arithmetical addition of several immanent analyses, leads to a copresence of voices which is also an absence of listening: several subjects are expressing themselves, but no one of them is taking his divergencies from the others into account. Anyone who accepts the principle of the shared search for truth is already practicing dialogic criticism.

Marc Bloch, one of the fathers of the "new history," used to say: "How much easier it is to condemn or praise Luther than to scrutinize his soul!" I have come to believe almost the opposite, except that I do not see why the two should be incompatible. If we have "scrutinized" well, we need not refrain from passing judgment, unless the object of study is so completely foreign to us that there is nothing left to say. If Luther continues to speak to us, we must continue to speak to him, and thus to agree or disagree with him. Let us not fool ourselves: our judgment will not derive from our knowledge. Our knowledge will help us to resurrect the voice of the other, whereas our own voice finds its source in ourselves, in the ethical responsibility we have taken on. I do not find this an easy task. I have written twice about Benjamin Constant, once in 1968 for *Critique* and again in 1983 for *Poétique*. The difference between the two studies and my preference for the second cannot be attributed simply to the fact that I did a lot of reading in the intervening fifteen years, or that in 1968 I found it easier to generalize; I find also that in my first text I do not have a distinct voice. I claim to be presenting Constant's thought, but naturally I want to say something myself as well, so I attribute my own ideas to Constant. The result is a hybrid voice, but a single one, in which our respective contributions are not clearly distinguished. In the more recent study, I made an effort both to remain more faithful to Constant and to contradict him. It is somewhat comparable to personal relationships: the illusion of fusion is sweet, but it is an illusion and it comes to a bitter end. The recognition of the other as other makes a better love possible.

It is possible to change our image of criticism in this way only if we transform our idea of literature at the same time. For two hundred years, the Romantics and their countless heirs have been ceaselessly reiterating that literature is a language that finds its end in itself. It is time to come (back) to the self-evident facts that we should never have forgotten: literature has to do with human existence, it is a discourse oriented toward—let us not be intimidated by the ponderous words—truth and morality. Literature is an unveiling of man and the world, Sartre said, and he was right. Literature would be nothing at all if it did not allow us to reach a better understanding of life.

If we have managed to lose sight of that essential dimension of literature, it is because we began by reducing truth to verification, and morality to moralism. The sentences of a novel do not aspire to be taken for factual truth, as do those of a history text; let us not belabor the obvious. The novel is not required—even assuming the task is within the realm of possibility—to describe the specific historical forms of a society; that is not where its truth lies. Nor of course is it a matter of saying that the author's ideas are necessarily correct. But literature is always an attempt to reveal to us "an unknown side of human existence," as Kundera says somewhere, and thus although it has no privileged access to truth, it never stops searching for it.

Literature and morality: "how disgusting!" my contemporary will exclaim. I myself, discovering around me a literature subordinated to politics, thought that it was essential to break every link and preserve literature from any contact with what is not literature. But the relation to values is inherent in literature: not only because it is impossible to speak of existence without referring to that relation, but also because the act of writing is an act of communication, which implies the possibility of understanding, in the name of common values. The writer's ideal may be interrogation, doubt, or denial; he incites his reader nonetheless to share this ideal and thus does not cease to be "moral." Propagandistic literature or the *roman à thèse* by no means exhausts the possible relationships between works and values; they may even be said to represent only an aberrant form of such a relationship: that of a dogmatic truth, held from the beginning, that one is merely seeking to illustrate. Yet a work of literature is not a sermon: the forms differ in that what is for the latter an a priori certainty can be for the former only a horizon.

Someone else will retort: at that price literature is no longer anything but the expression of ideas that we are expected to accept or contradict. But such a reaction presupposes that literature is a single thing. Now this is precisely what it is not: it is a formal game of its elements *and* at the same time an ideological entity (as well as many other things); it is not simply a quest for truth, but it is *also* a quest for truth. In this it is distinguished from the other arts, as Sartre and Bénichou remind us, since it "passes" through language, instead of being a structuring of a simple raw material such as sound, color, or movement; there can be no such thing as "abstract literature." We have at our disposal today a conceptual apparatus that suffices (no matter how obviously imperfect it is) to describe the structural properties of literature and to analyze its historical inscription. But we do not know how to speak of literature's other dimensions, and this is a gap we need to fill. Overly deterministic criticism makes the error of postulating that literary works are the expression, or the reflection, of ideology (of the "dominant" ideology, moreover); it then becomes a facile exercise to look for examples that prove the opposite. But if literature is not the reflection of an external ideology, this does not prove that it has no relationship at all to ideology: literature does not reflect an ideology, it is one. We have to know what literary works are stating, not *in order* to discover the spirit of the times or *because* we are already familiar with that spirit and are seeking new illustrations of it, but rather because the statement is essential to the works themselves.

And we come back once again to the proximity between literature and criticism. It is sometimes said that the former speaks of the world, the latter of books. But that is not true. First of all, the works themselves always speak about earlier works, or in any event imply them: the desire to write does not come from life but from other writings. Next, criticism must not, cannot, be limited to speaking about books; in its turn, it always has something to say about life. When it limits itself to structural description and historical reconstruction, it simply attempts to make its voice as inaudible as possible (even though it never entirely succeeds). Yet it can and must remember that it too is a quest for truth and values. The type of truth to which criticism and literature have access is of the same nature: the truth of things rather than of facts, the truth of unveiling and not the truth of equivalence (which the critic is acquainted with as well, but which constitutes only a preliminary truth for him). Many a wrong turn could have been avoided, in criticism as in history or anthropology, if it had only been recognized that, just as Dostoevsky is seeking to state the truth about man although one cannot declare that he possesses it, in the same way the critic is seeking to state the truth about Dostoevsky, with—at least in theory—the same chances of success; at the same time, and inevitably, he too speaks about man. As Sartre said, "prose is communication, a joint quest of truth; it is recognition and reciprocity";[2] but this definition can be applied, word for word, to criticism. Of course criticism and literature have their differences; in the current context, however, it seems to me more urgent to see what they have in common.

Dialogic criticism is standard in philosophy, where scholars are interested in authors for their ideas, but not very common in literature, where critics think it suffices to contemplate and admire. Now the forms themselves are bearers of ideology, and examples of literary criticism exist—although they are rare—that are not limited to analysis, but that argue with their authors, thereby demonstrating that dialogic criticism is just as possible in the literary field: René Girard disagrees with the Romantics, for example, and Leo Bersani enters into a polemic with the realists. In order to be understood, the language of forms requires a certain kind of listening (Ian Watt provided an excellent illustration of this); in its absence, we are forced to fall back upon the author's direct utterances or, worse, those of his characters. But just because some critics are deaf does not mean that literature ceases to speak. Even the least "moral" works take a stance with respect to human values and thus allow a confrontation with the position of the critic. The only case in which dialogic criticism is impossible is when the critic finds himself in complete agreement with his author: then no discussion is possible, and the dialogue ends up being replaced by an apologia. One may wonder whether such a perfect coincidence is really possible, but it is certain that even differences in degree are perceptible: it is easier for me to engage in dialogue (when I dare) with Diderot, whose ideas I disapprove of, than with Stendhal. I must say too, however, that personally I am even more ill at ease when the opposition is radical: war is not a search for understanding.

I should add that the critic who wants to enter into dialogue with his author should not forget that as soon as his own book is published he becomes an author in turn, and that a future reader will seek to enter into dialogue with him. The ideal of dialogic criticism is not the oracular formula that plunges the reader into stupefaction, followed by a bitter mix of admiration for the author and pity for oneself. Once he has become conscious of the dialogue in which he is engaged, the critic cannot remain ignorant of the fact that this particular dialogue is just one link in an uninterrupted chain, since the author was writing in response to other authors, and since one becomes an author oneself from that moment on. The form of one's writing itself is therefore not without importance, since this form must authorize a response, and not mere idolatry.

Is dialogic criticism more appropriate to our times than immanent criticism and dogmatic criticism? I have perhaps given the impression that I think so, by describing the relation between these latter as sequential: first came Patristic exegesis, then philology. But things are of course not so simple, both because societies are not perfectly homogeneous and because history does not unfold according to any linear schema. An "immanent" attitude toward art is found in Quintilian, and the "dogmatic" commentary did not die with the Church Fathers. The contemporary world, in particular, recognizes the plurality of options, and ("dogmatic") Christian or Marxist viewpoints are found side by side today with ("immanent") outlooks that are historical or structuralist in orientation. Human beings are never entirely determined by their milieu; their freedom is their defining characteristic; and I am a living illustration of the weakness of that determinism, since I have found myself in the span of just a few years attached more or less closely to each of the three forms of criticism that I have set out to distinguish here.

And yet it is clear, too, that even if individualism can be detected as far back as the writings of the Stoics, it takes on new vigor in the Renaissance and becomes dominant with Romanticism. The ideologies of a society are hierarchically articulated, and this articulation is significant: I do not believe that it is purely a matter of chance (a pure act of freedom on the part of certain individuals) that the idea of dialogic criticism, by this name or some other, comes to us here and how; nor do I believe that it has reached us because we are more intelligent than our predecessors. The events of the world around us are "favorable conditions" for this criticism rather than its "causes"; but I think I hear them echoing in it. Deliberately mixing the proximate and the remote, the fundamental and the derived, the trivial and the sublime, I shall cite the following: the current absence of any unanimously accepted doctrine; our increased familiarity with cultures other than our own, thanks to mass media and charter flights; the acceptance of decolonization, at least on the ideological level; an unprecedented development of technology; the new type of massacre that the mid-twentieth century has known; the rebirth (birth?) of the struggle for human rights.

I find another indication of this evolution in the contemporary transformations of literature itself (but here I am surely succumbing to a choice that derives from what I seek to find). What seems to me characteristic of this literature is not the inexhaustible autobiographical genre under which it is giving way, but the fact that it openly assumes its own heterogeneity, that it is at once fiction and pamphlet, history and philosophy, poetry and science. The writings of Solzhenitsyn and Kundera, Günter Grass and D. M. Thomas cannot be neatly packaged within previous conceptions of literature; they are neither "art for art's sake" nor "literature of commitment" (in the ordinary rather than the Sartrean sense); rather, they are works that know themselves for what they are, at once literary construction and search for truth.

Dialogic criticism has existed, of course, from time immemorial (like the other types), and if necessary the adjective can be dispensed with, so long as we recognize that the meaning of criticism always lies in transcending the opposition between dogmatism and skepticism. But our epoch—how much longer do we have?—seems to hold out some hope for this form of thought, if only we hurry to grasp it.

NOTES

1. I note that Sartre said the same thing, but with the intention of rejecting any universalist perspective. "Rousseau, the father of the French Revolution, and Gobineau, the father of racism, both sent us messages. And the critic considers them with equal sympathy" (*What Is Literature?*, trans. Bernard Frechtman [Gloucester, Mass.: Peter Smith, 1978], pp. 25–26).

2. *Saint Genet, Actor and Martyr*, trans. Bernard Frechtman (New York: George Braziller, 1963), p. 439.

Frank Lentricchia
1940–

Frank Lentricchia, Jr., has written scornfully of most of the theories of criticism that have prevailed in the universities over the past twenty-five years. He has challenged their chief theorists and created a reputation as one fiercely critical of professorial thinking (he himself is a professor) that weaves quietist, disengaged systems and theories when literature and criticism have the power as rhetoric to bring about social change. He was born on May 23, 1940, in Utica, New York. He took his B.A. at the Utica College of Syracuse University in 1962. A year later he received an M.A. from Duke University, staying on for his Ph.D., which he completed in 1966. He began teaching as an assistant professor of English and comparative literature at University of California–Los Angeles for two years; he moved to the university's Irvine campus in 1968, where he remained until 1982, having become, meanwhile, a full professor in 1976. He left Irvine for Rice University, Houston, where he was Autrey Professor of Humanities from 1982 to 1984. Lentricchia is presently professor of English at Duke University.

In the course of his career, Lentricchia has been moving toward mapping out a viable theory for American literary criticism; in challenging the positions of other theorists he has devoted much space in giving his account of their views. From the outset, he found himself at odds with the methods and assumptions of the New Critics. Politically, he was far to the left of them, and he had little regard for approaching a work of literature as an organic, separate aesthetic entity for "close reading." In recent years he has written several much-noticed books on the complications and shortcomings of the current literary scene. A bit of a brawler, perhaps, he has sought to deflate a number of the most established critical reputations of the day, aiming with a special zest at the "Yale Mafia"—Paul de Man, Geoffrey Hartman, J. Hillis Miller, and Harold Bloom. Lentricchia claims writers and critics have a historical role, that they are not mere aestheticizers, quietists, passive elements in the systems they elaborate in their theories. His own positions emerge from William James, Kenneth Burke, and Michel Foucault.

Lentricchia's first book, *The Gaiety of Language: An Essay on the Radical Poetics of W. B. Yeats and Wallace Stevens* (1968), manifested his own radicalism at a time when universities in America were still dominated by the New Criticism. *Robert Frost: Modern Poetics and the Landscapes of Self* (1975) studies Frost, oddly, as if from the critic's thinking about the language and ideas of Stevens. William James provides much of the philosophical framework for this book, which aims to revive Frost's poems from the limbo to which Winters and others had consigned them. With his second wife, Melissa

Christensen Lentricchia, he produced *Robert Frost: A Bibliography 1913–74* (1976).

After the New Criticism (1980) provides a revisionist account of the previous twenty years of American criticism. It opens with a moderately disdainful chapter on Northrop Frye and concludes with a harsh, combative chapter on Harold Bloom. Lentricchia's thesis, woven into discussions of numerous critics, faults American criticism for its antihistorical character and the "enervating aestheticism" found from the New Criticism to American deconstruction. Foucault's concept of discourse as "an act of power, a locus of power" suggests how things might be improved. *Criticism and Social Change* (1983) is an elaboration of this idea, a book offered as "required tools for the literary intellectual who would be a social force, who at his specific institutional site would begin a contribution to the formation of a community different from the one we live in." The intellectual hero of the book, Burke, is opposed by de Man, representative of "the debilitated literary mind," one who teaches "that there is nothing to be done." Burke, in contrast, "stands as a rare example of intellectual health—vigorously committed, always engaging the projects of aesthetics with the more significant project for living."

Lentricchia's most recent work, *Ariel and the Police* (1988), renews arguments with old enemies, and begins with a reading of Stevens's "Anecdote of the Jar" that aims at demonstrating the absurdity of New Critical method—"there is always something outside the text." Further discussion of Stevens links the "failure" of the long poems with the withdrawal of the poet from an engaged existence. In a chapter on William James, Lentricchia bitingly observes: "The new pragmatism . . . says in all but words: 'The unexamined life is the only life worth living.' Here at last, moving with the tides of the times, is the basis for a literary criticism of the eighties."

FROM
Criticism and Social Change

Part Five

I turn now to Burke's most provocative meditation on the writer as political force—his conceptual center as an intellectual, if it is possible to speak of a centered Burke. The following passage on Nietzsche's style will inform much of what I say on rhetoric, the subject of subjects in Burke.

> Nietzsche's later style is like a sequence of *darts*. Indeed, at first I tried to explain it to myself as a simple conversion of his fighting, hunting attitude into its behavioristic equivalent. His sentences are forever striking out at this or that, exactly like a man in the midst of game, or enemies. They leap with a continual abruptness and sharpness of naming, which seems to suggest nothing so much as those saltations by which cruising animals suddenly leap upon their prey. . . . But however much the state of his mental or neurological structure may account for this dartlike quality of his page, an equally important source of it is revealed in his world "perspective." Nietzsche, we learn in his *Will to Power,* was interested in the establishment of perspectives. It was part of his program to give us these repeatedly. And in trying to analyze just what he meant by them, I came upon reasons for relating his cult of perspectives to his dartlike style.[1]

I

In the scary, ironic discourse of Mafia dons (experts in these matters) the rhetorician is one who persuades us by making us an offer we believe we can't refuse. Persuading can seem friendly (a "friendly persuasion") or otherwise (as with a "persuader"—a gun, a knife, a whip, a piece of piano wire, or a word). In either instance rhetoric is a form of powerful action: darting, killing, drug dispensing, (doctor, pusher, hit-man, poisoner, healer). Each of these metaphors in Burke, with their immense history in rhetorical and literary theory, are figures for an essential process of representation involving teaching and writing in an action, to cite his two key words, of "identification" and "transformation." Burke's extended meditation on rhetoric—though intimately affiliated with the ancient traditions, as current poststructuralist writing on rhetoric is not—still very much shares with Nietzsche and the Yale neo-Nietzscheans the proposition that rhetoric does not sit upon the stabilizing foundation of "dialectic" in the classical Greek sense of that word. Like the darting saltations of Nietzsche's style, we cannot read rhetoric's force back to some logical base and thereby defer rhetoric by referring its linguistic violence to some legitimating source in reason. Rhetoric insists on presenting itself with stunning abruptness and discontinuity. Rhetoric is irreducible. And there is no alternative to it: "Wherever there is persuasion, there is rhetoric. And wherever there is 'meaning,' there is 'persuasion.'"[2]

Keeping in mind what Burke says about Nietzsche's later style, that it is "like a sequence of darts," maybe we should ask ourselves (more pointedly) what is the point of rhetoric? Of the texts that he takes up in the introductory sections of *A Rhetoric of Motives* Burke writes: "Since these texts involve an imagery of killing (as a typical text for today should) we note how, behind the surface, lies a quite different realm that has little to do with such motives. An imagery of killing is but one of many terminologies by which writers can represent the process of change. And while recognizing the sinister implications of a preference for homicidal and suicidal terms, we indicate that the principles of development or transformation ('rebirth') which they stand for are not strictly of such a nature at all."[3] The "point" of rhetoric (as persuasion) is to change its intended receivers, and killing one's auditors is certainly one way of changing them. But a terminology of killing is metaphoric for Burke, however literal it may be for underworld theorists of the subject (and their targets). To change or transform the object of rhetoric is the point of rhetoric, it always is. But Burke's metaphor for Nietzsche's stylistic effect of "darting" foregrounds rhetoric's intention to control and to dominate, to pin us to the wall. Moreover, he argues, Nietzsche's darts establish "perspectives"; they are modes of knowledge: not in its traditional, disinterested humanist definition, but knowledge as power. "Perspectives" are like "darts." To write is to know is to dominate. That is maybe too sinister a way of phrasing the rhetorical process. Burke permits us another phrasing. To write is to establish perspective by metaphor, by incongruity ("establish": fix, ordain, found permanently, as in the founding of governments or institutions). To make metaphor is to violate in one act the status quo of discourse and of society (and here Burke retends Marx and protends the Derrida of "White Mythology"). To make metaphor is to violate linguistic "propriety" and the "proper," conceptions which, as Marx insists, are intimately related to private property—mine, my own.[4] In the rhetoric of metaphor, language asserts its collective, classless potentiality as it moves against a stubborn, constellated series of notions like origin, privacy, ownership, virtue, the bourgeois subject, the liberal individual—all of which undergird the cultural staying power of capitalism. The rhetorical act in its metaphoric phase moves simultaneously against base, "property," and the habits and values, linguistic "manners," aligned with it in the superstructure. And against not just any social formation but, as the terms of Burke, Marx, and Derrida would indicate, in this convergence of theorists, against the dominant social formation in the West today. Burke insists that art conceived as rhetoric opens up radically divergent social functions for the writer. He may work, as in the writer's classical vocation, on behalf of a dominant hegemony by reinforcing habits of thought and feeling that help to sustain ruling power: at the stylistic level this means, among other things, that the writer sustains consensus and the social structure by reinforcing the metaphors of everyday life that are buried in clichés—and clichéd consciousness—by passing on the "truth" of dead metaphors, and naturalized conventions, like "free enterprise."⁵ Or he may work counter-hegemonically as a violator, in an effort to dominate and to re-educate (*inform*), to pin us to the wall, in order to assist in the birth of a critical mind by peeling off, one by one, and thus revealing to us for what they are, all bourgeois encrustations of consciousness. In the widest sense of the word, he would encourage cultural revolution.

This latter potentially disruptive, socially critical act of "transformation" does its work with the crucial assistance of a co-conspirator which Burke calls "identification." Transformation and identification are modes of rhetoric's deepest desire: to move from "the state of Babel, after the Fall," toward another "state"—political state and "state" of language—of perfect understanding and community, that recovery of paradise in which rhetoric ceases to have an occupation.⁶ Here we find ourselves in the ambiguous dream world of the visionary. No visionary in any active sense, Burke directs his rhetorical theory on behalf of the formation of a critical consciousness whose main work lies today, particularly in the United States, in the exposition of ideological formations of the advanced capitalist sort. Identification may be ultimately, and dangerously, "compensatory to division," as he puts it, but before we get to that place in history there is much undramatic work to be done.⁷

We can begin to get a hold on Burke's politically intriguing use of "identification" if we note a certain ambiguity that he does not bother to specify, much less clarify: identification *of*/identification *with*. "Identification with" operates at the mediating level where Burke situates rhetoric itself. It is conscious, as when we identify ourselves with our occupations; it is also elusively unconscious, and necessarily so under advanced capitalist norms of dispersion that encourage us to think of what we do as autonomous activity. Nevertheless, as Burke notes, the shepherd, though he thinks he works independently, for the good of the sheep, to protect them from harm, is linked to a project that is raising the sheep for market. The shepherd—writer, teacher—who needs to think that he runs his own show, that in his own special corner of culture he does "good," despite all the isolating specialization his act requires to be done "right," is "enrolled" (an important term for Burke) in a larger social action—unconsciously he is aligned rhetorically, he is identified with this larger action, just as he is always enrolled in (identified with), all democratic myths of the Adamic self to the contrary notwithstanding, a class or at least an "interested" socioeconomic "group."⁸ To exist socially is to be rhetorically aligned. It is the function of the intellectual as critical rhetor to uncover, bring into the light, and probe all such alignments. That is part of the work of ideological analysis. Only when such political work of identification is understood, when our various and devious "identities" are put on the table, when our involvements are brought thus bluntly before us, in all their repugnant detail: only then can the rhetorical work of transformation realistically begin.

"Identification with" requires that the critical rhetor perform the dangerous act of "identification of": the political work of ideological analysis presumes a power-enabling act of cognition—an identifying that necessarily entails a knowing and a mastering. If one of the marks of rhetoric from ancient times, as Burke notes, "is its use to *gain advantage,* of one sort or another," then his own working through the process of identification and transformation shows unmistakably that gaining advantage is synonymous with taking it.[9] The critical rhetor finds himself at the most delicate of all crossings, standing at a specific institutional site where any intellectual who teaches, whether as teacher in the conventional sense, or as writer, both dreads and longs to be, the place (this has been the burden of my argument) where intellectuals always already are. The dread of such a politically sensitive position has been expressed with maximum force by Foucault in *Discipline and Punish*. Modern society, in his narrative, is the full realization of knowledge-as-power-to-control. All our significant institutions are unified by an all pervasive carceral intentionality from which there is no escape; the prison is the microcosm of society, the exemplary institution because there individuals are openly known in order to be controlled, so that they may be utilized and commodified in the most productive manner possible. The "carceral continuum," as Foucault calls it, seems to be the logical finale of the socioeconomic enterprise of capitalism. Those of us generally characterized as humanist intellectuals often like to think we stand outside. Unlike technointellectuals—the sons of Frederick Taylor who manage our factories, universities, hospitals, and prisons—we, at any rate, do not work as engineers of the carceral system. Or so we must think. But Foucault will not exempt us: educators at all levels are for him prime examples of the channeling and application of knowledge/power.[10]

With his concept of intellection as rhetoricopolitical activity, Burke joins Foucault. Burke's intellectual "identifies" his audience in order to "transform" it. We want again to ask, to what end? But I do not think that we should ask that question in *a priori* fashion, as if "the intellectual" really represented an autonomous class, crystallized and separated out from socioeconomic matrices. To ask the question of the intellectual in that way is already to accept what Gramsci called the "traditional intellectual" on his own terms; it is to accept uncritically his idealistic vocation as a student of ideas and a keeper of culture, as if such vocation had never been severely tested by Marx and Engels in *The German Ideology*. The question will have to be rooted in what Foucault calls the "specific intellectual," working from a particular social and historical experience, within a specific place in the institutional network: the question must be so framed even though the intellectual (the academic intellectual in particular) will tend to regard himself as a cosmopolitan, universal figure, dispassionately attached *as intellectual* to the society in which he lives, speaking for the ages, and even though he will tend to think that when he serves culture he stands outside power—which is not the case, he will readily admit, when he pays taxes, votes, or buys groceries.

To come to cases: though we cannot ask the question Platonically, we can ask it specifically here of Kenneth Burke. We can ask whether Burke himself conceives of himself as an autonomous thinker; whether so self-deceived he permits himself to be appropriated for the better reinforcement of the disciplined society. Though there is no univocal answer to the question, I believe that Burke functioned for the most part as a critical intellectual whose rhetorical activity of identification and would-be transformation moves toward an emancipating ideal of sociopolitical self-awareness. Burke is mainly convinced that traditional American liberal ideals cannot make us free—that the liberal norm of autonomy in particular, as it defines us in our occupational identity and especially, I would add, as it defines teachers in traditional academic settings, is not only deceptive for the intellectual: it permits him to deceive the sheep as well. Thus do humanists help to fashion the hegemony that will keep us, and themselves, in the dark.

Burke's conception of himself as critical rhetor demands that he lay bare the hegemonic process in all its subtle and insidious ways. He says: "We are clearly in the region of rhetoric when considering the identification whereby a specialized activity makes one a participant in some social or economic class. 'Belonging' in this sense is rhetorical."[11] As he works this region of rhetoric, he is concerned not only to bring to the consciousness of his audience their identification as individuals with a "class" or, if that word is too Old World for Americans, then we must say their involvement, socially and economically, with an "interest" group. In the land of the new Adam and Eve, the isolato, as Melville called the American self—a darker measuring of that most happy fellow, the rugged individual—such consciousness is rarer than we think. Burke's purpose in identifying such consciousness and revealing to it its identifications is not to form social self-consciousness for its own sake or, in the current mode, to encourage a micro-politics. His goals are neither contemplative nor Foucauldian. The widening of consciousness is a necessary first step to a different kind of praxis, one that is not content merely to work its "autonomous" activity and then give up, refuse to take its work home, declaring its impotence with "that is not my field," and other statements which absolve us from the uses to which our work is put. Burke wants us to take our work home. His effort to undermine our feeling of autonomy, to make us feel responsible to the larger social project, to the social whole, is an effort to bring to birth, out of our fragmented existences, an organic identity that would be rooted in a critical power to coordinate and integrate the separate levels of our lives: to make us whole again beyond confusion. That is a redemptive project, one which would put us back in control, and shatter the image of Orwellian progress narrated in *Discipline and Punish*. Everything is "our business":

> If the technical expert, as such, is assigned the task of perfecting new powers of chemical, bacteriological, or atomic destruction, his morality *as technical expert* requires only that he apply himself to his task as effectively as possible. The question of what the new force might mean, as released into a social texture emotionally and intellectually unfit to control it, or as surrendered to men whose *specialty* is *professional killing*—well, that is simply "none of our business," as specialists, however great may be his misgivings as father of a family, or as citizen of his nation and of the world.[12]

It is always easy for humanists, too easy, to score ethical points off the myopia among technocrats and scientists. Burke won't indulge such self-righteousness; he won't let us off the hook. A *Rhetoric of Motives,* published in 1950, was mostly written in the late 1940s. In the passage I've just quoted on nuclear scientists and professional killers, we should feel the pressure of the Manhattan Project, the Cold War, and the anguish of Robert Oppenheimer. In the passage I am about to quote, Burke reflects on the literary-critical wars of the thirties and forties. Specialists in literary technology come off ethically not much better than specialists in atomic destruction: "So much progressive and radical criticism in recent years has been concerned with the social implications of art, that affirmations of art's autonomy can often become, by antithesis, a roundabout way of identifying oneself with the interests of political conservatism. In accordance with the rhetorical principle of identification, whenever you find a doctrine of 'nonpolitical' esthetics affirmed with fervor, look for its politics."[13]

II

In the title essay of *The Philosophy of Literary Form* Burke defines "symbolic action" by offering in its place a series of metonymic substitutions whose cumulative effect is to broaden immensely the scope of the term "literary" in his title. His key substitutions are "strategy," "magical decree," "scapegoat," "fetish," "name," and, father of them all, "representation." For Burke these nouns always need to be converted to their active verbal form—"decreeing," "scapegoating," "fetishizing," and so on, all of which are best understood by a term that must qualify as one of his favorites: "encompassment," writing as a technique of "encompassing," an attempt to master a situation, a will to power. Considered in such light, his traditional term for symbolic action, "representation," carries none of the freight that it is generally made to carry in the history of mimetic theories of art. Symbolic action as "representation" is an activity simply charged with power, an activity we can call aesthetic praxis provided that we understand the aesthetic against the grain of the highly specialized meaning that tends to dominate thought about literature and art since the late eighteenth century. Against the grain we retrieve a more classical sense of the aesthetic *as* the practical and *as* the rhetorical: the aesthetic as the sine qua non of the cultural economy.[14]

Burke says, "I feel it to be no mere accident of language that we use the same word for sensory, artistic, and political representation."[15] The inherent claim of any sort of representation, the basis, as the case may be, of its epistemological, or aesthetic, or sociopolitical authority (Burke would blur those categories), the basis of its coercive power is an ontological claim, used like a hammer, that some part of the whole *really does* stand in for the whole—participates in the whole. At the level of concept, we need a neo-Platonic sense of "participation" to grasp Burke's point; at the rhetorical level, either openly or (more frequently) covertly, representation appears under the figure of synecdoche, Burke's master trope for the part/whole relationship. The discourse of synecdoche asserts itself as a relationship of signifier and signified that is not arbitrary. To assent to the "truth" of a representation/synecdoche, then, is to assent to its profoundest claim: that of epistemological and ontological universality. And it is to assent necessarily and concomitantly to a profoundly repressive discourse. In the name of universality and truth, representation becomes a cover-up in two ways: it hides itself as an agency of specific political power, as a highly specified and structured social text, and in the same process it covers up social and cultural difference and conflict within the social text. Writing, as Derrida has argued, is unthinkable without repression—I choose to understand him to be making a statement about the inherent politics of writing.[16]

The theoretical text in the Western tradition most responsible for this complex sense of representation (though not consciously) is the *Poetics* of Aristotle—where we learn most of what we need to know about the deviousness of mimesis if we confront Aristotle with himself: if we place alongside the ninth chapter of the *Poetics*, in which the universality of "poetry" is argued at the expense of "history"—even as both are subordinated to philosophy: an unblemished mirror of the truth of universals—his fifteenth chapter (and related parts of the *Politics*) in which the proper representation of character, its "necessary" and "probable" mimesis according to the dictates of human nature, is stipulated by bringing forth the examples of women and slaves, one of which is said by nature to be inferior and the other, by the same eternal standard, is declared worthless. (All character typologies in the classical tradition should be read in the context of this source.) Aristotle is saying that if you would represent women and slaves in a fashion that would satisfy the conditions of human nature, if you want to persuade reason's tribunal, philosophy itself, then you must not give them the qualities appropriate only to a free male. Though it is his intention to tell us otherwise, at a certain level the text of the *Poetics*, because it is bound over to the larger cultural intentionality of his society, works against his ontological claim for the universal (and his claim for reason as ahistorical arbiter) and shows that representations are always culturally and politically specific, and in doing this the *Poetics* reveals, to our chagrin, that the material basis of its continuing cultural power resides in a slave-holding society. Yet as a "traditional" text, to come back to that difficult concept (which is how we have received it and how, according to the dominant paradigm of reading, we should understand it), its material basis is hidden by the eliding action of our tradition-making, beginning most forcefully in the Italian Renaissance, so that its universalist claims for mimesis are freed from the socially specific moment within which they were made. Against the traditional reading, I am making this claim: the *Poetics* says that "poetry" is better than "history" because it makes "reasonable" the specific "equipment for living" deployed by ruling-class Greek men in classical Athens.

One of Burke's strengths is that he understood the treachery of the traditionalist intellect early, and he knew it overtly. With ironic understatement of the issues involved he writes: "In theories of politics prevailing at different periods in history, there have been quarrels as to the precise vessel of authority that is to be considered 'representative' of the society as a whole . . . but all agree in assuming that there is *some* part representative of the whole, hence fit to stand for it."[17] The "agreement" that such is the case is the mask of a desire that it be so. Political and by implication aesthetic representations are revealed in their intentional force, as productions of a collective will to power when, in periods of social crisis, "an authoritative class, whose purpose and ideals had been generally considered as *representative* of the total society's purposes and ideals, becomes considered as *antagonistic*. Their class character, once felt to be a *culminating* part of the whole, is now felt to be a *divisive* part of the whole."[18] Under the pressure of Burke's analysis the term "representation" becomes a sign of the convergence of the political and the aesthetic, and of the complicity of the aesthetic with political power. The aesthetic is always traversed by power; never does it stand "outside" in a universal situated beyond the work of will. Again, however, and this cannot, I believe, be said too forcefully, the convergence of the political and the aesthetic is not necessarily a convergence of the aesthetic with the politically progressive (which, in different ways, is a sentimental argument sometimes made by both Lukács and Marcuse). We shouldn't forget the significance of the fifteenth chapter of the *Poetics* or, more dramatically, Burke's work on Hitler's artistry.

Hitler was a kind of medicine man, but then, as Burke reminds us, so are all poets.[19] The poet as medicine man, as political doctor: the diseases he would attend to infest the body politic; his medicine is a representation charged with power's purposiveness. To define representation in this way is to define it as rhetoric, and according to Burke aesthetic-rhetorical medicine has but two uses—it can be therapeutic or prophylactic. The common denominator in either function is that the aesthetic becomes a part of the *consolatio philosophiae*: "It would protect us. Let us remind ourselves, however, that implicit in the idea of protection there is the idea of something to be *protected against*. Hence, to analyze the element of *comfort* in beauty, without false emphasis, we must be less monistic, more 'dialectical,' in that we include also, as an important aspect of the recipe, the element of *discomfort* (actual or threatened) for which the poetry is 'medicine.'"[20] Burke explains that this dialectical sense of the aesthetic is to be retrieved from older theories of art that stress affect rather than interpretation. In ancient and Renaissance traditions, art exists as a type of cultural power, for the purpose of educating and moving, not for the purpose of interpretation. Beauty then should be taken in the context of the sublime (as a type of action) rather than in a nineteenth-century context of formalistic autonomy (as pure contemplation). In his proposal to replace our sense of beauty as "pure" representation by reading the beautiful through the impure category of the sublime (some "vastness of magnitude, power, or distance, disproportionate to ourselves"), Burke tells us that beauty's basis cannot be located monistically in an "in itself"—in some inert and isolated object or in a self conceived in its essential subjectiveness as prior to, or at least outside what we call society: "Confronting the poetic act in terms of the sublime and the ridiculous, we are disposed to think of the issue in terms *of a situation and a strategy for confronting or encompassing that situation,* a scene and an act, with each possessing its own genius, but the two fields interwoven."[21] For Burke, the beautiful understood as the sublime is an image of social struggle.

With a threat as its basis, beauty cannot be conceived monistically but only dialectically as always an act in the world, always involved in the administration of political medicine. Burke's Longinus, unlike Curtius's, is a theorist of aesthetic power.

Burke encapsulates his theory of poetic expression and in the process darkens his medical metaphor by appealing to the story of Perseus and the Medusa, a myth more central to poetics, from his point of view, than the story of Orpheus and his voyage to Hades: "Perseus who could not face the serpent-headed monster without being turned to stone, but was immune to this danger if he observed it to be a reflection in a mirror."[22] The mirror of Perseus does what Burke insists representation cannot help doing—it represents with a difference; it bears purpose; it is itself an act of power in that it controls the murderous Medusa and, performing this initial act, prepares for another: the decapitation of the Medusa. Burke would have us read the myth of Perseus as a tale of the political work of the aesthetic. It is a tale that tells us what he has told us in other, perhaps less striking ways—that literature makes something happen, that the literary is always the taking of position and simultaneously the exercising of position within and upon the social field. Thus: Hitler's rhetoric functioned as a representation of the German people, Jews and non-Jews alike; his representation bore a certain powerful purpose: it controlled the German people. By performing this initial act of power, it prepared for another—an act of genocide. And that act, whether viewed in its horrifying physical dimension, or in its not unhorrifying rhetorical dimension (these two cannot finally be separated) and all the preparatory acts that led up to it—including a certain reading of Nietzsche, as Derrida has suggested—let us not soften the point: this act of genocide and the acts which necessarily preceded it functioned, and continue to function, in the manner of the *consolatio philosophiae*: they functioned, and continue to function, for a certain audience, as therapy.

It is likely, I think, that many of us trained in literature, because of what that training did to us and pretty much continues to do to our students, it is likely that Burke's essay on Hitler will cause many of us so formed to make certain statements: "But *Mein Kampf* is not literature." Or: "*Mein Kampf* may be literature, but it is bad literature." The Burkean answer to these head-in-the-sand responses must be: "Not only is *Mein Kampf* literature; it was highly effective literature." If we need to believe otherwise, and literary people too often need to believe otherwise (I speak not from the outside on this matter); if we need to believe that literature is somehow always involved in a noble, humane cause, a position common on the literary left as well as the literary right and center (what else can be on our minds when we urge that our undergraduates read the classics of the Western tradition?), then let us at least be shaken by Burke's subversion of the sentiment that literature is inherently humane. Literature is inherently nothing; or it is inherently a body of rhetorical strategies waiting to be seized. And anybody can seize them. Literature is not Keats. The literary is never only the elite canon of great books; it is also what we call "minor" literature and "popular" literature. But it is more even than what this expanded definition would allow. It is all writing considered as social practice, all writing viewed in its material circumstances and in its purposiveness. It is power as representation. The literary is all around us, and it is always doing its work upon us. It bears the past in many complex ways, but it does its deed, makes its mark, marks us, here and now. The knowledge that the literary is present power (in Burke's sense of "present") cannot, of course, free us from power, though that knowledge is somewhat salutary especially because modern literary theory has not much wanted to know about power. We need to know that what is therapeutic or prophylactic for some is poison for others; that the literary cannot free itself from this double effect; that it is always efficacious, one way or another; that as writers and teachers we dispense drugs every day.

Of course no one wants to dispense poison to one's readers and students; one wants to be the good doctor. And in fact it is very difficult to define a role for the intellectual not grounded on that feeling—though Foucault has tried. It is probably not a simple matter of choosing not to dispense poison—were it so, the intellectual life would be a good deal simpler, and all honor would be ours. I'll put this personally: I have been tempted to offer Burke as the angel of modern criticism, an unambiguous good in the midst of all this bad. In more than one place in the preceding pages I have tried to resist this urge, but let me here bring this problem down to one case. My reader will have noticed the repeated occurrence of the figure of Babel in Burke's work—an image, variously, of linguistic divisiveness and chaos, hermeneutic solipsism, social struggle, the scene of rhetoric, the condition of exile from a unified, paradisal community, or even, for the antinomian soul, the Burkean soul, paradise itself. The figure occurs early and late in Burke's work. For reasons which I've explored, and won't bother to rehearse, he has considered the idea, sometimes with horror, other times with pleasure. What I have not yet mentioned, however, is that the figure of Babel occurs centrally in his essay on Hitler, whom Burke finds offering the German people, as an alternative to the many-voiced confusion of their parliament (a "vocal diaspora"), his single, mastering voice and presence, a unifying center interchangeable with Munich. The figure of Babel is an awful point of convergence: Hitler not as exterior bad from which we can protect ourselves by the proper cherishing of his negation, whoever or whatever that might be, but as figure himself of an ultimate impulse to essentialization inside any and all of our good angels. What has Burke found in Hitler if not a fun-house mirror reflection of tendencies within his own theories of interpretation? Assuming that Burke was well aware of the repeated figuration of Babel in his own writings, it is something of an astonishment that be undertook the essay on *Mein Kampf* at all. Having once undertaken it, it is to his credit that he did not bury the "familiar" figure he encountered in Hitler's book. Perhaps, then, there is yet another and finer quality of critical consciousness that this episode reveals: that finer quality, through its clarity, its accessibility, its refusal to revise its past, its refusal to pose as all-knowing, is nothing other than a quality that permits itself, the critical consciousness itself, *to be criticized*—the teacher become student, the critic become text, the doctor become patient. And perhaps that is the best one can give to one's students and readers: the means to resist oneself. Especially a criticism that would work for the alleviation of repression cannot afford to do less. It must make itself vulnerable; failure to do so will bring against its efforts the reactions of contempt which history always keeps waiting in the wings in readiness to expose false humanists.[23]

III

What is the rhetoric of *A Rhetoric of Motives*? Burke spoke of two purposes for writing the book: first, to bring rhetoric back into the literary against the effort of theoreticians of the aesthetic to banish rhetoric from the realm of the literary; second, to revise the traditional idea of rhetoric so that, newly conceived, it could stand between pure deliberate activity and the unconscious: "There is an intermediate area of expression that is not wholly deliberate, yet not wholly unconscious. It lies midway between aimless utterance and speech directly purposive."[24] "Speech directly purposive" stands, of course, as a definition of rhetoric in its classical, overtly political project, while "aimless utterance" signifies what the literary has become from Kant to de Man: discourse presumably apolitical, unrhetorical, without a design, as in the Kantian formula "purposiveness without purpose," or discourse, as in de Man's mode, whose designs incessantly subvert themselves—self-deconstructive writing, politics necessarily unfulfilled, frustrated rhetoric constantly turning against itself. Burkean rhetoric would occupy the space between the old rhetoric of pure will and the modernist and postmodernist aesthetic of antiwill: between a subject apparently in full possession of itself, and in full intentional control of its expression, and a subject whose relation to "its" expression is very problematic. (My use of the possessive "its" can be traced ultimately to a convention of thinking about expression and its source put to shame by philosophers as diverse as Kant, Nietzsche, Derrida, and Foucault.) Burke is giving rhetoric an unconscious, something unheard of in the ancient traditions, but in the process of doing so he is not going to lose sight of the conscious and the willful.

In the little fable of history as conversation that I am about to quote the conversants are simultaneously the innocent targets of history and its responsible executors, both subjected to the coercive power of the past and the accountable makers of the future. Similarly in Burke's theory of rhetoric: the rhetorician is the not-always-knowing carrier of historical and ideological forces, while at the same time he acts within and upon the present and thereby becomes an agent of change. Burke's metaphor of conversation, unlike Richard Rorty's, is from the beginning a metaphor of social text, of how that text makes us and of how we make *it*, both for ourselves and for the future. The primal scene of rhetoric is the unending conversation of history:

> Imagine that you enter a parlor. You come late. When you arrive, others have long preceded you, and they are engaged in a heated

discussion, a discussion too heated for them to pause and tell you exactly what it is about. In fact, the discussion had already begun long before any of them got there, so that no one present is qualified to retrace for you all the steps that had gone before. You listen for a while, until you decide that you have caught the tenor of the argument; then you put in your oar. Someone answers; you answer him; another comes to your defense; another aligns himself against you, to either the embarassment or gratification of your opponent, depending upon the quality of your ally's assistance. However, the discussion is interminable. The hour grows late, you must depart. And you do depart, with the discussion still vigorously in progress.[25]

Burke's domestic setting of rhetoric's historical scene is itself rhetorically shrewd. We are at home. Without flourish he sacrifices the usual Olympian grandeur that goes with such subjects in order to tell us that rhetoric and history are mostly just where we are, most of the time.

We enter a parlor and we are late—not by accident but by necessity. Others are already there, and they are so involved that they can't stop to fill us in. So we can't know what we would ideally like to know about the scene we've entered, but neither does anyone else, because no one was there, at the beginning, when the conversation started. No one is therefore qualified to "retrace" for us all the steps that have gone before. In fact, no one has ever been so qualified; strictly speaking, we aren't even allowed to say that the conversation "started." As in a dream, we find ourselves there: simply *there*. And we are late because, in dreams and in history, that is the way things are. We feel a pressure from the past exerting itself powerfully upon us through the conversation now taking place; whatever it is, nightmare or history, we are definitely in it. We didn't ask to be in it; we don't know what we think we need to know; and we can never know it. People make conversations, but this one is bigger than anybody. We feel burdened immensely; we are not the master.

Then we act; we just do. We *decide,* with what assurances Burke never says, because there are none to be given. We enter the conversation by putting in our "oar" (our "or"?). It matters not that no one in the room really knows, in the strict epistemological sense of "knowing," what is going on; or that no one who has ever been in the room ever knew. This is a conversation without epistemological "foundation" or "substance." The fact is that we are going to argue with one another, heatedly, and the argument is not going to come to a conclusion, ever, because more people, in similar states of historically burdened ignorance, are going to come into the room. The only thing that can come to conclusion is ourselves: "You must depart. And you do depart, with the discussion still vigorously in progress." Burke's fable for history has a double moral. History is a masterful, powerful process: it "makes" us, and yet, at the same time, at any moment in the process, our active willing "makes" the conversation, gives it the propulsive energy that forces it on. So even though we may feel "mastered," by putting in our oars we do two things: we help to shape our own experience of history *while providing the shape of things to come for those who will enter later,* after we are gone. Burke's fable is dialectical through and through. The scene of history and the scene of rhetoric are inseparable (in-"term"-inable).

Situated in a scene of history and willing that complicated, the rhetorical act as Burke understands it will imply other conditions no less fundamental, perhaps corollaries of its basic condition. Rhetoric's first condition constitutes something like an existential argument for freedom. Though he calls this a traditional principle of rhetoric, his point about freedom is compatible with Nietzsche's disposition, yet I do not see the new Nietzscheans paying any attention to it. In Burke's words: "Persuasion involves choice, will; it is directed to man only insofar as he is *free*. This is good to remember, in these days of dictatorship and near-dictatorship. Only insofar as men are potentially free, must the spellbinder seek to persuade them. Insofar as they *must* do something, rhetoric is unnecessary, its work being done by the nature of things, though often these necessities are not of a natural origin, but come from necessities imposed by man-made conditions . . . that sometimes [flow] from the nature of the 'free market.'"[26]

Determinism will permit no rhetoric. With its assumption of freedom, implicitly expressed in its every attempt to change the minds of others, rhetoric becomes the enemy, at least potentially, even of those perverse determinist schemes of thought and social organization that would employ rhetoric to defeat all willing. In Burke's provocative example, rhetoric itself subverts the naturalization of society, under the name of capitalism, that would submit us to the laws of political economy. Like Burke's antinomian aesthetic, rhetoric, rigorously pursued, will undermine any rigid and repressive scheme of living. Rhetoric is not the figural undoing of all action, as de Man claims in the name of Nietzsche: it is the very soul of action, potentially the good angel of change that could prevail against all determinist perversions of rhetoric. I do not say "it will," or "it must," because it is of the implicit nature of rhetoric to deny "it must" (even when it uses "it must" to accomplish its goals).

The second of rhetoric's conditions, Burke calls it "the characteristic invitation to rhetoric," involves a fundamental concern of social theory. Let us call it the potential for community. What characteristically invites rhetoric's activity is a social situation somewhere between pure identification of interests and absolute separation. In pure identification, while many kinds of human difference would remain, all differences of ideology would be resolved in a utopian commonality that would put us beyond the struggles that destroy the spirit. In utopian ideological identity there would be no need for rhetoric. "Likewise, there would be no strife in absolute separateness, since opponents can join battle only through a mediating ground that makes their communication possible, thus providing the first condition necessary for the exchange of blows." In absolute separateness there is no possibility for rhetoric. "But put identification and division ambiguously together, so that you cannot know for certain just where one ends and the other begins, and you have the characteristic invitation to rhetoric." In a world of agonistic stress, rhetoric would move inexorably toward the dream of perfect social organization, the achievement of which would cause rhetoric to self-destruct in the euphoria of real communion.[27]

But whose dream of community? Community founded, to cite Foucault's terms, upon a vertical, or a horizontal principle of human relations? Since the strategies of rhetoric are radically appropriable, since rhetoric as such favors no particular vision of community and the good life, those questions can have no *a priori* answers. Perfect community will require the elimination of the agon, but the word "elimination" is horribly ambiguous. Do we mean the "reconciliation" of agonistic elements through the healing power of a truly embracing human vision? Or do we mean "elimination" as exclusion, negation, exile, and murder? Since the dangerous game of rhetoric is open to all, since we are all always already involved: since, to come to an issue important to me, the historical fate and status of Marxism will not be decided by the irreversible narrative force of history (the appeal to teleology can only be a rhetorical ploy, a strategy perhaps worthy in times like ours, in the United States, when everything seems to be flowing the wrong way, when, therefore, we require patience and spiritual bracing—the appeal is not a reference to a promised end that must be), then the fate of Marxism will be decided by the active involvement of individuals in the great struggle of persuasion. To say this about the fate of socialism, that it will be decided in rhetorical war, is to say nothing especially specific to its vision. The fate of all visions, or nightmares, as the case may be, of the good life, will be similarly decided.

"Decided" is too weak: "chosen."

NOTES

1. Kenneth Burke, *Permanence and Change: An Anatomy of Purpose* (Los Altos, Calif.: Hermes Publications, 1954), p. 88.

2. Kenneth Burke, *A Rhetoric of Motives* (Berkeley and Los Angeles: University of California Press, 1969), p. 172.

3. Ibid., p. xiii.

4. *Permanence and Change,* p. 212.

5. Ibid., p. 40.

6. *A Rhetoric of Motives,* pp. 23, 146.

7. Ibid., p. 22.

8. Ibid., pp. 27–31, passim.

9. Ibid., p. 60.

10. See Frank Lentricchia, "Reading Foucault (Punishment, Labor, Resistance)," *Raritan* (Spring 1982), 5–32; (Summer 1982), 41–70.

11. *A Rhetoric of Motives,* pp. 27–28.

12. Ibid., p. 30.

13. Ibid., p. 28.

14. Kenneth Burke, *The Philosophy of Literary Form: Studies in Symbolic Action* (Berkeley and Los Angeles: University of California Press, 1973), pp. 1, 3–6, 18–19, 25–27, 109.

15. Ibid., p. 26.
16. Jacques Derrida, "Freud and the Scene of Writing," in *Writing and Difference*, trans. with an introduction by Alan Bass (Chicago: University of Chicago Press, 1978), p. 226.
17. *The Philosophy of Literary Form*, p. 26.
18. Ibid., p. 26n.
19. Ibid., pp. 61, 191.
20. Ibid., p. 61.
21. Ibid., p. 64.
22. Ibid., p. 63.
23. Ibid., pp. 191–220 ("The Rhetoric of Hitler's 'Battle'"), esp. p. 200.
24. *A Rhetoric of Motives*, p. xiii.
25. *The Philosophy of Literary Form*, pp. 110–11.
26. *A Rhetoric of Motives*, p. 50.
27. Ibid., p. 25.

Julia Kristeva
1941–

Julia Kristeva was born in Bulgaria in 1941. Her early training was in Russian and linguistics. In 1966 she went to Paris on a doctoral research fellowship. There her firsthand acquaintance with Marxist theory and practice as well as with the little-known work of Mikhail Bakhtin brought her to the attention of *Tel Quel*, the most prominent journal for the publication of structuralist criticism. She began publishing articles in *Tel Quel* in 1967, and later married its editor, the novelist Phillipe Sollers.

Kristeva's most important teacher during these early years was the renowned semiotician and critic Roland Barthes. Under his influence she was encouraged to pursue her interest in what she called "signifiance"—the process of how meaning is produced. Like Barthes she analyzed writing as a mode of production (of meaning) rather than as a mode of representation. She developed this approach in two works: *Semiotike* (1969) and her weighty doctoral thesis, *Revolution in Poetic Language: A Semiotic Approach to Literature* (published in 1980), which analyzes the processes and economies of meaning in modernist discourse.

"Word, Dialogue and the Novel" comes from this early phase of Kristeva's work. Written in 1966, published first in *Semiotike* and translated in *Desire in Language* (1980), it is a presentation and development of Bakhtin's theory of "linguistic dialogism." Whereas structuralism aims at a philosophical reduction of the literary sign to one fixed meaning, Bakhtin's approach opens up the literary text to a polyvalence more appropriate to its uniquely literary status. For Bakhtin the properly literary word or semantic unit must be seen as the locus of a plurality of dialogues occurring simultaneously on several different levels and extending in several different directions. The literary word represents a "dialogue among several writings: that of the writer, the addressee (or character) and the contemporary or earlier cultural context." That is to say that the meaning of a literary work is the constantly changing product of a series of dynamic relationships—between the writer and his cultural milieu, between the writer and his character(s), between the writer and his imagined reader(s), between the word chosen and the possible other words not chosen, and, perhaps most important, between the text and other texts, including other contemporary discourses, precursor texts, and rival texts. All these "others," however distant, are present in the literary work as the invisible interlocutors in response to whom the writer lifts his own voice. (This is the source of the now familiar concept of "intertextuality"—a term which Kristeva brought to Western Europe.)

For Bakhtin the greatest works of literature are those "polyphonic" novels (of Rabelais, Dostoevsky, Joyce) whose form is open enough to allow many of these different voices to speak at once. This sort of discourse, which Bakhtin calls "Menippean" in reference to an early form of Roman satire, is usually comic and has roots in the European folk traditions of carnival in which conventional "monologic," monolithic, and monotonous structures of authority are subverted and reversed. A serious consideration of Bakhtin's theory, Kristeva argues, would add a much-needed dynamism to structuralist approaches to literary language without necessarily abandoning structuralist ideas of objectivity and rigor.

In these earlier works Kristeva's concerns were explicitly political and revolutionary. But a trip to China with the *Tel Quel* group in April and May of 1974 disillusioned her with regard to communism as well as to the viability of large-scale political commitment. She turned increasingly toward what she saw as more private and particular issues of subjectivity—particularly the problem of feminine subjectivity in male-dominated discourses (as suggested in her 1977 book about her trip to China, *About Chinese Women*). The birth of her son in 1976 as well as her own involvement with psychoanalysis (first as analysand and then as analyst) contributed further to her shift toward psychological rather than political questions. Her more recent works, *Powers of Horror* (1982), *Tales of Love* (1987), and *In the Beginning Was Love: Psychoanalysis and Faith* (1987), draw upon her training in linguistics and semiotics to revive what she sees as neglected questions of speech, subjectivity, and emotion.

Word, Dialogue and Novel

If the efficacy of scientific approach in 'human' sciences has always been challenged, it is all the more striking that such a challenge should for the first time be issued on the very level of the structures being studied—structures supposedly answerable to a logic *other* than scientific.[1] What would be involved is the logic of language (and all the more so, of poetic language) that 'writing' has had the virtue of bringing to light. I have in mind that particular literary practice in which the elaboration of poetic meaning emerges as tangible, *dynamic gram*.[2] Confronted with this situation, then, literary semiotics can either abstain and remain silent, or persist in its efforts to elaborate a model that would be isomorphic to this other logic; that is, isomorphic to the elaboration of poetic meaning, a concern of primary importance to contemporary semiotics.

Russian Formalism, in which contemporary structural analysis claims to have its source, was itself faced with identical alternatives when reasons beyond literature and science halted its endeavors. Research was none the less carried on, recently coming to light in the work of Mikhail Bakhtin. His work represents one of that movement's most remarkable accomplishments, as well as one of the most powerful attempts to transcend its limitation. Bakhtin shuns the linguist's technical rigour, wielding an impulsive and at times even prophetic pen, while he takes on the fundamental problems presently confronting a structural analysis of narrative; this alone would give currency to essays written over forty years ago. Writer as well as 'scholar', Bakhtin was one of the first to replace the static hewing out of texts with a model where literary structure does not simply *exist* but is generated in relation to *another* structure. What allows a dynamic dimension to structuralism is his conception of the 'literary word' as an *intersection of textual surfaces* rather than a *point* (a fixed meaning), as a dialogue among several writings: that of the writer, the addressee (or the character) and the contemporary or earlier cultural context.

By introducing the *status of the word* as a minimal structural unit, Bakhtin situates the text within history and society, which are then seen as texts read by the writer, and into which he inserts himself by rewriting them. Diachrony is transformed into synchrony, and in light of this transformation, *linear history appears as abstraction*. The only way a writer can participate in history is by transgressing this abstraction through a process of reading-writing; that is, through the practice of a signifying structure in relation or opposition to another structure. History and morality are written and read within the infrastructure of texts. The poetic word, polyvalent and multi-determined, adheres to a logic exceeding that of codified discourse and fully comes into being only in the margins of recognized culture. Bakhtin was the first to study this logic, and he looked for its roots in *carnival*. Carnivalesque discourse breaks through the laws of a language censored by grammar and semantics and, at the same time, is a social and political protest. There is no equivalence, but rather, identity between challenging official linguistic codes and challenging official law.

THE WORD WITHIN THE SPACE OF TEXTS

Defining the specific status of the word as signifier for different modes of (literary) intellection within different genres or texts put poetic analysis at the sensitive centre of contemporary 'human' sciences—at the intersection of *language* (the true practice of thought)[3] with *space* (the volume within which signification, through a joining of differences, articulates itself). To investigate the status of the word is to study its articulations (as semic complex) with other words in the sentence, and then to look for the same functions or relationships at the articulatory level of larger sequences. Confronted with this spatial conception of language's poetic operation, we must first define the three dimensions of textual space where various semic sets and poetic sequences function. These three dimensions or coordinates of dialogue are writing subject, addressee and exterior texts. The word's status is thus defined *horizontally* (the word in the text belongs to both writing subject and addressee) as well as *vertically* (the word in the text is oriented towards an anterior or synchronic literary corpus).[4]

The addressee, however, is included within a book's discursive universe only as discourse itself. He thus fuses with this other discourse, this other book, in relation to which the writer has written his own text. Hence horizontal axis (subject-addressee) and vertical axis (text-context) coincide, bringing to light an important fact: each word (text) is an intersection of word (texts) where at least one other word (text) can be read. In Bakhtin's work, these two axes, which he calls *dialogue* and *ambivalence,* are not clearly distinguished. Yet, what appears as a lack of rigour is in fact an insight first introduced into literary theory by Bakhtin: any text is constructed as a mosaic of quotations; any text is the absorption and transformation of another. The notion of *intertextuality*[5] replaces that of intersubjectivity, and poetic language is read as at least *double*.

The word as minimal textual unit thus turns out to occupy the status of *mediator,* linking structural models to cultural (historical) environment, as well as that of *regulator,* controlling mutations from diachrony to synchrony, i.e., to literary structure. The word is spatialized: through the very notion of status, it functions in three dimensions (subject-addressee-context) as a set of *dialogical,* semic elements or as a set of *ambivalent* elements. Consequently the task of literary semiotics is to discover other formalisms corresponding to different modalities of word-joining (sequences) within the dialogical space of texts.

Any description of a word's specific operation within different literary genres or texts thus requires a *translinguistic* procedure. First, we must think of literary genres as imperfect semiological systems 'signifying beneath the surface of language but never without it': and secondly, discover relations among larger narrative units such as sentences, questions-and-answers, dialogues, etc., not necessarily on the basis of linguistic models—justified by the principle of semantic expansion. We could thus posit and demonstrate the hypothesis that *any evolution of literary genres is an unconscious exteriorization of linguistic structures at their different levels*. The novel in particular exteriorizes linguistic dialogue.[6]

WORD AND DIALOGUE

Russian Formalists were engrossed with the idea of 'linguistic dialogue'. They insisted on the dialogical character of linguistic communication[7] and considered the monologue, the 'embryonic form' of *common* language,[8] as subsequent to dialogue. Some of them distinguished between monological discourse (as 'equivalent to a psychic state')[9] and narrative (as 'artistic imitation of monological discourse').[10] Boris Eikhenbaum's famous study of Gogol's *The Overcoat* is based on such premises. Eikhenbaum notes that Gogol's text actively refers to an oral form of narration and to its linguistic characteristics (intonation, syntactic construction of oral discourse, pertinent vocabulary, and so on). He thus sets up two modes of narration, *indirect* and *direct,* studying the relationship between the two. Yet he seems to be unaware that before referring to an *oral* discourse, the writer of the narrative usually refers to the discourse of an *other* whose oral discourse is only secondary (since the other is the carrier of oral discourse).[11]

For Bakhtin, the dialogue-monologue distinction has a much larger significance than the concrete meaning accorded it by the Russian Formalists. It does not correspond to the *direct/indirect* (monologue/dialogue) distinction in narratives or plays. For Bakhtin, dialogue can be monological, and what is called monologue can be dialogical. With him, such terms refer to a linguistic infrastructure that must be studied through a *semiotics* of literary texts. This semiotics cannot be based on either linguistic methods or logical givens, but rather, must be elaborated from the point where they leave off.

> Linguistics studies 'language' and its specific logic in its *commonality* (*'obshchnost'*) as that factor which makes dialogical intercourse *possible,* but it consistently refrains from studying those dialogical relationships themselves . . . Dialogical relationships are not reducible to logical or concrete semantic relationships, which are in and of *themselves* devoid of any dialogical aspect . . . Dialogical relationships are totally impossible without logical and concrete semantic relationships, but they are not reducible to them; they have their own specificity.[12]

While insisting on the difference between dialogical relationships and specifically linguistic ones, Bakhtin emphasizes that those structuring a narrative (for example, writer/character, to which we would add subject of enunciation/subject of utterance) are possible because dialogism is inherent in language itself. Without explaining exactly what makes up this double aspect of language, he none the less insists that 'dialogue is the only sphere possible for the life of language'. Today we can detect dialogical relationships on several levels of language: first, within the *combinative* dyad, langue/parole; and secondly, within the systems either of langue (as collective, monological contracts as well as systems of correlative value actualized in dialogue with the other) or of parole (as essentially 'combinative', not pure creation, but individual formation based on the exchange of signs).

On still another level (which could be compared to the novel's ambivalent space), this 'double character of language' has even been demonstrated as syntagmatic (made manifest through extension, presence and metonymy) and systematic (manifested through association, absence and metaphor). It would be important to analyse linguistically the dialogical exchanges between these two axes of language as basis of the novel's ambivalence. We should also note Jakobson's double structures and their overlappings within the code/message relationship,[13] which help to clarify Bakhtin's notion of dialogism as inherent in language.

Bakhtin foreshadows what Emile Benveniste has in mind when he speaks about *discourse*, that is 'language appropriated by the individual as a practice'. As Bakhtin himself writes, 'In order for dialogical relationships to arise among [logical or concrete semantic relationships], they must clothe themselves in the word, become utterances, and become the positions of various subjects, expressed in a word.'[14] Bakhtin, however, born of a revolutionary Russia that was preoccupied with social problems, does not see dialogue only as language assumed by a subject; he sees it, rather, as a *writing* where one reads the *other* (with no allusion to Freud). Bakhtinian dialogism identifies writing as both subjectivity and communication, or better, as intertextuality. Confronted with this dialogism, the notion of a 'person-subject of writing' becomes blurred, yielding to that of 'ambivalence of writing'.

AMBIVALENCE

The term 'ambivalence' implies the insertion of history (society) into a text and of this text into history; for the writer, they are one and the same. When he speaks of 'two paths merging within the narrative', Bakhtin considers writing as a reading of the anterior literary corpus and the text as an absorption of and a reply to another text. He studies the polyphonic novel as an absorption of the carnival and the monological novel as a stifling of this literary structure, which he calls 'Menippean' because of its dialogism. In this perspective, a text cannot be grasped through linguistics alone. Bakhtin postulates the necessity for what he calls a *translinguistic* science, which, developed on the basis of language's dialogism, would enable us to understand intertextual *relationships;* relationships that the nineteenth century labelled 'social value' or literature's moral 'message'. Lautréamont wanted to write so that he could submit himself to a *high morality*. Within his practice, this morality is actualized as textual ambivalence: *The Songs of Maldoror* and the *Poems* are a constant dialogue with the preceding literary corpus, a perpetual challenge of past writing. Dialogue and ambivalence are borne out as the only approach that permits the writer to enter history by espousing an ambivalent ethics: negation as affirmation.

Dialogue and ambivalence lead me to conclude that, within the interior space of the text as well as within the space of *texts,* poetic language is a 'double'. Saussure's poetic *paragram* ('Anagrams') extends from *zero* to *two:* the unit 'one' (definition, 'truth') does not exist in this field. Consequently, the notions of definition, determination, the sign '=' and the very concept of sign, which presuppose a vertical (hierarchical) division between signifier and signified, cannot be applied to poetic language—by defining an infinity of pairings and combinations.

The notion of *sign* (Sr-Sd) is a product of scientific abstraction (identity-substance-cause-goal as structure of the Indo-European sentence), designating a vertically and hierarchically linear division. The notion of *double,* the result of thinking over poetic (not scientific) language, denotes 'spatialization' and correlation of the literary (linguistic) sequence. This implies that the minimal unit of poetic language is at least *double,* not in the sense of the signifier/signified dyad, but rather, in terms of *one and other*. It suggests that poetic language functions as a *tabular model,* where each 'unit' (this word can no longer be used without quotation marks, since every unit is double) acts as a multi-determined *peak*. The *double* would be the minimal sequence of a paragrammatic semiotics to be worked out starting from the work of Saussure (in the 'Anagrams') and Bakhtin.

Instead of carrying these thoughts to their conclusion we shall concentrate here on one of their consequences: the inability of any logical system based on a zero-one sequence (true-false, nothingness-notation) to account for the operation of poetic language.

Scientific procedures are indeed based upon a logical approach, itself founded on the Greek (Indo-European) sentence. Such a sentence begins as subject-predicate and grows by identification, determination and causality. Modern logic from Gottlob Frege and Giuseppe Peano to Jan Lukasiewicz, Robert Ackermann and Alonzo Church evolves out of a 0–1 sequence; George Boole, who begins with set theory, produces formulae that are more isomorphic with language—all of these are ineffective within the realm of poetic language, where 1 is not a limit.

It is therefore impossible to formalize poetic language according to existing logical (scientific) procedures without distorting it. A literary semiotics must be developed on the basis of a *poetic logic* where the concept of the *power of the continuum* would embody the 0–2 interval, a continuity where 0 denotes and 1 is implicitly transgressed.

Within this 'power of the continuum' from 0 to a specifically poetic double, the linguistic, psychic and social 'prohibition' is 1 (God, Law, Definition). The only linguistic practice to 'escape' this prohibition is poetic discourse. It is no accident that the shortcomings of Aristotelian logic when applied to language were pointed out by, on the one hand, twentieth-century Chinese philosopher Chang Tung-Sun (the product of a different linguistic heritage—ideograms—where, in place of God, there extends the Yin-Yang 'dialogue') and, on the other, Bakhtin (who attempted to go beyond the Formalists through a dynamic theorization accomplished in revolutionary society). With Bakhtin, who assimilates narrative discourse into epic discourse, narrative is a prohibition, a *monologism*, a subordination of the code to 1, to God. Hence, the epic is religious and theological; all 'realist' narrative obeying 0–1 logic is dogmatic. The realist novel, which Bakhtin calls monological (Tolstoy), tends to evolve within this space. Realist description, definition of 'personality', 'character' creation and 'subject' development—all are descriptive narrative elements belonging to the 0–1 interval and are thus *monological*. The only discourse integrally to achieve the 0–2 poetic logic is that of the carnival. By adopting a dream logic, it transgresses rules of linguistic code and social morality as well.

In fact, this 'transgression' of linguistic, logical and social codes within the carnivalesque only exists and succeeds, of course, because it accepts *another law*. Dialogism is not 'freedom to say everything', it is a *dramatic* 'banter' (Lautréamont), an *other* imperative than that of 0. We should particularly emphasize this specificity of dialogue as *transgression giving itself a law* so as radically and categorically to distinguish it from the pseudo-transgression evident in a certain modern 'erotic' and parodic literature. The latter, seeing itself as 'libertine' and 'relativizing', operates according to a principle of *law anticipating its own transgression*. It thus compensates for monologism, does not displace the 0–1 interval nor has anything to do with the architectonics of dialogism, which implies a categorical tearing from the norm and a relationship of non-exclusive opposites.

The novel incorporating carnivalesque structure is called *polyphonic*. Bakhtin's examples include Rabelais, Swift and Dostoevsky. We might also add the 'modern' novel of the twentieth century—Joyce, Proust, Kafka—while specifying that the modern polyphonic novel, although analogous in its status, where monologism is concerned, to dialogical novels of the past, is clearly marked off from them. A break occurred at the end of the nineteenth century: while dialogue in Rabelais, Swift and Dostoevsky remains at a representative, fictitious level, our century's polyphonic novel becomes 'unreadable' (Joyce) and interior to language (Proust, Kafka). Beginning with this break—not only literary but also social, political and philosophical in nature—the problem of intertextuality (intertextual dialogue) appears as such. Bakhtin's theory itself (as well as that of Saussure's 'Anagrams') can be traced historically to this break: he was able to discover textual dialogism in the writings of Mayakovsky, Khlebnikov and Andrei Bely, to mention only a few of the Revolution's writers who made the outstanding imprints of this scriptural break. Bakhtin then extended his theory into literary history as a principle of all upheavals and defiant productivity.

Bakhtin's term *dialogism* as a semic complex thus implies the double, language, and another logic. Using that as point of departure, we can outline a new approach to poetic texts. Literary semiotics can accept the word 'dialogism'; the logic of *distance* and *relationship* between the different units of a sentence or narrative structure, indicating a *becoming*—in opposition to the level of continuity and substance, both of which obey the logic of being and are thus monological. Secondly, it is a logic of *analogy* and *non-exclusive opposition,* opposed to monological levels of causality and identifying determination. Finally, it is a logic of the 'transfinite', a concept borrowed from Georg Cantor, which, on the basis of poetic language's 'power of the continuum' (0–2), introduces a second principle of formation: a poetic sequence is a 'next-larger' (not causally deduced) to all preceding sequences of the Aristotelian chain (scientific, monological or narrative). The novel's ambivalent space thus can be seen as regulated by two formative principles: monological (each following sequence is determined by the preceding one), and dialogical (transfinite sequences that are next-larger to the preceding causal series).[15]

Dialogue appears most clearly in the structure of carnivalesque language, where symbolic relationships and analogy take precedence over substance-causality connections. The notion of *ambivalence* pertains to the permutation of the two spaces observed in novelistic structure: dialogical space and monological space.

From a conception of poetic language as dialogue and ambivalence, Bakhtin moves to a re-evaluation of the novel's structure. This investigation takes the form of a classification of words within the narrative—the classification being then linked to a typology of discourse.

CLASSIFICATION OF WORDS WITHIN THE NARRATIVE

According to Bakhtin, there are three categories of words within the narrative.

First, the *direct* word, referring back to its object, expresses the last possible degree of signification by the subject of discourse within the limits of a given context. It is the annunciating, expressive word of the writer, the *denotative* word, which is supposed to provide him with direct, objective comprehension. It knows nothing but itself and its object, to which it attempts to be adequate (it is not 'conscious' of the influences of words foreign to it).

Second, the *object-oriented* word is the direct discourse of 'characters'. It has direct, objective meaning, but is not situated on the same level as the writer's discourse; thus, it is at some distance from the latter. It is both oriented towards its object and is itself the object of the writer's orientation. It is a foreign word, subordinate to the narrative word as object of the writer's comprehension. But the writer's orientation towards the word as object does not penetrate it but accepts it as a whole, changing neither meaning nor tonality; it subordinates that word to its own task, introducing no other signification. Consequently, the object-oriented word, having become the object of an another (denotative) word, is not 'conscious' of it. The object-oriented word, like the denotative word, is therefore univocal.

In the third instance, however, the writer can use another's word, giving it a new meaning while retaining the meaning it already had. The result is a word with two significations: it becomes *ambivalent*. This ambivalent word is therefore the result of a joining of two sign-systems. Within the evolution of genres, ambivalent words appear in Menippean and carnivalesque texts (I shall return to this point). The forming of two sign-systems relativizes the text. Stylizing effects establish a distance with regard to the word of another—contrary to *imitation* (Bakhtin, rather, has in mind *repetition*), which takes what is imitated (repeated) seriously, claiming and appropriating it without relativizing it. This category of ambivalent words is characterized by the writer's exploitation of another's speech—without running counter to its thought—for his own purposes; he follows its direction while relativizing it. A second category of ambivalent words, *parody* for instance, proves to be quite different. Here the writer introduces a signification opposed to that of the other's word. A third type of ambivalent word, of which the *hidden interior polemic* is an example, is characterized by the active (modifying) influence of another's word on the writer's word. It is the writer who 'speaks', but a foreign discourse is constantly present in the speech that it distorts. With this *active* kind of ambivalent word, the other's word is represented by the word of the narrator. Examples include autobiography, polemical confessions, questions-and-answers and hidden dialogue. The novel is the only genre in which ambivalent words appear; that is the specific characteristic of its structure.

THE INHERENT DIALOGISM OF DENOTATIVE OR HISTORICAL WORDS

The notion of univocity or objectivity of monologue and of the epic to which it is assimilated, or of the denotative object-oriented word, cannot withstand psychoanalytic or semantic analysis of language. Dialogism is coextensive with the deep structures of discourse. Notwithstanding Bakhtin and Benveniste, dialogism appears on the level of the Bakhtinian denotative word as a principle of every enunciation, as well as on the level of the 'story' in Benveniste. The story, like Benveniste's concept of 'discourse' itself, presupposes an intervention by the speaker within the narrative as well as an orientation towards the other. In order to describe the dialogism inherent in the denotative or historical word, we would have to turn to the psychic aspect of writing as trace of a dialogue with oneself (with another), as a writer's distance from himself, as a splitting of the writer into subject of enunciation and subject of utterance.

By the very act of narrating, the subject of narration addresses an other; narration is structured in relation to this other. (On the strength of such a communication, Francis Ponge offers his own variation of 'I think therefore I am': 'I speak and you hear me, therefore we are.' He thus postulates a shift from subjectivism to ambivalence.) Consequently, we may consider narration (beyond the signifier/signified relationship) as a dialogue between the *subject* of narration (S) and the *addressee* (A)—the other. This addressee, quite simply the reading subject, represents a doubly oriented entity: signifier in his relation to the text and signified in the relation between the subject of narration and himself. This entity is thus a dyad (A_1 and A_2) whose two terms, communicating with each other, constitute a code-system. The subject of narration (S) is drawn in, and therefore reduced to a code, to a non-person, to an *anonymity* (as writer, subject of enunciation) mediated by a third person, the *he/she* character, the subject of utterance. The writer is thus the subject of narration transformed by his having included himself within the narrative system; he is neither nothingness nor anybody, but the possibility of permutation from S to A, from story to discourse and from discourse to story. He becomes an anonymity, an absence, a blank space, thus permitting the structure to exist as such. At the very origin of narration, at the very moment when the writer appears, we experience emptiness. We see the problems of death, birth and sex appear when literature touches upon this strategic point that writing becomes when it exteriorizes linguistic systems through narrative structure (genres). On the basis of this anonymity, this zero where the author is situated, the *he/she* of the character is born. At a later stage, it will become a *proper name* (N). Therefore, in a literary text, O does not exist; emptiness is quickly replaced by a 'one' (a *he/she*, or a *proper name*) that is really twofold, since it is subject and addressee. It is the addressee, the other, exteriority (whose object is the subject of narration and who is at the same time represented and representing) who transforms the subject into an *author*. That is, who has the S pass through this zero-stage of negation, of exclusion, constituted by the author. In this coming-and-going movement between subject and other, between writer (W) and reader, the author is structured as a signifier and the text is a dialogue of two discourses.

The constitution of characters (of 'personality') also permits a disjunction of S into S_r (subject of enunciation) and S_d (subject of utterance). A diagram of this mutation would appear as diagram 1. This diagram incorporates the structure of the pronominal system[16] that

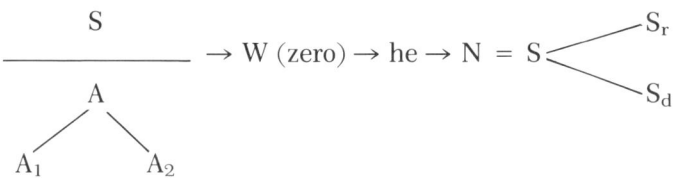

Diagram 1

psychoanalysts repeatedly find in the discourse of the object of psychoanalysis (see diagram 2).

$$\frac{\dfrac{\dfrac{I}{he_1}}{he_o}}{(some)\ one} \qquad \frac{\dfrac{\dfrac{S}{N}}{S_r}}{S_d}$$

Diagram 2

At the level of the text (of the signifier)—in the S_r–S_d relationship—we find this dialogue of the subject with the addressee around which every narration is structured. The subject of utterance, in relation to the subject of enunciation, plays the role of addressee with respect to the subject; it inserts the subject of enunciation within the writing system by making the latter pass through emptiness. Mallarmé called this operation 'elocutionary disappearance'.

The *subject of utterance* is both representative of the subject of enunciation and represented as object of the subject of enunciation. It is therefore commutable with the writer's anonymity. A *character* (a personality) is constituted by this generation of a double entity starting from zero. The subject of utterance is 'dialogical', both S and A are disguised within it.

The procedure I have just described in confronting narration and the novel now abolishes distinctions between signifier and signified. It renders these concepts ineffective for that literary practice operating uniquely within dialogical signifier(s). 'The signifier represents the subject for another signifier' (Lacan).

Narration, therefore, is always constituted as a dialogical matrix by the receiver to whom this narration refers. Any narration, including history and science, contains this dialogical dyad formed by the narrator in conjunction with the other. It is translated through the dialogical S_r/S_d relationship, with S_r and S_d filling the roles of signifier and signified in turns, but constituting merely a permutation of two signifiers.

It is, however, only through certain narrative structures that this dialogue—this hold on the sign as double, this ambivalence of writing—is exteriorized in the actual organization of poetic discourse on the level of textual literary occurrence.

TOWARDS A TYPOLOGY OF DISCOURSES

Bakhtin's radical undertaking—the dynamic analysis of texts resulting in a redistribution of genres—calls upon us to be just as radical in developing a typology of discourses.

As it is used by the Formalists, the term *'narrative'* is too ambiguous to cover all of the genres it supposedly designates. At least two different types of narrative can be isolated.

We have on the one hand *monological discourse,* including, first, the representative mode of description and narration (the epic); secondly, historical discourse; and thirdly, scientific discourse. In all three, the subject both assumes and submits to the rule of 1 (God). The dialogue inherent in all discourse is smothered by a *prohibition*, a censorship, such that this discourse refuses to turn back upon itself, to enter into dialogue with itself. To present the models of this censorship is to describe the nature of the differences between two types of discourse: the epic type (history and science) and the Menippean type (carnivalesque writings and novel), which transgresses prohibition. Monological discourse corresponds to Jakobson's systematic axis of language, and its analogous relationship to grammatical affirmation and negation has also been noted.

On the other hand, *dialogical discourse* includes carnivalesque and Menippean discourses as well as the polyphonic novel. In its structures, writing reads another writing, reads itself and constructs itself through a process of destructive genesis.

EPIC MONOLOGISM

The *epic*, structured at the limits of syncretism, illustrates the double value of words in their post-syncretic phase: the utterance of a subject ('I') inevitably penetrated by language as carrier of the concrete, universal, individual and collective. But in an epic, the speaker (subject of the epic) does not make use of another's speech. The dialogical play of language as correlation of signs—the dialogical permutation of two signifiers for one signified—takes place on the level of *narration* (through the denotative word, or through the inherency of the text). It does not exteriorize itself at the level of textual *manifestation* as in the structure of novels. This is the scheme at work within an epic, with no hint as yet of Bakhtin's problematic—the ambivalent word. The organizational principle of epic structure thus remains monological. The dialogue of language does not manifest itself except within a narrative infrastructure. There is no dialogue at the level of the apparent textual organization (historical enunciation/discursive enunciation); the two aspects of enunciation remain limited by the narrator's absolute point of view, which coincides with the wholeness of a god or community. Within epic monologism, we detect the presence of the 'transcendental signified' and 'self presence' as highlighted by Jacques Derrida.

It is the systematic mode of language (similarity, according to Jakobson) that prevails within the epic space. Metonymic contiguity, specific to the syntagmatic axis of language, is rare. Of course, association and metonymy are there as rhetorical figures, but they are never a principle of structural organization. Epic logic pursues the general through the specific; it thus assumes a hierarchy within the structure of substance. Epic logic is therefore causal, that is, theological; it is a *belief* in the literal sense of the word.

THE CARNIVAL: A HOMOLOGY BETWEEN THE BODY, DREAM, LINGUISTIC STRUCTURE AND STRUCTURES OF DESIRE

Carnivalesque structure is like the residue of a cosmogony that ignored substance, causality or identity outside its link to the whole, *which exists only in or through relationship*. This carnivalesque cosmogony has persisted in the form of an anti-theological (but not anti-mystical) and deeply popular movement. It remains present as an often misunderstood and persecuted substratum of official Western culture throughout its entire history; it is most noticeable in folk games as well as in medieval theatre and prose (anecdotes, fables and the *Roman de Renart*). As composed of distances, relationships, analogies and non-exclusive oppositions, it is essentially dialogical. It is a spectacle, but without a stage; a game, but also a daily undertaking; a signifier, but also a signified. That is, two texts meet, contradict and relativize each other. A carnival participant is both actor and spectator; he loses his sense of individuality, passes thorough a zero point of carnivalesque activity and splits into a subject of the spectacle and an object of the game. Within the carnival, the subject is reduced to nothingness, while the structure of *the author* emerges as anonymity that creates and sees itself created as self and other, as man and mask. The cynicism of this carnivalesque scene, which destroys a god in order to impose its own dialogical laws, calls to mind Nietzsche's Dionysianism. The carnival first exteriorizes the structure of reflective literary productivity, then inevitably brings to light this structure's underlying unconscious: sexuality and death. Out of the dialogue that is established between them, the structural dyads of carnival appear: high and low, birth and agony, food and excrement, praise and curses, laughter and tears.

Figures germane to carnivalesque language, including repetition, 'inconsequent' statements (which are none the less 'connected' within an infinite context) and non-exclusive opposition, which function as empty sets or disjunctive additions, produce a more flagrant dialogism than any other discourse. Disputing the laws of language based on the 0–1 interval, the carnival challenges God, authority and social law; so far as it is dialogical, it is rebellious. Because of its subversive discourse, the word 'carnival' has understandably acquired a strongly derogatory or narrowly burlesque meaning in our society.

The scene of the carnival, where there is no stage, no 'theatre', is thus both stage and life, game and dream, discourse and spectacle. By the same token, it is proffered as the only space in which language escapes linearity (law) to live as drama in three dimensions. At a deeper level, this also signifies the contrary: drama becomes located in language. A major principle thus emerges: all poetic discourse is dramatization, dramatic permutation (in a mathematical sense) of words. Within carnivalesque discourse, we can already adumbrate that 'as to mental condition, it is like the meanderings of drama' (Mallarmé). This scene, whose symptom is carnivalesque discourse, is the only dimension where 'theatre might be the reading of a book, its writing in operation'. In other words, such a scene is the only place where discourse attains its 'potential infinity' (to use David Hilbert's term), where prohibitions (representation, 'monologism') and their transgression (dream, body, 'dialogism') coexist. Carnivalesque tradition was absorbed into Menippean discourse and put into practice by the polyphonic novel.

On the omnified stage of carnival, language parodies and relativizes itself, repudiating its role in representation; in so doing, it provokes laughter but remains incapable of detaching itself from representation. The syntagmatic axis of language becomes exteriorized in this space and, through dialogue with the systematic axis, constitutes the ambivalent structure bequeathed by carnival to the novel. Faulty (by which I mean ambivalent), both representative and anti-representative, the carnivalesque structure is anti-Christian and anti-rationalist. All of the most important polyphonic novels are inheritors of the Menippean, carnivalesque structure: those of Rabelais, Cervantes, Swift, Sade, Balzac, Lautréamont, Dostoevsky, Joyce and Kafka. Its history is the history of the struggle against Christianity and its representation; this means an exploration of language (of sexuality and death), a consecration of ambivalence and of 'vice'.

The word 'carnivalesque' lends itself to an ambiguity one must avoid. In contemporary society, it generally connotes parody, hence a strengthening of the law. There is a tendency to blot out the carnival's *dramatic* (murderous, cynical and revolutionary in the sense of *dialectical transformation*) aspects, which Bakhtin emphasized, and which he recognized in Menippean writings or in Dostoevsky. The laughter of the carnival is not simply parodic; it is no more comic than tragic; it is both at once, one might say that it is *serious*. This is the only way that it can avoid becoming either the scene of law or the scene of its parody, in order to become the scene of its *other*. Modern writing offers several striking examples of this omnified scene that is both *law* and *others*—where *laughter* is silenced because it is not parody but *murder* and *revolution* (Antonin Artaud).

The epic and the carnivalesque are the two currents that formed European narrative, one taking precedence over the other according to the times and the writer. The carnivalesque tradition of the people is still apparent in personal literature of late antiquity and has remained, to this day, the life source reanimating literary thought, orienting it towards new perspectives.

Classical humanism helped dissolve the epic monologism that speech welded together so well, and that orators, rhetoricians and politicians, on the one hand, tragedy and epic, on the other, implemented so effectively. Before another monologism could take root (with the triumph of formal logic, Christianity and Renaissance humanism),[17] late antiquity gave birth to two genres that reveal language's dialogism. Situated within the carnivalesque tradition, and constituting the yeast of the European novel, these two genres are *Socratic dialogue* and *Menippean discourse*.

SOCRATIC DIALOGUE: DIALOGISM AS A DESTRUCTION OF THE PERSON

Socratic dialogue was widespread in antiquity: Plato, Xenophon, Antisthenes, Aeschines, Phaedo, Euclid and others excelled in it, although only the dialogues of Plato and Xenophon have come down to us. Not as much rhetorical in genre as popular and carnivalesque, it was originally a kind of memoir (the recollections of Socrates' discussions with his students) that broke away from the constraints of history, retaining only the Socratic process of dialogically revealing truth, as well as the structure of a recorded dialogue framed by narrative. Nietzsche accused Plato of having ignored Dionysian tragedy, but Socratic dialogue had adopted the dialogical and defiant structure of the carnivalesque scene. According to Bakhtin, Socratic dialogues are characterized by opposition to any official monologism claiming to possess a ready-made truth. Socratic truth ('meaning') is the product of a dialogical relationship among speakers; it is correlational and its relativism appears by virtue of the observers' autonomous points of view. Its art is one of *articulation* of fantasy, *correlation* of signs. Two typical devices for triggering this linguistic network are syncrisis (confronting different discourses on the same topic) and anacrusis (one word prompting another). The subjects of discourse are non-persons, anonyms, hidden by the discourse constituting them. Bakhtin reminds us that the 'event' of Socratic dialogue is of the nature of discourse: a questioning and testing, through speech, of a definition. This speech practice is therefore organically linked to the man who created it (Socrates and his students), or better, speech *is* man and his activity. Here, one can speak of a practice possessing a synthetic character; the process separating the *word* as act, as apodeictic practice, as articulation of difference from the *image* as representation, as knowledge and as idea was not yet complete when Socratic dialogue took form. But there is an important 'detail' to Socratic dialogism; it is the exclusive position of a subject of discourse that provokes the dialogue. In the *Apology* of Plato, Socrates' trial and the period of awaiting judgement determine his discourse as the confessions of a man 'on the threshold'. The exclusive situation liberates the word from any univocal objectivity, from any representative function, opening it up to the symbolic sphere. Speech affronts death, measuring itself against another discourse; this dialogue counts the *person* out.

The resemblance between Socratic dialogue and the ambivalent word of the novel is obvious.

Socratic dialogue did not last long, but it gave birth to several dialogical genres, including *Menippean discourse,* whose origins also lie in carnivalesque folklore.

MENIPPEAN DISCOURSE:
THE TEXT AS SOCIAL ACTIVITY

1   Menippean discourse takes its name from Menippus of Gadara, a philosopher of the third century BC. His satires were lost, but we know of their existence through the writings of Diogenes Laertius. The term was used by the Romans to designate a genre of the first century BC (Marcus Terentius Varro's *Satirae Menippeae*).

Yet the genre actually appeared much earlier; its first representative was perhaps Antisthenes, a student of Socrates and one of the writers of Socratic dialogue. Heraclitus also wrote Menippean texts (according to Cicero, he created an analogous genre called *logistoricus*); Varro gave it definite stability.

Other examples include Seneca the Younger's *Apocolocynthosis*, Petronius' *Satyricon*, Lucan's satires, Ovid's *Metamorphoses*, Hippocrates' *Novel*, various samples of Greek 'novels', classical utopian novels and Roman (Horatian) satire. Within the Menippean sphere there evolve diatribe, soliloquy and other minor genres of controversy. It greatly influenced Christian and Byzantine literature; in various forms, it survived through the Middle Ages, the Renaissance and the Reformation through to the present (the novels of Joyce, Kafka and Bataille). This carnivalesque genre—as pliant and variable as Proteus, capable of insinuating itself into other genres—had an enormous influence on the development of European literature and especially the formation of the novel.

Menippean discourse is both comic and tragic, or rather, it is *serious* in the same sense as is the carnivalesque; through the status of its words, it is politically and socially disturbing. It frees speech from historical constraints, and this entails a thorough boldness in philosophical and imaginative inventiveness. Bakhtin emphasizes that 'exclusive' situations increase freedom of language in Menippean discourse. Phantasmagoria and an often mystical symbolism fuse with macabre naturalism. Adventures unfold in brothels, robbers' dens, taverns, fairgrounds and prisons, among erotic orgies and during sacred worship, and so forth. The word has no fear of incriminating itself. It becomes free from presupposed 'values'; without distinguishing between virtue and vice, and without distinguishing itself from them, the word considers them its private domain, as one of its creations. Academic problems are pushed aside in favour of the 'ultimate' problems of existence: this discourse orients liberated language towards philosophical universalism. Without distinguishing ontology from cosmogony, it unites them into a practical philosophy of life. Elements of the fantastic, which never appear in epic or tragic works, crop forth here. For example, an unusual perspective from above changes the scale of observation in Lucan's *Icaromenippea*, Varro's *Endymion* and later in the works of Rabelais, Swift and Voltaire. Pathological states of the soul, such as madness, split personalities, daydreams, dreams and death, become part of the narrative (they affect the writing of Shakespeare and Calderón). According to Bakhtin, these elements have more structural than thematic significance; they destroy man's epic and tragic unity as well as his belief in identity and causality; they indicate that he has lost his totality and no longer coincides with himself. At the same time, they often appear as an exploration of language and writing: in Varro's *Bimarcus*, the two Marcuses discuss whether or not one should write in tropes. Menippean discourse tends towards the scandalous and eccentric in language. The 'inopportune' expression, with its cynical frankness, its desecration of the sacred and its attack on etiquette, is quite characteristic. This discourse is made up of contrasts: virtuous courtesans, generous bandits, wise men that are both free and enslaved, and so on. It uses abrupt transitions and changes; high and low, rise and fall, and misalliances of all kinds. Its language seems fascinated with the 'double' (with its own activity as graphic *trace*, doubling an 'outside') and with the logic of opposition replacing that of identity in defining terms. It is an all-inclusive genre, put together as a pavement of citations. It includes all genres (short stories, letters, speeches, mixtures of verse and prose) whose structural signification is to denote the writer's distance from his own and other texts. The multi-stylism and multi-tonality of this discourse and the dialogical status of its word explain why it has been impossible for classicism, or for any other authoritarian society, to express itself in a novel descended from Menippean discourse.

Put together as an exploration of the body, dreams and language, this writing grafts on to the topical: it is a kind of political journalism of its time. Its discourse exteriorizes political and ideological conflicts of the moment. The dialogism of its words *is* practical philosophy doing battle against idealism and religious metaphysics, against the epic. It constitutes the social and political thought of an era fighting against theology, against law.

2 Menippean discourse is thus structured as ambivalence, as the focus for two tendencies of Western literature: representation through language as staging, and exploration of language as a correlative system of signs. Language in the Menippean tradition is both representation of exterior space and 'an experience that produces its own space'. In this ambiguous genre appear, first, the *premises of realism* (a secondary activity in relation to what is lived, where man describes himself by making of himself an exhibition, finally creating 'characters' and 'personalities'); and secondly the *refusal to define* a psychic universe (an immediately present activity, characterized by images, gestures and word-gestures through which man lives his limits in the impersonal). This second aspect relates Menippean structure to the structure of dreams and hieroglyphic writing or, possibly, to the theatre of cruelty as conceived by Artaud. His words apply equally; Menippean discourse 'is not equal to individual life, to that individual aspect of life where characters triumph, but rather to a kind of liberated life that sweeps away human individuality and where man is no more than a reflected image.' Likewise, the Menippean experience is not cathartic; it is a festival of cruelty, but also a political act. It transmits no fixed message except that itself should be 'the eternal joy of becoming', and it exhausts itself in the act and in the present. Born after Socrates, Plato and the Sophists, it belongs to an age when thought ceases to be practice; the fact that it is considered as a *techne* shows that the *praxis-poiesis* separation has already taken place. Similarly, literature becoming 'thought' becomes conscious of itself as *sign*. Man, alienated from nature and society, becomes alienated from himself, discovering his 'interior' and 'reifying' this discovery in the ambivalence of Menippean writing. Such tokens are the harbingers of realist representation. Menippean discourse, however, knows nothing of a theological principle's monologism (or of the Renaissance man-God) that could have consolidated its representative aspect. The 'tyranny' it is subjected to is that of text (not speech as reflection of a pre-existing universe), or rather its own structure, constructing and understanding itself through itself. It constructs itself as a *hieroglyph,* all the while remaining a spectacle. It bequeaths this ambivalence to the novel, above all to the polyphonic novel, which knows neither law nor hierarchy, since it is a plurality of linguistic elements in dialogical relationships. The conjunctive principle of the different parts of Menippean dis-

course is certainly *similitude* (resemblance, dependence and therefore 'realism'), but also contiguity (analogy, juxtaposition and therefore 'rhetoric'—not in Benedetto Croce's sense of ornament, but rather, as justification through and in language). Menippean ambivalence consists of communication between two spaces:[18] that of the scene and that of the hieroglyph, that of representation *by* language, and that of experience *in* language, system and phrase, metaphor and metonymy. This ambivalence is the novel's inheritance.

In other words, the dialogism of Menippean and carnivalesque discourses, translating a logic of relations and analogy rather than of substance and inference, stands against Aristotelian logic. From within the very interior of formal logic, even while skirting it, Menippean dialogism contradicts it and points it towards other forms of thought. Indeed, Menippean discourse develops in times of opposition against Aristotelianism, and writers of polyphonic novels seem to disapprove of the very structures of official thought founded on formal logic.

THE SUBVERSIVE NOVEL

1 In the Middle Ages, Menippean tendencies were held in check by the authority of the religious text; in the bourgeois era, they were contained by the absolutism of individuals and things. Only modernity—when freed of 'God'—releases the Menippean force of the novel.

Now that modern, bourgeois society has not only accepted, but claims to recognize itself in the novel,[19] such claim can only refer to the category of monological narratives, known as realistic, that censor all carnivalesque and Menippean elements, whose structures were assembled at the time of the Renaissance. On the contrary, the Menippean, dialogical novel, tending to refuse representation and the epic, has only been tolerated; that is, it has been declared unreadable, ignored or ridiculed. Today, it shares the same fate as the carnivalesque discourse practised by students during the Middle Ages outside the Church.

The novel, and especially the modern, polyphonic novel, incorporating Menippean elements, embodies the effort of European thought to break out of the framework of causally determined identical substances and head towards another modality of thought that proceeds through dialogue (a logic of distance, relativity, analogy, non-exclusive and transfinite opposition). It is therefore not surprising that the novel has been considered as an inferior genre (by neo-classicism and other similar regimes) or as subversive (I have in mind the major writers of polyphonic novels over many centuries—Rabelais, Swift, Sade, Lautréamont, Kafka and Bataille—to mention only those who have always been and still remain on the fringe of official culture). The way in which European thought transgresses its constituent characteristics appears clearly in the words and narrative structures of the twentieth-century novel. Identity, substance, causality and definition are transgressed so that others may be adopted: analogy, relation, opposition, and therefore dialogism and Menippean ambivalence.[20]

Although this entire historical inventory that Bakhtin has undertaken evokes the image of a museum or the task of an archivist, it is none the less rooted in our present concerns. Everything written today unveils either the possibility or impossibility of reading and rewriting history. This possibility is evident in the literature heralded by the writings of a new generation, where the text is elaborated as *theatre* and as *reading*. Mallarmé, one of the first to understand the Menippean qualities of the novel (let it be emphasized that Bakhtin's term has the advantage of situating a certain kind of writing within history), said that literature 'is nothing but the flash of what should have been produced previously or closer to the origin'.

2   I would now suggest two models for organizing narrative signification, based on two dialogical categories: (1) Subject (S) $\rightleftarrows$ Addressee (A); and (2) Subject of enunciation $\rightleftarrows$ Subject of utterance.

The first model implies a dialogical relationship, while the second presupposes modal relationships within this dialogical formation. The first model determines genre (epic poem, novel) while the second determines generic variants.

Within the polyphonic structure of a novel, the first dialogical model (S $\rightleftarrows$ A) plays itself out entirely within the writing discourse; and it presents itself as perpetually challenging this discourse. The writer's interlocutor, then, is the writer himself, but as reader of another text. The one who writes is the same as the one who reads. Since his interlocutor is a text, he himself is no more than a text re-reading itself as it rewrites itself. The dialogical structure, therefore, appears only in the light of the text elaborating itself as ambivalent in relation to another text.

In the epic, on the other hand, A is an extra-textual, absolute entity (God or community) that relativizes dialogue to the point where it is cancelled out and reduced to monologue. With this in mind, it is easy to understand why not only the so-called 'traditional' novel of the nineteenth century, but also any novel with any ideological thesis whatsoever, tends towards an epic, thus constituting a deviation in the very structure of the novel; this is why Tolstoy's monologism is epic and Dostoevsky's dialogism novelistic.

Within the framework of the second model, several possibilities may be detected:

a   The subject of utterance (S_d) coincides with the zero degree of the subject of enunciation (S_r), which can be designated either by the 'he/she' non-person pronoun or a proper name. This is the simplest technique found at the inception of the narrative.

b   The subject of utterance (S_d) coincides with the subject of enunciation (S_r). This produces a first person narrative: 'I'.

c   The subject of utterance (S_d) coincides with the addressee (A). This produces a second person narrative: 'you': as for example with Raskolnikov's object-oriented word in *Crime and Punishment*. Michel Butor insistently explored this technique in *A Change of Heart*.

d   The subject of utterance (S_d) coincides both with the subject of enunciation (S_r) and the addressee (A). In such a case the novel becomes a questioning of writing and displays the staging of its dialogical structure. At the same time, the text becomes a reading (quotation and commentary) of an exterior literary corpus and is thus constructed as ambivalence. Through its use of personal pronouns and anonymous quotations, Philippe Sollers's *Drame* is an example of this fourth possibility.

A reading of Bakhtin therefore leads to the paradigm shown in figure 1.

I should finally like to insist on the importance of Bakhtin's concepts (on the status of the word, dialogue and ambivalence), as well as on the importance of certain new perspectives opened up through them.

By establishing the status of the word as *minimal unit* of the text, Bakhtin deals with structure at its deepest level, beyond the sentence and rhetorical

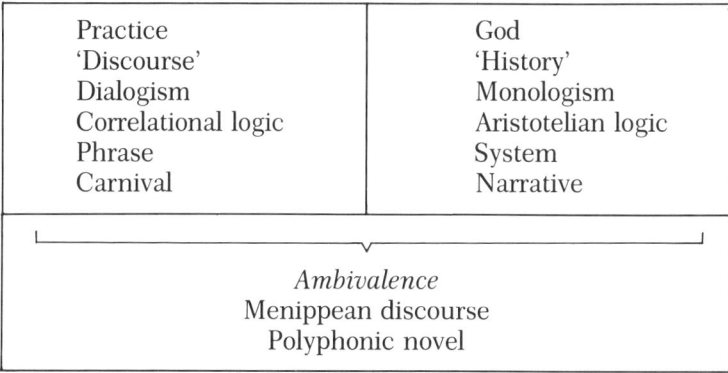

Figure 1

figures. The notion of *status* has added to the image of the text as a corpus of atoms that of a text made up of relationships, within which words function as quantum units. If there is a model for poetic language, it no longer involves lines or surfaces, but rather, *space* and *infinity*—concepts amenable to formalization through set theory and the new mathematics. Contemporary analysis of narrative structure has been refined to the point where it can delineate functions (cardinal or catalytic), and indices (as such or as information); it can describe the elaboration of a narrative according to particular logical or rhetorical patterns. Without gainsaying the undisputed value of this kind of research,[21] one might wonder whether the presuppositions of a metalanguage that sets up hierarchies or is heterogeneous to narrative do not weigh too heavily upon such studies. Perhaps Bakhtin's naïve procedure, centred on the word and its unlimited ability to generate dialogue (commentary of a quotation), is both simpler and more productive.

The notion of dialogism, which owed much to Hegel, must not be confused with Hegelian dialectics, based on a triad and thus on struggle and projection (a movement of transcendence), which does not transgress the Aristotelian tradition founded on substance and causality. Dialogism replaces these concepts by absorbing them within the concept of relation. It does not strive towards transcendence but rather toward harmony, all the while implying an idea of rupture (of opposition and analogy) as a modality of transformation.

Dialogism situates philosophical problems *within* language; more precisely, within language as a correlation of texts, as a reading-writing that falls in with non-Aristotelian, syntagmatic, correlational, 'carnivalesque' logic. Consequently, one of the fundamental problems facing contemporary semiotics is precisely to describe this 'other logic' without denaturing it.

The term 'ambivalence' lends itself perfectly to the current transitory stage of European literature—a coexistence (an ambivalence of 'the double of lived experience' (realism and the epic) and 'lived experience' itself (linguistic exploration and Menippean discourse)—a literature that will perhaps arrive at a form of thought similar to that of painting: the transmission of essence through form, and the configuration of (literary) space as revealing (literary) thought without 'realist' pretensions. This entails the study, through language, of the novel's space and of its transmutations, thereby establishing a close relationship between language and space, compelling us to analyse them as modes of thought. By examining the ambivalence of the spectacle (realist representation) and of lived experience (rhetoric), one might perceive the line where the rupture (or junction) between them takes place. That line could be seen as the graph of a motion through which our culture forsakes itself in order to go beyond itself.

The path charted between the two poles of dialogue radically abolishes problems of causality, finality, etc., from our philosophical arena. It suggests the importance of the dialogical principle for a space of thought much larger than that of the novel. More than binarism, dialogism may well become the basis of our time's intellectual structure. The predominance of the novel and other ambivalent literary structures; the communal, carnivalesque phenomena attracting young people; quantum exchanges; and current interest in the correlational symbolism of Chinese philosophy—to cite only a few striking elements of modern thought—all confirm this hypothesis.

NOTES

1. The point of departure of this essay lies in two books by Mikhail Bakhtin: *Rabelais and His World,* tr. Helene Iswolsky (Cambridge, Mass.: MIT Press, 1965), and *Problems of Dostoevsky's Poetics,* tr. R. W. Rotsel (Ann Arbor, Mich.: Ardis, 1973). Bakhtin died in 1975, the year of the publication of his collection of essays, *Voprosy literatury i estetiki* (Moscow), published in French as *Esthétique et théorie du roman* (Paris: Gallimard, 1978).

2. Derrida uses the word *gram* (from the Greek *gramma,* 'that which is written') to designate the irreducible material element of writing, as opposed to the vast amount

of extraneous connotations currently surrounding that word. See his *Of Grammatology*, tr. Gayatri Spivak (Baltimore, Md: Johns Hopkins University Press, 1976).

3. 'Language is as old as consciousness, language *is* practical consciousness that exists also for other men, and for that reason alone it really exists for me personally as well.' Karl Marx, *The German Ideology*, tr. S. Ryazanskaya, in *The Marx-Engels Reader*, ed. Robert C. Tucker (New York: Norton, 1972), p. 122. [The French translation quoted by Kristeva is less faithful to the German text, although, in the latter part of the sentence, the German word for 'genuine' does modify 'consciousness': '. . . auch für mich selbst echt existierende Bewuβtsein;' The French version begins 'Le langage *est* la conscience réelle . . .']

4. I shall refer to only a few of Bakhtin's notions in so far as they are congruent with the conceptions of Ferdinand de Saussure as related to his 'anagrams' (see Jean Starobinski, *Les Mots sous les mots*, Paris: Gallimard, 1971) and suggest a new approach to literary texts.

5. See Julia Kristeva, *La Révolution du langage poétique* (Paris: Seuil, 1974), pp. 59–60.

6. 'Indeed, when structural semantics refers to the linguistic foundations of discourse, it points out that 'an expanding sequence is recognized as the equivalent of a syntactically simpler communication' and defines 'expansion' as 'one of the most important aspects of the operation of natural languages'. A. J. Greimas, *Sémantique structurale* (Paris: Larousse, 1966), p. 72. I conceive of the notion of expansion as the theoretical principle authorizing me to study in the structure of genres an exteriorization (an expansion) of structures inherent to language.

7. E. F. Boudé, *K istorii velikoruskix govorov* (Towards a History of Russian Dialects) (Kazan: 1869).

8. L. V. Czerba, *Vostotchno-luzhickoe narechie* (The Eastern Loujiks' Dialect) (Petrograd: 1915).

9. V. V. Vinogradov, 'O dialogicheskoj rechi' (On Dialogical Discourse), in *Russkaja rech*, 1, p. 1440.

10. V. V. Vinogradov, *Poetika* (Moscow: Nauka, 1926), p. 33.

11. It seems that what is persistently being called 'interior monologue' is the most indomitable way in which an entire civilization conceives itself as identity, as organized chaos and finally, as transcendence. Yet this 'monologue' probably exists only in texts that pretend to reconstitute the so-called physical reality of 'verbal flux'. Western man's state of 'interiority' is thus a limited literary effect (confessional form, continuous psychological speech, automatic writing). In a way, then, Freud's 'Copernican' revolution (the discovery of the split within the subject) put an end to the fiction of an internal *voice* by positing the fundamental principles governing the subject's radical exteriority in relation to, and within, language.

12. Bakhtin, *Problems of Dostoevsky's Poetics*, pp. 151-2.

13. 'Shifters, Verbal Categories and the Russian Verb', in *Selected Writings II* (The Hague: Mouton, 1971), pp. 130–47.

14. Bakhtin, *Problems of Dostoevsky's Poetics*, p. 151.

15. I should emphasize that introducing notions of set theory into considerations on poetic language has only metaphorical value. It is legitimate to do so because one can draw an analogy between the Aristotelian logic/poetic logic relationship on the one hand, and the quantifiable/infinite relationship on the other.

16. See Luce Irigaray, 'Communication linguistique et communication speculaire', in *Cahiers pour l'Analyse*, 3 (May 1966), pp. 39–55.

17. I should like to stress the ambiguous role of Western individualism. Involving

the concept of identity, it is linked to the substantialist, causal and atomist thought of Aristotelian Greece and has strengthened throughout centuries this activist, scientistic or theological aspect of Western culture. On the other hand, since it is founded on the principle of a difference between the 'self' and the 'world', it prompts a search for mediation between the two terms, or for stratifications within each of them, in order to allow the possibility of a correlative logic based on the very components of formal logic.

18. It was perhaps this phenomenon that Bakhtin had in mind when he wrote, 'The language of the novel can be located neither on a surface nor on a line. It is a system of surfaces that intersect. The author as creator of everything having to do with the novel cannot be located on any of these linguistic surfaces. Rather, he resides within the controlling centre constituted by the intersection of the surfaces. All these surfaces are located at varying distances from that authorial centre' ('Šlovo o romane', in *Voprosy literatury*, 8 [1965], pp. 84–90). Actually, the writer is nothing more than the *linking* of these centres. Attributing a single centre to him would be to constrain him within a monological, theological position.

19. This point of view is shared by all theorists of the novel: A. Thibaudet, *Réflexions sur le roman* (Thoughts on the Novel) (Paris: Gallimard, 1938); Koskimies, 'Théorie des romans' (Theory of the Novel), in *Annales Academiae Scientarum Finnicae*, I, series B, 35 (1935), pp. 5–275; Georg Lukács, *Theory of the Novel* (Cambridge: MIT Press, 1971); and others.

An interesting perspective on the concept of the novel as dialogue is provided by Wayne Booth's *The Rhetoric of Fiction* (Chicago: University of Chicago Press, 1961). His ideas concerning the *reliable* and *unreliable writer* parallel some of Bakhtin's investigations into dialogism in the novel, although they do not posit any specific relationship between novelistic 'illusionism' and linguistic symbolism.

20. Such a mode shows up in modern physics as well as in ancient Chinese thought, as the two are equally anti-Aristotelian, anti-monological and dialogical. See S. I. Hayakawa, 'What Is Meant by Aristotelian Structure in Language', in *Language, Meaning and Maturity* (New York: Harper, 1959); Chang Tung-sun, 'A Chinese Philosopher's Theory of Knowledge', in S. I. Hayakawa, (ed.), *Our Language and Our World* (New York: Harper, 1959); Joseph Needham, *Science and Civilization in China*, vol. II (Cambridge: Cambridge University Press, 1965).

21. See the important collection of studies on narrative structure in *Communications*, 8 (1966), which includes contributions by Roland Barthes, A. J. Greimas, Claude Bremond, Umberto Eco, Jules Gritti, Violette Morin, Christian Metz, Tzvetan Todorov and Gérard Genette.

Elaine Showalter
1941–

Elaine Cottler Showalter was born on January 21, 1941, in Boston. Despite the opposition of her parents, who disapproved of her intellectual interests, she attended Bryn Mawr College, receiving a B.A. in 1962, and then did graduate work in English at Brandeis, from which she received an M.A. in 1964.

Showalter continued her graduate studies at the University of California–Davis. Research in the Victorian periodical holdings at the Davis, Berkeley, and U.C.L.A. libraries was the basis for her pioneering dissertation "The Double Critical Standard: Criticism of Women Writers in England 1845–1880," for which she was awarded a Ph.D. in 1970. That year she joined the faculty at Douglass College, Rutgers University. In 1978 she became a full professor at Rutgers; six years later she was appointed professor of English at Princeton, where her husband is a member of the French department.

Showalter's first book, based on her dissertation, was *A Literature of Their Own: British Women Novelists from Brontë to Lessing* (1977), but during the years preceding its publication Showalter had been establishing herself as a pioneering feminist critic, developing women's studies courses at Douglass, editing the first textbook on women in literature (*Women's Liberation and Literature*, 1971), and contributing the seminal essay "Women Writers and the Double Standard" to an important anthology of feminist writings, *Women in Sexist Society* (1971), edited by Vivian Gornick and Barbara Moran. Showalter's *A Literature of Their Own* was a ground-breaking study of the separate tradition of women's fiction in England, and established "gynocritics," an approach which focused on the historical and cultural contexts of women's writing, as the leading form of feminist criticism in the United States.

Guggenheim and Rockefeller fellowships as well as a stipend from the National Endowment for the Humanities enabled Showalter to concentrate on her next study, a two-volume feminist cultural history of psychiatry and women in nineteenth- and twentieth-century England. The first volume, *The Female Malady: Women, Madness, and English Culture 1830–1980*, published in 1985, identifies three distinctive and successive phases in the psychiatric treatment of "mad" women—Victorian, Darwinian, and Modern—and argues that the original model of male therapist controlling female patient has remained the same. The second volume, *Madness and the Victorian Imagination*, is scheduled for publication in 1990.

Showalter has edited *These Modern Women* (1978), an anthology of autobiographical essays by American women writers in the 1920s, and the important anthology *The New Feminist Criticism* (1985), which includes two previously published influential essays by Showalter: "Towards a Feminist Poetics" (1979) and "Feminist Criticism in the Wilderness" (1981). Her 1984 essay, "Women's Time, Women's Space: Writing the History of Feminist Criticism," is at once a review of modern criticism and a proclamation of gynocritics as the preeminent feminist approach to the study of literature.

Women's Time, Women's Space: Writing the History of Feminist Criticism

The history of literary criticism, according to Grant Webster's study, *The Republic of Letters*, obeys laws similar to those proposed by Thomas Kuhn for the structure of scientific revolutions. The paradigms or charters of successful critical revolutions make their way through predictable phases from the ideological period that produces them to the emergence of strong authority figures who dictate what will henceforth be "normal" criticism and who redefine the literary canon, and finally to their obsolescence in the face of new writers, new ideologies, and new generations. The career of the individual critic parallels the rise and fall of the critical charter, from apprenticeship to superannuation; and for those who are especially original, productive, and bold, it offers the chance to become what Webster calls a Man of Letters, whose lucrative activities are best defined by the list on Edmund Wilson's notorious postcard of what he would not do.[1]

Feminist criticism fits this model reasonably well in most respects. If we have not quite seen our heresy become orthodoxy, and if our Women of Letters are scattered all over the map rather than concentrated in major universities, yet we have done the profession some service and they know it; for a young critical school we have had an extraordinary degree of impact on the way literature is taught and read. If, as Gerry Graff has reminded us, "academic professionalism may require radical critical innovation as a condition of its expansion" as a "necessary spur to industrial growth,"[2] feminist criticism is obviously the most effective stimulant of the professional economy, since it has not only made it necessary to re-read the canon, but has also opened up for critical exploitation the vast, almost inexhaustible raw materials of women's texts.

But in many details feminist criticism seems like an anomaly in the history of modern criticism, and not only because it is gender-marked. We do not derive our charter from a single authority or a body of sacred theoretical texts. There is no Mother of Feminist Criticism, no fundamental work against which one can measure other feminisms. Feminist criticism has been rather a powerful movement than a unified theory, a community of women with a shared set of concerns but with a complex and resourceful variety of methodological practices and theoretical affiliations. In addition to having a broad social and intellectual base, feminist criticism is unusually wide in scope. It is not limited or even partial to a single national literature, genre, or century; it is interdisciplinary in theory and practice; it can handle Harlequin Books as well as *Paradise Lost*.

In writing the history of feminist criticism, we need to ask at the start therefore where it belongs in the republic of letters. Is feminist criticism a discourse of marginality, criticism in "a different voice" outside of modern criticism and motivated by other concerns? Is it rather, as some male theorists think, inside modern criticism, less a different phenomenon than a mutation of modernism, "a special-interest glamorization of mainstream discourse"?[3] Or is feminist criticism the women's space within modern criticism, the "maternal subtext" of patriarchal theory, the repository for the questions of literary value, social change, and personal experience that modern criticism has tried to banish or repress?[4] How would we have to rewrite the history of modern criticism and its meta-histories of dynastic struggle and change if feminist criticism were seen as part of it?

One way of writing the history of feminist criticism would be to situate it in women's time—that is, to emphasize its specificity by narrating its development in terms of the internal relationships, continuities, friendships, and institutions that shape the thinking and the writing of the last fifteen years.

In some sense the experiences and achievements of women have already been tacitly relegated to women's time in being hidden from history, obscured, or written out of the historical record. And from the masculinist point of view, women's time, like Miller time or the children's hour, may merely represent the pause in the day's occupations when serious business is set aside for a lighter entertainment, *le repos des professeurs*. Theorists of feminist historiography, however, such as Gerda Lerner, Joan Kelly-Gadol, Nancy Cott, and Elizabeth Fox-Genovese, have recuperated the concept of women's time as an essential model for writing the history of women. As they have explained, the process of restoring women's past to the historical record "is more than finding data about women and fitting it into the empty spaces within patriarchal history."[5] It demands that we challenge the temporal categories that have been adopted by traditional—that is, men's—history. Events and periods that are important to the development of male ideas and institutions may be negligible or irrelevant to women, and the temporal grid of men's history may filter out women's experiences, values, and achievements.

If we look at most male-authored histories of modern criticism, we will find that its periodization and conceptualization not only exclude feminist criticism but in a curious way negate it; one of the most commonplace and irritating ploys of this kind of mainstream critical history, in fact, is to condemn the apolitical nature of modern criticism and to issue a ringing call for a worldly, secular, oppositional critical practice, ignoring all the while the socially-based feminist criticism going on for fifteen years right under the author's nose. Presumably for Frank Lentricchia, Gerald Graff, and Edward Said, feminist criticism takes place in a women's time that is outside modernity.

But the "politics of exclusion," in Gayatri Spivak's term, are perhaps less problematic than the "politics of inclusion," which squeeze feminist criticism into an androcentric frame, distorting and devaluing its meaning.[6] Having omitted any reference at all to feminist criticism in *The Republic of Letters,* for example, Grant Webster now proposes in a sequel that we accommodate it to his Kuhnian model of critical change as a subcategory of the erotic revolution of the 1960s, a phenomenon not of criticism but of the counter-culture, and linked with the aesthetics of pornography and gay coming-out.[7]

The periodization of modern critical history in terms of New Criticism, structuralism, and post-structuralism also has unfortunate consequences for the history of feminist criticism, as Jonathan Culler has recently pointed out. In *On Deconstruction*, he argues:

> in mapping contemporary criticism as a struggle between New Critics, structuralists, and then post-structuralists, one would find it hard to do justice to feminist criticism, which has had a greater effect on the literary canon than any other critical movement and which has arguably been one of the most powerful forces of renovation in contemporary criticism. Though numerous post-structuralists are feminists (and vice-versa), feminist criticism is not post-structuralist, especially if post-structuralism is defined in its opposton to structuralism. To discuss feminist criticism adequately, one would need a different framework where the notion of post-structuralism was a product rather than a given.[8]

Generally speaking, of course, mainstream critical history has coped with the relationship between feminist criticism and these other movements by ignoring it. Most histories would locate the shift from structuralism to post-structuralism in the late 1960s, in the space between Roland Barthes' *Introduction to the Structural Analysis of Narratives* (1966) which appealed to a general grammar of narrative, and his *S/Z* (1970) which emphasized the self-contained difference of each text and rejected the idea of a system of narrative description. And they would point to the Johns Hopkins Conference on "The Structuralist Controversy and the Sciences of Man" in 1966, when Jacques Derrida first spoke to an audience of "Over one hundred humanists and social scientists from the U.S. and eight other countries."[9] But in a history of feminist criticism the Hopkins conference would occupy a minor place if it appeared at all, not only because, so far as I can determine, no women were invited to attend it; but also because the ideologies of structuralism were not the ones that galvanized women into an awareness that the time had come to speak out.

Looking at the question from the other side, Terry Eagleton has attempted to resolve the gender gap in the history of modern criticism by arguing that post-structuralism grew out of structuralism precisely as a response to the political demands and personal issues raised by the women's movement, the feminist insistence that neither Marxist economics nor the sciences of the text could explain the deeply held ideologies of gender. In *Literary Theory*, Eagleton asserts that for deconstructive theory and practice, the most blatant, influential, perdurable, and virulent of all the binary oppositions must be that of masculine and feminine.[10]

But feminists will be as startled by this news of their power as their structuralist brethren. Eagleton passes over the details of the gritty historical process by which structuralism *recognized* the relevance of feminist issues and adapted to them. From the enlightened perspective of Eagleton's current admirable pro-feminist stance, it may appear that all along there has been steady and welcome feminization of critical discourse, but feminists miss accounts of real confrontations between critical positions, such as the first feminist literary session at the Chicago MLA in 1970, or the presentation of the Marxist-Feminist Literature Collective, a small and short-lived English group whose members since have produced about ninety percent of the most important feminist criticism in Great Britain, at the Essex Conference on the Sociology of Literature in 1977. The abstractions of most official histories of criticism are too coarse to accommodate the false starts, the lucky breaks, the material pressures, the intellectual slog, or, least of all, the human drama that make up a living critical movement.

To do justice to the texture of this history, we need to begin by seeing feminist criticism from within and by defining its periodization within women's time, instead of as a subset of standard critical time. The history of feminist criticism is more than a history of ideas or institutions; it takes in events on many levels of women's daily lives. But to limit ourselves to women's time would be equally misleading, since feminist criticism is also constituted by the histories of the academy, the discipline, and modern criticism itself. Insofar as feminist criticism is a kind of women's writing, it is a double-voiced discourse that is influenced by both the muted and the dominant cultures, that operates at the juncture of two traditions, and that has both a Mother and a Father Time. In the second phase of this history, therefore, we need to trace the effects of modern criticism and especially modern theory upon feminist criticism as it evolved. But in the final phase, we must ask for a synchronization of women's time and critical time, a history of modern criticism to which feminist criticism has been restored, and thus a history with a different rhythm and shape.

Ideally, a history of feminist criticism would begin with interviews of pioneers in the field about how they became feminist critics. It would explain how Gilbert met Gubar, how Catherine Stimpson and Domna Stanton came to edit *Signs*, how the Bunting Institute became a critical community. It would include the voices of black and lesbian and Marxist feminist critics discussing the factors of race, sexuality, and class. In writing this essay, I did in fact speak to a number of feminist critics in the United States, England, and France, about their motives, influences, and careers; and their comments have guided me in constructing a historical outline. But space permits me to tell only one story; and it seems fair that it should be my own.

In 1968 I was a faculty wife with a small child trying to write what seemed to be a hopeless dissertation on the double critical standard applied to Victorian women novelists. The dissertation seemed doomed for several reasons. In the first place, by choosing to write on this unfashionable topic, I had labeled myself as a limited scholar with a narrow range of eccentric interests, like an ornithologist writing on Shelley; or worse, as a strident feminist to whom better-adjusted women professionals reacted, as Sandra Gilbert recalls in her own memoir of the period, "with a mixture of curiosity and scorn."[11] It was frightening to write a dissertation that seemed so different from the criticism I was reading in scholarly journals; there were very few precedents for what I wanted to say. And even if I finished it, I saw no professional future for myself. Two of the three colleges within commuting distance of my husband's job had told me that they did not hire women. After a disheartening period as the worst statistician ever employed by the Educational Testing Service, I had taken a part-time temporary instructorship teaching composition at Douglass, the women's college of Rutgers, a job I had been warned would never become regular. I had been living in Paris watching the police pull down the barricades of May 1968, and I had been part of the radical protest at the MLA that December, but I had not really connected the political turbulence of that extraordinary year with the questions I faced in my own work.

It was not until I joined the women's liberation movement in the spring of 1969 and began to teach a course on women and literature, that the personal became the critical, and that my passionate interest in women's writing began to define itself as feminist criticism. It was not isolation, discrimination, radical politics, the structuralist controversy, or an Oedipal rebellion against Cleanth Brooks that made women feminist critics, but the polemical force, activist commitment, powerful analysis, and sense of mutual endeavor that came out of the women's movement.

Something of the change in tone that distinguished feminist criticism from its pre-1968 precedents may be gathered by noting the ambivalence of purpose and the deprivation of political context that characterized the writing of even such major female precursors as Simone de Beauvoir, Queenie Leavis, and Mary Ellmann. Beauvoir, for example, refused to call *The Second Sex* a feminist work and would not acknowledge its ambitions to provide a systematic analysis of women's condition. Sartre, she insisted, was a philosopher, that is "somebody who truly builds a philosophical system"; she was only "someone who likes philosophy."[12] In England, Queenie Leavis's highly original essays on nineteenth-century women writers were produced in between the lines of F. R. Leavis's master *oeuvre*. After his death, Queenie Leavis admitted to an interviewer that she had actually written large parts of *The Great Tradition* and other books "without acknowledgment. I didn't mind at all. He was very grateful of course. I was more scholarly than he was, perhaps, because I like ferreting about in libraries. He didn't have time to go to the libraries."[13] If F. R. was the literary critic who built the system, she was simply someone who liked books and had time to go to libraries. Even Mary Ellmann's brilliant study, *Thinking about Women,* published in 1968, which anticipated and influenced the feminist critique of the next five years, revealed in its unassuming and offhand title the rejection or abdication of critical authority that made the construction of a feminist poetics historically impossible outside of a women's movement.

And yet there is a paradox in our history. While feminist criticism could not have existed without the galvanizing ideology and power of the women's movement, the women's movement would not have occurred without a generation of women who liked books—graduate students, assistant professors, editors, writers, faculty wives, highly educated products of the academic expansion of the 1960s—whose avid, devoted, socially-reinforced identifications with fictional heroines were coming into conflict with the sexist realities they encountered everyday.

Feminism spoke to our lived experience with the fierce urgency of a religious revelation, a Great Awakening. Sandra Gilbert is one of a number of feminist critics who have compared its beginnings to a conversion process, noting that:

> most feminist critics speak . . . like people who must bear witness, people who must enact and express in their own lives and words the revisionary sense of transformation that seems inevitably to attend the apparently simple discovery that the experiences of women in and with literature are different from those of men.[14]

Coming at a historical moment when the profession of literary studies in general seemed most sterile, pointless, and insecure, when for every Man of Letters there are one hundred English professors wishing they had gone to law school, the freshness and exuberance of feminist criticism, the sense of being embarked on a great intellectual journey, the conviction that what we were doing mattered in the world, the discovery of women's networks, indeed of sisterhood, made its early years as joyous as they were fruitful, and with Gissing's heroines of the 1890s we might have exclaimed, "Thank Heaven we are women."

If in its origins feminist criticism derived more from feminism than from criticism, we could argue that today the situation is reversed. Since 1975 a second wave has included many women, especially in French and Comparative Literature, who have come to feminist criticism via psychoanalytic, poststructuralist, or deconstructionist theory, rather than via the women's movement and women's studies. In the past year, several male theorists, especially those engaged in Marxist or black critical theory, have begun to write seriously about feminist criticism as well.[15] And more generally, even pioneering practitioners have been driven to ask theoretical questions and to accept the modern idea that there can be no practice without theory, even if theory is unformulated or incomplete.

The post-structural feminist critics see continental theory as the most powerful means to understanding the production of sexual difference in language, reading, and writing. They argue too that the categories of the woman reader, women's culture, and the woman's text, while politically useful, are unexamined and essentialist. From the perspective of some post-structuralist feminists the first phase of feminist criticism may be dismissed as theoretically naive, an American "flight towards empiricism" which assumes "an unbroken continuity between 'life' and 'text.'"[16] Only theory, they insist, can provide adequate answers to feminist questions and a position from which to discuss the whole of literature and culture, rather than one within a ghetto of female experience.

For some pioneering feminist critics, on the other hand, the glittering critical theories of Derrida, Althusser, and Lacan seem like golden apples thrown in Atalanta's path to keep her from winning the race. In the adaptation of continental theory to feminist practice they see the dictatorship of the dominant, the surrender of hard-won critical autonomy to a reigning language and style. The post-structuralist feminist, some would argue, is a rhetorical double agent, a little drummer girl who plays go-between in male critical quarrels.

In writing the history of feminist criticism, I want to avoid, however, such a hostile polarization of French and American feminist discourse, arid theory and crude empiricism, essentialism or obscurantism. In formulating or endorsing such hierarchical binary oppositions, we not only fall into the old dualistic traps, but genuinely misrepresent the much more complex and nuanced reality of feminist critical practice. American feminist criticism is as theoretically sophisticated as its continental sister, while the sheer brilliance and ambition of post-structuralist feminist writing has made its presence in the academy impossible for even the most unreconstructed critics to ignore. While feminist critical work will proceed on both fronts, this does not mean that we are torn by dissension, but rather that we are enriched by dialectical possibilities.

Since 1975, feminist criticism has taken two theoretical directions, that of the Anglo-American focus on the specificity of women's writing I have called *gynocritics*, and that of the French exploration of the textual consequences and representations of sexual difference that Alice Jardine has named *gynesis*.[17] These ought not to be taken as oppositional or exclusive terms either; in fact they describe tendencies within feminist critical theory rather than absolute categories. As such, however, they represent different emphases and perceptions of the role of feminist inquiry. Gynocritics is, roughly speaking, historical in orientation; it looks at women's writing as it has actually occurred and tries to define its specific characteristics of language, genre, and literary influence, within a cultural network that includes variables of race, class, and nationality.

Gynesis rejects, however, the temporal dimension of women's experience, what Julia Kristeva calles *le temps de femmes*, and seeks instead to understand the space granted to the feminine in the symbolic contract. "When evoking the name and destiny of women," Kristeva writes, "one thinks more of the *space* generating and forming the human species than of *time, becoming, or history*."[18] The problematic of women's space has had practical meanings, of course, for Anglo-American feminist inquiry as well; in social anthropology, where women's social maps and spatial domains have been topics for analysis; in the creative arts where "women's space" has become a code word for a feminist *salon des refusés;* and in literary theory where female space is the alternative linguistic and imaginative place from which women can speak. Gynesis goes beyond these, however, to repossess as a field of inquiry all the space of the Other, the gaps, silences, and absences of discourse and representation, to which the feminine has traditionally been relegated. As Alice Jardine explains, "the space 'outside' of the conscious subject has always connoted the feminine in Western thought—and any movement into alterity is a movement into that female space."[19] This space is most productively studied via theories of philosophy and psychoanalysis. In the texts of gynesis, very little attention is paid to women writers; even the concept of *écriture féminine* developed by the most influential critic of this school, Hélène Cixous, describes the symbolically or metaphorically feminine attributes of avant-garde writing rather than writing by women. Finally, some of the most prominent French theorists of gynesis, including Kristeva, Cixous, and Sarah Kofman, reject the label of "feminist," or even regard themselves as anti-feminist, seeing feminism in its activist mode as a liberal anachronism, or as "the final hysterization of middle-class women."[20]

Another very striking aspect of gynesis is its dependence on male masters and male theoretical texts. Although virtually all American feminist critics of the first wave were trained by men (as far as I know, I am one of the few in this group to have had a woman dissertation director), their graduate training occurred in a wide range of universities, and none became a disciple of a particular male teacher. It might be said that like the women of the Amahagger tribe described by Rider Haggard in *She*, pioneering American feminist critics "never pay attention to or even acknowledge any man as their father, even when their male parentage is perfectly well known."[21]

In contrast, Lacan's Ecole Freudienne, and especially his seminar of 1972–73 on "Femininity," played a central role in the development of gynesis, and Derrida has been an even more significant figure in its recent years. According to Stuart Schneiderman, Lacan's American disciple and client, the seminar called "Encore," "spoke to women in a way few psychoanalytic texts have ever done, and it exerted an important influence on French feminism."[22] In these teasing and gnomic lectures on feminine sexuality Lacan gave his fullest account of the symbolic construction of the feminine through language and representation and his most explicit attack on essentialist beliefs in the nature of Woman. "There is no such thing as *The* woman," he declared, "where the definite article stands for the universal."[23] Lacan's emphasis on the symbolic construction of sexual difference and his recasting of Freudian biologism in terms of language influenced a number of female theorists in several fields. By 1974, as Jane Gallop reports, Lacan had become the "ladies' man" of French feminism, the subject of a special issue of *L'Arc* with essays by Shoshana Felman, Catherine Clément, and Luce Irigaray, among others.[24] In 1974, too, Lacanian ideas were introduced to Anglo-American feminist thought by Juliet Mitchell in *Psychoanalysis and Feminism;* and recently Mitchell, along with Jacqueline Rose, translated Lacan's essays on feminine sexuality. Her readings of Freud and Lacan were further mediated for American feminists in two important reviews, the first by the structuralist anthropologist Sherry Ortner in *Feminist Studies*, and the second by Jane Gallop in the "Textual Politics" issue of *Diacritics* in 1976, which concluded with a call to feminist theory to "reexamine its ends in view of Lacanian psychoanalysis."[25]

The very strangeness and difficulty of Lacanian theory and of French feminist writing made it fascinating to many American feminists who began to encounter it in translations of Cixous, Kristeva, and Irigaray; in the review essays by Elaine Marks and Carolyn Burke published in the late 1970s in *Signs;* and in the collection *New French Feminisms,* edited by Marks and Isabelle de Courtivron which appeared in 1980.[26]

That Lacan was a man who, as Schneiderman sadly concedes, "loved women, but loved them too well and too much" has now become the topic of a certain brand of high Parisian scandal, as in the Philippe Sollers' *roman à clef, Femmes,* in which many of the leading women in French gynesic feminism play what one hopes are fantasy roles.[27] But well before these postmortem revelations, Derridean accusations of phallocentrism had seriously diminished Lacan's power as a theoretical force in gynesis. One factor in Derrida's ascendancy to the maître's throne has been his acclaimed regular trips to the United States to teach at Hopkins, Cornell, and Yale, whereas Lacan's American tour in 1975 was a near disaster. More importantly, poststructuralist feminists such as Gayatri Spivak have found in Derrida's critique of phallogocentrism and radical questioning of all discourse a "'feminization' of the practice of philosophy," and they believe that deconstruction is "an ultimately political practice," despite the skepticism of other critics, such as Christopher Norris, about Derrida's "curious equation" involving women, sexuality, and writing.[28]

The interest in women's writing, on the other hand, that is crucial to gynocritics preceded theoretical formulations and came initially from the feminist critic's own experience as a writer and from her identification with the anxieties and conflicts women writers faced in patriarchal culture. While modern criticism in general is a dialogue among critics because few contemporary writers have commanded the critic's attention, feminist criticism is again very different. Not only did Adrienne Rich, Tillie Olsen, Grace Paley, Audre Lorde, Anne Sexton, and Alice Walker command attention, they also shared the platforms at conferences and contributed to feminist journals. And gynocritics has been linked from the beginning with the enterprise of getting women into print. In the past decade, feminist publishing houses like the Feminist Press, éditions des femmes, and Virago Press, to name the top three in the U.S., France, and England, have among them brought out more than three hundred books.

But theoretical issues rapidly began to emerge from reading and research. The point at which the difference or specificity of women's writing was conceptualized as the focus of feminist criticism was, in my opinion, the single most important breakthrough in its history. While a critical paradigm alters as it evolves, in establishing itself it must make what Frye called an inductive leap, discovering a new object that can be charted by new laws. Although critics and writers had talked for centuries about women's writing, when feminist criticism set out to discover how it worked, to map the territory of the female imagination and the structures of the female plot, it was doing something completely new; it broke with previous ways of thinking about women's writing even if it had been dependent on them for its own development.[29]

One of these breaks was the rewriting of the literary history of women novelists in women's time, a deliberate strategic foregrounding of the continuities and inter-relations of a women's literary tradition. A second break was the hypothesis of nineteenth-century women's writing as a coded response to male images, influences, and texts, a form of protest against patriarchal literary authority. But the theoretical history of gynocritics developed in tempo with political changes in the women's movement and with the increasing power of women in the profession. When I wrote *A Literature of Their Own* in the early 1970s, I felt that it was crucial for my whole critical enterprise to construct a history with minimal dependence on, even minimal reference to, male authorities. When Gilbert and Gubar wrote *The Madwoman in the Attic* a few years later, they were freer to juxtapose feminist insights with masculine traditions and to make their own theory a feminist revision of Harold Bloom. Subsequently, developments in the fields of psychology, history, and anthropology about the construction of gender and sexual specificity have increased the theoretical complexity of gynocritical analyses that were never as innocent or unself-conscious as later arrivals have complained.

Since 1980, as feminist criticism in general has moved inexorably, book by book, back into standard critical time, its canon has undergone a parallel change. In the early 1970s, Kate Chopin's *The Awakening* was the most popular text in women's literature courses for reasons that were predominantly thematic. In the *Kate Chopin Newsletter,* now defunct, Emily Toth explained that Chopin raised "questions which are still being asked by women today."[30] One of the reasons *The Awakening* became the scripture of early feminist criticism was the resonance of "awakening" itself. Along with *Jane Eyre* and Toni Morrison's *The Bluest Eye*, Chopin's novel will be reprinted in full in the forthcoming *Norton Anthology of Women's Literature,* edited by Gilbert and Gubar, which will establish a feminist canon for the next generation.

But as the euphoria of awakening subsided and was replaced by a vision of the small, difficult changes and immense intellectual labors ahead, identification with Chopin and with women's condition shifted to less accessible and more problematic works. With Brontë, *Jane Eyre* gave way to *Villette*. With Eliot, *The Mill on the Floss,* beloved of Simone de Beauvoir, gave way first to *Middlemarch*, which posed the "woman question" in painfully relevant terms, and then to *Daniel Deronda,* beloved of no one, which seemed to be Eliot's most contradictory and divided study of women in patriarchal culture. In 1974, *Daniel Deronda* too was read in radical feminist circles as a guide to living, as Jane Alpert tells us in her autobiography *Growing Up Underground*. After four years as a political fugitive, Alpert was holed up in a room in Pittsfield, Massachusetts, deciding whether to surrender to the FBI:

> A bit of George Eliot's dialogue [she notes] kept echoing in my mind. "If you determine to face these hardships and still try," the composer Herr Klesmer says to the heroine, "you will have the dignity of a high purpose, even though you may have chosen unfortunately" . . . I decided—and George Eliot had as much to do with my choice as

anyone else—that I would take the high road. I was going to turn myself in.[31]

It is wonderful that Alpert should have had these high-minded meditations in Pittsfield, the headquarters of the American Renaissance, yet typical that in her moment of crisis she should not have turned to Hawthorne or Melville (although her lover, born Samuel Grossman, had renamed himself Melville in honor of the author of *Moby-Dick*) but to Eliot's stern moralism, making Pittsfield a place of as much allegorical resonance for an American feminist radical of the early 1970s as Middlemarch or St. Oggs had been for Eliot's heroines of the century before.

Since the late 1970s, though, feminist readings of *Daniel Deronda* show the impact of deconstruction, since the juxtaposition of the novel's two stories seems made to order for deconstructionist double-readings. The theories of Lacan and Foucault have also influenced readings such as Catherine Belsey's analysis of *Deronda* as "the history of an impossible resistance," in which "the text confers upon Gwendolen a kind of heroism in that she consistently resists her own hysterisation, refuses to identify with her own sexuality."[32]

To note that the interests and vocabularies of feminism and poststructuralism have coincided in the choice of this text brings me back to my original question: What is the relationship between feminist criticism and modern criticism? If we think of the history of feminist criticism as an antihistory of modern criticism, it will appear initially that modern theory has been a defensive reaction against the feminization of the profession. Northrop Frye has been the frankest in acknowledging the "dismal sexist symbology" which says that "the sciences, especially the physical sciences, are rugged, aggressive, out in the world doing things, and so symbolically male, whereas the literatures are narcissistic, intuitive, fanciful, staying at home and making the home more beautiful, but not doing anything serious and therefore symbolically female."[33] Frye's *Anatomy of Criticism* (1957) attempted to make the study of literature more serious and manly by structuring its principles scientifically like the laws of physics, biology, or mathematics.

When contemporary male theorists attempt to characterize the opposition against which their new paradigm asserts itself, they frequently resort to metaphors of the feminine. For Graff, the target of the New Criticism was the "genteel schoolmarm theory of literature."[34] Worse yet, as Eagleton scornfully remarks in *Criticism and Ideology,* traditional criticism is a "mere handmaiden to literature," a humble, quasi-domestic and undoubtedly ill-paid servant of the text.[35] Even when the metaphor appears to flatter women, as in Geoffrey Hartman's "Muse of Criticism," "more a governess than a muse, the stern daughter of books no longer read under trees and in the fields," in fact it implicitly excludes women from critical production, since it assumes that the critic will be a man.[36] Modern critical theory, however, has made strenuous efforts to get away from the feminine dependencies conjured up in the images of the schoolmarm, the governess, and the handmaiden, by joining forces with the tougher disciplines of linguistics, philosophy, and psychoanalysis.

Yet it is striking that within the past year or two, a number of distinguished literary theorists have begun to acknowledge that feminist criticism offers a paradigm for the kind of criticism they really want to do, that it seems to offer a way out of the labyrinth of indeterminacy, non-interference and self-referentiality post-structuralism has built for itself. For Terry Eagleton, for example, feminism is the closest we have come to a revolutionary critical practice that "challenges the separation of cultural criticism from cultural production."[37] For Barbara Hernnstein Smith, feminist criticism is the only approach centrally concerned with the issues of literary value and evaluation that have been banished from modern theoretical discourse.[38] Even Edward Said, in the single sentence that mentions feminist critics in his latest book, concedes that we have been the ones to open up the question of the political contexts of culture.[39]

This belated interest in feminist strategies, however, holds as many dangers as opportunities for our future. As Gayatri Spivak has warned, we must be wary of the "recuperation of the critical energies of feminism into the ruling ideology of Departments of English" and the possibility that this integration "might involve compromises . . . that might not let a feminism survive."[40] Insofar as the production of theory is now the business of modern criticism, there will be increased pressure on feminist criticism to accommodate itself more and more to the prevailing terminologies and systems, abandoning in the process the political priorities and the concerns for the personal that have made it so effective in the past.

As women have been the second sex, so the feminist critic has been historically the second reader, not only of dissertations but also of texts. But we are far from obsolescence; as critical movements go, we are not even in our prime, and feminist critics may be the first readers yet before our charter gives way to the inevitable mutations of history. Perhaps modern criticism, instead of graciously taking us into its historical embrace, will learn some lessons about itself from our anomalous movement, and will begin to question the myths of its own immaculate conception in the realms of pure and universal thought. At that point too, the power of gender will cease to be the special intellectual property of feminist criticism, and will be seen as a crucial determinant in the history of all forms of reading and writing. It may well turn out that in the critical histories of the future, these years will not be remembered as the Age of Structuralism or the Age of Deconstruction, but as the Age of Feminism. Wouldn't it be a surprise if, without having realized it, we have all been living in women's time?

NOTES

1. Grant Webster, *The Republic of Letters: A History of Postwar American Literary Opinion* (Baltimore: Johns Hopkins University Press, 1979), p. 33.

2. Gerald Graff, *Literature against Itself: Literary Ideas in Modern Society* (Chicago: University of Chicago Press, 1979), p. 95.

3. See Carol Gilligan, *In a Different Voice: Psychological Theory and Women's Development* (Cambridge: Harvard University Press, 1982); and Gayatri Chakravorty Spivak, "The Politics of Interpretations," *Critical Inquiry,* 9 (September 1982), 274.

4. See Coppélia Kahn, "Excavating 'Those Dim Minoan Regions': Maternal Subtexts in Patriarchal Literature," *Diacritics,* 12 (1982), 32–41.

5. Gerda Lerner, *The Majority Finds Its Past: Placing Women in History* (New York: Oxford University Press, 1979), p. 174.

6. Spivak, 276.

7. Grant Webster, "American Literary Criticism: A Bibliographical Essay," *American Studies International* (Autumn 1981), 18–20.

8. Jonathan Culler, *On Deconstruction* (Ithaca: Cornell University Press, 1983), p. 30.

9. See Frank Lentricchia, *After the New Criticism* (Chicago: University of Chicago Press, 1980), p. 157.

10. Terry Eagleton, *Literary Theory: An Introduction* (London: Basil Blackwell, 1983), pp. 148–50.

11. Sandra M. Gilbert, "Life Studies, or Speech after Long Silence," *College English,* 40 (April 1979), 849.

12. Margaret A. Simons and Jessica Benjamin, "Simone de Beauvoir: An Interview," *Feminist Studies,* 5 (Summer 1979), 338.

13. See P. J. M. Robertson, "Queen of Critics: The Achievement of Q. D. Leavis," *Novel,* 16 (Winter 1983), 141.

14. Gilbert, 850.

15. See for example, Terry Eagleton, *Literary Theory;* Wayne Booth, "Freedom of Interpretation: Bakhtin and the Challenge of Feminist Criticism," *Critical Inquiry,* 9 (September 1982), 45–76; Jonathan Culler, *On Deconstruction;* and Henry Louis Gates, Introduction to *Our Nig* by Harriet Wilson (New York: Vintage, 1983).

16. Mary Jacobus, "Is There a Woman in This Text?," *New Literary History,* 14 (Autumn 1982), 138.

17. Alice Jardine, "Gynesis," *Diacritics,* 12 (Summer 1982), 54–65.

18. Julia Kristeva, "Women's Time," *Signs,* 7 (Autumn 1981), 15.

19. Jardine, 59–60.

20. See Alice Jardine, "Introduction to Julia Kristeva's 'Women's Time,'" *Signs,* 7 (Autumn 1981), 11–12 and n. 12.

21. Rider Haggard, *She* (New York: Airmont, 1967), p. 76.

22. Stuart Schneiderman, *Jacques Lacan: The Death of an Intellectual Hero* (Cambridge: Harvard University Press, 1983), p. 30. See also the testimony of a French feminist who was there: Catherine Clément, *The Lives and Legends of Jacques Lacan,* trans. Arthur Goldhammer (New York: Columbia University Press, 1983), pp. 61–67.

23. Jacques Lacan, "God and the Jouissance of Woman," in *Feminine Sexuality: Jacques Lacan and the école freudienne,* eds. Juliet Mitchell and Jacqueline Rose (New York: Norton, 1983), p. 144.

24. Jane Gallop, *The Daughter's Seduction: Feminism and Psychoanalysis* (Ithaca: Cornell University Press, 1972), Chapter 3.

25. Sherry Ortner, "Oedipal Father, Mother's Brother and the Penis," *Feminist Studies,* 2 (1975), 176–82; and Jane Gallop, "The Ghost of Lacan, the Trace of Language," *Diacritics,* 5 (Winter 1975), 24.

26. Elaine Marks and Isabelle de Courtivron, eds., *New French Feminisms* (Amherst: University of Massachusetts Press, 1980).

27. Schneiderman, p. 30.

28. See Gayatri Spivak, "Displacement and the Discourse of Women," forthcoming; and Christopher Norris, *Deconstruction: Theory and Practice* (London: Methuen, 1982), p. 71.

29. In this paragraph I have adapted Juliet Mitchell's statement about the discovery of the unconscious in psychoanalysis, in *Psychoanalysis and Feminism* (New York: Pantheon, 1974), p. 322.

30. Emily Toth, "Why a *Kate Chopin Newsletter?*," *Kate Chopin Newsletter*, 1 (Spring 1975), 2.

31. Jane Alpert, *Growing Up Underground* (New York: Morrow, 1981), p. 355.

32. Catherine Belsey, "Re-reading the Great Tradition," in *Re-reading English*, ed. Peter Widdowson (New York and London: Methuen, 1982), pp. 132–33.

33. Northrop Frye, "Expanding Eyes," *Critical Inquiry*, 11 (1975), 201–2. I also discuss this passage in "Towards a Feminist Poetics," in *Women Writing and Writing about Women*, ed. Mary Jacobus (New York: Barnes and Noble, 1979), pp. 37–38.

34. Graff, p. 5.

35. Terry Eagleton, *Criticism and Ideology* (London: NLB, 1976), p. 11.

36. Geoffrey Hartman, *Criticism in the Wilderness* (New Haven: Yale University Press, 1980), p. 175.

37. Terry Eagleton, *Walter Benjamin, or Towards a Revolutionary Criticism* (London: Verso Editions and NLB, 1981), p. 99.

38. Barbara Hernnstein Smith, "Contingencies of Value," *Critical Inquiry*, 10 (September 1983), 7.

39. Edward Said, *The World, the Text, and the Critic* (Cambridge: Harvard University Press, 1983), p. 169.

40. Gayatri Spivak, "A Response to Annette Kolodny," unpublished essay, University of Texas, Austin. Thanks to Gayatri Spivak for sharing this work with me.

Shoshana Felman
1942–

For nearly twenty years the Israeli critic and scholar Shoshana Felman has been publishing from her base at Yale University books and articles exploring the relationship between literature and psychoanalysis. She was born in Tel Aviv on January 29, 1942. She received her B.A. and M.A. from the Hebrew University of Jerusalem in 1964 and 1966, with degrees in both French and English literature. She then studied at the University of Grenoble, in France, from 1967 to 1968, in preparation for a dissertation on Stendhal; in the two years following she sought to broaden the theoretical foundations of her thought by taking courses in philosophy, linguistics, psychology, and critical methodology, as well as literature, at the University of Geneva. She returned to Grenoble in 1970 to receive her Ph.D. *("Très honorable avec les félicitations du jury")*. Yale has been her academic home since 1970. She has been linked, almost inevitably, with some of the other "Yale School" critics, for her method is to bring to bear in her work the combined disciplines of philosophy, linguistics, psychoanalysis, and literary theory. Felman is currently (since 1986) Thomas E. Donnelly Professor in French and Comparative Literature.

Felman's first book was her doctoral dissertation, *La "Folie" dans l'oeuvre romanesque de Stendhal* (1971), a semantic and lexical study which draws the conclusion in its final chapters on *Armance* and *La Chartreuse de Parme* that in Stendhal one has not a synthesis of reason and madness, but a permanent tension between these two contradictory poles. She demonstrates how Stendhal's understatement derives from fear of hyperbole. Her second book, *La Folie et la chose littéraire* (1978), was translated into English as *Writing and Madness* (1985), containing eight of the twelve chapters of the French original. Here Felman demonstrates a method that is complex and, in the context of Lacan, emphatically psychoanalytic. (She was trained in psychoanalysis at the Western New England Institute for Psychoanalysis.) She recalls that "repression is defined by Freud as a 'failure of translation,'" and sets up a "dialogical perspective constituted by an intellectual exchange between America and France, between French and English, between the Gallic and the Anglo-Saxon contexts." Moreover, she performs "a two-level reading" that is "a reading of the text and a reading of its readings," the second part of which she defines as "the matter of transference." Felman's interest is in finding a point of difficulty and uncertainty regarding interpretation; she cites Lacan's axiom that "meaning indicates only direction, points only at the sense toward which it fails." The English version begins with a discussion of Foucault and Derrida, then provides essays on Gérard de Nerval, Flaubert, Balzac, Lacan, and Henry James ("Turning the Screw of Interpretation").

Le Scandale du corps parlant: Don Juan avec Austin, ou la séduction en deux langues (1980)—in translation *The Literary Speech Act: Don Juan with Austin, or Seduction in Two Languages* (1983)—is once more a "crossroads" of disciplines, languages, and theory. Felman discusses literary language as "performative" (one of J. L. Austin's terms), to be evaluated "not on the basis of *truth*, but *satisfaction*." Structured as "a meditation on promising," the book grows around the theme of the Don Juan myth with its dimensions of eroticism and pleasure, and its central figure who knows only how to promise. "Modern Don Juans, they know that truth is only an act. That is why they subvert truth and do not promise it, but *promise themselves to it*"—which Felman calls a logic of *scandal*. In a characteristic remark she observes that the task of the critic is "to articulate not what is said" but "what is happening" in the act of saying.

Felman's most recent book, *Jacques Lacan and the Adventure of Insight: Psychoanalysis in Contemporary Culture* (1987), is a study of the art (or act) of reading. She speaks of psychoanalysis "as, primarily, a revolutionary lesson . . . [modifying] both the interpretive stance and the very conception of the basic cultural act of reading." She draws on Freud and Lacan, and attempts to give an account of Lacan's "commitment to the triple reference—his persistent and creative use of the triple dimension of practice (clinical event), concept (theory), and metaphor (literature), in his multilayered and irreducibly complex account of all three together." She establishes Lacan's concept of the Oedipus complex (reconstructed "not as an answer but as the structure of a question") and asserts any reading, far from being simply factual, is metaphorical, "playing out its own literary resonances and deliberately operating at the level of a parable." There is, therefore, "no psychoanalytic understanding that can dispense with narrative or truly go beyond it." This is true in Lacan, she says, and, for that matter, Felman, too.

Felman is the contributor of many articles published in Europe and the United States. In addition to the books she has written, she is the editor of *Literature and Psychoanalysis: The Question of Reading—Otherwise* (1977). Two more books are in progress, *What Does a Woman Want? Reading and Sexual Difference* and *Testimony in History, Literature and Psychoanalysis*. She describes herself as intending to do more projects on feminist approaches to literature, on the creative interaction between psychoanalysis and literature, and on the relationship between theories of literature and film.

FROM

WRITING AND MADNESS

Jacques Lacan: Madness and the Risks of Theory (The Uses of Misprision)

—Meaning and Knowledge
—Grammar and Rhetoric
—A Shade of Enthusiasm
—The Status of Teaching: An Ethic of the Unconscious
—Knowledge Presumed to be a Subject: The Drop of Ink
—"Don't You See I'm Burning?" or Lacan and Philosophy

Meaning and Knowledge

"The truth pursued by science," writes Georges Bataille, "is true only on condition that it be devoid of meaning, and nothing can have meaning except insofar as it is fiction."[1] This proposition could define at once the doctrine and the difficulty of psychoanalysis, as a *practice*—and a *science*—of the *fiction* of the subject. "What is truth, if not a complaint?" says Lacan. Now, "it is not the *meaning* of the complaint that is important, but whatever might be found beyond that meaning, that might be definable as real." The "real," here, refers specifically to what is not dependent upon the idea the subject has of it: "that which is not affected by my thinking about it."[2] "There is no other truth," Lacan affirms, "than mathematicized truth, that is, *written* truth"; truth, in other words, "can hinge only on axioms: truth proceeds only from what has no meaning."[3] There is truth only where there is no meaning.

Does psychoanalysis, then, aspire to meaning—or to truth? What is the meaning *of* psychoanalysis? This question, whose urgency has become evident in the current field of theory (but we know—from psychoanalysis—that evidence is, precisely, that which is *least seen*), this now unavoidable question of *the meaning of psychoanalysis,* is in fact a contradiction in terms, since "meaning" is forever but a fiction and since it is psychoanalysis itself which has taught us that. But contradiction, as we know, is the mode of functioning par excellence of the unconscious, and consequently, also of the logic of psychoanalysis. To reckon with psychoanalysis is to reckon with contradiction, including its disequilibrium, without reducing it to the specular illusion of symmetry or of a dialectical synthesis. If, indeed, the specular illusion, the "Imaginary," to use the Lacanian term, is itself a constitutive principle of *meaning*, being precisely "that which *blocks* the decoding of the *Symbolic*," which in turn acts as a vehicle for the Real only by being "always encoded," then "the Imaginary is a dimension [*dit-mension,* a speech-dimension] as important as the others."[4] The Imaginary is an irreducible dimension because within language, the "sememe"—the semantic unit—is always occupied by the body: it makes up for the fact that there is nothing else to lead the body toward the Other. There is no *natural* relationship: the only relationship with the Other is by "the intermediary of what *makes sense* in language."⁵ We must not, then, resolve the contradiction, but resolve to accept it: we must articulate the question of the *meaning* of psychoanalysis on the basis of its own contradiction: we must consider this contradiction not as a contingent fact, but as the condition that makes possible the very question of psychoanalysis: of psychoanalysis *as a question*. Psychoanalysis introduces into the field of theory nothing less than the necessity of a new kind of articulation of its own question: the subversive urgency of psychoanalysis, its momentousness for culture, lies in the need it has brought out and in the henceforth irreversible search it has inaugurated for *a new status of discourse.*

If, by its most radical dimension, psychoanalysis subverts the very status of meaning, even while it is thereby constrained to call *itself* in question and to subvert *its own* meaning, it does so because, as Lacan says, "meaning *knows itself*": meaning is, above all else, that which is present to itself; it is therefore a form of knowledge—knowledge of self—of consciousness. Now, if Freud's discovery of the unconscious "makes sense" (we see here again the pervasive problem of meaning that language cannot eliminate, the problem of the apprehension by consciousness of the unconscious which escapes it), this "id" (this "it") which speaks yields a *language* which *knows*, but without any subject being able to assume such a knowledge or being able to know that he/she knows. Lacan makes it clear that we are in no way dealing with the myth of "non-knowledge" [*non-savoir*] that a superficial avant-garde used to its advantage: for not only is it not *sufficient* not to know; the very ability not to know is not granted to us,⁶ and cannot thus be taken for granted. What we are dealing with is a knowledge that is, rather, indestructible; *a knowledge which does not allow for knowing that one knows;*⁷ a knowledge, therefore, that is not supported by *meaning* which, by definition, *knows itself*. The subject can get a hold on this unconscious knowledge only by the intermediary of his *mistakes*—the effects of non-sense his speech registers: in dreams, slips of the tongue, or jokes.

"A question suddenly arises (. . .): in the case of the knowledge yielded solely by the subject's mistake, what kind of subject could ever be in a position to know it in advance?"⁸ The "subject who is presumed to know," that basic myth of Western culture, of the University, and of philosophic discourse, can only be "God Himself": a reflection in which the "knowledge" of consciousness contemplates itself, a phantom of potency produced by the narcissistic, self-inflating spell of the mirror. "Here he is, the God of the philosophers, dislodged from his latency in every theory. *Theoria,* might that not be the place in the world for the theo-logy?"⁹ The "subject presumed to know" lives in delusions and fantasies. By subverting this subject, psychoanalysis has radicalized a theory of non-transparency, a theory of what Baudelaire calls "the universal misunderstanding," and Proust "that perpetual error that we call, precisely, life." But within this theory, the position of psychoanalysis is itself problematic since it arises from the contradiction which determines its own discourse, namely: How can one construct a *theory* of the mistake essential to the very subject of theory as such? And if error is universal, how is one to escape error oneself? To what sort of listening or understanding can one appeal in a theory of radical *mis-understanding*? Lacan is fully aware of the untenable position he has nevertheless taken and taken on with an unparalleled intensity of effort and desire: "Retain at least what this text, which I have tossed out in your direction, bears witness to: my enterprise does not go beyond the act in which it is caught, and therefore, its only chance lies in its error—in its misprision [*elle n'a de chance que de sa méprise*]."[10] To my mind, the staggering originality of Lacan's work and discourse resides precisely in this untenable theoretical position. I would like, then, to attempt here an (overtly) brief meditation on this *méprise*—this misprision[11]—and on the significance of Lacan's gesture of giving it its chance.

Grammar and Rhetoric

Misprision, for Lacan, is of course an outgrowth of "the trickiness of the unconscious," which in language "is revealed by the rhetorical overload Freud shows it utilizes to make its argument":[12] the symptom functions like a metaphor, desire like a metonymy; the narcissistic mechanisms of defense and resistance employ all kinds of "tropes" and "figures of speech"—periphrasis, ellipsis, denial, digression, irony, litotes, etc.[13] A theory of misprision will thus be a theory of the *rhetoric* of the unconscious: "On the basis of the manifestations of the unconscious with which I deal as an analyst, I came to develop a theory of the effects of the signifier through which I rejoin the preoccupations of rhetoric."[14] Alongside this inquiry into rhetoric, there is in Lacan's work a second project, focusing on *grammar:* "Such are the structural conditions which determine—as *grammar*—the system of encroachments constitutive of the signifier."[15] The accomplishment of this double project should thus establish a *grammar of rhetoric*.

The logical coherence of such a project may seem self-evident. However, for a logician like Charles Sanders Peirce, the logical affiliation between rhetoric and grammar cannot be taken for granted: in fact, Peirce makes a distinction between "pure rhetoric" and "pure grammar." What he calls "pure rhetoric" is the well-known process by which one sign engenders another: a system of reference from sign to sign in which meaning is but another sign, requiring for its establishment the intervention of a *third* element which Peirce calls the *interpretant*. "Pure grammar," on the other hand, postulates the possibility of a continuous, binary relationship between sign and meaning not requiring the intervention of a third element. In general, we think of grammar as a logical system *par excellence* and, as such, identical to itself, universal, and generative, that is, inscribing the possibility of infinite combinations and transformations stemming from a *single, unified model* without the intervention of another model that would interfere with or subvert the first.[16] By contrast, rhetoric can be perceived only through a *discontinuity* that subverts or, at the very least, contradicts the logical *continuity* of the grammatical model. Rhetoric, to borrow out of context a Lacanian expression, always has an *"incongruous dimension* which analysts have not yet entirely given up because of their justified feeling that their conformism is of value only on the basis of that dimension."[17]

But if the grammatical model of continuity and the rhetorical model of discontinuity are not congruent, how are we to understand, as a whole, the Lacanian project of establishing a *grammar of rhetoric*? It would seem that Lacan's scientific project is to reduce the rhetorical mystifications of the unconscious to the rigor of a grammar. The unconscious as an operation and psychoanalysis as a science would, as a result, be modeled on two different epistemologies and would be distinguished from each other just as grammar is distinguished from rhetoric. "If the symptom is a metaphor, it is not a metaphor to say so," Lacan affirms.[18] To "grammaticalize" rhetoric would then be to formalize it, to abstract a concept from it, to state a theory of rhetoric in a language itself rid of rhetoric: it would be to make the uttering of a statement coincide perfectly with what is stated, concerning, but also contradicting, rhetoric itself which is precisely "the law by which the utterance of a statement can never be reduced to the statement itself of whatever discourse."[19] Man pursues his dream, Lacan says elsewhere, "and as he does, it sometimes happens that he wishes to stop dreaming."[20] By the same token, Lacan himself, at times, dreams of dreaming no more: "If all that is articulated in sleep only enters into analysis through its narration, doesn't this presuppose that the structure of narration does not succumb to sleep?"[21] The task Lacan assigns himself is to break away from sleep so as to talk about it, to break away from the very mechanisms of the unconscious in order to *say the unconscious itself*.

Is this project feasible? Lacan is the first to recognize and to affirm that one cannot *get out of* the unconscious; therefore, it is not possible to say the unconscious itself, it is not possible to free oneself from its fundamental function as deception in order to enunciate, without deceiving oneself, the absolute law of deception: "We don't even know if the unconscious has a being in itself, and (...) it is because one could not say *that's it* that it was named the 'it' [*id*]. In fact, one could only say of the unconscious, *that's not it*, or rather, *that's it, but not for real*."[22] Lacan formulates the same logical principle when he states "that no metalanguage can be spoken, or, more aphoristically, that there is no Other of the Other."[23] What, however, is a *grammar* (a formalized grammar) if not the epitome of metalanguage? Grammar is thus—and Lacan knows it—one more impossible desire: the desire to establish a norm, a rule of *correctness*, to avoid precisely the misprision inherent in the enterprise, to be for once a *non-dupe*. But who knows better than Lacan that "non-dupes err"?[24] Lacan's writing thus articulates the very torment which inhabits logic. And the chances taken by Lacan's text—what gives it a chance and what makes its chance ours—is the spark struck up in language by the inner tension of a discourse struggling with itself, struggling with its double, contradictory desire: the desire for grammar and its counterpart, the desire for rhetoric. It is precisely through this contradiction that Lacan's discourse rejoins the *Real*: "the real," says Lacan, "is the *impossible*."

A Shade of Enthusiasm

Lacan's language registers this contradictory desire both as a complication and as a simplification: on the one hand, as the ironic and sophisticated complication of a theory of misprision which excepts—in all conscience—neither its author nor its recipients; and on the other hand, as the affective simplification of the pathos of failure which pervades that discourse,[25] a pathos countered by the intensity of Lacan's affirmations and by the urgency of his enthusiasm. "The originality we are allowed," says Lacan, "is limited to the scrap of enthusiasm we have brought (. . .) to what Freud was able to name"[26] The urgency of the enthusiasm in Lacan's text serves to wrest affirmation from uncertainty, from the doubt occasioned by its own contradictions and complications. It manifests, in the very midst of logic, the function of desire,[27] that "function of haste"[28] necessary to produce an affirmation within a plural logic. Each time the urgency passes, the enthusiasm inevitably subsides again into a sense of failure, in recognition of its own inescapable naïveté, of the blindness of its own intoxication. Lacan takes stock—within his desire for *grammar*—of his own unconscious *rhetoric*. "A shade of enthusiasm is the surest trace to leave behind in a writing to make it dated—in the worst sense of the word." That is the way Lacan introduces nothing less than his famous Rome Report, "The Function and Field of Speech and Language in Psychoanalysis": "We wish to discuss," writes Lacan, "the subject put in question by this report, since putting the subject here in its place, at the place in which we ourselves have not failed to illustrate it, is but to do justice to the place where it lies in wait for us."[29] The movement of Lacan's text thus obeys the principle outlined by Bachelard: "Let us begin by admiring. Later, we shall see whether it will be necessary, through criticism or reduction, to organize our disappointment."[30]

"A shade of enthusiasm" is thus the surest trace to leave behind in a writing to make it dated. But what does "to make dated" mean here? When we are dealing with Lacan, it means, first of all, to mark a memorable date, to introduce a new articulation into cultural discourse, a "renewal of the alliance with Freud's discovery."[31] But since this innovation, this "renewal of the alliance" rallies specifically to an elusive structure, consisting in the linguistic articulation of the very mechanisms of repression through which truth escapes, modernity can be attained only within a radical dimension of loss. Modernity is precisely what gets lost: what gets lost in and through the very welling up of the enthusiasm of having discovered it. Enthusiasm thus becomes the hallmark of the "missed chance," that peculiar movement through which we move away from that toward which we want to go. "If it is true that psychoanalysis rests on a fundamental conflict, on an initial radical drama as far as everything that might be included under the heading psychical is concerned, the innovation to which I have referred (. . .) makes no claim to a position of exhaustiveness with respect to the unconscious, since it is, itself, an intervention in the conflict (. . .). This indicates that the cause of the unconscious (. . .) must be conceived as, fundamentally, a lost cause. And it is the only chance one has of winning it."[32]

This radical dimension of loss is, therefore, nothing other than the loss of the security of a metalanguage, the loss of a "claim to a position of exhaustiveness" which would precisely be the claim of *grammar:* we are faced, once again, with the inescapable dimension of *rhetoric,* that "stumbling block" which forces discourse to discover that it can only define rhetoric rhetorically, by participating in it, i.e., by stumbling, by elaborating not a grammar of rhetoric but a *rhetoric of rhetoric:* "Stumbling, faltering, splitting. In a spoken or written sentence something slips (. . .). It's there that something else is asking to be realized—something which appears as intentional, of course, but partaking of *a strange temporality.*"[33] This "strange temporality" is the lack of a present, the non self-presence characteristic of the rhetorical mode. It is also in this sense that the rhetoric of desire and enthusiasm is bound to be *dated:* for this rhetoric is not contemporaneous with its own statement. "There is no present," writes Mallarmé, "no—a present does not exist. (. . .) Ill-informed is he who would proclaim himself his own contemporary."[34]

To say that enthusiasm makes a text "dated" is to say that the enthusiasm has had a future that has come to point to it as past; that, from its own enthusiasm, the text has gleaned both more and less than it had expected; that urgency—both emotional and logical—has inscribed in language a vanishing point where the writing becomes *self-transgressive.* It is to say that the text—as it must—has organized our disappointment, has disappointed its own enthusiasm, subverted its own fantasy, and recanted the authority of its own rhetoric.

Inescapably, enthusiasm is what passes; it is, therefore, *nothing:* nothing, in any case, other than what is doomed—like us—to pass. "It is here that is inscribed that final *Spaltung* by which the subject articulates himself in the Logos, and on which Freud was beginning to write, giving us, at the ultimate point of a work that has the dimensions of being, the solution of the 'infinite' analysis, when his death applied to it the word Nothing."[35]

> Nothing, this foam, virgin verse
> Denoting only its cut.[36]

"A shade [*un rien*] of enthusiasm" has a good chance of amounting to the *nothingness* [*rien*] of enthusiasm. But isn't that the source, precisely, both of the misprision and of the chance inherent in psychoanalytic *transference*? "At that turning point where the subject experiences the collapse of the assurance provided him by that fantasy whereby each individual fashions his view of the Real, what becomes evident is that the hold of desire is *nothing* but the hold of an un-being."[37]

In the "transference of intensity"[38] constitutive of desire's repetitions and structuring not just psychoanalytic treatment but also "that perpetual error that we call, precisely, life," what seeks realization is a kind of metaphoric operation, a desire for analogy—for metaphor. But the result is, each time, the abortion of the specular analogy, the failure of the metaphor to attain and name its proper meaning. "If the psychoanalyst cannot respond to the demand, it is only because to respond to it would of necessity be to disappoint it, since what is demanded is, in any case, Something-Else; and *that is precisely what one must come to understand.*"[39] While the analyst, in the transferential operation, occupies the precise place of the "nothing" of enthusiasm, the place of the primordial partial object—*l'objet petit a*—which materalizes the non-being of desire, the end point of analysis—the naming of the Nothing—teaches the subject that the blind metaphor of his destiny is deprived of any proper meaning since all it can name is a metonymy (*l'objet petit a*). That is to say that the psychoanalyst, in playing the role of the non-proper (*non-propre*) (which the analysand deceives himself into reading as a proper name [*nom propre*]), occupies the radically other position of the pre-eminently rhetorical; and that the therapeutic goal is then to deconstruct the grammatical illusion of identity—of the proper—in order to reconcile the subject to his own rhetoric.

The Status of Teaching: An Ethic of the Unconscious

If transference is "the enacting of the reality of the unconscious,"[40] then, clearly, its manifestations will go beyond the strictly professional limits of psychoanalysis and become evident wherever effects of language are produced through regular interlocution: particularly, in the classroom situation. As Lacan points out, the transferential structure of the teaching relation is evoked in exemplary fashion in Plato's *Symposium:* "Who has expressed better than Alcibiades that the snares of love in transference have only one purpose, and that is to secure that of which he takes Socrates to be the unprepossessing container? But who knows better than Socrates that he bears only the meaning he engenders by containing this very *nothing?*"[41] The "Master" teacher, the illusory "subject presumed to know," occupies in the Real, like the analyst, the radically other position of the "*nothing*" of enthusiasm. However, far from challenging this instance of transference, teaching ought, rather, to assume it: "My seminar has been criticized precisely for playing, in relation to my audience, a role considered . . . dangerous, that of intervening in the transference. Now, far from denying it, I would regard this intervention as radical, as constitutive of the renewal of the alliance with Freud's discovery."[42] Lacan proposes here a praxis of teaching in which he puts himself against one of those three tasks declared by Freud to be impossible, since their effectiveness is based precisely on the mirage that governs their performance: psychoanalyzing, governing, educating. But here again, the impossible becomes for Lacan an imperative of the Real; and, in his view, the status of the unconscious is not ontological but *ethical:* "The status of the unconscious, which, as I have suggested, is so fragile on the ontic plane, is ethical. In his thirst for truth, Freud says, '*Whatever may happen, it is imperative to go there.*"[43] Lacan's practice of teaching, whose intensity derives at once from the pathos of a "vocation" and from the keenness of an intellectual awareness, from the "cruelty" (as Artaud would say) of a lucidity and of a rigor always striving toward that "extreme point of existence, the wager"[44]—embodies Lacan's quest not only for a new status of discourse, but also for a radically new kind of teaching.

It seems to me that this wager, which implicates us all, is the measure of Lacan's unprecedented move to confront psychoanalysis with its own madness, to push it—with all the risks involved—to the limits of its logical consequences.

"How are we to teach what psychoanalysis teaches us?" asks Lacan in a question posed not to the technicians of psychoanalytic treatment, but to the "practitioners of widely diverse disciplines."[45] What kind of teaching would assume in full consciousness its transferential function, assume, in other words, misprision with all its uses and abuses, with all its risks and possibilities? It would be, first of all, a teaching that would break with the mirror game of "the subject presumed to know," as well as with that false, narcissistic understanding inherent in all dual relationships; it would be a teaching based on a "firmer otherness,"[46] in which the "Master" would assume and articulate the radical *non-mastery* implied by the unconscious, making explicit his "rank"[47] (his position or his status) as the "nothingness of enthusiasm," so as to subvert fantasy and to "*transform the trap into a question.*"[48] It would be, consequently, an eminently ironic teaching, that is, once again, radically *rhetorical* (strategic): it would be, as Lacan puts it (speaking of Saussure, but his words apply to his own case as well), "a teaching worthy of the name, that one can come to terms with only in its own terms."[49] Such teaching would then mobilize the resources not so much of transparency as of obstacles: it would teach *about* and *through* misprision, about and through interpretive stumbling blocks and textual distortions: "Any return to Freud founding a teaching worthy of the name will occur only on that pathway where truth . . . becomes manifest in the revolutions of culture. That pathway is the only training we can claim to transmit to those who follow us. It is called—a style."[50]

But what is a style?

Knowledge Presumed to Be a Subject: The Drop of Ink

A "style," of course, is something that occurs in language; it is an event—or an advent—of textuality, that is, of writing. The writing of Lacan incorporates in turn the risk and the potential of misprision. It moves through the difficult and obstructed paths of desire. It writes, in Mallarmé's expression, "black on white," that is to say, darkening with the very inkwell of the unconscious, producing a *light* only by projecting *shadows* somewhere else.

> To write—
> The inkwell, crystal as a consciousness, with its drop,
> at the bottom, of shadows . . . casts the lamp aside.[51]

Lacan's writing, so like Mallarmé's, is not just well aware of its deliberate *literary* quality; it furthermore fully assumes its irreducible share of ambiguity, its irreducible involvement in that linguistic blindness which paradoxically *informs* flashes of clear-sightedness and insight. Misprision is, indeed, given its chance through the textual reverses suffered by the "subject presumed to know" [*le sujet supposé savoir*]: "I propose," Lacan says, "as a formula defining writing, the *knowledge presumed to be a subject [le savoir supposé sujet]*."[52] The fact that this aphoristic formula on writing's knowledge operates a playful chiasmus on Lacan's other well-known formula concerning knowledge; the fact that *le savoir supposé sujet* is a strict (syntactic and rhetorical) reversal of *le sujet supposé savoir,* is no gratuitous play on words: it suggests that what is at stake in writing is precisely a reversal, a subversion of subjective knowledge (of that knowledge which believes it knows itself), a subversion of the self and its self-knowledge. Writing's knowledge, then, although usually "presumed to be a subject"—believed to be an attribute of the (writing) subject—is nothing other in effect than the textual knowledge of what links the signifiers in the text (and not the signifieds) to one another: *knowledge that escapes* the subject but through which the subject is precisely constituted as the one who *knows how to escape*—by means of signifiers—his own self-presence: "The subject," says Lacan, "doesn't presume anything, he is presumed. Presumed, as we have taught, by the signifier which represents him to another signifier."[53]

If Lacan's writing lingers with so much emphasis and "insistence" on the opacity of the letter, on the *materiality* of the signifier in its puns and its anagrammatical surprises, it does so in order to try to "meet misprision in its own place,"[54] in that place of language where precisely writing is located: where we ourselves are being *played with*. This is the way Lacan's difficult writing—his "dis-spelling," as he puts it—should be understood: "The written as what means not-to-be-read" is "a demand for interpretation."[55] To interpret is to stumble on the *arbitrariness* of the sign so as to find out that chance, paradoxically, does not exist; to stumble on the arbitrariness of the sign so as to learn to interpret the *non-arbitrariness* of the connection between the signifiers. This, precisely, is what poets have always known: the insight into the non-arbitrariness of the arbitrary is constitutive of poetic knowledge in general, and specifically the poetic dimension inherent in Lacan's style. "And as Plato pointed out long ago, it is not at all necessary," says Lacan, "that the poet know what he is doing, in fact, it is preferable that he not know. That is what gives a primordial value to what he does. We can only bow our heads before it. . . . Freud always repudiated . . . the interpretation of art; what is called 'psychoanalysis of art' is to be avoided even more than the famous 'psychology of art' which is itself an insane notion. From art we should take seeds—take seeds for something else."[56]

Lacan does not indeed "interpret" poetry; he "takes seeds from it," incorporates it, writes it—and cites it. One of the reasons his texts are so difficult to approach is that he is (as he himself says about Freud) "an encyclopedia of the arts and muses."[57] But it is necessary to come to terms with this difficult, all but incomprehensible status of quotation—"the written as what means not-to-be-read"—in Lacan's texts. Lacan may quote Heidegger, for instance, while nonetheless keeping his distance from Heidegger's philosophic doctrine: "When I speak of Heidegger, or rather when I translate him, I at least make the effort to leave the speech he proffers us its sovereign significance."[58] *Sovereign significance* means that in the body of the text the quotation remains a foreign body; that it functions not as *meaning* (which "knows itself") but as a *signifier* which is always displaced, always imported from another text, another scene. Like the signifier, the quotation is incorporated into the text only through the unarticulated gap of its own displacement. The connection between the signifiers, the *articulation* between the various references quoted is what, by definition, can never be *thematized*, never be self-present in the text.

It is precisely this original stylistic feature of Lacan's text that philosophic discourse has refused to understand or to accept. Indeed, the unprecedented status of his quotations has been considered, by some philosophers, to be a major flaw. The "sovereign significance" that Lacan would like to leave, for example, to Heidegger's word, appears to these philosophers as a lack of seriousness, a philosophic "flippancy":

> One could say that his is clearly a way of not *reading* Heidegger's discourse, of avoiding or of refusing to read it. . . . One could also say that there is a certain flippancy (or excess cleverness) involved in this moving so flashily from one level to another and in "miraculously" resolving all the problems involved in the text's signifying process through a mere gesture of evocation.[59]

Upon encountering a writing as theoretically surprising, indeed as "flashy" as Lacan's, philosophic discourse—in a way specific to its reasoning—cannot but *miss the encounter* (all encounters are of course, in one way or another, missed: the difference here again is one of "style"). This particular philosophic way of missing the encounter—of giving form to "misprision"—here produces in effect, in a philosophically remarkable analysis, the "sovereign significance" of what might be called the *rigorist misunderstanding:* a radical misapprehension of the status of quotation in Lacan's works and, as a consequence, the rejection of his ellipsis and his "inarticulation," the rejection of his discourse as fundamentally a discourse *of the text*, "written as what means not-to-be-read." Philosophic discourse thus rejects Lacan's text insofar as the meaning of the latter can be neither reflected nor exhausted in its own self-knowledge, insofar precisely as the stake of its particular mode of *articulation* is to convey, put into play, and say the *maximum possible inarticulation*.

"Don't You See I'm Burning?" or Lacan and Philosophy

It is thus that, in their critical reading of Lacan's essay, "The Agency of the Letter in the Unconscious" (in which Lacan "transfers" the Freudian discovery onto Saussure), the philosophers have formulated the following critique: "The issue here is to articulate psychoanalysis with linguistics. . . . Yet this is precisely what is lacking . . . the articulation is missing."[60] Curiously enough, in (the very) place of what is missing, the critics find in Lacan's text a singular metaphor. Lacan writes:

> But haven't we felt for some time now that, having followed the pathways of the letter in search of the Freudian truth, we are getting very warm indeed, that something's burning all about us?[61]

The philosophers make the following comment: "But what this fire burns and lays waste here is nothing other, finally, than the articulation itself. At the place where the systematic linking of Saussure and Freud should take place, it burns, with the result that in this constitution of the science of the letter, we are in danger of having nothing left to decipher but ashes."[62]

What philosophy thus cannot accept is a discourse that *burns its way along,* skipping, in the process, its own logical (methodological) steps [*un discours qui brûle les étapes*]. For its part, philosophic discourse is defined by a demand for exhaustiveness of articulation—for *articulated,* thematized articulation. Even when philosophic discourse follows—as it currently does—more and more tortuous paths which, exhausting all possible detours and turns, "lead nowhere," it is still, despite all its denials, based on a fundamental demand for a linear course, requiring its progress to be uninterrupted and its detours to be kept in check; it is still based on a constitutive belief in the continuity (and exhaustiveness) of the Path. The paradox and the contradiction of contemporary philosophy reside in the fact that it attempts to express, by means of paths that are *continuous,* the radical nature of *discontinuity.* Lacan's position seems diametrically opposed to this: while it can be said that Lacan wishes to articulate the *continuity* of a logic and a mathematics of the unconscious, it is clear that he goes about it along paths remarkable for their *discontinuity.* These two positions, symmetrically contradictory and contradictorily asymmetrical, are symptomatic both of the difficulty and of the ambiguity of what is at stake in modern culture, namely, the search for a new status of discourse.

If contemporary psychoanalysis and philosophy both find themselves wrestling with the dramatic necessity, the ineluctable urgency, of breaking away from "Meaning," of radically "getting out of" the epistemology of presence and of consciousness, they are wrestling as well with the difficulty (the impossibility?) of raising their own discourse to the level of their discoveries and projects, of measuring up to the immeasurable demands, the unprecedented radicality, of the Freudian revolution. Rimbaud:

> —The mind is in authority, it insists that I remain in the West. It will have to be silenced if I am to end as I intended.[63]

Both Lacanian and ("post-phenomenological") philosophic discourse have thus produced "horrible toilers,"[64] engaged in rejecting the claims of both the "concept" and the "knowledge" it entails. This rejection, however, is articulated in two different ways: poetically by Lacan, discursively by the philosophers. Now, between philosophers and poets, the latter, paradoxically, are perhaps the least naïve. For if today's philosophers think they know that they don't know, the poets, for their part, know that they do know, but don't know what.

Lacan counters the philosophic, discursive variety of deconstruction with his own textual, rhetorical, and anagrammatical deconstruction. But, as we have seen, Lacan's (impossible) desire is to establish—rhetorically—a *grammar of rhetoric*. Conversely, philosophic discourse could be defined as the desire to exhaust the resources of grammar, in order to elaborate—*grammatically*—a radical *rhetoricity:* a rhetoric of rhetoric.

Hence, on the one hand, philosophic discourse reproaches Lacan for that moment of "denial" of radical "rhetoricity,"[65] when he seems to wish to pin down—to "arrest" or "immobilize"—the movement of rhetoric and metaphor (especially in his emphasis on the verb *to be:* "If the symptom *is* a metaphor, it is not a metaphor to say so"). But on the other hand, this same philosophic reading of Lacan's text in turn focuses on metaphor (in this case, Lacan's metaphor of fire: this "fire" of the Freudian truth "that is burning all about us") merely to arrest and immobilize it: the philosophic reading, in other words, inquires not into the "rhetoricity" of the metaphor, into its textual, rhetorical *functioning* in Lacan's writing, but rather into its *meaning,* its *proper* meaning. The metaphor is thus quickly pinned down, and its "closure" effected. "*It is well known* that Revelation is inscribed in letters of fire. Or, at any rate, that what is revealed is fire."[66]

By their own admission, these authors can learn from the "fire" metaphor only what is already "well known." And if it is indeed well known today that "God is dead," it is no less well known that "post-Nietzschean" philosophic discourse, for all that, still hasn't finished *killing* him off, killing off his ghost. Thus, the philosophic reading of Lacan's text rushes to the fire—to put it out. With the risk of fire averted, the (henceforth) philosophic path will be followed diligently, in the safety of a "comfortable pace"[67] that no longer "burns its way along."

To resolve this enigma of fire, Freud, however, proceeds quite differently, specifically in his discussion of the remarkable dream of a fire burning a corpse.[68] "And now we come upon a dream," Freud tells us (though it could just as well be said in reply to any philosophic reading), "and now we come upon a dream which raises no problem of interpretation and the meaning of which is obvious, but which, as we see, nevertheless retains the essential characteristics that differentiate dreams so strikingly from waking life and consequently call for explanation. It is only after we have disposed of everything that has to do with the work of interpretation that we can begin to realize the incompleteness of our psychology of dreams . . . Hitherto, . . . all the paths along which we have traveled have led us toward the light—toward elucidation and fuller understanding. But as soon as we endeavor to penetrate more deeply into the mental process involved in dreaming, every path will end in darkness. There is no possibility of *explaining* dreams . . . since to *explain* a thing means to *trace it back to something already known.*"[69]

Let us recall briefly the content and the circumstances of the dream in question, because the fire burning there will allow us to examine more fully the impact of the metaphor of fire on Freud's discovery, as well as its specific *rhetoricity* in Lacan's text. An old man had been engaged to keep vigil over the body of a child who had just died after a long illness; the father, worn out with fatigue, dozed off in the next room, and dreamed "that *his child was standing beside his bed, caught him by the arm and whispered to him reproachfully: 'Father, don't you see I'm burning?'* He [the father] woke up, noticed a bright glare of light from the next room, hurried into it and found the old watchman had dropped off to sleep and that the wrappings and one of the arms of his beloved child's dead body had been burned by a lighted candle that had fallen on them."[70]

Freud uses this dream to analyze, precisely, the question of awakening, and the dynamic relations between sleep and waking life. From this striking example, he concludes that if the dream, stimulated by the sleeper's perception of light from the real fire, nevertheless prolongs sleep despite the urgent need to awaken, it is because the dream functions not only to fulfill the father's wish to prolong his child's life but also to satisfy a bodily need, to integrate reality into the dream in order to fulfill the *wish to sleep*. Incited by the enigma of this dream, Freud proceeded, in his usual brilliant way, to ask a radical, unprecedented question: *What causes us to wake up?* and, by the same token, *What prevents awakening?*

In his usual brilliant way Lacan, in turn, picks up on Freud's question but displaces it somewhat, radicalizes it in a new way, by asking: "Where is *the reality* in this accident?"[71] I will translate the question thus: Is the reality of the desire that governs us and writes us of the order of the "fire" of our sleep, or of the order of the fire to which we awaken? Where exactly *is* the fire in this dream adventure? Which is the *real fire:* the one burning the living person in the dream, or the one burning, by metonymic repetition, the corpse in the next room and thus continuing, fatally and fantasmatically, to consume the body of a dead love? The rhetoricity of the Lacanian "fire," but also the rhetorical "burning" involved in every text, occurs precisely at the level of just such a missed encounter, of an *unarticulated* but dynamically metonymic, encounter between sleep and waking. Here, we can do no better than to quote Lacan, leaving to his writing its "sovereign significance": "Where is the reality in this accident, if not that something even more fatal is being repeated *by means of* reality, a reality in which the person who was supposed to be watching over the body still remains asleep, even when the father reemerges after having woken up? Thus the encounter, forever missed, has occurred between dream and awakening, between the person who is still asleep and whose dream we will never know and the person who has dreamt merely in order not to wake up.... It is only in the dream that this truly unique encounter can occur ... memorable encounter—for no one can say what the death of a child is, except the father *qua* father, that is to say, no conscious being. For the true formula of atheism is not *God is dead*—even by basing the origin of the function of the father upon his murder, Freud protects the father—the true formula of atheism is *God is unconscious.*"[72]

As we see here, the question Lacan asks is not the philosophic question, "What is the (im)*proper meaning* of the fire?" but rather a question I would call literary, the question par excellence of the textual, or of the rhetorical:

"Where is the fire that consumes, that burns us?" But this question is precisely one of undecidability—the very question of the undecidable—since the fire is of course burning in *both* rooms, in sleep and in waking life alike. The fire shifts in a dynamically metonymic burning that "catches all around us" only because *we don't know where it is*. "In this entirely sleeping world, only the voice is heard, *Father, can't you see I'm burning?* This sentence is itself a firebrand—of itself it brings fire where it falls—and one cannot see what is burning, for the flames blind us to the fact that the fire bears on the *Unterlegt*, on the *Untertragen*, on the real."[73]

Lacan's writing disconcerts us precisely because it is consumed by a "fire" that can never be *located* by the discourse of Meaning. Reading Lacan is like going through a Nervometer [*Pèse- Nerfs*];[74] it is like surrendering ourselves to a blindness that *works us over* and *thinks us through* without our necessarily ever achieving an exhaustive understanding of it. Thus it is that Lacan's text, whose singular articulation conveys the greatest possible degree of inarticulation, thinks beyond its means, and thinks *us* beyond ours.

> To bear down, according to the page, on the white, which inaugurates it, its simplicity, in itself, forgetful even of the title which would speak too loudly; and when there is aligned in a break, the least, disseminated break, chance vanquished word by word, indefectibly the white returns, gratuitous before, certain now, to conclude that nothing is beyond, and to authenticate silence.[75]

Lacan has effected in the current theoretical field an extremely subtle and complex *transferential operation*—in all the senses the word "transference" might possibly entail. To see that is to see, no doubt, that he is nothing but "the *Shade*"—the "*Nothing*"—of our own "enthusiasm"; but also, that he holds, in our cultural history, the undeniable "privilege of the Other": that he has given, that is, to psychoanalysis and to the field of culture and of theory precisely "*the gift of what he does not have;* namely, his love."[76]

NOTES

1. G. Bataille, "L'Apprenti sorcier," *Oeuvres complètes* (Paris: Gallimard, 1973), I, 526.
2. "Les Non-dupes errent" (seminar), April 23, 1974 (unpublished).
3. Ibid., February 11, 1973.
4. Ibid., November 13, 1973.
5. Ibid., June 11, 1974.
6. Ibid., April 23, 1974.
7. Ibid., February 2, 1974.
8. "La Méprise du sujet supposé savoir," *Scilicet*, no. I (1968), 38.
9. Ibid., p. 39.

10. Ibid., p. 41.

11. "A misunderstanding, a mistake (arch.)" (*Oxford English Dictionary*). This is the closest, and the only perfectly accurate, English equivalent to Lacan's word, *méprise*.

12. "La Méprise du sujet supposé savoir," p. 32.

13. "The Agency of the Letter in the Unconscious," *Ecrits: A Selection*, trans. A. Sheridan (New York: Norton, 1977), p. 156.

14. "La Métaphore du sujet," *Ecrits* (Paris: Seuil, 1966), p. 889.

15. "The Agency of the Letter," p. 152. Translation modified; emphasis added.

16. These comments, as well as the epistemological distinction between rhetoric and grammar, are based on the remarkable article by Paul de Man, "Semiology and Rhetoric," *Diacritics*, no. 3 (1973). Reprinted in *Allegories of Reading* (New Haven: Yale University Press, 1979).

17. "The Agency of the Letter," p. 152.

18. Ibid., p. 175.

19. "La Métaphore du sujet," p. 889.

20. "Les Non-dupes errent" (seminar), March 12, 1974.

21. "De la psychanalyse dans ses rapports avec la réalité," *Scilicet*, no. I, p. 35.

22. "La Méprise du sujet supposé savoir," p. 35.

23. "The Subversion of the Subject and the Dialectic of Desire in the Freudian Unconscious," *Ecrits: A Selection*, p. 311.

24. The title (translated) of Lacan's seminar of 1973–1974.

25. Cf. "La Psychanalyse: Raison d'un échec," *Scilicet*, no. I, pp. 42–50.

26. "Introduction to 'Scilicet,'" *Scilicet*, no. I (1968), 5–6.

27. Cf. Lacan's insistence on "the desire of the analyst" in *The Four Fundamental Concepts of Psychoanalysis*, trans. A. Sheridan (New York: Norton, 1977), p. 158.

28. Cf. "Le Temps logique et l'assertion de certitude anticipée," *Ecrits*, pp. 197–229.

29. "Du sujet enfin en question," *Ecrits*, p. 229.

30. Georges Bachelard, *La Poétique de l'espace* (Paris: P.U.F., 1958), pp. 197–198.

31. *The Four Fundamental Concepts*, p. 128.

32. Ibid., pp. 127–128.

33. Ibid., p. 25.

34. "L'Action restreinte," *Oeuvres complètes*, p. 372.

35. Lacan, "The Direction of the Treatment and the Principles of Its Power," *Ecrits: A Selection*, p. 277.

36. Mallarmé, "Salut," *Selected Poems*, trans. C. F. MacIntyre (Berkeley: University of California Press, 1957), p. 2.

37. Lacan, "Le Psychanalyste de l'école," *Scilicet*, no. I (1968), 25. My italics.

38. Cf. Freud, *The Interpretation of Dreams*, in the *Standard Edition* (London: Hogarth, 1956), V, 560, 562–563, 564: "I am now in a position to give a precise account of the part played in dreams by the unconscious wish . . . the psychology of the neuroses [shows us] that an unconscious idea as such is quite incapable of entering the preconscious and that it can only exercise any effect there by establishing a connection with an idea which already belongs to the preconscious, by *transferring its intensity* on to it and by getting itself 'covered' by it. Here we have the fact of 'transference' . . . It will be seen that the day's residues . . . not only borrow something from the unconscious . . . namely the instinctual force which is at the disposal of the repressed wish—but that they also offer the unconscious something indispensable—namely the necessary point of attachment for a transference."

39. Lacan, "La Psychanalyse: Raison d'un échec," p. 44. My italics.
40. Lacan, *The Four Fundamental Concepts*, p. 174.
41. Lacan, "Le Psychanalyste de l'école," p. 22.
42. *The Four Fundamental Concepts*, p. 128. Translation modified.
43. Ibid., p. 33. Translation modified.
44. Lacan, "La Raison d'un échec," p. 48.
45. Lacan, "La Psychanalyse et son enseignement," *Ecrits,* pp. 439, 440.
46. Ibid., p. 44.
47. Cf. Lacan's comments regarding the analyst: "This place that belongs to nobody . . . —the place of a rank to occupy, in semblance: the role of the analyst." "Les Non-dupes errent" (seminar), April 9, 1974.
48. On "transference," cf. *Ecrits,* p. 452.
49. *Ecrits: A Selection,* p. 149.
50. Lacan, "La Psychanalyse et son enseignement," p. 458.
51. Mallarmé, "L'Action restreinte, p. 370.
52. "Les Non-dupes errent" (seminar), April 9, 1974.
53. Lacan, "Le Psychanalyste de l'école," p. 19.
54. "De la psychanalyse dans ses rapparts avec la réalité," *Scilicet,* no. I (1968), 56.
55. Lacan, "Postface," *Les Quatre Concepts fondamentaux de la psychanalyse* (Paris: Seuil, 1973), p. 252. (This section does not appear in the English translation.)
56. "Les Non-dupes errent" (seminar), April 9, 1974.
57. "The Agency of the Letter, " pp. 169–170.
58. Ibid., p. 175.
59. J.-L. Nancy and P. Lacoue-Labarthe, *Le Titre de la lettre: Une Lecture de Lacan* (Paris: Galilée, 1973), pp. 136–137.
60. Ibid., pp. 84–85.
61. "The Agency of the Letter," quoted in ibid., p. 83.
62. Ibid., p. 86.
63. Rimbaud, "The Impossible," *Complete Works,* trans. P. Schmidt (New York: Harper & Row, 1967), p. 210. Translation modified.
64. Rimbaud, "Lettre dite du 'voyant,'" *Oeuvres* (Paris: Garnier, 1960), p. 346.
65. Nancy and Lacoue-Labarthe, *Le Titre de la lettre,* p. 149.
66. Ibid., p. 86. My italics.
67. Ibid., p. 96.
68. *The Interpretation of Dreams,* V, 509–511.
69. Ibid., pp. 510–511. My italics.
70. Ibid., p. 509. Freud's italics.
71. *The Four Fundamental Concepts,* p. 58.
72. Ibid., pp. 58–59. Translation modified.
73. Ibid., p. 59.
74. The implicit reference here is to a collection of prose poems by Artaud, entitled *Le Pèse-Nerfs* ("The Nervo-Meter").
75. Mallarmé, "Le Mystère dans les lettres," *Oeuvres,* p. 387.
76. Lacan, "The Signification of the Phallus," *Ecrits: A Selection,* p. 286.

Nina Auerbach
1943–

Nina Auerbach was born on May 24, 1943, in New York City. She attended the University of Wisconsin (B.A., 1964) and did graduate work at Columbia University (M.A., 1967; Ph.D., 1970). She has taught at Hunter College and California State University–Los Angeles, and since 1972 has been a member of the faculty at the University of Pennsylvania, where she is currently professor of English.

Auerbach, a Victorian specialist, has established herself as a leading feminist critic in the United States, beginning with the publication of her first book, *Communities of Women: An Idea in Fiction,* in 1978. Her second book, *Woman and the Demon: The Life of a Victorian Myth* (1982), explores the "other" Victorian myth of women—not the often voiced "angel in the house," but one that Auerbach sees as underlying it: woman as demonic and dangerous. The book attracted wide notice and was nominated for a National Book Critics Circle award in criticism.

Auerbach's next book, *Romantic Imprisonment: Women and Other Glorified Outcasts* (1985), is a collection of essays published betwen 1967 and 1983 which, taken collectively, traces a history of feminist criticism. Here Auerbach discusses Jane Austen, *Alice in Wonderland,* Dickens, the Brownings, George Eliot, the Brontës, Dorothy Sayers, and Ellen Terry, exploring both cultural myths and literary texts.

A frequent contributor of reviews and articles to scholarly publications, Auerbach also had essays included in *Toward a Poetics of Fiction* (1977, ed. Mark Spilka) and *Shakespeare's Sisters: Women Poets, Feminist Critics* (1979, ed. Sandra M. Gilbert and Susan Gubar). She is also the author of a biography of Ellen Terry (1987). Auerbach has received fellowships from the Ford Foundation, the Guggenheim Foundation, and the Radcliffe Institute.

WOMEN ON WOMEN'S DESTINY: MATURITY AS PENANCE

In searching for wings for women, feminist criticism may inadvertently be building new prisons. Three of our soundest and most searching feminist scholars have produced divergent books based on a single assumption: that properly understood, women writers create and inhabit an exclusively female context, out of which a "female tradition" can be extracted.[1] A corollary to this quest for a female literary tradition is that in these days of shifting trends and conflicting expectations, a perplexed female reader can turn only to other women to define her experience and evaluate it.

Literary men dare not cross these critical thresholds. Though Spacks, Moers, and Showalter have pruned angry rhetoric out of their scholarship, in their tacit exclusion of men from their cross-fertilizing sisterhoods, they are obeying the warning of an earlier, more bellicose generation of feminist critics. Kate Millett's *Sexual Politics* was our first and most urgent rallying cry,[2] warning its female readers away from the monsters which "classic" male writers had made of them. The gauntlet Millett flung at the traditional syllabus led easily to a sweeping dismissal of all fictional women created by men: "Our literature is not about women. It is not about men and women equally. It is . . . [about] not women but images of women [who] exist only in relation to the protagonist (who is male)."[3]

But in accepting too obediently the tenet that men mutilate their heroines to suit their own myopic needs, while even minor women writers reflect a certain truth of our experience, feminist criticism may itself be mutilating the women whose lives it wants to expand. For in excluding male visions from its canon, it may also be dismissing a faith in growth, freedom, and fun, of which women's worlds, in literature at any rate, are in general sadly deprived.

For from Fanny Burney's day to our own, women novelists have tended to cast a lugubrious and punitive glower over the lives of their heroines, lives into which male writers, no matter how overtly disapproving, often infuse a sense of option and power. Thackeray may insist intermittently that his Becky Sharp is a vixen to be shunned, but he endows her with the mobility to elude his definitions and to laugh at her own boundless role-playing with a freedom Jane Austen's similarly mobile Elizabeth Bennet is forbidden. Possibly because men have traditionally been raised to shape their own lives, while women are traditionally admonished to adjust to theirs; because a hero's vision of his life may be boundless, while a heroine's, conventionally, is predetermined by marriage, motherhood, and home; psychic and social boundaries tend to close quickly and ruthlessly in women's novels. Oddly, the omnipresence of feminism has only increased this pervasive literary entrapment.

Writing of a group of prize-winning stories by women, a recent critic "feels a kind of narrowing-down. The pure women-on-women story can eventually become an exercise in solipsism. The reader suspects that this intensive genre is on the way to creating new stereotypes of its own . . . a composite [of which] might look something like this": the author goes on to describe an educated and immobilized protagonist, trapped by men, children, and "irrelevant details" that obsess her. "Sometime back there, she has chosen the wrong life and now she doesn't know how to get out of it. . . . When she moves to take revenge on her life, she finds a self-destructive (often sexual) method."[4] One hopes this is not the only literary reflection to which our feminism will let us turn. Nor does this gloomy immobilization spring from women's new consciousness of discontent with old norms. Written in 1961, May Sarton's *The Small Room* poses a rhetorical question about an unorthodox life: "Is there a life more riddled with self-doubt than that of a woman professor, I wonder?" As a woman professor whose profession has been my most dependable cure for self-doubt, I can only meet this mournful definition of my life by pounding out "No! in thunder" with Leslie Fiedler, despite the fact that as a man, Fiedler is supposed to be incapable of defining my experience.

Of course we needed to turn to ourselves for a definition of ourselves; but at this point, I fear that one effect of feminist literary separatism will be our incarceration in a small room with an inflated specter of self-hate. Revealing and illuminating as women on women so often are, as a group, women writers tend to deny the flexibility, scope, and joy that are a vital dimension of all human life: the missing dimension that feminism first promised to restore. But now, the feminist ideal of the "woman-defined woman" threatens too often in our literature to turn into the "woman-destroyed woman" as well.

If one contemporary paradigm in women's literature is defined by immolation, paralysis, and madness, her Victorian counterpart was endowed with an often monstrously outsize nobility that led to her extinction, generally in the anonymity of an ambivalently defined marriage. Though contemporary critics have turned fruitfully back to the great Victorian women writers as role models, we need to remember the world they do not allow us: the world that makes possible a self-definition which male writers so often, and so enviably, assume.

Antigone, George Eliot's favorite heroine, seems to hover over our literary image of rebellious Victorian womanhood. Monumental in her rigid visionary insistence, her magnitude insures her defeat by the triviality of life-as-it-is—in contrast to such actual moral autocrats as Florence Nightingale and Queen Victoria, whose rigid self-insistence triumphed over surrounding pettiness. But art allows less than life might have to two of the most famous Victorian heroines: George Eliot's Dorothea Brooke in *Middlemarch* (1871–72) and Louisa May Alcott's Jo March in *Little Women* (1869–70). Both are endowed with all the fervor in their worlds, and both mature to renounce their early powers through penitential marriages which subdue them to commonality, although both Eliot and Alcott stubbornly fashioned unorthodox lives whose honor sprang out of defiance. As with so many women writers, the inevitability of defeat seems more literary than actual: the writer appropriates to herself all the joy of achievement, in life and in art, leaving her failed self to infect her heroines and edify her readers.

Though like the other characters in *Middlemarch,* Dorothea Brooke is "spiritually a-hungered," her destiny is defined exclusively by her two marriages and by the images of the prison and the maze that the book flings round her, hedging in her nobility and stature until "Dodo" seems a provincial female Minotaur immured in the labyrinth that is her novel. Though each marriage seems at first to promise purpose and meaning, each enmeshes her further and more finally: in its effects, her entombing marriage to the pedant Casaubon repeats itself in her subsequent marriage to his dashing cousin, Will Ladislaw. We learn early that Dorothea "likes giving up," and her marriages display this one talent she exercises fully.

The marriages are perceived, though, with increasing delicacy, in reiterated images of entombment. Dorothea's marriage to Casaubon is an incarceration which is literal, social, and spiritual at once, as "the still, white enclosure which made her visible world" where "her blooming full-pulsed youth stood . . . in a moral imprisonment which made itself one with the chill, colourless, narrowed landscape, with the shrunken furniture, the never-read books, and the ghostly stag in a pale fantastic world that seemed to be vanishing from the daylight."[5]

Mercurial and mobile, Will Ladislaw seems initially "like a lunette opened in the wall of her prison," and many critics still assume that Eliot intended, however unsuccessfully, to liberate Dorothea from her multiple crypts through a better marriage. Thus generations of female students have been admonished against immaturity by their male teachers when they chafe against her destiny; but the unmistakably elegiac tone of the novel's finale provides Dorothea with her final, and total, entombment, and the coffin is closed by George Eliot in her mask of the sibylline Wise Woman.

The finale's mournful emphasis on waste and erosion blends Dorothea's disastrous marriage to Casaubon with her supposedly triumphant marriage to Ladislaw, showing the common closure beneath their surface differences. As she submerges her ardor in "the common yearnings of womanhood," Dorothea loses even the mantle of grand defeat, embodying only "that element of tragedy that lies in the very fact of frequency": "But we insignificant people with our daily words and acts are preparing the lives of many Dorotheas, some of which may present a far sadder sacrifice than that of the Dorothea whose story we know" (p. 612). The ultimate burial of this Antigone is her assumption of the anonymity of Ismene: "Her full nature, like that river of which Cyrus broke the strength, spent itself on channels which had no great name on the earth. But . . . that things are not so ill with you and me as they might have been, is half owing to the number who lived faithfully a hidden life, and rest in unvisited tombs" (p. 613).

In her final revision, George Eliot banned Dorothea's uniqueness from survival even in the reader's memory, replacing it with her last, all-encompassing entombment. In manuscript, the final words and none of the implacability of "unvisited tombs," but restored Dorothea's most persistent attribute: "And that things are not so ill with you and me as they might have been is owing to the many of those who sleep in unvisited tombs, having lived a hidden life nobly."[6] This revision from "nobly" to "tombs" denies Dorothea's essence in perpetuity, forcing her into a common limbo touched only by the narrator's pitying, pervasive resignation. The turn of a phrase makes of her energy a forgotten irony, soothing the reader into agreeing that this last enclosure is the way of all aspiring flesh.

The lulling dreariness of Eliot's finale has often been used to epitomize her wisdom. It evokes more accurately a certain lugubrious pall that spreads over women writers when they create women's lives, even at the expense of its own material: for example, one wonders why Dorothea's many children neglect to visit her tomb. Moreover, though male Victorian writers similarly immolate their spirited heroines in marriage, they do not always let them go gentle into that good night. Hardy's Sue Bridehead must cope with the thundering wrath of Jude when she sacrifices herself to marriage: "That a woman-poet, a woman-seer, a woman whose soul shone like a diamond—whom all the wise of the world would have been proud of, if they could have known you—should degrade herself like this! I am glad I had nothing to do with Divinity—damn glad—if it's going to ruin you in this way!"[7] In *Middlemarch,* only the narrator has so exalted a vision of Dorothea's soul, and it is the narrator at the end who snuffs it out.

Similarly, in Henry James' *The Portrait of a Lady,* Ralph Touchett is the vehicle whereby Isabel Archer is reminded, not of life's constriction, but of its boundlessness. Like that of Hardy's Sue, her self-sacrifice in marrying Osmund is a free decision in a multitudinous world, while Dorothea's ultimate sacrifice is made to seem inevitable to the wise reader. Though women's heroines are repeatedly "ground in the very mill of the conventional," as Isabel is, few of them receive her bequest of the possibilities of space: "'You seemed to me to be soaring far up in the blue—to be sailing in the bright light, over the heads of men. Suddenly some one tosses up a faded rosebud—a missile that should never have reached you—and down you drop to the ground. It hurts me,' said Ralph audaciously, 'as if I had fallen myself!'"[8] I would argue, sadly, that there is something singularly unfemale in the joy of this vision, at least as far as fiction is concerned. A hundred years later, it seems our wings have still been clipped; but it remains a "perversity," to use both Hardy's and James' word, to deny the imagination of an open world of promise and power.

Though Hardy's Sue and James' Isabel both "fall" into grinding convention, their authors bestow on them some of the majesty of tragic choice; moreover, both are endowed with choric suitors to insist on their lambent possibilities had their vision been as large as life's promises. The potential buoyancy of the lives they abandon might seem to be embodied in Louisa May Alcott's stories for girls. For despite the tempering presence of Marmee and other cautionary adults, Alcott's tomboys are boisterously, joyfully ambitious, their hunger for games merging into plans for a triumphant future of "sailing in the bright light, over the heads of men." No doubt this insistence on life's promise and scope continues to make athletic, artistic Jo March in *Little*

Women an idealized self for girls today: Jo's scribbling, her impatience, her slang, above all her "romping," provide one of our few literary assurances that talent in a woman can burgeon out of sturdy good health.

The energy and fun of the first half of *Little Women* remove it from the ambience of *Middlemarch,* where "blooming full-pulsed youth" can move only from tomb to tomb. But the half-grotesque renunciation of Jo's marriage, together with the sense of inevitability that accompanies it, recalls the sacrificial consummation of Eliot's elegiac finale. Finally, Jo's romping and writing become embodied in her impossible wish to be a boy. She will not run off to Washington—seat of governmental power as well as escape from home—with her dashing comrade Laurie because the dream is inappropriate for "a miserable girl."[9] Shortly thereafter, she refuses Laurie himself and ultimately marries Professor Bhaer, the most Teutonic of Teutons, whose Spartan life is bare of the art, money, and vibrant physicality which life had seemed to promise Jo. His portliness precludes romping, and his Puritanism precludes writing: in deference to his horror at their effect on the young, she burns her published stories and denounces writing as "selfish." Destiny indulges her sacrifice equivocally; she becomes matriarch of her husband's boarding school, indefatigably tending the boys she can't be and indulging in secret her yearning love for the wildest ones.[10] In the final chapter, "Harvest Time," Marmee blesses her girls, who are now themselves chastened little mothers. This last emphasis on the seasonal cycle insists on the inexorability of Jo's destiny as strongly as had George Eliot's narrative voice of soothing, brooding wisdom. As in *Middlemarch,* the heroine is deprived of a fulminating Jude, or a visionary Ralph Touchett, to comment on the unnatural tragedy of her fall.

The adult and the adolescent classic concur in the message of their heroines' destinies: life, and the marriage with which it ends, are inevitable snuffings-out to which the strong submit. Both Dorothea and Jo are different characters at the end of their novels, more generalized and less vivid than they were. The end of their stories is less a ripening than a blurring into a common penitential destiny, whose assumed universality takes the edge from its betrayal. The traditional comic conclusion that Northrop Frye defines,[11] in which the flexibility of marriage and spring supplant winter's rigid authority, is streaked with tragedy in many women's novels, but the note of tragedy is secret, uncertain, rarely emerging to define itself as it does in corresponding novels by men. The rarity of Antigone's tragic fall is dubiously welded to the commonality of Frye's comic mythos, so that consummation unobtrusively turns to punishment, and the apparent liberation of life's continuity becomes its subtlest prison. The unstated yet implacable resignation which is so pervasive a part of women's literary voice rarely recomposes into heroic rebirth. Dorothea's nobility is extinguished in the final reality of her tomb. In the novel's vision, the closing epithalamium generates death rather than renewal of the spirit, a denial of the heroine's promise more profound than that in *The Portrait of a Lady,* where Ralph Touchett makes a final bequest of Isabel's rebirth, not vicariously through children, but in herself: "You will grow young again." Rarely do women endow their heroines with this resilience, or even with a prayer for it. They are doomed to grow up and leave the stage, though their author may play on till the end.

Today, women do seem as a class to be growing young again, going to school in life's promises as well as its prohibitions. In a decade of expansion, it seems needlessly, even wantonly, restrictive for us to reject what has at times bountifully been offered by literary men. But often to our loss we do. In George Gissing's late Victorian novel *The Odd Women* (1893), Rhoda Nunn rejects love to be a leader of women, her feminism exemplifying one of the few islands of elation in Gissing's dispirited novels. When she makes her final entrance there is no mention of tombs. Instead she exults: "The world is moving!"

For all her resolute anti-romance, Rhoda is one of the few women in fiction to be allowed a heroic identification of herself with her sweeping world. Her boundless identification of herself with space recalls the fluidity of Tennyson's Ulysses in his heroic boast: "I am a part of all that I have met." Though I can find no reason why this unity between the self and its world should be a masculine vision alone, in 1974 it was unequivocally rejected by one of Rhoda's literary descendants: the solitary, self-distrustful Jane Clifford in Gail Godwin's highly regarded novel, *The Odd Woman*.

Alone in a bleak world, trying to cling to an alien family, a self-absorbed lover she rarely sees, and a job whose slightest demands intimidate her, Jane combs desperately through Gissing's novel for a guide to life. But she ends up rejecting everything in it, last of all the heroine herself: "That left 'The world is moving!' 'How are you, Jane?' 'Oh, the world is moving!' She thought of Gerda [a caricatured feminist friend] burning her black candle, signing the death warrant for romantic love, now signing income tax forms for the employees of *Femme Sole*. She crossed off 'SUBLIMATION OF PERSONAL DESIRES AND FURIES INTO A "CAUSE."'"[12]

Depicted in Gissing's novel as a difficult triumph, Rhoda's breakthrough into the public sphere is sheer loss for Jane Clifford, who dismisses the achievement in knowing pseudo-Freudian jargon as "sublimation." But finally, entombed in her small room and her hopeless daydreams, Jane is a far grimmer and more static character than Rhoda was; moreover, her stubborn self-paralysis seems a more drastic insult to a contemporary woman's psyche than were Rhoda's mobility and courage. But as she sits alone with her notebook, scratching off one male-created woman after another by turning them into dismissive stereotypes, Jane Clifford is one image of our time, rejecting a literary endowment from men that might prove a rich inheritance in favor of the willed constriction of a very small room.

NOTES

1. Patricia Meyer Spacks, *The Female Imagination* (New York: Knopf, 1975); Ellen Moers, *Literary Women: The Great Writers* (New York: Doubleday, 1976);

Elaine Showalter, *A Literature of Their Own: British Women Novelists from Brontë to Lessing* (Princeton, N.J.: Princeton University Press, 1977).

2. Kate Millett, *Sexual Politics* (New York: Doubleday, 1970).

3. Joanna Russ, "Why Women Can't Write," in Susan Koppleman Cornillon, ed., *Images of Women in Fiction: Feminist Perspectives*, rev. ed. (Bowling Green, Ohio: Bowling Green University Popular Press, 1973), p. 5. See also Cynthia Griffin Wolff, "A Mirror for Men: Stereotypes of Women in Literature," *The Massachusetts Review* (1972), 13:207: "The stereotypes of women vary, but they vary in response to different masculine needs. . . . [Women] appear not as they are, certainly not as they would define themselves, but as conveniences to the resolution of masculine dilemmas." Wolff's article implicates women writers only in their collusion with masculine stereotypes; but five years later, I have come to the reluctant conclusion that women frequently "define themselves" in even more insidiously limited a fashion.

4. Robie Macauley in the *New York Times Book Review*, March 27, 1977, p. 7. See also Elin Schoen, "Kiss, Kiss, Kvetch, Kvetch: What's Ailing the New Belles of Letters?" *New York Magazine*, May 23, 1977, pp. 59–69, which excoriates the insult to female readers expected to identify with trapped and miserable heroines.

5. George Eliot, *Middlemarch* (1871–72; reprint, Cambridge, Mass.: Riverside Press, 1956), p. 202. Future references to this edition will appear in the text.

6. See Jerome Beaty, "Text of the Novel: A Study of the Proof," in Barbara Hardy, ed., Middlemarch: *Critical Approaches to the Novel* (New York: Oxford University Press, 1967), pp. 61–62.

7. Thomas Hardy, *Jude the Obscure* (1894–95; reprint, Boston: Houghton Mifflin, 1965), pp. 277–78.

8. Henry James, *The Portrait of a Lady* (1881; reprint, New York: New American Library, 1963), p. 318.

9. Spacks, in *The Female Imagination*, makes this point, p. 100.

10. For a fuller discussion of Jo's role throughout the March trilogy, see my *Communities of Women: An Idea in Fiction* (Cambridge, Mass: Harvard University Press, 1978), pp. 55–73.

11. See Northrop Frye, "The Mythos of Spring: Comedy" in *Anatomy of Criticism: Four Essays* (1957; reprint, New York: Atheneum, 1968), pp. 163–86.

12. Gail Godwin, *The Odd Woman* (1974; reprint, New York: Berkley Medallion Books, 1976), p. 246.

Terry Eagleton
1943–

Terence Francis Eagleton was born in 1943 in Salford, England, and earned M.A. and Ph.D. degrees at Trinity College, Cambridge University. He taught for several years at Cambridge before moving to Oxford University's Wadham College, where he has been fellow and tutor in poetry since 1969.

Preeminent as a Marxist critic in England, Eagleton has been praised for the accessibility of his writing as he relentlessly explores ideologies in literature with what one critic has called "grace, clarity, and force," as well as wit. Eagleton's early works were studies of New Left theology, but by the mid-1970s Eagleton was focusing on Marxist literary theory. *Myths of Power: A Marxist Study of the Brontës* (1975) was followed by *Marxism and Literary Criticism* (1976), a brief work which considers the author of a literary work as a producer and the relationships between literature and history. *Literary Theory: An Introduction* (1983), widely reviewed and quoted, declares literary criticism to be a political act and examines different schools of criticism and their related ideologies; every literary work, says Eagleton, is formed by ideology.

The Function of Criticism: From the Spectator *to Post-Structuralism* (1984) is both a history of English literary criticism and a polemical call to arms, urging that criticism become once again engaged in cultural politics. In 1986 a collection of Eagleton's previously published articles, *Against the Grain: Selected Essays 1975–1985*, appeared, and in 1987, a novel, *Saints and Scholars*.

Eagleton's other books include two studies of Shakespeare, *Shakespeare and Society* (1967) and *William Shakespeare* (1986); *Criticism and Ideology: A Study in Marxist Literary Theory* (1976); *Walter Benjamin; or, Towards a Revolutionary Criticism* (1981); and *The Rape of Clarissa: Writing, Sexuality and Class Struggle in Samuel Richardson* (1982). He has also edited books on Pope, Emily Brontë, and W. H. Auden.

FROM

LITERARY THEORY

CONCLUSION: POLITICAL CRITICISM

In the course of this book we have considered a number of problems of literary theory. But the most important question of all has as yet gone unanswered. What is the *point* of literary theory? Why bother with it in the first place? Are there not issues in the world more weighty than codes, signifiers and reading subjects?

Let us consider merely one such issue. As I write, it is estimated that the world contains over 60,000 nuclear warheads, many with a capacity a thousand times greater than the bomb which destroyed Hiroshima. The possibility that these weapons will be used in our lifetime is steadily growing. The approximate cost of these weapons is 500 billion dollars a year, or 1.3 billion dollars a day. Five per cent of this sum—25 billion dollars—could drastically, fundamentally alleviate the problems of the poverty-stricken Third World. Anyone who believed that literary theory was more important than such matters would no doubt be considered somewhat eccentric, but perhaps only a little less eccentric than those who consider that the two topics might be somehow related. What has international politics to do with literary theory? Why this perverse insistence on dragging politics into the argument?

There is, in fact, no need to drag politics into literary theory: as with South African sport, it has been there from the beginning. I mean by the political no more than the way we organize our social life together, and the power-relations which this involves; and what I have tried to show throughout this book is that the history of modern literary theory is part of the political and ideological history of our epoch. From Percy Bysshe Shelley to Norman N. Holland, literary theory has been indissociably bound up with political beliefs and ideological values. Indeed literary theory is less an object of intellectual enquiry in its own right than a particular perspective in which to view the history of our times. Nor should this be in the least cause for surprise. For any body of theory concerned with human meaning, value, language, feeling and experience will inevitably engage with broader, deeper beliefs about the nature of human individuals and societies, problems of power and sexuality, interpretations of past history, versions of the present and hopes for the future. It is not a matter of *regretting* that this is so—of *blaming* literary theory for being caught up with such questions, as opposed to some 'pure' literary theory which might be absolved from them. Such 'pure' literary theory is an academic myth: some of the theories we have examined in this book are nowhere more clearly ideological than in their attempts to ignore history and politics altogether. Literary theories are not to be upbraided for being political, but for being on the whole covertly or unconsciously so—for the blindness with which they offer as a supposedly 'technical', 'self-evident', 'scientific' or 'universal' truth doctrines which with a little reflection can be seen to relate to and reinforce the particular interests of particular groups of people at particular times. The title of this section, 'Conclusion: Political Criticism', is not intended to mean: 'Finally, a political alternative'; it is intended to mean: 'The conclusion is that the literary theory we have examined is political.'

It is not only, however, a matter of such biases being covert or unconscious. Sometimes, as with Matthew Arnold, they are neither, and at other times, as with T. S. Eliot, they are certainly covert but not in the least unconscious. It is not the fact that literary theory is political which is objectionable, nor just the fact that its frequent obliviousness of this tends to mislead: what is really objectionable is the nature of its politics. That objection can be briefly summarized by stating that the great majority of the literary theories outlined in this book have strengthened rather than challenged the assumptions of the power-system some of whose present-day consequences I have just described. I do not mean by this that Matthew Arnold supported nuclear weapons, or that there are not a good many literary theorists who would not dissent in one way or another from a system in which some grow rich on profits from armaments while others starve in the street. I do not believe that many, perhaps most, literary theorists and critics are not disturbed by a world in which some economies, left stagnant and lopsided by generations of colonial exploitation, are still in fee to Western capitalism through their crippling repayments of debts, or that all literary theorists would genially endorse a society like our own, in which considerable private wealth remains concentrated in the hands of a tiny minority, while the human services of education, health, culture and recreation for the great majority are torn to shreds. It is just that they would not regard literary theory as at all relevant to such matters. My own view, as I have commented, is that literary theory has a most particular relevance to this political system: it has helped, wittingly or not, to sustain and reinforce its assumptions.

Literature, we are told, is vitally engaged with the living situations of men and women: it is concrete rather than abstract, displays life in all its rich variousness, and rejects barren conceptual enquiry for the feel and taste of what it is to be alive. The story of modern literary theory, paradoxically, is the narrative of a flight from such realities into a seemingly endless range of alternatives: the poem itself, the organic society, eternal verities, the imagination, the structure of the human mind, myth, language and so on. Such a flight from real history is in part understandable as a reaction to the antiquarian, historically reductionist criticism which held sway in the nineteenth century; but the extremism of this reaction has been nevertheless striking. It is indeed the *extremism* of literary theory, its obstinate, perverse, endlessly resourceful refusal to countenance social and historical realities, which most strikes a student of its documents, even though 'extremism' is a term more commonly used of those who would seek to call attention to literature's role in actual life. Even in the act of fleeing modern ideologies, however, literary theory reveals its often unconscious complicity with them, betraying its elitism, sexism or individualism in the very 'aesthetic' or 'unpolitical' language it finds natural to use of the literary text. It assumes, in the main, that at the centre of the world is the contemplative individual self, bowed over its book, striving to gain touch with experience, truth, reality, history or tradition. Other things matter too, of course—this individual is in personal relationship with others, and we are always much more than readers—but it is notable how often such individual consciousness, set in its small circle of relationships, ends up as the touchstone of all else. The further we move from the rich inwardness of the personal life, of which literature is the supreme exemplar, the more drab, mechanical and impersonal existence becomes. It is a view equivalent in the literary sphere to what has been called possessive individualism in the social realm, much as the former attitude may shudder at the latter: it reflects the values of a political system which subordinates the sociality of human life to solitary individual enterprise.

I began this book by arguing that literature did not exist. How in that case can literary theory exist either? There are two familiar ways in which any theory can provide itself with a distinct purpose and identity. Either it can define itself in terms of its particular *methods* of enquiry; or it can define itself in terms of the particular *object* that is being enquired into. Any attempt to define literary theory in terms of a distinctive method is doomed to failure. Literary theory is supposed to reflect on the nature of literature and literary criticism. But just think of how many methods are involved in literary criticism. You can discuss the poet's asthmatic childhood, or examine her peculiar use of syntax; you can detect the rustling of silk in the hissing of the *s*'s, explore the phenomenology of reading, relate the literary work to the state of the class-struggle or find out how many copies it sold. These methods have nothing whatsoever of significance in common. In fact they have more in common with other 'disciplines'—linguistics, history, sociology and so on—than they have with each other. Methodologically speaking, literary criticism is a non-subject. If literary theory is a kind of 'metacriticism', a critical reflection on criticism, then it follows that it too is a non-subject.

Perhaps, then, the unity of literary studies is to be sought elsewhere. Perhaps literary criticism and literary theory just mean any kind of talk (of a certain level of 'competence', clearly enough) about an object named literature. Perhaps it is the object, not the method, which distinguishes and delimits the discourse. As long as that object remains relatively stable, we can move equably from biographical to mythological to semiotic methods and still know where we are. But as I argued in the Introduction, literature has no such stability. The unity of the object is as illusory as the unity of the method. 'Literature', as Roland Barthes once remarked, 'is what gets taught.'

Maybe this lack of methodological unity in literary studies should not worry us unduly. After all, it would be a rash person who would define geography or philosophy, distinguish neatly between sociology and anthropology or advance a snap definition of 'history'. Perhaps we should celebrate the plurality of critical methods, adopt a tolerantly ecumenical posture and rejoice in our freedom from the tyranny of any single procedure. Before we become too euphoric, however, we should notice that there are certain problems here too.

For one thing, not all of these methods are mutually compatible. However generously liberal-minded we aim to be, trying to combine structuralism, phenomenology and psychoanalysis is more likely to lead to a nervous breakdown than to a brilliant literary career. Those critics who parade their pluralism are usually able to do so because the different methods they have in mind are not all that different in the end. For another thing, some of these 'methods' are hardly methods at all. Many literary critics dislike the whole idea of method and prefer to work by glimmers and hunches, intuitions and sudden perceptions. It is perhaps fortunate that this way of proceeding has not yet infiltrated medicine or aeronautical engineering; but even so one should not take this modest disowning of method altogether seriously, since what glimmers and hunches you have will depend on a latent structure of assumptions often quite as stubborn as that of any structuralist. It is notable that such 'intuitive' criticism, which relies not on 'method' but on 'intelligent sensitivity', does not often seem to intuit, say, the presence of ideological values in literature. Yet there is no reason, on its own reckoning, why it should not. Some traditional critics would appear to hold that other people subscribe to theories while they prefer to read literature 'straightforwardly'. No theoretical or ideological predilections, in other words, mediate between themselves and the text: to describe George Eliot's later world as one of 'mature resignation' is not ideological, whereas to claim that it reveals evasion and compromise is. It is therefore difficult to engage such critics in debate about ideological preconceptions, since the power of ideology over them is nowhere more marked than in their honest belief that their readings are 'innocent'. It was Leavis who was being 'doctrinal' in attacking Milton, not C. S. Lewis in defending him; it is feminist critics who insist on confusing literature with politics by examining fictional images of gender, not conventional critics who are being political by arguing that Richardson's Clarissa is largely responsible for her own rape.

Even so, the fact that some critical methods are less methodical than others proves something of an embarrassment to the pluralists who believe that there is a little truth in everything. (This theoretical pluralism also has its political correlative: seeking to understand everybody's point of view quite often suggests that you yourself are disinterestedly up on high or in the middle, and trying to resolve conflicting viewpoints into a consensus implies a refusal of the truth that some conflicts can be resolved on one side alone.) Literary criticism is rather like a laboratory in which some of the staff are seated in white coats at control panels, while others are throwing sticks in the air or spinning coins. Genteel amateurs jostle with hard-nosed professionals, and after a century or so of 'English' they have still not decided to which camp the subject really belongs. This dilemma is the product of the peculiar history of English, and it cannot really be settled because what is at stake is much more than a mere conflict over methods or the lack of them. The true reason why the pluralists are wishful thinkers is that what is at issue in the contention between different literary theories or 'non-theories' are competing ideological strategies related to the very destiny of English studies in modern society. The problem with literary theory is that it can neither beat nor join the dominant ideologies of late industrial capitalism. Liberal humanism seeks to oppose or at least modify such ideologies with its distaste for the technocratic and its nurturing of spiritual wholeness in a hostile world; certain brands of formalism and structuralism try to take over the technocratic rationality of such a society and thus incorporate themselves into it. Northrop Frye and the New Critics thought that they had pulled off a synthesis of the two, but how many students of literature today read them? Liberal humanism has dwindled to the impotent conscience of bourgeois society, gentle, sensitive and ineffectual; structuralism has already more or less vanished into the literary museum.

The impotence of liberal humanism is a symptom of its essentially contradictory relationship to modern capitalism. For although it forms part of the 'official' ideology of such society, and the 'humanities' exist to reproduce it, the social order within which it exists has in one sense very little time for it at all. Who is concerned with the uniqueness of the individual, the imperishable truths of the human condition or the sensuous textures of lived experience in the Foreign Office or the boardroom of Standard Oil? Capitalism's reverential hat-tipping to the arts is obvious hypocrisy, except when it can hang them on its walls as a sound investment. Yet capitalist states have continued to direct funds into higher education humanities departments, and though such departments are usually the first in line for savage cutting when capitalism enters on one of its periodic crises, it is doubtful that it is only hypocrisy, a fear of appearing in its true philistine colours, which compels this grudging support. The truth is that liberal humanism is at once largely ineffectual, and the best ideology of the 'human' that present bourgeois society can muster. The 'unique individual' is indeed important when it comes to defending the business entrepreneur's right to make profit while throwing men and women out of work; the individual must at all costs have the 'right to choose', provided this means the right to buy one's child an expensive private education while other children are deprived of their school meals, rather than the rights of women to decide whether to have children in the first place. The 'imperishable truths of the human condition' include such verities as freedom and democracy, the essences of which are embodied in our particular way of life. The 'sensuous textures of lived experience' can be roughly translated as reacting from the gut—judging according to habit, prejudice and 'common sense', rather than according to some inconvenient, 'aridly theoretical' set of debatable ideas. There is, after all, room for the humanities yet, much as those who guarantee our freedom and democracy despise them.

Departments of literature in higher education, then, are part of the ideological apparatus of the modern capitalist state. They are not wholly reliable apparatuses, since for one thing the humanities contain many values, meanings and traditions which are antithetical to that state's social priorities, which are rich in kinds of wisdom and experience beyond its comprehension. For another thing, if you allow a lot of young people to do nothing for a few years but read books and talk to each other then it is possible that, given certain wider historical circumstances, they will not only begin to question some of the values transmitted to them but begin to interrogate the authority by which they are transmitted. There is of course no harm in students questioning the values conveyed to them: indeed it is part of the very meaning of higher education that they should do so. Independent thought, critical dissent and reasoned dialectic are part of the very stuff of a humane education; hardly anyone, as I commented earlier, will demand that your essay on Chaucer or Baudelaire arrives inexorably at certain pre-set conclusions. All that is being demanded is that you manipulate a particular language in acceptable ways. Becoming certificated by the state as proficient in literary studies is a matter of being able to talk and write in certain ways. It is this which is being taught, examined and certificated, not what you personally think or believe, though what is thinkable will of course be constrained by the language itself. You can think or believe what you want, as long as you can speak this particular language. Nobody is especially concerned about what you say, with what extreme, moderate, radical or conservative positions you adopt, provided that they are compatible with, and can be articulated within, a specific form of discourse. It is just that certain meanings and positions will not be articulable within it. Literary studies, in other words, are a question of the signifier, not of the signified. Those employed to teach you this form of discourse will remember whether or not you were able to speak it proficiently long after they have forgotten what you said.

Literary theorists, critics and teachers, then, are not so much purveyors of doctrine as custodians of a discourse. Their task is to preserve this discourse, extend and elaborate it as necessary, defend it from other forms of discourse, initiate newcomers into it and determine whether or not they have successfully mastered it. The discourse itself has no definite signified, which is not to say that it embodies no assumptions: it is rather a network of signifiers able to envelop a whole field of meanings, objects and practices. Certain pieces of writing are selected as being more amenable to this discourse than others, and these are what is known as literature or the 'literary canon'. The fact that this canon is usually regarded as fairly fixed, even at times as eternal and immutable, is in a sense ironic, because since literary critical discourse has no definite signified it can, if it wants to, turn its attention to more or less any kind of writing. Some of those hottest in their defence of the canon have from time to time demonstrated how the discourse can be made to operate on 'non-literary' writing. This, indeed, is the embarrassment of literary criticism, that it defines for itself a special object, literature, while existing as a set of discursive techniques which have no reason to stop short at that object at all. If you have nothing better to do at a party you can always try on a literary critical analysis of it, speak of its styles and genres, discriminate its significant nuances or formalize its sign-systems. Such a 'text' can prove quite as rich as one of the canonical works, and critical dissections of it quite as ingenious as those of Shakespeare. So either literary criticism confesses that it can handle parties just as well as it can Shakespeare, in which case it is in danger of losing its identity along with its object; or it agrees that parties may be interestingly analysed provided that this is called something else: ethnomethodology or hermeneutical phenomenology, perhaps. Its own concern is with literature, because literature is more valuable and rewarding than any of the other texts on which the critical discourse might operate. The disadvantage of this claim is that it is plainly untrue: many films and works of philosophy are considerably more valuable than much that is included in the 'literary canon'. It is not that they are valuable in different ways: they could present objects of value in the sense that criticism defines that term. Their exclusion from what is studied is not because they are not 'amenable' to the discourse: it is a question of the arbitrary authority of the literary institution.

Another reason why literary criticism cannot justify its self-limiting to certain works by an appeal to their 'value' is that criticism is part of a literary institution which constitutes these works as valuable in the first place. It is not only parties that need to be *made* into worthwhile literary objects by being treated in specific ways, but also Shakespeare. Shakespeare was not great literature lying conveniently to hand, which the literary institution then happily discovered: he is great literature because the institution constitutes him as such. This does not mean that he is not 'really' great literature—that it is just a matter of people's opinions about him—because there is no such thing as literature which is 'really' great, or 'really' anything, independently of the ways in which that writing is treated within specific forms of social and institutional life. There are an indefinite number of ways of discussing Shakespeare, but not all of them count as literary critical. Perhaps Shakespeare himself, his friends and actors, did not talk about his plays in ways which we would regard as literary critical. Perhaps some of the most interesting statements which could be made about Shakespearian drama would also not count as belonging to literary criticism. Literary criticism selects, processes, corrects and rewrites texts in accordance with certain institutionalized norms of the 'literary'— norms which are at any given time arguable, and always historically variable. For though I have said that critical discourse has no determinate signified, there are certainly a great many ways of talking about literature which it excludes, and a great many discursive moves and strategies which it disqualifies as invalid, illicit, non-critical, nonsense. Its apparent generosity at the level of the signified is matched only by its sectarian intolerance at the level of the signifier. Regional dialects of the discourse, so to speak, are acknowledged and sometimes tolerated, but you must not sound as though you are speaking another language altogether. To do so is to recognize in the sharpest way that critical discourse is power. To be on the inside of the discourse itself is to be blind to this power, for what is more natural and non-dominative than to speak one's own tongue?

The power of critical discourse moves on several levels. It is the power of 'policing' language—of determining that certain statements must be excluded because they do not conform to what is acceptably sayable. It is the power of policing writing itself, classifying it into the 'literary' and 'non-literary', the enduringly great and the ephemerally popular. It is the power of authority *vis-à-vis* others—the power-relations between those who define and preserve the discourse, and those who are selectively admitted to it. It is the power of certificating or non-certificating those who have been judged to speak the discourse better or worse. Finally, it is a question of the power-relations between the literary-academic institution, where all of this occurs, and the ruling power-interests of society at large, whose ideological needs will be served and whose personnel will be reproduced by the preservation and controlled extension of the discourse in question.

I have argued that the theoretically limitless extendibility of critical discourse, the fact that it is only arbitrarily confined to 'literature', is or should be a source of embarrassment to the custodians of the canon. The objects of criticism, like those of the Freudian drive, are in a certain sense contingent and replaceable. Ironically, criticism only really became aware of this fact when, sensing that its own liberal humanism was running out of steam, it turned for aid to more ambitious or rigorous critical methods. It thought that by adding a judicious pinch of historical analysis here or swallowing a non-addictive dose of structuralism there, it could exploit these otherwise alien approaches to eke out its own dwindling spiritual capital. The boot, however, might well prove to be on the other foot. For you cannot engage in an historical analysis of literature without recognizing that literature itself is a recent historical invention; you cannot apply structuralist tools to *Paradise Lost* without acknowledging that just the same tools can be applied to the *Daily Mirror*. Criticism can thus prop itself up only at the risk of losing its defining object; it has the unenviable choice of stifling or suffocating. If literary theory presses its own implications too far, then it has argued itself out of existence.

This, I would suggest, is the best possible thing for it to do. The final logical move in a process which began by recognizing that literature is an illusion is to recognize that literary theory is an illusion too. It is not of course an illusion in the sense that I have invented the various people I have discussed in this book: Northrop Frye really does exist, and so did F. R. Leavis. It is an illusion first in the sense that literary theory, as I hope to have shown, is really no more than a branch of social ideologies, utterly without any unity or identity which would adequately distinguish it from philosophy, linguistics, psychology, cultural and sociological thought; and secondly in the sense that the one hope it has of distinguishing itself—clinging to an object named literature—is misplaced. We must conclude, then, that this book is less an introduction than an obituary, and that we have ended by burying the object we sought to unearth.

My intention, in other words, is not to counter the literary theories I have critically examined in this book with a literary theory of my own, which would claim to be more politically acceptable. Any reader who has been expectantly waiting for a Marxist theory has obviously not been reading this book with due attention. There are indeed Marxist and feminist theories of literature, which in my opinion are more valuable than any of the theories discussed here, and to which the reader may like to refer in the bibliography. But this is not exactly the point. The point is whether it is possible to speak of 'literary theory' without perpetuating the illusion that literature exists as a distinct, bounded object of knowledge, or whether it is not preferable to draw the practical consequences of the fact that literary theory can handle Bob Dylan just as well as John Milton. My own view is that it is most useful to see 'literature' as a name which people give from time to time for different reasons to certain kinds of writing within a whole field of what Michel Foucault has called 'discursive practices', and that if anything is to be an object of study it is this whole field of practices rather than just those sometimes rather obscurely labelled 'literature'. I am countering the theories set out in this book not with a *literary* theory, but with a different kind of discourse—whether one calls it of 'culture', 'signifying practices' or whatever is not of first importance—which would include the objects ('literature') with which these other theories deal, but which would transform them by setting them in a wider context.

But is this not to extend the boundaries of literary theory to a point where any kind of particularity is lost? Would not a 'theory of discourse' run into just the same problems of methodology and object of study which we have seen in the case of literary studies? After all, there are any number of discourses and any number of ways of studying them. What would be specific to the kind of study I have in mind, however, would be its concern for the kinds of *effects* which discourses produce, and how they produce them. Reading a zoology textbook to find out about giraffes is part of studying zoology, but reading it to see how its discourse is structured and organized, and examining what kind of effects these forms and devices produce in particular readers in actual situations, is a different kind of project. It is, in fact, probably the oldest form of 'literary criticism' in the world, known as rhetoric. Rhetoric, which was the received form of critical analysis all the way from ancient society to the eighteenth century, examined the way discourses are constructed in order to achieve certain effects. It was not worried about whether its objects of enquiry were speaking or writing, poetry or philosophy, fiction or historiography: its horizon was nothing less than the field of discursive practices in society as a whole, and its particular interest lay in grasping such practices as forms of power and performance. This is not to say that it ignored the truth-value of the discourses in question, since this could often be crucially relevant to the kinds of effect they produced in their readers and listeners. Rhetoric in its major phase was neither a 'humanism', concerned in some intuitive way with people's experience of language, nor a 'formalism', preoccupied simply with analyzing linguistic devices. It looked at such devices in terms of concrete performance—they were means of pleading, persuading, inciting and so on— and at people's responses to discourse in terms of linguistic structures and the material situations in which they functioned. It saw speaking and writing not merely as textual objects, to be aesthetically contemplated or endlessly deconstructed, but as forms of *activity* inseparable from the wider social relations between writers and readers, orators and audiences, and as largely unintelligible outside the social purposes and conditions in which they were embedded.

Like all the best radical positions, then, mine is a thoroughly traditionalist one. I wish to recall literary criticism from certain fashionable, new-fangled ways of thinking it has been seduced by—'literature' as a specially privileged object, the 'aesthetic' as separable from social determinants, and so on—and return it to the ancient paths which it has abandoned. Although my case is thus reactionary, I do not mean that we should revive the whole range of ancient rhetorical terms and substitute these for modern critical language. We do not need to do this, since there are enough concepts contained in the literary theories examined in this book to allow us at least to make a start. Rhetoric, or discourse theory, shares with Formalism, structuralism and semiotics an interest in the formal devices of language, but like reception theory is also concerned with how these devices are actually effective at the point of 'consumption'; its preoccupation with discourse as a form of power and desire can learn much from deconstruction and psychoanalytical theory, and its belief that discourse can be a humanly transformative affair shares a good deal with liberal humanism. The fact that 'literary theory' is an illusion does not mean that we cannot retrieve from it many valuable concepts for a different kind of discursive practice altogether.

There was, of course, a reason why rhetoric bothered to analyze discourses. It did not analyze them just because they were there, any more than most forms of literary criticism today examine literature just for the sake of it. Rhetoric wanted to find out the most effective ways of pleading, persuading and debating, and rhetoricians studied such devices in other people's language in order to use them more productively in their own. It was, as we would say today, a 'creative' as well as a 'critical' activity: the word 'rhetoric' covers both the practice of effective discourse and the science of it. Similarly, there must be a reason why we would consider it worthwhile to develop a form of study which would look at the various sign-systems and signifying practices in our own society, all the way from *Moby-Dick* to the Muppet show, from Dryden and Jean-Luc Godard to the portrayal of women in advertisements and the rhetorical techniques of Government reports. All theory and knowledge, as I have argued previously, is 'interested', in the sense that you can always ask why one should bother to develop it in the first place. One striking weakness of most formalist and structuralist criticism is that it is unable to answer this question. The structuralist really does examine sign-systems because they happen to be there, or if this seems indefensible is forced into some rationale—studying our modes of sense-making will deepen our critical self-awareness—which is not much different from the standard line of the liberal humanists. The strength of the liberal humanist case, by contrast, is that it is able to say why dealing with literature is worth while. Its answer, as we have seen, is roughly that it makes you a better person. This is also the weakness of the liberal humanist case.

The liberal humanist response, however, is not weak because it believes that literature can be transformative. It is weak because it usually grossly overestimates this transformative power, considers it in isolation from any determining social context, and can formulate what it means by a 'better person' only in the most narrow and abstract of terms. They are terms which generally ignore the fact that to be a person in the Western society of the 1980s is to be bound up with, and in some sense responsible for, the kinds of political conditions which I began this Conclusion by outlining. Liberal humanism is a suburban moral ideology, limited in practice to largely interpersonal matters. It is stronger on adultery than on armaments, and its valuable concern with freedom, democracy and individual rights are simply not concrete enough. Its view of democracy, for example, is the abstract one of the ballot box, rather than a specific, living and practical democracy which might also somehow concern the operations of the Foreign Office and Standard Oil. Its view of individual freedom is similarly abstract: the freedom of any particular individual is crippled and parasitic as long as it depends on the futile labour and active oppression of others. Literature may protest against such conditions or it may not, but it is only possible in the first place because of them. As the German critic Walter Benjamin put it: 'There is no cultural document that is not at the same time a record of barbarism.' Socialists are those who wish to draw the full, concrete, practical applications of the abstract notions of freedom and democracy to which liberal humanism subscribes, taking them at their word when they draw attention to the 'vividly particular'. It is for this reason that many Western socialists are restless with the liberal humanist opinion of the tyrannies in Eastern Europe, feeling that these opinions simply do not go far enough: what would be necessary to bring down such tyrannies would not be just more free speech, but a workers' revolution against the state.

What it means to be a 'better person', then, must be concrete and practical—that is to say, concerned with people's political situations as a whole—rather than narrowly abstract, concerned only with the immediate interpersonal relations which can be abstracted from this concrete whole. It must be a question of political and not only of 'moral' argument: that is to say, it must be *genuine* moral argument, which sees the relations between individual qualities and values and our whole material conditions of existence. Political argument is not an alternative to moral preoccupations: it is those preoccupations taken seriously in their full implications. But the liberal humanists are right to see that there is a *point* in studying literature, and that this point is not itself, in the end, a literary one. What they are arguing, although this way of putting it would grate harshly on their ears, is that literature has a *use*. Few words are more offensive to literary ears than 'use', evoking as it does paperclips and hair-dryers. The Romantic opposition to the utilitarian ideology of capitalism has made 'use' an unusable word: for the aesthetes, the glory of art is its utter uselessness. Yet few of us nowadays would be prepared to subscribe to *that*: every reading of a work is surely in some sense a use of it. We may not use *Moby-Dick* to learn how to hunt whales, but we 'get something out of it' even so. Every literary theory presupposes a certain use of literature, even if what you get out of it is its utter uselessness. Liberal humanist criticism is not wrong to use literature, but wrong to deceive itself that it does not. It uses it to further certain moral values, which as I hope to have shown are in fact indissociable from certain ideological ones, and in the end imply a particular form of politics. It is not that it reads the texts 'disinterestedly' and then places what it has read in the service of its values: the values govern the actual reading process itself, inform what sense criticism makes of the works it studies. I am not going to argue, then, for a 'political criticism' which would read literary texts in the light of certain values which are related to political beliefs and actions; all criticism does this. The idea that there are 'non-political' forms of criticism is simply a myth which furthers certain political uses of literature all the more effectively. The difference between a 'political' and 'non-political' criticism is just the difference between the prime minister and the monarch: the latter furthers certain political ends by pretending not to, while the former makes no bones about it. It is always better to be honest in these matters. The difference between a conventional critic who speaks of the 'chaos of experience' in Conrad or Woolf, and the feminist who examines those writers' images of gender, is not a distinction between non-political and political criticism. It is a distinction between different forms of politics—between those who subscribe to the doctrine that history, society and human reality as a whole are fragmentary, arbitrary and directionless, and those who have other interests which imply alternative views about the way the world is. There is no way of settling the question of which politics is preferable in literary critical terms. You simply have to argue about politics. It is not a question of debating whether 'literature' should be related to 'history' or not: it is a question of different readings of history itself.

The feminist critic is not studying representations of gender simply because she believes that this will further her political ends. She also believes that gender and sexuality are central themes in literature and other sorts of discourse, and that any critical account which suppresses them is seriously defective. Similarly, the socialist critic does not see literature in terms of ideology or class-struggle because these happen to be his or her political interests, arbitrarily projected on to literary works. He or she would hold that such matters are the very stuff of history, and that in so far as literature is an historical phenomenon, they are the very stuff of literature too. What would be strange would be if the feminist or socialist critic thought analyzing questions of gender or class was merely a matter of academic interest—merely a question of achieving a more satisfyingly complete account of literature. For why should it be worth doing this? Liberal humanist critics are not merely out for a more complete account of literature: they wish to discuss literature in ways which will deepen, enrich and extend our lives. Socialist and feminist critics are quite at one with them on this: it is just that they wish to point out that such deepening and enriching entails the transformation of a society divided by class and gender. They would like the liberal humanist to draw the full implications of his or her position. If the liberal humanist disagrees, then this is a political argument, not an argument about whether one is 'using' literature or not.

I argued earlier that any attempt to define the study of literature in terms of either its method or its object is bound to fail. But we have now begun to discuss another way of conceiving what distinguishes one kind of discourse from another, which is neither ontological or methodological but *strategic*. This means asking first not *what* the object is or *how* we should approach it, but *why* we should want to engage with it in the first place. The liberal humanist response to this question, I have suggested, is at once perfectly reasonable and, as it stands, entirely useless. Let us try to concretize it a little by asking how the reinvention of rhetoric that I have proposed (though it might equally as well be called 'discourse theory' or 'cultural studies' or whatever) might contribute to making us all better people. Discourses, sign-systems and signifying practices of all kinds, from film and television to fiction and the languages of natural science, produce effects, shape forms of consciousness and unconsciousness, which are closely related to the maintenance or transformation of our existing systems of power. They are thus closely related to what it means to be a person. Indeed 'ideology' can be taken to indicate no more than this connection—the link or nexus between discourses and power. Once we have seen this, then the questions of theory and method may be allowed to appear in a new light. It is not a matter of starting from certain theoretical or methodological problems: it is a matter of starting from what we want to *do,* and then seeing which methods and theories will best help us to achieve these ends. Deciding on your strategy will not pre-determine which methods and objects of study are most valuable. As far as the object of study goes, what you decide to examine depends very much on the practical situation. It may seem best to look at Proust and *King Lear,* or at children's television programmes or popular romances or avant-garde films. A radical critic is quite liberal on these questions: he rejects the dogmatism which would insist that Proust is always more worthy of study than television advertisements. It all depends on what you are trying to do, in what situation. Radical critics are also open-minded about questions of theory and method: they tend to be pluralists in this respect. Any method or theory which will contribute to the strategic goal of human emancipation, the production of 'better people' through the socialist transformation of society, is acceptable. Structuralism, semiotics, psychoanalysis, deconstruction, reception theory and so on: all of these approaches, and others, have their valuable insights which may be put to use. Not all literary theories, however, are likely to prove amenable to the strategic goals in question: there are several examined in this book which seem to me highly unlikely to do so. What you choose and reject theoretically, then, depends upon what you are practically trying to do. This has always been the case with literary criticism: it is simply that it is often very reluctant to realize the fact. In any academic study we select the objects and methods of procedure which we believe the most important, and our assessment of their importance is governed by frames of interest deeply rooted in our practical forms of social life. Radical critics are no different in this respect: it is just that they have a set of social priorities with which most people at present tend to disagree. This is why they are commonly dismissed as "ideological', because 'ideology' is always a way of describing other people's interests rather than one's own.

No theory or method, in any case, will have merely one strategic use. They can be mobilized in a variety of different strategies for a variety of ends. But not all methods will be equally amenable to particular ends. It is a matter of finding out, not of assuming from the start that a single method or theory will do. One reason why I have not ended this book with an account of socialist or feminist literary theory is that I believe such a move might encourage the reader to make what the philosophers call a 'category mistake'. It might mislead people into thinking that 'political criticism' was another sort of critical approach from those I have discussed, different in its assumptions but essentially the same kind of thing. Since I have made clear my view that all criticism is in some sense political, and since people tend to give the word 'political' to criticism whose politics disagrees with their own, this cannot be so. Socialist and feminist criticism are, of course, concerned with developing theories and methods appropriate to their aims: they consider questions of the relations between writing and sexuality, or of text and ideology, as other theories in general do not. They will also want to claim that these theories are more powerfully explanatory than others, for if they were not there would be no point in advancing them as theories. But it would be a mistake to see the particularity of such forms of criticism as consisting in the offering of alternative theories of methods. These forms of criticism differ from others because they define the object of analysis differently, have different values, beliefs and goals, and thus offer different kinds of strategy for the realizing of these goals.

I say 'goals', because it should not be thought that this form of criticism has only one. There are many goals to be achieved, and many ways of achieving them. In some situations the most productive procedure may be to explore how the signifying systems of a 'literary' text produce certain ideological effects; or it may be a matter of doing the same with a Hollywood film. Such projects may prove particularly important in teaching cultural studies to children; but it may also be valuable to use literature to foster in them a sense of linguistic potential denied to them by their social conditions. There are 'utopian' uses of literature of this kind, and a rich tradition of such utopian thought which should not be airily dismissed as 'idealist'. The active enjoyment of cultural artefacts should not, however, be relegated to the primary school, leaving older students with the grimmer business of analysis. Pleasure, enjoyment, the potentially transformative effects of discourse is quite as 'proper' a topic for 'higher' study as is the setting of puritan tracts in the discursive formations of the seventeenth century. On other occasions what might prove more useful will not be the criticism or enjoyment of other people's discourse but the production of one's own. Here, as with the rhetorical tradition, studying what other people have done may help. You may want to stage your own signifying practices to enrich, combat, modify or transform the effects which others' practices produce.

Within all of this varied activity, the study of what is currently termed 'literature' will have its place. But it should not be taken as an *a priori* assumption that what is currently termed 'literature' will always and everywhere be the most important focus of attention. Such dogmatism has no place in the field of cultural study. Nor are the texts now dubbed 'literature' likely to be perceived and defined as they are now, once they are returned to the broader and deeper discursive formations of which they are part. They will be inevitably 'rewritten', recycled, put to different uses, inserted into different relations and practices. They always have been, of course; but one effect of the word 'literature' is to prevent us from recognizing this fact.

Such a strategy obviously has far-reaching institutional implications. It would mean, for example, that departments of literature as we presently know them in higher education would cease to exist. Since the government, as I write, seems on the point of achieving this end more quickly and effectively than I could myself, it is necessary to add that the first political priority for those who have doubts about the ideological implications of such departmental organizations is to defend them unconditionally against government assaults. But this priority cannot mean refusing to contemplate how we might better organize literary studies in the longer term. The ideological effects of such departments lie not only in the particular values they disseminate, but in their implicit and actual dislocation of 'literature' from other cultural and social practices. The churlish admission of such practices as literary 'background' need not detain us: 'background', with its static, distancing connotations, tells its own story. Whatever would in the long term replace such departments—and the proposal is a modest one, for such experiments are already under way in certain areas of higher education—would centrally involve education in the various theories and methods of cultural analysis. The fact that such education is not routinely provided by many existing departments of literature, or is provided 'optionally' or marginally, is one of their most scandalous and farcical features. (Perhaps their other most scandalous and farcical feature is the largely wasted energy which postgraduate students are required to pour into obscure, often spurious research topics in order to produce dissertations which are frequently no more than sterile academic exercises, and which few others will ever read.) The genteel amateurism which regards criticism as some spontaneous sixth sense has not only thrown many students of literature into understandable confusion for many decades, but serves to consolidate the authority of those in power. If criticism is no more than a knack, like being able to whistle and hum different tunes simultaneously, then it is at once rare enough to be preserved in the hands of an elite, while 'ordinary' enough to require no stringent theoretical justification. Exactly the same pincer movement is at work in English 'ordinary language' philosophy. But the answer is not to replace such dishevelled amateurism with a well-groomed professionalism intent on justifying itself to the disgusted taxpayer. Such professionalism, as we have seen, is equally bereft of any social validation of its activities, since it cannot say why it should bother with literature at all other than to tidy it up, drop texts into their appropriate categories and then move over into marine biology. If the point of criticism is not to interpret literary works but to master in some disinterested spirit the underlying sign-systems which generate them, what is criticism to do once it has achieved this mastery, which will hardly take a lifetime and probably not much more than a few years?

The present crisis in the field of literary studies is at root a crisis in the definition of the subject itself. That it should prove difficult to provide such a definition is, as I hope to have shown in this book, hardly surprising. Nobody is likely to be dismissed from an academic job for trying on a little semiotic analysis of Edmund Spenser; they are likely to be shown the door, or refused entry through it in the first place, if they question whether the 'tradition' from Spenser to Shakespeare and Milton is the best or only way of carving up discourse into a syllabus. It is at this point that the canon is trundled out to blast offenders out of the literary arena.

Those who work in the field of cultural practices are unlikely to mistake their activity as utterly central. Men and women do not live by culture alone, the vast majority of them throughout history have been deprived of the chance of living by it at all, and those few who are fortunate enough to live by it now are able to do so because of the labour of those who do not. Any cultural or critical theory which does not begin from this single most important fact, and hold it steadily in mind in its activities, is in my view unlikely to be worth very much. There is no document of culture which is not also a record of barbarism. But even in societies which, like our own as Marx reminded us, have no time for culture, there are times and places when it suddenly becomes newly relevant, charged with a significance beyond itself. Four such major moments are evident in our own world. Culture, in the lives of nations struggling for their independence from imperialism, has a meaning quite remote from the review pages of the Sunday newspapers. Imperialism is not only the exploitation of cheap labour-power, raw materials and easy markets but the uprooting of languages and customs—not just the imposition of foreign armies, but of alien ways of experiencing. It manifests itself not only in company balance-sheets and in airbases, but can be tracked to the most intimate roots of speech and signification. In such situations, which are not all a thousand miles from our own doorstep, culture is so vitally bound up with one's common identity that there is no need to argue for its relation to political struggle. It is arguing against it which would seem incomprehensible.

The second area where cultural and political action have become closely united is in the women's movement. It is in the nature of feminist politics that signs and images, written and dramatized experience, should be of especial significance. Discourse in all its forms is an obvious concern for feminists, either as places where women's oppression can be deciphered, or as places where it can be challenged. In any politics which puts identity and relationship centrally at stake, renewing attention to lived experience and the discourse of the body, culture does not need to argue its way to political relevance. Indeed one of the achievements of the women's movement has been to redeem such phrases as 'lived experience' and 'the discourse of the body' from the empiricist connotations with which much literary theory has invested them. 'Experience' need now no longer signify an appeal away from power-systems and social relations to the privileged certainties of the private, for feminism recognizes no such distinction between questions of the human subject and questions of political struggle. The discourse of the body is not a matter of Lawrentian ganglions and suave loins of darkness, but a *politics* of the body, a rediscovery of its sociality through an awareness of the forces which control and subordinate it.

The third area in question is the 'culture industry'. While literary critics have been cultivating sensibility in a minority, large segments of the media have been busy trying to devastate it in the majority; yet it is still presumed that studying, say, Gray and Collins is inherently more important than examining television or the popular press. Such a project differs from the two I have outlined already in its essentially defensive character: it represents a critical reaction to someone else's cultural ideology rather than an appropriation of culture for one's own ends. Yet it is a vital project nevertheless, which must not be surrendered to a melancholic Left or Right mythology of the media as impregnably monolithic. We know that people do not after all believe all that they see and read; but we also need to know much more than we do about the role such effects play in their general consciousness, even though such critical study should be seen, politically, as no more than a holding operation. The democratic control of these ideological apparatuses, along with popular alternatives to them, must be high on the agenda of any future socialist programme.

The fourth and final area is that of the strongly emergent movement of working-class writing. Silenced for generations, taught to regard literature as a coterie activity beyond their grasp, working people over the past decade in Britain have been actively organizing to find their own literary styles and voices. The worker writers' movement is almost unknown to academia, and has not been exactly encouraged by the cultural organs of the state; but it is one sign of a significant break from the dominant relations of literary production. Community and cooperative publishing enterprises are associated projects, concerned not simply with a literature wedded to alternative social values, but with one which challenges and changes the existing social relations between writers, publishers, readers and other literary workers. It is because such ventures interrogate the ruling *definitions* of literature that they cannot so easily be incorporated by a literary institution quite happy to welcome *Sons and Lovers,* and even, from time to time, Robert Tressell.

These areas are not alternatives to the study of Shakespeare and Proust. If the study of such writers could become as charged with energy, urgency and enthusiasm as the activities I have just reviewed, the literary institution ought to rejoice rather than complain. But it is doubtful that this will happen when such texts are hermetically sealed from history, subjected to a sterile critical formalism, piously swaddled with eternal verities and used to confirm prejudices which any moderately enlightened student can perceive to be objectionable. The liberation of Shakespeare and Proust from such controls may well entail the death of literature, but it may also be their redemption.

I shall end with an allegory. *We* know that the lion is stronger than the lion-tamer, and so does the lion-tamer. The problem is that the lion does not know it. It is not out of the question that the death of literature may help the lion to awaken.

Leslie Brisman
1944–

Leslie Brisman was born on May 22, 1944, in New York City. A graduate of Columbia University (B.A., 1965), where he majored in philosophy, Brisman then studied English at Cornell, receiving an M.A. in 1966 and a Ph.D. in 1969. Since 1969 Brisman has been a member of the faculty of Yale University, where he teaches Milton and Romanticism as well as the Bible as literature. In addition to numerous essays, he has published two major studies of Miltonic poetry and its influence, *Milton's Poetry of Choice and Its Romantic Heirs* (1973) and *Romantic Origins* (1978).

Brisman's subtle and complex readings of Miltonic and post-Miltonic poetry (which include the Romantics and Wallace Stevens) are perhaps best described as Freudian-phenomenological. They approach poetry in terms of a Bergsonian and existentialist concept of temporality and a Freudian concept of the psyche. To write or to read Miltonic poetry, Brisman argues, is to experience an arrest of ordinary, historical contingency. Poetry enables consciousness to pass from the "sick hurry" of facticity to a slower, more pleasurable apprehension of transcendence and its correlatives—beauty, sublimity, and freedom. This passage, however, is not easily achieved. The pleasure of freedom implies the burden of choosing. In the free moment of arrest, not only do all the potentialities of consciousness become accessible to the poet, but all its uncertainties as well—including questions of selfhood and voice, desire and loss, presence and absence of divinity, guilt and redemption, and, not least important, anxieties about the Oedipal nay-saying authority of previous poets. But if a poet is strong and mature enough, Brisman argues, these potentially disastrous confusions become salutary complexities, which the poet might even willfully appropriate as an opportunity for exercising his capability. A strong poet like Milton or Stevens "assumes the role of chooser." He characteristically pauses at the "experience of alternatives" in order to attain the fullest possible consciousness of his options. In the best poems this lingering becomes a distinct form of poetic pleasure—"the hovering over the 'or' in Milton or Stevens . . . points not to weak indecisiveness but to potency, the hovering becomes seminal, the abyss, a womb of time." Thus Milton's hesitations become the experienced richness of his allusions, while Keats's consideration of his poetic options feels like a sweet kind of "amorous delay." For these poets the anxiety of influence becomes an opportunity for revision not accessible to those who are unwilling to linger and listen to past voices: "The power of choice is reconceived as that which holds alternatives in protracted arrest and creates, out of the abyss between them, out of the will to encounter the abyss, a second will more wise."

FROM

MILTON'S POETRY OF CHOICE AND ITS ROMANTIC HEIRS

AFTERWORD

The nothingness was a nakedness, a point

Beyond which thought could not progress as thought.
He had to choose. But it was not a choice
Between excluding things. It was not a choice

Between, but of.
—Wallace Stevens, "Notes toward a Supreme Fiction"

Georges Poulet has said that Bergson's originality lay "in his affirmation that duration is something other than history or a system of laws; that it is free creation."[1] I have been arguing that such is Milton's originality: his poetry conveys a sense of duration "so to interpose a little ease" in historical sequentiality; on the basis of this freedom he establishes an intimacy between poetry and its subject matter, between poetic process and the processes of free creation—the Father's creation of the Son, the Son's creation of the cosmos, man's creation of history, the poet's creation of moments of choice in which the reader can share the sense of potentiality.

Bypassing the contingencies of time, the poetics of choice itself seems to draw later poets into the circle of these analogies. Beyond "history or a system of laws," the romantic poet, turning to Milton, finds a source of "free creation." Not that a shared poetic denies literary history; Milton is not, like fallen Adam, to be "brought down / To dwell on even ground now with thy Sons" (*Paradise Lost,* XI.347–348). The distance remains; only it can be consciously turned from a matter of temporality into a metaphor for imaginative space. The distance is thus "willed" in both directions, both senses: decreed by Milton's historicity, desired by the romantic seeking poetic voice. If we think in terms of a bequest rather than a burden, we open ourselves to discover both the salubriousness of the relation to the past and the element of volition in entering that relationship. The emphasis must be both on second *will*, the conscious, controlled turning to a Miltonic way, and on *second* will as the matured submissiveness to a voice that must seem to come from outside. At moments, volition itself seems to be held in indefinite abstraction between poets: not only does a romantic reach back, but authoritative voice seems to reach forward, arresting time, to touch the trembling ears of the listener in another life and another time.

A poet's distance from voice is measured by the uneasy resemblance of voice to moral prohibition; his closeness, by the feeling that literary history has this dimension of family history. In "Lycidas," Milton invokes the angel of prohibition, and achieves poetic voice in the grand domestication of that angel's concern: "Look homeward Angel now, and melt with ruth." In "To William Wordsworth," Coleridge finds "the Angel of the vision" in Wordsworth's hopeful spirit; he recounts how *The Prelude* sang "Of Duty, chosen Laws controlling choice," and turned Miltonic sublimity, "summoned homeward," into the egotistical sublime. Awe at the uncanny and attachment to the canny, the *heimlich,* are brought together in these spiritual homecomings, and in similar encounters, from Adam's with Michael to Stevens' discovery of the necessary angel.

Looking at Stevens makes us see Michael's bequest as poetry's estate:

> Yet always there is another life,
> A life beyond this present knowing,
> A life lighter than this present splendor,
> Brighter, perfected and distant away,
> Not to be reached but to be known,
> Not an attainment of the will
> But something illogically received,
> A divination, a letting down
> From loftiness, misgivings dazzlingly
> Resolved in dazzling discovery.
> There is no map of paradise.[2]

If we let frail thought dally with the false surmise of Milton's presence behind these lines, we can hear not an imitation but an echo, not an attainment of the will—at least no primary will—but something illogically received. In Stevens' terms, one apprehends an order not imposed but discovered; it is not a discovery by horizontal, "Allegro" exploration—"Straight mine eye hath caught new pleasures"—but by a vertical, "Penseroso" descendentalism, making poetry capture the fallen Adam and Eve's new knowledge of "A life beyond this present knowing." Lingering a moment longer, one discovers the arrest of the present through structured repetitions, and the silence arrested in song between the conclusion of the long sentence and the quick expression of the awareness of what cannot be written in poetry, cannot be turned into structure: "There is no map of paradise." One cannot lay out in space what is so essentially experienced in time, what is apprehended only as it is being lost, "a letting down/From loftiness."

Such is the "letting down" with which Milton too expresses the dazzling experience when visionary poetry re-enters ongoing time:

> Let us descend now therefore from this top
> Of Speculation; for th' hour precise
> Exacts our parting hence.
> [*PL,* XII.588–590]

The first enjambment keeps us poised, looking back to the root meaning of "Speculation" as "outlook," looking forward as we descend from the pointedness of "top" down the syllabic steps of the longer word. Another way: for the moment, we catch the elegant Latinate word as the grandness of the past—and, simultaneously, the "degeneration" in the descent out of Eden caught in this Anglo-Saxon "top"—and the awareness that higher voice is now looked back upon as mere speculation. The second enjambment captures in its precision all the pathos of the "parting hence." "We do not know what 'the hour precise' is, but the fact that it has been determined helps us to return to a different scale of experience."[3] The passing of time marks the new awareness of human life; one shares with the poet the descent from artistic splendor to dazzling discovery of experience beyond pattern, beyond second-hand representation as narrative past. The real resolving of "misgivings" is not in any statement, however angelic, of the justice of God's ways, but in the awareness of the difference between pattern and life, an awareness it is Milton's greatest achievement to express in such verse.

The "letting down from loftiness" within Miltonic verse is a model for experiencing the handing down of loftiness that is poetic influence. The poet's vision and revision, turning on a moment of confrontation with higher voice, is like the reader's sight and insight, turning on moments of arrested temporality. In these confrontations the poetry of choice becomes the poetry of the sublime, where grandeur is discovered in facing origins and the moment of creation is re-created now. The process of choice leads to a fork in the road where alternatives are simultaneously present; and since Oedipus' revision of his journey to Thebes, the crossroads have represented the challenge to one's unity of being posed by the recognition that one has been "generated."

Pausing over the intersection till it becomes a pleasance, the poet discovers an interposed ground the vision of which redeems him from both the haste of repudiation and the narrowness of back recoiling on himself. The way is the wait. Milton himself repeatedly demonstrates how the old footsteps point the way to open spaces rather than traumatic intimidation. When Satan seems to tread in Odysseus' shadow, the ghostlier demarcations produce keener sounds, and his voyage takes on the quality of what Poulet calls "free creation"; poised between the overtones of possible literary allusion, we experience an arrested moment of choice. When Satan re-enters paradise, he pauses in a revery that can stand for the romantic brooding over the choice to tread in Milton's shadow. Rapt beyond himself, Satan is caught by this vision of the earth's beauty: "Seat worthier of Gods, as built / With second thoughts, reforming what was old" (*PL*, IX. 100–101). He feels excluded not only from heaven but from the earth as "revision" of heaven; and he feels doubly excluded from this product of second thoughts which has, without him, overcome the problem of loss. His question, "For what God after better worse would build?" may be said to haunt the post-Miltonic poet. But unlike Satan, the romantic comes to see revision as his own work. The more lovely the objects of nature appear to Satan, the more he feels, "I in none of these / Find place or refuge." The romantic, casting out the Satan or selfhood, finds his place or refuge in second thoughts, the labor of reforming his old conception of his literary self.

If a poet is strong enough to get past the solipsistic resignation to the mind as its own place, he assumes the role of chooser, and pausing to confront a poetic father, asserts his right of way. In Stevens' terms he says "yes" to the "no!" of authoritative voice, and in saying "yes" he says farewell. This exchange and the sense of new departure are all myth, to be sure, but the strong poet creates the myth of origin with which he grapples. He takes on a Miltonic blindness, choosing re-vision over the primary vision of the fact that these confrontations are a matter of "false surmise." Rapt in Keatsian "embalmed darkness," the poet transcends the easy daylight demystifications, and finds a choice inaudible to those untuned to voices "heard / In ancient days," invisible to those afraid to reimagine the giant.

Acknowledging his version of those daylight awarenesses ("My house has changed a little in the sun,") Wallace Stevens goes on to his version of the choice:

> It must be visible or invisible,
> Invisible or visible or both:
> A seeing and unseeing in the eye.
> ["Notes toward a
> Supreme Fiction"]

Helen Vendler speaks generally of Stevens' use of "or" as a "device for hovering over the statement rather than making it."[4] What is recreated thus as a habit of speech points to the creative nature of poetic language. Like the hovering over statement in Stevens and Milton is the image of hovering over an abyss. The experience of alternatives points not to weak indecisiveness but to potency; the hovering becomes seminal, the abyss, a womb of time. In a parody of creative movement, Sin and Death "Flew diverse, and with Power (thir Power was great) / Hovering upon the Waters" (*PL,* X. 284–285). One may wish to find here the power that Wordsworth identifies with imagination itself; the difference in that Sin bridges the chaos, while poets like Wordsworth and Stevens make a dwelling of the abyss, not spanning it but brooding on it till it brings forth new imaginative life. The abyss of consciousness opens to reveal, beyond the awareness of loss, the awareness of new worlds. Poetry thus participates in the divine illuminative power, recreating in each new imagining the creative moment when Holy Spirit "Dove-like [sat] brooding on the vast Abyss / And [made] it pregnant" (*PL,* I. 21–22).

Imaging an abyss, the conscious will "dissolves, diffuses, dissipates, in order to recreate." Reading Milton, we must see the divine will participating in these recreations, enacting the revisionary power of "secondary imagination." In the begetting of the Second Person, in second thoughts producing this earth, in the revision of history with the Fall, in every expression of the Word become words, creativity is made manifest. For the poet, God's participation is the basis of the complex analogies between aesthetic and religious experience, the reason aesthetic and ethical choice are one; for the critic, the conception of Divinity sharing Milton's poetry of choice extends the possibilities for seeing Milton sharing a poetics with romantic heirs. To attempt to come to terms with

Milton on the ground that poetry and theology are separate things and that the reader can accept the one while overlooking the other does this poet, perhaps more than any other, extreme violence. The only option is to see every choice of word as a moral choice, every musical echo as an echo of heavenly music, every proper arrest as an apprehension of the presence of God. One need not, of course, be a believer in Miltonic or any other doctrine, but one must believe in the absolute unity of the doctrine and the poetry, a unity of earthly and heavenly song in which every note is a note toward a supreme fiction. Fiction and faith form a continuum in which false surmise is an imaginative equivalent of transcendence, in which every "perhaps" points to the essential romantic insight that we live beyond ourselves, in possibility.

Leone Vivante cites Milton's Sonnet XXIII to illustrate how much the supreme fiction that is poetry depends on the beauty of the sense of possibility:

> Her face was veiled; yet to my fancied sight
> Love, sweetness, goodness, in her person shined
> So clear as in no face with more delight.

"There is not one single thing with distinct outlines," he notes, and we may think of Wordsworth's description of the Miltonic "indefinite abstraction" as we apprehend the face of Katherine (or an indefinite abstraction of Mary, or of woman more generally). "The 'white,' and the 'clear,' all these terms express here the (in tendency) self- and form-transcending value of deep original freedom; that is, of the active principle in its *potential* intensity, and in its primal character."[5] This is just the relation between "original freedom" and a poetry of choice, one which reaches toward moments of abstraction when alternatives exist as potentialities, when we come upon something forever in the realm of possibility. In "Notes toward a Supreme Fiction," Stevens muses:

> To discover an order as of
> A season, to discover summer and know it,
>
> To discover winter and know it well, to find,
> Not to impose, not to have reasoned at all,
> Out of nothing to have come on major weather,
>
> It is possible, possible, possible. It must
> Be possible.

More prosaically Sartre says that the goal of art must be to restore to the event its freshness and unforeseeability, to "recover this world by giving it to be seen as it is, but as if it had its source in human freedom"[6] If one takes as subject the event of literary composition itself, then one may want ultimately to interpret poetic influence as something neither to be evaded nor imposed, but a process profoundly dependent on a forgetting and a recovery, a new will to come upon a crossroads and "discover an order." What happens in poetic composition is thus analogous to, if not expressed by, what happens in reading

Miltonic verse. To confront each choice in its presentness, *as if* order were not already there, to come upon the world of time as a discovery, not an imposition—such is the achievement of Milton's poetry of choice.

NOTES

1. Georges Poulet, *Studies in Human Time,* trans. Elliott Coleman (Baltimore, 1956), p. 35.
2. Wallace Stevens, "The Sail of Ulysses," in *Opus Posthumous* (New York, 1957), pp. 101–102.
3. Laurence Stapleton, "Perspectives on Time in *Paradise Lost,*" *Philological Quarterly* 56 (1966), p. 747.
4. Helen Hennessy Vendler, *On Extended Wings: Wallace Stevens' Longer Poems* (Cambridge, Mass., 1969), p. 37.
5. *English Poetry and Its Contribution to the Knowledge of a Creative Principle* (New York, 1950), pp. 73–74.
6. Jean-Paul Sartre, *What Is Literature?,* trans. Bernard Frechtman (New York, 1949), p. 57.

Alice Walker
1944–

Alice Walker, in her fiction, poetry, and essays, speaks with devastating clarity on what she calls "womanist" issues. Although she is not an academic literary theorist, she is a person who is "living by the word" and she has written powerfully about the values of writing. She was born in Eatonton, Georgia, on February 9, 1944, to Willie Lee and Minnie Tallulah (Grant) Walker, poor sharecroppers. She was the youngest of five boys and three girls, and as a child was by her own description solitary and timid. She attended Spelman College in Atlanta for two years, and completed her B.A. at Sarah Lawrence College in 1965. At Sarah Lawrence she came "to understand how alone woman is, because of her body," and she said of her writing at that time, "Writing poetry is my way of celebrating that I have not committed suicide the evening before." While working in Mississippi on voter-registration drives and the creation of black studies programs she published her first book of poems, *Once* (1968), and began, with the support of a National Endowment for the Arts grant, her first novel, *The Third Life of Grange Copeland* (1970).

Walker's perception of the civil rights movement in the South was that it would fail utterly if it did not seek to achieve feminist as well as racial objectives. As a writer she found that black women who wrote about the relationship between sexism and racism were felt to be a threat not only to literary norms in white society but in black as well—consequently, they were scorned or ignored. During her Mississippi years she gathered folklore from black women and noted the details of their everyday lives. She has spoken frequently of the importance of finding her "maternal ancestors." Her successful attempt to save the works of Zora Neale Hurston from oblivion was a major step in a process that involved looking back to her own mother (whose artistry was expressed in her garden), to black women writers who preceded her, and to the women who passed on to her folklore that connected her with past generations of women and put her in touch with her African heritage. It is from her ancestors that Walker says she finds the animism that informs much of her work with "a belief that makes it possible to view all creation as living, and being inhabited by spirit."

Her books of poems include *Once* (1968); *Revolutionary Petunias & Other Poems* (1973); *Good Night, Willie Lee, I'll See You in the Morning* (1979). They are concerned with finding the terms for love relationships that are healthy and allow individuals to be self-cherishing. Walker's fiction includes the short-story collections *In Love and Trouble: Stories of Black Women* (1973) and *You Can't Keep a Good Woman Down* (1981). Much of their material is topical and the writing polemical in tone. *The Color Purple* (1982), her third novel, achieved a popular success that overshadows most of her other works. Perhaps it reveals with most power and concentration Walker's ability to present lives shaped by terrible forms of abuse that can be transformed by caring. *The Temple of My Familiar* (1989), her fourth novel, deals more diffusely with reincarnations in various forms and history going back many generations. It is a depiction of Walker's theory of animism that she speaks of in a way that suggests that some of her meanings are literal, not to be taken as fantasy.

Walker's nonfiction includes *Langston Hughes* (1974). She edited *I Love Myself When I Am Laughing: A Zora Neale Hurston Reader* (1979). Two collections of her essays, articles, reviews, and statements have been published: *In Search of Our Mothers' Gardens: Womanist Prose* (1983) and *Living by the Word* (1988). In the earlier collection she begins with offerings of definitions for "womanist": "a black feminist or feminist of color"; one who is "outrageous, audacious, courageous, or *willful*"; also, "a woman who loves other women, sexually and/or nonsexually"; finally, "Womanist is to feminist as purple to lavender." Hurston—writer, anthropologist, "all-around black woman"—is the most important figure in these works. Walker tells of her first glimpse of Hurston in a footnote, and of a long effort to find her that ends in a moment "when the pain . . . is . . . a threat to one's existence," as she locates her grave in a field of weeds. The title essay provides the central statement about the womanist writer and her own experience. The key figure for Walker is her mother, the forebears she seeks are maternal ones, and the essay echoes Woolf's *A Room of One's Own*. Elsewhere in the collection, in anticipation of the title of her second collection of essays, Walker announces the seriousness of the business of writing: "It is, in the end, the saving of lives that we writers are about."

The Black Writer and the Southern Experience

My mother tells of an incident that happened to her in the thirties during the Depression. She and my father lived in a small Georgia town and had half a dozen children. They were sharecroppers, and food, especially flour, was almost impossible to obtain. To get flour, which was distributed by the Red Cross, one had to submit vouchers signed by a local official. On the day my mother was to go into town for flour she received a large box of clothes from one of my aunts who was living in the North. The clothes were in good condition, though well worn, and my mother needed a dress, so she immediately put on one of those from the box and wore it into town. When she reached the distribution center and presented her voucher she was confronted by a white woman who looked her up and down with marked anger and envy.

"What'd you come up here for?" the woman asked.

"For some flour," said my mother, presenting her voucher.

"Humph," said the woman, looking at her more closely and with unconcealed fury. "Anybody dressed up as good as you don't need to come here *begging* for food."

"I ain't begging," said my mother; "the government is giving away flour to those that need it, and I need it. I wouldn't be here if I didn't. And these clothes I'm wearing was given to me." But the woman had already turned to the next person in line, saying over her shoulder to the white man who was behind the counter with her, "The *gall* of niggers coming in here dressed better than me!" This thought seemed to make her angrier still, and my mother, pulling three of her small children behind her and crying from humiliation, walked sadly back into the street.

"What did you and Daddy do for flour that winter?" I asked my mother.

"Well," she said, "Aunt Mandy Aikens lived down the road from us and she got plenty of flour. We had a good stand of corn so we had plenty of meal. Aunt Mandy would swap me a bucket of flour for a bucket of meal. We got by all right."

Then she added thoughtfully, "And that old woman that turned me off so short got down so bad in the end that she was walking on *two* sticks." And I knew she was thinking, though she never said it: Here I am today, my eight children healthy and grown and three of them in college and me with hardly a sick day for years. Ain't Jesus wonderful?

In this small story is revealed the condition and strength of a people. Outcasts to be used and humiliated by the larger society, the Southern black sharecropper and poor farmer clung to his own kind and to a religion that had been given to pacify him as a slave but which he soon transformed into an antidote against bitterness. Depending on one another, because they had nothing and no one else, the sharecroppers often managed to come through "all right." And when I listen to my mother tell and retell this story I find that the white woman's vindictiveness is less important than Aunt Mandy's resourceful generosity or my mother's ready stand of corn. For their lives were not about that pitiful example of Southern womanhood, but about themselves.

What the black Southern writer inherits as a natural right is a sense of *community*. Something simple but surprisingly hard, especially these days, to come by. My mother, who is a walking history of our community, tells me that when each of her children was born the midwife accepted as payment such home-grown or homemade items as a pig, a quilt, jars of canned fruits and vegetables. But there was never any question that the midwife would come when she was needed, whatever the eventual payment for her services. I consider this each time I hear of a hospital that refuses to admit a woman in labor unless she can hand over a substantial sum of money, cash.

Nor am I nostalgic, as a French philosopher once wrote, for lost poverty. I am nostalgic for the solidarity and sharing a modest existence can sometimes bring. We knew, I suppose, that we were poor. Somebody knew; perhaps the landowner who grudgingly paid my father three hundred dollars a year for twelve months' labor. But we never considered ourselves to be poor, unless, of course, we were deliberately humiliated. And because we never believed we were poor, and therefore worthless, we could depend on one another without shame. And always there were the Burial Societies, the Sick-and-Shut-in Societies, that sprang up out of spontaneous need. And no one seemed terribly upset that black sharecroppers were ignored by white insurance companies. It went without saying, in my mother's day, that birth and death required assistance from the community, and that the magnitude of these events was lost on outsiders.

As a college student I came to reject the Christianity of my parents, and it took me years to realize that though they had been force-fed a white man's palliative, in the form of religion, they had made it into something at once simple and noble. True, even today, they can never successfully picture a God who is not white, and that is a major cruelty, but their lives testify to a greater comprehension of the teachings of Jesus than the lives of people who sincerely believe a God *must* have a color and that there can be such a phenomenon as a "white" church.

The richness of the black writer's experience in the South can be remarkable, though some people might not think so. Once, while in college, I told a white middle-aged Northerner that I hoped to be a poet. In the nicest possible language, which still made me as mad as I've ever been, he suggested that a "farmer's daughter" might not be the stuff of which poets are made. On one level, of course, he had a point. A shack with only a dozen or so books is an unlikely place to discover a young Keats. But it is narrow thinking, indeed, to believe that a Keats is the only kind of poet one would want to grow up to be. One wants to write poetry that is understood by one's people, not by the Queen of England. Of course, should she be able to profit by it too, so much the better, but since that is not likely, catering to her tastes would be a waste of time.

For the black Southern writer, coming straight out of the country, as Wright did—Natchez and Jackson are still not as citified as they like to think they are—there is the world of comparisons; between town and country, between the ugly crowding and griminess of the cities and the spacious cleanliness (which actually seems impossible to dirty) of the country. A country person finds the city confining, like a too tight dress. And always, in one's memory, there remain all the rituals of one's growing up: the warmth and vividness of Sunday worship (never mind that you never quite believed) in a little church hidden from the road, and houses set so far back into the woods that at night it is impossible for strangers to find them. The daily dramas that evolve in such a private world are pure gold. But this view of a strictly private and hidden existence, with its triumphs, failures, grotesqueries, is not nearly as valuable to the socially conscious black Southern writer as his double vision is. For not only is he in a position to see his own world, and its close community ("Homecomings" on First Sundays, barbecues to raise money to send to Africa—one of the smaller ironies—the simplicity and eerie calm of a black funeral, where the beloved one is buried way in the middle of a wood with nothing to mark the spot but perhaps a wooden cross already coming apart), but also he is capable of knowing, with remarkably silent accuracy, the people who make up the larger world that surrounds and suppresses his own.

It is a credit to a writer like Ernest J. Gaines, a black writer who writes mainly about the people he grew up with in rural Louisiana, that he can write about whites and blacks exactly as he sees them and *knows* them, instead of writing of one group as a vast malignant lump and of the other as a conglomerate of perfect virtues.

In large measure, black Southern writers owe their clarity of vision to parents who refused to diminish themselves as human beings by succumbing to racism. Our parents seemed to know that an extreme negative emotion held against other human beings for reasons they do not control can be blinding. Blindness about other human beings, especially for a writer, is equivalent to death. Because of this blindness, which is, above all, racial, the works of many Southern writers have died. Much that we read today is fast expiring.

My own slight attachment to William Faulkner was rudely broken by realizing, after reading statements he made in *Faulkner in the University*, that he believed whites superior morally to blacks; that whites had a duty (which at their convenience they would assume) to "bring blacks along" politically, since blacks, in Faulkner's opinion, were "not ready" yet to function properly in a democratic society. He also thought that a black man's intelligence is directly related to the amount of white blood he has.

For the black person coming of age in the sixties, where Martin Luther King stands against the murderers of Goodman, Chaney, and Schwerner, there appears no basis for such assumptions. Nor was there any in Garvey's day, or in Du Bois's or in Douglass's or in Nat Turner's. Nor at any other period in our history, from the very founding of the country; for it was hardly incumbent upon slaves to be slaves and saints too. Unlike Tolstoy, Faulkner was not prepared to struggle to change the structure of the society he was born in. One might concede that in his fiction he did seek to examine the reasons for its decay, but unfortunately, as I have learned while trying to teach Faulkner to black students, it is not possible, from so short a range, to separate the man from his works.

One reads Faulkner knowing that his "colored" people had to come through "Mr. William's" back door, and one feels uneasy, and finally enraged that Faulkner did not burn the whole house down. When the provincial mind starts out *and continues* on a narrow and unprotesting course, "genius" itself must run on a track.

Flannery O'Connor at least had the conviction that "reality" is at best superficial and that the puzzle of humanity is less easy to solve than that of race. But Miss O'Connor was not so much of Georgia, as in it. The majority of Southern writers have been too confined by prevailing social customs to probe deeply into mysteries that the Citizens Councils insist must never be revealed.

Perhaps my Northern brothers will not believe me when I say there is a great deal of positive material I can draw from my "underprivileged" background. But they have never lived, as I have, at the end of a long road in a house that was faced by the edge of the world on one side and nobody for miles on the other. They have never experienced the magnificent quiet of a summer day when the heat is intense and one is so very thirsty, as one moves across the dusty cotton fields, that one learns forever that water is the essence of all life. In the cities it cannot be so clear to one that he is a creature of the earth, feeling the soil between the toes, smelling the dust thrown up by the rain, loving the earth so much that one longs to taste it and sometimes does.

Nor do I intend to romanticize the Southern black country life. I can recall that I hated it, generally. The hard work in the fields, the shabby houses, the evil greedy men who worked my father to death and almost broke the courage of that strong woman, my mother. No, I am simply saying that Southern black writers, like most writers, have a heritage of love and hate, but that they also have enormous richness and beauty to draw from. And, having been placed, as Camus says, "halfway between misery and the sun," they, too, know that "though all is not well under the sun, history is not everything."

No one could wish for a more advantageous heritage than that bequeathed to the black writer in the South: a compassion for the earth, a trust in humanity beyond our knowledge of evil, and an abiding love of justice. We inherit a great responsibility as well, for we must give voice to centuries not only of silent bitterness and hate but also of neighborly kindness and sustaining love.

Barbara Johnson
1947–

Barbara Johnson was born in Boston in 1947. After graduating from Oberlin College she did graduate work at Yale, studying under Paul de Man. From 1977 to 1982 Johnson taught in the French department at Yale. She is currently on the faculty of Harvard University, where she is a professor of French and comparative literature.

Johnson began to establish her present reputation as a leading "second-generation" deconstructionist in the 1970s as a contributor to scholarly journals. The understanding of deconstruction in the United States had heretofore been hampered to some extent by the preoccupation of its major proponents, notably de Man and Jacques Derrida, with the analysis of often unfamiliar texts. Johnson chose to apply deconstructionist theory to the works of more accessible writers, like Melville and Molière. A collection of these early essays was published in book form in 1980 as *The Critical Difference*.

In her preface to this book, Johnson addresses head-on the charge by many critics that deconstruction is a form of nihilistic reductionism. Deconstruction, she writes, is "not an annihilation of all values and differences; it is an attempt to follow the subtle, powerful effects of differences already at work within the illusion of a binary opposition. . . . Difference is a form of *work* to the extent that it *plays* beyond the control of any subject: it is, in fact, that without which no subject could ever be constituted."

Later she writes that "*deconstruction* is not synonymous with *destruction*. . . . It is in fact much closer to the original meaning of the word *analysis*. . . . The deconstruction of a text does not proceed by random doubt or arbitrary subversion, but by the careful teasing out of warring forces of signification within the text itself." Reading is, for Johnson, a process of "identifying and dismantling differences by means of other differences that cannot be fully identified or dismantled." A significant "difference" is gender, and Johnson has made sexual difference an important focus of deconstruction. "It seems to me," she has written "that women are all trained, to some extent, to be deconstructors. There's always a double message, and there's always a double response. The difficulty, for women, is unlearning self-repression and ambiguation and conciliation, and reaching affirmation."

Johnson's second collection of essays, *A World of Difference*, was published in 1987 and considers works by, among others, Wordsworth, Poe, Baudelaire, Mallarmé, Thoreau, Mary Shelley, Hurston, and Gwendolyn Brooks. Here Johnson addresses the politics of deconstruction and answers charges that it is conservative, even apolitical. Although deconstruction appears to argue that the meaning of language is ultimately undecidable, Johnson maintains that this very "undecidability" of language can be read as a political statement.

Johnson is a translator as well as a critic. At the request of Derrida, she prepared the first English translation of his *Dissemination* (1972), which was published in the United States in 1981.

FROM

A WORLD OF DIFFERENCE

NOTHING FAILS LIKE SUCCESS[1]

As soon as any radically innovative thought becomes an *ism,* its specific groundbreaking force diminishes, its historical notoriety increases, and its disciples tend to become more simplistic, more dogmatic, and ultimately more conservative, at which time its power becomes institutional rather than analytical. The fact that what is loosely called deconstructionism is now being widely institutionalized in the United States seems to me both intriguing and paradoxical, but also a bit unsettling, although not for the reasons advanced by most of its opponents. The questions I shall ask are the following: How can the deconstructive impulse retain its *critical* energy in the face of its own success? What can a reader who has felt the surprise of intellectual discovery in a work by Jacques Derrida or Paul de Man do to remain in touch not so much with the content of the discovery as with the intellectual upheaval of the surpise? How can that surprise be put to *work* in new ways?

I would like to begin by examining briefly two types of accusations commonly directed *against* deconstruction: the literarily conservative, which accuses deconstruction of going too far, and the politically radical, which accuses deconstruction of not going far enough. The first type comes from well-established men of letters who attempt to defend their belief in the basic communicability of meanings and values against what is said to be the deconstructionists' relativism, nihilism, or self-indulgent love of meaninglessness. What I shall try to determine is not whether misunderstanding is a mere accident or the inevitable fate of reading, but rather what the relation is between deconstruction and the type of logic on which these opponents' accusations of relativism and solipsism are based. Consider the following sentences taken from well-known critiques of deconstruction:

> In revisionist criticism the first consequence of calling discourse itself into question is the proposition that all criticism amounts to misreading, and thus one reading is as legitimate as another.

> But if all interpretation is misinterpretation, and if all criticism (like all history) of texts can engage only with a critic's own misconstruction, why bother to carry on the activities of interpretation and criticism?

> In the absence of any appeal to such a coercive reality to which the plurality of subjectivities can be referred, all perspectives become equally valid.

> Certainty and piety of all kinds are systematically undermined in favor of a universal relativism of values and judgment. Just as the revisionists are led to reduce the act of criticism to a given critic's subjective

preference, so do professors relegate judgment of all sorts to the students' subjective preferences.

What Deconstruction urges is not a new system of thought but skepticism toward all the old ways, which are construed as really only one way.[2]

The logic behind such utterances is the logic of binary opposition, the principle of noncontradiction, often thought of as the very essence of Logic as such. The arguments can be reduced to the following logical formulas:

1. If all readings are misreadings, then all readings are equally valid.
2. If there is no such thing as an objective reading, then all readings are based on subjective preferences.
3. If there is no absolute truth, then everything is relative.
4. To criticize is to be skeptical; to put in question is to dismiss.

In other words, if not absolute, then relative; if not objective, then subjective; if you are not for something, you are against it. Now, my understanding of what is most radical in deconstruction is precisely that it questions this basic logic of binary opposition, but not in a simple, binary, antagonistic way. Consider the following passage from Derrida's *Dissemination:*

It is thus not simply false to say that Mallarmé is a Platonist or a Hegelian. But it is above all not true. And vice versa.[3]

Instead of a simple "either/or" structure, deconstruction attempts to elaborate a discourse that says *neither* "either/or," *nor* "both/and" nor even "neither/nor," while at the same time not totally abandoning these logics either. The very word *deconstruction* is meant to undermine the either/or logic of the opposition "construction/destruction." Deconstruction is both, it is neither, and it reveals the way in which both construction and destruction are themselves not what they appear to be. Deconstruction both opposes and redefines; it both reverses an opposition and reworks the terms of that opposition so that what was formerly understood by them is no longer tenable. In the case of the much-publicized opposition between speech and writing, deconstruction *both* appears to grant to writing the priority traditionally assigned to speech *and* redefines "writing" as *différance* (difference/deferment) so that it can no longer simply mean "marks on a page" but can very well also refer to those aspects of spoken speech (nonimmediacy, the nontransparency of meaning, the gap between signifier and signified) that are normally occulted by traditional notions of what speech is. In the case of the opposition between objectivity and subjectivity, deconstruction *seems* to locate the moment of meaning-making in the nonobjectivity of the act of reading rather than in the inherent givens of a text, but then the text seems already to anticipate the reading it engenders, and at the same time the reader's "subjectivity" is discovered to function something like a text, that is, something whose conscious awareness of meaning and desire is only one aspect of a complex unconscious signifying system which determines consciousness as one of its several effects. To imply that subjectivity is structured like a machine, as Paul de Man does in his essay "The Purloined Ribbon,"[4] is both to subvert the opposition between subject and object (since a machine is considered to be an object) and to displace the traditional notion of what a subject is. If the original opposition between subject and object corresponds, as Gerald Graff would have it, to the opposition between the pleasure principle and the reality principle,[5] what deconstruction shows is that there is *something else involved* that puts in question the very separability of the pleasure principle and the reality principle, something that continuously generates effects that can be explained by neither. Freud called this something the death instinct, but this death instinct is to be understood as what ceaselessly escapes the mastery of understanding and the logic of binary opposition by exhibiting some "other" logic one can neither totally comprehend nor exclude. It is the attempt to *write with* this "other" logic that produces the appearance of obscurity in many deconstructive texts. Any statement that *affirms* while using a logic different from the logic of binary opposition will necessarily not conform to binary notions of "clarity."

Hence, if deconstruction focuses on the act of reading rather than on the objective meaning of a text, this in no way entails any greater degree of self-indulgence than the belief in conventional values does: on the contrary, at its best it undoes the very comforts of mastery and consensus that underlie the illusion that objectivity is situated somewhere outside the self. Thus, the incompatibility between deconstruction and its conservative detractors is an incompatibility of logics. While traditionalists say that a thing cannot be both A and not-A, deconstructors open up ways in which A is necessarily but unpredictably already different from A.

Now we come to the second type of critique of deconstruction, which accuses it of not giving up to its own claims of radicality, of working with too limited a notion of textuality, and of applying its critical energy only within an institutional structure that it does not question and therefore confirms.[6] This charge, which judges deconstruction against its own claims to an unflagging critical stance, is one which deconstruction must in fact continuously make against itself. Any discourse that is based on the questioning of boundary lines must never stop questioning its own. To reserve the deconstructive stance solely for literary criticism without analyzing its institutional underpinnings and economic and social relations with the world is to decide where the boundaries of the very critique of boundaries lie. To read a text apart from the historical and biographical conditions and writings that participate in its textual network is to limit a priori the kinds of questions that can be asked. Why, therefore, do some deconstructors tend to avoid going beyond the limits of the literary text?

There are, I think, three reasons for this unwarranted restriction. The first is entailed by the current institutionalization of deconstruction: the more it becomes entrenched as the self-definition of some literary critics in their opposition to other literary critics, the more it will resist problematizing the institutional conditions of literary criticism as such. The other two reasons spring out of an oversimplified understanding of certain aspects of deconstructive theory. To say, as Derrida has said, that there is nothing outside the text is not to say that the reader should read only one piece of literature in isolation from history, biography, and so on. It is to say that *nothing* can be said to be *not* a text, subject to the différance, the nonimmediacy, of presence or meaning. Even the statement that there is nothing outside the text cannot be taken to be the absolute certainty it appears to be, since it has to include itself in its own consequences. If there is nothing outside the text, then how can *any* locus of research or action be considered a priori as illegitimate?

The final reason for the conservatism of some forms of deconstruction is more pervasive: in questioning the nature of knowledge and causality, deconstruction has often given nothing but negative help in the attempt to read literature or philosophy *with* history and biography. In saying that history is a fiction, a text subject to ideological skewings and mystifications, and that it cannot be relied upon as a source of objective knowledge, deconstructive theory sometimes seems to block all access to the possibility of reading explicitly "referential" documents in conjunction with literary or speculative texts. Yet in practice we find Derrida drawing upon Freud's life and letters in his analysis of *Beyond the Pleasure Principle* (in *La Carte Postale*), and de Man often beginning an article with a historical account that in some way doubles the rhetorical problem he is about to discuss. The question, then, is how to use history and biography *deconstructively,* how to seek in them not answers, causes, explanations, or origins, but new questions and new ways in which the literary and nonliterary texts alike can be made to read and rework each other.

I would now like to outline a few general remarks about how to avoid becoming too comfortable in the abyss. To go back to the original objection that "if all readings are misreadings, then all readings are equally valid," how is it possible to maintain that some readings are better than others in a way that cannot be entirely reduced to a binary opposition? Since it is obvious that no deconstructor actually thinks all readings are equally valid, what kind of evaluation does deconstruction permit?

The sentence "all readings are misreadings" does not *simply* deny the notion of truth. Truth is preserved in vestigial form in the notion of error. This does not mean that there is, somewhere out there, forever unattainable, the one true reading against which all others will be tried and found wanting. Rather, it implies (1) that the reasons a reading might consider itself *right* are motivated and undercut by its own interests, blindnesses, desires, and fatigue, and (2) that the *role* of truth cannot be so simply eliminated. Even if truth is but a fantasy of the will to power, *something* still marks the point from which the imperatives of the not-self make themselves felt. To reject objective truth is to make it harder to avoid setting oneself up as an arbitrary arbiter. Therefore, the one imperative a reading must obey is that it follow, with rigor, what puts in question the kind of reading it thought it was going to be. A reading is strong, I would therefore submit, to the extent that it encounters and propagates the surprise of otherness. The impossible but necessary task of the reader is to set herself up to be surprised.

No methodology can be relied on to generate surprise. On the contrary, it is usually surpise that engenders methodology. Derrida brings to his reader the surprise of a nonbinary, undecidable logic. Yet comfortable undecidability needs to be surprised by its own conservatism. My emphasis on the word *surprise* is designed to counter the idea that a good deconstructor must constantly put his own enterprise into question. This is true, but it is not enough. It can lead to a kind of infinite regress of demystification, in which ever more sophisticated subtleties are elaborated within an unchanging field of questions.

How, then, can one set oneself up to be surprised by otherness? Obviously, in a sense, one cannot. Yet one can begin by transgressing one's own usual practices, by indulging in some judicious time-wasting with what one does not know how to use, or what has fallen into disrepute. What the surprise encounter with otherness should do is lay bare some hint of an ignorance one never knew one had. Much has been made of the fact that "knowledge" cannot be taken for granted. But perhaps rather than simply questioning the nature of knowledge, we should today reevaluate the static, inert concept we have always had of ignorance. Ignorance, far more than knowledge, is what can never be taken for granted. If I perceive my ignorance as a gap in knowledge instead of an imperative that changes the very nature of what I think I know, then I do not truly experience my ignorance. The surprise of otherness is that moment when a new form of ignorance is suddenly activated as an imperative. If the deconstructive impulse is to retain its vital, subversive power, we must therefore become ignorant of it again and again. It is only by forgetting what we know how to do, by setting aside the thoughts that have most changed us, that those thoughts and that knowledge can go on making accessible to us the surprise of an otherness we can only encounter in the moment of suddenly discovering we are ignorant of it.

DECONSTRUCTION, FEMINISM, AND PEDAGOGY[7]

It is better to fail in teaching what should not be taught than to succeed in teaching what is not true.
—Paul de Man

The old folks say, "It's not how little we know that hurts so, but that so much of what we know ain't so."
—Toni Cade Bambara

The purpose of this chapter is to attempt to articulate deconstruction and feminism in terms of pedagogical theory and practice, to make a link, in a sense, between "what is not true" and "what ain't so." My remarks will be based on two texts: (1) an essay by Paul de Man (from which the first epigraph is taken) entitled "The Resistance to Theory," which first appeared in an issue of *Yale French Studies* called *The Pedagogical Imperative: Teaching as a Literary Genre,* and (2) a recent collection of essays on pedagogy edited by Margo Culley and Catherine Portuges entitled *Gendered Subjects: The Dynamics of Feminist Teaching.*[8]

I will begin by reinserting the first epigraph into its original context. Speaking about the question of whether theory and scholarship are compatible, de Man writes:

> A question arises only if a tension develops between methods of understanding and the knowledge which those methods allow one to reach. If there is indeed something about literature, as such, which allows for a discrepancy between truth and method, between *Wahrheit* and *Methode,* then scholarship and theory are no longer necessarily compatible; as a first casualty of this complication, the notion of "literature as such" as well as the clear distinction between history and interpretation can no longer be taken for granted. For a method that cannot be made to suit the "truth" of its object can only teach delusion. . . . These uncertainties are manifest in the hostility directed at theory in the name of ethical and aesthetic values. . . . The most effective of these attacks will denounce theory as an obstacle to scholarship and, consequently, to teaching. It is worth examining whether, and why, this is the case. For if this is indeed so, then it is better to fail in teaching what should not be taught than to succeed in teaching what is not true. (*PI,* p. 4)

In order to make some headway with this assertion, we might examine the ways in which the essay itself functions pedagogically. What, if anything, does the essay teach? Interestingly, it opens by placing itself under the sign of failure. "This essay was not originally intended to address the question of teaching directly, although it was supposed to have a didactic and an educational function—which it failed to achieve" (*PI,* p. 3). The essay itself, in other words, can be read as an *enactment* of the failure to teach that it promotes. De Man explains that the essay was commissioned to provide a summary of recent work in literary theory for an MLA volume entitled *Introduction to Scholarship in Modern Languages and Literatures.* "I found it difficult to live up, in minimal good faith, to the requirements of this program, and could only try to explain, as concisely as possible, why the main theoretical interest of literary theory consists in the impossibility of its definition. The Committee rightly judged that this was an inauspicious way to achieve the pedagogical objectives of the volume and commissioned another article." It is not pedagogically auspicious, it seems, to be sent on a mission of scholarship and to come back with a tale of impossibility. Yet it is the value of such a failure to teach that de Man is asserting as the moral of his pedagogical tale. What is of pedagogical interest for him is precisely what resists pedagogical mastery.

Feminist theories of pedagogy, too, involve a critique of masterful meaning and an interest in the resistance to reductive appropriation. One of the most visible differences, however, lies in the status of the pedagogical subject. De Man makes a clear case for teaching as an impersonal rather than an interpersonal phenomenon: "Overfacile opinion notwithstanding, teaching is not primarily an intersubjective relationship between people but a cognitive process in which self and other are only tangentially and contiguously involved. The only teaching worthy of the name is scholarly, not personal" (*PI*, p. 3). When de Man ultimately concludes that the resistance to theory is ineradicable because theory is its own self-resistance, that self-resistance is also a form of resistance to the very notion of a self.

The title *Gendered Subjects,* on the other hand, indicates a move to reverse the impersonalization that de Man radicalizes and to reintroduce the personal, or at least the positional, as a way of disseminating authority and decomposing the false universality of patriarchally institutionalized meanings. Not only has female personal experience tended to be excluded from the discourse of knowledge, but the realm of the personal itself has been coded as female and devalued for that reason. In opposition, therefore, many of the essays of the volume consciously assume a first-person autobiographical stance toward the question of pedagogical theory: this is how it looks *to me* as the only black woman in an English department, or as a male feminist, or as a teacher of feminist theory. This is where I am positioned in the institutions of pedagogy. Explicitly speaking from *where one is* turns out to allow for an expansion rather than a contraction of the range of pedagogical experiences available. While de Man urges maximum abstraction, Michele Russell, for one, exhorts us to "use everything":

> The size and design of the desks, for example. They are wooden, with one-sided stationary writing arms attached. The embodiment of a poor school. Small. Unyielding. Thirty years old. Most of the black women [students] are ample-bodied. . . . Sitting there for one hour—not to mention trying to concentrate and work—is a contortionist's miracle, or a stoic's. It feels like getting left back.
>
> With desks as a starting-point for thinking about our youth in school, class members are prompted to recall the mental state such seats encouraged. They cite awkwardness, restlessness, and furtive embarrassment. When they took away our full-top desks with interior compartments, we remember how *exposed* we felt. . . . We talk about all the unnecessary, but deliberate, ways the educational process is made uncomfortable for the poor. . . . We remember that one reason many of us stopped going to school was that it became an invasion of privacy. (*GS*, p. 163)

The constraints of positionality here *literally* become the access route to a whole rethinking of the educational enterprise. This, too, is a story of the pedagogical recuperation of a failure of teaching, but in a very different sense from de Man's.

I find both these versions of the resistance to pedagogy equally compelling and equally difficult to put into genuine—as opposed to apparent—practice. Both versions involve an imperative not to lose, but rather to work through, that resistance. The question I want to ask here is whether there is a *simple* incompatibility between the depersonalization of deconstruction and the re-personalization of feminism, or whether each is not in reality haunted by the ghost of the other.

The personal in fact returns in de Man in two very different ways. On the one hand, he has always been and is increasingly being lionized as the embodiment of the great teacher: the recent issue of *Yale French Studies* entitled *The Lesson of Paul de Man* (1985) opens by saying, "He was never not teaching." Testimonials repeatedly assert that it was precisely his way of denying personal authority that engendered the unique power of his personal authority. What is not clear, of course, is whether his personal impact should be seen as a sign of the success or of the failure of his pedagogical project as he conceived it. Another sign of this paradox is the function of proper names in the present essay: the name of de Man occupies a focal position that no proper name assumes—and this is part of the point—in the feminist collective volume, however personal the narratives. (Is it by chance, moreover, that he should be named "the Man"?)

The other return of the personal in de Man's work takes a rhetorical form. Even a cursory perusal of his essays reveals that their insistant rhetorical mode—in the service of their irony, paradoxes, and chiasmuses—is personification. In the absence of a personal agent of signification, the rhetorical entities themselves are constantly said to "know," to "renounce," or to "resign themselves" in the place where the poet or critic as subject has disappeared. It is as though the operations of personhood could not be eliminated but only transferred—which does not necessarily imply that their rightful place is within the self. Rather, it implies that personification is a trope available for occupancy by either subjects or linguistic entities, the diffference between them being ultimately indeterminable, if each is known only in and through a text. The teacher, in any event, becomes neither impersonal nor personal: the agent of pedagogy is a personification.

What the transfer of personhood to rhetorical entities does enable de Man to achieve, however, is an elimination of sexual difference. By making personhood the property of an "it," de Man is able to claim a form of universality which can be said to inhere in language itself, and which is not directly subject to ordinary feminist critique, however gender-inflected language can in fact be shown to be. The analysis of the rhetorical operations of self-resistance is, as de Man asserts, irrefutable in its own terms. But the question *can* be asked why de Man's discourse of self-resistance and uncertainty has achieved such authority and visibility, while the self-resistance and uncertainty of *women* has been part of what has insured their lack of authority and their invisibility. It would seem that one has to be positioned in the place of power in order for one's self-resistance to be valued. Self-resistance, indeed, may be one of the few viable postures remaining for the white male establishment.

But does this imply that the task of feminism would be the overcoming of self-resistance? In many of the essays in *Gendered Subjects*, this would seem to be the case. A typical essay (this one by Susan Stanford Friedman) begins: "I chose to address the issue of feminist pedagogy in a personal narrative not only because the cornerstone of that pedagogy has been the validation of experience, but also because my own evolution as a teacher in a university setting over the last twelve years illuminates a pedagogical problem we all must face" (*GS*, p. 203). What is interesting about this attempt at personalization is how quickly it slides into an assumption of generalizability ("a problem we all must face"). The recourse to "experience" is always, in these essays, a double-edged sword. On the one hand, it would be impossible to deny that female experience has been undervalidated. On the other hand, the moment one assumes one knows what female experience is, one runs the risk of creating another reductive appropriation—an appropriation that consists in the reduction of experience *as* self-resistance. While deconstructive discourse may be in danger of overvaluing self-resistance, feminist discourse may be in danger of losing self-resistance as a source of insight and power rather than merely of powerlessness. While de Man's writing is haunted by the return of personification, feminist writing is haunted by the return of abstraction. The challenge facing both approaches is to recognize these ghosts not as external enemies but as the uncannily familiar strangers that make their own knowledge both possible and problematic.

NOTES

1. This chapter was originally written for a session at the 1980 MLA Convention organized by the Society for Critical Exchange on the topic "The Future of Deconstruction." While I would want to argue some of the points a bit differently now (and perhaps with different examples), the basic thrust of the essay seems to me to be, if anything, even more relevant today. In the years since this essay was written, many more critiques of deconstruction have appeared, both from the left and from the right, but I leave the references as they were in 1980. Some of the later material will present itself in this book in dialogue with other chapters.

2. Peter Shaw, "Degenerate Criticism," *Harper's*, October 1979, p. 97; M. H. Abrams, "The Deconstructive Angel," *Critical Inquiry*, Spring 1977, p. 434; Gerald Graff, *Literature against Itself* (Chicago: University of Chicago Press, 1979), p. 39; Shaw, "Degenerate Criticism," p. 93; and Denis Donoghue, "Deconstructing Deconstruction," *New York Review of Books*, June 12, 1980, p. 37.

3. Jacques Derrida, *Dissemination*, trans. Barbara Johnson (Chicago: University of Chicago Press, 1981), p. 207.

4. Paul de Man, "The Purloined Ribbon," in *Glyph 1: Johns Hopkins Textual Studies* (Baltimore: Johns Hopkins University Press, 1977). (Reprinted as "Excuses" in *Allegories of Reading* [New Haven: Yale University Press, 1979].)

5. Graff, *Literature against Itself*, p. 65.

6. Cf., for example, Jeffrey Mehlman, "Teaching Reading," *Diacritics*, Winter 1976; Gayatri Chakravorti Spivak and Michael Ryan, "Anarchism Revisited," *Diacrit-*

ics, Summer 1978; John Brenkman, "Deconstruction and the Social Text," *Social Text* 1 (Winter 1979); and Edward Said, "Reflections on Recent American 'Left' Literary Criticism," *Boundary 2* 8, no. 1 (1979), reprinted in *The World, the Text, and the Critic* (Cambridge: Harvard University Press, 1983).

7. This chapter was conceived as a contribution to a session of the 1985 MLA Convention organized by Thaïs Morgan entitled "Postpedagogy."

8. Paul de Man, "The Resistance to Theory," in *The Pedagogical Imperative,* ed. Barbara Johnson (New Haven: Yale University Press, 1982), hereafter referred to as *PI; Gendered Subjects,* ed. Margo Culley and Catherine Portuges (Boston: Routledge & Kegan Paul, 1985), hereafter referred to as *GS.*

Henry Louis Gates, Jr.
1950–

Henry Louis Gates, Jr., is one of several black critics who have recently taken on the task of redefining both black literary history and literary history itself. He was born on September 16, 1950, in Keyser, West Virginia. He took a B.A. in history at Yale University in 1973. On Mellon and Ford Foundation fellowships he went to Clare College, Cambridge, where his tutor was the writer Wole Soyinka, who influenced him to turn from history to literature and led him to Yoruba literature and interpretative modes that would figure prominently in Gates's work. Gates received his M.A. from Cambridge in 1974. Back in the United States, he worked, spent a month at Yale Law School, but took an instructorship in English, and upon completion of his Ph.D. from Cambridge in 1979 became assistant professor of English literature and director of the undergraduate Afro-American studies program at Yale.

At Yale, with support from grants from the National Endowment for the Humanities and the Ford Foundation, he began and directed the Black Periodical Fiction Project, whose purpose was to recover black fiction buried in nineteenth-century periodicals. He continued that project at Cornell University, where since 1985 he has been professor of English, African studies, and comparative literature.

Gates's work as an editor demonstrates the scope of his interests and critical intentions, which are to get in print and make accessible the "lost" works of black writers, to present in collections of essays theories for a literary criticism, and to aid scholarly work on writers such as Wole Soyinka. Over a mere ten years his accomplishments in this area have been extraordinary and valuable. He wrote the foreword to Charles T. Davis's *Black Is the Color of the Cosmos: Essays on Afro-American Literature and Culture 1942–1981* (1982). In 1983 he republished Harriet Wilson's *Our Nig; or, Sketches from the Life of a Free Black,* the first novel published by a black person in the United States and virtually unknown until Gates's rediscovery of it. An anthology of critical essays, *Black Literature and Literary Theory*, followed in 1984. With Davis, Gates edited and wrote the introduction to *The Slave Narrative* (1985). A collection of his essays, *"Race," Writing, and Difference,* was published in 1986, and in that same year, with James Gibbs and Ketu H. Katrak, Gates published *Wole Soyinka: A Bibliography of Primary and Secondary Sources.* He has edited *In the House of Osugbo: Critical Essays on Wole Soyinka* and *The Classic Slave Narratives* (both 1987). Gates is series editor of the thirty-volume *Oxford-Schomburg Library of Nineteenth-Century Black Women's Writings.*

A 1983 essay by Gates in *Critical Inquiry,* "On 'The Blackness of Blackness': A Critique of the Sign and the Signifying Monkey," laid the groundwork for a critical trilogy. The first of these, *Figures in Black: Words, Signs, and the "Racial" Self* (1987), sets out "to experiment by letting contemporary theories (Russian Formalism, French Structuralism, Anglo-American Practical Criticism, among others) inform my close readings of black texts." Gates speaks of his feelings about this project as being complex and charged, that his sense of his own "marginality" prevents him from falling into "what I think of as the embarrassment of conversion." Moreover, while "explicating white texts was a delightful . . . academic exercise . . . , analyzing black texts, on the contrary, was both extraordinarily personal and political for me." He intends "to demonstrate the relationship of literary theory to Afro-American literature" and to address the question "How 'white' is literary theory?" Furthermore, his purpose is "naming indigenous black principles of criticism and applying these to explicate our own texts." In the second book, *The Signifying Monkey: A Theory of Afro-American Literary Criticism* (1988), Gates advances beyond what he established in the first and narrows the focus. "[It had been] my hope that I had at last located with the African Afro-American traditions a system of rhetoric and interpretation that could be drawn upon both as *figures* for a genuinely 'black' criticism and as *frames* through which I could interpret, or 'read,' theories of contemporary literary criticism." The task he sets himself here is "to locate and identify how the 'black tradition' had theorized about itself." In close readings of Ralph Ellison's work and Ishmael Reed's "revisionary techniques of parody and pastiche" Gates develops the theory of "signifyin(g)" as basic to the experience of black literature and the method whereby "the black tradition had theorized about itself." Signifyin(g) is to be found in jazz, in the *Narrative of the Life of Frederick Douglass, An American Slave,* Reed's *Mumbo Jumbo,* and Walker's *The Color Purple,* and in African literature in "Esu's double voice." It is built upon "the implications of doubled voices upon strategies of writing" that are indigenous to the tradition, both "for patterns of revision from text to text and for modes of figuration at work within the text." The third book of this critical trilogy is to be called *Black Letters and the Enlightenment.*

FROM

FIGURES IN BLACK

LITERARY THEORY AND THE BLACK TRADITION

III

Unlike almost every other literary tradition, the Afro-American literary tradition was generated as a response to eighteenth- and nineteenth-century allegations that persons of African descent did not, and could not, create literature. Philosophers and literary critics, such as Hume, Kant, Jefferson, and Hegel, seemed to decide that the absence or presence of a written literature was the signal measure of the potential, innate humanity of a race. The African living in Europe or in the New World seems to have felt compelled to create a literature both to demonstrate implicitly that blacks did indeed possess the intellectual ability to create a written art and to indict the several social and economic institutions that delimited the humanity of all black people in Western cultures.

So insistent did these racist allegations prove to be, at least from the eighteenth to the early twentieth centuries, that it is fair to describe the subtext of the history of black letters as this urge to refute the claim that because blacks had no written traditions they were bearers of an inferior culture. The relationship between European and American critical theory, then, and the development of African and Afro-American literary traditions, can readily be seen to have been ironic indeed. Even as late as 1911, when J. E Casely-Hayford published *Ethiopia Unbound* (called the first African novel), that pioneering author felt compelled to address this matter in the first two paragraphs of his text. "At the dawn of the twentieth century," the novel opens, "men of light and leading both in Europe and in America had not yet made up their minds as to what place to assign to the spiritual aspirations of the black man.... Before this time, it had been discovered that the black man was not necessarily the missing link between man and ape. It has even been granted that for intellectual endowments he had nothing to be ashamed of in an *open* competition with the Aryan or any other type." *Ethiopia Unbound*, it seems obvious, was concerned to settle the matter of black mental equality, which had remained something of an open question for two hundred years. Concluding this curiously polemical exposition of three paragraphs, which precedes the introduction of the novel's protagonist, Casely-Hayford points to "the names of men like [W. E. B.] Du Bois, Booker T. Washington, [Edward Wilmot] Blyden, [Paul Laurence] Dunbar, [Samuel] Coleridge-Taylor, and others" as prima facie evidence of the sheer saliency of what Carter G. Woodson once termed "the public Negro mind." These were men, the narrative concludes, "who had distinguished themselves in the fields of activity and intellectuality," men who had demonstrated conclusively that the African's first cousin was indeed the European rather than the ape.

That the presence of a written literature could assume such large proportions in several Western cultures from the Enlightenment to this century is only as curious as the fact that blacks themselves, as late as 1911, felt the need to speak the matter silent, to end the argument by producing literature. Few literary traditions have begun or been sustained by such a complex and ironic relation to their criticism: allegations of an absence led directly to a presence, a literature often inextricably bound in a dialogue with its potentially harshest critics.

In Spanish and English, in Latin and French, in German and Dutch, the writings of blacks in the Enlightenment came under scrutiny not primarily literary, giving rise to an implicit theory of writing itself, at least of black writing, and its relation to what we have come to think of as the innate rights of a people to political freedom. Indeed, we can only begin to understand the resistance to theory in the Afro-American tradition if we qualify these terms somewhat and call this tendency the resistance to *Western* theory. Black writers and critics, since Amo, have been forced to react against an impressive received tradition of Western critical theory which not only posited the firm relation among writing, "civilization," and political authority, but which also was called upon by various Western men of letters to justify various forms of enslavement and servitude of black people. It is no surprise that black people have been theory-resistant. Because the history of this relationship between blacks and theory involves many Western philosophers, because its threads of influence have not been defined before, and because it has had such a determining effect upon black critics and writers since the eighteenth century, I have sketched its contours to begin to suggest its implications. Let us next consider how black writers and critics reacted to the racism of Western writings about the relationship between the written arts and the status of the black human being.

Hume, Kant, Jefferson, and Hegel's stature demanded response: from black writers, refutations of white doubts about their very capacity to imagine great art and hence to take a few giant steps up the Great Chain of Being; from would-be critics, encyclopedic and often hyperbolic replies to these disparaging generalizations. The critical responses include Thomas Clarkson's Prize Essay, written in Latin at Cambridge in 1785 and published as *An Essay on the Slavery and Commerce of the Human Species, Particularly the African* (1788), and the following rather remarkable volumes: Gilbert Imlay's *A Topographical Description of the Western Territory of North America* (1793); the Marquis de Bois-Robert's two-volume *The Negro Equalled by Few Europeans* (1791); Thomas Branagan's *Preliminary Essay on the Oppression of the Exiled Sons of Africa* (1804); the Abbé Grégoire's *An Enquiry concerning the Intellectual and Moral Faculties, and Literature of Negroes* . . . (1808); Samuel Stanhope Smith's *An Essay on the Causes of the Variety of the Human Complexion and Figure in the Human Species* (1810); Lydia Maria Child's *An Appeal in Favor of That Class of Americans Called Africans*

(1833); B. B. Thatcher's *Memoir of Phillis Wheatley, a Native American and a Slave* (1834); Abigail Mott's *Biographical Sketches and Interesting Anecdotes of Persons of Color* (1838); R. B. Lewis's *Light and Truth* (1844); Theodore Hally's *A Vindication of the Capacity of the Negro Race* (1851); R. T. Greener's urbane long essay in *The National Quarterly Review* (1880); Joseph Wilson's rather ambitious *Emancipation: Its Course and Progress from 1481 B.C. to A.D. 1875* (1882); William Simmon's *Men of Mark* (1887); Benjamin Brawley's *The Negro in Literature and Art* (1918); and Joel A. Rodgers's two-volume *The World's Great Men of Color* (1946). There are well over 150 encyclopedias of black intellection, published to disprove racist aspersions cast upon the mind of "the race."

Even more telling for our purposes here is that the almost quaint authenticating signatures and statements that prefaced Wheatley's book became, certainly through the period of Dunbar and Chesnutt and even until the middle of the Harlem Renaissance, fixed attestations of the "specimen" author's physical blackness. This sort of authenticating color description was so common to these prefaces that many late nineteenth- and early twentieth-century black reviewers, particularly in the *African Methodist Episcopal Church Review*, the *Southern Workman*, the *Voice of the Negro*, *Alexander's Magazine* and *The Colored American*, adopted it as a political as well as rhetorical strategy to counter the intense and bitter allegations of African inferiority popularized by journalistic accounts and "colorations" of social Darwinism. Through an examination of a few of these prefaces, I have tried to sketch an ironic circular thread of interpretation that commences in the eighteenth century but does not reach its fullest philosophical form until the decade between 1965 and 1975: the movement from blackness as a physical concept to blackness as a metaphysical concept. Indeed, this movement became the very text and pretext of the "Blackness" of the recent Black Arts movement, a solidly traced hermeneutical circle into which we all found ourselves drawn.

The confusion of realms, of art with propaganda, plagued the Harlem Renaissance in the twenties. A critical determination—a mutation of principles set in motion by Matthew Arnold's *Culture and Anarchy*, simplified thirty years later into Booker T. Washington's "toothbrush and bar of soap" and derived from Victorian notions of "uplifting" spiritual and moral ideals that separated the savage (noble or not) from the realm of culture and the civilized mind—meant that only certain literary treatments of black people could escape community censure. The race against social Darwinism and the psychological remnants of slavery meant that each piece of creative writing became a political statement. Each particular manifestation served as a polemic: "another bombshell fired into the heart of bourgeois culture," as *The World Tomorrow* editorialized in 1921. "The black writer," said Richard Wright, "approached the critical community dressed in knee pants of servility, curtseying to show that the Negro was not inferior, that he was human, and that he had a gift comparable to other men." As early as 1921, W. E. B. Du Bois wrote of this in the *Crisis*:

Negro art is today plowing a difficult row. We want everything that is said about us to tell of the best and highest and noblest in us. We insist that our Art and Propaganda be one. We fear that evil in us will be called racial, while in others it is viewed as an individual. We fear that our shortcomings are not merely human.[1]

And as late as 1925, even as sedate an observer as Heywood Broun argued that only through art would the Negro gain freedom: "A supremely great negro artist," he told the New York Urban League, "who could catch the imagination of the world, would do more than any other agency to remove the disabilities against which the negro now labors." Further, Broun remarked that this artist–redeemer could come at any time, and he asked his audience to remain silent for ten seconds to imagine that coming![2] Ambiguity in language, then, and "feelings that are general" (argued for as early as 1861 by Frances E. W. Harper) garnered hostility and suspicion from the critical minority; ambiguity was a threat to "knowing the lines." The results for a growing black literature were disastrous, these perorations themselves dubious. Black literature came to be seen as a cultural artifact (the product of unique historical forces) or as a document that bore witness to the political and emotional tendencies of the Negro victim of white racism. Literary theory became the application of a social attitude.

By the apex of the Harlem Renaissance, then, certain latent assumptions about the relationships between art and life had become prescriptive canon. In 1925, Du Bois outlined what he called "the social compulsion" of black literature, built as it was, he contended, on "the sorrow and strain inherent in American slavery, on the difficulties that sprang from emancipation, on the feelings of revenge, despair, aspiration, and hatred which arose as the Negro struggled and fought his way upward."[3] Further, he made formal the mechanistic distinction between "method" and "content," the same distinction that allowed James Weldon Johnson to declare with glee that, sixty years after slavery, all that separated the black poet from the white was "mere technique"! Structure, by now, was atomized. Form was merely a surface for a reflection of the world, the world here being an attitude toward race; form was a repository for the disposal of ideas; message was not only meaning but value; poetic discourse was taken to be literal, or once removed; language lost its capacity to be metaphorical in the eyes of the critic; the poem approached the essay, with referents immediately perceivable; literalness precluded the view of life as allegorical; and black critics forgot that writers approached things through words, not the other way around. The functional and didactic aspects of formal discourse assumed primacy in normative analysis. The confusion of realms was complete: the critic became social reformer, and literature became an instrument for the social and ethical betterment of the black person.

So, while certain rather conservative notions of art and culture wove themselves into F. R. Leavis's *Scrutiny* in Cambridge in the thirties, blacks borrowed whole the Marxist notion of base and superstructure and made of it, if you will, race and superstructure. Here, as in Wright's "Blueprint for Negro

Literature," for example, race in American society was held to determine the social relations that determine consciousness, which in turn determines actual ideas and creative works. "In the beginning was the deed," said Trotsky in an attack on the Formalists; now the deed was *black*. The brilliant critical work of Sterling Brown and Zora Neale Hurston ran counter to these trends but did not predominate.

This notion of race and superstructure became, during the forties and fifties, in one form or another the mode of criticism of black literature. As would be expected, critics urged the supremacy of one extraliterary idea after another, as Ralph Ellison challenged Richard Wright on one front and James Baldwin on another. But race as the controlling mechanism in critical theory reached its zenith of influence and mystification when LeRoi Jones metamorphosed himself into Imamu Baraka and his daishiki-clad, Swahili-named "harbari gani" disciples "discovered" they were black. With few exceptions, black critics employed blackness-as-theme to forward one argument or another for the amelioration of the Afro-American's social dilemma. Yet the critical activity altered little, whether that message was integration or whether it was militant separation. Message was the medium; message reigned supreme; form became a mere convenience or, worse, a contrivance.

The commonplace observation that black literature with very few exceptions has failed to match pace with a sublime black music stems in large measure from this concern with statement. Black music, by definition, could never utilize the schism between form and content, because of the nature of music. Black music, alone of the black arts, has developed free of the imperative, the compulsion, to make an explicit political statement. Black musicians, of course, had no choice: music groups masses of nonrepresentational material into significant form; it is the audible embodiment of form. All this, however, requires a specific mastery of technique, which cannot be separated from "poetic insight." There could be no "knowing the lines" in the creation of black music, especially since the Afro-American listening audience had such a refined and critical aesthetic sense. Thus, Afro-America has a tradition of masters, from Bessie Smith through John Coltrane, unequaled perhaps in all of modern music. In literature, however, we have no similar development, no sustained poignancy in writing. In poetry, where the command of language is indispensable if only because poetry "thickens" language and thus draws attention from its referential aspect, we saw in the sixties the growth of what the poet Ted Joans calls the "Hand-Grenade" poets, who concern themselves with futile attempts to make poetry preach, which poetry is not capable of doing so well. And the glorification of this poetry (especially the glorification of Baraka and Don Lee's largely insipid rhetoric), in which we feel the unrelenting vise of the poet's grip upon our shoulders, became the principal activity of the "New Black" critic. The suppositions on which this theory of criticism rests are best explicated through a close reading of four texts that, conveniently, treat poetry, literary history, and the novel.

Stephen Henderson's *Understanding the New Black Poetry* is the first attempt at a quasi-formalistic analysis of black poetry.[4] It is of the utmost importance to the history of race and superstructure criticism because it attempts to map a black poetic landscape, identifying inductively those unique cultural artifacts that critics, "especially white critics," have "widely misunderstood, misinterpreted, and undervalued for a variety of reasons—aesthetic, cultural, and political." Henderson's work is seminal insofar as he is concerned with discrete uses of language, but in the course of his study he succumbs to the tendency of advancing specific ideological prerequisites.

Henderson readily admits his bias: he equates aesthetics and ethics. "Ultimately," he says, "the 'beautiful' is bound up with the truth of a people's history, as they perceive it themselves." This absolute of truth Henderson defines in his fifth definition of what "black poetry is chiefly": "Poetry by any identifiably Black person whose ideological stance vis-à-vis the history and aspirations of his people since slavery [is] adjudged by them to be 'correct.'" Hence, an ideal of truth, which exists in fact for the black poet to find, is a "Black" truth. And "Black" is integral to the poetic equation, since "if there is such a *commodity* as 'blackness' in literature (and I assume that there is), it should somehow be found in concentrated or in residual form in the poetry" (emphasis added).

Had Henderson elaborated on "residual form" in literary language, measured formally, structurally, or linguistically, he would have revolutionized black literary criticism and brought it into the twentieth century. But his theory of poetry is based on three sometimes jumbled broad categories that allow the *black* critic to define "norms" of blackness." The first of these is an oversimplified conception of *theme:* "that which is spoken of, whether the specific subject matter, the emotional response to it, or its intellectual formulation." The second is *structure,* by which Henderson intends "chiefly some aspects of the poem such as diction, rhythm, figurative language, which goes into the total makeup." (At times, he notes, "I use the word in an extended sense to include what is usually called genre.") His third critical tool, the scale by which he measures the "commodity" he calls "Blackness," is *saturation*. He means by this "several things, chiefly the communication of 'Blackness' and fidelity to the observed or intuited truth of the Black Experience in the United States."

Now, the textual critic has problems with Henderson's schema not only because it represents an artificial segmentation of poetic structure (which can never, in fact, be explicated as if one element existed independently of the rest) but also because that same scheme tends to be defined in terms of itself and hence is tautological. Henderson defines *theme,* for example, as "perhaps the simplest and most apparent" of the three. By *theme,* however, he means a poem's paraphrased level of "meaning." To illustrate this, he contrasts a George Moses Horton quatrain with a couplet from Countee Cullen. The "ambiguity" of the former lines, he concludes, defined for us insofar as "it might evoke a sympathetic tear from the eye of a white [Jewish] New York professor meditating upon his people's enslavement in ancient Egypt, does make it a less precise kind of ["Black"] statement than Cullen's, because in the latter the irony cannot be appreciated without understanding the actual historical debasement of the African psyche in America." Thus, the principal corollary to the theorem of "black themes" is that the closer a theme approaches cultural exclusivity, the closer it comes to a higher "fidelity." Moreover, Henderson allows himself to say, had Shakespeare's Sonnet 130 "been written by an African at Elizabeth's court, would not the thematic meaning change?" That leap of logic is difficult to comprehend, for a poem is above all atemporal and must cohere at a symbolic level, if it coheres at all. Perhaps Henderson's problem is the poetry prompting his theory; he has only followed that poetry's lead and in that way left himself open to Wittgenstein's remonstration: "Do not forget that a poem, even though it is composed in the language of information, is not used in the language of giving information."

The most promising of Henderson's categories is *structure*, and yet it is perhaps the most disappointing. By *structure*, he means that "Black poetry is most distinctly Black" whenever "it derives its form from two basic sources, Black speech and Black music." At first glance, this idea seems exciting, since it implies a unique, almost intangible use of language peculiar to Afro-Americans. On this, one could build—nay, one *must* build—that elusive "Black Aesthetic" the race and superstructure critics have sought in vain. But Henderson's understanding of speech as referent is not linguistic; he means a literal referent to nonpoetic discourse and unfortunately makes no allowances for the manner in which poetic discourse differs from prosaic discourse or "instances" of speech. He provides us with an elaborate and complicated taxonomy of reference to speech and to music, yet unaccountably ignores the fact that the "meaning" of a word in a poem is derived from its context within that poem, as well as from its context in our actual, historical (un)consciousness. But a taxonomy is a tool to knowledge, not knowledge itself. The use of language is not a stockpile of referents or forms, but an activity.

Henderson remarks with some astonishment that "Black speech in this country" is remarkable in that "certain words and constructions seem to carry an inordinate charge of emotional and psychological weight." These he calls "mascon" words, borrowing the acronym from NASA, where it is employed to describe a massive concentration of matter beneath the lunar surface. What he is describing, of course, is not unique to black poetic discourse; it is common to all poetic uses of language in all literatures and is what helps to create ambiguity, paradox, and irony. This, of course, has been stated adamantly by the "practical critics" since the twenties—those same "New Critics" Henderson disparages. These usages, however, do make black poetic language unique and argue strongly for a compilation of a black dictionary of discrete examples of specific signification, where "Black English" departs from "general usage." They are not, I am afraid, found only in the language of black folks in this country. Had Henderson identified some criteria by which we could define an oral tradition in terms of the "grammar" it superimposes on nonliterary discourse, then shown how this comes to bear on literary discourse, and further shown such grammars to be distinctly black, then his contribution to our understanding of language and literature would have been no mean thing indeed.

His final category, *saturation,* is the ultimate tautology: poetry is "Black" when it communicates "Blackness." The more a text is saturated, the "Blacker" the text. One imagines a daishiki-clad Dionysus weighing the saturated, mascon lines of Countee Cullen against those of Langston Hughes, as Paul Laurence Dunbar and Jean Toomer are silhouetted by the flames of our own black Hades. The blacker the berry, the sweeter the juice.

Should it appear that I have belabored my reading of this theory, it is not because it is the weakest of the three theories of black literature. In fact, as I will try to show, Henderson's is by far the most imaginative of the three and has, at least, touched on areas critical to the explication of black literature. His examination of form is the first in a race and superstructure study and will most certainly give birth to more systematic and less polemical studies. But the notions implicit and explicit in Henderson's ideas were shared by Houston A. Baker, Jr., and Addison Gayle as well.

In the first essay of *Long Black Song: Essays in Black American Literature and Culture,* Houston A. Baker proffers the considerable claim that black culture, particularly as measured through black folklore and literature, serves in intent and effect as an "index" of "repudiation" not only of white Western values and white Western culture but of white Western literature as well.[5] "In fact," he writes, "it is to a great extent the culture theorizing of whites that has made for a separate and distinctive black American culture. That is to say, one index of the distinctiveness of black American culture is the extent to which it repudiates the culture theorizing of the white Western world." Repudiation, he continues, "is characteristic of black American folklore; and this is one of the most important factors in setting black American literature apart from white American literature." Further, "black folklore and the black American literary tradition that grew out of it reflect a culture that is distinctive both of white American and of African cultures, and therefore neither can provide valid standards by which black American folklore and literature may be judged." A text becomes "blacker," it surely follows, to the extent that it serves as an index of repudiation. Here we find an ironic response to Harold Bloom's *Anxiety of Influence* in what we could characterize as an "animosity of influence."

Baker discusses this notion of influence between black and white American culture at length. "Call it black, Afro-American, Negro," he writes, "the fact remains that there is a fundamental, qualitative difference between it and white American culture." The bases of this "fundamental, qualitative difference" are, first, that "black American culture was developed orally or musically for many years"; second, that black American culture was characterized by a "collective ethos"; and, finally, that "one of [black American culture's] most salient characteristics is an index of repudiation." Oral, collectivistic, and repudiative, Baker concludes, "each of these aspects helps to distinguish black American culture from white American culture."

These tenets suggest that there must be an arbitrary relationship between a sign and its referent, indeed that all meaning is culture-bound. Yet what we find elaborated here are rather oversimplified, basically political criteria, which are difficult to verify, partly because they are not subject to verbal analysis (that is, can this sense of *difference* be measured through the literary uses of language?), partly because the thematic analytical tools employed seem to be useful primarily for black naturalist novels or for the mere paraphrasing of poetry, partly because the matter of influence is almost certainly too subtle to be traced in other than close textual readings, and finally because Baker's three bases of "fundamental, qualitative difference" seem to me too unqualified. There is so much more to Jean Toomer, Zora Hurston, Langston Hughes, Sterling Brown, Ralph Ellison, Leon Forrest, Ishmael Reed, Toni Morrison, and Alice Walker than their "index of repudiation," whatever that is. Besides, at least Toomer, Ellison, and Reed have taken care to discuss the complex matter of literary ancestry, in print and without. It is one of the ironies of the study of black literature that our critical activity is, almost by definition, a comparative one, since many of our writers seem to be as influenced by Western masters, writing in English as well as outside it, as they are by indigenous, Afro-American oral or even written forms. That the base for our literature is an oral one is certainly true; but, as Millman Parry and Albert Lord have amply demonstrated, so is the base of the whole of Western literature, commencing with the Hebrews and the Greeks. Nevertheless, Baker does not suggest any critical tools for explicating the oral tradition in our literature, such as the formulaic studies so common to the subject. Nor does he suggest how folklore is displaced in literature, even though, like Henderson, he does see it at "the base of the black literary tradition." The claim that black culture is characterized by a collective ethos most definitely demands some qualification, since our history, literary and extraliterary, often turns on a tension, a dialectic, between the private perceptions of an individual and the white public perceptions of that same individual.

Nor does Baker's thought-provoking contention that black imaginative culture is deprived of the American frontier stand to prove this thesis:

> When the black American reads Frederick Jackson Turner's *The Frontier in American History*, he feels no regret over the end of the Western *frontier*. To black America, frontier is an alien word; for, in essence, all frontiers established by the white psyche have been closed to the black man. Heretofore, later, few have been willing to look steadily at America's past and acknowledge that the black man was denied his part in the frontier and his share of the nation's wealth.

At least Ralph Ellison has written extensively on the fact of the frontier (physical and metaphysical) and its centrality to his sensibility, and Ishmael Reed uses the frontier again and again as a central trope.

Part of the problem here is not only Baker's exclusive use of thematic analysis to attempt to delineate a literary tradition but also his implicit stance that literature functions primarily as a cultural artifact, as a repository for ideas. "It is impossible to comprehend the process of transcribing cultural values," he says (in his essay "Racial Wisdom and Richard Wright's *Native Son*"), "without an understanding of the changes that have characterized both the culture as a whole and the lives of its individual transcribers." Further, "Black American literature has a human immediacy and a pointed relevance which are obscured by the overingenious methods of the New Criticism, or any other school that attempts to talk of works of art as though they had no creators or of sociohistorical factors as though they did not filter through the lives of individual human beings." (How ironic this sentence seems today, since Baker by his own admission is now a post-structuralist critic.[6]) Here we find the implicit thesis in *Long Black Song,* the rather Herderian notion of literature as primarily the reflection of ideas and experiences outside it. It is not, of course, that literature is unrelated to culture, to other disciplines, or even to other arts; it is not that words and usage somehow exist in a vacuum or that the literary work of art occupies an ideal or reified, privileged status, the province of some elite cult of culture. It is rather that the literary work of art is a system of signs that may be decoded with various methods, all of which assume a fundamental relationship between form and content and all of which demand close reading. Baker seems to be reading black texts in a particular fashion for other than literary purposes. In *Singers of Daybreak: Studies in Black American Literature,* he suggests these purposes. "What lies behind the neglect of black American literature," he asserts, "is not a supportable body of critical criteria that includes a meaningful definition of *utile* and *dulce,* but a refusal to believe that blacks possess the humanity requisite for the production of works of art."[7] Baker finds himself shadow-boxing with the ghostly judgments of Jefferson on Phillis Wheatley and Ignatius Sancho; his blows are often telling, but his opponent's feint is deadly.

If Baker's early pre-theoretical criticism taught us more about this attitude toward being black in white America than it did about black literature, then Addison Gayle, Jr., in *The Way of the New World,* does not even teach us that.[8] Gayle makes no bones about his premises:

> To evaluate the life and culture of black people, it is necessary that one live the black experience in a world where substance is more important than form, where the social takes precedence over the aesthetic, where each act, gesture, and movement is political, and where continual rebellion separates the insane from the sane, the robot from the revolutionary.

Gayle's view of America, and of the critic, means that he can base his "literary judgments" on some measure of ideology; and he does. Regrettably, he accuses James Baldwin of "ignorance of black culture." His praise of John A. Williams seems predicated on an affinity of ideology. He praises John Killens's *And Then We Heard the Thunder* because Killens "creates no images of racial degradation." For Gayle, the "central flaw" of the protagonist in *Invisible Man* ("an otherwise superb novel") is "attributable more to Ellison's political beliefs than to artistic deficiency." In Gayle, we see race and superstructure criticism at its basest: not only is his approach to literature deterministic, but his treatment of the critical activity demonstrates an alarming disrespect for the diversity of the black experience itself and for the subtleties of close textual criticism.

What is wrong with employing race and superstructure as a critical premise? This theory of criticism sees language and literature as reflections of "Blackness." It postulates "Blackness" as an entity, rather than as metaphor or sign. Thus, the notion of a signified black element in literature retains a certain impressiveness insofar as it exists in some mystical kingdom halfway between a fusion of psychology and religion on the one hand and the Platonic Theory of Ideas on the other. Reflections of this "Blackness" are more or less literary according to the ideological posture of the critic. Content is primary over form and indeed is either divorced completely from form, in terms of genesis and normative value, or else is merely facilitated by form as a means to an end. In this criticism, rhetorical value judgments are closely related to social values. This method reconstitutes message, when what is demanded is an explication of a literary system.

The race and superstructure critics would have us believe that the function of the critic is to achieve an intimate knowledge of a literary text by re-creating it from the inside: critical thought must become the thought criticized. Only a black man, therefore, can think (hence, rethink) a black thought. Consciousness is predetermined by culture and color. These critics, in Todorov's phrase, "recreate" a text either by repeating its own words in their own order or by establishing a relationship between the work and some system of ideas outside it. They leave no room for the idea of literature as a system. Normative judgments stem from how readily a text yields its secrets or is made to confess falsely on the rack of "black reality."

Yet perceptions of reality are in no sense absolute; reality is a function of many variables. Writers present models of reality rather than a description of it, though obviously the two may be related variously. In fact, fiction often contributes to cognition by providing models that highlight the nature of things precisely by their failure to coincide with received ideas of reality. Such, certainly, is the case in science fiction. Moreover, the thematic studies so common to black criticism suffer from a similar fallacy. Themes in poetry, for instance, are rarely reducible to literal statement; literature approaches its richest development when its "presentational symbolism" (as opposed by Suzanne Langer to its "literal discourse") cannot be reduced to the form of a literal proposition. Passages of creative discourse cannot be excerpted and their meaning presented independent of context. For Ralph Ellison, for example, invisibility was not a matter of not being seen but rather a refusal to run the gamut of one's own humanity.

"Blackness," as these critics understand it, is weak in just the decisive area where practical criticism is strong: in its capacity to give discrete accounts of consciousness rather than a scheme or a generalization. And the reason for this weakness is not difficult to discern; it lies in the received formula of race and superstructure, which reduces far too readily to the simple repetition of ideology. The critical method, then, is reductionist; literary discourse is described mechanically by classifications that find their ultimate meaning and significance somewhere else, outside the texts at hand.

Ultimately, black literature is a verbal art like other verbal arts. "Blackness" is not a material object, an absolute, or an event, but a trope; it does not have an "essence" as such but is defined by a network of relations that form a particular aesthetic unity. Even the slave narratives offer the text as a world, as a system of signs. The black writer is the point of consciousness of his or her language. If the writer does embody a "Black Aesthetic," then it can be measured not by content but by a complex structure of meanings. The correspondence of content between a writer and his or her world is less significant to literary criticism than is a correspondence of organization of structure, for a relation of content may be a mere reflection of prescriptive, scriptural canon, such as those argued for by Baker, Gayle, and Henderson. A relation of structure, on the other hand, according to Raymond Williams, "can show us the organizing principles by which a particular view of the world, and from that the coherence of the social group which maintains it, really operates in consciousness." If there is a relationship between social and literary "facts," it must be found here.[9]

To paraphrase René Wellek, black literature may well be dark, mysterious, and foreboding, but it is certainly not beyond careful scrutiny and fuller understanding. The tendency toward thematic criticism implies a marked inferiority complex: afraid that our literature cannot sustain sophisticated verbal analysis, we view it from the surface merely and treat it as if it were a Chinese lantern with an elaborately wrought surface, parchment-thin but full of hot air. Black critics enjoyed such freedom in our discipline that we found ourselves with no discipline at all. This set of preconceptions brought readers and writers into a blind alley. Literary images, even black ones, are combinations of words, not of absolute or fixed things. The tendency of black criticism toward an ideological absolutism, with its attendant inquisition, had to come to an end. A literary text is a linguistic event; its explication must be an activity of close textual analysis. Simply because Bigger Thomas kills Mary Dalton and tosses her body into a furnace, *Native Son* is not necessarily a "blacker" novel than *Invisible Man*—Gayle notwithstanding. We urgently need to direct our attention to the nature of black figurative language, to the nature of black narrative forms, to the history and theory of Afro-American literary criticism, to the fundamental relation of form and content, and to the arbitrary relationships between the sign and its referent. Finally, we must begin to understand the nature of intertextuality, that is, the nonthematic manner by which texts—poems and novels—respond to other texts. After all, all cats may be black at night, but not to other cats.

IV

Black literature and its criticism, then, have been put to uses that were not primarily aesthetic; rather, they have formed part of a larger discourse on the nature of the black and his or her role in the order of things. The integral relation between theory and literary text, therefore, which so often in other traditions has been a sustaining relation, in our tradition has been an extraordinarily problematical one. The relationship among theory, tradition, and integrity within the black literary tradition has not been, and perhaps cannot be, a straightforward matter at all.

Let us consider the etymology of the word *integrity,* which I take to be the keyword in the subject of the relationship between the black tradition and theory. *Integrity* is a curious keyword to address in a period of bold and sometimes exhilarating speculation and experimentation, two other words that aptly characterize literary criticism generally, and Afro-American criticism specifically, at the present time. The Latin origin of the English word, *integritas,* connotes wholeness, entireness, completeness, chastity, and purity, most of which are descriptive terms that made their way frequently into the writings of the American "New Critics," who seem not to have cared particularly for or about the literature of Afro-Americans. Two of the most common definitions of *integrity* elaborate upon the sense of wholeness, derived from the Latin original. Let me cite these here, as taken from the *Oxford English Dictionary:*

1. The condition of having no part or element taken away or wanting; undivided or unbroken state; material wholeness, completeness, entirety; something undivided; an integral whole.
2. The condition of not being marred or violated; unimpaired or uncorrupted condition; original perfect state; soundness.

It is the second definition of *integrity*—that is to say, connoting the absence of violation and corruption, the preservation of an initial wholeness or soundness—which I would like to consider in this deliberation upon theory and the black tradition, or more precisely upon that relationship which ideally should obtain between Afro-American literature and the theories we fabricate to account for its precise nature and shape.

It is probably true that critics of Afro-American literature (which, by the way, I employ as a less ethnocentric designation than "the black American critic") are more concerned with the complex relationship between literature and literary theory than we have ever been before. There are many reasons for this, not the least of which is our increasingly central role in the profession, precisely when our colleagues in other literatures are engulfed in their own extensive debates about the intellectual merit of so very much theorizing. Theory, as a second-order reflection upon a primary gesture such as literature, has always been viewed with deep mistrust and suspicion by those scholars who find it presumptuous and perhaps even decadent when criticism claims the right to stand as discourse on its own, as a parallel textual universe to literature. Theoretical texts breed other, equally decadent theoretical responses, in a creative process that can be remarkably far removed from a poem or a novel.

For the critic of Afro-American literature, this process is even more perilous precisely because the large part of contemporary literary theory derives from critics of Western European languages and literatures. Is the use of theory to write about Afro-American literature, we might ask rhetorically, merely another form of intellectual indenture, a form of servitude of the mind as pernicious in its intellectual implications as any other form of enslavement? This is the issue raised, for me at least, not only by the notion of the word *integrity* in this context but also by my own work in critical theory over the last ten years. Does the propensity to theorize about a text or a literary tradition mar, violate, impair, or corrupt, the soundness of an "original perfect state" of a black text or of the black tradition? This is the implied subject of this book, which I try to address in several ways.

To be sure, this matter of criticism and integrity has a long and ironic history in black letters. It was Hume, we recall, who called the Jamaican poet of Latin verse, Francis Williams, "a parrot who merely speaks a few words plainly"; and Phillis Wheatley has for far too long suffered from the spurious attacks of black and white critics alike for being the original *rara avis* of a school of so-called mockingbird poets, whose use and imitation of received European and American literary conventions has been regarded, simply put, as a corruption itself of a "purer" black expression, privileged somehow in black artistic forms such as the blues, Signifyin(g), the spirituals, and the Afro-American dance. Can we, as critics, escape the mockingbird trap? Can we signify only as critical monkeys?

These are some of the questions that have been debated heatedly by critics of Afro-American literature in the past few years. For example, a conference of twenty-eight college professors, grouped together at Yale for two weeks during the summer of 1977, prefaced their summarizing statement (which outlined the nature and function of black literary criticism) with the premise that "Afro-American literature is, above all, an act of language." The conference itself, funded by the National Endowment for the Humanities, sponsored by the Modern Language Association, and jointly directed by Robert Burns Stepto, Assistant Professor of English at Yale, and Dexter Fisher, then Program Coordinator of the MLA's Commission on Minority Literatures, seemed determined to refute certain received notions of the relationship between black art and black social and political status within American society. Among these presuppositions are the following formulations: that black literature is primarily raw data or cultural artifact for the social scientist determined to explicate the "true nature" of black people; that there is a correlation between a people's artistic excellence and its political authority; and, especially, that the corpus of creative writing by Africans and Afro-Americans, dark and mysterious and foreboding as it might be, is not open to legitimate literary analysis by critics of any "intellectual complexion" employing all of the remarkably sophisticated tools of explication now at their disposal. Further and most crucially, the conference seemed to argue, just as we read and reread Joyce's *Ulysses* more to discover the art of the novel than to remark at the manners and morals of a Dublin Jew, so too must we read the works of black authors as discrete manifestations of form and genre and as implicit commentaries on the white literature of similar structure. The conference itself, in short, represented an attempt to take the "mau-mauing" out of the black literary criticism that defined the "Black Aesthetic Movement" of the sixties and transform it into a valid field of intellectual inquiry once again.

That the conference boldly and successfully addressed these matters is as remarkable as the very need to speak at all. Only ten years ago, the shared polemic of black criticism was that "blackness" existed as some mythical and mystical absolute, an entity so subtle, sublime, and unspeakable that only the "very black" racial initiate could ever begin to trace its contours, let alone force it to utter its darkest secrets. As I have argued above, our critics' hermeneutical circle was a mere tautology; only black people could think black thoughts, and therefore only the black critic could rethink, and hence criticize, a black text.

Not only the theory but also the practice of black literature has, for two hundred years, grown stunted within these dubious ideological shadows. The content of a black work of art has, with few but notable exceptions, assumed primacy in normative analysis, at the expense of the judgment of form. What's more, many black writers themselves seem to have conceived their task to be the creation of an art that reports and directly reflects brute, irreducible, and ineffable "black reality," a reality that in fact was often merely the formulaic fictions spawned by social scientists whose work intended to reveal a black America dehumanized by slavery, segregation, and racial discrimination, in a one-to-one relationship of art to life. Black literacy, then, became far more preoccupied with the literal representation of social content than with literary form, with ethics and thematics rather than poetics and aesthetics. Art, therefore, was argued implicitly and explicitly to be essentially referential. This theory assumed, first of all, that there existed a common, phenomenal world, which could be reliably described by the methods of empirical historiography or else by those of empirical social science. It assumed, second, that the function of the black writer was to testify to the private world of black pain and degradation, determined by a pervasive white and unblinking racism. Not only would creative writing at last make visible the face of the victimized and invisible black person, but it would also serve notice to the white world that individual black people had the requisite imagination to create great art and therefore to be "equal," an impetus, again, that we have traced to the eighteenth century.

To signify upon Henry James, the House of Black Fiction has many windows, but many are cracked and jagged. Haunted by archetypal Running Men who wrestle in dream-and-nightmare sequences with the unmediated Specter of White Racism, our House of Black Fiction is strewn with dead rats and cockroaches that feed off the ashen-pale bodies of dumb and, of course, wealthy white girls. Only the odor of chittlins and collard greens, steaming on gas burners, mitigates the certain stench of death. Nowhere can the critic unravel James's "figure in the carpet," and not only because "the city's" welfare checks are too paltry to afford the luxury. And the kitchen linoleum is worn thin, we fear, from overuse, buried, we suspect, beneath a growing mound of garbage, and purchased, we assume, on some usurious Easy Payment Plan. It is a house in tatters, created by novelists who fail to realize that by the very act of writing—the language of which is not reality but a system of signs—they commit themselves to the construction of coherent, symbolic worlds related to but never relegated to be merely plausible reproductions of the real world, not even the nightmare land of the inner city.

V

If theories of race and superstructure criticism did not prove to be fertile grounds in which Afro-American criticism could blossom, it nevertheless remains incumbent upon critics of black literature to extend their pioneering search *within the black idiom* for principles of criticism.

The Afro-American literary tradition has not yet produced a coherent theory of the texts that comprise it. We have benefited little from this absence of theories that are specific to black texts. What a fecund field awaits our attention. Perhaps the last black scholar to write a purely theoretical text was Amo, one of the first persons of African descent to publish a book in a European language. Amo may well have been the first, and remains one of the few, writers of African descent to theorize about the integrity of literature as an ideal institution. Amo was concerned, moreover, with the nature of analysis, of interpretation itself, rather than with containing an ideological stance about oppression in the guise of criticism. True, there are ideological presuppositions implicit in any critical judgment; for Amo, we recognize his explicit formalism as a reaction against eighteenth-century correlations between the race of an author and the value of his or her work. The import, if not the stance, of his work does reflect the world of ideas and economic relations that surround him. Nevertheless, Amo's treatise is a philosophical discourse upon the role of the reader as he or she interacts with text and author to produce meaning.

To underscore Amo's formalism is not merely to emphasize his uniqueness in a critical tradition that, consistently since Amo and until the last half-decade, has privileged the political function of a work of art at the expense of what it has described as sterile flirtation with "decadent" or "bourgeois" or "white" notions of art for art's sake. To underscore Amo's concern for the text is to emphasize the irony of eighteenth-century European theorizing about the nature and function of writers of African descent publishing texts in European languages. As I hope I have demonstrated above, these Enlightenment theorists privileged the fact of public writing—the literacy of literature, as it were—as the signal criterion for demonstrating the innate mental equality of the African with the European. Contrary to our assumptions that the Western philosophical tradition privileged the spoken over the written text, close readings of the evidence suggest strongly that the written word was privileged, not only above the spoken word but among all of the other representational arts as well. Had polyrhythms in music been privileged, for instance, our history in the West could have been a drastically different one. But it was the literacy of literature that, arbitrarily, was used as a commodity to measure the black's humanity. Amo, we know, was acutely aware of all of this. For Amo, as we have seen, was the very product of one such Enlightenment experiment designed to measure the mental capacity of the African by his ability to master the European arts and letters.

How are we to escape this trap of our own literature mastery, as well as the trap of the mindless imitation of the monkey? Are we doomed as critics of a noncanonical literature merely to cut monkeyshines, or can signifying monkeys decode the signs that comprise our black structures of literature? It seems to me that finding metaphors for black literary relations from within the Afro-American tradition, and combining these with that which is useful in contemporary literary theory, is the challenge of Afro-American literary history. At least two other critics of black literature have developed meaningful metaphors of Afro-American literary history. Houston A. Baker, Jr., and Robert Burns Stepto have defined "repudiation" and "authentication," respectively, as metaphors of literary history.[10]

Baker's theory of repudiation establishes an inverse relationship between a nonblack text and its black repudiation. This repudiation is essentially thematic, epistemological, and ontological. Baker's metaphor for literary relationships between black and white texts concerns itself with the signified, and not especially with the signifier. Stepto's metaphor of authentication draws upon strategies of legitimacy employed by black authors and their white "prefacers," since Phillis Wheatley published her poems in 1773, to attest to the claims of authorship of the black subject. Stepto's work traces this theme of "authorial control," of subject—object dialectics, from its most patent form in the slave narratives to Ralph Ellison's subtle refiguration in *Invisible Man*. Above all else, Stepto is concerned with the capacity of a narrator to tell his or her own tale.

Both Baker and Stepto, curiously enough, have developed metaphors of literary history that are implicitly ideological and antagonistic, turning as they do on notions of power and autonomy, which we may read as themes of racial and individual selfhood. If only in these broad senses, the two metaphors share similar presuppositions about the will to power as the will to write. I have tried to supplement these creative theories by locating a metaphor for literary history that arises from within the black idiom exclusively, that is not dependent upon black-white power or racial relations, and that is essentially rhetorical. I call it critical signification, and I take it from the black rhetorical strategy called Signifyin(g). *Signifyin(g)* is a rhetorical strategy that is indigenously black and that derives from the Signifying Monkey tales. The figure of the Signifying Monkey, in turn, is the profane counterpart of Esu-Elegbara, the Yoruba sacred trickster who is truly Pan-African, manifesting himself among the Cubans, the Haitians, and the Fon as Legba, among the Brazilians as Exu, among the believers of Vodun as Papa Legba, and among the believers of Hoodoo as Papa LaBas. Hermes is his closest Western counterpart. As Hermes is to hermeneutics, so is Esu to the black art of interpretation, *Esu-'tufunaalo*.

I use Esu as the metaphor for the critical activity of interpretation and Signifyin(g) as my metaphor for literary history because these are idiomatically black. I have not had to strain or reinterpret these figures. The discursive, or signifying, structures from which I take them define them in these ways: Esu the Yoruba call the figure of indeterminacy and the figure of interpretation. Signifyin(g) is a uniquely black rhetorical concept, entirely textual or linguistic, by which a second statement or figure repeats, or tropes, or reverses the first. Its use as a figure for intertextuality allows us to understand literary revision without resource to thematic, biographical, or Oedipal slayings at the crossroads; rather, critical signification is tropic and rhetorical. Indeed, the very concept of Signifyin(g) can exist only in the realm of the intertextual relation.

We are able to trace such complex intertextual Signifyin(g) relations by explicating what I like to think of as the Discourse of the Black Other in the eighteenth and early nineteenth centuries. By "Discourse of the Black" I mean to say the literature that persons of African descent created as well as the nonblack literature that depicts black characters. The phrase, then, suggests both how blacks figured language and how blacks and their blackness were figured in Western languages, especially in English and French. I am speaking here of the black as both subject and object of literature.

Because the discourse of the black occupied a fundamental polemical place in the fight against slavery, literary historians have tended to dismiss or ignore the hundreds of poems, plays, and novels about blacks that Europeans and Americans published between the seventeenth and the mid-nineteenth centuries. This literature contains only a few noble blacks, and even these are rendered ambiguously. Aphra Behn renders Oronooko, for example, as a noble African, but only at the expense of his fellow Africans: they are short, while he is tall; they speak an African language, while he speaks French; they have African features, while his are aquiline; they are weak and cowardly, while he is strong. The "Dying Negro" poems made popular by the English Romantics attempt to elicit pity and sentiment for the insufferable plight of the unfortunate slave. These, too, like the noble Negro tales, draw upon received racist images of the African, even if they intend to arouse the conscience of the European.

We can think of the slave narratives as a reaction to these sentimental figurations. The generic expectations of this aspect of the discourse of the black had a profound effect on the shape of that discourse which we call the slave's narrative, as did the sentimental novel and more especially the particularly American transmutation of the European picaresque. The slave narratives, in turn, spawned their formal antithesis, the Confederate romance. It is useful to think of this curious, dialectical relation of the slave narratives to the confederate romance as that of repetition and reversal. It is as if the figure of the North Star in the slave narratives becomes the figures of moonbeams and magnolia blossoms in the plantation novel. Structurally, the two modes of figuration are opposite, mirror images, in a relation of archetype and stereotype. Furthermore, all of those so-called illegitimate slave narratives, anathema to the historian, are merely novels that refigure tropes and conventions of both genres, often masking themselves as authentic first-person slave narratives, both pro- and anti-slavery, such as Mattie Griffiths's *Autobiography of a Fe-*

male Slave, or Richard Hildreth's *Archy Moore* and my absolute favorite, *Peculiar,* published in 1863, the protagonist of which is called Peculiar Institution.

The hundreds of slave narratives and Confederate romances published before 1865 have been documented and analyzed by scholars such as Charles Nichols, Marion Wilson Starling, Margaret Young Jackson, Frances Smith Foster, John W. Blassingame, Vernon Loggins, John Herbert Nelson, Sterling A. Brown, and Jean Fagan Yellin. Moreover, Charles T. Davis, Leslie Fielder, and Harry Levin have explicated the interplay of figures of light and darkness in the works of Hawthorne, Melville, and Poe. No one, to my knowledge, has yet discussed the relationship among the slave narratives, the Confederate romance, and the American Romantics, which we may think of as the three terms of the dialectic—thesis, antithesis, synthesis—wherein the themes of black and white, common to the bipolar moment in which the slave narratives and the plantation novel oscillate, inform the very structuring principles of the great gothic works of Hawthorne, Melville, and Poe. The intertextual relations that obtain here are formal ones; indeed, the use of the power of blackness as a structuring principle in many ways assumes the function of any mythic structure, reconciling the two otherwise irreconcilable forces. Narration here is the trick of mediation.

We can illustrate this set of relationships in literary history by considering that curious relationship between the figures of Harlequin and the American Minstrel Man. Many scholars have discussed myths of origins of Harlequin which attribute the blackness of his mask and its patently "negroid" features to the mask of blackness of the African. Marmontel wrote in 1787 that "it is likely that an African slave was the first model for this character." Florian, a few years later, argued that "the most realistic opinion is that [Harlequin] was originally an African slave. His black face and shaved head seem to indicate this." Harlequin's tricolored clothing, moreover, Florian attributes to the clothing of this same orphaned African by three sons of a cloth merchant, who pieced together "three half-ells" to clothe the stranger. Ducharte, writing in this century, suggests that "the ancient Harlequin was a phallophore, and, inasmuch as some of the phallophores of the ancient theatre played the part of African slaves, it is thought that Harlequin might be their direct descendant," thereby explaining his black mask. Harlequin's authentic mask, he continues, suggests "a cat, a satyr, and the sort of negro that the Renaissance painter portrayed." When we recall that early Harlequin figures wore a phallus, the connections between him and Western representations of the African are even stronger.[11]

These are all, of course, myths of origins. Nevertheless, the visual evidence does suggest at least the myth of an African connection with the origins of Harlequin's mask, in terms of both its features and its color. So stylized did Harlequin's role become that he could simply point to one of the black patches on his suit and become invisible, a trope that has become central to the black literary tradition. ⟨. . .⟩

Critical signification is a useful concept in explaining ⟨. . .⟩ black-white relations. The relation of Phillis Wheatley's poetry to that of Milton and Pope, and to the aesthetic theories of Kant and Hume, is a Signifyin(g) relation. The intertextual relationship between the slave narrative as a body of discourse and its counter-genre, the Confederate romance or the plantation novel, is also a relation of Signifyin(g) structures. The body of literature through which we define the New Negro Renaissance repeats and reverses the racist presuppositions of turn-of-the-century American pseudo-science and social Darwinism. Minstrel Man and Bones's bifurcated presence is a signification upon the half-black, half-white mask of Harlequin, as mediated through the dozen harlequinades in which a wizard transforms a black slave into Harlequin and sets him free. It is through such formal textual relations that we begin to understand the arbitrariness of both the signifier and the signified, the latter of which divides reality arbitrarily, culture by culture, language by language, discourse by discourse. But it is this very chiastic imperative in Afro-American literature that helps us to understand the tautology at the heart of Black Aesthetic criticism and the need of subsequent critics of black literature to relate their project to what is vaguely known as contemporary literary theory.

In the final chapter of this book, on the Signifying Monkey and on *Mumbo Jumbo*, I supplement my analysis of race and superstructure with an analysis of the idea of a transcendent signified, a belief in an essence called blackness, a presence our tradition has tried of late to will into being, in order to negate two and a half millennia of its figuration as an absence. As healthy politically as such a gesture was, as revealing as it was in this country and abroad of the very arbitrariness of the received sign of blackness itself, we must also criticize the idealism, the notion of essence, implicit in even this important political gesture. To think of oneself as free simply because one can claim—one can utter—the negation of an assertion is not to think deeply enough. *Négritude* already constituted such a claim of blackness as a transcendent signified, of a full and sufficient presence; but to make such a claim, to feel the necessity to make such a claim, is already to reveal too much about perceived absence and desire. It is to take the terms of one's assertion from a discourse whose universe has been determined by an Other. Even the terms of one's so-called spontaneous desire have been presupposed by the Other. I render this critique of blackness as a transcendent signified in order to help break through the enclosure of negation.

The enclosure of negation is only one trap. That sort of intellectual indenture, which we might call, after Jean Price-Mars, "bovarysme collectif," is quite another, and equally deadly, trap. Jules de Gaultier, expanding upon Price-Mars, defines bovarysme as the phenomenon of being "fated to obey the suggestion of an external milieu, for lack of auto-suggestion from within."[12] The challenge of black literary criticism is to derive principles of literary criticism from the black tradition itself, as defined in the idiom of critical theory but also in the idiom that constitutes the language of blackness, the Signifyin(g) difference that makes the black tradition our very own. To borrow mindlessly, or to vulgarize, a critical theory from another tradition is to satisfy de Gaultier's definition of bovarysme; but it is also to satisfy, in the black idiom, Ishmael

Reed's definition of "The Talking Android." The sign of the successful negotiation of this precipice of indenture, of slavish imitation, is that the black critical essay refers to two contexts, two traditions, the Western and the Black. Each utterance, then, is "double-voiced."

In a 1925 review of James Weldon Johnson's *The Book of American Negro Spirituals,* W. E. B. Du Bois argued that evidence of critical activity is a sign of a tradition's sophistication, since criticism implies an awareness of the process of art itself and is a second-order reflection upon those primary texts that define a tradition and its canon. Insofar as we, critics of the black tradition, master our craft, we serve both to preserve our own traditions and to shape their direction. All great writers demand great critics. The imperatives of our task are clear.

The chapters of this book, ranging from theoretical to practical criticism, exemplify various modes of reading. The black literary and critical traditions need all sorts of close readings; the body of practical criticism that enabled new theories of reading to emerge in the Western tradition has yet to be created in the black traditions. The tradition needs readings of several kinds before it can move into the mainstream of critical debate in the profession. Such a move, it seems to me, is a desirable one, since ultimately our subject is literary discourse and not the blackness of blackness. Nevertheless, I am not advocating a new form of de Gaultier's "bovarysm," in which we seek to imitate, from the critics we have decided to be most "like," "all that can be imitated, everything exterior, appearance, gesture, intonation, and dress." To do so would be to repeat the mistake of a neo-Romantic poet such as Countee Cullen, for whom form was a container into which he could pour a precious and black content. Rather than proselytizing for one warring faction of criticism or another, or vulgarizing this or that theory by reducing it to summary or method, this book seeks to encourage a plurality of readings, as various as the discrete texts in our literary tradition, and as black. These essays address issues fundamental to critical theory and to the nature of black literary discourse. My subject is the interpretation of literature.

This book attempts to achieve its unity from the stress each chapter brings to bear upon the play of the signifier, and from the belief that, as René Girard puts it,

> great writers apprehend intuitively and concretely, through the medium of their art, if not formally, the system in which they were first imprisoned together with their contemporaries. Literary interpretation must be systematic because it is the continuation of literature. It should formalize implicit or already half explicit systems.... The value of a critical thought depends not on how cleverly it manages to disguise its own systematic nature or on how much literary substance it really embraces, comprehends, and makes articulate. The goal may be ambitious but it is not outside the scope of literary criticism. Failure to reach it should be condemned but not the attempt. Everything else has already been done.[13]

In an essay called "For Whom Does One Write?" collected in *What Is Literature?* Jean-Paul Sartre asks none too rhetorically, "To whom does Richard Wright address himself?" Sartre's answer helps us to answer our own central question, "For Whom Does the Critic of Black Literature Write?"

> Each of Wright's works contains what Baudelaire would have called "a double simultaneous postulation"; each word refers to two contexts; two forces are applied simultaneously to each phrase and determine the incomparable tension of his tale. Had he spoken to the whites alone, he might have turned out to be more prolix, more didactic, and more abusive; to the negroes alone, still more elliptical, more of a confederate and more elegiac. In the first case, his work might have come close to satire; in the second, to prophetic lamentations. Jeremiah spoke only to the Jews. But Wright, a writer for a split public, has been able to maintain and go beyond this split. He has made it the pretext for a work of art.[14]

How does this split readership affect the work of criticism? The most obvious way, it seems to me, is in exactly what one can take for granted. While a reader from within the black tradition might need no footnote on T. Thomas Fortune, *Cane,* or *Signifying,* that same reader may need data about "The Lyrical Ballads," "East Coker," or John Donne. The problem is compounded by the need I feel to establish the very texts I explicate, to make available to the reader *my* text milieu. Only footnoting and extensive quotation works only where a readership shares familiarity with a common body of texts. Not even other critics of black texts share the sort of familiarity we assume when interpreting canonical texts; we are still in the process of recovering and establishing the texts in the tradition, a process necessarily preceding canon formation.

What we are able to assume about our readers is related to the complex matter of "originality." How "original" is the use of contemporary theory to read black texts? Perhaps only critics who are familiar with black texts can ascertain this, since only they understand the received interpretations that serve as discourse on that text. What is "original" about Edward Said's use of poststructuralist theory to analyze representations of "the Oriental" is his "application"; indeed, the application of a mode of reading to explicate a black text changes both the received theory and received ideas about the text. When this occurs, the results are "original."

We write, it seems to me, primarily for other critics of literature. Through shared theoretical presuppositions, the arduous process of "cultural translation," if not resolved, is most certainly not hindered. To maintain yet go beyond this split text milieu is our curse and, of course, our challenge, as is the fact that we must often resurrect the texts in our tradition before we can begin to explicate them. To render major contributions to contemporary theory's quest to "save the text," in Hartman's phrase, is our splendid opportunity. Unlike critics in almost every other literary tradition, almost all that we have to say about our literature is new. What critics of the Western tradition can make an even remotely similar claim? Jeremiah could speak only to the Jews; we, however, must address two audiences, the Jews and the Babylonians, whose interests are distinct yet overlapping in the manner of interlocking sets.

I would say that the most conscious presupposition of my work is that one repeats, as it were, in order to produce a black and critical difference, to echo Barbara Johnson. As Said argues in "On Repetition" about Marx's narrative strategy in the *Eighteenth Brumaire of Louis Bonaparte,* Marx's intention is "not to validate Bonaparte's claims but to give facts by emending their apparent direction." We are able to achieve difference through repetition, as Ralph Ellison put it, we "change the joke and slip the yoke." Marx himself in *Eighteenth Brumaire* states the process in this way: "The beginner who has learned a new language always retranslates it into his mother tongue: he can only be said to have appropriated the spirit of the new language and to be able to express himself in it freely when he can manipulate it without reference to the old, and when he forgets his original language while using the new one." Does this sort of repetition, Said asks at the end of his essay, "enhance or degrade a fact?" His creative response bears repetition here: "But the question brings forth consciousness of two where there had been repose in one; and such knowledge of course, like procreation, cannot really be reversed. Thereafter the problems multiply. Naturally or not, filiatively or affiliatively, is the question." The speculative and interpretive chapters of this book chart one critic's adventure through the jungle of criticism, as he wrestles eagerly with that dense and compelling terrain, and with Said's rhetorical question.[15]

If I had to define my relationship to contemporary criticism, I would turn, as I frequently do, to Ralph Ellison. As Ellison said to Ishmael Reed in an interview published in 1978:

> So that's the way it continues to go: anywhere I find a critic who has an idea or concept that seems useful, I grab it. Eclecticism is the word. Like a jazz musician who creates his own style out of the styles around him, I play by ear.[16]

Although all theory is text-specific and can tend to break down when mechanically applied outside its own tradition, other aspects of theory are more broadly relevant than to one text milieu. Free indirect discourse is free indirect discourse, no matter in what literary tradition it appears. Just as Zora Neale Hurston, for example, imitated the story-telling devices of the black oral tradition, so too is her lyrical novel, *Their Eyes Were Watching God* (1937), drawn after the manner of Flaubert and Woolf. Her text, in this sense, is double-voiced. The critic of her text, moreover, must also be double-voiced. The challenge of the critic of comparative black literature is to allow contemporary theoretical developments to inform his or her readings of discrete black texts but also to generate his or her own theories from the black idiom itself. The challenge of theorists generally is to realize that what we have for too long called "the tradition" is merely one tradition of several and that we have much to learn from the systematic exploration of new canons. That which unites those of us whose canonical texts differ is the shared concern with theory that arises from these texts. It is here that we are to find common ground; it is here that we can bridge text milieus. It is here that the hegemony of the Western tradition at last can be seen to be the arbitrary and ideological structures that it is.

I end this chapter with a quote from great blues artist Junior Parker: "Anybody can boil up some greens, but a good cook—a good one—has a special way of seasoning 'em that ain't like nobody else's. So anybody can do it, but it's only somebody who can do it their own way."[17] I have tried to do it my own way; this, after all, is the imperative of all literary criticism. Perhaps critics of other literatures can find something useful in my metaphors of Esu and signification for interpretation and literary history.

NOTES

1. W. E. B. DuBois, "Negro Art," *Crisis* 22 (June 1921): 55–56.
2. *New York Times*, January 26, 1925, p. 3.
3. W. E. B. DuBois,"The Social Origins of American Negro Art," *Modern Quarterly* 3 (Autumn 1925): 53.
4. *Understanding the New Black Poetry* (New York: Morrow, 1972). All subsequent citations are from pp. 3–69.
5. *Long Black Song* (Charlottesville: University of Virginia Press, 1972).
6. See Baker's very important book, *Blues, Ideology, and Afro-American Literature: A Vernacular Theory* (Chicago: University of Chicago Press, 1984).
7. *Singers of Daybreak* (Washington, D.C.: Howard University Press, 1974).
8. *The Way of the New World* (Garden City, N.Y.: Doubleday, 1975).
9. Raymond Williams, "Base and Superstructure in Marxist Cultural Theory," *New Left Review* 82 (December 1973): 3–16.
10. Baker's theory of repudiation is found in *Long Black Song*. See note 5. Stepto's theory of "authentication" is elaborated in *From Behind the Veil: A Study of Afro-American Narrative* (Urbana: University of Illinois Press, 1979). Baker's brilliant theory of the black vernacular, the blues idiom, and its relation to literary structure is fundamentally related to my theory of signifying. Although Baker graciously acknowledges my influence on his work, I would argue that ours is a reciprocal relationship.
11. See the article "Arlequin" and "Marmontel" in *The Oxford Companion to French Literature,* edited by Sir Paul Harvey and J. E. Heseltine (Oxford: Clarendon Press, 1959), pp. 27, 456. Marmontel's theory of the origins of Harlequin's blackness is found in his collection of essays, *Eléments de littérature* (1787). See also Pierre Louis Ducharte, *The Italian Comedy,* trans. Randolph T. Weaver (New York: Dover, 1966), chapters 2 and 4, and pp. 124, 135.
12. Jules de Gaultier, cited in René Girard, *Deceit, Desire, and the Novel: Self and Other in Literary Structure*, trans. Yvonne Frecerro (Baltimore: Johns Hopkins University Press, 1965), p. 5.
13. Girard, p. 3.
14. Jean-Paul Sartre, *What Is Literature?* (London: Methuen, 1970), pp. 57–59.

15. Edward Said, "On Repetition," in *The World, The Text, and the Critic* (Cambridge: Harvard University Press, 1983), pp. 111–26.

16. Ralph Ellison, "The Essential Ellison (Interview)," *Y'Bird* 1, no. 1 (1978): 130–59.

17. Quoted in Charles Keil, *Urban Blues* (Chicago: University of Chicago Press, 1966), p. 169.

BIBLIOGRAPHY

GENERAL

Arac, Jonathan. *Critical Genealogies: Historical Situations for Postmodern Literary Studies*. New York: Columbia University Press, 1987.

Atkins, G. Douglas, and Laura Morrow, eds. *Contemporary Literary Theory*. Amherst: University of Massachusetts Press, 1989.

Attridge, Derek; Bennington, Geoff; and Young, Robert, eds. *Post-Structuralism and the Question of History*. Cambridge: Cambridge University Press, 1987.

Bagwell, J. Timothy. *American Formalism and the Problem of Interpretation*. Houston: Rice University Press, 1986.

Barr, Marleen S., and Richard Feldstein, eds. *Discontented Discourses: Feminism/Textual Intervention/Psychoanalysis*. Urbana: University of Illinois Press, 1989.

Benstock, Shari, ed. *Feminist Issues in Literary Scholarship*. Bloomington: Indiana University Press, 1987.

Bercovitch, Sacvan, ed. *Reconstructing American Literary History*. Cambridge, MA: Harvard University Press, 1986.

Berman, Art. *From the New Criticism to Deconstruction: The Reception of Structuralism and Post-Structuralism*. Urbana: University of Illinois Press, 1988.

Bruss, Elizabeth W. *Beautiful Theories: The Spectacle of Discourse in Contemporary American Criticism*. Bloomington: Indiana University Press, 1982.

Eagleton, Terry. *Literary Theory: An Introduction*. Minneapolis: University of Minnesota Press, 1983.

Ellis, John M. *Against Deconstruction*. Princeton: Princeton University Press, 1989.

Jay, Gregory S., and David L. Miller, eds. *After Strange Texts: The Role of Theory in the Study of Literature*. University: University of Alabama Press, 1985.

Melville, Stephen W. *Philosophy beside Itself: On Deconstruction and Modernism*. Minneapolis: University of Minnesota Press, 1986.

Merrell, Floyd. *Deconstruction Reframed*. West Lafayette, IN: Purdue University Press, 1985.

Natoli, Joseph, ed. *Tracing Literary Theory*. Urbana: University of Illinois Press, 1987.

Norris, Christopher. *Deconstruction and the Interests of Theory*. Norman: University of Oklahoma Press, 1989.

Showalter, Elaine, ed. *The New Feminist Criticism*. New York: Pantheon, 1985.

Spanos, William V.; Bové, Paul A.; and O'Hara, Daniel, eds. *The Question of Textuality: Strategies of Reading in Contemporary American Criticism*. Bloomington: Indiana University Press, 1982.

Stimpson, Catharine R. *Where the Meanings Are: Feminism and Cultural Spaces*. New York: Methuen, 1988.

Tompkins, Jane P., ed. *Reader-Response Criticism: From Formalism to Post-Structuralism*. Baltimore: Johns Hopkins University Press, 1980.

RAYMOND WILLIAMS

Barnett, Anthony. "Raymond Williams and Marxism: A Rejoinder to Terry Eagleton." *New Left Review* No. 99 (1976): 47–64.

Bilan, R. P. "Raymond Williams: From Leavis to Marx." *Queen's Quarterly* 87 (1980): 211–23.
Donoghue, Denis. "Raymond Williams." In *England, Their England*. New York: Knopf, 1988, pp. 351–58.
Eagleton, Terry. "Mutations of Critical Ideology." In *Criticism and Ideology*. London: NLB, 1976, pp. 11–43.
Giddens, Anthony. "Literature and Society: Raymond Williams." In *Profiles and Critiques in Social Theory*. Berkeley: University of California Press, 1982, pp. 133–43.
Gorak, Jan. *The Alien Mind of Raymond Williams*. Columbia: University of Missouri Press, 1988.
Higgins, John. "Raymond Williams and the Problem of Ideology." In *Postmodernism and Politics,* ed. Jonathan Arac. Minneapolis: University of Minnesota Press, 1986, pp. 112–22.
Hoggart, Richard. Review of *Culture and Society 1780–1950*. *Essays in Criticism* 9 (1959): 171–79.
Johnson, Lesley. "Raymond Williams." In *The Cultural Critics*. London: Routledge & Kegan Paul, 1979, pp. 150–73.
Macdonald, Dwight. Review of *The Long Revolution*. *Encounter* 16 (June 1961): 79–84.
Parrinder, Patrick. "The Accents of Raymond Williams." *Critical Quarterly* 26 (1984): 47–57.
———. *The Failure of Theory*. New York: Barnes & Noble, 1987.
Thompson, E. P. Review of *The Long Revolution*. *New Left Review* No. 9 (1961): 24–33; No. 10 (1961): 34–39.
Ward, J. P. *Raymond Williams*. Cardiff: University of Wales Press, 1981.
Watkins, Evan. "Raymond Williams and Marxist Criticism." In *The Critical Act: Criticism and Community*. New Haven: Yale University Press, 1978, pp. 141–57.
Williams, Raymond. *Politics and Letters: Interviews with* New Left Review. London: NLB, 1979.

JACQUES DERRIDA

Carlshamre, Staffan. *Language and Time: An Attempt to Arrest the Thought of Jacques Derrida*. Goteborg: Acta Universitatis Gothoburgensis, 1986.
Carroll, David. *Paraesthetics: Foucault, Lyotard, Derrida*. New York: Methuen, 1987.
de Man, Paul. "The Rhetoric of Blindness: Jacques Derrida's Reading of Rousseau." In *Blindness and Insight: Essays in the Rhetoric of Contemporary Criticism*. New York: Oxford University Press, 1971, pp. 102–41.
De Neef, A. Leigh. *Traherne in Dialogue: Heidegger, Lacan, and Derrida*. Durham, NC: Duke University Press, 1988.
Finas, Lucette, et al. *Ecarts: Quatre Essais à propos de Jacques Derrida*. Paris: Fayard, 1973.
Gasché, Rodolphe. *The Tain of the Mirror: Derrida and the Philosophy of Reflection*. Cambridge, MA: Harvard University Press, 1986.

Hartman, Geoffrey H. *Saving the Text: Literature, Derrida, Philosophy*. Baltimore: Johns Hopkins University Press, 1981.

Harvey, Irene E. *Derrida and the Economy of Différance*. Bloomington: Indiana University Press, 1986.

Johnson, Barbara. "Translator's Introduction" to *Dissemination* by Jacques Derrida. Chicago: University of Chicago Press, 1981, pp. vii–xxxiii.

Kofman, Sarah. *Lectures de Derrida*. Paris: Éditions Galilée, 1984.

Krupnick, Mark, ed. *Displacement: Derrida and After*. Bloomington: Indiana University Press, 1983.

Llewelyn, John. *Derrida on the Threshold of Sense*. New York: St. Martin's Press, 1986.

Magliola, Robert. *Derrida on the Mend*. West Lafayette, IN: Purdue University Press, 1984.

Megill, Allan. *Prophets of Extremity: Nietzsche, Heidegger, Foucault, Derrida*. Berkeley: University of California Press, 1985.

Muller, John P., and William J. Richardson, eds. *The Purloined Poe: Lacan, Derrida, and Psychoanalytic Reading*. Baltimore: Johns Hopkins University Press, 1988.

Norris, Christopher. *Derrida*. Cambridge, MA: Harvard University Press, 1987.

Rapaport, Herman. *Heidegger and Derrida: Reflections on Time and Language*. Lincoln: University of Nebraska Press, 1989.

Sallis, John, ed. *Deconstruction and Philosophy: The Texts of Jacques Derrida*. Chicago: University of Chicago Press, 1987.

Smith, Joseph H., and William Kerrigan, eds. *Taking Chances: Derrida, Psychoanalysis, and Literature*. Baltimore: Johns Hopkins University Press, 1984.

Staten, Henry. *Wittgenstein and Derrida*. Lincoln: University of Nebraska Press, 1984.

ANGUS FLETCHER

Bloom, Harold. Review of *Allegory*. *Yale Review* 54 (1964–65): 147–49.

———. Review of *The Prophetic Moment*. *Virginia Quarterly Review* 47 (1971): 477–80.

Bullough, Geoffrey. Review of *Allegory*. *English Language Notes* 4 (1966–67): 157–60.

Davis, B. E. C. Review of *The Prophetic Moment*. *Review of English Studies* 23 (1972): 333–35.

Drake, Ben. Review of *The Transcendental Masque*. *Modern Language Quarterly* 34 (1973): 102–5.

Frank, Armin Paul. Review of *Allegory*. *Modern Philology* 64 (1966–67): 382–84.

Halewood, William H. Review of *Allegory*. *Journal of English and Germanic Philology* 64 (1965): 712–14.

Hawkes, Terence. Review of *Allegory*. *Renaissance News* 18 (1965): 340–42.

Hollander, Robert. Review of *Allegory*. *Southern Review* 4 (1968): 756–62.

Mackenzie, Manfred. Review of *Allegory*. *Essays in Criticism* 14 (1964): 397–401.

Maclean, Hugh. Review of *The Prophetic Moment*. *Journal of English and Germanic Philology* 71 (1972): 243–46.

Unsigned. Review of *Allegory*. *Times Literary Supplement*, 10 June 1965, p. 465.

LEO BERSANI

Collerye, Anne de. Review of *Marcel Proust*. *New York Review of Books*, 11 November 1965, p. 5.

Culler, Jonathan. Review of *A Future for Astyanax*. *Yale Review* 66 (1976–77): 592–98.

Donoghue, Denis. Review of *A Future for Astyanax*. *New York Times Book Review*, 26 September 1976, p. 27.

Goodheart, Eugene. Review of *Baudelaire and Freud*. *Partisan Review* 47 (1980): 132–35.

Hindus, Milton. Review of *Marcel Proust*. *Virginia Quarterly Review* 42 (1966): 158–62.

Howard, Richard. Review of *The Death of Stéphane Mallarmé*. *Yale Review* 72 (1982–83): 108–12.

Lang, Candace. Review of *Baudelaire and Freud*. *MLN* 95 (1980): 1092–97.

Solomon-Godeau, Abigail. Review of *Forms of Violence*. *New York Times Book Review*, 6 October 1985, p. 32.

Taylor, Paul. Review of *A Future for Astyanax*. *Essays in Criticism* 30 (1980): 247–55.

Teleky, Richard. Review of *A Future for Astyanax*. *University of Toronto Quarterly* 47 (1977–78): 90–92.

Wing, Nathaniel. Review of *Baudelaire and Freud*. *Diacritics* 9 (Winter 1979): 13–27.

Unsigned. Review of *Balzac to Beckett*. *Times Literary Supplement*, 30 April 1971, p. 509.

SUSAN SONTAG

Braudy, Leo. Review of *Under the Sign of Saturn*. *New Republic*, 20 November 1980, pp. 43–46.

Bromwich, David. Review of *Under the Sign of Saturn*. *New York Times Book Review*, 23 November 1980, p. 11.

Brooks, Peter. Review of *Against Interpretation*. *Partisan Review* 33 (1966): 439–43.

DeMott, Benjamin. Review of *Against Interpretation*. *New York Times Book Review*, 23 January 1966, p. 5.

Dennis, Nigel. Review of *Illness as Metaphor*. *New York Review of Books*, 20 July 1978, pp. 18, 20.

Gilman, Richard. Review of *Styles of Radical Will*. *New Republic*, 3 May 1969, pp. 23–28.

Goodheart, Eugene. "The 'Radicalism' of Susan Sontag." In *Pieces of Resistance*. Cambridge: Cambridge University Press, 1987, pp. 46–55.

Kermode, Frank. Review of *Under the Sign of Saturn*. *New York Review of Books*, 6 November 1980, pp. 42–43.

Koch, Stephen. "On Susan Sontag." *Triquarterly* 7 (Fall 1966): 153–60.

Mazzocco, Robert. Review of *Against Interpretation*. *New York Review of Books*, 9 June 1966, pp. 22–23.

Ostriker, Alicia. Review of *Against Interpretation*. *Commentary* 41 (June 1966): 83–84.

Parini, Jay. Review of *A Barthes Reader*. *Hudson Review* 36 (1983–84): 411–19.
Raban, Jonathan. Review of *Against Interpretation*. *New Statesman*, 12 December 1969, p. 866.
Solotaroff, Theodore. "Interpreting Susan Sontag." In *The Red Hot Vacuum*. New York: Atheneum, 1970, pp. 261–68.
Sypher, Wylie. Review of *Against Interpretation*. *Book Week*, 30 January 1966, p. 2.

FREDRIC JAMESON

Arac, Jonathan. "Fredric Jameson and Marxism." In *Critical Genealogies: Historical Situations for Postmodern Literary Studies*. New York: Columbia University Press, 1987, pp. 261–79.
Bergonzi, Bernard. Review of *Fables of Aggression*. *Times Literary Supplement*, 31 October 1980, p. 1215.
Compagnon, Antoine. Review of *The Political Unconscious*. *Times Literary Supplement*, 28 August 1981, p. 984.
Culler, Jonathan. Review of *Marxism and Form*. *Modern Language Review* 69 (1974): 599–601.
———. Review of *The Prison-House of Language*. *Yale Review* 62 (1972–73): 290–96.
Donoghue, Denis. Review of *Fables of Aggression*. *New York Review of Books*, 29 April 1982, pp. 28–30.
Dowling, William C. *Jameson, Althusser, Marx*. Ithaca: Cornell University Press, 1984.
Eagleton, Terry. "Fredric Jameson: The Politics of Style." In *Against the Grain*. London: Verso, 1986, pp. 65–78.
Erlich, Victor. Review of *The Prison-House of Language*. *Modern Language Quarterly* 34 (1973): 344–48.
Ferguson, Francis C. Review of *The Prison-House of Language*. *Partisan Review* 41 (1974): 310–14.
Fish, Stanley. Review of *The Prison-House of Language*. *Novel* 6 (1972–73): 283–87.
Gelber, Andrew. Review of *The Political Unconscious*. *MLN* 97 (1982): 1228–31.
Poster, Mark. Review of *The Political Unconscious*. *Nineteenth-Century Fiction* 36 (1981–82): 252–56.
Watkins, Evan. "Dialectic and Form." In *The Critical Act: Criticism and Community*. New Haven: Yale University Press, 1978, pp. 158–87.
Wellek, René. Review of *Marxism and Form*. *Yale Review* 62 (1972–73): 119–26.

EDWARD W. SAID

Bayley, John. Review of *The World, the Text, and the Critic*. *New York Times Book Review*, 27 February 1983, p. 11.
Bové, Paul A. Review of *The World, the Text, and the Critic*. *Contemporary Literature* 26 (1985): 91–106.
Brombert, Victor. Review of *Orientalism*. *American Scholar* 48 (1978–79): 532–33, 536, 538, 540, 542.

Cain, William E. Review of *The World, the Text, and the Critic*. *Virginia Quarterly Review* 60 (1984): 181–88.
Donoghue, Denis. Review of *The World, the Text, and the Critic*. *New Republic*, 18 April 1983, pp. 30–33.
Ehrenpreis, Irvin. Review of *The World, the Text, and the Critic*. *New York Review of Books*, 19 January 1984, pp. 37–39.
Hourani, Albert. Review of *Orientalism*. *New York Review of Books*, 8 March 1979, pp. 27–30.
Howard, Anthony. Review of *Covering Islam*. *New York Times Book Review*, 26 July 1981, p. 7.
Lodge, David. Review of *The World, the Text, and the Critic*. *Times Literary Supplement*, 4 May 1984, p. 487.
Tanner, Tony. Review of *Beginnings*. *Times Literary Supplement*, 20 August 1976, p. 1026.
Watkins, Evan. "The Politics of Literary Criticism." In *The Question of Textuality*, eds. William V. Spanos, Paul A. Bové, and Daniel O'Hara. Bloomington: Indiana University Press, 1982, pp. 31–38.

SANDRA M. GILBERT & SUSAN GUBAR

Abraham, Julie. Review of *No Man's Land*, Volume 1. *Nation*, 2–9 July 1988, p. 27.
Ashton, Rosemary. Review of *The Madwoman in the Attic*. *Times Literary Supplement*, 8 August 1980, p. 901.
Auerbach, Nina. Review of *The Madwoman in the Attic*. *Victorian Studies* 23 (1979–80): 505–7.
Banta, Martha. Review of *No Man's Land*, Volume 1. *American Literature* 60 (1988): 463–65.
Dinnage, Rosemary. Review of *The Madwoman in the Attic*. *New York Review of Books*, 20 December 1979, p. 6.
Ferguson, Moira. Review of *The Madwoman in the Attic* and *Shakespeare's Sisters*. *Prairie Schooner* 54 (1980–81): 81–83.
Froula, Christine. Review of *No Man's Land*, Volume 1. *New York Times Book Review*, 7 February 1988, p. 12.
Godwin, Gail. Review of *The Norton Anthology of Literature by Women*. *New York Times Book Review*, 28 April 1985, p. 13.
Hardy, Barbara. Review of *No Man's Land*, Volume 1. *Times Literary Supplement*, 3–9 June 1988, p. 621.
Kendrick, Walter. Review of *No Man's Land*, Volume 2. *New York Times Book Review*, 19 February 1989, p. 9.
Kolodny, Annette. Review of *The Madwoman in the Attic*. *American Literature* 52 (1980): 128–32.
Rose, Phyllis. Review of *The Norton Anthology of Literature by Women*. *Atlantic Monthly* 256 (August 1985): 88–91.
Schreiber, LeAnne. Review of *The Madwoman in the Attic*. *New York Times Book Review*, 9 December 1979, p. 11.

Spacks, Patricia Meyer. Review of *The Madwoman in the Attic. Yale Review* 69 (1979–80): 266–70.
Taliaferro, Frances. Review of *The Madwoman in the Attic. Harper's* 259 (December 1979): 78–79.

STANLEY E. FISH

Bilan, R. P. Review of *Is There a Text in This Class? University of Toronto Quarterly* 51 (1981–82): 102–12.
Bogue, Ronald L. Review of *Is There a Text in This Class? Criticism* 23 (1981): 177–80.
Donoghue, Denis. Review of *Is There a Text in This Class? Times Literary Supplement*, 8 May 1981, p. 507.
Gallagher, Catherine. Review of *Is There a Text in This Class? MLN* 96 (1981): 1168–71.
Graff, Gerald. Review of *Is There a Text in This Class? New Republic*, 14 February 1981, pp. 36–38.
Martz, Louis L. Review of *The Living Temple. Renaissance Quarterly* 33 (1980): 300–303.
Rendall, Steven. Review of *Is There a Text in This Class? Diacritics* 12 (Winter 1982): 49–56.
Sisson, C. H. Review of *The Living Temple. Times Literary Supplement*, 29 September 1978, p. 1075.
Williamson, C. F. Review of *The Living Temple. Review of English Studies* 31 (1980): 461–66.
Wollheim, Richard. Review of *Is There a Text in This Class? New York Review of Books*, 17 December 1981, pp. 64–66.

TZVETAN TODOROV

Bruns, Gerald L. Review of *Theories of the Symbol. Comparative Literature* 35 (1983): 286–89.
Cocking, J. M. Review of *The Poetics of Prose. French Studies* 35 (1981): 101–3.
Culler, Jonathan. Review of *The Fantastic. Yale Review* 63 (1973–74): 439–47.
Donoghue, Denis. Review of *Mikhail Bakhtin. Raritan* 5, No. 2 (Fall 1985): 107–19.
Frow, John. Review of *Introduction to Poetics. Journal of Aesthetics and Art Criticism* 41 (1982–83): 112–13.
Hult, David. Review of *Symbolism and Interpretation. MLN* 98 (1983): 765–71.
Morgan, Thais E. Review of *Introduction to Poetics. Semiotica* 57 (1985): 125–76.
Norris, Christopher. Review of *Introduction to Poetics. Modern Language Review* 78 (1983): 636–37.
O'Brien, William A. Review of *Theories of the Symbol. MLN* 97 (1982): 1295–98.

FRANK LENTRICCHIA

Altieri, Charles. Review of *After the New Criticism*. *Philosophy and Literature* 6 (1982): 210–11.

Baldick, Chris. Review of *Criticism and Social Change*. *Times Literary Supplement*, 22 June 1984, p. 707.

Cain, William F. Review of *After the New Criticism*. *Western Humanities Review* 35 (1981): 192–94.

Conant, Oliver. Review of *Criticism and Social Change*. *Virginia Quarterly Review* 61 (1985): 366–76.

Hawkes, Terence. Review of *After the New Criticism*. *Times Literary Supplement*, 17 April 1981, p. 444.

Henderson, Greig E. Review of *Criticism and Social Change*. *University of Toronto Quarterly* 54 (1984–85): 303–12.

Levine, George. Review of *After the New Criticism*. *College English* 43 (1981): 146–60.

Norris, Christopher. Review of *After the New Criticism*. *Essays in Criticism* 32 (1982): 89–93.

O'Hara, Dan. Review of *After the New Criticism*. *Contemporary Literature* 23 (1982): 109–13.

Parker, Andrew. Review of *After the New Criticism*. *Diacritics* 11 (Fall 1981): 57–73.

JULIA KRISTEVA

Arac, Jonathan. Review of *Desire in Language*. *Modern Fiction Studies* 28 (1982–83): 723–25.

Chase, Cynthia. Review of *Desire in Language* and *Powers of Horror*. *Criticism* 26 (1984): 193–201.

Jacobus, Mary. "Dora and the Pregnant Madonna." In *Reading Woman: Essays in Feminist Criticism*, ed. Mary Jacobus. New York: Columbia University Press, 1986, pp. 137–93.

McCannell, Juliet Flower. Review of *Desire in Language* and *Powers of Horror*. *Semiotica* 62 (1986): 325–55.

Mall, James. Review of *Desire in Language*. *Journal of Aesthetics and Art Criticism* 40 (1981–82): 93–94.

Morton, Donald. Review of *Revolution in Poetic Language*. *Western Humanities Review* 40 (1986): 91–97.

Radford, Jean. Review of *The Kristeva Reader*. *New Statesman*, 31 October 1986, p. 28.

Taylor, Marc C. "Woman: Julia Kristeva." In *Altarity*. Chicago: University of Chicago Press, 1987, pp. 151–83.

Warner, Marina. Review of *Chinese Women*. *Times Literary Supplement*, 22 April 1977, p. 491.

Yaeger, Patricia S. Review of *Revolution in Poetic Language*. *Contemporary Literature* 27 (1986): 246–56.

ELAINE SHOWALTER

Auerbach, Nina. Review of *A Literature of Their Own*. *Nineteenth-Century Fiction* 32 (1977–78): 340–45.

Bick, Suzann. Review of *The Female Malady*. *Antioch Review* 44 (1986): 242–43.
Cahill, Daniel J. Review of *A Literature of Their Own*. *Contemporary Literature* 19 (1978): 128–31.
Colby, Vineta. Review of *A Literature of Their Own*. *Modern Philology* 77 (1979–80): 357–60.
Gubar, Susan. Review of *A Literature of Their Own*. *Victorian Studies* 22 (1978–79): 90–92.
Jackson, Rosemary. Review of *A Literature of Their Own*. *Encounter* 49 (July 1977): 67–70.
Mitchell, Juliet. Review of *A Literature of Their Own*. *Times Literary Supplement*, 1 July 1977, p. 798.
Moglen, Helen. Review of *A Literature of Their Own*. *Yale Review* 67 (1977–78): 150–57.
Reed, John R. Review of *The Female Malady*. *Victorian Studies* 30 (1986–87): 410–11.
Spacks, Patricia Meyer. Review of *The Female Malady*. *New Republic*, 28 April 1986, p. 34.
———. Review of *A Literature of Their Own*. *New York Times Book Review*, 27 March 1977, p. 12.
Storr, Anthony. Review of *The Female Malady*. *New York Times Book Review*, 19 January 1986, p. 7.

SHOSHANA FELMAN

Carroll, Robert C. Review of *La Folie et la chose littéraire* and *La Scandale du corps parlant*. *MLN* 96 (1981): 897–905.
Chaitin, Gilbert D. Review of *La Folie et la chose littéraire*. *Comparative Literature* 33 (1981): 389–92.
Culler, Jonathan. Review of *La Scandale du corps parlant*. *Times Literary Supplement*, 13 June 1980, p. 662.
Gill, Gillian C. Review of *Writing and Madness*. *Journal of Aesthetics and Art Criticism* 45 (1986–87): 314–16.
Godin, Henri. Review of *La Folie et la chose littéraire*. *Modern Language Review* 75 (1980): 651–52.
Gorman, David. Review of *The Literary Speech Act*. *Philosophy and Literature* 8 (1984): 140–41.
Knapp, Bettina L. Review of *Writing and Madness*. *Nineteenth-Century French Studies* 14 (1985–86): 405–6.
Knutson, Harold C. Review of *La Scandale du corps parlant*. *Modern Language Review* 76 (1981): 963–64.
Schneider, Monique. Review of *La Scandale du corps parlant*. *Diacritics* 11 (Fall 1981): 27–38.
Steig, Michael. Review of *Writing and Madness*. *Queen's Quarterly* 92 (1985): 857–59.

NINA AUERBACH

Brown, Julia Prewitt. Review of *Communities of Women*. *American Scholar* 48 (1978–79): 129–32.

Donoghue, Denis. Review of *Romantic Imprisonment*. *New Republic*, 10 March 1986, p. 30.
Gordon, Marcia. Review of *Romantic Imprisonment*. *Novel* 19 (1985–86): 278–82.
Goreau, Angeline. Review of *Romantic Imprisonment*. *New York Times Book Review*, 5 January 1986, p. 5.
Levine, George. Review of *Woman and the Demon*. *New York Times Book Review*, 9 January 1983, p. 8.
Showalter, Elaine. Review of *Communities of Women*. *Criticism* 21 (1979): 172–74.
Spacks, Patricia Meyer. Review of *Woman and the Demon*. *New Republic*, 28 February 1983, pp. 34–35.
Uglow, Jennifer. Review of *Woman and the Demon*. *Times Literary Supplement*, 15 April 1983, p. 384.
Vicinus, Martha. Review of *Communities of Women*. *Nineteenth-Century Fiction* 33 (1978–79): 387–91.

TERRY EAGLETON

Bayley, John. Review of *Literary Theory*. *Times Literary Supplement*, 10 June 1983, p. 587.
Bergonzi, Bernard. "The Terry Eagleton Story." In *The Myth of Modernism and Twentieth Century Literature*. New York: St. Martin's Press, 1986, pp. 188–209.
Butler, Marilyn. Review of *The Rape of Clarissa*. *Times Literary Supplement*, 12 November 1982, p. 1241.
Casey, John. Review of *Criticism and Ideology*. *Times Literary Supplement*, 20 May 1977, p. 606.
Donoghue, Denis. Review of *Literary Theory*. *New York Review of Books*, 8 December 1983, pp. 43–45.
Greenblatt, Stephen. Review of *William Shakespeare*. *New Republic*, 10 November 1986, p. 42.
Lerner, Laurence. Review of *Myths of Power*. *Encounter* 45 (July 1975): 60–66.
Mitchell, Stanley. Review of *Marxism and Literary Criticism*. *Times Literary Supplement*, 21 January 1977, p. 76.
Slaughter, Cliff. "Conclusions: Literature and Dialectical Materialism." In *Marxism, Ideology and Literature*. New York: Humanities Press, 1980, pp. 197–213.
Strickland, Geoffrey. Review of *Criticism and Ideology* and *Marxism and Literary Criticism*. *Encounter* 49 (July 1977): 86–91.
Unsigned. Review of *Exiles and Emigrés*. *Times Literary Supplement*, 23 October 1970, p. 1219.

LESLIE BRISMAN

Bullough, Geoffrey, Review of *Milton's Poetry of Choice*. *English* 23 (1974): 113–15.
Burden, Dennis H. Review of *Milton's Poetry of Choice*. *Review of English Studies* 31 (1980): 211–16.

Gill, Stephen. Review of *Romantic Origins*. *Times Literary Supplement*, 21 December 1979, pp. 166–67.
Hughes, Daniel. Review of *Romantic Origins*. *Studies in Romanticism* 18 (1979): 316–22.
Reiman, Donald H. Review of *Romantic Origins*. *Keats-Shelley Journal* 28 (1979): 161–64.
Swingle, L. J. Review of *Romantic Origins*. *Journal of English and Germanic Philology* 78 (1979): 139–41.
Tave, Stuart M. Review of *Romantic Origins*. *Yearbook of English Studies* 11 (1981): 290–93.
Wagenknecht, David. Review of *Milton's Poetry of Choice*. *Studies in Romanticism* 14 (1975): 85–91.
Wittreich, Joseph Anthony, Jr. Review of *Milton's Poetry of Choice*. *Journal of English and Germanic Philology* 73 (1974): 435–39.

ALICE WALKER

Benet, Mary Kathleen. Review of *In Search of Our Mothers' Gardens*. *Times Literary Supplement*, 20 July 1984, p. 818.
Bloom, Harold, ed. *Alice Walker*. New York: Chelsea House, 1989.
Clark, Beverly Lyon. Review of *In Search of Our Mothers' Gardens*. *Modern Fiction Studies* 30 (1984): 334.
Davis, Thadious M. "Alice Walker's Celebration of Self in Southern Generations." In *Women Writers of the Contemporary South*, ed. Peggy Whitman Prenshaw. Jackson: University Press of Mississippi, 1984, pp. 39–53.
Okri, Ben. Review of *In Search of Our Mothers' Gardens*. *New Statesman*, 22 June 1984, p. 24.
Perrin, Noel. Review of *Living by the Word*. *New York Times Book Review*, 5 June 1988, p. 42.
Pryse, Marjorie. "Zora Neale Hurston, Alice Walker, and the Ancient Power of Black Women." In *Conjuring: Black Women, Fiction, and the Literary Tradition*, eds. Marjorie Pryse and Hortense Spillers. Bloomington: Indiana University Press, 1985, pp. 1–24.
Stade, George. "Womanist Fiction and Male Characters." *Partisan Review* 52 (1985): 264–70.
Vigderman, Patricia. Review of *In Search of Our Mothers' Gardens*. *Nation*, 17 December 1983, p. 635.
Washington, Mary Helen. "An Essay on Alice Walker." In *Sturdy Black Bridges: Visions of Black Women in Literature*, eds. Roseann P. Bell, Bettye J. Parker, and Beverly Guy-Sheftall. Garden City, NY: Doubleday (Anchor), 1979, pp. 133–49.

BARBARA JOHNSON

Cain, William E. Review of *The Critical Difference*. *Comparative Literature* 34 (1982): 369–71.

Coughlin, Ellen K. Review of *A World of Difference*. *Chronicle of Higher Education*, 12 August 1987, p. 7.

Kenner, Hugh. Review of *The Critical Difference*. *Harper's* 263 (August 1981): 66.

Mackinnon, Lachlan. Review of *The Critical Difference*. *Times Literary Supplement*, 8 January 1982, p. 34.

Norris, Christopher. Review of *The Critical Difference*. *Modern Language Review* 78 (1983): 381–83.

Palmer, Richard E. Review of *The Critical Difference*. *Philosophy and Literature* 5 (1981): 244–45.

Scholes, Robert. Review of *The Critical Difference*. *Yale Review* 72 (1982–83): 105–8.

Starr, Peter T. Review of *The Critical Difference*. *MLN* 96 (1981): 1163–68.

HENRY LOUIS GATES, JR.

Bhabha, Homi K. Review of *Black Literature and Literary Theory*. *Poetics Today* 8 (1987): 181–87.

Blount, Marcellus. Review of *Figures in Black*. *Southern Review* 24 (1988): 462–72.

Eagleton, Terry. Review of *Black Literature and Literary Theory*. *New York Times Book Review*, 9 December 1984, p. 45.

Kinnamon, Keneth. Review of *Figures in Black*. *American Literature* 60 (1988): 483–84.

Weixlmann, Joe. "Black Literary Criticism at the Juncture." *Contemporary Literature* 27 (1986): 48–62.

Werner, Craig. Review of *Figures in Black*. *Modern Fiction Studies* 34 (1988): 125–35.

Wideman, John. Review of *The Signifying Monkey*. *New York Times Book Review*, 14 August 1988, p. 3.

Editor's Note to Glossary and Index

A glossary and three indexes conclude our series, *The Art of the Critic*. The *Glossary of Critical Terms* should be interpreted very literally as containing only definitions of technical terms pertaining to criticism or critical theory, as opposed to terms that have a more purely literary signification (e.g., novel). Along with basic definitions, the glossary provides quotations from the works of those critics who created or utilized the terms; these works have in most instances been reprinted in our series. In some cases a history of the term, noting its changes of usage over time, has been supplied.

The *Index to Critics* provides an alphabetical list of the 213 critics reprinted in our series, while the *Index to Works* indexes the 395 works or portions of works reprinted. A comprehensive *Index to Names and Titles* concludes the volume, and contains references to all actual persons (not mythological figures or fictional characters) and titles significantly mentioned throughout the eleven volumes of the series. Harold Bloom's introductions to each volume are indexed, but the biographies preceding the reprinted selections are not. All references in the three indexes are to volume and page; e.g., an index entry reading "4:426" refers to Volume 4, page 426 of the series.

—S. T. Joshi

GLOSSARY OF CRITICAL TERMS

AESTHETICISM. A doctrine of the later nineteenth century whereby the role of the critic is to perceive, and make perceptible to others, elements of beauty and pleasure in both art and life. In the "Preface" to *The Renaissance* (1873) Walter Pater writes: "The aesthetic critic . . . regards all the objects with which he has to do, all works of art, and the fairer forms of nature and human life, as powers or forces producing pleasurable sensations, each of a more or less peculiar or unique kind. This influence he feels, and wishes to explain, analysing it, and reducing it to its elements. . . . The function of the aesthetic critic is to distinguish, analyse, and separate from its adjuncts, the virtue by which a picture, a landscape, a fair personality in life or in a book, produces this special impression of beauty or pleasure, to indicate what the source of that impression is, and under what conditions it is experienced." Other important aesthetic critics are Oscar Wilde, Lionel Johnson, and Ernest Dowson. Contemporary critics censured this approach as leading to immoralism or unrestrained hedonism, while later critics—especially those who, like I. A. Richards and W. K. Wimsatt, wished to establish criticism on a more "scientific" basis—disapproved of aestheticism on the grounds that it is vague, subjective, and relativistic.

AFFECTIVE FALLACY. A term created by W. K. Wimsatt and Monroe Beardsley in their essay "The Affective Fallacy" (1946; in *The Verbal Icon*, 1954), referring to "a confusion between the poem and its *results* (what it *is* and what it *does*). . . . It begins by trying to derive the standard of criticism from the psychological effects of the poem and ends in impressionism and relativism." The objects of attack were principally such critics of the early twentieth century as George Saintsbury and Sir Arthur Quiller-Couch, whose criticism focuses upon the emotions inspired by works of literature. "The report of some readers . . . that a poem or story induces in them vivid images, intense feelings, or heightened consciousness, is neither anything which can be refuted nor anything which it is possible for the objective critic to take into account." Reader-response critics have taken issue with this stance for its failure to acknowledge that literary works do not exist as independent objects but only insofar as they are actually read (see **READER-RESPONSE CRITICISM**).

AFRO-AMERICAN LITERATURE, CRITICISM OF. A recent movement that seeks to champion writing by Afro-Americans as authentic contributions to American literature. Through the influence of such critics as Henry Louis Gates, Jr., Houston A. Baker, Jr., Robert B. Stepto, Barbara Christian, and others, Afro-American writing in the novel (Zora Neale Hurston, Richard Wright, James Baldwin, Toni Morrison, Alice Walker), poetry (Sterling Brown, Ishmael Reed, Jay Wright), prose nonfiction (Frederick Douglass, W. E. B. Du Bois), and other genres has been recognized. Gates argues that the criticism of Afro-American literature is still at a very early stage: "W. E. B. Du Bois argued that evidence of critical activity is a sign of a tradition's sophistication, since criticism implies an awareness of the process of art itself and is a second-order reflection upon those primary texts that define a tradition and its canon. Insofar as we, critics of the black tradition, master our craft, we serve both to preserve our own traditions and to shape their direction. All great writers demand great critics. The imperatives of our task are clear. . . . Unlike critics in almost every other literary tradition, almost all that we have to say about our literature is new. What critics of the Western tradition can make an even remotely similar claim?" (*Figures in Black*, 1987).

ALEXANDRIANISM. A literary movement in Greece during the third and second centuries B.C., which stressed subjectivity, intellectualism, allusiveness, and repudiation or reinterpretation of older literary modes and schools of thought. The period saw the emergence of the first professional literary critics and scholars, among them Zenodotus (who compiled critical editions of Homer, Hesiod, and Pindar), Callimachus (lyric poet who catalogued the Library at Alexandria), Eratosthenes, Aristophanes of Byzantium, and Aristarchus. Parallels have been drawn between the Alexandrian age and the Modernist movement of the early twentieth century (see **MODERNISM**).

ALLEGORY. A narrative in which the surface events and characters stand for abstract ethical or philosophical concepts. Notable examples of allegory are Edmund Spenser's *The Faerie Queene* and John Bunyan's *The Pilgrim's Progress*. In *Allegory: The Theory of a Symbolic Mode* (1964), Angus Fletcher reinterprets allegory in terms of Freud's psychoanalytic theory, and in the process provides a radical reinterpretation of both allegory and psychoanalytic criticism: "It is apparent that psychoanalytic theory has brought us to our final point about *theme,* that allegory always demonstrates a degree of inner conflict, which we call 'ambivalence.' . . . No psychobiography of authors is required, though it can become a useful control, when the works they create correspond to known patterns. Only the pattern itself needs to be considered in this rather idealized criticism. If one wanted to go further and write psychobiography, one could, but the personal history of the author's life and character is not a requisite of a psychoanalytic criticism, however interesting it may be on its own merits, as long as that criticism remains focused on the formal properties of works." Allegory must be clearly distinguished from the use of *symbols,* in which there is no direct correlation between the literal and the metaphorical signification of all narrative elements.

AMBIGUITY. A use of language in which either more than one meaning is suggested or in which there is doubt as to what meaning is being suggested. William Empson, in *Seven Types of Ambiguity* (1930), felt that the conception was central to the way literature operated. His seven types of ambiguity are as follows: "First-type ambiguities arise when a detail is effective in several ways at once. . . . In second-type ambiguities two or more alternative meanings are fully resolved into one. . . . The condition for third-type ambiguity is that two apparently unconnected meanings are given simultaneously. . . . In the fourth type the alternate meanings combine to make clear a complicated state of mind in the author. . . . The fifth type is a fortunate confusion, as when the author is discovering his idea in the act of writing . . . In the sixth type what is said is contradictory or irrelevant and the reader is forced to invent interpretations. . . . The seventh type is that of full contradiction, marking a division in the author's mind." Although Empson frequently probed the putative state of the author's mind (most clearly evident in his fourth, fifth, and seventh types), his conception of ambiguity was adopted, along with those of irony and paradox, as central tenets in the New Criticism's methodology of studying a literary work as an independent object.

ANXIETY OF INFLUENCE. In the critical theory of Harold Bloom, the notion that a "strong" poet engages (perhaps unconsciously) in a quasi-Oedipal struggle with a significant precursor, whom he must overcome in order to carve out a place for himself in literature; in the process the later poet "misreads" or distorts the earlier poet so that his own work can claim to be innovative and significant. Bloom writes in *The Anxiety of Influence* (1973): "Poetic Influence,—when it involves two strong, authentic poets,—always proceeds by a misreading of the prior poet, an act of creative correction that is actually and necessarily a misinterpretation. The history of fruitful poetic influence, which is to say the main tradition of Western poetry since the Renaissance, is a history of anxiety and self-saving caricature, of distortion, of perverse, wilful revisionism without which modern poetry as such could not exist." The idea appears to have been anticipated by W. Jackson Bate in *The Burden of the Past and the English Poet* (1970), but without the psychological framework, derived from the psychopathology of Sigmund Freud, employed by Bloom. Feminist critics have criticized the idea for its apparent inapplicability to women writers.

ARCHETYPAL CRITICISM. Criticism that focuses on tracing the "archetypes" or myth-patterns thought to be present in all literary work. Some archetypal critics draw upon the psychological theories of Carl Gustav Jung, who related the archetype to his notion of the collective unconscious (see **PSYCHOANALYTICAL CRITICISM**). Other critics do not use a specifically Jungian model, tracing archetypes in works of a given genre (e.g., pastoral). Northrop Frye treats the subject exhaustively in the third essay in *Anatomy of Criticism* (1957), "Archetypal Criticism: Theory of Myths."

ART FOR ART'S SAKE. A concept associated with the Aestheticism of the later nineteenth century (see **AESTHETICISM**), referring to the belief that art must be produced without regard to political, social, or ethical concerns. Oscar Wilde, drawing upon Poe's notion of "pure poetry" (see **PURE POETRY**), stated in the preface to *The Picture of Dorian Gray* (1891): "The artist is the creator of beautiful things. . . . No artist desires to prove anything. . . . No artist has ethical sympathies.... Vice and virtue are to the artist materials for an art.... All art is quite useless." In evolving this concept Wilde and others were combating the prevailing bourgeois didacticism of the late Victorian period, where the social and moral "usefulness" of art as guide to conduct was stressed.

BATTLE OF THE ANCIENTS AND MODERNS. A controversy originating in the later seventeenth century concerning the relative merits of ancient (i.e., Greek and Latin) authors and contemporary authors, conducted by such critics as Charles de Saint-Evremond, Sir William Temple, Bernard le Bovier Fontenelle, Thomas Rymer, Richard Bentley, and others. Saint-Evremond took the side of the "moderns," affirming that the advance of morals from ancient times (largely due to the influence of Christianity) necessitated the creation of a new literature to reflect it. Rymer took the opposite approach, asserting in *The Tragedies of the Last Age* (1678) that "our poets have forc'd another way to the wood; a by-road, that runs directly cross to that of Nature, Manners and Philosophy which gain'd the Ancients so great veneration." The controversy was wittily treated by Jonathan Swift in *The Battel of the Books* (1704).

BIOGRAPHICAL CRITICISM. Criticism that studies the relationship between art and the life of the artist. Literary biography had its origins in the Alexandrian age of Greece (see **ALEXANDRIANISM**), and, although recently under attack from several critical methodologies (see **DECONSTRUCTION; INTENTIONAL FALLACY; NEW CRITICISM**), it remains a vigorously pursued discipline. C. A. Sainte-Beuve, in his *Causeries du lundi* (1851–62) and other works, was a pioneer in biographical criticism in the depth and richness of his synthesis of the artist's life and work, as was Leslie Stephen in his *Studies of a Biographer* (1898–1902). Leon Edel (*Henry James,* 1953–72), W. Jackson Bate (*John Keats,* 1963; *Samuel Johnson,* 1977), Richard Ellmann (*Oscar Wilde,* 1987), and others have continued the tradition. Edel defends the practice of biography in *Writing Lives: Principia Biographica* (1984).

CANON. A body of texts deemed worthy of study and preservation on account of their historical importance and the breadth of human experience they embody. Although the notion of the canon continues to have its supporters (see Allan Bloom, *The Closing of the American Mind,* 1987), it has been attacked by feminist critics for being patriarchal, by black critics for being racist, by Marxist critics for representing reactionary political ideals, and by such critics as Leslie A. Fiedler for its general exclusion of works not customarily thought to come under its scope (e.g., science fiction, fantasy, detective fiction).

CATHARSIS. Literally, Greek for "purgation." The term served as a focal point in Aristotle's theory of tragedy: "A tragedy ... is the imitation of an action that is serious and also, as having magnitude, complete in itself; ... with incidents arousing pity and fear, wherewith to accomplish its catharsis of such emotions" (*Poetics* 1449b). The notion is thought to represent Aristotle's rebuttal to

Plato's belief that certain works of art unhealthily stimulate the emotions and ought therefore to be banned (*Republic,* Book 10).

CLASSICISM. The maintenance of traditions and modes of expression evolved by the Greek and Latin writers of classical antiquity. Classicism was an important component of the European Renaissance of the fourteenth and fifteenth centuries. Boccaccio, in *The Genealogy of the Gentile Gods* (1350–63), defended the study of classical mythology against charges that pagan writers and myths would be a corrupting influence upon Christians. Erasmus did the same in *The Antibarbarians* (1520). By the sixteenth century, voices began to be raised against the possibly stifling effect of following classical models too rigidly. Giovanni Battista Giraldi Cintio, in *On the Composition of Romances* (1554), protested against judging modern tragedies on strictly Aristotelian principles, and Joachim Du Bellay, in *The Defence and Illustration of the French Language* (1549), acknowledged the general superiority of ancient literature but makes a claim for the aesthetic powers of the French language. Classicism gained new life in the later seventeenth and eighteenth centuries in England with John Dryden, Alexander Pope, and Samuel Johnson (see **NEOCLASSICISM**).

DADAISM. A movement of the early twentieth century which expressed opposition and hostility to what it believed to be the excessive rationalism and moral bankruptcy of the prevailing bourgeois culture, a view inspired largely by the cultural devastation of World War I. Dadaist works of art and literature used radical, experimental, and seemingly irrational modes of expression to convey contempt for the rigidity of conventional art and civilization. In *A Dada Manifesto* (1918) Tristan Tzara writes: "So DADA was born of a desire for independence, of a distrust of the community. Those who belong to us keep their freedom. We don't recognize any theory." Dadaism was eventually superseded by Surrealism (see **SURREALISM**), which incorporated many of its theories and methodologies.

DECADENCE. A movement of the late nineteenth century in France and England that rejected bourgeois notions of progress and social conformity and asserted the value of refined sensations and freedom from artificial social constraints. In critical theory the movement saw the dominance of aestheticism and the art for art's sake credo (see **AESTHETICISM; ART FOR ART'S SAKE**).

DECONSTRUCTION. A critical school growing out of poststructuralism (see **POSTSTRUCTURALISM**) originated by Jacques Derrida and elaborated by such of his disciples as Paul de Man, Barbara Johnson, the later J. Hillis Miller, Jonathan Culler, and others. Derrida, adopting and extending Ferdinand de Saussure's notion of the arbitrariness of the signifier and the signified (see **STRUCTURALISM**), maintains that there is no correspondence between language and the "real" world, so that the "play" of language is infinite—there is no end to the implications or resonances of a given word. Derrida coins the term *différance* (meaning both "difference" and "deferral") to denote that a word gains meaning only through its difference from other words, so that one must "defer" any definitive meaning to the word. Deconstructive practice therefore consists in taking the "conventional" interpretation of a text and "subverting" it—showing that the text can be interpreted to mean the opposite of what it purports to mean. Derrida's theories were first expressed in *De la grammatologie* (1967) and expanded in many other works. Theoreticians have pointed out weaknesses or demonstrable errors in deconstructive theory and practice. Derrida's belief in the "infinite" play of language would suggest that a word has no determinate meaning, something contrary to the actual usage of language. Derrida's desire to "subvert" the standard interpretation of a text is said to have emerged in the context of a rigidly hierarchical and authoritarian academic environment existing in France up to the 1960s; since such an environment does not exist in English-speaking countries, where pluralism is the rule, deconstruction has not "traveled" well, and can rarely find a "standard" interpretation of a text to subvert. The lack of correspondence between language and reality has been anticipated by many linguistic philosophers of this century, of whose work Derrida appears ignorant. The willful obscurantism of much deconstructionist writing has also alienated many readers and critics. See further John M. Ellis, *Against Deconstruction* (1989).

DIALOGIC CRITICISM. A concept evolved in the recent critical theory of Tzvetan Todorov and representing a sort of fusion between hermeneutics (the study of the historical circumstances in which a literary work is written) and ethical criticism (the study of the ethical presuppositions of a literary work). As Todorov writes in *Literature and Its Theorists* (1984), "Dialogic criticism speaks not about literary works but to them, or rather with them; it refuses to eliminate either of the two voices involved. The text under study is not an object that must be taken in hand by a 'metalanguage,' but rather a discourse that is met by the critic's own; the author is a 'thou' and not a 'he,' an interlocutor with whom one discusses human values. . . . It is time to come (back) to the self-evident facts that we should never have forgotten: literature has to do with human existence, it is a discourse oriented toward—let us not be intimidated by the ponderous words—truth and morality. . . . Literature would be nothing at all if it did not allow us to reach a better understanding of life."

DIDACTICISM. The belief that literature ought to inculcate moral values. Plato asserted that writers "should imitate from youth upward only those characters which are suitable to their profession—the courageous, temperate, holy, free, and the like; but they should not depict or be skillful at imitating any kind of illiberality or baseness, lest the fruit of imitation should be reality" (*Republic*, Book 3). Aristotle laid much less stress on the didactic function of art, but the view was widely held throughout the Renaissance up to the Romantic period. In the preface to *All for Love* (1678) John Dryden praised Shakespeare's *Antony and Cleopatra* for "the excellency of the moral. . . . The chief persons represented were famous patterns of unlawful love; and their end accordingly was unfortunate." Jeremy Collier attacked the Restoration stage on account of its "immorality and profaneness." In *Biographia Literaria* (1817) Samuel Taylor Coleridge commenced the revolt on didacticism by claiming that "a poem is that species of composition, which is opposed to works of science, by proposing for its *immediate* object pleasure, not truth," a distinction echoed by Edgar Allan Poe in his criticism of Longfellow: "We would define in brief the Poetry of words as the *Rhythmical Creation of Beauty*. Beyond the limits of beauty its province does not extend. Its sole arbiter is Taste. With the Intellect or with the Conscience it has only collateral relations. It has no dependence, unless incidentally, upon either Duty or *Truth*." Matthew Arnold is thought to have reinstated the didactic principle, but his position is more complicated than that. In the preface to *The Poems of Wordsworth* (1879) he stated: "Some kinds of poetry are in themselves lower kinds than others. The ballad kind is a lower kind; the didactic kind, still more, is a lower kind." Later in the same work he wrote: "poetry is at bottom a criticism of life; ... the greatness of a poet lies in his powerful and beautiful application of ideas to life,—to the question: How to live? ... The question, *how to live*, is itself a moral idea; and it is the question which most interests every man, and with which, in some way or other, he is perpetually occupied. A large sense of course is to be given to the term *moral*." Didacticism is not to be confused with ethical criticism (see **ETHICAL CRITICISM**).

DISINTERESTEDNESS. Matthew Arnold's notion that criticism should follow "the law of its own nature, which is to be a free play of the mind on all subjects which it touches," as he writes in "The Function of Criticism at the Present Time" (1864). "By steadily refusing to lend itself to any of those ulterior, political, practical considerations about ideas, which plenty of people will be sure to attach to them, which perhaps ought often to be attached to them, which in this country at any rate are certain to be attached to them quite sufficiently, but which criticism has really nothing to do with. Its business is ... simply to know the best that is known and thought in the world, and by in its turn making this known, to create a current of true and fresh ideas." Although Arnold's specific object of attack was the partisan and narrowly political nature of the periodical criticism and reviews of his day, Marxist critics would contend that this goal of a "pure" criticism without political overtones is inherently unachievable. Arnold also stressed disinterestedness in another way: "Our personal affinities, likings, and circumstances, have great power to sway our estimate of this or that poet's work, and to make us attach more importance to it as poetry than in itself it really possesses" ("Introduction" to *The English Poets,* 1880). This position led indirectly to the "objective" criticism of I. A. Richards and Northrop Frye.

DISSOCIATION OF SENSIBILITY. A conception in the critical theory of T. S. Eliot, who in "The Metaphysical Poets" (1921) defines it as follows: "The poets of the [early] seventeenth century ... possessed a mechanism of sensibility which could devour any kind of experience. They are simple, artificial, difficult, or fantastic, as their predecessors were. ... In the seventeenth century a dissociation of sensibility set in, from which we have never recovered." This dissociation was "aggravated" by the two premier poets of the middle to late seventeenth century, Milton and Dryden. "The language went on and in some respects improved. . . . But while the language became more refined, the feeling became more crude."

DRAMATIC UNITIES. The rules that a drama must observe in its representation of time, setting, and action. In the *Poetics* (1451a) Aristotle laid down only the most general notions of unity, stressing that in a drama "the story, as an imitation of action, must represent one action, a complete whole, with its several incidents so closely connected that the transposal or withdrawal of any one of them will disjoin and dislocate the whole." Aristotle made no specifications as to the number of acts in a drama (Greek drama was not divided into acts), but stated that the following were commonly found in tragedies: "Prologue, Episode, Exode, and a choral portion, distinguished into Parode and Stasimon" (*Poetics* 1452b). It was Horace who, in the *Ars Poetica,* claimed that a drama must have five acts. These rules were elaborated upon by the French Neoclassic playwrights and theorists of the seventeenth century. In his *Discourses* (1660) Pierre Corneille identified "the three unities of action, time, and place." The unity of action is similar to Aristotle's notion of a single and complete action; the unity of time (i.e., that a drama must represent actions that occur in the course of a single day) is something Corneille claimed to find in Aristotle, although in the *Poetics* (1449b) Aristotle merely says that, as an empirical rule, "tragedy endeavours to keep as far as possible within a single circuit of the sun"; the unity of place is derived from the unity of time, and states that actions must take place in locales "to which a man may go and return in twenty-four hours." Many of these rules are summed up in Nicolas Boileau's *L'Art poétique* (1674). Samuel Johnson was among the first to rebel against the stifling effect of these unities, claiming that spectators do not mistake the action depicted on the stage for real events: "Imitations produce pain or pleasure, not because they are mistaken for realities, but because they bring realities to mind. . . . It is therefore evident, that the action is not supposed to be real, and it follows that between the acts a longer or shorter time may be allowed to pass, and that no more account of space or duration is to be taken by the auditor of a drama, than by the reader of a narrative, before whom may pass in an hour the life of a hero, or the revolutions of an empire" (*Preface to Shakespeare,* 1765).

ETHICAL CRITICISM. The analysis of literature on the basis of its ethical presuppositions. Although ethical criticism can be traced to Plato, it must be differentiated from didacticism (see **DIDACTICISM**), in that ethical critics do not look to literature for the inculcation of any specific ethical beliefs but merely focus on ethical issues present in literary work; as such, ethical criticism is properly a subset of philosophical criticism (see **PHILOSOPHICAL CRITICISM**). Wayne C. Booth defends the practice in *The Company We Keep: An Ethics of Fiction* (1988), while Tobin Siebers, in *The Ethics of Criticism* (1988), maintains that all critical theory and practice is inherently (if at times covertly) ethical even when it takes the forms of New Criticism, Formalism, and deconstruction, which claim to be concerned solely with language and not with any ethical issues involved with the text. See also **DIALOGIC CRITICISM**.

FANCY. A quality of mind inferior to imagination (see **IMAGINATION**), in the critical theory of Samuel Taylor Coleridge. In *Biographia Literaria* (1817) Coleridge defines fancy as follows: "Fancy . . . has no other counters to play with, but fixities and definites. The Fancy is indeed no other than a mode of Memory emancipated from the order of time and space; while it is blended with, and modified by that empirical phenomenon of will, which we express by the word choice. But equally with the ordinary memory the Fancy must receive all its materials ready made from the law of association."

FEMINIST CRITICISM. Criticism that affirms that women writers or female perspectives and outlooks have been ignored by both literary figures and by critics, and seeks to display the unique insights provided by women writers and the frequently unconscious male chauvinism embedded in many standard works of literature. Feminist thought can be traced to antiquity, but one of the pioneer works of feminist literary criticism was Virginia Woolf's *A Room of One's Own* (1929). Two decades later Simone de Beauvoir wrote *The Second Sex* (1949), primarily a tract exposing the general oppression of women but containing keen insights into the treatment of women in the work of D. H. Lawrence, Paul Claudel, André Breton, and others. Feminist literary criticism emerged as a genuine and permanent force in modern criticism in the 1970s, with such works as Ellen Moers's *Literary Women* (1976), Elaine Showalter's *A Literature of Their Own* (1977), and Sandra M. Gilbert and Susan Gubar's *The Madwoman in the Attic* (1979). Other important feminist critics are Nina Auerbach, Shoshana Felman, Adrienne Rich, Hélène Cixous, Julia Kristeva, and Patricia Meyer Sparks. Gilbert and Gubar have commenced a projected three-volume study of women's writing in the twentieth century, *No Man's Land* (1988–   ), and have edited *The Norton Anthology of Literature by Women: The Tradition in English* (1985). See also **RE-VISION**.

FORMALISM. A theory of criticism originating with such Russian critics as Boris Eikhenbaum, Victor Shklovsky, Roman Jakobson, and M. M. Bakhtin, which stressed the "formal" linguistic aspects of a literary work and gave attention to what separates literary and nonliterary writing. Both Eikhenbaum ("The Theory of the Formal Method" [1926]) and Bakhtin (*The Formal Method in Literary Scholarship* [1928]) attempt to refute charges that the Formalists focused excessively on the linguistic and structural features of a text and paid no attention to broader historical, psychological, and philosophical issues. Formalism, in its less theoretical aspects, is a component of many types of "close reading" critical approaches.

FREUDIAN CRITICISM. A branch of psychoanalytic criticism (see **PSYCHOANALYTIC CRITICISM**) specifically utilizing the theories of Sigmund Freud in the interpretation of literature. Freud himself saw his theories of repression, sublimation, and the Oedipus complex functioning in many works of literature, and in "The Theme of the Three Caskets" (1913) he interpreted *King Lear* as follows: "One might say that the three inevitable relations man has with woman are here represented: that with the mother who bears him, with the companion of his bed and board, and with the destroyer." Freud's disciple Ernest Jones continued this manner of interpretation in *Hamlet and Oedipus* (1949), and many other critics have used Freudian theory in varying degrees, among them Edmund Wilson (*The Wound and the Bow*, 1941), Lionel Trilling ("Freud and Literature" in *The Liberal Imagination*, 1950), and others. For Harold Bloom's adaptation of the Oedipus complex, see **ANXIETY OF INFLUENCE**.

FUGITIVES, THE. A group of Southern writers and critics headed by John Crowe Ransom, Allen Tate, Robert Penn Warren, and Donald Davidson, who in the 1920s advocated a return to traditionalism and literary classicism. The Fugitives published a journal, *The Fugitive* (1922–25), as well as a symposium, *I'll Take My Stand: The South and the Agrarian Tradition* (1930), in which they voiced their views. These critics were the nucleus of the New Criticism (see **NEW CRITICISM**).

GENRE. A categorization of literary works by form (novel, short story, poem, drama, etc.) or by content ("mainstream" literature, science fiction, fantasy, romance, historical fiction, etc.). The notion of genre has recently come under criticism for its excessive rigidity and its concomitant failure to deal adequately with works (e.g., the novels of Thomas Pynchon) that appear to disregard or cross standard genre distinctions.

HERMENEUTICS. The science of interpretation, usually involving the reconstruction of the historical context of a work so that its original orientation and purpose can be understood. Hermeneutics originated in the early nineteenth century with Friedrich Schleiermacher (1768–1834) and was developed by Wilhelm Dilthey (1833–1911). In this century, Hans Georg Gadamer made a significant break with traditional hermeneutics: whereas older thinkers believed that the interpreter must suppress his own prejudices and adopt as much as possible the worldview of the creator of the text in question, Gadamer believed that such an attempt was not even possible and also unprofitable: the interpreter must engage in a dialogue with the text so that both the text and the interpreter can be transformed. As Gadamer writes in *Truth and Method* (1960): "A person who imagines that he is free of prejudices, basing his knowledge on the objectivity of his procedures and denying that he is himself influenced by historical circumstances, experiences the power of the prejudices that unconsciously dominate him. . . . Historical consciousness in seeking to understand tradition must not rely on the critical method with which it approaches its sources, as if this preserved it from mixing its own judgments and prejudices. It must, in fact, take account of its own historicality. To stand within a tradition does not limit the freedom of knowledge but makes it possible." E. D. Hirsch, Jr., however, argues for a return to the older hermeneutical method (see **INTERPRETATION**). See also **DIALOGIC CRITICISM**.

HISTORICISM. The practice of interpreting a literary work in the context of the social, political, and cultural milieu in which it was produced; the attempt to ascertain contemporary reactions to a work in order to understand its original purpose and function. Historicism, which enters into the methodologies of many critical schools, is thought to have been opposed by the New Critics (see **NEW CRITICISM**), but they only rejected it insofar as the actual work under discussion tended to be forgotten by critics who paid more attention to the historical circumstances of its composition. Historicism is an important component of both hermeneutics and Marxist criticism.

IMAGINATION. In the critical theory of Samuel Taylor Coleridge, a quality of mind, superior to fancy (see **FANCY**), that is principally responsible for the creation of poetry; it is analogous to the creative power of God. In *Biographia Literaria* (1817) Coleridge writes: "The Imagination then, I consider either as primary, or secondary. The primary Imagination I hold to be the living Power and prime Agent of all human Perception, and as a repetition in the finite mind of the eternal act of creation in the infinite I AM. The secondary Imagination I consider as an echo of the former, co-existing with the conscious will, yet still as identical with the primary in the *kind* of its agency, and differing only in *degree,* and in the *mode* of its operation. It dissolves, diffuses, dissipates, in order to re-create; or where this process is rendered impossible, yet still at all events it struggles to idealize and to unify. It is essentially *vital,* even as all objects (*as* objects) are essentially fixed and dead." See also Leigh Hunt's *Imagination and Fancy* (1844).

INTENTIONAL FALLACY. A term created by W. K. Wimsatt and Monroe Beardsley in their essay "The Intentional Fallacy" (1946; in *The Verbal Icon,* 1954), referring to the apparent fallacy of judging a work of literature in reference to how closely it approximates or fulfills the author's intention. Wimsatt and Beardsley claim that "the design or intention of the author is neither available nor desirable as a standard for judging the success of a work of literary art." It is not available because intention, being a private psychological function, is incapable of being precisely determined by any other mind; it is not desirable because a work must stand or fall on the actual meaning in the text and not what the author may have meant by it: "A poem can *be* only through its *meaning* . . . yet it *is,* simply *is,* in the sense that we have no excuse for inquiring what part is intended or meant." Many critics now question the soundness of this view, and intentionalism of various sorts has returned to critical theory (see, e.g., **MEANING**). The concept of the intentional fallacy appears to be roughly analogous to what, in deconstruction, is called the "metaphysics of 'presence,'" where again the author's control of his text once it is written is questioned.

INTERIORITY. In the critical theory of Georges Poulet, a phenomenon whereby the act of reading revivifies a consciousness that exists in the literary work, which then subsumes or informs the consciousness of the reader. In "Criticism and the Experience of Interiority" (in *The Language of Criticism and the Sciences of Man,* ed. Richard Macksey and Eugenio Donato, 1970), Poulet writes: "And so the work forms the temporary mental substance which fills my consciousness; and it is moreover that consciousness, the *I*-subject, the continued consciousness of what is, revealing itself within the interior of the work. Such is the characteristic condition of every work which I summon back into existence by placing my own consciousness at its disposal." This "consciousness" is not identical with the author of the work: "Whatever may be the sum of the information I acquire on Baudelaire or Racine, in whatever degree of intimacy I may live with their genius, I am aware that this contribution does not suffice to illuminate for me its own inner meaning, in its formal perfection, and in the subjective principle which animates it, the particular work of Baudelaire or of Racine the reading of which now absorbs me. At this moment what matters to me is to live, from the inside, in a certain identity with the work and the work alone."

INTERPRETATION. In the critical theory of E. D. Hirsch, Jr., a term that denotes the ascertaining of the "meaning" of a text (see **MEANING**). In *Validity in Interpretation* (1967), Hirsch defines interpretation as "the construction of textual meaning as such; it explicates those meanings, and only those meanings, which the text explicitly or implicitly represents." The conception is contrasted to criticism, which "builds on the results of interpretation; it confronts textual meaning not as such, but as a component within a larger context. . . . The object of criticism . . . is . . . meaning in its bearing on something else (standards of value, present concerns, etc.) and this object may therefore be called the *significance* of the text."

IRONY. A use of language in which meanings other than, and usually antipodal to, that of the surface meaning of the words are suggested. The concept became central to the theory of poetry evolved by the New Criticism. In "Irony as a Principle of Structure" (1949; in *Literary Opinion in America,* ed. Morton Dauwen Zabel [rev. ed. 1951]), Cleanth Brooks writes: "Irony, taken as the acknowledgment of the pressures of context, is to be found in poetry of every period and even in simple lyrical poetry." Robert Penn Warren writes in "Pure and Impure Poetry" (1942): "The poet . . . proves his vision by submitting it to the fires of irony—to the drama of his structure—in the hope that the fires will refine it."

LITERARY HISTORY. The tracing of the historical development of literature as a whole or of facets or genres of literature. Literary history had its origins in antiquity, and the gathering of information about the lives of authors began in the Alexandrian age. Among the first works of literary history known to us is a lost work by Eratosthenes (c. 275–c. 194 B.C.), *On Old Comedy.* Thomas Warton's *History of English Poetry* (1774–81) and Samuel Johnson's *Lives of the Poets* (1779–81) gave much impetus to literary history, and it was widely practiced throughout the nineteenth century, especially by Hippolyte Taine (*Histoire de la littérature anglaise,* 1863–64), George Saintsbury (*A Short History of English Literature,* 1898; *A History of Criticism,* 1900–04), and many others. Although the very practice of literary history has been attacked by the New Critics, Northrop Frye, and others, René Wellek (whose *History of Modern Criticism* [1955–86] is regarded as a landmark) defends it in "Literary Theory, Criticism, and History" (in *Concepts of Criticism,* 1963) in an explicit response to Frye: "Literary theories, principles, criteria cannot be arrived at *in vacuo:* every critic in history has developed his theory in contact (as has Frye himself) with concrete works of art which he has had to select, interpret, analyze and, after all, to judge. The literary opinions, rankings, and judgments of a critic are buttressed, confirmed, developed by his theories, and the theories are drawn from, supported, illustrated, made concrete and plausible by works of art. The relegation, in Frye's *Anatomy of Criticism,* of concrete criticisms, judgments, evaluations to an arbitrary, irrational, and meaningless 'history of taste' seems to me as indefensible as the recent attempts to doubt the whole enterprise of literary theory and to absorb all literary study into history."

LOGOCENTRISM. A term created by Jacques Derrida in the context of his critical theory of deconstruction (see **DECONSTRUCTION**), and referring to what Derrida feels is the erroneous belief that the meaning of a word can be ascertained independently of the structure of the language in which the word is used. In other contexts the term appears to be used to denote the apparently erroneous belief that the meaning of a word can be definitively determined by its user (what Derrida calls the "metaphysics of 'presence'"). Critics of deconstruction observe that the first meaning is little different from the philosophical conception of *essentialism,* the belief that words denote real categories of meaning existing outside of language. The second meaning appears very similar to the intentional fallacy (see **INTENTIONAL FALLACY**).

LOGOLOGY. A term created by Kenneth Burke, literally meaning "words about words" and used by Burke as an umbrella term for all linguistic discussions: "Here is the realm of dictionaries, grammar, etymology, philology, literary criticism, rhetoric, poetics, dialectics—all that I like to think of as coming to a head in the discipline I would want to call 'Logology'" (*The Rhetoric of Religion,* 1961).

MARXIST CRITICISM. Criticism that employs the sociopolitical theories of Karl Marx (1818–1883) and seeks to reveal the underlying, frequently unconscious, ideological biases embedded in literary works. Among the leading Marxist critics (although perhaps they would not all be happy with the label) are Raymond Williams, Walter Benjamin, Georg Lukács, Fredric Jameson, and Terry Eagleton. A literal adherence to Marxist critical theory would lead to the assertion that all human institutions, including literature, are governed by the "means of production"—the fundamental socioeconomic forces that shape society—and that no literary work can escape from reflecting in some capacity the prevailing ideology of the society. More flexible Marxist critics grant a greater element of autonomy to literature, but still emphasize the degree to which political and ideological concerns enter into the very fabric of literary and even critical writing; Eagleton, in *Literary Theory* (1983), criticizes literary theoreticians for failing to acknowledge the political assumptions they make: "Literary theories are not to be upbraided for being political, but for being on the whole covertly or unconsciously so—for the blindness with which they offer as a supposedly 'technical', 'self-evident', 'scientific' or 'universal' truth doctrines which with a little reflection can be seen to relate to and reinforce the particular interests of particular groups of people at particular times." From a slightly different perspective, Frank Lentricchia (*Criticism and Social Change*, 1983) and Edward W. Said (*The World, the Text, and the Critic*, 1983) urge critics to become more conscious of their sociopolitical environment and to address a broader range of political issues in their writing.

MEANING. In his *Letter to Can Grande* (c. 1316) Dante distinguishes two types of meaning: "The first meaning is the one obtained through the letter; the second is the one obtained through the things signified by the letter. The first is called literal, the second allegorical or moral or anagogical." Although many critics have employed the term in various contexts, two technical uses of it occur in the critical theories of I. A. Richards and E. D. Hirsch, Jr. In *Practical Criticism* (1929) Richards suggests that meaning has four subcategories: 1) sense (what the speaker is saying), 2) feeling (the speaker's attitude to what he is saying), 3) tone (the speaker's attitude to his listener), and 4) intention (the speaker's aim, "*conscious or unconscious,* the effect he is endeavouring to promote"). Hirsch equates the term with *Sinn,* deriving the usage from the linguistic theories of Edmund Husserl and Gottlob Frege. For Hirsch, meaning is what the author meant in writing a text, and is unchanging. The author's meaning is not identical to his "intention," and so escapes the intentional fallacy (see **INTENTIONAL FALLACY**); it is the "content" of the author's intention. The task of interpretation is to ascertain the meaning of a text (see **INTERPRETATION**).

MIMESIS. Literally, Greek for "imitation." Plato maintained that the actual world is only an inferior imitation of ideal "forms" (*ideai*), and that art is an inferior imitation of the actual world, so that it is twice removed from reality: "All poetical imitations are ruinous to the understanding of the hearers, unless as an antidote they possess the knowledge of the true nature of the originals" (*Republic*, Book 10). Aristotle in the *Poetics* also affirmed that artists are "imitators," but with some important differences. Aristotle believed that "imitation is natural to man from childhood," so that artistic imitation answers a deep-seated need in the individual. The artist does not imitate (or represent) objects, as Plato believed, but "actions," and mimesis will be of value insofar as the representation is true and leads to a catharsis in the reader or spectator (see **CATHARSIS**). In *Mimesis: The Representation of Reality in Western Literature* (1953) Erich Auerbach undertakes a history of mimesis from antiquity to the present; Auerbach sees a radical shift in mimetic representation in the "realist" movement of the early nineteenth century (see **REALISM**), where "ordinary" people were portrayed for the first time in literature.

MODERNISM. A literary and critical movement of the early twentieth century, principally associated with James Joyce, Virginia Woolf, T. S. Eliot, Ezra Pound, T. E. Hulme, and others. Although a very diverse movement, its focus is the notion that there was a radical break in culture at this time (as Woolf says in "Mr. Bennett and Mrs. Brown" [1924], "on or about December, 1910, human character changed"), requiring radically different forms of expression. The increased complexity of modern life demands a corresponding complexity of thought and diction in literature. Eliot writes in "The Metaphysical Poets" (1921): "We can only say that it appears likely that poets in our civilization, as it exists at present, must be *difficult*. Our civilization comprehends great variety and complexity, and this variety and complexity, playing upon a refined sensibility, must produce various and complex results. The poet must become more and more comprehensive, more allusive, more indirect, in order to force, to dislocate if necessary, language into his meaning." Eliot and Pound sought to exemplify this complexity through their allusive poetry, Joyce and Woolf through their stream-of-consciousness novels, and Hulme through his recommendation to slough off the constraints of formal meter and the creation of an "impressionist poetry" to reflect the "modern conception of the poetic spirit, this tentative and half-shy manner of looking at things" ("A Lecture on Modern Poetry" [c. 1908]).

NEGATIVE CAPABILITY. A term coined by John Keats in a letter to George and Thomas Keats (December 22, 1817): "I had not a dispute but a disquisition with [Sir Charles Wentworth] Dilke, on various subjects; several things dovetailed in my mind, and at once it struck me what quality went to form a Man of Achievement especially in Literature and which Shakespeare possessed so enormously—I mean *Negative Capability*, that is when a man is capable of being in uncertainties, Mysteries, doubts, without any irritable reaching after fact and reason . . . This pursued through Volumes would perhaps take us no further than this, that with a great poet the sense of Beauty overcomes every other consideration, or rather obliterates all consideration."

NEOCLASSICISM. A movement of the seventeenth and eighteenth centuries that emphasized adherence to "classical" (i.e., Greek and Latin) standards of literary expression. Neoclassicists claimed to find in the ancients such conceptions as decorum, unity (leading to the adoption of the dramatic unities [see **DRAMATIC UNITIES**]), universality, and objectivity. John Dryden, in the "Preface to the *Aeneis*" (1697), enunciates many principles of neoclassical critical thought in speaking of Vergil: "I had also studied Virgil's design, his disposition of it, his manners, his judicious management of the figures, the sober retrenchments of his sense, which always leaves somewhat to gratify our imagination, on which it may enlarge at pleasure; but, above all, the elegance of his expressions and the harmony of his numbers." It was a lack of unity and harmony that Samuel Johnson claimed to be the principal failing of the metaphysical poets: "As they were wholly employed on something unexpected and surprising, they had no regard to that uniformity of sentiment which enables us to conceive and to excite the pains and the pleasure of other minds" ("Life of Cowley," *Lives of the Poets* [1779–81]). A reaction to these tenets in the late eighteenth century led to the Romantic movement (see **ROMANTICISM**), whereas a reaction to Romanticism in the early twentieth century led to a partial return to such qualities as impersonality and objectivity in the work of T. S. Eliot, Ezra Pound, and others (see **MODERNISM**).

NEW CRITICISM. A school of criticism associated with such British critics as I. A. Richards, F. R. Leavis, and William Empson, and such American critics as T. S. Eliot, Cleanth Brooks, Robert Penn Warren, John Crowe Ransom, Allen Tate, and W. K. Wimsatt. Reacting to the emphasis on biographical and historical study in later nineteenth-century criticism, the New Critics stressed that a literary work is an independent object that must be examined without reference to authorial intention or historical circumstances. Adopting Richards's belief that literature presented "pseudo statements" (i.e., statements not subject to verification by reference to the facts of nature), the New Critics claimed that literature embodied a kind of "knowledge" different from but not inferior to the knowledge provided by scientific inquiry. Although many theoretical presuppositions of the New Criticism have subsequently been attacked (can a literary work really be regarded as independent of its authorial source and the historical circumstances of its creation? What is the actual nature of the "knowledge" supplied by literature?), and although the New Critics were accused of being politically reactionary and indifferent to literature as a social force, the New Criticism's practice of "close reading" (a very careful study of the actual text of a work, in place of vague generalities or impressionistic criticism) has been incorporated into most subsequent critical methodologies. See also **AMBIGUITY; IRONY; PARADOX.**

OBJECTIVE CORRELATIVE. A term coined by T. S. Eliot in his essay "Hamlet and His Problems" (1919): "The only way of expressing emotion in the form of art is by finding an 'objective correlative'; in other words, a set of objects, a situation, a chain of events which shall be the formula of that *particular* emotion; such that when the external facts, which must terminate in sensory experience, are given, the emotion is immediately evoked." Eliot claimed that *Hamlet* is "an artistic failure" because it fails to find this objective correlative: "Hamlet (the man) is dominated by an emotion which is inexpressible, because it is in *excess* of the facts as they appear. And the supposed identity of Hamlet with his author is genuine to this point: that Hamlet's bafflement at the absence of objective equivalent to his feelings is a prolongation of the bafflement of his creator in the face of his artistic problem."

PARADOX. In the critical theory of Cleanth Brooks and the New Critics generally, a central component of poetry. As Brooks writes in "The Language of Paradox" (in *The Well Wrought Urn*, 1947), "there is a sense in which paradox is the language appropriate and inevitable to poetry. It is the scientist whose truth requires a language purged of every trace of paradox; apparently the truth which the poet utters can be approached only in terms of paradox." Paradox is not merely something the poet uses to convey his message; it is inherent in the very nature of poetry: "even the apparently simple and straightforward poet is forced into paradoxes by the nature of his instrument."

PARNASSIANS, THE. A group of poets in later nineteenth-century France who rebelled against the dominant Romanticism and realism of the period and who advocated the art for art's sake credo (see **ART FOR ART'S SAKE**); their name was derived from a series of volumes, *Le Parnasse contemporain,* containing poetry by members of the group. Théophile Gautier, an early proponent of art for art's sake, was looked upon as a precursor of the Parnassians, whose leading figures were Charles-Marie-René Leconte de Lisle, José Maria de Hérédia, Anatole France, Paul Verlaine, and Stéphane Mallarmé. An important tenet of the movement was the poet's freedom to write in an individual and personal style; Mallarmé writes in "Crisis in Poetry" (1886–95): "For the first time in the literary history of any nation, along with the general and traditional great organ of orthodox verse which finds its ecstasy on an ever-ready keyboard, any poet with an individual technique and ear can build his own instrument, so long as his fluting, bowing, or drumming are accomplished—play that instrument and dedicate it, along with others, to Language." See also **SYMBOLISM**.

PATHETIC FALLACY. A term coined by John Ruskin in *Modern Painters*, Volume 3 (1856), to refer to the attribution of human feelings to nonhuman objects. Ruskin did not, however, consider this poetic device to be universally fallacious. In commenting on a passage in Charles Kingsley's *Alton Locke,* "They rowed her in across the rolling foam— / The cruel, crawling foam," Ruskin remarks: "The foam is not cruel, neither does it crawl. The state of mind which attributes to it these characters of a living creature is one in which the reason is unhinged by grief." But later Ruskin states: "Now so long as we see that the *feeling* is true, we pardon, or are even pleased by, the confessed fallacy of sight which it induces: we are pleased, for instance, with those lines of Kingsley's . . . not because they fallaciously describe foam, but because they faithfully describe sorrow. But the moment the mind of the speaker becomes cold, that moment every such expression becomes untrue, as being for ever untrue in the external facts. And there is no greater baseness in literature than the habit of using these metaphorical expressions in cold blood."

PHENOMENOLOGICAL CRITICISM. Criticism that is founded upon the philosophy of Edmund Husserl (1859–1938) and others. Husserl regarded the Kantian distinction between "phenomena" (objects as the mind perceives them) and "noumena" (objects as they "really" are) as artificial and unverifiable, and asserted that consciousness is always "intentional," i.e., directed toward some "object"; there is as a result an inextricable union between the "object" and the mind that "intends" it. Roman Ingarden (1893–1970) was among the first to apply Husserl's theories to literature. Ingarden believed that a literary work is "intentional" in the sense that it embodies the intentional acts of the author (which are not identical to "authorial intention" in the usual sense). The reader then "concretizes" the text by re-experiencing the work in his own consciousness, filling in the "places of indeterminancy" in a text (a process similar to Wolfgang Iser's theory of the ideal reader [see **READER-RESPONSE CRITICISM**]). See Ingarden's *The Literary Work of Art* (1931). The phenomenological approach to literature was adopted and modified by members of the so-called Geneva School, whose leading figures were Georges Poulet, Marcel Raymond, Jean-Pierre Richard, and the early J. Hillis Miller (for Poulet, see **INTERIORITY**). E. D. Hirsch, Jr., has also made use of Husserl's phenomenology (see **MEANING**).

PHILOSOPHICAL CRITICISM. The analysis of the philosophical foundations of a literary work. The philosophical analysis of literature may be thought to have had its origin in Aristotle, who in the *Poetics* (1415b) writes: "The distinction between historian and poet is not in the one writing prose and the other verse—you might put the work of Herodotus into verse, and it would still be a species of history; it consists really in this, that the one describes the thing that has been, and the other a kind of thing that might be. Hence poetry is something more philosophic and of graver import than history, since its statements are of the nature rather of universals, whereas those of history are singulars." In the nineteenth century Leslie Stephen (1832–1904) did much philosophical criticism, including such essays as "Wordsworth's Ethics" (1876) and others gathered in his *Hours in a Library* (1874–79). In "Philosophy and the Form of Fiction" (in *Fiction and the Figures of Life,* 1970), William H. Gass argues for a fundamental similarity between philosophy and literature ("Novelist and philosopher are both obsessed with language, and make themselves up out of concepts. Both, in a way, create worlds"), but argues that the philosophical analysis of fiction must be conducted with care and subtlety: "The philsophical analysis of fiction has scarcely taken its first steps. Philosophers continue to interpret novels as if they were philosophies themselves, platforms to speak from, middens from which may be scratched important messages for mankind; they have predictably looked for content, not form; they have regarded fictions as ways of viewing reality and not as additions to it." See also **ETHICAL CRITICISM.**

POSTMODERNISM. A nebulous term for a period of literary and cultural history succeeding Modernism (see **MODERNISM**) and commencing roughly in the

1960s. Postmodernism appears to be an umbrella term for a broad-based rejection of many of the fundamental tenets of Modernism, and has had a number of ramifications for critical theory. T. S. Eliot's notion of "impersonality" and the New Criticism's emphasis on the literary work as an independent aesthetic object have given way to a renewed interest in the political, social, or ethical relevance of literature and criticism, whether in a Marxist context (Fredric Jameson, Terry Eagleton) or otherwise (Edward W. Said, Frank Lentricchia, Wayne C. Booth). The fundamentally empiricist approach of New Criticism and structuralism, as well as Northrop Frye's attempt to establish criticism on a "scientific" basis, has yielded to the skepticism of poststructuralism (Michel Foucault, Jacques Lacan) and deconstruction (Jacques Derrida and his followers). A reaction to what was seen as the chauvinism and Eurocentrism of the Modernists has led to a broadening of interest in literature of all types, including women's writing (see **FEMINIST CRITICISM**), black literature (Henry Louis Gates, Jr.), non-European writing (Edward W. Said, Ihab Hassan), and, in general, a breakdown in the notion of a recognizable "canon" of literary classics (see **CANON**), as genre fiction (science fiction, fantasy, detective fiction) and the mass media have come under critical scrutiny (Susan Sontag, Gore Vidal, Leslie A. Fiedler, Richard Poirier). See further *Postmodernism and Politics,* ed. Jonathan Arac (1986); Ihab Hassan, *The Postmodern Turn* (1987).

POSTSTRUCTURALISM. A diverse movement growing out of the logical difficulties perceived in structuralism (see **STRUCTURALISM**) and associated with such thinkers as Michel Foucault, Jacques Lacan, and Jacques Derrida; Derrida's theory of deconstruction (see **DECONSTRUCTION**) is now the dominant poststructuralist critical theory. Structuralism had rested upon Ferdinand de Saussure's analysis of the *sign* as consisting of a *signifier* (a verbal sound) combined with a *signified* (the "concept" to be expressed); but Saussure's vagueness as to what the "concept" actually is, coupled with the perception that the signified is not independent of language but merely more words, led to a radical skepticism that rejected entirely the referential theory of language (as Saussure had not quite done). It is impossible to determine any logical relation between language and the "real" world; all that is left is an infinite "play" of language, where meanings are never exhausted. The notion of the "self" is itself a product of language, and Foucault studies this phenomenon in *The Order of Things* (1966) and *The Archeology of Knowledge* (1969). For Lacan, see **PSYCHOANALYTIC CRITICISM;** for Derrida, see **DECONSTRUCTION.**

PRACTICAL CRITICISM. A type of criticism that focuses upon the emotions directly felt by a reader from a literary work, without reference to the historical background of the work or other features "external" to it. D. H. Lawrence's comment in "John Galsworthy" (in *Scrutinies,* ed. Edgell Rickword [1928]) is thought to encapsulate the method of practical criticism: "Literary criticism can be no more than a reasoned account of the effect produced upon the critic by the book he is criticising." Practical criticism claims to function without theoretical presuppositions, although critical theorists maintain that such presuppositions are covertly present in any sort of critical writing; in particular, the methodology of practical criticism appears susceptible to the affective fallacy (see **AFFECTIVE FALLACY**). In *Practical Criticism* (1929) I. A. Richards records the results of an experiment whereby a series of poems from standard authors, with the authors' names not indicated, were given to undergraduates for analysis.

PRE-RAPHAELITES. A group of artists of the late nineteenth century, led by Dante Gabriel Rossetti, William Holman Hunt, John Everett Millais, and others, who sought to recapture the style of medieval painting prior to Raphael (1483–1520). The movement was vigorously defended by John Ruskin in *Modern Painters* (1843–60) and *Pre-Raphaelitism* (1851), and the artists influenced such writers as William Morris, Christina Rossetti, and others. The Pre-Raphaelites were violently attacked by Max Nordau in *Degeneration* (1895) for their purported subversion of morality; George Bernard Shaw responded to Nordau in "The Sanity of Art" (1895).

PSYCHOANALYTIC CRITICISM. Criticism that employs various psychological or psychoanalytic theories in the interpretation of literature. Freudian criticism seeks to apply the theories of Sigmund Freud to literature (see **FREUDIAN CRITICISM**). Jungian criticism applies the theories of Carl Gustav Jung (1875–1961), who asserted that all human consciousness draws upon a "collective unconscious" that shapes our view of the world. Jungian criticism is interested in tracing in literature and art the archetypes or universal symbols representative of the collective unconscious (see **ARCHETYPAL CRITICISM**). More recently, Jacques Lacan has melded psychoanalysis and structuralism and evolved the view that the structure of the unconscious is analogous to the structure of language, so that the analysis of language will provide insights into unconscious states. Other noted psychoanalytic critics are Julia Kristeva, Shoshana Felman, and Harold Bloom (see **ANXIETY OF INFLUENCE**). For Angus Fletcher's use of psychoanalytic criticism, see **ALLEGORY**.

PSYCHOLOGY OF FORM. In the critical theory of Kenneth Burke, the idea that an element of a literary work must gain its relevance not from the intrinsic interest of its content (which Burke labels "the psychology of information") but from its function in the work itself. In *Counter-Statement* (1931) Burke writes: "In information, the matter is intrinsically interesting.... In art, ... the matter is interesting by means of an extrinsic use, a function. Consider, for instance, the speech of Mark Antony, the 'Brutus is an honorable man.' Imagine in the same place a very competently developed thesis on human conduct, with statistics, intelligence tests, definitions; imagine it as the finest thing of the sort ever written, and as really being at the roots of an understanding of Brutus. Obviously, the play would simply stop until Antony had finished. For in the case of Antony's speech, the value lies in the fact that his words are shaping the future of the audience's desires, not the desires of the Roman populace, but the desires of the pit. This is the psychology of form as distinguished from the psychology of information." The idea appears related to Poe's notion of the unity of effect (see **UNITY OF EFFECT**).

PURE POETRY. Defined by Robert Penn Warren in "Pure and Impure Poetry" (1942) as follows: "The pure poem tries to be pure by excluding, more or less rigidly, certain elements which might qualify or contradict its original impulse. In other words, the pure poems want to be, and desperately, all of a piece." Warren believes that this position, ascribed by many critics to Edgar Allan Poe (for whose opposition of "truth" and "beauty" see **DIDACTICISM**), has in fact been espoused in varying forms by many theorists, including Sir Philip Sidney, John Dryden, Percy Bysshe Shelley, and others. Warren asserts that many poets have desired the exclusion from poetry of such things as ideas, irony, unbeautiful material, logical transition, and other features perhaps more closely associated with prose, but claims that "impure" poetry embodying these and other features may be more truly reflective of the complexity of human existence.

READER-RESPONSE CRITICISM. The analysis of a reader's response to a literary text. The movement was originated by Hans Robert Jauss, who coined the term *Rezeptionsästhetik* ("aesthetic of reception") to denote the "horizon of expectations" against which a work is both written and read. It was Jauss's claim that a defining quality of literature was the degree to which it expanded or confounded a reader's expectations. Jauss's work was taken up by Wolfgang Iser, who evolved the notion of the "implied reader" (see *The Implied Reader: Patterns of Communication in Prose Fiction*, 1974) or "ideal reader," as opposed to the "real reader." Iser writes: "The real reader is invoked mainly in studies of the history of responses, i.e., when attention is focused on the way in which a literary work has been received by a specific reading public" (*The Act of Reading,* 1976). The ideal reader, on the other hand (which Iser admits is "a purely fictional being"), is one for whom the text is written and who can supply the gaps and indeterminacies that always exist in a text and so can "actualize" it. Stanley E. Fish gives still greater weight to the reader. He rejects the notion that "meanings can be specified independently of the activity of reading"; criticism, therefore, should be concerned with "the structure of the reader's experience rather than any structures available on the page" ("Interpreting the *Variorum*," 1976). Meaning does not reside *in* a text, but is a result of the interaction of text and reader. This interaction, however, will not lead to an infinity of diverse interpretation, because there are "interpretive communities" that govern or limit the interpretations any given reader makes on a text. Fish has been attacked for his assertion that "positivist" or "formalist" critics are tied to the belief that a text has only "one" meaning (something that has almost never been asserted in modern criticism), and other reader-response critics have been attacked for believing that it is impossible to ascertain whether one reader's interpretation of a text is "better" or more accurate than another's.

REALISM. A movement of the early nineteenth century that stressed the portrayal of ordinary people and the workings of their daily lives, generally with an emphasis upon middle- or lower-class individuals, who had hitherto been ignored in literature. Realism is generally associated with the novel in France (Honoré de Balzac) and England (Charles Dickens, George Elliot, William Makepeace Thackeray). In the later nineteenth century the concept was extended into *Naturalism,* which argued that the novelist was essentially a scientist depicting the biologically determined nature of human life; Emile Zola was a leading practitioner of this form, and his influence can be felt in the work of Theodore Dreiser, Sinclair Lewis, and others. In the twentieth century many writers found the purely realistic novel to be too confining a mode, and the introduction of stream-of-consciousness (Virginia Woolf, James Joyce), fantasy (Franz Kafka, Jorge Luis Borges, Thomas Pynchon), and other elements has expanded modern conceptions of the novel. Such writers as Saul Bellow, John Updike, and Bernard Malamud, however, continue writing in a predominantly realist manner. In "French Letters: Theories of the New Novel" (1967) Gore Vidal defends the "traditional novel" against attacks by those who advocate the "New Novel" (in which radical innovations of style, form, and technique are sought). Directing his argument against Alain Robbe-Grillet, Vidal writes: "It is worrisome to be told that a man can create a world from nothing when that is the one thing he cannot begin to do, simply because, no matter how hard he tries, he cannot dispose of himself. Even if what he writes is no more than nouns and adjectives, who and what he is will subconsciously dictate order."

RE-VISION. A term coined by Adrienne Rich and defined as "the act of looking back, of seeing with fresh eyes, of entering an old text from a new critical direction" but applied specifically to a feminist reading of literature and, more generally, a feminist approach to life. As Rich writes in "When We Dead Awaken: Writing as Re-vision" (1971; in *On Lies, Secrets, and Silence,* 1979): "Re-vision . . . is for women more than a chapter in cultural history: it is an act of survival. Until we can understand the assumptions in which we are drenched we cannot know ourselves. And this drive to self-knowledge, for women, is more than a search for identity: it is part of our refusal of the self-destructiveness of male-dominated society."

ROMANTICISM. A movement of the late eighteenth and early nineteenth centuries in Germany, England, and France, born of a reaction to what were seen as the stifling literary and critical theories of neoclassicism (see **NEOCLASSICISM**). Romanticism emphasized such qualities as subjectivity, spontaneity, reunification with the natural world, and interest in less refined states of consciousness (e.g., childhood, as in Wordsworth's "Ode: Intimations of Immortality") or culture (e.g., the Middle Ages, as in the novels of Sir Walter Scott). Wordsworth summed up the Romantic conception of poetry by defining it as "the spontaneous overflow of powerful feelings" ("Preface" [1800] to *Lyrical Ballads*). Shelley, in "A Defence of Poetry" (1821), wrote: "Poetry is indeed something divine. It is at once the centre and circumference of knowledge; it is that which comprehends all science, and that to which all science must be referred." This elevation of poetry above science and philosophy led to the Romantics' sense of the aesthetic and moral superiority of the artist and his freedom from the constraints of conventional society (as in the figure of Lord Byron). By the turn of the twentieth century this "bardolatry," as it was derisively termed, led to the New Critics' championing of the poem at the expense of the poet. The Romantics also stressed the idea of originality, a quality in art not previously given much importance; as W. Jackson Bate notes in *The Burden of the Past and the English Poet* (1970), this stance eventually led to the sense of a "burden of the past" wherein the artist was overwhelmed by the difficulty of saying anything new or fresh in light of the enormous amount of literature already written. Bate sees this notion continuing to haunt modern literature; Harold Bloom interprets it somewhat differently in his conception of the anxiety of influence (see **ANXIETY OF INFLUENCE**).

SECULAR CRITICISM. In the critical theory of Edward W. Said, a type of criticism that eschews the political irrelevance of abstract critical theory and engages in political, social, and ethical issues. As Said writes in his "Introduction: Secular Criticism" (in *The World, the Text, and the Critic*, 1983): "Criticism in short is always situated; it is skeptical, secular, reflectively open to its own failings. This is by no means to say that it is value-free. Quite the contrary, for the inevitable trajectory of critical consciousness is to arrive at some acute sense of what political, social, and human values are entailed in the reading, production, and transmission of every text. To stand between culture and system is therefore to stand *close to* . . . a concrete reality about which political, moral, and social judgements have to be made and, if not only made, then exposed and demystified."

SEMIOTICS/SEMIOLOGY. The study of "signs." A sign is interpreted very widely to mean not only language but bodily gestures, clothing, and anything else that communicates a "meaning" to an individual or to a culture. Semiotics as a philosophical discipline was founded in the late nineteenth century by C. S. Peirce (1839–1914), and Ferdinand de Saussure initiated the linguistic study of signs. Saussure, who defined the sign as the union of *signifier* and *signified* (see **STRUCTURALISM**), also made a fundamental distinction between *parole* (a single word used by an actual speaker) and *langue* (the whole framework of a language that underlies and makes possible the use of *paroles*). Semioticians are concerned with *langue* not only in the sense of linguistic structures that shape the actual use of language but with other hierarchical structures in society. Semiotics has tended to be subsumed under the more developed theory of structuralism.

SOCIOLOGICAL CRITICISM. Criticism that studies the relationship between literature and society. Sociological criticism is thought to have had its origins in the work of Madame de Staël, who in such works as *De la littérature considerée* *dans ses rapports avec les institutions sociales* (1800) and *De l'Allemagne* (1810) traced the differences between French and German literature to differences in the sociological characteristics of the two nations. Sociological criticism focuses upon such issues as the relation of the author to society, the social standing of readers, the history of taste, and the like. Many literary critics object to sociological criticism on the grounds that it diminishes the literary work as an autonomous aesthetic entity, but sociological critics counter that the literary work can never be autonomous in any event. See also **HISTORICISM; MARXIST CRITICISM**.

STRUCTURALISM. A movement, growing out of Russian Formalism and the anthropology of Claude Lévi-Strauss and associated with such French critics as Tzvetan Todorov and Roland Barthes, that sought to apply the linguistic theories of Ferdinand de Saussure (1857–1913) to the study of literature. Saussure asserted that all knowledge is dependent upon language; nothing can be known unless it is formulated into language. Meaning results when a *signifier* (a verbal sound) and a *signified* (the "concept" to be expressed) unite into the *sign* (a word); but the sign does not "denote" anything in the world but is only a concept in the mind. A sign is "arbitrary" in that there is no logical connection between the sound of the word and the concept it signifies. All signs gain meaning only in the context of a given linguistic "structure." (It is, however, a mistake to assert that Saussure completely rejected the "referential" theory of language; i.e., that language refers to entities in the real world.) Just as Lévi-Strauss studied the structure of myth (see "The Structural Study of Myth," in *Structural Anthropology,* 1958), the structuralists are concerned with studying the elements and rules of language in an effort to ascertain both the functioning of language in human society and the structure of human consciousness, which is shaped by language. Structuralism has gradually given way to poststructuralism (see **POSTSTRUCTURALISM**), and both Todorov and Barthes appear to have moved away from the structuralist theories they had adopted in their early work.

SUBLIME. Defined by "Longinus" in *On Sublimity* (first century A.D.) as "a kind of eminence or excellence of discourse. It is the source of the distinction of the very greatest poets and prose writers and the means by which they have given eternal life to their own fame. For grandeur produces ecstasy rather than persuasion in the hearer; and the combination of wonder and astonishment always proves superior to the merely persuasive and pleasant." Longinus identifies five sources of sublimity: 1) the power to conceive great thoughts; 2) strong and inspired emotion; 3) certain kinds of figures; 4) noble diction; and 5) dignified and elevated word-arrangement. In the eighteenth century Edmund Burke modified Longinus somewhat in *A Philosophical Enquiry into the Origin of Our Ideas of the Sublime and Beautiful* (1756). Burke contrasted the sublime and the beautiful, associating the latter merely with pleasure but saying of the former: "Whatever is fitted in any sort to excite the ideas of pain and danger, that is to say, whatever is in any sort terrible, or is conversant about terrible objects, or operates in a manner analogous to terror, is a source of the *sublime;* that is, it is productive of the strongest emotion which the mind is capable of feeling. I say the strongest emotion, because I am satisfied the ideas of pain are much more powerful than those which enter on the part of pleasure." See also Immanuel Kant, "The Beautiful and the Sublime" (1764); Friedrich Schiller, "On the Sublime" (1793).

SURREALISM. A literary and artistic movement of the early twentieth century, largely in France, that grew out of and subsumed Dadaism (see **DADAISM**). The Surrealists wished to revise or alter our habitual notions of reality through seemingly illogical juxtapositions, use of dreams, madness, and hallucination, and other ostensibly irrational or antirational techniques. André Breton, the major spokesman of the movement, wrote in *The Manifesto of Surrealism* (1924): "Surrealism is based on the belief in the superior reality of certain forms of previously neglected associations, in the omnipotence of dream, in the disinterested play of thought. It tends to ruin once and for all all other psychic mechanisms and to substitute itself for them in solving all the principal problems of life."

SUSPENSION OF DISBELIEF. A term coined by Samuel Taylor Coleridge to denote the reader's acquiescence in the depiction of unusual phenomena in literature. In *Biographia Literaria* (1817), ch. 14, Coleridge speaks of the plan of the *Lyrical Ballads,* "in which it was agreed that my endeavours should be directed to persons and characters supernatural, or at least romantic; yet so as to transfer from our inward nature a human interest and a semblance of truth sufficient to procure for these shadows of imagination that willing suspension of disbelief for the moment, which constitutes poetic faith." This conception has often been used as a goal for the writer of supernatural fiction, who must write in such a fashion as to convince the reader momentarily of the reality of the unreal. In "Notes on Writing Weird Fiction" (c. 1932) H. P. Lovecraft writes: "One cannot . . . present an account of impossible, improbable, or inconceivable phenomena as a commonplace narration of objective acts and conventional emotions. Inconceivable events and conditions have a special handicap to overcome, and this can be accomplished only through the maintenance of a careful realism in every phase of the story *except* that touching on the one given marvel."

SYMBOLISM. A late nineteenth-century movement, mostly in France, that sought to use words as "symbols" representing an occult, nonrational mode of knowledge. The movement drew upon the work of William Blake and Charles Baudelaire, and its leading practitioners were Gérard de Nerval, Stéphane Mallarmé, and others. Symbolism has left its influence upon such later writers as Yeats, Joyce, and Eliot. Arthur Symons's *The Symbolist Movement in Literature* (1899) is an early account of the movement.

TEXTUAL CRITICISM. The study of the transmission of a text and the establishment of an accurate version of a text. Textual criticism had its origins in antiquity, when scholars produced critical editions of Homer, Hesiod, and others (see **ALEXANDRIANISM**). In the Middle Ages textual criticism was conducted by the writing of "glosses" or explanatory notes in the margins of manuscripts and in the ascertaining of possibly spurious lines or passages. In the Renaissance this activity was intensified in the critical work done on ancient and biblical texts by Julius Caesar Scaliger, Richard Porson, and others. In this century A. E. Housman was a leading textual scholar of classical texts. Shakespearean textual studies commenced in the early eighteenth century with Lewis Theobald, Samuel Johnson, and others, and continues to this day. In the twentieth century textual criticism (frequently conducted in conjunction with bibliography) has gained in breadth and sophistication under the leadership of W. W. Greg, Fredson T. Bowers, and many others. Bowers defends textual criticism as a valuable component of literary criticism in "Textual Criticism and the Literary Critic" (1959).

TOUCHSTONES. In the critical theory of Matthew Arnold, those great works of poetry that help us to judge the merits of poetry in general. As Arnold writes in his "Introduction" to *The English Poets* (1880), "There can be no more useful help in discovering what poetry belongs to the class of the truly excellent, and can therefore do us most good, than to have always in one's mind lines and expressions of the great masters, and to apply them as a touchstone to other poetry." Arnold feels that the distinguishing qualities or "marks" of great poetry are inherently indefinable: "But if we are asked to define this mark and accent in the abstract, our answer must be: No, for we should thereby be darkening the question, not clearing it."

UNITY OF EFFECT. A concept popularized by Edgar Allan Poe (although Poe himself, in his review of Longfellow [1842], attributes the notion of "the unity or totality of interest" to August Wilhelm von Schlegel), whereby every component of a literary work must have a direct bearing upon the climax or *dénouement* of the work. Poe writes in "The Philosophy of Composition" (1846): "Nothing is more clear than that every plot, worth the name, must be elaborated to its *dénouement* before anything be attempted with the pen. It is only with the *dénouement* constantly in view that we can give a plot its indispensable air of consequence, or causation, by making the incidents, and especially the tone at all points, tend to the development of the intention."

INDEX TO CRITICS

Abrams, M. H. 10:141
Addison, Joseph 4:25
Adorno, Theodor W. 9:295
Aristophanes 1:7
Aristotle 1:145
Arnold, Matthew 7:179
Ascham, Roger 2:185
Auden, W. H. 9:533
Auerbach, Erich 8:477
Auerbach, Nina 11:309
Augustine, St. 1:435
Bacon, Sir Francis 3:1
Bakhtin, Mikhail 9:109
Barthes, Roland 9:679
Bataille, Georges 10:3
Bate, W. Jackson 10:219
Baudelaire, Charles 7:127
Beauvoir, Simone de 9:589
Belinskii, V. G. 6:571
Benjamin, Walter 8:433
Bentley, Eric 10:191
Bersani, Leo 11:91
Blackmur, R. P. 9:311
Blake, William 5:119
Blanchot, Maurice 10:105
Bloom, Harold 10:601
Boccaccio, Giovanni 2:1
Boileau-Despréaux, Nicolas 3:289
Booth, Wayne C. 10:309
Bowers, Fredson T. 10:81
Brecht, Bertolt 8:613
Breton, André 8:583
Brisman, Leslie 11:339
Brooks, Cleanth 9:497
Browning, Robert 7:3
Burke, Edmund 4:281
Burke, Kenneth 9:181
Campion, Thomas 2:499
Carew, Thomas 3:509
Carlyle, Thomas 6:297
Castelvetro, Lodovico 2:211

Chapman, George 2:477, 3:119
Chernyshevsky, Nikolai 7:315
Cicero 1:221
Coleridge, Samuel Taylor 5:397
Collier, Jeremy 3:661
Congreve, William 3:661
Corneille, Pierre 3:261
Cowley, Abraham 3:245
Croce, Benedetto 8:103
Daniel, Samuel 2:521
Dante 1:493
Davenant, Sir William 3:197
de Man, Paul 10:259
Demetrius 1:211
Dennis, John 3:661
De Quincey, Thomas 6:103
Derrida, Jacques 11:33
Diderot, Denis 4:307
Dionysius of Halicarnassus 1:277
Donatus 1:425
Drayton, Michael 3:137
Dryden, John 3:357
Du Bellay, Joachim 2:139
Eagleton, Terry 11:319
Edel, Leon 10:129
Eikhenbaum, Boris 8:317
Eliot, George 7:105
Eliot, T. S. 8:391
Emerson, Ralph Waldo 6:381
Empson, William 9:473
Erasmus, Desiderius 2:85
Esslin, Martin 10:237
Euanthius 1:425
Felman, Shoshana 11:291
Fiedler, Leslie A. 10:205
Fielding, Henry 4:239
Fish, Stanley E. 11:197
Flaubert, Gustave 7:153
Fletcher, Angus 11:71
Foucault, Michel 10:453
Freud, Sigmund 8:33

Frye, Northrop 9:635
Fulgentius 1:479
Gadamer, Hans Georg 10:21
Gascoigne, George 2:241
Gates, Henry Louis, Jr. 11:365
Gay, John 4:89
Gilbert, Sandra M. 11:167
Giraldi Cintio, Giovanni Battista 2:121
Girard, René 10:347
Goethe, Johann Wolfgang von 5:55
Goldsmith, Oliver 4:249
Gorgias of Leontini 1:3
Gray, Thomas 4:355
Guarini, Giambattista 2:453
Gubar, Susan 11:167
Harington, Sir John 2:379
Hartman, Geoffrey 10:541
Harvey, Gabriel 2:357
Hassan, Ihab 10:371
Hazlitt, William 5:569
Hegel, G. W. F. 5:225
Heine, Heinrich 6:347
Herder, Johann Gottfried 5:95
Hermogenes 1:399
Hirsch, E. D., Jr. 10:485
Hobbes, Thomas 3:197
Hölderlin, Friedrich 6:3
Hollander, John 10:575
Horace 1:263
Hulme, T. E. 8:199
Hunt, Leigh 6:61
Iser, Wolfgang 10:433
James, Henry 7:507
Jameson, Fredric 11:121
Jeffrey, Francis 5:505
Johnson, Barbara 11:353
Johnson, Samuel 4:401
Jonson, Ben 3:71
"K., E." 2:263
Kant, Immanuel 5:3
Kazin, Alfred 10:177
Keats, John 6:249
Keble, John 6:209
Kenner, Hugh 10:333
Kermode, Frank 10:291
Kleist, Heinrich von 6:21
Knight, G. Wilson 9:135
Kristeva, Julia 11:251
Lacan, Jacques 9:265
Lamb, Charles 5:661
Lawrence, D. H. 8:241
Leavis, F. R. 9:51
Lentricchia, Frank 11:233
Leopardi, Giacomo 6:361
Lessing, Gotthold Ephraim 5:17
Levin, Harry 10:161
Lévi-Strauss, Claude 9:613
Longinus 1:323
Lukács, Georg 8:261
Mallarmé, Stéphane 7:479
Mazzoni, Jacopo 2:313
Meredith, George 7:235
Meres, Francis 2:487
Mill, John Stuart 6:485
Miller, J. Hillis 10:513
Milton, John 3:165
Minturno, Antonio 2:169
Montaigne, Michel Eyquem de 2:251
Nashe, Thomas 2:357
Newman, John Henry 6:209
Nietzsche, Friedrich 7:543
Novalis (G. F. P. von Hardenberg) 5:349
Ortega y Gasset, José 8:221
Pater, Walter 7:405
Peacock, Thomas Love 6:129
Petrarch 2:65
Plato 1:79
Plotinus 1:417
Plutarch 1:361
Poe, Edgar Allan 6:505
Poirier, Richard 10:395
Pope, Alexander 4:133
Poulet, Georges 10:51
Pound, Ezra 8:305
Proclus 1:467
Puttenham, George 2:333
Quintilian 1:285

INDEX TO CRITICS

Ransom, John Crowe 9:3
Rapin, René 3:331
Reynolds, Henry 3:137
Rich, Adrienne 10:589
Richards, I. A. 8:521
Robinson, Henry Crabb 5:525
Ruskin, John 7:21
Rymer, Thomas 3:549
Said, Edward W. 11:139
Saint-Evremond, Charles de 3:275
Sainte-Beuve, Charles-Augustin 6:465
Sartre, Jean-Paul 9:417
Scaliger, Julius Caesar 2:157
Schiller, Friedrich 5:153
Schlegel, Friedrich von 5:357
Schopenhauer, Arthur 6:141
Scott, Sir Walter 5:323
Shaftesbury, Anthony Ashley Cooper, Third, Earl of 4:3
Shaw, George Bernard 8:3
Shelley, Percy Bysshe 6:169
Shklovsky, Victor 8:557
Showalter, Elaine 11:275
Sidney, Sir Philip 2:271
Sontag, Susan 11:105
Spitzer, Leo 8:361
Staël, Madame de 5:183
Steele, Sir Richard 4:25
Stendhal (Henri Beyle) 6:29
Stevens, Wallace 8:143
Swift, Jonathan 4:97
Swinburne, Algernon Charles 7:347
Tasso, Torquato 2:399
Tate, Allen 9:217
Temple, Sir William 3:615
Todorov, Tzvetan 11:219
Tolstoy, Leo 7:267
Trilling, Lionel 9:377
Trissino, Giangiorgio 2:105
Tzara, Tristan 8:349
Valéry, Paul 8:123
Vico, Giambattista 4:183
Vidal, Gore 10:413
Walker, Alice 11:347
Walton, Izaak 3:509
Warren, Robert Penn 9:451
Webster, John 3:119
Wellek, René 10:67
Whitman, Walt 7:79
Wilde, Oscar 7:649
Williams, Raymond 11:3
Wilson, Edmund 9:23
Wimsatt, W. K. 9:555
Winters, Yvor 9:227
Woolf, Virginia 8:169
Wordsworth, William 5:269
Yeats, W. B. 8:69
Young, Edward 4:365

INDEX TO WORKS

Act of Reading, The (Iser) 10:435
Address to the Reader by the Tragedy of Orbecche, An (Giraldi Cintio) 2:123
Advancement of Learning, The (Bacon) 3:3
Adventurer, The (Johnson) 4:426
Age of Elizabeth, The (Hazlitt) 5:646
Agon: Revisionism and Critical Personality (Bloom) 10:622
Allegory (Fletcher) 11:73
Anatomy of Criticism (Frye) 9:637
Ancient and Modern (Goethe) 5:65
Anima Poetae (Coleridge) 5:399
Annotations to Boyd's Dante (Blake) 5:130
Annotations to Wordsworth's Excursion (Blake) 5:148
Annotations to Wordsworth's Poems (Blake) 5:146
Antibarbarians, The (Erasmus) 2:87
Anxiety of Influence, The (Bloom) 10:605
Apology for Dido, The (Giraldi Cintio) 2:126
Apology for Poetry, An (Sidney) 2:273
Apology for Smectymnuus (Milton) 3:180
Appendix to the "Preface" (Wordsworth) 5:300
Appreciations (Pater) 7:413
Ars Poetica (Horace) 1:265
Art and Objective Truth (Lukács) 8:278
Art of English Poetry, The (Puttenham) 2:333
Art of Fiction, The (James) 7:511
Art of Poetry, The (Boileau-Despréaux) 3:289
Arte Poetica, L' (Minturno) 2:171

Artificial Comedy of the Last Century, The (Lamb) 5:663
Athenaeum, The (Schlegel) 5:357
Axel's Castle (Wilson) 9:25
Baudelaire (Eliot) 8:414
Beautiful and the Sublime, The (Kant) 5:5
Belief and the Suspension of Disbelief (Abrams) 10:143
Beyond Formalism (Hartman) 10:543
Biographia Literaria (Coleridge) 5:406
Black Writer and the Southern Experience, The (Walker) 11:349
Blindness and Insight (de Man) 10:261
Book: A Spiritual Instrument, The (Mallarmé) 7:486
Brief Apology for Poetry, A (Harington) 2:381
Burden of the Past and the English Poet, The (Bate) 10:221
Byron and Wordsworth (Hazlitt) 5:619
Characters of Dramatic Writers Contemporary with Shakespeare (Lamb) 5:687
Commendation of Sidney, A (Nashe) 2:367
Common Pursuit, The (Leavis) 9:84
Company We Keep, The (Booth) 10:311
Compendium of Tragicomic Poetry, The (Guarini) 2:455
Concerning Humor in Comedy (Congreve) 3:665
Conjectures on Original Composition (Young) 4:367
Conversations with Drummond (Jonson) 3:79

Conversations with Eckermann (Goethe) 5:73
Counter-Statement (Burke) 9:183
Crisis in Poetry (Mallarmé) 7:489
Critic as Artist, The (Wilde) 7:653
Critic as Host, The (Miller) 10:513
Critic as Innovator: A Paracritical Strip in X Frames, The (Hassan) 10:373
Criticism (James) 7:526
Criticism and Social Change (Lentricchia) 11:235
Criticism and the Experience of Interiority (Poulet) 10:53
Criticism in the Wilderness (Hartman) 10:555
Cultural Criticism and Society (Adorno) 9:297
Dada Manifesto, A (Tzara) 8:351
Day of the Leopards (Wimsatt) 9:582
De Inventione (Cicero) 1:221
De Oratore (Cicero) 1:231
De Vulgari Eloquentia (Dante) 1:497
Decay of Lying, The (Wilde) 7:700
Deceit, Desire, and the Novel (Girard) 10:347
Dedicatory Letter to Volpone, The (Jonson) 3:76
Defence and Illustration of the French Language, The (Du Bellay) 2:141
Defence of Helen, A (Gorgias of Leontini) 1:5
Defence of Poetry, A (Shelley) 6:186
Defense of Rhyme, A (Daniel) 2:523
Dehumanization of Art, The (Ortega y Gasset) 8:221
Detached Thoughts on Books and Reading (Lamb) 5:669
Dialogue on Poetry (Schlegel) 5:369
Discourse concerning the Original and the Progress of Satire, A (Dryden) 3:405
Discourses, The (Corneille) 3:263

Discourses on the Heroic Poem (Tasso) 2:401
Dostoevsky and Parricide (Freud) 8:56
Dyer's Hand, The (Auden) 9:535
Eagle's Nest (Ruskin) 7:64
Elegy upon the Death of John Donne, An (Carew) 3:511
Emerson (Poe) 6:558
Endymion & Lamia (Jeffrey) 5:517
Enneads, The (Plotinus) 1:419
Epilogue to the Satires, The (Pope) 4:178
Epistle to Henry Reynolds (Drayton) 3:139
Essay of Dramatic Poesy, An (Dryden) 3:418
Essay on Criticism, An (Pope) 4:135
Essay on Epitaphs, An (Johnson) 4:401
Essay, Supplementary to the Preface (Wordsworth) 5:304
Essay upon Ancient and Modern Learning, An (Temple) 3:617
Essays, The (Goldsmith) 4:251
Evolution of Literature, The (Mallarmé) 7:481
Expense of Greatness, The (Blackmur) 9:313
Fiction, Fair and Foul (Ruskin) 7:66
Figure of Echo, The (Hollander) 10:577
Figure of the Youth as Virile Poet, The (Stevens) 8:145
Figures in Black (Gates) 11:367
Folk Poetry and Poets' Poetry (Croce) 8:111
Fools of Time (Frye) 9:658
Fors Clavigera (Ruskin) 7:57
Four Ages of Poetry, The (Peacock) 6:131
Four Letters (Harvey) 2:370
French Letters: Theories of the New Novel (Vidal) 10:415
Frogs, The (Aristophanes) 1:9

INDEX TO WORKS 439

Function of Criticism, The (Eliot) 8:399
Function of Criticism at the Present Time, The (Arnold) 7:215
Function of Criticism Today, The (Kazin) 10:179
Function of Language in Psychoanalysis, The (Lacan) 9:267
Future for Astyanax, A (Bersani) 11:93
Genealogy of the Gentile Gods, The (Boccaccio) 2:6
General Censure, A (Nashe) 2:359
Great Tradition, The (Leavis) 9:63
Grounds of Criticism in Tragedy, The (Dryden) 3:379
Guardian, The (Addison and Steele) 4:38
Hamlet (Mallarmé) 7:504
Hawthorne's Twice-Told Tales (Poe) 6:559
Henry James (Blackmur) 9:340
Hero as Poet, The (Carlyle) 6:323
Homer's Contest (Nietzsche) 7:547
Humour (Freud) 8:52
I Meet August Wilhelm Schlegel (Heine) 6:351
Idler, The (Johnson) 4:430
Imagination of the Sign, The (Barthes) 9:681
Impartial Critic, The (Dennis) 3:686
Imperial Theme, The (Knight) 9:161
In Praise of the New Poet ("E. K.") 2:265
Institutio Oratoria (Quintilian) 1:287
Interpreting the Variorum (Fish) 11:199
Introduction to Genesis (Eliot) 7:107
Introduction to The English Poets (Arnold) 7:195
Introductory Remarks on Popular Poetry (Scott) 5:325
Ion (Plato) 1:86

Jew in Search of a Son: Joyce's Ulysses, *The* (Blackmur) 9:326
Language as Gesture (Blackmur) 9:362
Laokoon (Lessing) 5:19
Laws (Plato) 1:136
Leaves from a Note-book (Eliot) 7:115
Lecture on Modern Poetry, A (Hulme) 8:213
Lectures on Art (Ruskin) 7:55
Letter concerning Enthusiasm, A (Shaftesbury) 4:5
Letter to a Young Poet, A (Swift) 4:120
Letter to Can Grande della Scala (Dante) 1:531
Letters (Whitman) 7:96
Liberal Imagination, The (Trilling) 9:379
Life of Dante, The (Boccaccio) 2:3
Life of John Donne, The (Walton) 3:514
Linguistics and Literary History (Spitzer) 8:363
Literary Theory (Eagleton) 11:321
Literary Theory, Criticism, and History (Wellek) 10:69
Literature and Evil (Bataille) 10:5
Literature and Its Theorists (Todorov) 11:221
Literature of Knowledge and the Literature of Power, The (De Quincey) 6:123
Lives of the Poets, The (Johnson) 4:495
Long Revolution, The (Williams) 11:5
Longfellow (Poe) 6:548
Madwoman in the Attic, The (Gilbert and Gubar) 1:171
Making of Verse, The (Gascoigne) 2:241
Man of Letters in the Modern World, The (Tate) 9:219

Manifesto of Surrealism, The (Breton) 8:585
Marriage of Heaven and Hell, The (Blake) 5:123
Mechanic Muse, The (Kenner) 10:333
Metaphysical Poets, The (Eliot) 8:406
Milton (Coleridge) 5:505
Milton's Poetry of Choice and Its Romantic Heirs (Brisman) 11:341
Minturno, or On Beauty (Tasso) 2:435
Modern Fiction (Woolf) 8:192
Modern Painters III (Ruskin) 7:34
Montaigne; or, The Skeptic (Emerson) 6:439
Moralia (Plutarch) 1:363
Music and Literature (Mallarmé) 7:495
Mythomystes (Reynolds) 3:144
Nature of Poetic Art, The (Proclus) 1:469
New Bearings in English Poetry (Leavis) 9:53
New Science, The (Vico) 4:183
Nietzsche, Genealogy, History (Foucault) 10:469
Note on Poetry, A (Tzara) 8:359
Notes on Form in Art (Eliot) 7:111
Notes on the Illustrations to Dante (Blake) 5:150
Observations in the Art of English Poetry (Campion) 2:501
Observations on English Metre (Gray) 4:357
Of Grammatology (Derrida) 11:37
Of Heroic Plays (Dryden) 3:361
Of Tragedy Ancient and Modern (Saint-Evremond) 3:277
On Art (Hegel) 5:227
On Books (Montaigne) 2:253
On Books and Reading (Schopenhauer) 6:145
On Christian Doctrine (Augustine) 1:437

On Comedy (Donatus) 1:431
On Commonplace Critics (Hazlitt) 5:571
On Criticism (Goethe) 5:68
On Drama (Euanthius) 1:427
On Edgar Poe (Baudelaire) 7:129
On Familiar Style (Hazlitt) 5:589
On Germany (Staël) 5:185
On Homer (Chapman) 2:479
On Homer's Poetry & On Virgil (Blake) 5:145
On Literary Composition (Dionysius of Halicarnassus) 1:279
On Love (Shelley) 6:184
On Poetry (Temple) 3:640
On Poetry in General (Hazlitt) 5:574
On Shakespeare (Coleridge) 5:464
On Shelley (Browning) 7:7
On Simple and Sentimental Poetry (Schiller) 5:155
On Style (Demetrius) 1:213
On the Composition of Romances (Giraldi Cintio) 2:130
On the Death of Coleridge (Lamb) 5:700
On the Defense of the Comedy of Dante (Mazzoni) 2:315
On the Difference between Writing and Speaking (Hazlitt) 5:604
On the Genealogy of Morals (Nietzsche) 7:554
On the Idea of Comedy (Meredith) 7:237
On the Knocking at the Gate in Macbeth (De Quincey) 6:105
On the Marionette Theatre (Kleist) 6:23
On the Origin of Language (Herder) 5:97
On the Poems of the Ancients (Saint-Evremond) 3:283
On the Poetics (Castelvetro) 2:213
On the Present State of Wit (Gay) 4:91

On the Process of the Poetic Mind (Hölderlin) 6:7
On the Prose-Style of Poets (Hazlitt) 5:594
On the Sublime (Longinus) 1:325
On the Sublime (Schiller) 5:174
On the Sublime and Beautiful (Burke) 4:283
On Tolstoy (Chernyshevsky) 7:319
On Tristram Shandy (Shklovsky) 8:559
On Truth and Lie (Nietzsche) 7:551
On Types (Hermogenes) 1:401
On Vergil (Fulgentius) 1:481
Orator (Cicero) 1:256
Palladis Tamia (Meres) 2:489
Paradox of Acting, The (Diderot) 4:307
Per Amica Silentia Lunae (Yeats) 8:93
Phaedrus (Plato) 1:81
Philosophy and the Form of Fiction (Gass) 10:357
Philosophy of Composition, The (Poe) 6:539
Philosophy of Shelley's Poetry, The (Yeats) 8:71
Pleasure of the Text, The (Barthes) 9:685
Poet, The (Emerson) 6:423
Poetica (Trissino) 2:107
Poetics (Aristotle) 1:149
Poetics (Scaliger) 2:159
Poetry and Abstract Thought (Valéry) 8:125
Poetry and Imagination (Emerson) 6:383
Poetry, with Reference to Aristotle's Poetics (Newman) 6:232
Political Unconscious, The (Jameson) 11:123
Politics and Literature (Sartre) 9:436
Pornographic Imagination, The (Sontag) 11:107

Practical Criticism (Richards) 8:523
Praeterita (Ruskin) 7:74
Preface and Conclusion to The Renaissance (Pater) 7:407
Preface to All for Love (Dryden) 3:370
Preface to Gondibert (Davenant) 3:201
Preface to Homer (Hobbes) 3:239
Preface to Joseph Andrews, The (Fielding) 4:241
Preface to Leaves of Grass (Whitman) 7:81
Preface to Longinus (Boileau-Despréaux) 3:317
Preface to Lyrical Ballads *(1800)* (Wordsworth) 5:271
Preface to Lyrical Ballads *(1802)* (Wordsworth) 5:283
Preface to Madame Bovary (Baudelaire) 7:141
Preface to Paradise Lost (Milton) 3:169
Preface to Prometheus Unbound (Shelley) 6:180
Preface to Rapin (Rymer) 3:551
Preface to Samson Agonistes (Milton) 3:170
Preface to Sejanus (Jonson) 3:73
Preface to Sylvae (Dryden) 3:393
Preface to the Aeneis (Dryden) 3:462
Preface to The Alchemist (Jonson) 3:75
Preface to The Ambassadors (James) 7:530
Preface to The Cutter of Coleman Street (Cowley) 3:255
Preface to The Dictionary (Johnson) 4:445
Preface to the Fables (Dryden) 3:489
Preface to The Fall of Islam (Shelley) 6:173
Preface to the Iliad, *The* (Chapman) 3:123

Preface to the Iliad, *The* (Pope) 4:152
Preface to the Odyssey, *The* (Chapman) 3:130
Preface to The Plays of William Shakespeare, *The* (Johnson) 4:463
Preface to the Poems (Cowley) 3:247
Preface to The Poems of Wordsworth (Arnold) 7:181
Preface to The White Divel (Webster) 3:121
Problems for the Modern Critic of Literature (Winters) 9:229
Proclamation without Pretention, A (Tzara) 8:358
Proposal for Correcting, Improving, and Ascertaining the English Tongue (Swift) 4:109
Public Address (Blake) 5:134
Pure and Impure Poetry (Warren) 9:453
Quantity and Quality (Bentley) 10:193
Quotation and Originality (Emerson) 6:412
Rabelais and His World (Bakhtin) 9:111
Racine and Shakespeare (Stendhal) 6:31
Rambler, The (Johnson) 4:407
Rationale of Verse, The (Poe) 6:507
Reason of Church Government, The (Milton) 3:173
Reflections on Aristotle (Rapin) 3:333
Reflections on Longinus (Boileau-Despréaux) 3:324
Relation of the Poet to Day-Dreaming, The (Freud) 8:37
Reminiscences of Blake (Robinson) 5:527
Reminiscences of Coleridge, Wordsworth, and Lamb (Robinson) 5:533
Renewal of Literature, The (Poirier) 10:397

Reply to Davenant (Hobbes) 3:231
Republic (Plato) 1:97
Rhetoric (Aristotle) 1:179
Rhetoric of Religion, The (Burke) 9:192
Rhythm and Imagery in English Poetry (Empson) 9:480
Romantic School, The (Heine) 6:352
Romanticism and Classicism (Hulme) 8:201
Room of One's Own, A (Woolf) 8:173
Rousseau's Confessions (Sainte-Beuve) 6:475
Sacred Poetry (Keble) 6:213
Salon of 1859, The (Baudelaire) 7:148
Sanity of Art, The (Shaw) 8:5
Sartor Resartus (Carlyle) 6:316
Scenes from the Drama of European Literature (Auerbach) 8:479
Schoolmaster, The (Ascham) 2:187
Second Sex, The (Beauvoir) 9:591
Selected Aphorisms (Novalis) 5:351
Selected Essays (Bacon) 3:39
Selected Letters (Flaubert) 7:155
Selected Letters (Keats) 6:251
Selected Letters (Petrarch) 2:67
Sense of an Ending, The (Kermode) 10:293
Sentimental-Poetry (Schiller) 5:170
Sesame and Lilies (Ruskin) 7:51
Shakespeare ad Infinitum (Goethe) 5:57
Shakespeare; or, The Poet (Emerson) 6:453
Short Organum for the Theatre, A (Brecht) 8:617
Short View of the Immorality and Profaneness of the English Stage (Collier) 3:672
Short View of Tragedy, A (Rymer) 3:581
Shouldn't We Abolish Aesthetics? (Brecht) 8:615

INDEX TO WORKS 443

Signs of the Times (Carlyle) 6:299
Sincerity and Authenticity (Trilling) 9:394
Soul and Form (Lukács) 8:263
Space of Literature, The (Blanchot) 10:107
Spectator, The (Addison and Steele) 4:41
Spirit of Romance, The (Pound) 8:305
Spirit of the Age, The (Hazlitt) 5:621
State of Modern Poetry, The (Jeffrey) 5:520
Stones of Venice, The (Ruskin) 7:23
Storyteller, The (Benjamin) 8:435
Strange News (Nashe) 2:376
Structural Study of Myth, The (Lévi-Strauss) 9:615
Studies in Classic American Literature (Lawrence) 8:243
Supplement to Aristotle's Poetics (Goethe) 5:70
Suspiria de Profundis (De Quincey) 6:109
Symbolism of Poetry, The (Yeats) 8:87
Tale-Writing: Nathaniel Hawthorne (Poe) 6:565
Taste and the Reproduction of Art (Croce) 8:105
Tatler, The (Addison and Steele) 4:29
Tatler, The (Swift) 4:105
Textual Criticism and the Literary Critic (Bowers) 10:83
Theatre of the Absurd, The (Esslin) 10:239
Theme of the Three Caskets, The (Freud) 8:44
Theory of the Formal Method, The (Eikhenbaum) 8:319
Thoughts and Notes on Russian Literature (Belinskii) 6:575
Thoughts on Poetry and Its Varieties (Mill) 6:489
Timber, or Discoveries (Jonson) 3:92

To Criticize the Critic (Eliot) 8:422
Toward a More Feminist Criticism (Rich) 10:591
Tractate of Education, A (Milton) 3:183
Tradition and the Individual Talent (Eliot) 8:393
Tragedies of Shakespeare, The (Lamb) 5:674
Tragedies of the Last Age, The (Rymer) 3:563
Transcendental Aesthetic (Kant) 5:6
Tritical Essay, A (Swift) 4:101
Truth and Method (Gadamer) 10:21
Twilight of the Idols (Nietzsche) 7:629
Two or Three Ideas (Stevens) 8:160
Usefulness of the Stage, The (Dennis) 3:706
Validity in Interpretation (Hirsch) 10:487
Verbal Analysis, The (Empson) 9:475
Verbal Icon, The (Wimsatt) 9:557
Walter Scott and La Princesse de Clèves (Stendhal) 6:58
Well Wrought Urn, The (Brooks) 9:499
What Is a Classic? (Sainte-Beuve) 6:467
What Is an Author? (Foucault) 10:455
What Is Art? (Tolstoy) 7:269
What Is Literature? (Sartre) 9:419
What Is Poetry? (Hunt) 6:63
What Was Literature? (Fiedler) 10:207
Wheel of Fire, The (Knight) 9:137
Why Literary Criticism Is Not an Exact Science (Levin) 10:163
William Blake (Swinburne) 7:349
Wisdom of the Ancients, The (Bacon) 3:45
Wit and Humor (Hunt) 6:100
Women on Women's Destiny:

Maturity as Penance (Auerbach) 11:311

Women's Time, Women's Space: Writing the History of Feminist Criticism (Showalter) 11:277

Word, Dialogue and Novel (Kristeva) 11:253

Wordsworth's *Excursion* (Jeffrey) 5:511

Wordsworth's *Poems* (Jeffrey) 5:507

Work of Art in the Age of Mechanical Reproduction, The (Benjamin) 8:453

World as Will and Idea, The (Schopenhauer) 6:152

World of Difference, A (Johnson) 11:355

World, the Text, and the Critic, The (Said) 11:141

World's Body, The (Ransom) 9:5

Wound and the Bow, The (Wilson) 9:37

Writing and Madness (Felman) 11:293

Writing Lives (Edel) 10:131

Zibaldone, The (Leopardi) 6:365

Index of Names and Titles

A la recherche du temps perdu (Proust), 9:65, 328, 461; 10:302, 348, 351, 409, 561; 11:55–56, 153

"A propos of the Kreutzer Sonata" (Leskov), 8:441, 450

A Rebours (Huysmans), 8:418

Aaron's Rod (Lawrence), 10:157

Abaris (Heracleides), 1:363

Abbas, Joachim, 9:334

Abelard, Pierre, 9:341

Abignac, abbé d', 3:277

Abraham, Karl, 10:465; 11:75

Abrams, M. H., 5:x; 6:viii; 9:xiii; 10:449, 515, 520, 522, 632; 11:172

Absalom and Achitophel (Dryden), 3:408, 503; 4:537, 543; 9:260

Absalom Senior (attrib. to Settle), 4:537

Absalon (Watson), 2:197–98

Acconci, Vito Hannibal, 10:386

Achebe, Chinua, 10:313

Achilleid (Statius), 2:130

Ackermann, Robert, 11:257

Ad Herennium (attrib. to Cicero), 8:484, 488

Adam Bede (Eliot), 11:213

Adamov, Arthur, 9:436; 10:239–41, 252

Adams, Henry, 9:255, 313–25, 350, 536; 10:403

Addison, Joseph, 3:484n.24; 4:93, 95, 263, 385–92, 513; 5:330; 6:84, 324; 7:208; 9:573; 10:94

Adelphoi (Terence), 2:114, 200; 3:429; 7:249

Adler, Alfred, 9:608

Adonais (Shelley), 6:67

Adone (Marino), 3:336, 346, 474, 559

Adorno, Theodor W., 11:108, 127

Adrian VI, Pope, 5:160

Adventures of Huckleberry Finn (Twain), 9:38; 10:210, 311–12

Adversus Marcionem (Tertullian), 8:488–89, 491, 496

Adversus Nationes (Arnobius), 8:499

Advertisements for Myself (Mailer), 10:610

Aelian (Claudius Aelianus), 3:128

Aeneid (Vergil), 1:481–82, 517, 521; 2:21, 29, 33, 41, 76, 110, 175, 255–56, 360; 3:237, 243–44, 278, 283, 285, 324, 339–40, 395–97, 409, 412, 430, 432, 462–88, 492, 502, 643, 649; 4:21, 31, 53–60, 70, 262, 276, 279, 301, 421, 544; 5:145; 7:422; 8:388–89n.15, 484, 508–11; 9:250; 10:580; 11:76

Aeschines, 1:200, 218–19, 234, 291, 339

Aeschylus, 1:ix, 45–73, 152, 164, 168, 270, 337, 366, 386, 390, 395, 427, 432; 3:171, 269, 302, 339, 350, 386, 423, 463, 566, 585, 587, 594, 719, 723, 726, 745; 4:255; 5:374; 6:235; 7:233, 476; 8:397; 10:25–26, 30, 48n.17; 11:vii

Aesop, 1:363; 2:18, 20, 255, 266, 292, 296, 360–61, 367, 369; 3:21, 635, 649; 4:192–93

"Aesthetic Poetry" (Pater), 7:xxiv

Afranius, Lucius, 1:429; 3:425

Africa (Petrarch), 2:57; 3:336

African Methodist Episcopal Church Review, 11:369

"After Apple-Picking" (Frost), 10:320

After Babel (Steiner), 10:376, 393

After Strange Gods (Eliot), 9:102, 104–6; 11:155

"After the Burial" (Lowell), 9:470n.3

After the New Criticism (Lentricchia), 10:637

"After the Storm" (Hemingway), 9:41

"Afternoon of a Faun" (Mallarmé). *See* "Après-midi d'un faune, L'"

Against Aristogiton (attrib. to Demosthenes), 1:343–44

Against Interpretation and Other Essays (Sontag), 10:416

Against Midias (Demosthenes), 1:340

Agamemnon (Aeschylus), 3:269; 6:235; 8:397

Agathon, 1:16, 156, 161, 164

Age of Innocence, The (Wharton), 9:242–43, 249

Age of Suspicion, The (Sarraute), 10:417

Agellius, 3:557

Agnostos Theos (Norden), 10:569

Agrippa, Cornelius, 2:384

Agrippa, Menenius, 3:228

Ahania (Blake), 7:394n.7

Aids to Reflexion (Coleridge), 5:566–67; 7:440–41

Aiken, Conrad, 10:189

Aimeric de Belenoi, 1:525

Ainsworth, William Harrison, 5:565

Ajax (Augustus), 3:170

Ajax (Sophocles), 2:462; 3:114–15, 265, 272, 348; 6:233

Akhmatova, Anna, 8:338; 11:222

Alaham (Brooke), 5:695
Alaric (Scudéry), 3:324–25, 467
Alastor (Shelley), 10:527, 532
Albanzani, Donato, 2:75
Alcaeus, 2:266; 3:109, 252
Alcestis (Euripides), 1:49; 3:188
Alchemist, The (Jonson), 3:309, 440, 442, 447, 676; 5:696
Alcibiades, 3:111; 8:274
Alcibiades II (attrib. to Plato), 1:473–74
Alcidamas, 1:183–84
Alcott, Louisa May, 11:312, 314
Aldington, Richard, 8:426
Aldrich, Thomas Bailey, 9:33
Aldrovandus (Ulisse Aldrovandi), 7:709
Alemani, Antonio, 2:117
Alembert, Jean le Rond d', 7:247, 276
Alexander of Aphrodisias, 2:323
Alexander the Great, 1:217; 3:13–15, 97, 621–22, 659, 724
Alexander, Franz, 9:389
Alexander, Sir William, 3:81
"Alexander's Feast" (Dryden), 5:626; 6:244
Alexander's Magazine, 11:369
"Alexandrite, The" (Leskov), 8:444, 451
Alexis, 1:373
Alger, Horatio, 9:649
Alison, Sir Archibald, 10:222–23
All for Love; or, The World Well Lost (Dryden), 4:536–37
All's Well That Ends Well (Shakespeare), 5:697; 9:169–70
Allegory (Fletcher), 10:579
Allegory of Love, The (Lewis), 11:88n.30
"Allegro, L'" (Milton), 4:525–26; 11:199, 342
Allen, Grant, 7:283
Allonnes, Olivier Revault d', 10:384
Alpert, Jane, 11:286–87
"Alpine Idyll, An" (Hemingway), 9:48
"Altar of the Dead, The" (James), 9:346, 351, 357–58; 10:399
Althusser, Louis, 11:125, 131, 143, 283
Alton Locke (Kingsley), 7:40
Amadis (Tasso), 3:346
Amadis de Gaule (anon.), 2:285
Ambassadors, The (James), 7:531; 9:245–46, 249, 343, 347, 350, 355–57, 360
Amber Witch, The (Meinhold), 7:470
Ambrose, St., 3:18, 152, 527; 9:190
Amelia (Fielding), 9:65
American, The (James), 9:71, 355
American Mercury, The, 10:186
American Scene, The (James), 9:343, 357; 10:399
American Scholar, The, 10:408

Ami Fritz, L' (Erckmann-Chatrian), 7:264
Aminta (Tasso), 2:472; 3:400
Amintas (Watson), 2:363–64
Ammianus Marcellinus, 8:516n.17
Amo, 11:382
"Among School Children" (Yeats), 10:96
Amour fou, L' (Breton), 9:603–4
Amours de Gaul (Bussy), 3:636
Amphitryo (Plautus), 2:114, 300, 455, 467; 3:86
Anacreon, 1:345, 410; 3:339, 511
"Anagrams" (Saussure), 11:257–58
"Analysis Terminable and Interminable" (Freud), 9:402
Anatomy of Criticism (Frye), 9:ix–x; 10:71, 172–73, 390; 11:84–85n.14, 287
Anatomy of Nonsense (Winters), 9:524
Anaxagoras, 1:318; 10:26
Ancient India (Bohlen), 7:109
Ancient Legendary Tales (Hartshorne), 5:347–48
And Then We Heard the Thunder (Killens), 11:376
Anders, Günther, 10:557
Anderson, Perry, 11:162
Anderson, Sherwood, 9:105
Andrewes, Lancelot, 3:526; 8:427; 11:153–54
Andrey Kolosov (Turgenev), 7:319
Andreyev, Leonid, 8:297
Andria (Terence), 1:227, 433; 2:470–71; 3:271; 7:249
Andromache (Euripides), 2:127; 3:340
Andromaque (Racine), 11:93–94, 102n.1
Andromeda (Euripides), 1:14
Andromède (Corneille), 3:265, 271, 442
Andronicus, Livius, 1:430–31
Androtion, 1:184
"Angel, The" (Blake), 7:373
Anna Karenina (Tolstoy), 11:107
"Annabel Lee" (Poe), 9:31
Anselm, St., 9:197–98
Antheus (Agathon), 1:156
Anthropology (Kroeber), 11:62n.2
Anti-Cato (Caesar), 3:15
Antichrist, Der (Nietzsche), 7:625–26nn.108, 110
Antidosis (Isocrates), 1:203
Antidotes against Poisons (Nicander), 1:365
Antigone (Sophocles), 1:160; 3:384, 687, 697
Antimachus, 1:186
Anti-Oedipe, L' (Deleuze and Guattari), 10:385; 11:95–96, 136
Antipater, 3:243
Antiphanes, 6:415
Antiphon, 1:279, 414

INDEX OF NAMES AND TITLES

Antiquary, The (Scott), 5:641
Antiquierheit des Menschen, Die (Anders), 10:557
Antisthenes, 1:184, 214, 391; 11:266
Antoninus, Marcus Aurelius, 3:12, 620
Antoninus Pius, 3:11
Antonio and Mellida (Marston), 5:689
Antonioni, Michelangelo, 10:416
Antonius, M. (Mark Antony), 1:237
Antony and Cleopatra (Shakespeare), 8:181, 183; 9:164, 173, 176–80, 527, 665, 670
Anxiety of Influence, The (Bloom), 11:374
Apelles, 1:256; 3:42, 110, 338
Apocolocynthosis (Seneca the Younger), 11:267
Apollinaire, Guillaume, 8:596, 611n.10
Apollodorus, 1:307
Apollonius Rhodius, 1:347; 3:337, 557, 561
Apologia (Pico della Mirandola), 3:149, 152
Apologia adversus Hieronymus (Rufinus), 8:498
Apology for Poetry (Sidney), 2:xii–xiv, 382; 3:145, 484n.29; 11:7–9
Apology of Socrates (Plato), 2:217
Appeal in Favor of That Class of Americans Called Africans (Child), 11:368–69
Appian, 3:370
Appreciations (Pater), 7:xxiv
"Après-midi d'un faune, L'" (Mallarmé), 7:484
Apuleius, Lucius, 2:19, 299; 8:49, 51n.10; 9:xiii
Aquilius, Manius, 1:246–47
Aquinas, St. Thomas, 2:407–8, 411; 7:678; 8:506, 514; 9:10, 330; 10:173, 609
Aquino, Rinaldo d', 1:518
Arabian Nights, 7:74, 252; 10:456, 458
Aragon, Louis, 8:599, 605
Arator, 8:498
Aratus, 1:238, 333, 343; 3:187
Arbuthnot, John, 4:168–77
Arc, L', 11:284
Arcadia (Sidney), 2:xii; 3:145, 476; 5:697
Arcane 17 (Breton), 9:604, 606
Archilochus, 1:86, 203, 266, 334–35, 347, 375, 390; 3:109, 337, 647; 5:373, 394n.6
Archy Moore (Hildreth), 11:385
Archytas, 1:192
Arendt, Hannah, 1:xiv
Areopagitica (Milton), 4:519; 10:330
Aretino, Pietro, 2:118; 3:145
Argonautica (Apollonius Rhodius), 1:347; 3:557
Ariel Poems (Eliot), 11:154
Arimaspea (Aristeas), 1:333

Ariosto, Ludovico, 2:126, 131, 133, 136, 172, 175–77, 179, 254–55, 390–97, 420, 422–23, 432–35; 3:145, 173, 203, 336, 341, 346, 348, 362–63, 462, 467, 553, 558–59, 654; 5:168, 378; 8:37
Aristarchus, 1:274, 381; 3:viii
Aristides, 1:406
Aristippus, 1:218–19, 318
Ariston, 1:363
Aristophanes, 1:ix–xi, 151, 182, 351, 386, 427; 2:116, 160; 3:111–12, 336, 422, 425, 503, 594, 676, 734, 740; 7:238, 249, 256, 262, 717; 9:650; 10:643; 11:vii
Aristophon, 1:368
Aristotle, 1:xv, 233, 235, 260, 345, 380, 390, 482; 2:xiii, 5, 17–18, 60, 67, 108, 110, 113, 115, 124, 126–30, 135–36, 150, 163, 165–67, 173, 182, 195–96, 213, 216, 219, 221–22, 227–30, 233–36, 257, 277, 282, 284–85, 294, 296, 300, 303, 317, 319–21, 323, 325, 327–28, 330, 386, 393, 404, 409, 412, 420, 425, 441, 453–54, 457, 459–66, 469, 471–72; 3:viii, xii, 5, 8, 13, 18–19, 25–27, 30–31, 103, 107–8, 110–12, 127–28, 151–52, 170, 174, 187–89, 266–69, 272, 277, 279, 317, 326, 333–55, 372, 379–80, 386, 390–91, 415, 422–23, 426–28, 433–34, 451, 454, 463–64, 502, 551, 555, 564, 566, 580–81, 612, 646–47, 676, 678–79, 690–93, 695–96, 698–99, 701, 704, 712, 724, 729–30, 734, 740, 750; 5:38–39, 70–72, 291; 6:232–34, 236–37, 243; 7:114, 201, 205, 548, 646–47, 661, 681, 683; 8:147–48, 158, 218, 281, 291, 298, 301, 481, 487, 515n.4, 618–19; 9:xii, 5–22, 208, 235–36, 239, 391–92, 395, 561, 572, 575, 644–45, 661, 674; 10:26–28, 32, 37, 45, 143, 148, 167–69, 200–201, 211, 215, 227, 230, 298, 320, 323n.6, 359, 363, 459, 464, 565, 570, 634; 11:vii, ix, 5–7, 17, 53, 63n.4, 241, 269, 272, 274n.17
Arlotto, Pievano, 2:118
Armstrong, John, 4:267
Arnaut, Daniel, 8:309–11, 313, 315
Arnheim, Rudolf, 8:461
Arnobius, 8:499
Arnold, Matthew, 5:xix; 7:xiii, 658, 705; 8:95, 266, 399, 403, 422–23; 9:ix, 32, 54–56, 58–59, 99–101, 103, 234, 380, 561, 577, 637, 641–43, 650–52; 10:71, 134–35, 144, 164, 170, 182, 185–86, 208–9, 377, 390, 544, 564, 566–68, 605, 623, 632, 645; 11:147–50, 152, 162, 322
Arnould, Sophie, 4:345
Arnoux, Alexandre, 8:460

Arp, Hans, 10:386
Arrabal, Fernando, 10:240
Ars Amatoria (Ovid), 2:32; 3:297; 8:485
Ars Poetica (Horace), 1:432, 517, 532; 2:83, 200–201, 467; 3:86, 337, 342, 347, 349, 365, 423, 467, 698, 737; 4:218, 227, 291; 5:237–38; 8:147; 10:168
Ars Poetica (MacLeish), 9:638
"Art as Device" (Shklovsky), 8:327
"Art of Fiction, The" (James), 10:186
Art of Love (Ovid). *See Ars Amatoria*
Art of Memory, The (Yates), 10:431
Art of Preserving Health, The (Armstrong), 4:267
Art religieux du 12eme siècle en France, L' (Male), 8:519n.43
Artaud, Antonin, 9:438–39, 441–42, 447–48; 10:245; 11:42, 265, 268
Artist as Critic, The (Wilde, ed. Ellmann), 10:376
"As I Ebb'd with the Ocean of Life" (Whitman), 10:630
As You Like It (Shakespeare), 9:166, 169, 177
Ascham, Roger, 3:4
Asclepiades, 1:237
Ash Wednesday (Eliot), 9:566; 10:97; 11:154–55
Asimov, Isaac, 10:211
Asinaria (Plautus), 2:165
Assassinat du Pont-Rouge, L' (Rousseau), 7:143
Assommoir, L' (Zola), 7:704
Astronomica (Manilius), 8:485
"Asya" (Turgenev), 7:330–48
Atala (Chateaubriand), 7:474
Atget, Eugène, 8:459
Athalie (Racine), 3:327, 697; 11:94
Athanasius, 2:408
Athenaeum, The, 8:426
Athenaeus, 3:346
Atlantic Monthly, The, 9:342; 10:189
Atlantica (Rudbeck), 4:195
"Attachment to the World" (Schlegel), 203–4
Attis [Poem 63] (Catullus), 8:484
Atwood, Margaret, 11:179–80
Aubigné, Agrippa d', 8:384n.7
Auden, W. H., 6:x; 9:222–23, 488; 10:134–35
Audubon, John James, 6:267, 294n.75
Auerbach, Erich, 2:x–xi; 10:74, 78–79, 170–71, 173; 11:144–47, 150, 153, 157, 159, 163, 172, 193n.1
Augustine, St. (Aurelius Augustinus), 2:25, 27, 39, 60, 95, 98, 206; 3:18, 152, 161, 535, 735; 6:401; 8:367, 481, 493–97, 586; 9:189, 192–93, 206, 220–21, 326, 330, 537; 10:361, 577; 11:214, 223
Augustus (C. Octavius), 1:451; 3:101, 111, 170, 233, 638, 659
Aulularia (Plautus), 2:114
Aurelian (L. Domitius Aurelianus), 3:318
Aurelius, Marcus. *See* Antonius, Marcus Aurelius
Aureng-Zebe (Dryden), 3:482
Aurifex, L., 1:254
Aurora Leigh (Browning), 7:xlii
Auslander, Joseph, 9:527
Ausonius (D. Magnus Ausonius), 3:655
Austen, Jane, 7:257; 8:175, 182, 188; 9:63–68, 71; 11:180–83, 186–87, 311
Autobiography (Mill), 9:74
Autobiography of a Female Slave (Griffiths), 11:384–85
Avantures de Télémaque fils d'Ulysse, Les (Fénelon), 4:245n.4
Avare, L' (Molière), 5:86
"Avenge O Lord thy slaughtered saints" (Milton), 11:202–3
Aventures de Sophie, Les (Claudel), 9:602
Averroes, 9:333–34
Avitus, Bishop of Vienne, 8:498
Awakening, The (Chopin), 11:286
Awkward Age, The (James), 9:72, 354
Axël (Villiers de l'Isle-Adam), 8:92; 10:341
Axiochus (attrib. to Plato), 2:254
Azaria and Hushai (attrib. to Settle), 4:537

Babbitt, Irving, 8:424–26; 9:229–30; 10:392
Babbitt (Lewis), 10:92, 96
"Babes in the Wood," 5:280, 298
Babylonians, The (Aristophanes), 1:182
Bacchae (Euripides), 6:235–36; 9:583, 661
Bacchylides, 1:347, 396; 3:337
Bachelard, Gaston, 10:549, 552; 11:99, 190, 297
Bacon, Sir Francis, 2:x; 3:vii–ix, xi–xiv, 84, 102–3, 636, 720; 4:382; 5:141, 576, 604; 6:64, 99, 124, 402; 9:388, 646; 10:24–25, 30, 166, 173, 175, 459
Bacon, Sir Nicholas, 3:106
Bailey, Benjamin, 6:251–53
Baillet, Adrien, 8:153
Baillie, Joanna, 8:175
Bain, Alexander, 8:535
Bajazet (Racine), 11:93
Baker, Houston A., Jr., 11:374–76, 378, 383
Baker, Sir Richard, 3:553
Bakhtin, Mikhail, 11:126, 226, 253–60, 262–63, 265–67, 270–71, 272n.1, 274n.18

INDEX OF NAMES AND TITLES

Balanchine, George, 9:366
"Balcon, Le" (Baudelaire), 8:419; 11:58
Balcony, The (Genet), 9:440
Bald Prima Donna, The (Ionesco). See
    Cantatrice chauve, La
Bald, R. C., 10:85, 87
Baldus (Coccaius), 3:412
Baldwin, James, 10:x, 415; 11:371, 376
Balint, Michael, 9:278
Ball, A. H. R., 7:xlvii
"Ballad on a Wedding" (Suckling), 6:80–81
Ballads and Sonnets (Rossetti), 7:467
Balzac, Honoré de, 7:68, 356, 393n.5, 706,
    712; 8:100, 285, 294, 297, 377; 9:342,
    347, 351, 357; 10:460; 11:56, 265
Bambara, Toni Cade, 11:359
"Banal Story" (Hemingway), 9:41
"Bantams in Pine-Woods" (Stevens), 9:373
Baraka, Imamu Amiri (LeRoi Jones), 9:584;
    11:371
Barbarian Within, The (Ong), 10:390
Barbey d'Aurevilly, Jules, 7:134, 142; 9:687
Bard, The (Gray), 4:x, 582–83; 5:399
Bardi, Giovanni, 8:87
Barfield, Owen, 10:568, 617
Barlaam, 2:55–56
Barlaam and Josaphat (anon.), 6:353–54
Barnes, Djuna, 9:78
Barraclough, Geoffrey, 10:77
Barrault, Jean-Louis, 9:446
Bart, Pauline, 11:177
Barth, John, 10:369, 416
Barthes, Roland, 10:264, 378, 382, 385, 423,
    644; 11:102n.5, 279, 323
Bartholomew Fair (Jonson), 3:440, 449, 494,
    668
Bartole, 3:326
Bartram, William, 5:463
Barzun, Jacques, 9:385; 10:183
Basil, St., 2:95
Basilides, 10:628
Bataille, Georges, 9:689; 11:112, 114, 267,
    269, 293
Bateson, F. W., 9:470n.4, 566; 10:499–501,
    506–8, 543–45
Batrachomyomachia (Homer), 2:153
Battaile of Agincourt, The (Drayton), 3:146
Battel of the Books, The (Swift), 3:xv
Batteux, Charles, 7:276
Baudelaire, Charles, 7:392n.3, 679, 705;
    8:166, 234, 289, 412, 414–21, 427, 429,
    598; 9:30–32, 189, 221, 330, 381; 10:5–
    20, 57, 170, 427; 11:58, 294, 388
Baudelaire and the Symbolists (Quennell),
    8:414

Baudouin, Charles, 9:187
Baumgarten, Alexander Gottlieb, 5:20; 7:283;
    9:573; 10:145
Beach Boys, The, 10:313
Beardsley, Monroe, 10:439–40, 503
Beare, Robert, 10:91, 97
"Beast in the Jungle, The" (James), 9:346,
    358
Beatles, The, 10:322
Beaujour, Michel, 9:585
Beaumont, Francis, 3:81–82, 121, 142, 433,
    445–46, 563, 677; 5:309, 481, 697–98;
    10:94
Beaumont, Sir John, 6:83, 402
Beauvoir, Simone de, 10:299; 11:185, 191,
    281, 286
Beccari, Agostin de', 2:472–73
Becker, Philipp August, 8:364–65, 382–83n.2
Beckett, Samuel, 9:436, 449; 10:175, 240,
    242, 247, 251, 256, 358, 362–63, 456, 616
Beethoven, Ludwig van, 7:290, 302; 8:30n.2,
    226; 10:234, 322
Beginnings: Intention and Method (Said),
    10:387; 11:161
Being and Nothingness (Sartre), 9:399, 401
Being and Time (Heidegger). See *Sein und
    Zeit*
Belchamber (Sturgis), 9:75
Belinsky, V. I., 10:170
Bell, Clive, 9:66
Bell, Currer (Charlotte Brontë), 8:178
Bell, Gertrude, 8:182
"Belle Dame sans Merci, La" (Keats), 9:56
Belle Hélène, La (Offenbach), 8:46
Bellegarde, abbé (Jean Baptiste Morvan de
    Bellegarde), 4:243
Bellini, Giovanni, 7:714
Bellow, Saul, 10:415, 420–21
"Bells for John Whiteside's Daughter"
    (Ransom), 9:459, 467
Bellum Belgicum (Strada), 4:271–72
Belsey, Catherine, 11:287
Bembo, Pietro, 2:125, 176, 303; 3:145, 173
"Bench of Desolation, The" (James), 9:358
Benda, Julien, 11:142, 151–52
Benediction (Baudelaire), 8:418
Bénichou, Paul, 11:226, 228
Benito Cereno (Melville), 9:243–44
Benjamin, Walter, 9:394; 10:315, 382–83;
    11:126, 134, 141, 331
Bennett, Arnold, 8:192, 445
Bentham, Jeremy, 9:570; 10:144, 167; 11:150
Benveniste, Emile, 11:256, 260
Benvenuto of Imola, 8:508
Beowulf, 9:669

Béranger, Pierre-Jean de, 7:157
Bérénice (Racine), 11:93
Berenson, Bernard, 10:184
Bergson, Henri, 8:145–46, 212, 367; 9:201–2, 419, 424; 11:341
Berkeley, George, 10:361
Berlin, Isaiah, 10:75; 11:222–23
Bernard, Emile, 8:149
Bernard, J. J., 9:445
Bernard, Jessie, 11:177
Bernays, Jacob, 9:7
Bernhardt, Sarah, 8:153
Berni, Francesco, 2:118
Bernini, Giovanni Lorenzo, 6:148
Berrichon, Paterne, 9:430
Berryman, John, 10:610
Bersani, Leo, 11:229
Bertran de Born, 1:515
Bertrand, Aloysius, 7:475; 8:598
Besant, Walter, 7:511–25, 695
Bessborough, Lady, 8:180–81
Bettelheim, Bruno, 10:313
Beyond Good and Evil (Nietzsche), 7:559–60, 590
Beyond the Pleasure Principle (Freud), 7:x; 9:288, 391, 407; 10:565; 11:97, 358
Bhagavad Gita, 9:660
Bible, The, 1:437–65; 3:254; 5:652–54; 6:413–14; 7:29, 108, 132, 229, 421, 465, 609; 8:421, 489–96, 499–501, 505–8, 518n.33; 9:xv–xvii, 515, 645; 10:582, 585, 615; 11:42, 214
Biely, Andrei, 8:321, 325, 561; 11:258
Bijoux indiscrets, Les (Diderot), 8:281–82
Billy Budd (Melville), 9:243–44
Bimarcus (Varro), 11:267
Binswanger, Paul, 10:263
Binyon, Laurence, 9:61
Biographia Literaria (Coleridge), 7:440, 442; 9:562; 10:155, 166; 11:11
Biographical Sketches and Interesting Anecdotes of Persons of Color (Mott), 11:369
Biographie Universelle, 7:183
Bion, 1:374
Birds, The (Aristophanes), 7:249
Birkenhead, Frederick Edwin Smith, Earl of, 8:179
Birth of the Child, The (Norden), 10:569
Birth of Tragedy, The (Nietzsche), 7:627, 647; 9:10, 661; 10:210, 285; 11:68n.57
Black, Max, 10:641
Black, William, 7:703
Black Arrow, The (Stevenson), 7:703
Black Book, The (Durrell), 9:78

"Black Forest" (Breton), 8:594
Blacklock, Thomas, 4:300
Blackmore, Sir Richard, 3:502–4; 4:279; 9:238, 653; 10:71, 229
Blackmur, R. P., 9:5, 230, 232–33; 10:381–83, 563, 565
Blacks, The (Genet), 9:437
Blake, William, 3:484n.24; 5:527–32, 541; 6:392; 7:xlvi–xlvii, 64, 349–404, 423, 476; 8:72, 77, 82, 84–85, 88; 9:ix, xi, xiv, 26, 221, 330, 380, 410, 463, 502; 9:546; 10:11, 155, 173, 185, 216, 550, 555, 569, 584–85, 587, 607, 610–11, 614–19, 623, 645; 11:x
Blanchot, Maurice, 10:61–63, 261, 263, 266, 284, 286, 298; 11:41
Blassingame, John W., 11:385
Bleak House (Dickens), 7:69; 9:492; 10:399
Blessed Damozel, The (Rossetti), 7:463–64, 467
Blindness and Insight (de Man), 10:380, 567
Blithedale Romance, The (Hawthorne), 7:519
Bloch, Ernst, 8:448; 11:126–27
Bloch, Marc, 11:227
Blok, Aleksandr, 8:325, 343
Bloody Brother; or, Rollo, Duke of Normandy (Fletcher et al.), 3:384, 563–64
Bloom, Allan, 10:324n.13
Bloom, Harold, 10:137, 378, 520, 522, 568, 581, 588n.9; 11:172–76, 181–82, 184, 286, 374
"Blueprint for Negro Literature" (Wright), 11:370–71
Bluest Eye, The (Morrison), 11:286
Blyden, Edward Wilmot, 11:367
Boas, Franz, 9:615
Boccaccio, Giovanni, 2:vii, 74, 82–83, 116, 124, 176, 228, 230–31, 254–55, 461; 3:333, 346, 477, 490, 493–94, 496; 4:499, 501–2, 636; 5:377; 7:458; 8:95; 9:129–30
Bodily Changes in Pain, Hunger, Fear and Rage (Cannon), 9:575
Bodin, Jean, 2:261
Body and Mind, (Mauldsey), 11:194n.12
Boece, Hector, 4:198
Boeckh, August, 10:488
Boehme, Jakob, 5:390; 8:93; 10:441
Boethius (Anicius Manlius Severinus Boethius), 1:533; 2:44–45, 177, 285–86, 323, 405; 8:487, 515n.4
Bogatyrev, Peter, 8:573
Bohlen, Peter von, 7:109–10
Boiardo, Matteo Maria, 2:131, 175, 177; 3:336, 467; 9:453
Boileau, Nicolas (Nicolas Boileau-Despreaux),

3:410, 412–13, 740–46; 4:32, 160; 5:189; 6:54–55, 95; 11:63n.4
Bolingbroke, Henry St. John, Viscount, 6:441, 470
Bonaventure, St., 7:678
Bond, Donald, 10:94–95
Bonefonius (Jean Bonnefons), 3:80, 85, 339
Book of American Negro Spirituals, The (Johnston), 11:387
Book of Categories (attrib. to Augustine), 8:487
Book of Heroes, 6:354
Book of Myths (Fulgentius), 2:39
Boole, George, 10:361; 11:257
Booth, Wayne C., 10:515; 11:274n.19
Borges, Jorge Luis, 10:369, 605, 619
Borgia, Caesar, 8:97
Borinage (film), 8:462
Boris Godunov (Pushkin), 7:290
Bosanquet, Bernard, 9:7, 16, 22n.1
Boskind-Lodahl, Marlene, 11:189
Bossuet, Jacques-Bénigne, 7:230, 261; 8:506
Bostonians, The (James), 9:71, 357–58
Boswell, James, 4:x–xv; 7:709; 10:131, 135–39
Botticelli, Sandro, 7:xix
Bouguereau, William-Adolphe, 8:5
Bourgeois gentilhomme, Le (Molière), 6:50
Bourget, Paul, 7:704
Bouvard et Pécuchet (Flaubert), 9:28–29; 10:566
Boyd, Henry, 5:130–33
Boyer, Claude, abbé, 3:581
Boyhood (Tolstoy), 7:319, 325–27
Boys and Girls Together (Saroyan), 10:415
Bradley, A. C., 8:527; 9:393n.1; 10:78, 146–47
Bradley, F. H., 8:422, 427; 10:361
Bradley, Henry, 8:145
Brain, Sir Russell, 11:16
Brambletye House (Smith), 6:239
Brancusi, Constantin, 8:306
Brand, Max, 10:217
Brand (Ibsen), 9:29
Brandes, Georg, 8:11
Braut von Messina, Die (Schiller), 8:282
Breaking of the Vessels, The (Bloom), 9:xv
Break-up of Britain, The (Nairn), 11:134
Brecht, Bertolt, 8:472n.11; 9:439–41, 552, 690; 10:241–42, 246, 254
Breme, Luigi Arborio Gattinara di, 6:365, 379n.1
Bremond, abbé, 9:462; 10:549
Breton, André, 8:475n.25; 9:425, 602–10; 10:118

"Bride of Abydos, The" (Byron), 7:211
Bride of Corinth, The (Goethe), 5:200
Bridge, The (Crane), 10:585, 633
Bridges, Robert, 8:145; 9:85
Bridgman, Laura, 9:202
Brik, Osip, 8:325, 334–35, 337, 343
British Quarterly Review, The, 7:223
Britten, Benjamin, 10:587
Briusov, Valery Iakovlevich, 8:321
Broken Heart, The (Ford), 5:694–95
"Broken Love" (Blake), 7:374
Bromwich, David, 5:xii–xiii; 10:401
Brontë, Charlotte, 9:79; 11:180–81, 185–86, 189, 286. *See also* Bell, Currer
Brontë, Emily, 9:79; 11:97, 180–81, 183, 186–87
Bronze Horseman, The (Pushkin), 7:327
Brook, Peter, 9:443; 10:174
Brooke, Lord (Fulke Greville), 5:695
Brooke, Rupert, 9:60, 62
Brooks, Cleanth, 9:230, 232–33, 235, 576; 10:71–72, 146, 150, 156, 499–501, 506–7, 543–45, 547, 632; 11:281
Brooks, Peter, 10:306
Brooks, Van Wyck, 9:71
Brothers Karamazov, The (Dostoevsky), 7:626; 8:56, 59, 63–64
Broun, Heywood, 11:370
Brown, Charles, 6:289–90
Brown, Hugo, 9:161, 164, 170
Brown, Norman O., 9:409, 413; 11:95–96
Brown, Sterling, 11:371, 375, 385
Brown, Thomas, 5:118n.7
Browne, Sir Thomas, 5:493; 6:401
Browne, William, 3:142
Browning, Elizabeth Barrett, 7:xlii; 10:136; 11:180–81
Browning, Oscar, 8:179–80
Browning, Robert, 7:656, 683, 695; 8:12, 410–11, 429; 9:32, 59–60, 463
Bruce, Sir John, 5:343
Bruno, Giordano, 7:687; 10:619
Brunswick, Ruth Mack, 9:283
Brustein, Robert, 9:583
Brutus, L., 1:232
Brutus, M. Junius, 1:289
Brutus (Cicero), 2:200, 204
Buber, Martin, 9:xvi, 197; 10:569; 11:45, 66n.34
Bubu de Montparnasse (Philippe), 8:370–71
Buchan, Peter, 5:346–47
Buchanan, George, 2:197; 3:89, 265
Buckley, Samuel, 10:94
Bucolics (Petrarch). *See Eclogues*
Bucolics (Vergil). *See Eclogues*

Budaeus (Guillaume Budé), 2:191
Buffon, Georg-Louis Le Clerc, comte de, 8:369, 389n.15; 10:455; 11:53
Bulgarin, Faddei Venediktovich, 8:343
Bunyan, John, 6:82, 392; 7:26; 8:153, 265; 10:400; 11:76, 186
Buonaparte, Lucien, 5:316
Burckhardt, Jacob, 7:645; 8:157, 264
Burden, Chris, 10:386
Bürger, Gottfried August, 5:198–200, 314–15
Burke, Carolyn, 11:285
Burke, Edmund, 5:xvi, 578–79, 597, 599–600, 607–9, 613–15, 619; 6:412; 7:220, 276; 9:574
Burke, Kenneth, 8:384n.7; 9:vii–ix, 362; 10:568, 632, 635, 641; 11:vii, 141, 235–47
Burnand, Sir Francis Cowley, 7:710
Burne-Jones, Sir Edward, 8:86, 94
Burnet, Gilbert, 3:721
Burnet, John, 10:87
Burnet, Thomas, 7:452
Burney, Fanny, 9:65; 11:311
Burns, Robert, 5:79–80; 6:218–20; 7:75, 193, 205, 208–12; 8:88; 9:651
Burroughs, John, 11:110
Burroughs, William S., 10:422, 430
Burton, Robert, 10:173
Bush, Douglas, 11:200
Bussy, Roger de Rabutin Bussy-Rabutin, comte de, 3:636
Bussy d'Ambois (Chapman), 3:303; 5:697
Butcher, S. H., 9:6–7, 14, 19
Butler, Samuel, 3:293
Butor, Michel, 9:684; 10:305–6, 416, 550
Buzzati, Dino, 10:240
Byatt, A. S., 10:295
Byron, George Gordon, Lord, 5:89, 91–92, 603, 619–20, 624–25, 628; 6:vii, 138, 241–44, 259, 263, 272, 277, 369, 470–71; 7:74–75, 211, 217, 449, 472–73, 605; 8:419, 430, 535; 9:26, 30, 35; 11:189
Byron's Conspiracy (Chapman), 5:697
Byron's Tragedy (Chapman), 5:697
"Byzantium" (Yeats), 10:99

Cabanis, Pierre Jean Georges, 6:440
Cabell, James Branch, 10:93
Caecilius Statius, 1:266
Caecilius. *See* Calactinus, Caecilius
Caepio, Q. Servilius, 1:249
Caesar, C., 3:425
Caesar, C. Julius, 1:451; 2:50, 198, 207, 209–10, 259–60, 439; 3:15–16, 102, 451, 458, 643, 659, 705; 6:36
Cage, John, 10:417

Caillot, M., 4:340, 352n.44
Caine, Hall, 7:703
Calactinus, Caecilius, 1:325, 327, 329, 345–46; 3:317, 320, 327, 425
Calamus (Whitman), 8:252
Calderón de la Barca, Pedro, 3:435; 5:84, 86, 219; 6:193; 11:267
"Caliban upon Setebos" (Browning), 8:12
Callimachus, 3:viii, 148, 174, 339
Callisthenes, 1:326; 3:13–14
Callistratus, 1:202
Callixenus, 1:406
Calprenède, Gauthier de la, 3:365
Camden, William, 3:85, 90
Camões, Luis de, 3:343, 349
Campbell, O. J., 10:85
Campbell, Thomas, 6:138
Campion, Thomas, 3:79
Camus, Albert, 9:676; 10:240, 249, 255, 297, 301, 418, 423, 426
"Canary for One, A" (Hemingway), 9:48
Candide (Voltaire), 7:60
Candy (Southern and Hoffenberg), 11:107
Canfield, Dorothy, 9:573
Canguilhem, Georges, 11:43–44
Cannaccio, Giovanni, 2.118
Cannon, W. B., 9:575
"Canonization, The" (Donne), 9:503–9, 526–27
Cantatrice chauve, La (Ionesco), 9:448
Canterbury Tales, The (Chaucer), 2:248; 3:490, 493–94, 496–98; 5:134, 626; 7:203–4; 6:65; 9:580; 10:342–43
Cantor, Georg, 10:467; 11:259
Cantos (Pound), 9:253–54; 10:210; 11:74
"Cape Hatteras" (Crane), 10:584
Capek, Karel, 9:188
Capitaine Fracasse, Le (Gautier), 7:474
"Capital of the World, The" (Hemingway), 9:47
Caporali, Cesare, 3:145
Capture of Miletus (Phrynichus), 1:342
Carbo, C. Papirius, 1:233
Carcinus, 1:161–62, 201
Carlyle, Thomas, 5:82–83; 7:xvi, 77, 226, 259, 632, 636–37, 709; 8:178–79; 9:560–61, 650; 10:74, 623–24, 634
Carmichael, Mary, 8:182–85, 187–90
Carmina (Paulinus of Nola), 8:498
Carneades, 1:234–35, 313, 483
Caro, Hannibal, 3:395–96, 471
Carpetbaggers, The (Robbins), 11:107
Carroll, Lewis, 6:viii
Carte Postale, La (Derrida), 11:358
Casanova, Jacques, 7:709

INDEX OF NAMES AND TITLES

Case Is Altered, The (Jonson), 5:695–96
Case of Wagner, The (Nietzsche), 11:68n.63
Casely-Hayford, J. E., 11:367
Cassandra (Schiller), 5:194
Cassirer, Ernst, 10:498
Castelvetro, Ludovico, 3:188; 4:222; 11:7
Castiglione, Baldassare, 2:116
Castle of Indolence, The (Thomson), 5:314
Catiline (Jonson), 3:364, 435, 443–44, 446, 563
Cato (Addison), 4:386–88; 6:77
Cato the Elder (M. Porcius Cato "Censorius"), 1:266, 289, 309, 313, 321, 363, 385, 450; 2:207; 3:186, 319, 731; 8:512
Cato the Younger (M. Porcius Cato Uticensis), 1:298; 2:294; 3:48; 8:509–10
Catullus (C. Valerius Catullus), 2:255–56; 3:339, 414, 495; 8:313, 484, 515n.10
Caucasian Chalk Circle, The (Brecht), 8:638
Caudwell, Christopher, 11:18
Causabon, Isaac, 3:317, 405, 410, 641, 643
Causeries du lundi (Sainte-Beuve), 7:470
Cavalcanti, Guido, 8:95, 410, 417
Cave, Terence, 2:xv–xvi
Caylus, Claude-Philippe de Tubières, comte de, 5:36, 38–41, 43
Caylus, Madame de, 6:477–78
Cebes, 3:186
Cecil, Lord David, 9:65–67, 81n.17
Cedrenus, Adam, 3:127
Celestial Hierarchy (Dionysius the Areopagite), 2:40
Céline, Louis-Ferdinand, 8:377
Cellini, Benvenuto, 7:653, 709
Celsus (A. Cornelius Celsus), 1:287, 293, 307; 3:22, 187; 8:486
Cenci, The (Shelley), 6:289; 7:18
Centaur (Chaeremon), 1:150
Ceremonial Songs of Spring (Anichkov), 8:571
Cervantes, Miguel de, 2:xi; 3:636; 5:378–79; 7:262; 8:296, 329, 332; 9:131; 10:294, 353; 11:265
Cestius, 3:97, 101
Cézanne, Paul, 8:148–49, 352; 9:185; 10:120
Chaeremon, 1:150, 170, 193
Chairs, The (Ionesco), 10:254
Chaloner, Sir Thomas, 3:106
Chamfort, 5:361
Champfleury (Jules Husson), 7:142
Champollion, Jean-Francois, 9:270
Chance (Conrad), 9:73, 344
Chang Tung-Sun, 11:258
Chanson de Roland (Turoldus), 7:199; 8:119n.3

Chanticleer (Rostand), 9:445
Chants de Maldoror, Les (Lautréamont), 10:117; 11:97
Chapelain, Jean, 3:467, 559
Chapman, George, 3:79, 81–83, 121, 142, 303, 476; 4:164; 5:697; 6:433; 7:206–7, 367; 8:406, 409; 9:664, 666, 670; 10:579
Char, René, 10:8, 119–21, 123–24
Characters and Caricaturas (Hogarth), 4:246n.8
Characters of Men (Pope). See *Moral Essays*
Characters of Shakespear's Plays (Hazlitt), 5:xv
Charles I (King of England), 6:127n.1
Charles II (King of England), 9:548
Charles V (Titian), 8:226
Charmadas, 1:234, 240–42
Chase, Stuart, 9:503
Chasse spirituelle, La (attrib. to Rimbaud), 10:459
Chateaubriand, François René, vicomte de, 6:478; 7:429, 474; 8:226, 598; 9:30, 432
Chateaubriand et ses amis (Sainte-Beuve), 8:422
Chateaubrun, Jean Baptiste Vivienne de, 5:30–31
Chatelet, François, 10:384
Chatiments (Hugo), 7:402n.32
Chatterton, Thomas, 6:259; 7:16
Chaucer, Geoffrey, 2:vii, xiv, 202, 245, 248, 265, 298, 355, 377–78, 393; 3:93, 96, 140, 145, 300, 413, 490, 493–502, 553, 720; 4:xii; 5:134, 584, 611, 626; 6:65, 70–71, 80, 201, 225, 456; 7:55, 203–6, 211, 261, 392n.2, 468; 8:311; 9:258, 651; 10:136, 342, 491
Chaumont, Father, 5:100
Cheese and the Worms, The (Ginzburg), 10:397
Cheke, Sir John, 2:189, 194, 197, 199, 201, 206
Chekhov, Anton, 8:196, 343; 10:326–27
Chemins de la liberté, Les (Sartre), 10:298
Chénier, Joseph-Marie de, 6:47–48
Cherniss, Harold, 8:385n.10
Cheselden, William, 5:102
Chesler, Phyllis, 11:177
Chesnutt, Charles W., 11:369
Chesterton, G. K., 8:216; 9:499
"Chevauchée d'Yeldis" (Vielé-Griffin), 9:32
Chevrillon, André, 9:72
"Chevy Chase," 5:330
Chicago, Judy, 11:183
"Child in the House, The" (Pater), 7:xxiv
"Child of Elle, The" (anon.), 5:341

Childe Harold's Pilgrimage (Byron), 6:241–43, 470
Childhood (Tolstoy), 7:319, 325–27
"Children in the Wood," 5:429
"Chimère, La" (Flaubert), 7:719
Choephoroe (Aeschylus), 1:162
Choerilus, 1:196
Choise of Emblemes (Whitney), 10:579
Chomsky, Noam, 10:466, 608; 11:163
Chopin, Fryderyk Franciszek, 7:654
Chopin, Kate, 11:286
Chrétien de Troyes, 7:202
Christ Suffering (attrib. to Nazianzen), 3:170
Christabel (Coleridge), 5:633; 6:67–68, 92–94; 7:452; 9:484
Christiansen, B., 8:331
Christopherson, John, 10:99
Chronicle, The (Cowley), 4:512
Chrysippus, 1:235, 311, 388, 392, 482; 2:94; 3:21, 30, 45, 341
Chrysostom, St. John, 11:44
Chukovsky, Kornei Ivanovich, 8:321
Chung Yung (Confucius), 8:548–52, 555n.23
Church, Alonzo, 11:257
Church and State Review, 7:228
Churchill, Winston, 9:548
Churchyard, Thomas, 3:140
Cibber, Colley, 4:561–62
Cicero (M. Tullius Cicero), 1:289, 292–93, 297, 301, 303–4, 308, 310–12, 316, 318, 321, 334–35, 431, 489; 2:14, 31, 42, 48, 71, 94–95, 97, 116–17, 133, 148, 150, 154, 161, 177, 189–91, 193, 199–200, 203–5, 207–9, 257–59, 266, 289, 301–2, 321, 341, 359, 421; 3:4, 23–25, 29, 33, 48, 101–2, 104, 187–88, 242, 249, 258, 395, 419, 493, 582, 643, 719, 722, 730–31, 735–36, 740; 4:47, 207–8, 210, 253, 258, 260, 266, 337; 5:32; 7:229, 426, 709; 8:479, 482–84, 486, 509; 9:683; 10:335; 11:266
Cid, Le (Corneille), 3:264, 269–70, 273, 447, 551, 583; 10:169; 11:50
Cid, The, 9:249–50
"Cimetière marin, Le" (Valéry), 8:140; 9:250
Cinna (Corneille), 3:266, 268, 270–73, 447; 11:50
Cino da Pistoia, 1:505, 508, 511, 515, 518; 8:95, 410
Cinthio, Giraldi. *See* Giraldi Cintio, Giovanni Battista
Cistolaria (Plautus), 1:490
City of God (Augustine). *See De Civitate Dei*
Civil Wars, The (Daniel), 5:434–35

Civilization and Its Discontents (Freud), 9:403–7, 409
Civilization of the Greeks, The (Burckhardt), 7:645
Cixous, Hélène, 11:284–85
Clairon, Mlle., 4:312, 317–19, 328–29, 347n.5
Clarissa (Richardson), 5:585; 6:59; 9:65; 11:324
Clark, Sir Kenneth, 7:xliii; 10:196–97
Clarke, Bartholomew, 2:395
Clarkson, Thomas, 11:368
Claudel, Paul, 8:153; 9:447–48, 597–602, 608–10; 11:54, 56–58, 61, 67n.51
Claudian (Claudius Claudianus), 3:395
Claudius, Matthias, 5:214
Clausen, Jan, 10:593
Clauserus (Conrad Clauser), 2:303
"Clean, Well-Lighted Place, A" (Hemingway), 9:42
Cleanthes, 1:311, 388, 391
Clement of Alexandria, 4:198, 200
Clément, Catherine, 11:284
Cleombrotus, 1:218
Cleopatra, 2:439; 7:708
Cleophon, 1:150, 167, 186
Cleveland, John, 3:419, 430–31; 4:504; 8:407, 413
Clitarchus, 1:220, 326
Clitomachus, 1:234
Cloister and the Hearth, The (Reade), 7:706
Closing of the American Mind, The (Bloom), 10:324n.11
Clouds, The (Aristophanes), 4:257; 7:249
Clutton-Brock, Arthur, 8:402
Cobbe, Frances Power, 7:229
Coccaius, Merlin, 3:412
Cochin, Henry, 7:183
Cocktail Party, The (Eliot), 10:98
Cocteau, Jean, 9:438; 10:195
Coeur simple, Un (Flaubert), 7:175
Colenso, John William, 7:228, 233n.2
Coleridge, Mary Elizabeth, 11:185
Coleridge, Samuel Taylor, 3:xvi; 5:vii–xii, xix, 271, 283, 533–45, 562, 565–67, 601–2, 628–36, 700; 6:vii, 78, 80, 85, 92, 98, 138, 254, 417; 7:xvi, xxv, xlv, 16, 41, 75, 181, 206, 218, 438–57, 668; 8:146, 208, 211–12, 405, 422–23, 426, 429, 432, 545–46; 9:xiv, 30, 33, 58, 64, 195, 208, 214, 222, 380, 467, 484, 500–502, 508, 561, 565, 572, 574; 10:65, 77, 152, 155–57, 166–67, 175, 186, 199, 228, 232, 405, 548–50, 568, 608–9, 619, 624–25; 11:11, 18, 20, 190, 367

Coleridge, Sara Fricker, 5:vii–x
Coleridge on Imagination (Richards), 10:155, 167
"Coleridge's Writings" (Pater), 5:ix, xii
Colet, Louise, 7:155, 159, 166
Collected Poems (Yeats), 10:96, 100
Collections, The (Paul of Perugia), 2:56
College English, 10:387–88
Collier, Jeremy, 3:503–4, 706–52
Collingwood, R. G., 10:41–42, 44–45
Collins, William, 4:580–81; 5:xvii, 314, 579; 6:136; 8:410; 9:463; 10:614
"Colloquy of Monos and Una, The" (Poe), 7:130–32
Colonne, Guido delle, 1:518
Color Purple, The (film), 10:313
Colored American, The, 11:369
Coltrane, John, 11:371
Columbus, Christopher, 8:185
Columella (L. Junius Moderatus Columella), 3:186; 8:486
"Come In" (Frost), 10:584
Comédie humaine, La (Balzac), 7:712; 8:285
Comedy of Errors, The (Shakespeare), 9:168
Comment c'est (Beckett), 10:302
Commentary, 10:408
Communist Manifesto, The (Marx and Engels), 10:464
"Composed upon Westminster Bridge" (Wordsworth), 9:500
Composition of Lyric Verse, The (Zhirmunsky), 8:335
"Compulsory Heterosexuality and Lesbian Experience" (Rich), 10:595
Comte, Auguste, 7:633; 9:594; 10:429
Comus (Milton), 4:527–28; 6:400; 7:660; 9:93; 10:583; 11:199, 207
"Concerning the Education of the Human Race" (Lessing), 6:358
Conder, Josiah, 6:213–14
Condillac, Etienne Bonnot de, 10:281, 285
Conditioned Reflexes (Pavlov), 8:554n.21
Condolle, A. de, 8:319
Condorcet, Marie Jean Antoine Nicolas Caritat, marquis de, 10:136
Confessio Amantis (Gower), 11:78
Confessions (Augustine), 9:193, 206
Confessions, Les (Rousseau), 6:475–77, 480–82, 484; 7:412, 473–74; 10:270
Confessions of an English Opium-Eater (De Quincey), 6:109–12, 116
Confucius, 3:623; 8:548–52, 554n.19
Congreve, William, 3:480; 4:247n.15; 5:663–65, 668; 6:84; 7:243–46; 9:354, 557

"Connection of Devices of Plot Formation with General Devices of Style, The" (Shklovsky), 8:329
Connolly, Cyril, 9:330
Conquest of America: The Question of the Other, The (Todorov), 10:403
Conquest of Granada, The (Dryden), 3:382; 4:536
Conrad, Joseph, 8:192; 9:63, 72–76, 344; 10:313, 421; 11:143, 155
Considerations sur les moeurs (Duclos), 6:51
Consolatio Philosophiae (Boethius), 1:533; 2:44
Constable, John, 7:700; 8:205; 10:230
Constant, Benjamin, 8:598; 11:227
Constitution of the Lacedaemonians (Xenophon), 1:327
Conteur, Le (Picard), 6:47
Conti, Armand, Prince de, 3:352
Continentia Vergiliana (Fulgentius), 8:499
Contra Faustinum (Augustine), 8:495
Contrat social, Le (Rousseau), 9:431; 10:285
Conversations with Goethe (Eckermann), 9:115–16
Coomaraswamy, Ananda K., 9:558–59
Cooper, David, 9:413
Cooper's Hill (Denham), 3:470
Copernicus, Nicholas, 3:410, 630; 7:615; 9:392
Corax, 1:241
Corbière, Tristan, 8:412, 418, 429
Cordemoy, Geraud de, 10:466
Coriolanus (Shakespeare), 5:xviii; 9:173, 177–79, 389, 665–66, 673–74
Corneille, Pierre, 3:277, 321–22, 361, 424–25, 433, 436–37, 439, 442–44, 447, 449, 452, 463, 551, 583, 693, 695, 726; 4:337; 5:222; 6:60; 7:251; 8:264, 296; 9:447; 10:169; 11:50–51, 53–54, 63n.4, 66–67n.43
Cornford, F. M., 10:173
Cornucopian Text, The (Cave), 2:xv
Corot, Camille, 7:686, 700
Correggio, Antonio, 9:116
Correspondant, Le, 7:183
Correspondence with Friends (Gogol), 8:342
Corsair, The (Byron), 6:369
Cortázar, Julio, 10:385
Cott, Nancy, 11:278
"Cotter's Saturday Night, The" (Burns), 7:209
Cotton, Charles, 3:656
Coulter, James A., 1:xix
Counterfeiters, The (Gide), 10:157, 323n.7
Counter-Statement (Burke), 9:vii

Country and the City, The (Williams), 11:158
Country Wife, The (Wycherley), 3:674, 684; 7:238
"Coup de dés, Un" (Mallarmé), 10:632
Couples (Updike), 10:320
"Course of a Particular, The" (Stevens), 7:xvii
Cousin, Victor, 7:280
Covering Islam (Said), 11:161
Cowley, Abraham, 3:314, 364, 399, 401–2, 413, 421, 470, 473, 476–77, 499–500, 555–57, 566, 579, 720; 4:x, 51, 495–519; 5:310, 438, 441; 8:406–8, 412; 10:580
Cowper, William, 5:302–3, 593; 6:113, 136–37, 218–19, 246; 7:261; 10:614
Crabbe, George, 6:242
"Cradle Song" (Blake), 7:363, 395n.9
Craft of Fiction, The (Lubbock), 10:135
Crane, Hart, 9:315; 10:583–85, 633
Crane, R. S., 9:232–39, 245, 248
Crane, Ralph, 10:94
Crantor, 3:341
Crashaw, Richard, 8:406, 409, 412
Crates, 1:153, 215; 2:165
Cratinus, 1:427; 3:740
Cratylus (Plato), 4:199; 10:556
Crawford, F. Marion, 7:703
Crawley, Rawdon, 7:713
"Crazy Jane and the Bishop" (Yeats), 9:374
"Crazy Jane on God" (Yeats), 9:374
"Creation" (Du Bartas). *See* "Semaine, La"
Creative Evolution (Bergson). *See Evolution créatrice, L'*
Creech, Thomas, 3:475
Crépet, Jacques, 8:416
Cresphontes (Euripides), 1:160
Crillon, Comte de, 6:417
Crisis, The, 11:369
"Critic as Artist, The" (Wilde), 10:377
"Critic as Artist as Wilde, The" (Ellmann), 7:xxxiv
Critical Essays (Barthes), 10:382
Criticism and Ideology (Eagleton), 11:287
Criticism in Antiquity (Russell), 1:vii
Criticism in the Wilderness (Hartman), 10:623
Critics and Criticism (Crane), 9:236
Critic's Notebook, The (Stallman), 10:380
Critique de l'Ecole des femmes (Molière), 7:261
Critique et vérité (Barthes), 10:382
Critique of Dialectical Reason (Sartre), 11:131
Critique of Judgment, The (Kant), 10:146; 11:40

Critique of Political Economy, A (Marx), 8:298
Critique of Pure Reason (Kant), 11:40
Critique on Goethe, A (Schubarth), 5:65
Critolaus, 1:234
Croce, Benedetto, 9:559; 11:152, 269
Cromwell, Oliver, 4:534
"Cross Country Snow" (Hemingway), 9:48
Cruche Cassée, La (Greuze), 8:115
Cry of the Royal Blood (anon.), 10:580
"Crystal Cabinet, The" (Blake), 7:388
Ctesias, 1:279
Ctesiphon, 1:291
"Cuchulain's Fight with the Sea" (Yeats), 10:88
Culex (attrib. to Vergil), 2:76
Cullen, Countee, 11:372–73, 387
Culler, Jonathan, 11:279
Culture and Anarchy (Arnold), 11:147–49, 152, 369
Cunningham, Allan, 5:532
Cunningham, J. V., 9:241
"Cupid" (Blake), 7:372
Curtius, E. R., 11:243
Curtius, Q., 2:283
Custine, Astolphe Louis Leonard, marquis de, 7:142
Custom of the Country, The (Fletcher), 3:503
Cuvier, Georges Leopold Chrétien Frédéric Dagobert, baron, 10:455, 465
Cuyp, Aelbert Jacobsz, 7:715
Cyclops (Euripides), 2:455, 467
Cymbeline (Shakespeare), 8:204
Cynthia's Revels (Jonson), 10:587
Cypria, 1:169
Cyprioe (Dicaeogenes), 1:162
Cyropaedia (Xenophon), 2:130; 3:729

Dacier, André, 3:405, 467, 691–93, 696, 698–704, 724, 737–38
Daemon of the World, The (Shelley), 10:532, 535
"Daffodils" (Wordsworth), 7:435
Daisy Miller (James), 9:349
Damon, S. Foster, 9:330
Dampier, Sir William, 3:474
Daniel, Arnaut, 1:515, 523, 526
Daniel, Samuel, 3:79, 81–82, 141, 146, 454; 5:434–35, 456
Daniel Deronda (Eliot), 7:706; 9:70–71; 11:286–87
D'Annunzio, Gabriele, 9:35
Dante Alighieri, 2:vii, 3–5, 21, 47, 55, 69–74, 108, 136, 176, 315–32, 391, 408, 413–14; 3:145, 203, 333, 343, 346; 5:130–33, 150,

377, 423, 456, 586–88; 6:46, 48, 66, 68, 70, 97, 196, 200, 229, 325, 327–37, 341, 343, 345, 377, 410; 7:23–25, 40–41, 43, 54, 200, 465, 473, 677; 8:91, 93, 95–97, 107, 109, 308–10, 315, 376, 384n.7, 396–97, 410, 414, 416–17, 419–20, 427, 430, 507–14, 519–20nn.49–52; 9:34, 220, 251–53, 324, 329, 468–69, 515, 602, 638, 642; 10:153–55, 569, 583; 11:viii
Dante le théologien (Mandonnet), 8:519n.42
Darkness (Andreyev), 8:297
Darkness at Noon (Koestler), 9:75; 11:221
Darwin, Charles, 7:xx, 282, 637–38, 698; 8:202; 9:392, 480; 10:455
Darwin, Erasmus, 7:282
da Tempo, Antonio, 2:108
Daudet, Alphonse, 7:704
Daughter of Heth, The (Black), 7:705
D'Avenant, Sir William, 3:231, 293, 361–62, 554–55, 720; 5:444; 9:527
David, Jacques-Louis, 6:48
David Copperfield (Dickens), 7:538
Davideis (Cowley), 3:252, 364, 413, 555–57; 4:515–16; 10:580
Davies, Sir John, 3:82, 85; 5:415
Davis, Charles T., 11:385
Dawn, The (Nietzsche), 7:590
Day, John, 3:81
"Day-Dream, The" (Coleridge), 6:85
De Actibus Apostolorum (Arator), 8:498
De Amicitia (Cicero), 3:731
De Analogia (Caesar), 3:15, 102
De Anima (Aristotle), 2:330
De Antiquitatibus Romanorum (Varro), 2:206
De Apparatu Linguae Latinae (Riccius), 2:192
De Audendis Poetis (Plutarch), 3:717
De Baptismo (Tertullian), 8:491
De Bello Civili (Caesar), 2:209
De Bello Gallico (Caesar), 2:209
de Brunne, Robert. *See* Mannyng, Robert, of Brunne
De Catechizandis Rudibus (Augustine), 8:493
De Civitate Dei (Augustine), 2:206; 8:493–96
De Differentiis Topicis (Boethius), 2:405
De Div. Quaest. ad Simplicianum (Augustine), 8:497
De Divinatione (Cicero), 8:483
De Finibus (Cicero), 2:154
De Fuga in Persecutione (Tertullian), 8:490–91
De Genesi ad Litteram (Augustine), 8:496
De Gloria Atheniensium (Plutarch), 3:717
De Imitatione Christi (Thomas à Kempis), 7:633

De la grammatologie (Derrida), 10:270, 274, 283–85; 11:150
de la Motte, Antoine Houdar. *See* Houdar de la Motte, Antoine
De Lingua Latina (Varro), 2:205; 8:480
De Natura Deorum (Cicero), 2:341; 4:253; 8:483
De Natura et Usu Literarum (Malinckrodt), 4:194
De Nobilitate Literata et de Amissa Dicendi Ratione (Sturmius), 2:191
De Oratore (Cicero), 1:316; 2:190; 8:484
De Pace (Isocrates), 1:202
De Partu Virginis (Sannazaro), 3:349
De Prima Scribendi Origine (Hugo), 4:194
De Profundis (Wilde), 7:xxxiii
De Republica (Augustine), 3:735
De Resurrectione Carnis (Tertullian), 8:490, 492
De Senectute (Cicero), 3:731, 735
De Spectaculis (Tertullian), 3:750
De Spiritu et Littera (Augustine), 8:495
De Trinitate (Augustine), 8:494, 506
De Viris Illustribus (Jerome), 10:462
De Vita Beati Martini (Severus), 8:498
De Vulgari Eloquentia (Dante), 2:108, 414
"Dead, The" (Joyce), 10:408
Dead Souls (Gogol), 8:561
"Death, a Voyage" (Donne), 4:507
Death in the Afternoon (Hemingway), 9:41–43, 45
Death in Venice (Mann), 11:153
Death of a Salesman (Miller), 9:241
Death of the Past, The (Plumb), 9:395
Death on a Pale Horse (West), 6:253, 291n.12
Debauched Hospodar, The (Apollinaire), 11:107
Debray, Regis, 10:407
Debussy, Claude, 8:223, 231–32
Decameron (Boccaccio), 2:81–82, 254; 3:493; 9:129–30
"Decay of Lying: An Observation, The" (Wilde), 7:xxxii; 10:316, 377, 632
"Deception, The" (Leskov), 8:439–40
De Chirico, Giorgio, 8:661n.10
Declamations (Seneca the Elder), 2:73
Deemster, The (Caine), 7:705
Defence of Lady Chatterley, The (Lawrence), 9:592
Defence of Poesie (Sidney). *See Apology for Poetry*
Defence of Poetry, A (Shelley), 1:xi; 6:vii–xi; 7:397n.14; 8:72; 10:616; 11:9–10
Defence of Ryme, A (Daniel), 3:454

Defoe, Daniel, 7:709; 9:79n.3
Degas, Edgar, 8:131
Deirdre of the Sorrows (Synge), 8:94
"Dejection: An Ode" (Coleridge), 5:viii; 7:449
Dekker, Thomas, 3:121; 5:654, 689, 693, 699; 10:94
Delacroix, Eugène, 11:48
Deleuze, Gilles, 7:x; 10:385–86; 11:95–96, 102n.6
Deliacus (Hyperides), 1:405
Delille, abbé, 6:46
"Dell, The" (Coleridge), 7:450
Delteil, Joseph, 8:599
Demades, 1:217–18, 258
de Man, Paul, 10:x, 380–81, 567, 626, 631–32, 636; 11:vii–viii, 245, 247, 355, 359–63
Demetrius of Phalerum, 1:218, 259; 2:425, 467; 3:342, 344; 4:266, 277
Democracy (Adams), 9:318–21
Democrates, 1:184
Democritus, 1:233–34, 247, 252, 271; 3:51, 54, 63, 150–51, 623; 8:515n.8; 10:256
Democritus of Chios, 1:189
Demosthenes, 1:184, 214–16, 236, 241, 258, 283, 291, 310–11, 318, 326, 334–36, 338–41, 343–45, 347–49, 351, 401–2, 404–5, 407–8, 411; 2:386; 3:4, 26, 29, 110, 128, 188, 228, 320, 396, 493, 583, 719, 722, 726
Denham, Sir John, 3:314, 413, 421, 496, 720; 4:500, 516
Denis, Maurice, 8:206
Dennis, John, 4:480
"Denys l'Auxerrois" (Pater), 7:xxiv
Dépit amoureux, Le (Molière), 4:320
De Quincey, Thomas, 5:xii; 6:193; 7:414, 441, 447; 9:30
Derrida, Jacques, 10:267–89, 381, 522, 559–60, 562–63; 11:vii, 68nn.56, 60, 102–3n.6, 135n.2, 143, 150, 236, 241, 243, 245, 263, 272n.2, 279, 283–85, 355, 357–59
Desbordes-Valmore, Marceline Felicité Josephe, 8:598
Descartes, René, 3:277, 630; 5:407; 7:xlvii; 8:xii, 120n.8, 153, 389n.17; 9:26, 219–20, 546; 10:viii, 118, 429, 616–18; 11:49
Desnos, Robert, 8:599, 605, 611n.9
Desportes, Philippe, 3:145
"Destiny of Nations, The" (Coleridge), 7:451
Deussen, Paul, 7:624n.86
Deux gendres, Les (Etiènne), 6:42
Dewey, John, 8:385n.10
Diable amoureux, Le (Cazotte), 7:131

Diacritics, 11:284
Diaghilev, Sergei, 10:195
Dialektik der Aufklärung (Adorno and Horkheimer), 9:302; 11:127
"Dialogue between a Pilgrim and Time" (Townshend), 8:413
"Dialogue of Self and Soul, The" (Marvell), 11:78
Dialogue on Poetry (Fracastoro), 2:402
Dialogues (Perrault), 3:326
Dialogues (Plato), 11:152
Diana of the Crossways (Meredith), 8:183
"Diaphaneitè" (Pater), 7:xv
Dicaeogenes, 1:162
Dichtung und Wahrheit (Goethe), 9:111
Dickens, Charles, 7:57, 695, 706; 8:21; 9:73–75, 253, 342, 347, 492, 495; 10:135, 211, 217, 365, 416; 11:189–90
Dickinson, Emily, 7:xxxii; 9:574, 655; 10:183, 409; 11:171, 176, 178, 180–84, 186–90, 193
Dickson, Carter, 10:217
Dictionary of Accepted Ideas (Flaubert), 10:566
Didascalicon (Hugo of St. Victor), 11:145–46
Diderot, Denis, 6:59; 7:276; 8:281–82, 289, 296; 9:379–80; 10:55; 11:225, 229
Diez, Friedrich, 8:365, 369, 375–76
Digest (Justinian), 8:486
Diliad (Nicochares), 1:150
Dilthey, Wilhelm, 8:375; 10:23, 33, 512n.30, 549
Dio Cassius, 3:73, 370
Dio Chrysostom, 2:95; 4:199
Diodorus, 1:234
Diodorus Siculus, 3:618
Diogenes, 1:215, 373, 487; 3:13
Diogenes Laertius, 2:259; 3:187; 10:458; 11:266
Dionysius Chalcus, 1:182
Dionysius of Alexandria, 3:187
Dionysius of Halicarnassus, 2:108, 110, 191, 206; 3:252, 325
Dionysius of Syracuse, 3:6
Dionysius the Areopagite, 2:40, 407
Disciple, Le (Bourget), 7:705
"Disciple, The" (Wilde) 7:xxxvi
Discipline and Punish (Foucault), 11:238–39
Discours de la méthode (Descartes), 8:120n.8, 153
Discours sur l'origine de l'inégalité (Rousseau) 10:270, 273, 280, 282
Discourse on Cromwell, A (Cowley), 5:441
Discourse on Metaphysics (Leibniz), 11:52
Discovery of the Mind, The (Snell), 1:ix

Disraeli, Benjamin, 9:79n.1
Dissémination, La (Derrida), 11:62n.3, 356
Dissertation upon Laughter, A (anon.), 4:247n.12
Dissertations and Discussions (Mill), 11:151
Divina Commedia, La (Dante), 1:531–32; 2:47, 55, 215–32; 4:221; 5:130–33, 150–51; 6:46, 327, 329–35; 7:24, 26, 28, 61, 213nn.5–6, 473, 475, 677; 8:93, 95, 109, 308, 396, 420, 507–14, 519–20nn.50–52; 9:250, 253, 468–69, 522; 10:153–54, 157, 569; 11:76
Divinae Institutiones (Lactantius), 8:492
Divine Weeks and Works, The (Du Bartas, tr. Sylveter), 10:580
"Doctor and the Doctor's Wife, The" (Hemingway), 9:48
Doctor Faustus (Marlowe), 5:688
Dolet, Etienne, 2:154; 9:127
Dolon, 1:172
"Domination of Black" (Stevens), 10:581
Dominic, St., 7:678
Domitian, 7:701
Don Juan (Byron), 6:272, 470; 9:566
Don Juan (Musset), 7:165
Don Quixote (Cervantes), 3:636, 638–39, 656; 5:378–79, 694; 7:262, 560; 8:106, 329, 332, 438, 446, 561, 576; 9:131; 10:347–50, 352–53
Don Sanche d'Aragon (Corneille), 3:264, 271
Don Sebastian (Dryden), 3:673, 681
Donato, Eugenio, 10:383
Donatus, Aelius, 9:241
Donne, John, 3:79, 80–82, 86, 90, 93, 409, 411, 421, 511–48; 4:500–505, 508–12; 5:437, 492; 6:402; 8:406, 409–13, 427, 429–30, 543, 546; 9:54, 461, 503–10, 512, 515, 519, 525–30, 563–64, 567, 648; 10:71, 87, 101, 131, 398, 545; 11:9, 153–54, 189
Doppia Favola (Mascardi), 3:410
Doré, Gustave, 7:60
Dorrie, H., 10:48n.17
Dos Passos, John, 9:353
Dostoevsky, Fyodor, 7:626n.113, 641; 8:56–68, 244, 298, 342–43, 441, 450; 9:100, 286, 342, 381; 10:48–49, 351–53, 421; 11:74, 175, 229, 258, 265, 270
Dostoevsky and Gogol (Tynianov), 8:342
Double Dealer, The (Congreve), 3:674
Doubrovsky, Serge, 10:390
Doubt and Certainty in Science (Young), 11:14–16, 18–19
Doudan, Xavier, 8:152
Douglas, Lord Alfred, 7:xxxiii

Douglas, Gavin, 8:426
Douglas, Norman, 9:80n.11
Douglass, Frederick, 11:351
Draco, 4:192
Dracula (Stoker), 10:210, 214
Drake, James, 3:497
Dramas, Fields, and Metaphors (Turner), 10:374
Drame (Soller), 11:271
Drapier's Letters, The (Swift), 4:551
Drayton, Michael, 3:79, 81–82
"Dream of Oblomov, The" (Goncharov), 8:561
"Dreigroschenprozess, Der" (Brecht), 8:472n.16
Dreiser, Theodore, 10:398
Dreyer, Carl Theodor, 8:473n.18
Driesen, Otto, 9:126
Droz, Gustave, 7:122
Drummond, William, 3:142; 9:461
"Drum-Taps" (Whitman), 7:xxxii; 8:252
Dryden, John, 3:xi, xiv–xv, 314, 587, 675–77, 679, 689–93, 733, 745; 4:45, 51–52, 165, 385–87, 492–93, 497, 512, 536–48, 571–72, 576; 5:141, 309, 313, 473, 603, 626; 6:86–87, 89–91, 95, 136, 244; 7:203–7, 397–98, 413; 8:410–12, 422–23; 9:54, 260, 334, 461, 507, 642; 10:147, 227, 496, 579, 609; 11:330
Dryden's Satire on His Muse (attrib. to Somers), 4:537
Du Bartas, Guillaume de Salluste, seigneur, 3:79–80, 142, 203, 291, 338; 5:308; 10:580
Du Bellay, Joachim, 2:xiii, 261; 7:xviii, 409
Du Bois, W. E. B., 11:351, 367, 369–70, 387
Du Bos, Charles, 10:59
Du Bos, Jean Baptiste, abbé, 4:291; 10:275, 277, 279, 285
Dublin Review, The, 7:223
Dubrovsky (Pushkin), 7:320
Ducasse, Curt, 9:561
Duchamp, Marcel, 10:386
Ducharte, Pierre Louis, 11:385
Duchess of Malfi, The (Webster), 5:693; 9:671
Duclos, Mlle, 4:325, 350n.27
Duhamel, Georges, 8:467–68
Dühring, E., 7:564–66, 597
Dumas, Alexandre, 7:149
Dumesnil, Mlle, 4:312, 348n.7
Dunbar, Paul Laurence, 11:367, 369, 374
Dunbar, William, 9:374
Dunbar-Nelson, Alice, 10:594–95
Dunciad, The (Pope), 4:561–62; 7:56
Duns Scotus, 2:330

Dupont, Pierre, 10:459
Durand, Jacques, 10:459
Dürer, Albrecht, 3:42; 7:26; 8:516n.15; 10:303
D'Urfey, Thomas, 3:734
"During Wind and Rain" (Hardy), 10:581
Durkheim, Emile, 9:615; 11:130–32, 136n.13
Durrell, Lawrence, 9:78
Durtain, Luc, 8:474n.214
Dvořák, Antonin, 7:654, 659
Dyer, Sir Edward, 2:356; 3:82
Dynamics of Literary Response, The (Holland), 11:213

Eagleton, Terry, 11:279–80, 287–88
Early Victorian Novelists (Cecil), 9:65
Eastman, Max, 9:462–63, 573, 576–77
Eatanswill Independent, The, 7:57
Ecclesiazusae (Aristophanes), 3:336
Eckermann, Johann Peter, 7:697; 9:115–16
Eckhart, Meister, 10:256
Eclogues (Gay), 5:213
Eclogues (Petrarch), 2:47, 57
Eclogues (Vergil), 1:481, 486–87, 489; 2:20, 346; 3:139, 400, 469, 471, 473, 477, 480, 641–42; 8:309
Eclogues (Vida), 4:272
Ecole des femmes, L' (Molière), 7:243, 250, 261; 8:364–65
Ecole des maris (Molière), 7:250
Ecrits intimes (Baudelaire), 10:13
Eddington, Arthur S., 8:528
Edelstein, Ludwig, 8:385n.10
"Eden Bower" (Rossetti), 7:468
Edgeworth, Maria, 6:239–40
Edinburgh Review, The, 5:534, 539; 7:223
Education of Henry Adams, The (Adams), 9:321–23; 10:403
Education sentimentale, L' (Flaubert), 8:446; 9:29; 10:262
Edward the Second (Marlowe), 5:688
Egerton, Alice, 10:583
Egerton, Sir Thomas, 3:106
Egmont (Goethe), 5:91
Egoist, The (Meredith), 8:426; 9:69
Ehrenreich, Barbara, 11:178
Ehrmann, Jacques, 9:585
Eichner, Hans, 11:178
Eighteenth Brumaire of Louis Bonaparte (Marx), 11:389
Eikhenbaum, Boris, 11:255
"Einleitung in die Propylaen" (Goethe), 8:387n.13
Einstein, Albert, 8:618
Eisagogikos (Galen), 2:161

Elective Affinities, The (Goethe), 5:90, 211–13
Electra (Euripides), 6:234
Electra (Sophocles), 1:170; 3:336, 701–3
Elegant and Witty Epigrams (Harington), 10:545
"Elegy on Prince Henry" (Donne), 9:564
Elegy Written in a Country Churchyard (Gray), 4:585; 6:94; 8:411, 418; 9:235–36, 502
Eleoi (Thrasymachus), 1:180
Eliade, Mircea, 11:85n.16
Eling, Ingewald, 4:194
Eliot, George, 7:523, 633, 706; 8:178; 9:63, 65–68, 70–71, 74, 76–77; 10:134, 302, 416; 11:181–82, 185–86, 286–87, 312–15, 324
Eliot, T. S., 7:xvii–xviii; 8:554n.21; 9:xiii, 5, 35–36, 61–62, 78, 84–107, 188, 221, 230, 232, 327, 362, 373, 381, 394, 397, 465–66, 475–77, 502, 519, 564–67, 577, 648; 10:134–35, 143, 146, 149, 155, 179, 181–82, 185–86, 208, 210, 252, 340, 376, 392; 400–401, 410, 491, 497, 504, 563–64, 584, 605, 607–8, 611, 623, 644; 10:71, 87, 91, 93, 97–101; 11:76, 153–56, 172, 193n.1, 322
Elizabeth I (Queen of England), 3:12, 84, 140, 724, 738–39
Elliott, George P., 11:108
Ellis, Edwin, 8:99
Ellison, Ralph, 10:x; 11:371, 375–77, 383, 389
Ellmann, Mary, 11:281
Ellmann, Richard, 7:xxxiv–xxxv; 10:323n.7, 376
"Eloise to Abelard" (Pope), 4:575
Elton, G. R., 9:395
Eluard, Paul, 8:598–99
Elyot, Sir Thomas, 2:362; 3:106
Emancipation: Its Course and Progress from 1481 B.C. to A.D. 1875 (Wilson), 11:369
Emerson, Ralph Waldo, 1:xvii; 7:xv, 96, 637, 663, 701; 8:xi, 254; 9:vii–ix, 204; 10:186, 222, 233, 398, 405, 409, 558, 569–71, 587, 609, 611, 615, 623–34, 638–39, 641; 11:vii–viii
Emile (Rousseau), 6:378; 10:270
Emile Zola (Hemmings), 11:87n.26
Emilia Galotti (Lessing), 6:357
Emma (Austen), 8:182; 9:67; 11:181
Emotions and the Will, The (Bain), 8:535
Empedocles, 1:149, 365, 367; 2:165, 319, 321, 325; 3:63, 128, 232, 335; 5:376; 9:288
Empedocles on Etna (Arnold), 9:58

Emperor and Galilean (Ibsen), 8:16; 9:639
Emploi du temps, L' (Butor), 10:306
Empson, William, 8:423; 372, 542; 10:72–73, 97, 99–100, 167, 342, 607, 621, 623
En Route (Huysmans), 8:418
"Enchanted Pilgrim, The" (Leskov), 8:448
Encounters (Goffman), 10:201
Encyclopädie (Boeckh), 10:488
Encyclopädie der philosophischen Wissenschaften in Grundrisse, Die (Hegel), 10:29
Endymion (Keats), 5:517–19; 6:260; 7:xxv, 694; 10:234, 558
Endymion (Varro), 11:267
Enemy of the People, An (Ibsen), 8:32n.5
Engels, Friedrich, 8:278, 281, 286, 288, 291, 297, 301; 11:238
English, Deirdre, 11:178
English Traveller, The (Heywood), 5:691
English Utilitarians and India, The (Stokes), 11:150
Enjoyment of Poetry, The (Eastman), 9:573
Ennius (Q. Ennius), 1:260, 266, 270; 2:42, 117, 163; 3:93, 218, 494, 496
Enquiry concerning Political Justice, An (Godwin), 8:71–72
Enquiry concerning the Intellectual and Moral Faculties, and Literature of Negros . . ., An (Gregoire), 11:368
"Ensorcelée, L'" (Barbey d'Aurevilly), 7:142
ENTRÉE DES MEDIUMS (Breton), 8:594
Entwistle, William James, 8:388–89n.15
Enzensberger, Hans Magnus, 10:391
Epicene; or, The Silent Woman (Jonson), 3:440, 442, 445, 447–50, 667, 676
Epicharmus, 1:153; 3:128
Epictetus, 3:415
Epicurus, 1:318, 364, 395, 397, 489; 3:40, 54, 241, 326, 401, 623–24, 626, 638, 658, 694; 11:ix–x
Epipsychidion (Shelley), 8:79, 82, 84; 10:527, 529–33
Epistle to Damasus (Jerome), 2:37
Epistles (Phalaris), 3:635
Epistles (Plato), 10:38
Epistles (Seneca), 2:257
Epistula ad Pisones (Horace). *See Ars Poetica*
Epistulae (Augustine), 8:493
Epistulae (Leo the Great), 8:498
Epistulae (Seneca), 8:516n.15
Epistulae ex Ponto (Ovid), 3:481; 8:485
Epos (Steinthal), 8:199n.2
Epstein, Jean, 8:411
Erasmus, Desiderius, 2:189, 191, 194, 290, 362; 8:373

Eratosthenes, 1:347; 3:337
Erigone (Eratosthenes), 1:347
Erikson, Erik, 11:190
Ernout, Alfred, 8:515n.7
Eros and Civilization (Marcuse), 9:409
"Error in *The Ambassadors*, An" (Young), 9:246
Essai sur l'origine des connaissances humaine (Condillac), 10:281
Essai sur l'origine des langues (Rousseau), 10:267, 270, 273, 275–77, 280–85
"Essai sur le Beau" (André), 7:276
Essay concerning Human Understanding, An (Locke), 5:537–38
Essay of Dramatick Poetry, An (Dryden), 4:540
Essay on Criticism, An (Pope), 4:569–72
Essay on Grace and Dignity (Schiller), 5:218
Essay on Man, An (Pope), 4:577–78; 9:463, 502
Essay on Poetry, An (Mulgrave), 3:399, 482
Essay on the Causes of the Variety of the Human Complexion and Figure in the Human Species, An (Smith), 11:368
Essay on the Genius and Writings of Pope, An (Warton), 9:54, 573
Essay on the Nature and Principles of Taste (Reid), 7:282
Essay on the Novel (Lukács). *See Theory of the Novel, The*
"Essay on the Philosophy of Art" (Ker), 7:283
Essay on the Slavery and Commerce of the Human Species, Particularly the African, An (Clarkson), 11:368
Essay on Translated Verse, An (Roscommon), 3:393, 399
Essays (Montaigne), 2:xiv, xvii; 6:443–44; 8:265; 9:433
Esther (Adams), 9:318, 320–23
Esther (Racine), 3:695, 697
Esthétique, L' (Veron), 7:282
Eternal Ones of the Dream, The (Roheim), 11:85n.18
Ethical Relativity (Westermarck), 9:571
Ethics (Aristotle). *See Nicomachean Ethics*
Ethics and Language (Stevenson), 9:568
Ethics of Reading, The (Miller), 10:315
Ethiopia Unbound (Casely-Hayford), 11:367
Etranger, L' (Camus), 10:297, 300, 418, 426
Etre et le néant, L' (Sartre), 10:297, 305
Eucherius (Bishop of Lyons), 8:497
Eugene Onegin (Pushkin), 7:289, 327; 8:333
Eugenie (Goethe), 5:91
Eugénie Grandet (Balzac), 10:304
Eumenides (Aeschylus), 7:61

Eunapius, 3:317
Eunuchus (Terence), 2:299; 3:265, 425, 428–30, 438, 668; 7:248–49; 8:479
Euphorion (Götze), 8:288n.14
Eupolis, 1:427; 3:734, 740; 4:256
Eureka (Poe), 7:130
Euripides, 1:x, 14–16, 45–73, 89, 163–64, 168, 182, 198, 281, 336–37, 351–52, 368, 370–72, 375–76, 378–79, 383, 386, 391–93, 396–97, 485, 491; 2:vii, 127, 129, 160, 295, 299, 425, 455, 460, 467; 3:109, 111, 121, 170–71, 174, 188, 218, 267, 269, 281, 336, 340, 342–43, 345, 348, 350–51, 372, 380, 384, 423, 425, 428, 463, 563, 566, 569, 579, 586, 686, 697, 719, 724, 730; 5:374; 6:44, 246, 233–36; 7:241; 9:583, 662; 11:vii
Eusebius, 1:461; 2:17
Eustathius, 3:128, 242
Evagrius Ponticus, 2:437
Evans, R. H., 5:342
Evans, T., 5:342
Eve of St. Mark, The (Keats), 6:278–80
Evelyn, John, 3:400
Evening's Love; or, The Mock Astrologer, An (Dryden), 3:674–77, 680–81
Evergreen (Ramsay), 5:336
"Everlasting Gospel, The" (Blake), 7:374
Every Man in His Humor (Jonson), 3:446, 668
Everyman, 9:663
Evidences of Christianity (Paley), 7:705
Evolution créatrice, L' (Bergson), 8:145; 9:201
Excursion, The (Wordsworth), 5:xiii, 148–49, 444, 446–63, 511, 625; 7:185, 194; 9:463
Exequy (King), 8:407–8
"Experience" (Emerson), 10:405, 638, 641
"Experiment in Criticism" (Eliot), 10:392

Fable, A (Faulkner), 10:189
Fables (Aesop), 1:363; 3:635
Fabricius, 1:315
"Facts in the Case of M. Valdemar" (Poe), 9:686
Faerie Queene, The (Spenser), 2:xiii; 3:145, 413, 467, 477; 5:308, 433–34, 582–83, 656; 6:70, 83–85, 97, 225–27, 231; 7:26, 28, 30; 9:251, 253, 463; 10:403, 577, 613; 11:88n.27
Fair Maid of Perth, The (Scott), 5:92–93
Fair Quarrel, A (Middleton and Rowley), 5:691–92
Fairfax, Edward, 3:79, 293, 489, 496; 10:579
Fairy Tales (Grimms), 8:47, 51n.10

Faithful Shepherdess, The (Fletcher), 3:385, 444, 455; 5:699
Faliscus, Cincius, 1:432
Fanny Hill (Cleland), 11:107
Fanon, Frantz, 11:183
Fantasia of the Unconscious (Lawrence), 9:105
"Far Field, The" (Roethke), 10:610
Farewell to Arms, A (Hemingway), 9:40–41, 46, 48
"Farewell to Arms for Queen Elizabeth, A" (attrib. to Peele), 10:579
"Farewell to Nancy" (Burns), 7:211
Fargue, Léon-Paul, 8:598
Farquhar, George, 5:663
Fasti (Ovid), 2:179; 3:493; 8:485
Father and Son (Gosse), 8:423
"Fathers and Sons" (Hemingway), 9:42
Faulkner, William, 9:248, 344; 10:89, 189, 406, 427; 11:351–52
Faulkner in the University (Faulkner), 11:351
Faust (Goethe), 6:408; 7:213; 8:101, 470n.4; 10:551; 11:81, 89–90n.41
Faust (Turgenev), 7:325–26, 332
Fearful Symmetry (Frye), 9:ix; 10:569
"Fears in Solitude" (Coleridge), 7:450
Fechner, Otto, 9:574
Feipel, Louis N., 10:92
Fekete, John, 11:159
Felman, Shoshana, 11:284
Female Imagination, The (Spacks), 11:184
Feminary, 10:594
Feminist Studies, 10:595; 11:284
Femmes (Sollers), 11:285
"Femmes damnées" (Baudelaire), 9:189
Femmes savantes, Les (Molière), 7:242, 250
Fénelon, François de Salignac de la Mothe-, 4:245n.4
Fénichel, Otto, 9:392; 11:79, 86–87nn.24–25
Ferenczi, Sándor, 11:95
Ferguson, Margaret W., 2:xiii
Fernandat, René, 8:153
Fernandez, Ramon, 10:392
Ferry, David, 10:405
Festus (Sextus Pompeius Festus), 8:486, 516n.14
Feu qui reprend mal, Le (Bernard), 9:446
Feuerbach, Ludwig, 7:581, 622n.52; 9:305; 11:64–65n.23, 130
Fichte, Johann Gottlieb, 5:534–35; 6:147–48, 359; 7:277–78; 9:205; 10:482
Ficino, Marsilio, 9:413
"Fidelity" (Wordsworth), 5:440
Fiedler, Leslie A., 10:380; 11:312, 385

Field, Nathan, 10:94
Fielding, Henry, 5:475; 7:60, 257–58; 9:64–65, 574
Fifth Column, The (Hemingway), 9:46–48
"Figure in the Carpet, The" (James), 9:349, 354
Filastrius, 8:498
Fin-de-Siècle Vienna: Politics and Culture (Schorske), 8:ix
Finer Grain, The (James), 9:343, 361
Finlay, John, 5:346
Finnegans Wake (Joyce), 9:78, 87; 10:vii, 242, 302, 343, 357, 420
"First Anniversary, The" (Donne), 9:564
Fish, Stanley E., 10:342, 443–45; 11:160
Fisherman, The (Goethe), 5:196
Fitzgerald, F. Scott, 10:87, 93, 190, 422
Flaubert, Gustave, 7:141–51, 418, 420, 422–26, 519–20, 669, 706, 719; 8:145, 178–79, 257, 377, 423; 9:28–29, 67–68, 70–71, 342, 347, 351–52, 394, 419, 436; 10:171, 262, 420–21, 457, 566; 11:37, 41, 58, 61, 63n.4, 68n.63, 389
Flecknoe, Richard, 3:293, 583
Fleming, Ian, 10:415
Fletcher, Angus, 3:viii; 10:579
Fletcher, Ian, 7:xxvi
Fletcher, John, 3:79, 81–82, 121, 248, 346, 361, 375, 381, 384–85, 390, 431, 433, 438–39, 444–46, 451, 453, 455, 503, 563, 677; 5:309, 481, 697–99; 6:402; 10:viii, 85, 94
Fletcher, Phineas, 11:79
Fleurs de mal, Les (Baudelaire), 8:414–15, 417; 10:6, 13–14, 16, 18
Fleury, André Hercule de, 7:228
Fliess, Robert, 9:275
Florian, Jean Pierre Claris de, 11:385
Florian Geyer (Hauptmann), 8:294
Floridante (Tasso), 3:346
Flower and the Leaf, The (anon.), 3:502
Focillon, Henri, 8:148–50; 10:65; 11:41
Folz, Hans, 8:517n.28
Fontenelle, Bernard Le Bovier de, 10:136
Foote, Samuel, 7:256
For a New Novel (Robbe-Grillet), 10:417
"For Children. The Gates of Paradise" (Blake), 7:382, 391
For Lancelot Andrewes (Eliot), 8:424
"For Whom Does One Write?" (Sartre), 11:388
For Whom the Bell Tolls (Hemingway), 9:49–50
Ford, Ford Madox, 9:82nn.19–20, 38, 73, 344
Ford, John, 5:693–95; 8:427

Forme et signification (Rousset), 11:40–41, 46, 49, 66n.37, 67nn.43, 49
Formulae Spiritualis Intelligentiae (Eucherius), 8:497
Forrest, Leon, 11:375
"Forsaken Garden, A" (Swinburne), 8:553n.12
Forster, E. M., 9:76; 10:304
Fortunatus (Massinger and Decker), 5:699
Foster, Frances Smith, 11:385
Foucault, Michel, 9:413; 10:384, 639–40; 11:vii–viii, 102n.3, 143, 149, 157, 238–39, 244–45, 248, 287, 329
Foundations of Aesthetics, The (Ogden, Richards, and Wood), 8:554n.21; 9:480, 573; 10:165
"Four Ages of Poetry, The" (Peacock), 6:vii, 193, 201, 206
Four Quartets (Eliot), 9:87; 10:252; 11:155
Fourier, Charles, 6:451; 7:132; 9:606, 687
Fox, Charles James, 5:613–14; 6:390
Fox, George, 6:451
Fox, The (Jonson). See *Volpone; or, The Fox*
Fox-Genovese, Elizabeth, 11:278
"Fra Lippo Lippi" (Browning), 7:656
Fracastoro, Girolamo, 2:402
Fragment of an Agon (Eliot). See *Sweeney Agonistes*
Frame Analysis (Goffman), 10:373
France, Anatole, 8:313
"France: An Ode" (Coleridge), 7:451
Francis of Assisi, St., 7:678; 8:97
Francis of Barberino, 2:55
Frankenstein (Shelley), 10:339
Frankl, Victor, 10:200
Franklin, Benjamin, 7:134
Frazer, Sir James George, 9:480, 615
Frege, Gottlob, 10:488, 490; 11:257
French Revolution: A History, The (Carlyle), 7:709; 8:178
Freud, Sigmund, 2:viii, xiv; 5:xvi; 7:x, xii; 8:vii–xi, 384n.7, 589, 595; 9:vii–viii, xviii, 185, 203, 268–93, 379–93, 397–409, 412, 419, 480, 622, 624, 675; 10:x, 136–37, 215, 421, 464–67, 565–68, 610, 616, 623–26, 629, 635, 640–41; 11:vii–viii, 13, 48, 63n.3, 73–75, 78, 84n.12, 88n.36, 96–97, 123–24, 155, 172–75, 256, 273n.11, 284, 294, 297–300, 302–5, 328, 357–58
Freud, Biologist of the Mind (Sulloway), 8:x
Freud's Discovery of Psychoanalysis: The Politics of Hysteria (McGrath), 8:ix
"Friar of Orders Grey" (Beaumont and Fletcher), 6:67

Friedlander, Paul, 1:xi; 8:514n.1
Friedman, Arthur, 10:95
Friedman, Susan Stanford, 11:363
Friedrich, Caspar David, 10:389
Friend, The (Coleridge), 5:634; 7:440–41
"Friends of the Friends, The" (James), 9:351
Frisch, Karl von, 9:273
Frogs, The (Aristophanes), 2:160; 7:262; 9:650
Froissart, Jean, 7:709
Fromm, Erich, 9:409
Fromont jeune et Risler aîné (Daudet), 7:175
Frontier in American History, The (Turner), 11:375
"Frost at Midnight" (Coleridge) 5:vii; 6:78
Frost, Robert, 9:458; 10:193, 320, 398, 401, 409, 584
Fry, Paul H., 1:xiv–xv, xvii–xviii; 3:xiv–xv; 6:vii, ix
Fry, Roger, 10:133, 136, 323n.11
Frye, Northrop, 9:ix–xviii; viii; 10:70–71, 172–73, 175, 207, 264, 390, 441, 552, 569–70, 607; 11:84–85n.14, 130, 157, 226, 285, 287, 315, 325, 328
Fugitive, The, 10:400
Fulgentius (Fabius Planciades Fulgentius), 2:39; 8:499
"Function and Field of Speech and Language in Psychoanalysis, The" (Lacan), 11:297
"Function of Criticism at the Present Time, The" (Arnold), 10:377
"Function of Criticism, The" (Eliot), 9:648
Fundamental Concepts in the History of Art (Wolfflin), 8:235
Future of an Illusion, The (Freud), 9:404
Future of Poetry, The (Graves), 9:484
Fyfe, William Hamilton, 8:147

Gaines, Ernest J., 11:351
Gainsborough, Sir Thomas, 7:247, 429, 694
Galatea (Cervantes), 5:378–79
Galba, Servius, 1:233
Galen, 2:161; 3:150, 311, 463
Galerie du palais, La (Corneille), 11:50
Galileo Galilei, 8:617–18, 629–30; 10:360, 465–67
Gallatin, Albert, 9:318
Gallop, Jane, 11:284
Galsworthy, John, 8:192–93
"Gambler, the Nun and the Radio, The" (Hemingway), 9:44
Gance, Abel, 8:456, 459–60
"Garden, The" (Marvell), 9:490; 11:9
"Garden of Love" (Blake), 7:370
Gardiner, Stephen, 3:106

Gardner, John, 10:322n.2
Gargantua and Pantagruel (Rabelais), 9:113
Garrick, David, 4:322, 350n.22
Garvey, Marcus, 11:351
Gascoigne, George, 2:356, 363; 3:140
Gaspard de la nuit (Bertrand), 7:475
Gass, William H., 10:415
Gassendi, Pierre, 3:277
Gaudentius (Bishop of Brescia), 8:497
Gaultier, Jules de, 11:386–87
Gaussin, Mlle, 4:319, 348n.14
Gautier, Théophile, 7:189, 429, 470, 473–74, 679, 691; 8:377, 417; 9:27
Gay, John, 5:213; 6:91–92
Gay Science, The (Nietzsche), 7:612, 618, 626n.110; 10:469, 632
Gayle, Addison, Jr., 11:374, 376, 378
Gebir (Landor), 5:541
Geist als Widersacher der Seele, Der (Klages), 10:243
Gelber, Jack, 10:240
Gellius, Aulus, 2:164; 3:151, 162; 8:480, 486
Gémier, Firmin, 9:445
Gendered Subjects: The Dynamics of Feminist Teaching (ed. Culley and Portuges), 11:360–61, 363
Genet, Jean, 9:436–41, 448, 687; 10:171, 240
Genettes, Madame Roger des, 7:171
Génie du Christianisme, Le (Chateaubriand), 7:474
George III (King of England), 5:536–37
George, Stefan, 8:299, 385–86n.10
Georgics (Vergil), 1:427, 481; 2:21, 41; 3:335, 344, 397, 412, 414, 471, 473, 477–78, 480, 649; 4:275; 5:49
Gérard de Nerval, 8:91, 596–97; 9:30, 33, 381, 432–33, 567, 603
German Ideology, The (Marx and Engels), 11:238, 273n.3
Germinal (Zola), 7:704; 10:179
"Gerontion" (Eliot), 9:85; 10:100; 11:154
Gerusalemme liberata (Tasso), 2:xiii, 383; 3:145, 364, 467, 489, 557, 559, 573; 10:579
Gesta Romanorum, 8:44
Ghisilieri, Guido del, 1:509, 525
Ghosts (Ibsen), 8:626; 10:199
Gibbon, Edward, 7:259
Gide, André, 8:157, 377; 9:326, 433; 10:157, 171, 304, 323n.7, 417; 11:38, 56, 68n.63
Gielgud, Sir John, 10:196
Gifford, William, 10:85
Gil Blas (Le Sage), 5:214; 7:538
Gilbert, Sandra, 11:280–82, 286
Gilbert, W. S., 7:xiv

Gilgamesh, Epic of, 9:660
Gilman, Charlotte Perkins, 11:171, 187–88, 191–93
Gilman, Richard, 9:394
Gilson, Etienne, 8:519n.41
Ginnekin, Jacobus van, 9:685
Ginsberg, Allen, 10:190
Ginzburg, Carlo, 10:397
Gioconda, La (Leonardo), 7:407; 8:470n.2
"Gioconda, La" (Pater), 7:xvi
Giorgione (Giorgio Barbelli), 7:668, 688
Giraldi Cintio, Giovanni Battista, 3:587–88; 7:458
Girard, René, 11:229, 387
Giraudoux, Jean, 9:429
Giraut de Borneil, 1:503, 515
Girl in a Cornfield (Bouguereau), 8:5
Gissing, George, 11:282, 316
"Give me your patience, sister, while I frame" (Keats), 6:273–74
Glas (Derrida), 10:560, 562; 11:103n.6
Glasgow, Ellen, 9:248
Glaucon, 1:173, 179
Glossary j'y serre mes gloses (Leiris), 9:423
Glover, Edward, 9:275
Go Tell It on the Mountain (Baldwin), 10:x
Gobineau, Joseph-Arthur, comte de, 9:431; 11:231n.1
"God and the Bayadère, The" (Goethe), 5:195–96
"God Rest You Merry, Gentlemen" (Hemingway), 9:42
Godard, Jean-Luc, 11:330
Godelier, Maurice, 11:136
Godfrey of Boulogne (Tasso). See *Gerusalemme liberata*
Godwin, Gail, 11:316
Godwin, William, 5:634–35; 8:71
Goethe, Johann Wolfgang von, 5:195, 200, 209–13, 351, 380, 535; 6:339, 358–59, 408, 421, 469; 7:191, 213, 216–19, 224, 251, 259, 264, 470, 472, 477, 573, 582, 608, 642–43, 646, 661, 697; 8:22, 87, 98, 101, 115, 119n.1, 272, 383–84n.7, 387n.13; 9:111–19, 185, 288, 379, 515; 10:77, 182, 194, 201, 221, 230, 234, 421; 11:81, 178, 189
Goetz von Berlichingen (Goethe), 5:83; 6:358–59; 7:470
Goffman, Erving, 10:201, 373
Gogol, Nikolai, 7:319; 8:329, 333, 342
Gold Rush, The (film), 8:460
Goldberg, Rube, 10:641–42
Golden Ass, The (Apuleius), 9:xiii
Golden Bough, The (Frazer), 9:564

Golden Bowl, The (James), 9:343, 346, 348, 355–56, 359; 11:94
"Golden Net, The" (Blake), 7:373–74
"Golden Stair, The" (Rossetti), 7:711
Golden Treasury, The (Palgrave), 7:162
Golding, Arthur, 2:356, 363
Goldsmith, Oliver, 5:614; 6:136; 7:473; 8:410; 10:95
Gombrich, E. H., 10:578
Gómez de la Serna, Rámon, 8:233
Goncourt, Edmond de, 7:523; 10:420
Goncourt, Jules de, 10:420
Gondibert (D'Avenant), 3:293, 311, 364, 554; 6:83
Gonzalo de Berceo, 8:506
Good Soldier, The (Ford), 9:344
Good Woman of Setzuan, The (Brecht), 9:440
Goode, T. C., 8:506
Goodman, Paul, 11:108, 119
"Goody Blake and Harry Gill" (Wordsworth), 5:279, 297
Gorboduc (Norton and Dorset), 2:298
Gordon, D. J., 10:578
Gorgias, 1:180, 183–84, 187, 196, 202, 204, 243, 282, 326, 364; 2:166; 3:344; 4:207–8; 10:635–37
Gorgias (Plato), 1:234, 395; 7:549
Gorky, Maxim, 8:292, 297–98, 447
Gorp, Johannes van, 4:195
Gospel of Truth, 10:628
Gosse, Edmund, 8:423, 429
Gotthelf, Jeremias, 8:437, 448
Gottlieb, Annie, 11:176, 181
Gotto of Mantua, 1:526
Götze, A., 8:388n.14
Götzenberger, Jakob, 5:528, 530, 532
Gourmont, Remy de, 8:314, 405, 426; 9:35, 606; 10:379
Government Inspector, The (Gogol), 7:319
Gower, John, 2:355; 3:93, 140, 495
Gozzi, Carlo, conte, 5:85
Graff, Gerald, 11:277–78, 287, 357
Grammar of Motives, A (Burke), 9:viii
Grammatica (Voss), 4:194
Grammatology (Derrida). See *De la grammatologie*
Grammont, Maurice, 8:338
Gramsci, Antonio, 11:152, 238
Granville-Barker, Harley, 10:174
Grass, Günter, 11:230
Graves, Robert, 9:481–82, 484–85
Gravity's Rainbow (Pynchon), 10:403–4
Gray, Cecil, 8:180
Gray, Thomas, 4:x, 582–85; 5:276, 288, 301,

399, 427, 432–33, 599–600; 6:136, 403; 7:208; 8:409–11; 9:235–36, 502
Great Code, The (Frye), 9:xii, xiv–xvi
Great Expectations (Dickens), 8:21
Great Gatsby, The (Fitzgerald), 10:190; 11:107
"Great Good Place, The" (James), 9:354
Greco, El (Dominicos Theotocopuli), 9:365
Greek Studies (Pater), 7:xxiv
Green Hills of Africa (Hemingway), 9:43, 47, 49
Greene, Graham, 9:344
Greene, Robert, 2:370–71, 376, 378; 9:374
Greene, Thomas M., 2:vii–x; 3:x–xi
Greener, R. T., 11:369
"Greenland" (Montgomery), 6:218
Greg, W. R., 8:180
Greg, W. W., 10:95
Gregory of Tours, 8:508
Gregory, Pope, 2:3; 3:10; 8:499
Greimas, A. J., 11:131, 273n.6
Greuze, Jean-Baptiste, 8:115; 9:421
Grey, Zachary, 4:486
Grierson, Herbert J. C., 8:406, 413, 429; 10:87
Griffiths, Mattie, 11:384–85
Grimm, Jacob, 5:309; 8:378
Grimme, Hubert, 8:472n.10
Gröber, Gustav, 8:386n.10
Groethuysen, Bernhard, 8:506
Grotius, Hugo, 3:265, 552
Growing Up Underground (Alpert), 11:286–87
Grube, G. M. A., 1:xii
Guardian, The (Cowley), 3:247, 255
Guarini, Giovanni Battista, 3:80, 90, 145, 346, 400, 410; 5:378
Guattari, Félix, 10:385–86; 11:95
Gubar, Susan, 11:280, 286
Guevara, Antonio de, 3:636; 8:384n.7
Guibbory, Achsah, 3:ix, xi–xii
Guicciardini, Francesco, 2:261
Guide to the Lakes (Wordsworth), 7:181
Guido, 8:309–10, 315–16n.4
Guido of Florence, 1:525–26
Guinizelli, Guido, 1:503, 509, 518; 8:309, 410
Guittone of Arezzo, 1:520
Guizot, François Pierre Guillaume, 6:34
Gulliver's Travels (Swift), 9:28, 645; 10:213, 338; 11:79
Gundolf, Friedrich, 8:363
"Gusev" (Chekhov), 8:196
Guy Mannering (Scott), 7:71
Guyau, Jean-Marie, 7:270, 281; 8:216
Gwinner, Wilhelm von, 7:605, 625

H. D. (Hilda Doolittle), 11:183, 187, 196n.35
Hadrian, 3:11, 650
Haggard, H. Rider, 11:284
Hales, John, 3:445
Hall, Joseph, 3:90
Hall, R. A., 8:387n.10
Hallam, Henry, 6:419
Halle, Adam de la, 9:119–20, 122–23
"Halloween" (Burns), 7:209
Hamilton, William, of Bangour, 6:400
Hamlet (Shakespeare), 3:388; 4:267–71, 468; 5:468, 482, 537, 675–79, 685; 6:69, 263, 459; 7:157, 165, 200, 676; 8:63–64, 153; 9:137–60, 161, 171, 175–78, 180, 183, 186, 189, 332, 370–72, 375, 387–89, 639, 665, 667, 672, 674, 676; 10:viii, 77, 83, 86–87, 211, 329; 11:viii, 74
"Hamlet and His Problems" (Eliot), 8:427; 9:577
Hammett, Dashiell, 9:519
Hamsun, Knut, 8:611n.10
Hanmer, Sir Thomas, 4:483–84
Hanno, 7:709
Hanslick, Eduard, 9:568
Hard Times (Dickens), 9:74
Hardy, Alexandre, 3:720
Hardy, Thomas, 8:430–31; 9:76, 104, 649, 658; 10:171, 401, 515, 581–82; 11:314
Hardyng, John, 2:355
Harington, Sir John, 3:79, 496; 10:545
Harley, Robert, 4:548–49
"Harlot's House, The" (Wilde), 10:582
Harper, Frances E. W., 11:370
Harrison, G. B., 10:85
Harrison, Jane, 8:182
"Hart-Leap Well" (Wordsworth), 5:534
Hartley, David, 5:400, 402, 537; 9:562; 10:166, 340
Hartman, Geoffrey, 9:583; 10:579, 623; 11:287, 388
Hartmann, Eduard von, 7:280
Hartmann, Nicolai, 10:48n.34
Hartshorne, Charles Henry, 5:347–48
Harvey, Gabriel, 2:265, 364
Harvey, William, 3:630, 643; 11:79
Hassan, Ihab, 10:568
Hauff, Wilhelm, 8:452
Hauptmann, Gerhart, 8:293–94
Havelock, Eric, 1:xii
Hawes, Stephen, 11:88n.30
Hawthorne, Nathaniel, 7:519; 8:244, 254; 9:243, 342, 347, 649; 10:368, 400; 11:76, 175, 287, 385
Hay, John, 9:317
Haydn, Robert, 10:545

Haydon, Benjamin Robert, 6:251, 254, 259, 281
Hayne, Thomas, 4:203
Hazard, Paul, 10:549; 11:62n.1
Hazlitt, William, 3:xvi; 4:vii; 5:xii–xxii, 539–40, 544, 563; 6:82, 255, 259; 10:152, 186, 228, 230–31, 613, 622–23; 11:vii
Heart of Midlothian, The (Scott), 6:641; 7:61–62; 9:80n.5
Heath, James, 5:134–35
Heath, John, 3:101
Heautontimoroumenos (Terence), 2:200, 296; 3:428; 7:250
Hebel, Johann Peter, 8:437, 442, 447, 450
Hebraicae Quaestiones (Jerome), 2:40
Hecataeus, 1:343, 414
Hecuba (Euripides), 3:348, 724
Hecyra (Terence), 1:429; 2:109, 114; 7:248–49
Hefner, Hugh, 10:336
Hegel, G. W. F., 6:147–48; 7:277, 283; 8:119, 120n.11, 279, 281, 284, 291–93, 471–72n.10; 9:205, 209, 269–70, 297, 306, 379–80, 411, 575; 10:28–29, 31–32, 40, 379, 393, 482, 549, 583; 11:59, 65n.23, 117, 128, 130, 132, 271–72, 356, 367–68
Hegemon, 1:150
Heidegger, Martin, 8:386n.10; 9:202–3, 205, 671; 10:28–29, 283, 521, 558–63; 11:vii, 46, 66n.35, 130, 301–2
Heilbrun, Carolyn, 11:184
Heimann, Moritz, 8:446
Heine, Heinrich, 7:251, 264, 472; 8:120n.13, 301
Heinsius, Daniel, 3:265, 405, 407–8, 467, 552
Helen (Gorgias), 10:635
Helen (Isocrates), 1:196
Helen in Egypt (H. D.), 11:196n.35
Heliodorus, 2:278
Hellas (Shelley), 8:82
Helle (anon.), 1:160
Heller, Erich, 9:544; 10:182
Helmont, Mercurius van, 8:519n.43
Hemingway, Ernest, 9:37–50, 248, 344, 353; 10:157, 398, 610
Hemmings, F. W. J., 11:87n.26
Hemsterhuis, Franciscus, 7:276; 8:277
Henderson, Stephen, 11:371–75, 378
Henri IV (Legouvé), 6:45
Henry Esmond (Thackeray), 7:427, 706; 10:515
Henry IV (Shakespeare), 4:viii–ix, 316; 5:63, 469; 7:59; 9:162–64, 166–67, 389; 10:87, 329

Henry V (Shakespeare), 9:162, 164–67, 664, 673
Henry VI (Shakespeare), 6:455; 9:162, 171, 667, 672, 674
Henry VIII (Shakespeare), 6:455; 9:664, 668, 676
Heracleides, 1:363
Heracles (Euripides), 8:265; 9:662
Heraclitus, 1:185, 384, 482; 2:287, 437; 3:128; 8:98; 11:ix, 266
Héraclius (Corneille), 3:266, 270, 272–73
Herbart, Johann Friedrich, 7:279
Herbert, Edward, Lord, 3:80; 8:408, 410, 412
Herbert, George, 3:536–37; 8:406, 408, 412, 430; 9:515; 10:72–73, 398, 546
Hercules Furens (Seneca), 3:339
Herd, David, 5:342–43
Herder, J. G., 10:569
Hérédia, José Maria de, 9:27
Hermagoras, 1:228, 287
Hermes Trismegistus, 10:459–60
Hermogenes, 3:4, 188, 317, 319
Hernani (Hugo), 7:475
Herodian, 3:435
Herodotus, 1:156, 213, 283, 328, 335, 340–41, 343–44, 350, 352, 413–14; 2:225, 274, 325; 3:129, 618, 622; 6:146; 8:439; 9:19
Heroides (Ovid), 3:414; 8:485
Herrick, Robert, 8:211; 9:453, 529
Hertz, Neil, 1:xviii; 10:641
Hesiod, 1:86, 116, 126, 330, 335, 375–76, 378, 383, 392, 395; 2:163, 323, 408; 3:142, 147, 149, 153, 156–57, 162, 187, 229, 313, 647; 7:548
Hessus, Eobanus, 3:125, 133
Hesychius, 2:406
Heywood, John, 3:82, 89
Heywood, Thomas, 3:121, 254; 5:690–91
Hicks, Sir William Joynson, 8:186
Hieronymo Is Mad Again (Jonson), 5:694
Higginson, Thomas Wentworth, 7:xxxii
Hilbert, David, 11:264
Hildreth, Richard, 11:385
"Hills Like White Elephants" (Hemingway), 9:48
Hinman, Charlton, 10:174
Hints on Insanity (Millar), 11:194n.12
Hippocrates, 2:161, 438; 3:81, 150, 326, 620, 624; 10:168, 460, 464
Hippolytus (Euripides), 6:234
Hippolytus (Seneca), 3:345
"Hippolytus Veiled" (Pater), 7:xxiv
Hipponax, 1:220
Hirt, Johann Friedrich, 5:239–41

"His Toy, His Dream, His Rest" (Berryman), 10:610
Histoire amoureuse des Gaules. See *Amours de Gaul*
Histoire d'O, L' (Réage), 11:97, 107, 110, 115–17
Histoire de l'oeil (Bataille), 11:107, 112, 114
Histoire de la folie (Foucault), 9:413
Historia Linguae Graecae (Eling), 4:194
Historia Naturalis (Pliny the Elder), 3:131; 7:709
Historia Scholastica (Petrus Comestor), 8:519n.42
"Historicism Once More" (Pearce), 10:74
History and Class Consciousness (Lukács), 11:153
History of Aesthetic (Bosanquet), 9:7, 16
History of Criticism, A (Saintsbury), 10:169
History of Criticism in the Italian Renaissance, A (Weinberg), 10:169
History of England (Macaulay), 9:242, 249–50
History of England (Trevelyan), 8:173
History of Granada (Hita), 3:366
History of Modern Criticism, A (Wellek), 10:71, 74–75, 169–70
History of Russian Literature (Pypin), 8:341
History of the Fine Arts in Greece (Meyer), 5:239
History of the League, The (Maimbourg, tr. Dryden), 3:393
History of the Royal Society, The (Sprat), 10:335, 337, 339, 342
Hitler, Adolf, 9:303, 396, 425; 11:242–44
Hobbes, Thomas, 3:201, 363, 397, 490, 492, 630; 4:165; 6:38, 70–71; 9:193; 10:144–45, 166
Hobsbaum, Philip, 10:437
Hobsbawm, Eric, 11:151
Hogarth, William, 4:243, 246n.8
Hokusai, 7:717
Holbein, Hans, 7:706, 718
Hölderlin, Friedrich, 10:119–20
Holland, Norman N., 10:441; 11:213, 321
"Holy Fair" (Burns), 7:209
Holy Living and Holy Dying (Taylor), 5:537
Holy Sonnets (Donne), 10:87
Holyday, Barton, 3:407, 409, 415–16
Home and Foreign Review, 7:223
"Home" (Chekhov), 10:326–27
Homer, 1:viii, xvii, 86–93, 95, 97–103, 106, 111, 115–16, 121–22, 126, 149–50, 152, 155, 161, 164, 169–70, 173–74, 191, 200, 213, 215, 272–73, 283, 303, 329–33, 335–36, 340, 343, 347, 349, 353, 364, 366–71, 374, 376–89, 393–95, 427, 471–72, 475–77, 483–84, 490; 2:18, 29, 42, 53, 59, 83, 109–10, 130–34, 136, 148, 153, 163–64, 173–79, 192, 222, 227, 294, 323–24, 335, 347, 405, 479–85; 3:10, 13–14, 21, 79, 93, 109, 112, 114–15, 123–35, 142, 147–49, 151, 156, 161–63, 174, 181, 191, 201–2, 204, 211, 218, 221, 229, 235, 239–41, 243–46, 284, 287, 303, 307–8, 313, 320, 325, 335–39, 341–43, 346, 348, 363, 366, 374, 382–83, 394–95, 409, 413, 447, 463, 465, 476–77, 482, 489, 491–93, 495, 553, 555, 645, 647, 649; 4:211–38, 241, 261, 264, 274, 276–78, 316, 371–79, 544, 576; 5:22–23, 41–46, 50–54, 130–31, 145, 150, 167–69, 172, 325–27, 361, 373, 586; 6:72, 77, 96, 191, 200, 246; 7:38, 41, 44, 199, 215, 399n.21, 547–50, 582, 660, 668; 8:48, 80, 292, 296, 561; 9:17, 56, 185, 249–51, 458, 484, 669; 10:147, 459, 464, 579–81, 609, 613; 11:vii–viii
Honest Whore, The (Dekker), 5:689
Hooke, Robert, 10:337
Hooker, Richard, 3:81, 106; 11:154
Hopkins, Anne, 11:178
Hopkins, Ezekiel, 3:456
Hopkins, Gerard Manley, 8:154; 9:58, 103, 519; 10:608; 11:153
Horace (Q. Horatius Flaccus), 1:298, 304, 432, 517, 532; 2:22, 34, 83, 124, 126, 135, 163–64, 166, 173, 200, 255, 388, 401, 415, 420, 422, 467; 3:77, 79–81, 86, 107, 109, 111–12, 121, 126, 188, 218, 249–50, 258, 267, 272, 284, 286, 299, 314–15, 321, 324–25, 333–34, 337, 339, 341–42, 346–47, 349, 364–65, 373, 375, 383, 391, 393, 395, 400–401, 406–11, 421–23, 425–28, 430, 432, 434, 437, 449, 456, 465, 467, 469, 471, 491, 493, 495–96, 503, 580, 583, 588–89, 638, 646, 649, 655, 659, 675–76, 678, 697–98, 700, 709, 737–38, 740, 743; 4:65, 218, 227, 256, 258–59, 275, 373; 5:37–38, 49, 237, 264, 376, 447; 6:373; 8:147, 308, 313; 10:168, 545, 610, 642
Horace (Corneille), 3:263, 268, 271–72, 274, 321
"Horatian Ode upon Cromwel's Return from Ireland, An" (Marvell), 9:466; 10:72
Horkheimer, Max, 11:127
Horton, George Moses, 11:372
Hotson, Leslie, 10:174
Houdar de la Motte, Antoine, 4:161
House Beautiful (Stevenson), 7:436, 469
House of Life, The (Rossetti), 7:467

INDEX OF NAMES AND TITLES

Housman, A. E., 9:60, 103, 483–84, 520, 560, 574
"How Gogol's 'Overcoat' Is Made" (Eikhenbaum), 8:333
Howells, William Dean, 9:340; 10:186
Hoy, Cyrus, 10:94
Huckleberry Finn (Twain). *See Adventures of Huckleberry Finn*
Hudibras (Butler), 3:411, 656; 6:94–95
Hudson, W. H., 8:192
Hughes, Langston, 11:374–75
Hugo of St. Victor, 11:145–46
Hugo, Herman, 4:194
Hugo, Victor, 5:89; 6:402; 7:166, 174, 402n.32, 426–27, 429, 472–75, 481, 489, 632; 8:204, 377, 598; 9:29, 32; 10:vii
Huizinga, Johan, 11:85n.15
Hull, Gloria T., 10:594–95
Hulme, T. E., 8:405, 421, 426; 9:492
"Human Abstract, The" (Blake), 7:361
Human, All Too Human (Nietzsche), 10:469–70, 482
Humbolt, Alexander von, 10:466
Hume, David, 5:xix; 9:489; 10:32, 221, 223, 225, 363, 610; 11:367–68, 380, 386
Hunt, Leigh, 6:255, 444; 8:95
Hunt, William Holman, 8:22
Hurd, Richard, 10:145
Hurston, Zora Neale, 10:x; 11:371, 375, 389
Husserl, Edmund, 10:23–25, 488, 492–95, 508–9; 11:44, 59–60
Hutcheson, Francis, 7:275–76
Huxley, Aldous, 8:473–74n.20; 9:459, 508; 10:257
Huxley, Thomas Henry, 7:568, 622n.27
Huygens, Christiaan, 9:284
Huysmans, Joris-Karl, 8:377, 418–19; 9:29
Huysum, Jacobus van, 5:48
"Hymn before Sun-Rise, in the Vale of Chamouni" (Coleridge), 5:ix
"Hymn of Apollo" (Shelley), 6:xi
"Hymn to Nature" (Goethe), 9:288
Hyperides, 1:236, 258, 338, 347–48, 405
Hyperion (Keats), 7:49n.15; 8:411; 9:99; 10:224

"I am of Ireland" (Yeats), 9:376
I and Thou (Buber), 10:569
Iakubinsky, Lev, 8:323–25, 337, 345n.1, 346n.23
Iamblichus, 3:149, 152
Ibsen, Henrik, 8:10–11, 16, 22, 27, 29, 32n.5; 9:28–29, 35, 381, 639; 10:199, 203, 242
Icaromenippea (Lucan), 11:267

Idea of a University, The (Newman), 7:418
"Idea of Order at Key West, The" (Stevens), 10:644
Ideal Husband, An (Wilde), 7:xxxv
"Idealistic Extensions of Linguistics" (Entwistle), 8:388–89n.15
Idées et les lettres, Les (Gilson), 8:519n.41
Ideologie und Utopie (Mannheim), 10:75
Idiom of Poetry, The (Pottle), 9:463–64, 517, 521
Idiot, The (Dostoevsky), 10:353
"Idiot Boy, The" (Wordsworth), 5:420
Idler, The (Johnson), 7:76
"Igitur" (Mallarmé), 10:53
Iliad (Homer), 1:viii, 93, 102, 152, 155, 161, 164, 169, 174, 331–32, 427; 2:41, 59, 130, 164, 174–75, 177, 227; 3:127, 128, 140, 151, 237, 240, 283, 285, 306, 324–25, 463–64, 467, 489, 491, 493, 502, 649; 4:53, 55–56, 58, 152–67, 196, 198, 217, 221, 223, 227, 229–32, 241, 264, 274, 276, 576–77; 5:22–23, 167; 6:72–77; 7:28, 213n.3, 476; 9:239, 253, 660, 664, 669; 10:397
Iliad (Homer, tr. Chapman), 3:81
Illuminations (Rimbaud), 11:95, 100–101, 103n.6
Illusions perdues (Balzac), 7:705; 8:297
Image, L' ("Berg"), 11:101, 107
Imaginary Conversations (Landor), 7:xxiv; 8:95
Imaginary Portraits (Pater), 7:xxiv, xxxii
Importance of Being Earnest, The (Wilde), 7:xxxii, xxxv–xxxvi
"In Ampezzo" (Stickney), 10:586
"In Duty Bound" (Perkins), 11:187–88
In Our Time (Hemingway), 9:37
In the Matter of J. Robert Oppenheimer (Kipphardt), 9:443–44
"Incidents in the Life of My Uncle Arly" (Lear), 6:viii
"Incipit Poema Lyrica de Staffa tractans" (Keats), 6:276
Indépendance Belge, L', 7:149
Indian Emperor, The (Dryden), 3:387, 456
"Indian Jugglers, The" (Hazlitt), 5:xix
Indian Queen, The (Dryden), 3:456
Inès de Castro (anon.) 4:325
"Infant Joy" (Blake), 7:359
"Infant Sorrow" (Blake), 7:368
Inge, Dean, 8:179
Inquiry into Meaning and Truth, An (Russell), 8:152
Inspector General, The (Gogol), 8:333, 572

"Instincts and Their Vicissitudes" (Freud), 11:97
Instituta Laconica (Plutarch), 3:717
Instituta Regularia Divinae Legis (Junilius), 8:497
Institutio Oratoria (Quintilian), 8:487
"Intellectual Crisis, The" (Valéry), 8:xii
Intent of the Artist, The (ed. Centeno), 9:367
"Intentional Fallacy, The" (Wimsatt and Beardsley), 10:503
"Interesting Men" (Leskov), 8:441
Interpretation of Dreams, The (Freud), 8:ix; 10:216, 464; 11:63n.3, 73, 84n.12; 307n.38
Introduction to Genesis (Bohlen), 7:109
Introduction to Metrics (Zhirmunsky), 8:337
Introduction to Scholarship in Modern Languages and Literatures (MLA), 11:360
Introduction to the Structural Analysis of Narratives
(Barthes), 11:279
Introductory Lectures on Psychoanalysis (Freud), 9:379
Invective contra Medicum (Petrarch), 2:26, 57
Invisible Man (Ellison), 10:x; 11:376–78, 383
"Invitation au voyage, L'" (Baudelaire), 8:420
Invitée, L' (Beauvoir), 10:298
"Invocation of the Wind" (Taliessin), 6:404–5
Io (Euripides), 2:127
Ion of Chios, 1:347; 3:337
Ion (Plato), 1:471; 2:160, 163, 296
Ionesco, Eugene, 9:447–48; 10:240, 250–54, 256
Iphicrates, 1:198
Iphigeneia in Aulis (Euripides), 1:160–63, 485, 491; 2:126, 233
Iphigenia (Goethe), 5:81
Iphigenie (Racine), 4:316; 6:37
Irenaeus, 8:515n.4; 9:198
Irigaray, Luce, 11:284–85
"Irony as a Principle of Structure" (Brooks), 10:543
Irving, Washington, 9:342
Is There a Text in This Class? (Fish), 11:165
Iser, Wolfgang, 10:378
Isocrates, 1:187, 191, 196, 202–3, 220, 327, 341, 349, 413; 2:166, 401; 3:189
"It Must Be Abstract" (Stevens), 8:xi
Italia liberata dai Goti (Trissino), 2:133, 422
"Italian Journey" (Goethe), 9:112, 116
"Ivan Fyodorovich Shpoinka and His Aunt" (Gogol), 8:568
Ivan the Terrible, 9:128
Ivanhoe (Scott), 5:93, 620, 642

Ivanov, Vjaceslav Ivanov, 8:321
Ivory Tower, The (James), 9:343
Ivy-Wife, The (Hardy), 10:515, 518

Jack (Daudet), 7:175, 704
Jackson, Margaret Young, 11:385
Jacobi, F. H., 5:451–52
Jaeger, Werner, 1:xiv
Jakobson, Roman, 8:322–23, 337–38, 345, 573; 10:264
James, Henry, 7:703; 8:426; 9:63, 68–74, 245–47, 258, 315, 340–61, 394, 649; 10:134–35, 183, 185–86, 323n.4, 363, 368, 398–400, 549–52; 11:111, 155, 222, 314, 381
James, Henry, Sr., 9:341, 345; 10:570–71
James, William, 8:145–46, 154–55; 9:ix, 142, 341, 344–46, 361; 10:361, 562, 624–25, 638–39; 11:viii, 118
James Joyce (Levin), 9:326
Jameson, Fredric, 10:304, 312
Jamieson, Robert, 5:345–47
Jane Eyre (Brontë), 11:189, 191, 286
Janet, Pierre, 9:278–79
Janssen, Johannes, 7:606
Jardine, Alice, 11:283–84
Jarrell, Randall, 10:189
Jarry, Alfred, 8:598; 10:618–19
Javolenus, 8:486
Jealousy (film), 10:423
Jeanne d'Arc (Dreyer), 8:473n.18
Jeanneret, Maurice, 8:516n.18
Jefferson, Thomas, 9:220; 11:367–68
Jefferson and Madison (Adams), 9:255
Jeffrey, Francis, 5:534; 9:35; 10:223–25, 236n.2
Jephtha (Buchanan), 2:197
Jeremiah, 8:517n.26
Jerome, St., 2:37, 39–40, 47, 68, 95, 98, 102; 3:99; 8:517n.25; 10:462–63, 569
Jerusalem (Blake), 7:379, 384, 396n.11; 10:555, 584–85, 615
Jesperson, Otto, 11:88n.31
Jesus Ben Sirah (Ecclesiasticus), 4:vii
Jeu de la feuillée (Halle). See *Play in the Bower, The*
Jew of Malta, The (Marlowe), 5:688; 9:667
Joachim of Floris, 9:209
Joans, Ted, 11:371
John of the Cross, St., 10:256
Johnson, Barbara, 11:389
Johnson, James Weldon, 11:370
Johnson, Samuel, 1:xv; 3:xvi; 4:vii–xv; 5:280, 297–98, 301–2, 310–12, 314, 317; 5:495, 589, 594, 596, 614, 626, 649; 6:221–24,

321; 7:75–77, 216; 8:180, 407–10, 412, 422–23, 425–26, 430, 432; 9:31, 65, 221, 525; 10:131, 135–37, 152, 169–70, 223, 225, 230, 233, 235, 320, 578–80, 605, 609–10, 613; 10:623; 11:vii
Jokes and the Unconscious (Freud), 10:536
"Jolly Beggars, The" (Burns), 7:212
"Jolly Corner, The" (James), 9:345, 358
Jonathan Wild (Fielding), 7:258; 9:64–65
Jones, Ernest, 9:271, 387–89; 10:78; 11:74
Jones, Inigo, 3:84, 87
Jones, LeRoi. *See* Baraka, Imamu Amiri
Jonson, Ben, 2:ix; 3:121, 141, 248, 309, 364, 366, 375, 381, 384–85, 425–27, 433, 435, 438–40, 442, 444–48, 451–52, 455, 457, 459, 551, 563, 580, 582, 666–67, 676–79; 4:244, 384–85, 477, 500; 5:678, 694–97; 6:64, 95, 398, 402, 458; 8:406, 409; 9:260–61, 461, 673; 10:viii, 546, 587, 609
Jordan, Thomas, 3:583
Joseph Andrews (Fielding), 9:64
Josephus, Flavius, 3:123; 4:195
Jouffroy, Théodore Simon, 7:280
Journal to Stella (Swift), 11:74
Journaux intimes (Baudelaire), 8:415, 420; 10:15
Joyce, James, 8:194–95, 233, 384n.7, 431; 9:35–36, 78, 184, 246–48, 326–40, 382; 10:vii, 91, 210, 242, 248, 293, 343, 357, 399, 401, 404–5, 420–21, 427, 429, 581; 11:155, 258, 265, 267
Jude the Obscure (Hardy), 9:76; 11:153, 314–15
Julian and Maddalo (Shelley), 7:17–18; 8:73
Julius Caesar (Shakespeare), 3:563; 5:482, 484; 9:161, 166, 171–72, 174–75, 177–80, 665–66, 670, 673, 675; 10:201, 410
Jung, Carl Gustav, 9:616; 10:248; 11:13–14
Junger, Ernst, 10:521
Junilius, 8:497
Junius, 7:16
Justin Martyr, 3:618
Justine (Sade), 10:331
Juvenal (D. Junius Juvenalis), 2:34; 3:79, 81, 114, 230, 299–300, 375, 401, 405–10, 415–16, 426, 432, 503; 6:242

Kabbalah and Criticism (Bloom), 10:568
Kafka, Franz, 9:326, 382, 582, 586; 10:111, 157, 428, 457; 11:73–74, 265, 267, 269
Kahn, Gustave, 8:215
Kain, Richard, 9:326–27
Kainich (Turgenev), 7:319
"Kalewipoeg" (Estonian folk song), 8:44–45
Kames, Henry Home, Lord, 7:276

Kant, Immanuel, 2:xiii; 5:218, 359, 365, 407, 534; 6:138, 147–48; 7:277, 445, 585, 593, 615, 642; 8:153; 9:205, 306; 10:32, 46, 146, 150, 152, 166, 170, 361, 380, 437; 11:40–41, 245, 367–68, 386
Kant and the Question of Metaphysics (Heidegger), 11:66n.35
Kapital, Das (Marx), 10:464
Kaplan, Justin, 10:629
Kapp, Ernst, 10:37
Kassner, Rudolf, 8:271
Kate Chopin Newsletter, 11:286
Kater Murr (Hoffmann), 8:568
Kean, Edmund, 6:253, 268
Keats, George, 6:253–56, 258–59, 267–88
Keats, Georgiana, 6:267–88
Keats, John, 5:517–19; 6:66; 7:xxv, 43, 49; 8:84, 95, 178–79, 181, 207, 397, 411; 9:35, 56–58, 89–90, 99; 9:411, 489, 509–10, 512, 530, 574, 638, 675; 10:149–51, 224, 228, 231, 234, 558, 572, 587, 612–13, 642–43; 11:190, 350
Keats, Thomas, 6:253–56, 258–59
Keep the Aspidistra Flying (Orwell), 11:81
Keller, Helen, 9:202
Kelly-Gadol, Joan, 11:278
Kemble, John, 5:667–68
Kennedy, A. G., 9:230
Kenyon Review, The, 10:380
Ker, W. P., 7:283; 8:405, 423
Kermode, Frank, 10:391, 428; 11:172, 193n.1
"Key-Note, The" (Rossetti), 11:181
Khlebnikov, Velimir, 8:322, 338; 11:258
Khor (Turgenev), 7:319
Kierkegaard, Soren, 8:265; 9:208, 548; 10:562, 566, 609, 612
Killens, John, 11:376
King, Henry, 3:527, 532, 536, 539, 544; 8:406–7, 411–12
King, Martin Luther, Jr., 11:351
King, Stephen, 10:211
King and No King, A (Beaumont and Fletcher), 3:381, 384–85, 438, 563–64
King Arthur (Dryden), 3:745
King John (Shakespeare), 9:163, 169, 667, 675
King Lear (Shakespeare), 4:45; 5:xvii, 64, 207, 577, 579, 682–83, 689; 6:65, 67, 83, 193, 255, 392; 7:673; 8:45–46, 49–51, 639; 9:139, 149–50, 157–58, 171–72, 175, 368–69, 387, 659, 665, 674; 10:151–52, 174, 197, 202–4
"*King Lear* or *Endgame*" (Kott), 10:174
"King Malcolm and Sir Colvin." *See* "Sir Caulin"

"King's Tragedy, The" (Rossetti), 7:468
Kingsley, Charles, 7:43
Kipling, Rudyard, 7:695; 8:447
Kisses, The (Secundus), 2:254
Kizer, Carolyn, 11:185
Klages, Ludwig, 10:243
Klein, Melanie, 10:465; 11:101
Kleist, Heinrich von, 5:49
Klopstock, Friedrich Gottlieb, 5:354, 501–3
Kluckhohn, Clyde, 11:147
Knight, Edward, 10:94
Knight, G. Wilson, 8:423. 427; 10:621
Knight, William, 7:272, 282–83
Knights, L. C., 8:423
Kock, Charles Paul de, 7:143; 8:423
Koestler, Arthur, 9:75; 11:221–23
Kofman, Sarah, 11:284
Koheleth (Ecclesiastes), 4:vii
Kökeritz, Helge, 10:84
Komet, Der (Paul), 10:352
Konig, Josef, 10:436
Körner, Theodor, 5:74
Korzybski, Count, 9:568
Kostelanetz, Richard, 10:388
Kotik Latayev (Biely), 8:561
"Kotin the Provider and Platonida" (Leskov), 8:449
Kott, Jan, 10:174, 301
Koyre, Alexandre, 9:284
Kralik, Richard, 7:270, 273
Kraus, Karl, 8:vii; 9:299
Kristeva, Julia, 10:384; 11:283–85
Kroeber, A. L., 11:62n.2, 147
Kruchonykh, Alexei Eliseevich, 8:322
Kubla Khan (Coleridge), 7:446; 9:30, 562–63
Kugel, James, 10:588n.9
Kuhn, Helmut, 10:511n.10
Kuhn, Thomas S., 10:374, 641; 11:277
Kundera, Milan, 11:227, 230
Kunstgeschichte ohne Namen (Wolfflin), 8:320

La Bruyère, Jean de, 6:49; 7:164
La Chaussée, Nivelle de, 4:322, 350n.21
La Fayette, Madame de, 10:417
La Fontaine, Jean de, 3:688; 7:121, 245; 9:432
La Loubere, Simon de, 5:100
La Rochefoucauld, Duc de, 3:636; 9:26, 29
La Rochelle, Drieu, 10:313
La Touche, Rose, 7:xl
Là-Bas (Huysmans), 8:418
Laberius, Decimus, 8:516n.18

Lacan, Jacques, 9:447; 11:viii, 262, 283–85, 287, 293–306, 308n.47
La Condamine, Pierre de, 5:100
Lactantius (L. Caelius Firmianus Lactantius), 8:492, 498
Ladies' Home Journal, 9:649
Lady Chatterley's Lover (Lawrence), 8:431
"Lady Macbeth of Mzensk" (Leskov), 8:449
Lady of the Lake, The (Scott), 7:59, 77; 10:223
Lady Oracle (Atwood), 11:179
Laelius, C., 1:232
Laet, Jan de, 4:198
LaFarge, John, 9:342
Lafontaine, August, 6:359
Laforgue, Jules, 7:490; 8:412, 418–19, 427, 429–30
Laing, Malcolm, 5:316
Laing, R. D., 9:408, 413; 11:95
Lalane, Pierre de, 3:345
Lamb, Charles, 5:534–36, 542, 544, 562–66, 591, 659; 6:420; 7:441; 8:429; 9:385; 10:228
Lamb, Mary, 5:535
"Lamb, The" (Blake), 7:359
Lambert, Johann Heinrich, 5:100
"Lamia" (Keats), 5:517–19; 6:270
Lamoignon, Guillaume de, 3:746
Lance, The, 7:703
Landino, Cristoforo, 2:304
Landor, Walter Savage, 5:541, 545; 6:417; 7:xxiv, 245, 698; 8:94, 101
Lang, Andrew, 9:55–56
Langbaine, Gerard, 3:319
Langer, Suzanne, 11:377
Language and Responsibility (Chomsky), 11:164n.1
Language as Gesture (Blackmur), 10:382
Language Habits in Human Affairs (Lee), 9:570
Language of Poetry, The (Stauffer), 9:512
Languages of Criticism and the Sciences of Man, The (Donato), 10:383
Languages of Criticism and the Structure of Poetry, The (Crane), 9:235
Langue des tablettes d'éxecration latines, La (Jeanneret), 8:516n.18
Lanham, Richard, 2:xii–xiii
Lanson, Gustave, 8:374, 389–90n.18
"Laodamia" (Wordsworth), 5:624; 7:192, 707
Laon and Cythna (Shelley), 6:254, 291n.16; 8:72–74, 78, 81–82; 10:527, 534
Lao-tzu, 10:256
Lapouge, Gilles, 10:384
Lassalle, Ferdinand, 8:301

Lasserre, Pierre, 8:201
Last Man, The (Shelley), 10:553n.1
Last Year at Marienbad (film), 10:423–24
Latimer, Hugh, 11:154
Latin Mystique, Le (Gourmont), 8:314
Latini, Brunetto, 7:202
Latter-Day Pamphlets (Carlyle) 7:226
Lauderdale, Richard Maitland, Earl of, 3:479
Laughton, Charles, 8:630
Laus Amoris (Rossetti), 7:711
Lautréamont, Comte de (Isidore Ducasse), 8:605; 11:97, 256–58, 265, 269
Lawrence, D. H., 8:430–31; 9:67, 74, 76–78, 102–7, 493–95, 574, 591–97, 600, 608, 666; 10:157, 193, 400–401, 404–5, 571; 11:155
"Lawrence of virtuous father virtuous son" (Milton), 11:199–200
Laws (Plato), 1:344, 472–75; 2:316, 319
Lay of the Last Minstrel, The (Scott), 7:77
Le Bossu, René, père, 3:380, 382, 462, 468, 471
le Carré, John, 10:211
Le Clerc, Jean, 3:471
Le Kain, M., 4:318, 326, 348n.13
Le Moyne, Pierre, le père, 3:467, 560
Lear, Edward, 6:viii; 10:245
Leary, Timothy, 10:198
Leatherstocking Tales, The (Cooper), 10:210
Leaves of Grass (Whitman), 7:96; 10:630
Leavis, F. R., 8:423, 431; 10:312, 400–401, 439, 563; 11:156, 281, 328, 370
Leavis, Q. D., 11:281
Leçon, La (Ionesco), 9:447
Leconte de Lisle, Charles Marie Rene, 7:167; 9:27–29
Lee, Don, 11:371
Lee, Sir Henry, 10:579
Lee, Irving, 9:570
Lee, Nathaniel, 4:43
Lee, Vernon, 8:182
"Leech-Gatherer, The" (Wordsworth), 5:534
Lefebvre, Tannegui, 3:319, 321
Lefranc, Abel, 8:373
Leibniz, Gottfried Wilhelm, baron von, 5:365, 406; 8:519n.43; 9:573; 11:42–44, 49, 51–52, 57, 65n.25, 66n.30
Leicester, Philip Sidney, Earl of, 3:499–500
Leiris, Michel, 9:423
Leivick, Halzer, 10:642
Lenin, V. I., 8:278–80, 287–88, 290–92, 299–300, 345; 9:45
Lenore (Bürger), 5:198–99
Lentricchia, Frank, 10:637, 639; 11:278
Leo the Great, 8:498

Leon, Derrick, 7:xxxviii
Leonardo da Vinci, 5:67; 7:xxi; 8:474–75nn.22–23; 9:386
"Leonardo da Vinci" (Pater), 7:xxv
Leonardo Poe Mallarmé (Valéry), 8:xi
Leontius. *See* Pilatus, Leontius
Lermontov, Mikhail Iurevich, 7:320–21; 8:325
Lerner, Gerda, 11:278
Leskov, Nikolai, 8:435–452
Leslie, Charles, 5:346
Lesser, Simon, 10:441
Lessing, Doris, 11:ix, 181
Lessing, Gotthold Ephraim, 5:451–52; 6:357–58; 7:251; 8:264, 296, 298; 10:70
Lesson, The (Ionesco). *See Leçon, La*
"Lesson of the Master, The" (James), 9:349
Letter on Humanism (Heidegger), 10:558
Letter on the Theatre (Sade), 9:431
Letter to a Lady on Her Marriage (Swift), 4:553
Letter to a Noble Lord (Burke), 5:615
Letter to Can Grande (Dante), 10:153
"Letter to My Father" (Kafka), 11:73–74
"Letter to the October Club" (Swift), 4:548–49; 5:548–49
Letters on the Aesthetic Education of Man (Schiller), 5:218
Lettres d'un voyageur (Sand), 7:634
Leucippus, 8:515n.8
Lévêque, Charles, 7:243, 281
Leveson-Gower, Lord Granville, 8:181
Leviathan (Hobbes), 8:523; 9:193
Levin, Harry, 9:326–27, 330; 10:186; 11:385
Levinas, Emmanuel, 11:68n.56
Lévi-Strauss, Claude, 9:683; 10:269–70, 390, 418, 530; 11:48–49, 150
Lévy-Bruhl, Lucien, 9:279; 10:9
Lewis, C. S., 9:557, 572, 579; 10:215, 439, 607, 613; 11:88n.30, 324
Lewis, Janet, 9:244
Lewis, Sinclair, 10:92–93, 96
Lewis, Wyndham, 9:102–7, 495
Lewy, Ernst, 8:383
Leyland (Newton), 2:364
Liber de Haeresibus (Filastrius), 8:498
Liber Temporum (Eusebius), 2:17
Liberal Imagination, The (Trilling), 10:185
Lichtenberg, George Christoph, 6:149; 9:284; 10:612
Licymnius, 1:193, 195
Liddell, Alice, 10:583
Life against Death (Brown), 9:409; 11:96
Life and Letters (Gosse), 8:429
Life of Albert Gallatin, The (Adams), 9:318

Life of Forms in Art, The (Focillon), 8:148
Life of Galileo (Brecht), 8:634–35, 638–39
"Life of Gray" (Johnson), 4:x
Life of Johnson (Boswell), 4:x, xiii–xv; 5:310; 7:709
"Life of Waller" (Johnson), 6:221–24
"Life of Yalden" (Johnson), 4:ix
Life's Adventure (Carmichael), 8:182–85, 187–90
Light and Truth (Lewis), 11:369
Light in Troy, The (Greene), 2:vii–viii
Lille, Alain de, 8:502
Lily, William, 3:186
"Lines to a Young Ass" (Coleridge), 7:452
"Lines to Joseph Cottle" (Coleridge), 7:449
Linnaeus (Carl von Linné), 10:455
Linnell, John, 5:530, 532
Lipps, Theodor, 8:283
Lipsius, Justus, 3:108
Liszt, Franz, 7:632; 8:9
Literary Criticism: A Short History (Wimsatt and Brooks), 10:335
"Literary Fact" (Tynianov), 8:345
Literary Fiction and Reality (Kermode), 10:428
Literary Microcosm, The (Coulter), 1:xix
Literary Mind, The (Eastman), 9:462, 573
Literary Theory (Eagleton), 11:279
Literature and Dogma (Arnold), 7:705
Literature and Revolution (Trotsky), 10:552
"Literature as Knowledge" (Tate), 9:233–34
Literature of Their Own, A (Showalter), 11:286
"Literaturkritik und Literaturgeschichte" (Milch), 10:70
Littérature de l'âge baroque en France, La (Rousset), 11:63n.7
"Little Black Boy, The" (Blake), 7:359
"Little Boy Lost" (Blake), 7:395n.11
Little Iliad, 1:169
Little Women (Alcott), 11:312, 314–15
Littré, Emile, 11:39
Lives of the Philosophers (Diogenes Laertius), 10:458
Lives of the Poets (Johnson), 4:ix; 7:216; 8:425
Living Corpse, The (Tolstoy), 9:366
Livius Andronicus, 3:719–20, 726, 731, 736
Livre irréalisé (Mallarmé), 11:57
Livy (T. Livius), 1:297, 300, 302–3; 2:164, 198; 3:93, 731–32, 736; 4:21
Lobeck, Christian August, 7:645–46
Lobgesang auf den Heiligen Anno (anon.), 6:353–54

Locke, John, 3:721; 4:49–50, 53, 298; 9:253, 489; 10:166, 563
Lockhart, John Gibson, 9:35
Lodge, Henry Cabot, 9:317
Loggins, Vernon, 11:385
Logische Untersuchungen (Husserl), 10:492
Lohengrin, 6:354
Lolita (Nabokov), 10:157
Long Black Song: Essays in Black American Literature and Culture (Baker), 11:374, 376
"Long Way Round to Nirvana, A" (Santayana), 10:565
Longinus, 1:xvi–xviii; 3:xi, 188, 317–29, 341–42, 386, 388, 493; 4:78, 230, 265–66, 278; 6:vii–viii; 9:462, 559, 573; 10:216, 628; 11:vii–viii, 243
Lope de Vega, 3:346
Lord, Albert, 11:375
Lord Jim (Conrad), 10:313
Lorde, Audre, 11:285
Lost Girl, The (Lawrence), 9:74
Lost Illusions (Balzac). *See Illusions perdues*
Louis XIV (King of France), 7:241
Louis-Philippe, King, 7:143
Love for Love (Congreve), 3:673; 7:245
Love in the Western World (Rougemont), 11:85n.15
"Love Song of J. Alfred Prufrock, The" (Eliot), 9:567; 11:154
Love Triumphant (Dryden), 3:674, 682, 684
Lovejoy, A. O., 10:76, 550
"Lover neither dead nor alive, A" (Cowley), 4:507
"Lover's heart, a hand grenado, A" (Cowley), 4:507
Love's Labour's Lost (Shakespeare), 6:78; 9:169–70
"Love's Nocturn" (Rossetti), 7:465
"Love's Secret" (Blake), 7:371
Lowell, James Russell, 9:470n.3
Lowes, John Livingston, 9:562–63
Lubbock, Percy, 9:82n.18
Lucan (M. Annaeus Lucanus), 2:29, 76, 164, 236, 255, 419; 3:80, 90, 145, 218, 232, 241–42, 278–79, 312, 333, 363, 373, 395, 426, 474, 555, 646, 650; 4:279
Lucas, F. L., 8:191n.1
Lucas, Prosper, 11:87n.26
Lucian, 3:128, 157, 348, 635, 650; 4:380; 7:687
Lucilius, C., 1:238; 3:111, 299, 407, 432, 496
Lucinde (Schlegel), 9:381
Lucretius (T. Lucretius Carus), 2:116, 255, 466; 5:376, 395n.21; 3:96, 107, 153, 187,

232, 258, 281, 283, 335, 375, 393, 395, 397–400, 496, 626, 643, 649; 4:22–23, 302; 7:xxi; 8:479, 481–82, 515nn.7–8; 10:618–19
"Lucy Gray" (Wordsworth), 7:191
Lukács, George, 8:445; 10:261–63, 284, 286, 392; 11:131, 135n.2, 141, 155, 242
Lukasiewicz, Jan, 11:257
Lust's Dominion; or, The Lascivious Queen (Marlowe), 5:687–88
Luther, Martin, 3:3; 6:200, 440; 7:230, 580, 610; 8:13–14; 9:546; 11:227
"Luther's Wedding" (Wagner), 7:580
Lutrin, Le (Boileau), 3:412
"Lycidas" (Milton), 4:525; 7:413; 9:332; 10:78, 84, 564, 585, 588n.10, 623; 11:199, 209–10, 212–14, 341–42
Lycon (Ariston), 1:363
Lycophron, 1:183; 3:326, 423
Lycosthenes, Conrad, 7:709
Lycurgus, 1:236; 3:659
Lydgate, John, 2:265, 355; 3:495
"Lyke-Wake Dirge" (anon.), 10:587
Lyly, John, 9:190
Lynceus (Theodectes), 1:163
Lyotard, Jean-François, 10:385–86
Lyrical Ballads (Coleridge and Wordsworth), 5:vii, 271, 324, 411–13, 416–25, 442–44; 507, 511, 534, 621–24, 7:446, 452; 9:101, 501, 513, 639; 10:339, 341
Lysias, 1:84–85, 215, 258, 346–48, 410, 413
Lysippus, 3:110

Mac Flecknoe (Dryden), 9:260
Macaulay, Thomas Babington, 7:181; 9:242, 247, 249, 254–55; 11:150
Macbeth (Shakespeare), 5:87, 484, 683–86, 692; 6:33, 48, 105–8; 9:149–50, 158, 169, 171–72, 176–78, 188–89, 236, 239–40, 243, 245, 256–61, 368–72, 478, 491, 525, 527, 665, 674, 676; 11:74
MacCaffrey, Isabel G., 3:ix
MacCarthy, Desmond, 8:422, 430; 10:132
McGrath, William J., 8:ix–x
Machiavelli, Niccolo, 3:21, 636, 728–29, 734; 6:195; 7:251, 644; 9:667, 673
Mackail, J. W., 8:527
Mackenzie, Sir George, 3:413
Macklin, Charles, 4:346
MacLeish, Archibald, 9:638
MacLuhan, Marshall, 10:416
Macpherson, James, 5:315–17
Macrobius, 3:326, 425, 451, 557
Madame Bovary (Flaubert), 7:141–51, 168, 418; 8:145, 178; 9:29, 70, 360; 10:347–48, 350, 358, 421; 11:58, 98
"Madame de Mauves" (James), 9:71
Madame Edwarda (Bataille), 11:107
Madeleine Férat (Zola), 11:87n.26
Mademoiselle de Belle-Isle (Béranger), 7:157
Madwoman in the Attic, The (Gilbert and Gubar), 11:286
Maeterlinck, Maurice, 8:82, 92, 94; 9:35
Magic Mountain, The (Mann), 9:328
Magnus, Johannes, 4:195
Magnus, Olaus, 4:195; 7:709
Magny, Claude-Edmond, 10:304, 417
Mahomet, 6:343–44
Maid (Chapelain). See *Pucelle, La*
Maid's Tragedy, The (Beaumont and Fletcher), 3:384, 442, 563, 567–79; 5:697
Mailer, Norman, 10:415, 610
Maimonides, Moses, 9:333–34
Maino, Jason, 3:326
Making of an Orator, The (Cicero). See *De Oratore*
Malade imaginaire, La (Molière), 5:86
Mâle, Emile, 8:506
Malherbe, François de, 3:470, 551; 8:135
Mallarmé, Stéphane, 7:481; 8:xii, 131, 154, 230–32, 418, 430, 458, 598; 9:29, 32–36, 220, 222, 436, 544; 10:53, 117–18, 263, 302, 342–43, 388, 458, 556, 563, 631–32; 11:43, 63n.4, 153, 262, 264, 270, 298, 300, 356
Mallinckrodt, Bernard von, 4:194
Mallock, W. H., 7:xiv
Malory, Sir Thomas, 6:405; 7:709
Malraux, André, 9:430, 433, 593, 609; 10:79, 123, 568, 609
Man Who Loved Children, The (Stead), 11:107
Man without Qualities, The (Musil), 10:293
Mandeville, Sir John, 7:710
Mandonnet, Père, 8:513–14, 519n.42
Mandragola, La (Machiavelli), 7:251
Manfred (Byron), 6:244
Manilius, C., 3:187, 475, 493
Manilius, M., 8:485
Mankind, Nation and Individual (Jesperson), 11:88n.31
Mann, Klaus, 8:157
Mann, Thomas, 9:326, 328, 382–83, 575; 10:235n.1
Mannheim, Karl, 10:75; 11:132
Mantegna, Andrea, 7:676
Manutius (Paulo Manuzio), 3:319
Manzoni, Alessandro, 5:75
Map of Misreading, A (Bloom), 10:634

Map of Time, The (Guibbory), 3:xii
Marcel, Gabriel, 10:199
Marcellus, M., 1:236
Marcuse, Herbert, 8:ix; 9:409–12; 11:95
"Margaret" (Wordsworth), 7:194
Marginalia (Poe), 7:131
Margites (attrib. to Homer), 1:152
Mariamne (Fenton), 6:78
"Marianne's Dream" (Shelley), 8:86
Marie Stuart (Lebrun), 6:37
Marina (Eliot), 9:91; 10:91
Marinetti, Fillipo, 8:469–70
Marino Faliero (Byron), 5:89
Marino, Giambattista, 3:203, 333, 336, 338, 346, 474, 559, 561
Maritain, Jacques, 8:155; 9:226
Marius, C., 1:237, 247
Marius the Epicurean (Pater), 7:x, xviii–xix, xxiv
Marivaux, Pierre de, 11:54, 67
Markham, Gervase, 3:81
Marks, Elaine, 11:285
Marlowe, Christopher, 3:141; 5:687–88; 7:367; 8:409, 427; 9:658, 666–67, 673; 10:405
Marmontel, Jean François, 11:385
Marriage à la Mode (Dryden), 3:379
Marriage of Heaven and Hell, The (Blake), 7:387, 395n.9
Marriage of Sir Gawain, The (anon.), 5:341
Marston, John, 3:81–83; 5:689–90
"Martha Ray" (Wordsworth), 7:707
Martial (M. Valerius Martialis), 2:256; 3:79–81, 107, 122, 130, 145, 420, 425, 473–74, 503, 655; 8:516n.14
Martin, Wendy, 11:179
Martz, Louis, 10:585
Marvell, Andrew, 8:406, 409, 411–12; 9:466–67, 490–92, 529, 567, 668; 10:72, 490–91, 495, 545–46, 587; 11:9
Marx, Karl, 7:622n.52; 8:278–80, 291–92, 295–96, 298–301, 453; 9:45, 305, 379, 480; 10:169, 378, 409, 455, 464–65, 467; 11:vii–viii, x, 123–26, 129–35, 162–63, 230, 236, 238, 248, 273n.3, 282, 328, 336, 370, 389
Mascardi, Agostino, 3:410
Masefield, John, 9:180
Maske Presented at Ludlow Castle, A (Milton). *See Comus*
Masque of Anarchy, The (Shelley), 8:73
Massacre of Guernica, The (Greuze), 9:421
Massignon, Louis, 11:147
Massinger, Philip, 5:699; 10:85, 94
Master and Man (Tolstoy), 10:78

Masterpiece, The (Zola), 8:297
Matabletica (Van den Berg), 7:xlvii
Matthiessen, F. O., 9:565–66; 10:98
"Maud-Evelyn" (James), 9:351, 354
Maudsley, Henry, 8:24–25; 11:194n.12
Maule's Curse (Winters), 9:69
Maupassant, Guy de, 7:176, 703
Mauriac, François, 10:300, 302
Maurras, Charles, 8:201, 426
Maxims (La Rochefoucauld), 9:26
Mayakovsky, Vladimir, 8:322, 338; 11:258
Mazzoni, Jacobo, 2:406–7
Meaning of Meaning, The (Richards and Ogden), 9:568; 10:165
Measure for Measure (Shakespeare), 7:457–63; 9:158, 168–69, 172–74; 10:viii–x
Medal, The (Dryden), 4:537
Medal Reversed, The (Settle), 4:537–38
Medea (Euripides), 1:161, 173; 2:174; 3:563; 6:234
Meillet, Antoine, 8:515n.7
Mein Kampf (Hitler), 11:243
Meinhold, Wilhelm, 7:433, 470
Meistersinger, Die (Wagner), 7:580
Mela, Pomponius, 3:187
Mclanippides, 1:189
Melanthius, 1:371
Melantius (Fletcher), 3:384
Melodies of Life, The (Schlegel), 5:204–6
Melville, Herman, 8:248–49, 254, 258; 9:242–44, 315, 649; 10:98, 400, 404; 11:287, 385
Memoir of Phillis Wheatley, a Native American and a Slave (Thatcher), 11:369
Memoirs (Du Bellay), 2:261
Memoirs (Rochefoucauld), 3:636
Men of Mark (Simmon), 11:369
Men without Women (Hemingway), 9:39, 48
Menaechmi (Plautus), 2:114
Menander, 1:369, 373, 379, 428; 2:319, 466; 3:111, 425, 741, 752; 5:85–86; 7:241, 248
Mencken, H. L., 9:42; 10:186
Ménechmes, Les (Regnard), 6:54
Menedemus, 1:240–41
Menippus, 11:266
"Mental Traveller, The" (Blake), 7:389
Menteur, Le (Corneille), 3:264, 273
Merchant of Venice, The (Shakespeare), 5:xvii; 8:44–45, 49; 9:169, 179; 11:74
Meredith, George, 7:656, 695, 705; 8:183; 9:60, 69, 76, 103; 10:171
Merezhkovsky, Dmitry Sergeevich, 8:321
Mérimée, Prosper, 5:88–89; 7:466
Merleau-Ponty, Maurice, 9:420, 683; 10:548; 11:44

Merrill, Stuart, 9:32
Merry Devil of Edmonton, The (anon.), 5:690
Merry Wives of Windsor, The (Shakespeare), 3:381, 445; 9:169
"Mesmeric Revelation" (Poe), 7:130
Messiah (Klopstock), 5:501–2
Metamorphoses (Ovid), 1:498; 2:130, 179, 363; 3:249, 333, 339, 414, 489, 649; 8:485; 10:581; 11:267
Metamorphoses du cercle, Les (Poulet), 10:549
Metaphysical Lyrics and Poems of the Seventeenth Century: Donne to Butler (ed. Grierson), 8:406
Metaphysical Poetry (Grierson), 8:429
Metaphysics (Aristotle), 1:533; 2:5, 409; 8:481, 515n.8; 9:9; 10:26, 37
Metman, Eva, 10:247
Metrodorus, 1:234
Meyer, Hans Heinrich, 5:238, 240
Meyer-Lübke, Wilhelm, 8:364–65, 368, 372, 382n.2
"Michael" (Wordsworth), 5:419–20; 7:192
Michaels, Fern, 10:211
Michelangelo Buonarroti, 2:224; 5:67; 7:16, 37, 419; 8:236
Michelet, Jules, 7:632; 9:31, 617; 10:136
Mickle, William Julius, 5:342
Middle Span, The (Santayana), 8:387–88n.13
"Middle Years, The" (James), 9:349
Middlemarch (Eliot), 11:286, 312–15
Middleton, Thomas, 3:81; 5:691–92, 699; 8:407, 427
Midnight Birds (ed. Washington), 10:597
Midsummer Night's Dream, A (Shakespeare), 6:459; 7:64; 8:21; 9:169; 11:12
Midsummer Night's Dream, A (film), 8:460
Milbourne, Luke, 3:500, 502, 504
Milch, Werner, 10:70
Miles Gloriosus (Plautus), 3:336, 668
Military Tales (Tolstoy), 7:319, 327
Mill, James, 9:74; 11:150
Mill, John Stuart, 7:445, 632; 9:74, 380, 572, 638; 10:144, 330; 11:150
Mill on the Floss, The (Eliot), 11:286
Millais, Sir John Everett, 7:xxxix; 8:22
Millar, John, 11:194n.12
Millay, Edna St. Vincent, 11:179
Miller, Henry, 9:78
Miller, J. Hillis, 10:315, 322n.4, 632; 11:172–76
Millett, Kate, 10:592; 11:311
Milthalter, Julius, 7:272
Milton, John, 3:xiii–ix, xiv, 402, 413, 467, 473, 489; 4:53–83, 262–63, 272–73, 292, 304, 379, 497, 500, 517–534; 5:xi–xii, xiv; 5:123, 141, 310–11, 316, 409, 445, 477, 499–504, 537, 596, 603, 609, 625, 650, 652, 688; 6:66–67, 82–83, 90–91, 98, 136, 199–200, 204, 226, 228–29, 246, 265, 399–400; 7:xlvi, 26, 52–54, 183, 192, 200, 207; 8:410–12, 427, 430, 532; 9:xvii, 54, 84–102, 238, 250–51, 253, 324, 515, 518–19, 648, 652–53; 10:71–72, 84, 224, 330, 405, 439, 564, 566, 568, 577–82, 585–86, 605–8, 610, 612–14, 616–17, 623, 634; 11:viii, 172, 186, 199–201, 324, 335, 341–46, 386
Milton (Blake), 7:399n.21; 10:585, 615
Mimesis: The Representation of Reality in Western Literature (Auerbach), 2:x; 10:173; 11:144–47, 159, 193n.1
Mince, Sir John, 3:656
Minstrelsy of the Scottish Border, The (ed. Scott), 5:325
Mirogorod (Gogol), 7:319
Mirror and the Lamp, The (Abrams), 5:x
Mirror for Magistrates, A (anon.), 2:298
"Mirror for Men: Stereotypes of Women in Literature, A" (Wolff), 11:317n.3
Misanthrope, Le (Molière), 7:242–43, 247–48, 262
Miscellanies (Clement of Alexandria), 4:198
Miser, The (Molière). See *Avare, L'*
Misérables, Les (Hugo), 7:426
Misogynes (Menander), 7:248
Mr. Isaacs (Crawford), 7:705
"Mrs. Battle's Opinion on Whist" (Lamb), 5:591
Mistress; or, Love-Verses, The (Cowley), 3:251; 4:512–13
Mitchell, Juliet, 11:173–74, 284
Mitchell, S. Weir, 11:171, 191, 193
Mitford, Mary Russell, 8:175
Mizener, Arthur, 9:522–23, 529–30
Mnesarchus, 1:234, 240
Moby-Dick (Melville), 8:248–49; 9:253; 10:331, 399; 11:330–31
Mock Tempest, The (Duffet), 3:293
Models and Metaphors (Black), 10:641
Modern Century, The (Frye), 10:569
Modern Love (Meredith), 9:60
Modern Painters (Ruskin), 7:xvi, xix, xxxix, xl, xliii, xlvi–xlvii, 62; 8:207–8
Modern Poetry and the Tradition (Brooks), 9:514–15, 522
Modern Theme, The (Ortega y Gasset), 8:233
Modification, La (Butor), 10:550
Moers, Ellen, 11:187, 311
Moissi, Alessandro, 9:366–67

Molé, M., 4:319, 349n.17
Molière (Jean Baptiste Poquelin), 3:439, 450, 657, 726, 740; 4:320; 5:83–84, 86–87; 6:41–43, 48–50, 53–54, 95, 469, 471; 7:237, 241, 242–46, 249–50, 261–62; 8:364; 9:31
"Mon Coeur mis a nu" (Baudelaire), 8:420
Mona Lisa (Leonardo). *See Gioconda, La*
Mondrian, Piet, 9:684
Monet, Claude, 8:5
Monk, The (Lewis), 8:591–92
Monkhouse, William, 5:563–64
"Monody on the Death of Chatterton" (Coleridge), 5:630
Monro, Harold, 9:53
"Mont Blanc" (Shelley), 8:73, 81
Mont-Saint-Michel (Adams), 9:321–22
Montaigne, Michel de, 2:viii–xi, xiv–xvii; 3:vii–viii, 40, 371, 636; 6:443–52, 471, 476; 7:698; 8:265, 270, 384n.7, 409, 439; 9:432–33; 10:viii, 200
Montesquieu, Charles le Secondat, baron de, 7:174
Montfaucon, Bernard de, 5:26; 8:519n.43
Montgomery, James, 6:218; 9:638
Montherlant, Henri de, 9:591, 594, 600, 608–9
Montménil (Montmesnil), M., 4:328, 351n.32
Monty Python and the Holy Grail (film), 10:572
Moore, G. E., 10:165
Moore, George, 8:214; 9:67–68, 462
Moore, Marianne, 9:365, 486–87; 10:340
Moore, Thomas, 6:viii, 138, 246, 400; 7:605
Moral Essays (Plutarch), 2:257
Moral Essays (Pope), 4:560
More, Sir George, 3:516–18, 531, 543
More, Henry, 5:418
More, Paul Elmer, 8:422, 425; 9:18, 326; 10:181, 392
More, Sir Thomas, 2:202, 281, 347, 362, 395, 503; 3:105, 514, 583
Moreno, J. L., 10:200
Morgante, Il (Pulci), 3:346
Morgante maggiore (Pulci), 8:376
Morise, Max, 5:599, 605
Morley, Henry, 10:95
Mornings in Mexico (Lawrence), 9:105
Morris, William, 7:xiv, xx, 700, 718; 8:28–29, 94; 9:56, 60
Morrison, Toni, 11:375
Mort de Henri IV, La (Legouvé), 6:45
"Morte amoureuse, La" (Gautier), 7:474
Morte Darthur, Le (Malory), 6:405–6
Mortimer, Raymond, 8:153

Moses, Paul, 10:311–13
Mostellaria (Plautus), 2:165
Motives of Eloquence, The (Lanham), 2:xii
Motley, John Lothrop, 9:255
Mots, Les (Sartre), 10:297
"Moyen Age et l'histoire, Le" (Gilson), 8:519n.41
Mozart, Wolfgang Amadeus, 8:8; 9:366
Much Ado About Nothing (Shakespeare), 9:166, 168, 170, 177, 187
Muller, Adam, 7:277
Muller, Herbert, 9:468–69, 514–16, 575
Müller, Karl Ottfried, 6:417
Munera Pulveris (Ruskin), 7:xl, xlvi; 9:641
Muratori, Lodovico Antonio, 7:276
Murder in the Cathedral (Eliot), 8:427; 10:87, 100
Murdoch, Iris, 10:294–95, 298, 300–301
Muret, Marc-Antoine, 3:319
Murger, Henri, 7:473–74
Murray, Henry, 11:74
Murry, John Middleton, 8:400–402, 426; 9:104, 576, 649; 10:143, 149
Musaeus, 2:166, 347; 3:142, 156–57
"Muse of Criticism, The" (Hartman), 11:287
Muse's Elysium, The (Drayton), 6:80
Musil, Robert, 10:293
Musset, Alfred de, 7:134, 165; 9:30, 32
Mustapha (Boyle), 3:456
Mustapha (Brooke), 5:695
Mustapha (Orrery), 3:379
Myers, F. W. H., 7:718
Myers, L. H., 9:80n.6
Mysians, The (Aeschylus), 1:171
Mysteries of Udolpho, The (Radcliffe), 10:464
Mystic Theology (Dionysius), 2:407
Myth of Sisyphus, The (Camus), 10:240, 255
Myth of the Eternal Return, The (Eliade), 11:85n.16
Mythologies (Fulgentius), 1:487
Mythomystes (Reynolds), 3:viii; 7:xlvi

Nabokov, Vladimir, 10:134, 157; 11:110
Nairn, Tom, 11:133–34
Naive and Sentimental Poetry (Schiller), 5:81
Napoleon Bonaparte, 7:642, 697
Nashe, Thomas, 3:141; 8:88
Nasica, P. Cornelius Scipio, 2:117
Nation, The, 9:342
Native Son (Wright), 10:x; 11:378
Natural History (Pliny). *See Historia Naturalis*
Naturales Quaestiones (Seneca), 3:187
Nature (Emerson), 9:204; 10:409
"Nature" (Goethe), 9:117, 119

INDEX OF NAMES AND TITLES 479

Nature of the Physical World, The
　(Eddington), 8:528
Naugerius (Fracastoro), 2:402
Nauman, Bruce, 10:386
Nausée, La (Sartre), 10:296–300, 302–6
Nazianzen, Gregory, 3:152, 170
Necker, Jacques, 4:323, 350n.25; 5:207;
　6:417
Negro Equalled by Few Europeans, The
　(Bois-Robert), 11:368
Negro in Literature and Art, The (Brawley),
　11:369
Nekrasov, Nikolai Alekseevich, 7:333
Nelson, John Herbert, 11:385
Nest of Gentlefolk, A (Turgenev), 8:561
"Neue Denken, Das" (Rosenzweig),
　8:386n.10
New Criterion, The, 10:408
New Criticism in France, The (Doubrovsky),
　10:390
"New Feminist Criticisms: Exploring the
　History of the New Space, The" (Pratt),
　11:195n.31
New French Feminisms (ed. Marks and
　Courtivron), 11:285
New Republic, The (Mallock), 7:xiv
New Wonder: A Woman Never Vext, A
　(Rowley), 5:692
New York Times, The, 10:78
New Yorker, The, 10:186
Newcomes, The (Thackeray), 7:713
Newman, John Henry, 7:418, 653; 9:642
Newton, Sir Isaac, 3:721; 6:403; 7:380;
　8:185; 9:26; 10:165, 226, 337–38, 366,
　466–67
Newton, Thomas, 2:364
Nibelungenlied, 6:354
Nicander of Colophon, 1:238, 365; 3:187
Nichols, Charles, 11:385
Nicholson, Marjorie, 10:548
Nicochares, 1:150
Nicomachean Ethics (Aristotle), 2:328, 461;
　9:11
Nicomède (Corneille), 3:270
Nicostratus, 1:413
Niebuhr, Reinhold, 9:226
Nietzsche, Friedrich, 1:vii–viii, xii–xiii; 2:viii;
　3:viii; 6:viii; 7:vii–xii; 8:203, 230, 274;
　9:vii–viii, xiv, 10, 301, 379, 396, 406–7,
　413, 436, 661–62, 665–66, 668, 676,
　685–87; 10:14, 33, 193, 195, 210, 239,
　261, 283, 285, 361, 377, 383, 457, 469–84,
　521, 523–24, 566, 620, 623–26, 631–34;
　11:vii–viii, 68nn.57, 61, 63, 98, 123,
　235–36, 243, 245, 247, 264, 266

Nietzsche as Philosopher (Danto), 7:620n.1
"Night" (Blake), 7:359
Night Thoughts (Young), 6:241; 8:597
Nightingale, Florence, 8:181; 11:312
Nightwood (Barnes), 9:78
Nijinski, Waslaw, 8:609; 9:366
Nineteen Eighty-Four (Orwell), 9:495
"Nineteenth Psalm" (Addison), 7:465
Ninth Symphony (Beethoven), 7:302
Nodier, Charles, 8:437
Norbanus, C., 1:246
Nordau, Max, 8:11, 17–18, 20–30, 32nn.4–5
Norden, Eduard, 10:569
Norris, Christopher, 11:285
Norris, Frank, 9:243
North American Review, The, 7:530–36;
　9:317
Norton Anthology of Women's Literature, The
　(ed. Gilbert and Gubar), 11:286
Nostromo (Conrad), 9:75; 10:408; 11:153,
　155
Notebooks (Coleridge), 5:x
Notes of a Billiard Marker (Tolstoy), 7:319,
　323, 325, 327
"Notes on a Case of Obsessional Neurosis"
　(Freud), 11:88–89n.36
"Notes toward a Supreme Fiction" (Stevens),
　6:viii; 7:xvii; 8:xi; 11:341, 344–45
Notre Dame de Paris (Hugo), 5:89
Nouveau, Germain, 8:598
Nouvelle Héloïse, La (Rousseau), 7:143;
　10:273, 279, 282, 285, 567
Novalis, 7:411; 9:381
Novel (Hippocrates), 11:267
Novum Organum (Bacon), 3:102; 10:173, 459
Noyes, Alfred, 9:61
Numa Pompilius, 1:511
Nymphidia (Drayton), 6:80

O'Brien, Flann, 10:369
O'Connor, Flannery, 11:352
O'Shaughnessy, Arthur, 8:89; 9:55
Obermann (Senancour), 7:474
Obiter Dicta (Birrell), 7:676
Observations (Breme), 6:365
Observations on Horace His Art of Poetry
　(Jonson), 3:73
Octavia (attrib. to Seneca), 9:663
Octopus, The (Norris), 9:243
Odd Woman, The (Godwin), 11:316
Odd Women, The (Gissing), 11:316
"Ode" (Herbert), 8:408, 410
"Ode: Intimations of Immortality"
　(Wordsworth), 5:xxi, 530; 7:xxxvii, xliii,
　707; 9:101; 10:155–56; 11:190

"Ode concerning Wit" (Cowley), 3:399
"Ode for the Confederate Dead" (Tate), 10:581
"Ode Occasion'd by the Death of Mr. Thomson" (Collins), 5:314
"Ode on a Distant Prospect of Eton College" (Gray), 4:582; 5:276, 288, 427, 432–33
"Ode on a Grecian Urn" (Keats), 10:149–51, 642–43
"Ode on Chatterton" (Coleridge). See "Monody on the Death of Chatterton"
"Ode on Melancholy" (Keats), 7:xxxiii
"Ode on the Death a Favorite Cat" (Gray), 4:582
"Ode on the Recollections of Childhood" (Wordsworth), 7:434
"Ode on the Singing of Mrs. Arabella Hunt" (Congreve), 6:84
"Ode on the Spring" (Gray), 4:582
"Ode to a Nightingale" (Keats), 8:397
"Ode to Adversity" (Gray), 4:582
"Ode to Autumn" (Keats), 9:489
"Ode to Liberty" (Shelley), 8:82
"Ode to Naples" (Shelley), 7:18; 8:72–73
Odes (Cowley), 3:470
Odes (Horace), 3:321, 709
Odes (Ronsard), 3:80
Odyssey (Homer), 1:93, 152, 155, 159, 163, 169–71, 174, 184, 331–32, 427, 476; 2:30, 41, 110, 130–32, 174–75, 177, 227; 3:127–28, 130–35, 151, 240, 283, 285, 324–25, 335, 463, 492, 555; 4:58, 60, 199, 217, 221, 226–27, 229–32, 241, 274, 276, 278–79; 5:130–31; 7:476; 9:185, 522
"Odyssey, The" (Lang), 9:55
Oedipus (Carcinus), 1:201
Oedipus (Dryden and Lee), 3:379, 691, 693
Oedipus at Colonus (Sophocles), 3:384; 5:70; 6:233, 246
Oedipus Rex (Sophocles), 1:157, 159, 161–62, 170, 174, 347; 2:126, 128–29, 455, 462, 464; 3:271, 281, 339, 375, 382–83, 690, 697; 4:46; 6:235, 246; 8:63, 626; 9:13; 10:147, 199–200
Oeil vivant, L' (Starobinski), 10:269
"Of Books" (Montaigne), 2:viii–ix, xiv
Of Education (Milton), 3:xiv
"Of Experience" (Montaigne), 2:xvi–xvii
"Of His Mistress Bathing" (Cowley), 4:505
Of Human Bondage (Maugham), 10:357
"Of Mere Being" (Stevens), 8:xii
"Of Pleasing, An Epistle to Sir Richard Temple" (Congreve), 4:247n.15
"Of Studies" (Bacon), 2:x

"Of the Education of Children" (Montaigne), 2:xv
Offenbach, Jacques, 8:46
Ogden, C. K., 9:480, 568, 573; 10:165
Ogilby, John, 3:394, 396, 502
"Oh Soul Thou Pleasest Me" (Whitman), 10:89–90
Ohnet, Georges, 7:669
Old Ballads, Historical and Narrative (ed. Evans), 5:342
Old Batchelor, The (Congreve), 3:674
Old Curiosity Shop, The (Dickens), 7:73
Old Fortunatus (Dekker), 5:689
Old Law (Massinger, Middleton, and Rowley), 5:699
Old Mortality (Scott), 5:641; 7:70
Olsen, Tillie, 11:285
Olson, Elder, 9:231, 237, 478–79
Olympic (Gorgias), 1:196
Olympica, 8:153
Ombilic des limbes, L' (Artaud), 11:42
"On a Sun-Dial" (Hazlitt), 5:xxi
On Christian Doctrine (Augustine), 11:214
On Czech Verse (Jakobson), 8:337
On Deconstruction (Culler), 11:279
On First Principles (Origen), 8:448
"On Going a Journey" (Hazlitt), 5:xx
On Liberty (Mill), 10:330; 11:150–51
"On Life" (Shelley), 8:78, 81
"On Mrs. Corbet, Who Died of a Cancer in Her Breast" (Pope), 4:579–80
"On Modern Comedy" (Hazlitt), 10:230
On Moral Fiction (Gardner), 10:322n.2
"On Poetry and Transrational Language" (Shklovsky), 8:324
"On Repetition" (Said), 11:389
"On Rhythmic-Syntactic Figures" (Brik), 8:334–35
On Simple and Sentimental Poetry (Schiller), 5:218
"On Sitting Down to Read *King Lear* Once Again" (Keats), 6:255–56
"On Sounds in Verse Language" (Iakubinsky), 8:323
On Sublimity (Calactinus), 1:325
On the Alliance (Isocrates). See *De Pace*
On the Crown (Demosthenes), 1:338
"On the Fear of Death" (Hazlitt), 5:xxi
"On the Feeling of Immortality in Youth" (Hazlitt), 5:xxi
On the Fortune of the Romans (Plutarch), 2:419
On the Genealogy of Morals (Nietzsche), 7:viii–ix; 10:469–70

INDEX OF NAMES AND TITLES

"On the History of European Nihilism" (Nietzsche), 7:618
"On the Morning of Christ's Nativity" (Milton), 8:532
On the Origin of Species (Darwin), 7:698; 9:27
"On the Periodical Essayists" (Hazlitt), 5:xv
On the Remedies of Fortune (Petrarch), 2:57
On the Solitary Life (Petrarch), 2:57
On the Sublime (Longinus), 3:317–29; 9:572–73, 575; 10:216
On the Vulgar Tongue (Dante). *See De Vulgari Eloquentia*
"On Westminster Bridge" (Wordsworth), 9:512–13
"One Child of One's Own" (Walker), 10:595
Onesto degli Onesti (Onesto Bolognese), 1:509
Ong, Walter J., 10:390
Opera and Drama (Wagner), 7:583
Opinion publique, L' (film), 8:460
Oppenheimer, Robert, 8:618; 11:240
Oppian, 3:187
Orator (Cicero), 2:359; 4:207
Orcagna (Andrea de Cione), 7:459
Order of Things, The (Foucault), 10:455
Oresteia (Aeschylus), 9:659
Orestes (Euripides), 1:161, 173, 281; 3:266; 6:234
Orientalism (Said), 10:403; 11:161
Origen, 2:48; 3:152, 174; 8:448, 492–93, 503, 517n.26
Origin of Geometry, The (Husserl), 11:44
Origin of Harlequin, The (Driesen), 9:126
Origines de la France bourgeoise, Les (Groethuysen), 8:506
Orlando (Woolf), 10:136
Orlando Furioso (Ariosto), 2:174, 256, 294, 390–97, 414, 422–23, 434–35; 3:336, 346; 6:70–71
Orlando Innamorato (Boiardo), 9:453
Orphan, The (Otway), 3:674
Ortega y Gasset, José, 8:233; 10:294–95
Ortner, Sherry, 11:284
Orwell, George, 9:495; 11:80
Oscar Wilde (Ellmann), 10:323n.7
Ossian (James Macpherson), 5:588; 6:82
Ostrovsky, Alexander Nikolaevich, 7:290
Otage, L' (Claudel), 11:58
Othello (Shakespeare), 3:563–64, 587–613; 5:475–76, 577, 683; 6:34, 48; 7:673; 8:397, 626; 9:158, 172, 175, 177–78, 244, 362, 375; 9:665
"Other Side of the Mirror, The" (Coleridge), 11:185

Otto (Fletcher), 3:384
Otway, Thomas, 4:43; 5:650
Outline of Psychoanalysis, An (Freud), 8:viii
Overbury, Sir Thomas, 3:81–82
Overcoat, The (Gogol), 8:333; 11:255
Ovid (P. Ovidius Naso), 1:498; 2:32, 130–32, 179, 254, 363, 393; 3:108, 142, 145, 147, 153, 249, 297, 333, 339, 387, 394–97, 401, 413–14, 430–31, 452, 459, 471, 481, 489, 493–95, 499–500, 502, 646, 649, 716; 4:52; 8:309, 313–14, 484–85, 515n.13; 10:581
Owen, John, 3:82, 474
Owen, Richard, 6:401
Oxford Book of Modern Verse, The (ed. Yeats), 7:xvi

Pagello, Bartolomeo, 2:117
"Pains of Sleep, The" (Coleridge), 7:446
"Palace of Art, The" (Tennyson), 9:57
Palamedes (Gorgias), 10:635
Pale Fire (Nabokov), 10:415
Paleface (Lewis), 9:104–5
Paleotti, Camillo, 2:319
Paley, Grace, 11:285
Paley, William, 7:705
Palgrave, Francis Turner, 7:182
Palimpsest (H. D.), 11:183
Pall Mall Gazette, 7:522–23, 525
Palme (Valéry), 8:xii
Panaetius, 1:234, 239
Panegyricus (Isocrates), 1:187, 202, 327, 349
Panegyricus ad Messalam (Propertius), 8:484
Panhypocrisiade (Lemercier), 6:56n.21
Paolo, Padre, 3:636
"Paquet de lettres, Un" (Droz), 7:122
Paradise Lost (Milton), 3:xiv, 402, 580; 4:53–83, 292, 304, 521–34; 5:xi, 123, 141, 310–11, 406, 445, 477, 499–504; 6:67, 82–83, 90–91, 199–200, 204, 228–29; 7:660; 9:87–88, 91–98, 250, 487, 515, 669; 10:405, 439, 505, 568, 577–78, 580, 586, 605, 612; 11:viii, 277, 341–44
Paradise Lost and Its Critics (Waldock), 9:92
Paradise Regained (Milton), 4:532; 7:192; 10:556, 605–6
Parallel betwixt Painting and Poetry, A (Dryden), 3:477
Parcival, 6:354
Parerga et Paralipomena (Schopenhauer), 8:275–76
Paria, Le (Delavigne), 6:31
Parker, Junior, 11:389
Parkman, Francis, 9:254; 10:398
Parmenides, 1:365; 11:ix

Parmenides (Plato), 10:37
Parmeno, 1:368
"Paroles d'un conservateur à propos d'un perturbateur" (Hugo), 7:402n.32
Parry, Milman, 11:375
Parsifal (Wagner), 7:580–82; 8:7
Partage de midi (Claudel), 9:598
Pascal, Blaise, 2:ix; 7:245, 414, 601; 8:153, 378, 424, 445; 9:220–21, 223, 274, 320, 323, 429, 433; 10:552, 619
"Passage to India" (Whitman), 10:89–90, 585
Passetyme of Pleasure, The (Hawes), 11:78
Pasternak, Boris, 11:222
Pastor Fido, Il (Guarini), 2:454, 471, 473; 3:80, 400, 410
Pastorals (Pope), 4:272–73
Pastorals (Theocritus), 1:347
Pastorals (Vergil). *See Eclogues*
Pater, Walter, 5:viii–x; 7:x–xxxi, xxxiii, xxxvi, 660, 671, 681, 687, 716; 8:414; 9:59, 67, 367, 462, 560; 10:377, 399, 572, 606, 619, 623, 626; 11:viii, ix
Paterculus, Velleius, 3:123, 128
Paterson (Williams), 10:294, 298
Patience (Gilbert and Sullivan), 7:xiv
Patmore, Coventry, 11:189
Paul of Perugia, 2:55–56
Paul, St., 2:100–101; 7:53
Paul, Jean, 5:535; 10:352
Paulhan, Jean, 11:116
Paulinus of Nola, 8:498
Pausanias, 3:158; 9:622
Payn, James, 7:703
Peacock, Thomas Love, 6:vii–viii, 201; 9:80n.11
Peano, Giuseppe, 11:257
Pearce, Roy Harvey, 10:74
Pedrolo, Manuel de, 10:240
Peele, George, 10:579
Peer Gynt (Ibsen), 9:29, 639
Peirce, Charles Saunders, 8:542; 11:295
Péladan, Joséphiu, 8:26
Pélerinage de Charlemagne, Le, 8:364
Pemberton, Henry, 10:338
Pendennis (Thackeray), 8:195
Penjon, Auguste, 9:573
Penn, William, 8:153
Penrose, Roland, 9:480–81
"Penseroso, Il" (Milton), 4:525–26; 11:342
Pepys, Samuel, 5:335; 7:654
Per Amica Silentia Lunae (Yeats), 7:xiv; 10:643
Percy, Thomas (Bishop of Dromore), 5:314–15, 330, 336–38, 340–42

Percy, Thomas (Bishop of Dromore's nephew), 5:341
Père Goriot (Balzac), 7:68l; 8:294
Peregrine Pickle (Smollett), 7:262
Performing Self, The (Poirier), 10:400
Peri Hypsous (Longinus). *See On the Sublime*
Pericles, 1:184, 203, 318; 3:110; 8:178
"Pericles and Aspasia" (Landor), 5:567–68
Periplus (Hanno), 7:709
Peristephanon (Prudentius), 8:498
Perkins, David, 10:227
Perkins, Maxwell, 10:184
Perrault, Charles, 3:324, 326
Persae (Aeschylus), 1:56; 3:585
Perse, St.-John (Alexis Saint-Léger Léger), 8:598; 9:223
Persians (Timotheus), 1:390
Persius (A. Persius Flaccus), 2:34; 3:81, 299, 406–7, 409–11, 415, 493
Personal Heresy, The (Lewis and Tillyard), 9:557
Pèse-nerfs, Le (Artaud), 11:42
Peter Bell (Wordsworth), 7:194, 707
Peter the Great, 9:128
Petra, Gabrielle della, 3:319
Petrarch (Francesco Petrarca), 2:vii–viii, 8, 21, 26, 41, 43, 47, 56, 108, 124, 136, 145, 172, 176, 202, 256, 355, 461, 529; 3:80, 145, 218, 336, 490, 493, 553, 580, 654; 4:221, 496; 5:377; 6:97; 9:505
Petronius (T. Petronius Arbiter), 3:80–81, 363, 401, 421, 426, 650; 5:415; 6:131; 8:423, 516n.14
Petrus Comestor, 8:519n.42
Peveril of the Peak (Scott), 6:239
Peyre, Henri, 10:164, 171
Pflaum, H., 8:506
Phaedo (Plato), 2:319, 326; 3:128; 8:385n.10
Phaedrus (Plato), 1:187, 470–72; 2:163, 295, 322; 9:413; 10:267
Phaer, Thomas, 2:356, 363
Phalareus, 3:188
Phalaris, 3:635, 642, 659
Phänomenologie des Geistes, Die (Hegel), 10:28; 11:55, 65n.23, 67n.50
Pharsalia (Lucan), 3:278, 333, 363
Phayer, Thomas. *See* Phaer, Thomas
Phèdre (Racine), 4:272; 9:240, 243, 260
Phenomenology of Perception, The (Merleau-Ponty), 9:420
Pherecides, 3:647
Phidias, 1:423; 7:712
Philaster (Beaumont and Fletcher), 3:446; 5:698
Philebus (Plato), 2:161

Philip (Isocrates), 1:203
Philippe, Charles-Louis, 8:370–71, 375
Philippe de Commines, 2:261
Philistus, 1:351
Philo, 7:681; 8:502–3
Philoctetes (Aeschylus), 1:168
Philoctetes (Sophocles), 2:127; 6:233–34; 7:476
"Philologie der Weltliteratur" (Auerbach), 11:145
Philosophe sans le savoir (Sedaine), 4:323
Philosophical Inquiry into the Origin of the Ideas of the Sublime and the Beautiful (Burke), 7:276
Philosophical Investigations (Wittgenstein), 10:562
Philosophical Review of Reform, The (Shelley), 8:73
"Philosophy of Composition, The" (Poe), 10:588n.11
Philosophy of History (Hegel), 8:471–72n.10
Philosophy of Literary Form, The (Burke), 8:384n.7; 11:240
Philosophy of Rhetoric, The (Richards), 9:492
Philosophy of Symbolic Forms, The (Cassirer), 10:498
Philosophy of the Beautiful (Knight), 7:283
Philostratus, 2:323–24; 3:341
Philoxenus, 1:150, 363; 5:375, 395n.18
Phinidae (Timotheus), 1:162
Phocyllides, 3:232, 649
Phoenissae (Euripides), 2:460; 6:234
Phoenix (Lawrence), 9:105
Phoenix and the Turtle, The (Shakespeare), 9:508–10; 11:78
Phormio (Terence), 7:249
Phormis, 1:153
Phrynichus, 1:12, 42, 51, 342
"Physick and Chirurgery for a Lover" (Cowley), 4:506
Physics (Aristotle), 1:523; 3:277; 8:515n.8
Physiological Aesthetics (Allen), 7:283
Piaget, Jean, 10:10
Pibrach, Guy de Faur, seigneur de, 3:232
Picard, Louis, 6:47
Picard, Raymond, 10:423
Picasso, Pablo, 9:423–24, 480–81; 10:251
Piccolomini, Alessandro, 2:405, 427n.17
Piccolomini (Goethe), 5:83
Pico della Mirandola, 3:148–49, 152–53, 156–57, 514, 637
Picon, Gaeton, 11:40
Pictet, Adolphe, 7:281
Pidal, Menéndez, 8:119n.3

Pièces sur l'art (Valéry), 8:453
Piercy, Marge, 11:186
Pierre; or, The Ambiguities (Melville), 11:74
Piers Ploughman (Langland), 2:355; 3:182
Pieyre de Mandiargues, André, 11:116
Pilatus, Leontius, 2:15–17, 56, 59
Pilgrim's Progress, The (Bunyan), 5:584–85; 6:82; 7:28; 11:186
Pindar, 1:347, 366, 372, 407–8; 2:288, 295; 3:81, 147, 174, 218, 252, 337, 339, 353, 401–2, 454, 470, 476, 649; 4:236, 373, 514–15; 5:438; 7:218, 549; 9:xvii; 10:635–36
Pindaric Odes (Cowley), 3:252; 5:310, 438
Pinget, Robert, 10:416
Pinkerton, John, 5:343–44
Pinter, Harold, 10:240
"Piper, The" (Blake), 7:359
Pirandello, Luigi, 8:224, 462; 10:197, 200
Piranesi, Giovanni Battista, 8:150; 10:641–42
Pisander, 2:131
Piso, M., 1:243
Pitt, William, 5:613
Pius IX, Pope, 7:230
Plain Dealer, The (Wycherley), 3:672, 684, 705, 717; 7:243
Plain Tales from the Hills (Kipling), 7:695
Plath, Sylvia, 11:185, 187
Plato, 1:viii, xi–xv, xvii, xix–xx, 184, 213, 215, 218–19, 234, 241, 247, 261, 318, 327–28, 334–36, 342, 344, 346–49, 364, 367, 380, 385, 395, 401, 405–7, 412–13, 455, 462, 470–77, 482, 484, 487; 2:11, 28, 31, 41–44, 94–95, 150, 160–63, 165, 182, 188, 196, 216–17, 219–20, 233, 258, 274, 285, 289, 291, 294–96, 316–20, 322–24, 326, 328, 335, 347, 386, 407; 3:19, 23, 26, 29–30, 93, 108, 112, 123, 128, 147–49, 151–52, 156, 181, 187–89, 229–30, 279, 320, 325, 385, 400, 621, 624, 676, 729, 749; 4:199, 266; 5:242, 390, 457; 6:viii, 198; 7:xx, 8, 439, 465, 548–49, 627n.118, 639, 644, 661, 681, 687, 690, 702, 719; 8:xi, 147, 214–15, 265, 270, 273–75, 289, 385n.10, 427, 505, 515n.4; 9:xii, 12–14, 16–17, 196, 205, 211, 214, 247, 270, 288, 330, 347, 430, 550, 560, 572, 606, 661; 10:26, 34–41, 44, 143, 146, 155–56, 167–68, 208, 235, 267, 318, 321–22, 338, 359, 361, 470, 480, 518, 523, 556, 558, 570, 628, 634, 637; 11:vii–ix, 5–7, 11, 15, 17, 47, 59, 68n.60, 111, 189, 238, 266, 299, 301, 356, 377
Plautus (T. Maccius Plautus), 1:266, 270, 429, 490; 2:18, 93, 114–15, 165–66, 199–200, 228, 255, 299–300, 455, 467;

3:86, 93, 110–12, 142, 336, 384, 425, 432, 503, 668, 675, 731; 8:749; 11:63n.4
Play in the Bower, The (Halle), 9:119–20, 122–23
Playboy of the Western World, The (Synge), 8:94
Pleasure of the Text, The (Barthes), 10:382
Pleasures of Hope, The (Campbell), 6:241
Pliny the Elder (C. Plinius Secundus), 3:131, 187, 326, 647; 7:709; 8:486
Pliny the Younger (C. Plinius Caecilius Secundus), 2:258; 3:11, 79, 81, 90; 5:39; 8:486
Plot Unfolding (Shklovsky), 8:332, 340
Plotinus, 1:xviii–xix
Plowman's Tale, The (attrib. to Chaucer), 3:496
Plumb, J. H., 9:395–96
Plumed Serpent, The (Lawrence), 9:596
Plutarch, 2:xv–xvii, 253, 256–59, 294–96, 319, 325, 352, 381, 383–85, 419; 3:12, 123, 127, 186–87, 370, 716, 734–35; 8:98, 395; 9:673; 10:26
Plutus (Aristophanes), 3:676
Podhoretz, Norman, 10:415
Poe, Edgar Allan, 7:129–140; 8:175, 408, 447, 452, 598; 9:30–33, 220–22, 381, 461–62, 686; 10:146, 186, 211, 400, 504, 588n.11; 11:189–90, 385
Poema (Avitus of Vienne), 8:498
Poems (Lautréamont), 11:257
Poems (Wordsworth), 5:146–47, 507–10
"Poems of Our Climate, The" (Stevens), 7:xii; 10:625, 642
Poésie d'aujourd-hui, La (Epstein), 8:411
"Poet, The" (Emerson), 10:398, 587, 633
Poet as Citizen and Other Papers, The (Quiller-Couch), 9:5
Poetaster, The (Jonson), 5:696
Poetical Works (Wordsworth), 10:340
Poetics (Aristotle), 1:180–81, 204; 2:108, 115, 126, 317, 319, 323, 327, 404, 459, 469; 3:188, 277, 423, 580, 696, 724, 734, 740; 4:245n.3; 5:70–72; 6:232–33; 7:661; 8:147, 298; 9:5, 7, 11–12, 19, 645; 10:143, 148, 168–69; 11:241–42
Poetics of Space, The (Bachelard), 11:190
"Poetry and Morals" (Wimsatt), 10:148
Poetry and Repression (Bloom), 10:645
Poetry Direct and Oblique (Tillyard), 11:88n.27
"Poetry for Poetry's Sake" (Bradley), 10:146
Poetry, Language, Thought (Heidegger), 11:63n.4
Poetry of Architecture, The (Ruskin), 7:xxxix

Poggioli, Renato, 10:391
Poirier, Richard, 10:570–71
Polanyi, Karl, 10:375
Political Unconscious, The (Jameson), 10:312
Politics (Aristotle), 2:327; 3:730; 5:71; 8:481; 9:8, 11; 11:241
Poliziano, Angelo, 3:145, 151
Pollio, C. Asinius, 1:297; 2:260
Pollock, Jackson, 10:187
Polo, Marco, 7:709
Polybius, 3:724
Polyeucte (Corneille), 3:265, 272, 274; 4:325; 11:50, 53
"Polyeucte, or the Ring and the Helix" (Rousset), 11:50–59
Polygnotus, 1:88, 154
Polyidus, 1:162
Polyolbion (Drayton), 3:79, 146
Pompée (Corneille), 3:265, 269, 272, 274, 322
Pompeius, Sextus, 1:237
Pompilius, Numa, 1:232
Ponge, Francis, 11:260
"Poor Man's Hymn" (Conder), 6:214
Pope, Alexander, 4:x–xi, 261, 272–73, 385, 388, 482–83, 498–99, 557–80; 5:xvii, 49, 309 10, 312–14, 579; 6:136, 239, 245–46, 470; 7:41, 47, 55–56, 206, 238; 8:206; 9:28–29, 31, 54, 453, 502, 510, 518–20, 530; 10:168, 580, 609, 642, 645; 11:386
Popper, Leo, 8:263–77
Popular Ballads and Songs (Jamieson), 5:345–47
Porché, François, 8:416
Porcina, M. Aemilius, 1:233
Porphyry, 3:317; 8:79–81, 83–84
Porta, Giambattista della, 3:497
Portrait of a Lady, The (James), 9:69–71, 343, 346, 350, 352, 355–57; 11:314–15
"Portrait of a Lady" (Eliot), 9:85
Portrait of the Artist as a Young Man, A (Joyce), 8:195; 9:330, 340; 10:405
Portraits contemporains (Sainte-Beuve), 7:xxiv
Port-Royal (Sainte-Beuve), 8:422
Posa, Marquis, 9:299
Posterior Analytics (Aristotle), 10:26
Posthumous Poems (Shelley), 10:96
Potebnia, Aleksandr Afanas'evich, 8:325–30, 340
"Potebnia" (Shklovsky), 8:328
Pottle, Frederick A., 9:463–66, 517–21
Poulantzas, Nicos, 11:133
Poulet, Georges, 10:261, 263, 266, 284, 286, 548–52; 11:46, 100, 102n.6, 225, 341, 343
Pound, Ezra, 7:xv, xxi; 8:426; 9:59, 90, 105,

229–30, 232, 247, 253–54, 492; 10:210, 340, 401, 409; 11:74, 155
Powys, T. F., 9:79n.3
Practical Criticism (Richards), 9:102, 568, 575; 10:165
Praeterita (Ruskin), 7:xvii, xxxix–xli, xliii
Pratt, Annis V., 11:195n.31
Praxiteles, 7:712
Praz, Mario, 10:578
Pre-Capitalist Modes (Hindess and Hirst), 11:137
Précieuses ridicules, Les (Molière), 7:243
Pre-Established Harmony (Leibniz), 5:631
Preface à la vie d'ecrivain (Flaubert), 11:37, 63n.4
Preface to Plato (Havelock), 1:xii
Preface to Shakespeare (Johnson), 4:xi
Preliminary Essay on the Oppression of the Exiled Sons of Africa (Branagan), 11:368
Prelude, The (Wordsworth), 7:xxxix, 185, 435, 446, 449; 9:476; 10:166, 405, 548; 11:342
"Preludes" (Eliot), 10:584
"Present Function of Criticism, The" (Tate), 9:234
Price-Mars, Jean, 11:386
Priestley, J. B., 9:64
Priestley, Joseph, 10:221
Primitive Rebels (Hobsbawm), 11:151
Primitivism and Decadence (Winters), 9:577
Prince, The (Machiavelli). See *Principe, Il*
Prince Athanase (Shelley), 8:83–84
Princess, The (Tennyson), 9:454; 10:586
Princess Casamassima, The (James), 9:74, 357–58
Princesse de Clèves, La (La Fayette), 6:58
Principe, Il (Machiavelli), 3:728; 7:644
Principia (Newton), 6:126
Principia Ethica (Moore), 10:165
Principles of Literary Criticism, The (Richards), 8:552n.5, 554n.21; 9:573; 10:165
Principles of Psychology, The (James), 10:562
Prior, Matthew, 8:406
Prioress's Tale, The (Chaucer), 7:204
Prisons (Piranesi), 8:150
Private Thoughts (Descartes), 10:617
Pro Q. Roscio (Cicero), 8:483
Pro Rabirio (Cicero), 1:293
Pro S. Roscio (Cicero), 8:483
Pro Vareno (Cicero), 1:293
Problem of Form in Poetry, The (Walzel), 8:335
Problem of Verse Language, The (Tynianov), 8:338

"Problem of Verse Rhythm, The" (Tomashevsky), 8:336–37
"Problèmes de l'esthétique contemporaine, Les" (Guyau), 7:270
Problems (Aristotle), 2:425, 441; 3:152
Problems of Dostoevsky's Poetics (Bakhtin), 11:272n.1
Proclus, 1:xix; 2:319; 8:85
Proculus, 8:486
Proculus, Artorius, 1:305
Prodicus of Ceos, 1:116, 197; 2:323
Prodigal Son, The (Greuze), 9:421
Prodigiorum et Ostentorum Chronicon (Lycosthenes), 7:709
Professeur Taranne, Le (Adamov), 10:252
Progress of Poesy, The (Gray), 4:x
"Progress of the Soul" (Donne), 5:437
"Prologue" to *The Pilgrim* (Dryden), 6:94
Prometheus Bound (Aeschylus), 3:339; 6:234; 10:25–26
Prometheus Unbound (Shelley), 7:212; 8:71, 74, 76–77, 79;
Promos and Cassandra (Giraldi Cintio), 7:458, 460, 462
Propertius (Sextus Propertius), 3:339; 5:376, 395n.20; 8:484, 515nn.10, 13
Propp, Vladimir, 9:683
Prose Style of Samuel Johnson, The (Wimsatt), 4:xiv
Protagoras, 1:116, 164, 185; 3:128; 10:634–37
Prothymus, Minucius, 1:432
Protogenes, 3:338; 5:38–39
Proudhon, Pierre Joseph, 9:594
Proust, Marcel, 8:184, 233; 9:35, 326, 328, 351, 381, 675, 687; 10:139, 171, 182, 186, 293, 348–52, 416–17, 419–21, 427, 457, 561; 11:54–58, 98, 101, 258, 294, 333, 337
Provincial Letters (Pascal), 9:429
Provok'd Wife, The (Vanbrugh), 3:673–74
Prudentius, 8:498, 502, 518n.36
Pseudo-Martyr (Donne), 3:515, 526, 529
Psyche (Shadwell), 6:85
Psychoanalysis and Aesthetics (Baudouin), 9:187
Psychoanalysis and Feminism (Mitchell), 11:284
Psychoanalytic Theory (Fénichel), 11:86–87nn.24–25
Psychomachia (Prudentius), 8:502
Psychopathology of Everyday Life, The (Freud), 8:465; 9:269; 10:536
Ptolemy, 3:618
Pucelle, La (Chapelain), 3:467

Pulci, Luigi, 3:336, 346, 467; 8:376
Purcell, Henry, 9:482
Purchas, Samuel, 7:452
"Purloined Ribbon, The" (de Man), 11:357
Purple Island, The (Fletcher), 11:79
"Pursuit Race, A" (Hemingway), 9:39
Pushkin, Alexander, 7:289, 319–20; 8:325, 333, 561
"Pushkin's Iambic Pentameter" (Tomashevsky), 8:336
Putnam, G. H., 8:306
Puttenham, George, 10:577
Pynchon, Thomas, 10:403
Pypin, A. N., 8:341
Pyramus and Thisbe (Théophile), 3:346
Pyrrho, 1:318
Pythagoras, 3:94, 149, 152, 189, 556, 620, 623–24, 647, 649; 10:635; 11:116, 233, 395, 455, 482
Pythagoras Leontinus, 5:26
"Pythie, La" (Valéry), 8:141

Quarles, Francis, 3:254, 472
Quarterly Review, 7:223
Quatre-vingt-treize (Hugo), 7:474
Queen Mab (Shelley), 8:73–74; 10:527–28
Queen of the Air, The (Ruskin), 7:xvi, xl, xlvi, xlviii
Quennell, Peter, 8:414
Question of Palestine, The (Said), 11:161
"Questioning the Concept of Literature" (Rivière), 11:111
Quiller-Couch, Sir Arthur, 8:423; 9:5–6, 8, 14
Quillinan, Edward, 5:567
Quinault, Philippe, 3:439
Quinault-Dufresne, M., 4:325–26, 328, 351n.28
Quinet, Edgar, 7:474
Quintessence of Ibsenism, The (Shaw), 8:10
Quintilian (M. Fabius Quintilianus), 2:20, 70, 93, 102, 115, 161–62, 191, 201, 215; 3:610, 679; 3:79, 81, 93, 97, 111, 186, 242, 319, 337, 343, 345; 4:278; 8:486–88, 515n.11; 10:584; 11:230
Quodlibets (Haydn), 10:545

R.U.R. (Capek), 9:188
Rabbe, Alphonse, 8:598
Rabelais, François, 2:xi, 254; 3:584, 592, 602, 636; 7:237, 245, 262; 8:373–77, 387n.12; 9:31, 111–34; 11:87n.26, 265, 267, 269
Rabelais and His World (Bakhtin), 11:272n.1
Racan, Honorat de Bueil, seigneur de, 3:334; 8:135

"Racial Wisdom and Richard Wright's *Native Son*" (Baker), 11:375
Racine, Jean, 3:327–28, 384, 581, 695–97, 699, 727; 4:272, 316, 329; 6:31–38, 44–45, 47, 59; 7:471; 8:183, 201, 203, 296, 384n.7, 412, 418, 423; 9:26, 28, 31, 187, 260, 429, 445; 10:vii–viii, 57, 201; 11:93–95, 102n.1
Racine and Shakespeare (Stendhal), 7:475
Radcliffe, Ann, 10:464–65; 11:187
Rainbow, The (Lawrence), 9:78
Ralegh, Sir Walter, 2:356; 3:79, 82, 84, 106, 720; 6:97; 7:710
Rambler, The (Johnson), 4:vii, xiv–xv; 7:76
Rameau, Jean-Philippe, 10:285
Rameau's Nephew (Diderot), 9:379
Ramsay, Allan, 5:336
Ramus, Peter, 2:360
Randolph, John, 9:318
Rank, Otto, 8:44; 11:75
Ranke, Leopold von, 7:606; 10:31
Ransom, John Crowe, 9:230, 232, 236, 459, 515, 525–28; 10:74, 84, 146–47, 400, 563
Rape of Lucrece, The (Shakespeare), 9:171
Rape of the Lock, The (Pope), 4:558, 574–75; 6:89–90; 7:238
Raphael (Raffaello Santi), 5:66–67; 8:472n.10
Rapin, René, 3:381, 390, 485n.42, 551, 566, 678
Rasselas (Johnson), 4:vii; 10:230
"Rätsel des Schönen" (Mithalter), 7:272
Ravaisson-Mollien, Félix, 7:281
Ray, Gordon, 10:135
Raymond, Marcel, 10:63–65, 284, 549; 11:46
Raynouard, François, 8:375
Reach of Criticism, The (Fry), 1:xiv; 3:xiv
Read, Sir Herbert, 8:554n.21; 9:494; 10:380; 11:13–14
Reade, Charles, 7:706
Reader, the Text, the Poem, The (Rosenblatt), 10:318
Readie and Easie Way to Establish a Free Commonwealth, The (Milton), 3:viii
Reading of George Herbert, A (Tuve), 10:73
Réage, Pauline, 11:116
Reason in Madness (Tate), 9:233
Recent Russian Poetry (Iakubinsky), 8:337
Record, The, 7:228
Red and the Black, The (Stendahl). See *Rouge et le noir, Le*
Ree, Paul, 10:469–70
Reed, Ishmael, 11:375, 386–87, 389
Reflections on History (Burckardt), 8:157

INDEX OF NAMES AND TITLES

Reflexions sur le ridicule, et sur les moyens de l'éviter (Bellegarde), 4:247n.11
Regnard, Jean-François, 6:38
Regnier, Henri de, 7:485, 490
Regnier, Mathurin, 3:327
Reid, Thomas, 7:282
Reinhardt, Max, 8:460
Relapse, The (Vanbrugh), 3:673, 684; 5:669
"Relation of the Poet to Day-dreaming, The" (Freud), 11:74, 84n.12
Religio Medici (Browne), 5:493
Religion and the Rise of Capitalism (Tawney), 10:404
Religiose Disputation in der europäischen Dichtung des Mittelalters, Die (Pflaum), 8:506
Religious Duty (Renan), 7:229
Reliques of Ancient English Poetry (Percy), 5:314–15, 317, 336–38, 340–42
Rembrandt van Rijn, 9:365
Remedium Amoris (Ovid), 3:716
Remembrance of Things Past (Proust). *See A la recherche du temps perdu*
Remorse (Coleridge), 5:634
Renaissance, The (Pater), 7:xiii, xviii, xix–xxxv
Renan, Ernest, 7:183, 228, 270–71, 632, 666, 688, 698; 10:170; 11:147
René (Chateaubriand), 7:474
Representative Government (Mill), 11:151
Representative Men (Emerson), 8:xi
Republic (Plato), 1:184, 335, 395, 473–74, 477; 2:42, 163, 188, 316–19; 3:749; 6:viii; 7:719; 10:143; 11:6–7
Republic of Letters, The (Webster), 11:277–79
"Researching Alice Dunbar-Nelson" (Hull), 10:594
"Resistance to Theory, The" (de Man), 11:359–60
"Resolution and Independence" (Wordsworth), 7:193
"Resurrection, The" (Cowley), 3:252
Resurrection of the Word, The (Shklovsky), 8:326
Retreat from the Word, The (Steiner), 10:244
Retrospective Review, The, 7:701
Retrouvailles, Les (Adamov), 10:252
Returne from Parnassus, The (anon.), 5:658–59
Revaluation (Leavis), 9:86, 99
Revenger's Tragedy, The (Tourneur), 5:693
Reverdy, Pierre, 8:594–95, 598, 604
Revolt of Islam, The (Shelley), 6:259; 10:527, 535

Revolution française, La (Quinet), 7:474
Revolution sans modèle, La (Chatelet, Lapouge, and Allonnes) 10:384
Revue de Paris, 7:142
Revue des Deux Mondes, 7:223
Reynolds, Henry, 3:viii; 7:xlvi
Reynolds, John Hamilton, 6:257–59, 261–65
Reynolds, Sir Joshua, 5:281, 298–99; 7:38, 429, 694; 10:229
Rhetoric (Aristotle), 1:533; 2:110, 115; 3:342; 9:11; 10:167, 323n.6
Rhetoric (Cicero), 2:71
"Rhetoric of Blindness, The" (de Man), 10:x
Rhetoric of Fiction, The (Booth), 10:317–18, 321; 11:274n.19
Rhetoric of Motives, A (Burke), 11:236, 240, 245
Rhetoric of Religion, The (Burke), 9:viii; 10:568, 635, 641
Ricci, Bartolomeo, 2:192–93
Ricciboni, M., 4:339, 352n.41
Ricciboni, Mme, 4:339, 352n.42
Rich, Adrienne, 11:174, 186–87, 191, 285
Richard, Jean-Pierre, 10:60–61; 11:47, 57, 62n.1, 66n.38; 11:100, 102n.6
Richard II (Shakespeare), 5:688; 9:162, 168, 664, 672
Richard III (Shakespeare), 5:681; 9:664, 669; 10:84–85
Richards, I. A., 8:423; 9:56, 102, 476, 480, 492, 502, 561, 568, 573, 575–77; 10:143–45, 149, 152, 155–56, 163–67, 171, 175; 11:156
Richardson, Dorothy, 9:246, 344
Richardson, Samuel, 5:585, 688; 6:59; 7:258; 9:65; 10:217; 11:324
Richelieu, Armand Jean du Plessis, duc de, 3:433, 440–41, 551, 583, 656, 724, 726
Richmond, Bruce, 8:426
Richter, Jean-Paul, 5:215–16; 7:251; 10:118
Ricoeur, Paul, 8:ix; 11:125–26
Rieff, Philip, 8:ix
Riegl, Alois, 8:456
Riffaterre, Erwin, 10:443–44
Rigaltius, Nicolas Ligault, 3:405
Rilke, Rainer Maria, 9:544; 10:107, 119–21
Rimbaud, Arthur, 8:594, 598; 9:29, 221, 381, 425, 430, 432, 606; 10:56, 110, 459; 11:303
Rimbaud, Isabelle, 9:430
Rime of the Ancient Mariner, The (Coleridge), 5:vii, 411, 534, 633; 7:452–57; 8:542–43; 9:502, 563, 565; 10:157
Rinehart, Mary Roberts, 9:519

Rise of the Dutch Republic, The (Motley), 9:255
Risler (Daudet). See *Fromont jeune et Risler aîné*
Ritson, Joseph, 5:336–42, 344–45
Rival Ladies, The (Dryden), 3:454
Rivière, Jacques, 10:59; 11:111
Road to Xanadu, The (Lowes), 9:562
Robbe-Grillet, Alain, 9:684; 10:296, 300, 302, 305, 416–30
Robbers, The (Schiller), 9:301
Robbins, Harold, 10:211
Robert Elsmere (Ward), 7:703, 705
Robertson, J. M., 8:427
Robespierre, François-Maxmilian-Joseph de, 7:712
Robin Hood (ed. Ritson), 5:344
Robinson, Henry Crabb, 7:400n.26
Robinson Crusoe (Defoe), 5:584–85; 10:338
Rochester, John Wilmot, Earl of, 3:376n.11, 377nn.13, 23, 25, 401, 495
Rock, The (Eliot), 10:93
Roderick (Southey), 6:241
Roderick Hudson (James), 9:71, 74
Rodogune (Corneille), 3:263, 270–73
Roe, John, 3:81–82
Roethke, Theodore, 10:610
Róheim, Géza, 11:75, 85n.18
Rollo (Fletcher et al.) See *Bloody Brother; or, Rollo, Duke of Normandy, The*
"Roman Carnival" (Goethe), 9:118
Roman de la Rose, 3:553; 8:502, 509
Roman de Renart, 11:264
Romancero: Teorias y investigaciones, El (Pidal), 8:119n.3
Romantische Schule, Die (Heine), 7:472; 8:120n.13
Romeo and Juliet (Shakespeare), 5:421, 470–82, 676; 6:80; 7:457; 9:40, 166, 168–69, 508, 665
Romola (Eliot), 7:706
Romuald ou la vocation (Custine), 7:142
Ronsard, Pierre de, 3:80, 145, 470, 654; 7:468; 9:31
Roosevelt, Franklin Delano, 9:320
Roosevelt, Theodore, 9:319–20
Root and the Flower, The (Myers), 9:80n.6
Rorty, Richard, 7:xi; 10:624–25, 637–75; 11:245
Roscommon, Wentworth Dillon, Earl of, 3:393, 396, 399, 473
Rose, Jacqueline, 11:284
"Rose Aylmer" (Landor), 9:459, 467
"Rose Tree, The" (Blake), 7:369
Rosenberg, Harold, 10:374–75, 386

Rosenblatt, Louise, 10:318
Rosenthal, A. M., 9:584
Rosenzweig, Franz, 8:386n.10
Rosmersholm (Ibsen), 9:28
Rosmonda (Ruscelli), 2:126
Rossetti, Christina, 11:180–81, 187
Rossetti, Dante Gabriel, 7:xiv, 463–69, 692, 711; 8:22, 29
Roth, Leon, 8:153
Rouge et le noir, Le (Stendhal), 7:418, 695; 10:348
Rougemont, Denis de, 11:85n.15
Rousseau, Jean-Jacques, 5:169; 7:63, 133, 247, 411, 429, 473–75, 653, 712; 6:378, 475–84; 8:178; 9:380, 411, 431–33, 594; 10:62, 267–89, 567, 615; 11:131, 231n.1
Roussel, Albert-Charles-Paul-Marie, 8:598
Roussel, Raymond, 10:425
Rousset, Jean, 10:63–65; 11:40–42, 45–59, 62n.1, 67n.51, 68n.55
Roux, Saint-Paul, 9:425
Rowe, Nicholas, 4:482
Rowland, Samuel, 10:546
Rowley, William, 5:691–93, 699; 10:94
Rowse, A. L., 10:174
Roxburghe, John, Duke of, 5:335
Rozanov (Shklovsky), 8:342–43
Rubinstein, Artur, 7:676
Rudbeck, Olaf, 4:195
Rudin (Turgenev), 7:332
Rufinus, 8:498
Rufinus, Cornelius, 1:315
Ruge, Arnold, 7:279
"Ruined Cottage, The" (Wordsworth), 9:88
Ruscelli, Girolamo, 2:126
Ruskin, John, 7:xv, xxxvi–xxxvii, xxxix, xli–xlviii, 226–27, 670, 688; 8:22, 207–8, 212; 9:ix, 579, 641–42; 10:377, 424, 563–64, 572, 623–24; 11:vii
Russell, Bertrand, 8:152, 534; 10:165, 358, 639
Russell, D. A., 1:vii
Russell, Michele, 11:361
Russian Versification (Tomashevsky), 8:336
Rymer, Thomas, 3:375, 381, 384, 490, 686–705

S/Z (Barthes), 11:102n.5, 279
Sackville-West, Edward, 10:134
Sacred Fount, The (James), 9:357, 359
Sacred Wood, The (Eliot), 9:86; 10:376
"Sacrifice, The" (Herbert), 10:72
Sacrificio (Beccari), 2:472
Sacrificio de la misa, El (Gonzalo de Berceo), 8:506

Sade, Donatien Alphonse François, marquis de, 8:598; 9:431, 685, 687–88; 10:457; 11:265, 269
Sagesse (Verlaine), 7:481
"Sagt es niemand" (Goethe), 9:114
Sahlins, Marshall, 11:123–24, 130
Said, Edward W., 10:387, 403; 11:278, 288, 388–89
"Sailing to Byzantium" (Yeats), 9:88
"Sailor Boy, The" (Tennyson), 9:566
"Sailor's Mother, The" (Wordsworth), 5:430–31; 7:191
"St. Crispin to Mr. Gifford" (Lamb), 5:544
Saint Louis (Le Moine), 3:467
St. Petersburg (Biely), 11:110
"Saint Teresa" (Crashaw), 8:409
St. Victor, Richard, 8:313
Saint-Evremond, Charles de Saint-Denis, sieur de, 3:485n.42, 688, 695, 712; 9:429
Sainte-Pierre, Bernardin de, 6:479
Saint-Pol-Roux (Paul Roux), 8:591, 598
Saint-Simon, Louis de Rouvroy, duc de, 9:602, 606
Sainte-Albine, Rémond de, 4:339
Sainte-Beuve, Charles Augustin, 7:xxiv, 195, 248, 408, 470, 472, 477, 632; 8:422; 10:182, 186
Saintsbury, George, 8:423; 9:559, 573; 10:169
Salammbô (Flaubert), 7:706
Salinger, J. D., 10:189
Sallust (C. Sallustius Crispus), 1:483; 2:206–9, 259; 3:93, 145, 152
Salon of 1859, The (Baudelaire), 10:427
Samson Agonistes (Milton), 6:400; 7:183, 660; 9:94
Sanctuary (Faulkner), 10:89
Sand, George, 7:433, 632, 634; 9:381
Sandys, Sir Edwin, 3:106
Sandys, George, 3:142, 456, 489; 10:581
Sannazaro, Giacomo, 2:286; 3:145, 349; 4:513
Santayana, George, 8:387–88n.13; 9:73, 75, 315, 339, 347, 572; 10:232
Sappho, 1:332–33; 3:642, 647; 4:266; 8:311
Sar Peladan, 7:282
Sarasin, Jean-François, 3:345
Sarraute, Nathalie, 10:416–24, 426–28, 430, 566
Sarton, May, 11:185, 312
Sartre, Jean Paul, 9:202, 399–402; 10:5–14, 16, 18, 171, 249, 296–306, 379-80, 570; 11:228–30, 231n.1, 345, 388
Satirae Menippeae (Varro), 11:266
Satires (Donne), 3:409

Satires (Horace), 3:406
Saturday Review, The, 10:185
Saturday Review, The (London), 7:710
Satyricon (Petronius), 11:267
Saussure, Ferdinand de, 9:617; 10:465, 502–3, 577; 11:257, 300, 302–3
Savile, Sir Henry, 3:106
Saving the Appearances (Barfield), 10:568
Scaevola, P. Mucius, 1:321
Scaliger, Julius Caesar, 2:221, 290, 295, 303, 481; 3:88, 109, 111, 128, 243, 348, 405, 467, 557–58; 10:545
Scarlet Letter, The (Hawthorne), 8:244, 254; 9:243
Scarron, Paul, 3:412, 656; 11:48
Scènes de la vie de jeunesse (Murger), 7:474
Schasler, Max, 7:273–74
Schelling, Friedrich Wilhelm Joseph von, 5:534–35; 6:147–48, 359; 7:278, 442–43; 8:288
Schiller, Friedrich von, 5:76–77, 81, 86, 90–91, 193, 218, 535; 6:47; 7:277, 418, 632; 8:282, 296, 298, 366, 444, 631; 9:301, 380
Schlegel, August Wilhelm von, 5:87–88, 203–6, 218–22; 6:342, 351, 359–60; 8:236, 277; 9:381; 10:70; 11:63n.4
Schlegel, Friedrich von, 5:220–21; 6:359–60; 7:277; 8:236, 272; 10:34, 70
Schleiermacher, Friedrich Ernst Daniel, 8:375, 378, 385n.10
Schneiderman, Stuart, 11:284–85
"Scholar-Gipsy, The" (Arnold), 9:99–100
School for Scandal, The (Congreve), 5:665, 667
"School of Giorgione, The" (Pater), 7:xxiii
Schopenhauer, Arthur, 7:xii, 279–80, 583, 589, 605, 638–39; 8:16, 276, 288; 9:379, 381, 392, 658; 10:202, 470, 623
Schorske, Carl E., 8:ix
Schrade, L., 8:507
Schubarth, Karl Ernst, 5:65
Schwab, Raymond, 11:147
Schwartz, Delmore, 10:96, 189
Schwartzkogler, Rudolph, 10:386
Science and Criticism (Muller), 9:575
Science and Poetry (Richards), 8:554 nn.18, 21; 9:568; 10:144, 152, 165
Science and Sanity (Korzybski), 9:568
Science and the Modern World (Whitehead), 9:26
Scornful Lady, The (Beaumont and Fletcher), 3:438, 445
Scott, Sir Walter, 5:92–94, 542, 545, 594, 603, 636–45; 6:vii, 31, 58–60, 138, 246,

259; 7:57–59, 61, 71, 75, 77, 117, 181, 425, 470, 472–73; 9:64, 80n.5, 347, 565; 10:223, 225, 293
Scottish Historical and Romantic Ballads (Finlay), 5:346
Scrutiny, 10:400; 11:370
Scudéry, Madeleine de, 3:324, 467, 501
Scylla (Timotheus), 1:161
Searle, John, 10:459
Seasons, The (Thomson), 5:312–14
"Sebastian Van Storck" (Pater), 7:xxiv, xxxii
Secchia rapita, La (Tassoni), 3:412, 656
"Second Coming, The" (Yeats), 10:182
Second Defence of the English People, A (Milton), 10:580
Secret Agent, The (Conrad), 9:73–74
Secret Love; or, The Maiden Queen (Dryden), 4:536
Secular Scripture, The (Frye), 9:xi–xii
Secundus, Johannes, 2:254
Sedaine, M., 4:323
Sedulius, 8:498, 516n.18
Segrais, Jean Regnauld de, 3:468, 471, 473, 476, 478; 4:52
Sein und Zeit (Heidegger), 10:559, 561
Sejanus (Jonson), 3:84, 89, 435, 443–44, 446; 10:viii
Selden, John, 3:81, 90, 580, 636
Select Ballads (ed. Pinkerton), 5:343–44
Selections from Modern Poets (ed. Squire), 9:53, 60
Selections from the Ancient Dramatists Made at the British Museum (Lamb), 5:566
"Self-Reliance" (Emerson), 10:398, 609, 625
Selkirk, Alexander, 5:302
"Semaine, La" (Du Bartas), 5:308
Semantique structurale (Greimas), 11:273n.6
"Semiology and Rhetoric" (de Man), 11:307n.16
Sempronius, Aulus, 1:254
Sénancour, Etienne de, 7:429, 474
Seneca the Elder (L. Annaeus Seneca), 2:73; 8:486
Seneca the Younger (M. Annaeus Seneca), 1:511, 532; 2:xv–xvii, 43, 123, 253, 256–57, 298, 361; 3:6, 108, 142, 145, 170, 187, 263, 267, 339, 341, 345, 363, 373, 426, 431, 452, 457–58, 474, 582, 650, 694, 716, 718; 7:632; 8:486; 9:662, 669
Sensation and Intuition: Studies in Psychology and Aesthetics (Sully), 7:284
Sense of an Ending, The (Kermode), 11:193n.1
Sense of the Past, The (James), 9:343
"Sensitive Plant, The" (Shelley), 8:75

Sentences (Duns Scotus), 2:330
Sentimental Journey, A (Sterne), 8:567–68
Séraphita (Balzac), 8:100
Serenade (Britten), 10:587–88
Sermones (Augustine), 8:494–95
Serre, Jehan de, 3:583
Serres, Michel, 10:466
Servius Tullius, 4:191
Sesame and Lilies (Ruskin), 7:xvii, xlvi; 10:563–64
Sessions, Roger, 9:367
Sette giorni (Tasso), 3:145
Settle, Elkanah, 3:300, 311; 4:537
Sevastopol Sketches (Tolstoy), 7:319
Seven Beauties (film), 10:313
Seven Lamps of Architecture, The (Ruskin), 7:xxxix
Seven Types of Ambiguity (Empson), 9:372, 478; 10:99
Seventeenth Century Background, The (Willey), 9:250; 10:335
Severus, Cassius, 1:297
Sévigné, Marie de Rabutin-Chantal, marquise de, 6:50
Sexton, Anne, 11:171, 179–80, 285
Sexual Politics (Millett), 10:592, 597; 11:311
Shadwell, Thomas, 3:311; 6:85–86; 9:260
Shaftesbury, Anthony Ashley Cooper, Third Earl of, 4:242, 246n.6; 5:311; 7:275; 8:289; 9:236
Shairp, John Campbell, 7:2156
Shakespeare, William, 2:xi; 3:vii–viii, 79, 82, 101, 121, 248, 361, 364, 370, 375, 379, 381, 384–85, 388–90, 431, 434, 443–45, 447, 451, 455, 563, 582, 586–613, 643, 657, 677, 688, 705; 4:viii–xiii, 45, 263–64, 267–71, 273, 279–80, 373, 384–85, 463–94; 5:x–xi, xv, xvii, 57–65, 75, 84, 87, 167, 219, 278, 292, 295, 309–10, 379–80, 464–98, 536–37, 577–79, 586, 626, 648, 650, 656–57, 674–90, 692, 695, 697–98; 6:31–38, 44–45, 47–48, 54, 59, 67–68, 70–71, 80, 91, 96, 136, 193, 226, 263, 325, 327, 337–45, 392–93, 398, 408, 410, 417, 444, 454–64, 470–71; 7:61, 75, 157–58, 165, 183, 200, 218, 232, 241, 249, 261, 290, 356, 417, 443–44, 448, 457–63, 504–6, 663, 673, 683, 686, 693, 704–5, 708, 710–11; 8:viii, 21–22, 44–47, 49–51, 63–64, 87–89, 91, 97, 153, 173–78, 181, 183–84, 188, 203–4, 264, 296, 298, 311, 384n.7, 395, 397, 407, 417, 427, 430; 9:19, 31–32, 54, 131, 137–80, 183, 188–89, 241, 253, 256–60, 271, 324, 368–73, 375–76, 387–89, 430, 446, 453, 478, 491, 493, 507–9, 515–16, 518, 521, 526–29,

544, 548, 577, 579–80, 638–39, 641–42, 650–52, 658–77; 10:vii–viii, 77, 83–87, 94, 136, 151–53, 174, 197–98, 200–204, 211, 222, 242, 250, 329–30, 405, 410, 459, 480, 491, 546–47, 557, 571, 610; 11:viii, x, 12, 189, 267, 326–27, 335, 337
Shankara, 7:602
Shapiro, Barbara, 10:335
Shaw, George Bernard, 9:326, 379, 652; 10:242
She (Haggard), 11:284
"She dwelt among the untrodden ways" (Wordsworth), 10:543
Sheale, Richard, 5:330
Shelburne Essays (More), 8:422
Shelley, Mary, 8:71, 75, 79, 84; 10:96, 339, 553n.1; 11:181, 183, 186, 190
Shelley, Percy Bysshe, 1:xi; 2:428n.39; 6:vii–xi, 67, 98, 254, 259, 288–89, 291n.16; 7:xi, xiii, xxv, 7–19, 212, 218, 368, 389, 429, 449, 682, 694; 8:10, 71–86, 95, 147–48, 411, 419; 9:32, 58, 381, 454, 462, 580, 648, 652–54; 10:71, 96, 165, 520–22, 525–38, 605, 607–8, 616, 626, 642; 11:viii, 9–10, 12–13, 180, 321
Shepheardes Calender, The (Spenser), 2:298; 3:81, 401; 10:588n.10
Sheridan, Richard Brinsley, 5:665; 7:244
Shirley, James, 5:699; 10:94
Shirley (Brontë), 11:189
Shklovsky, Viktor, 8:324, 326–33, 340
"Short Happy Life of Francis Macomber, The" (Hemingway), 9:47–49; 10:157
Short View of Tragedy, A (Rymer), 3:686–705
Showalter, Elaine, 11:175, 184, 311
Shropshire Lad, A (Housman), 9:62
Sibylline Leaves (Blake), 7:399n.21
"Sick Rose, The" (Blake), 10:587
Sickingen (Lassalle), 8:301
Sidney, Sir Philip, 2:xii–xiv, 268, 356, 367–70, 372, 382, 389, 396, 484n.29, 556–57, 636, 650; 3:viii–ix, xi, 79, 81–82, 85, 90, 93, 106, 141, 145, 477; 4:470; 5:330, 697; 9:461, 586; 10:165, 547; 11:7–10
Sidonia the Sorceress (Meinhold), 7:470
Siege of Rhodes, The (D'Avenant), 3:361–62, 454, 456
Signs, 10:595; 11:280, 285
Silanion, 1:368
Silent Woman, The (Jonson). *See Epicene; or, The Silent Woman*
Silius Italicus, 2:130; 3:130
"Silken Tent, The" (Frost), 10:584
Simillimi, I (Trissimo), 2:114, 118

Simmel, Georg, 11:155
Simon, Claude, 10:416
Simonides, 1:337, 364; 2:295; 3:647, 649; 5:19; 7:549
"Simple Enquiry, A" (Hemingway), 9:39
Simpson, N. F., 10:240
Simylus, 3:109
Sincerity and Authenticity (Trilling), 10:331n.5, 377
Sinclair, Upton, 8:290
Singer, Isaac Bashevis, 10:363
Singers of Daybreak: Studies in Black American Literature (Baker), 11:376
Singleton, Charles S., 8:383n.5
Sinister Wisdom, 10:591
"Sir Caulin" (anon.), 5:341
"Sir Eger, Sir Graham, and Sir Gray-Steel" (anon.), 6:65
Sir Tristem (Thomas of Erceldoune), 5:329
"Sirens, The" (Binyon), 9:61
"Sister Helen" (Rossetti), 7:468
"Six Swans, The" (Grimms), 8:47
Skelton, Sir John, 2:355
Slatoff, Walter, 10:435
Slighted Maid, The (Stapylton), 3:379
"Slumber did my spirit seal, A" (Wordsworth), 10:499, 506, 543
Small Room, The (Sarton), 11:312
Smith, Barbara Hernnstein, 10:592, 595, 598; 11:288
Smith, Bessie, 11:371
Smith, Frederick Edwin. *See* Birkenhead, Earl of
Smith, Lillian, 10:593
Smith, Sir Thomas, 3:106
Smollett, Tobias, 7:262
Snapshots (Robbe-Grillet), 10:417
Snell, Bruno, 1:ix–x; 10:643; 11:vii
Snodgrass, DeWitt, 11:179
Snow, C. P., 10:187, 306
"Snow Man, The" (Stevens), 7:xvii
"Snows of Kilimanjaro, The" (Hemingway), 9:47–48
Snowstorm, The (Tolstoy), 7:319, 323
Snyder, E. D., 9:54
Social Contract, The (Rousseau). *See Contrat social, Le*
Society the Redeemed Form of Man (James), 9:345, 352
"Sociology of Knowledge, The" (Wolf), 8:386n.10
Socrates, 1:73, 149, 198, 200, 203, 218–19, 233, 237, 271, 310, 327, 365, 367, 373, 471–72, 474–75, 477; 2:43, 52, 162; 3:19, 24, 112, 128–29, 186, 308, 319, 344, 448,

566, 623, 676, 730; 4:257, 386; 7:210, 586, 627n.118; 8:266, 273–74, 385n.10; 9:269, 413, 560, 674; 10:35, 37–38, 473, 558; 11:152, 265–66, 299
Sodom (Earl of Rochester), 11:107
Sofonisba (Trissino), 2:109, 126
Soft Machine, The (Burroughs), 10:430
"Sohrab and Rustum" (Arnold), 9:58
Solger, K. W. F., 7:278
Solinus, C. Julius, 3:187
Sollers, Philippe, 11:285
Solomon, Simeon, 8:95
Solon, 1:236; 2:42; 3:647, 659
Solzhenitsyn, Alexander, 11:230
Some Do Not (Ford), 9:344
"Some Notes on the Nature of English Poetry" (Mizener), 9:522
Somnium Scipionis (Cicero), 9:683
Son of Woman (Murry), 9:104
Sonata Appassionata (Beethoven), 7:676
"Song for St. Cecilia's Day" (Dryden), 4:545
"Song of Liberty, A" (Blake), 7:398n.16
Song of Myself (Whitman), 10:582, 628–29
Song of Roland, The, 8:329; 9:249–50
Song of the Bell, The (Schiller), 5:193
Songs of Innocence and Experience (Blake), 7:357–59, 362–63, 367–68, 396n.12; 8:92
Songs of Maldoror, The (Lautréamont). *See Chants de Maldoror, Les*
"Sonnet XX" (Milton), 11:202
"Sonnet XXIII" (Milton), 11:345
Sonnets (Milton), 4:528
Sonnets (Shakespeare), 10:405, 546
Sonnets (Wordsworth), 5:534
Sons and Lovers (Lawrence), 9:76, 595; 11:337
Sontag, Susan, 10:383, 416–17, 420–22, 429–31
Sophist (Plato), 1:474; 2:317–18, 323, 407; 10:523
Sophists, The (Untersteiner), 10:634
Sophocles, 1:16, 46, 73, 151–52, 161–62, 174, 196, 198, 200–201, 203, 326, 337, 342, 347, 364, 366, 372–73, 375–76, 383, 391; 2:127, 129, 455, 460, 462, 464; 3:110, 114–15, 171, 174, 188, 265, 272, 281, 302, 336–37, 339–41, 343, 348, 351, 375, 382, 384, 423, 425, 463, 563, 566, 579, 584, 681, 686–87; 3:691–93, 701–3, 719–723, 726, 738; 4:255; 5:21, 23, 26, 30, 33–34, 75, 374; 6:44, 233–34, 246; 7:218, 476; 8:63; 9:622; 10:147, 199, 202–3
Sophron, 1:149

Sorrows of Young Werther, The (Goethe), 5:209; 6:358–59
"Soul of Man under Socialism, The" (Wilde), 7:xxxv–xxxvi
Soulier de satin, Le (Claudel), 9:601; 11:58
Sound and the Fury, The (Faulkner), 10:189
"Sound Repetitions" (Brik), 8:335
Soupault, Philippe, 8:596, 598, 605
Southern Workman, 11:369
Southey, Robert, 5:vii, 538–40, 544–45, 562–64, 602; 6:vii–viii, 138, 240–41; 10:229
Southwell, Robert, 3:82
Souvenirs (Caylus), 6:477–78
Spacks, Patricia Meyer, 11:184, 311
Spain (Auden), 9:488
Spanish Fryar, The (Dryden), 3:674, 682–83, 689
Spanish Rogue, The (Duffett), 5:696
Spark, Muriel, 10:295–96
Spectator, The, 4:95; 9:64, 573; 10:94–95
Speght, Thomas, 3:506n.39
Spence, Joseph, 4:300; 5:34–35
Spencer, Herbert, 7:283, 568, 710
Spengler, Oswald, 9:302
Spenser, Edmund, 2:xiii, 265–69, 365, 372, 377; 3:203–4, 291, 293, 314, 363, 401, 413, 467, 470–71, 473, 476–77, 479, 489, 496, 553–54, 566, 654, 720; 3:viii–ix, 79, 81, 93, 140, 145; 5:308–9, 379, 433–34, 656; 6:70–71, 83–85, 97, 225–28, 231; 7:25, 30, 32, 38; 9:54, 99, 251–53, 374, 642; 10:403–4, 577, 583, 586, 588n.10, 613; 11:76, 88n.27, 335
Speroni, Sperone, 3:395
Spinoza, Benedict, 5:386–91, 632; 7:571, 639, 642, 680, 687; 8:205, 310, 427; 9:117, 203–4, 320; 11:226
Spirit of Laws, The (Montesquieu), 9:431
Spitzer, Leo, 11:46
Spivak, Gayatri, 11:278, 285, 288
Spoils of Poynton, The (James), 9:343, 350, 357
Spondanus (Jean de Sponde), 3:124–25, 127
Spranger, Eduard, 10:512n.31
Sprat, Thomas, 3:721; 10:335–37, 339–41
"Spring" (Kleist), 5:49
Spring and All (Williams), 10:582
Sprinker, Michel, 10:313
Spurgeon, Caroline, 10:84
Squire, J. C., 9:53, 60
Staël, Anne-Louise-Germaine Necker, Madame de, 8:152–53
Stalin, Joseph, 8:299
Stallman, R. W., 10:380

Stanyhurst, Richard, 2:376
Stapilton, Richard, 3:127
Stapylton, Sir Robert, 3:408, 415–16
Star in the East; with Other Poems, The (Conder), 6:213–14
"Star in the East, The" (Conder), 6:213–14, 216–17
Starling, Marion Wilson, 11:385
Starobinski, Jean, 10:62–63, 268–69, 284
Staseas, 1:244
Statius (P. Papinius Statius), 2:130; 3:109, 202, 214, 230, 248, 338, 363, 462, 474, 559, 561; 8:510
Stauffer, Donald, 9:512–14, 516
"Steel Flea" (Leskov), 8:441
Steele, Sir Richard, 4:92–95; 10:94
Steevens, George, 5:310
Stein, Gertrude, 11:110
Steiner, George, 10:244, 376, 393, 431–32; 11:108
Steinthal, Heymann, 8:119n.2
Stekel, William, 11:80
Stendhal (Henri Beyle), 7:418, 468, 475, 477, 585, 641, 695; 8:588; 9:381, 432, 608–10; 10:348–52, 418, 459; 11:229
Stephen, Leslie, 9:79n.3
Stephen Hero (Joyce), 9:330
Stepto, Robert Burns, 11:383
Sterling, John, 6:444
Sternbald (Tieck), 5:213–14
Sterne, Laurence, 5:215; 6:185; 7:121, 259; 8:195, 329, 332–33, 559–82; 9:489; 10:87, 133, 187, 409, 551, 581–82, 607, 612–14; 11:87n.25
Sterne's Tristram Shandy *and the Theory of the Novel* (Shklovsky), 8:332
Sternhold, Thomas, 3:456
Stesichorus, 1:192, 335; 2:349; 3:642, 647, 649, 659; 2:xvii; 6:viii; 7:xii–xiii, xli; 8:xi–xii; 9:373; 10:617, 622, 625, 634, 642–45; 11:viii–ix, 341–42, 344
Stevenson, C. L., 9:568–70
Stevenson, Robert Louis, 7:523, 703, 713; 8:452; 9:60; 10:132
Sthenelus, 1:167
Stickney, Trumbull, 10:585
Stilo, L. Aelius, 3:110
Stimpson, Catharine, 11:184, 280
Stobaeus, John, 3:109
Stockdale, Percival, 9:520
Stoker, Bram, 10:214
Stokes, Eric, 11:150
Stoll, E. E., 9:557–58; 10:77
Stone, I. F., 11:163
Stone Guest, The (Pushkin), 7:327

Stones of Venice, The (Ruskin), 7:xix–xx, xxxix
"Stopping by Woods on a Snowy Evening" (Frost), 9:458
Story of O, The (Réage). See Histoire d'O, L'
Stothard, Thomas, 5:134–35; 7:473
Stow, John, 3:89
Stowey, Nether, 7:447
Strachey, Lytton, 9:68; 10:133, 136, 139
Strada, Famiano, 4:271
Strange, Sir Robert, 5:136, 143
Stranton, Donna, 11:280
Strassburg, Gottfried von, 6:354
Strauss, Richard, 8:30–31n.2
Stravinsky, Igor, 8:224
"Stream's Secret, The" (Rossetti), 7:465
Strindberg, August, 10:202, 242
Stromates (Clement of Alexandria), 10:458
Structure of Scientific Revolutions, The (Kuhn), 10:374, 641
Struve, Burkhard Gotthelf, 8:281
Stuart, Daniel, 5:544
Stucken, E., 8:44
"Study of Poetry, The" (Arnold), 10:144, 567
Sturgis, Howard, 9:75
Sturmius, Joannes (Johann Sturm), 2:191–92
"Style" (Pater), 7:xxvi
Suckling, Sir John, 3:421, 445; 4:500, 512; 5:658; 6:80–81
Suetonius (C. Suetonius Tranquillus), 2:68; 3:81; 5:364; 7:709
Suite du Menteur, La (Corneille), 3:273
Suivante, La (Corneille), 3:264–65
Suleiman, Susan, 10:313
Sullivan, Sir Arthur, 7:xiv
Sulloway, Frank J., 8:x
Sully, James, 7:284
Sulpicius, Servius, 1:321; 8:498
Summa Theologica (Aquinas), 2:407–8; 9:10
"Summer Night, A" (Arnold), 9:58
Sun Also Rises, The (Hemingway), 9:38, 40–42, 48
Supplement to Natural History (Buffon), 11:53
Suppliants (Euripides), 3:269, 342
Surrey, Henry Howard, Earl of, 2:202, 208, 355, 395; 3:106, 140
Süssmilch, Johann Peter, 5:116
Swedenborg, Emanuel, 5:128, 150, 527–28; 6:387–89, 435; 7:681
Sweeney Agonistes (Eliot), 9:362
Swift, Jonathan, 3:xv; 4:x–xi, 373, 388, 548–57; 7:259; 8:26, 598; 9:28, 190, 334; 10:337; 11:74, 79, 160–62, 265, 267, 269
Swinburne, Algernon Charles, 7:xv–xvi;

8:414, 419, 429; 9:56–57, 59, 62; 10:157, 376
Sylvester, Joshua, 3:79, 142; 10:580
Sylvie (Gérard de Nerval), 9:433
Symbolism (Bely), 8:321
"Symbolism in Painting" (Yeats), 8:88
Symbolist Movement in Literature, The (Symons), 8:87–88; 10:341–42
Symons, Arthur, 8:87–88; 10:341–42, 420
Symphonie en blanc majeur (Gautier), 7:691
Symposiacum (Plutarch), 3:717
Symposium (Plato), 1:412; 2:163, 165, 295; 7:549; 11:299
Symposium (Xenophon), 1:412
Synge, J. M., 8:94
Systasis (Galen), 2:161

Tacitus (Cornelius Tacitus), 3:7, 10, 33, 58, 73, 79, 81, 89, 732; 4:198, 200–201; 5:364; 7:709
Taine, Hippolyte, 7:281, 606; 9:27
Tale of a Tub, A (Swift), 4:x–xi
Tales from Olden Times (Leskov), 8:450
Tales from the Poets, 1:363
Tales of Belkin (Pushkin), 8:561
Tales of the Hall (Crabbe), 6:242
Taliessin, 6:404–5
Talma, François-Joseph, 6:35, 37, 55n.3
"Tam Glen" (Burns), 7:121
"Tam o' Shanter" (Burns), 7:212
Tamburlaine the Great; or, The Scythian Shepherd (Marlowe), 5:687–88
Tancred of Salerno (Boccaccio), 7:458
Tannhäuser (Wagner), 7:672
Tarleton, Richard, 2:371, 378
Tartarin de Tarascon (Daudet), 7:175
Tartuffe (Molière), 5:83; 6:42, 469; 7:238, 242–43, 250, 262, 689
Tarzan of the Apes (Burroughs), 10:210
Task, The (Cowper), 6:219
Tasso, Bernardo, 3:346
Tasso, Torquato, 2:xiii, 383, 472, 530; 3:145, 174, 188, 203, 218, 305, 341, 348–49, 363, 365–66, 395, 400, 413, 553–54, 556–61, 566, 573, 579, 654; 6:205, 367, 377; 8:106; 10:579–80; 11:7, 10–11
Tassoni, Alessandro, 3:412
Tate, Allen, 9:230, 232–34, 236; 10:147, 400, 581
Tatler, The, 9:64
Tawney, R. H., 10:404
Taylor, Charles, 10:96
Taylor, Frederick, 11:238
Taylor, Jeremy, 5:471, 603; 6:138
Taylor, John, 6:259–61

Taylor, John, the Water-Poet, 3:101, 458
Taylor, Thomas, 6:400
Tea-Table Miscellany, The (Ramsay), 5:336
Telemachus (Fénelon), 4:241
Teleny (Wilde), 11:107
Telesias (Carneades), 1:483
Tempest, The (Dryden), 4:536
Tempest, The (Shakespeare), 3:385, 564; 5:484, 656–57, 684–85; 7:708; 9:651
Temple; or, Sacred Poems and Ejaculations, The (Herbert), 3:536
Temps Modernes, Les, 9:422
Tennyson, Alfred, Lord, 7:43, 181; 8:92, 179, 181, 410–11, 430; 9:28, 56–58, 62, 89, 99, 454, 483, 566, 576, 648; 10:71, 586–87; 11:190
"Tension in Poetry" (Tate), 9:234
Tentation de Saint Antoine, La (Flaubert), 7:147, 155; 9:29
Terence (P. Terentius Afer), 1:225, 227, 427–29, 433; 2:18, 40, 63, 109, 114, 199–200, 255, 296, 299, 454–55, 466, 470; 3:93, 111, 218, 265, 271, 309–10, 326, 379, 425, 428–29, 438, 659, 668, 675, 683, 705, 736; 7:248–49; 8:479
Tereus (Sophocles), 1:162; 2:174
Tertullian (Q. Septimus Florens Tertullianus), 3:749–50; 8:488–91, 496, 499
Teseid (Boccaccio), 2:176
Tess of the D'Urbervilles (Hardy), 9:76
Testament of Beauty, The (Bridges), 9:60, 85
Teucer (Sophocles), 1:199
Thackeray, William Makepeace, 7:58, 427; 9:75; 10:134–35, 515; 11:311
Thais (Menander), 1:369
Thales, 3:620
"Thanksgiving Ode" (Wordsworth), 7:194
Thasos, 1:150
Thayer, Tiffany, 9:519
Theaetetus (Plato), 3:128
Theatre and Its Double, The (Artaud), 9:438, 441
Theatre of the Greeks, The (ed. Buckham), 6:232–33
Thebaid (Statius), 3:462
Their Eyes Were Watching God (Hurston), 10:x; 11:389
"Theme of the Three Caskets, The" (Freud)
Theobald, Lewis, 4:483, 526, 561
Theocritus, 1:347, 407, 410; 2:113, 472; 3:187, 296, 393, 395, 400–401, 646
Theodamas, 1:184
Theodectes, 1:162–63
Theodicy: Essays on the Goodness of God, the

Freedom of Man, and the Origin of Evil (Leibniz), 11:43
Théodore (Corneille), 3:263
"Theodore and Honoria" (Dryden), 6:90
Theodorus, 1:192, 195, 327, 368
Theognis, 1:365, 374, 473–74; 3:232, 649
Théophile de Viau, 3:338, 346
Theophilus, 3:749
Theophrastus, 1:233, 235, 258, 345; 2:221; 4:277
Theopompus, 1:213–14, 345, 353
Theory of Knowledge (Fichte), 5:388, 396n.58
Theory of Literature (Wellek and Warren), 10:69, 71, 171, 489
Theory of the Avant-Garde, The (Poggioli), 10:391
Theory of the Beautiful (Todhunter), 7:283
Theory of the Novel, The (Lukács), 8:445; 10:261
Thérèse Raquin (Zola), 11:87n.26
"Theses on the Philosophy of History" (Benjamin), 11:123
Thespis, 1:396, 431
Thierry and Theodoret (Fletcher), 5:698–99
Thinking about Women (Ellmann), 11:281
This Side of Paradise (Fitzgerald), 10:87, 93
Thody, Philip, 10:302
Thomas Carlyle (Froude), 7:636–37
Thomas, D. M., 11:230
Thomas, Dylan, 9:231
Thomas, Edward, 10:401
Thomas of Erceldoune (Thomas the Rhymer), 5:329, 333, 338
Thompson, E. P., 11:162
Thomson, J. A. K., 10:173
Thomson, James, 4:273; 5:312–14; 6:137
Thorburn, J. M., 9:62n.3
Thoreau, Henry David, 9:542; 10:215, 398
"Thorn, The" (Wordsworth), 5:420
Thorndike, A. H., 10:85
"Those Wrecked by Success" (Freud), 11:74
Thoughts on French Affairs (Burke) 7:221
Thrasymachus, 1:180, 187; 2:166
Three Songs about Lenin (film), 8:462
"Three Years She Grew" (Wordsworth), 10:564
Through the Looking-Glass (Carroll), 10:583
Thucydides, 1:279, 336, 341, 343, 350, 408, 413–14; 2:207–8, 347; 3:30; 7:644
Thus Spake Zarathustra (Nietzsche), 7:viii, 624; 10:239, 285
Thyestes (Carcinus), 1:161
Thyestes (Seneca), 9:662
Tiberius, 3:590; 7:716
Tibullus, Albius, 3:297, 339

Tieck, Ludwig, 5:213–14, 364, 535; 6:330; 7:472; 9:381
"Tiger, The" (Blake), 7:361
Tillich, Paul, 10:295
Tillotson, John, 3:721
Tillyard, E. M. W., 9:93, 96, 557, 561; 11:87–88n.27
Timaeus, 1:327–28
Timaeus (Plato), 1:405
Timanthes, 5:25–26
Timber; or, Discoveries (Jonson), 3:vii, x–xii, 425, 447
Time and Western Man (Lewis), 9:104
Times Literary Supplement, The, 8:426; 9:485; 10:99, 171
Times, The, 7:223
Timomachus, 5:28
Timon of Athens (Shakespeare), 6:54; 9:158, 170, 172, 175, 180, 660, 665
Timotheus, 1:150, 374, 390
"Tintern Abbey" (Wordsworth), 5:vii; 6:265; 7:xxxvii–xl, 434; 10:617
Tintoretto (Jacapo Robusti), 9:425; 10:65
Tisias, 1:241
Titian (Tiziano Vecellio), 6:357; 8:226; 9:365
Titurel, 6:354
Titus Andronicus (Shakespeare), 9:171, 662; 665
"To a Lady, Who Wrote Poesies for Rings" (Cowley), 4:502
"To Autumn" (Keats), 9:99
"To Destiny" (Cowley), 8:406
To Have and Have Not (Hemingway), 9:44–45
"To His Coy Mistress" (Marvell), 8:409, 411; 9:567; 10:338
"To Light" (Cowley), 4:x
"To Sleep" (Keats), 10:587
"To the Author of *The Robbers*" (Coleridge), 5:633–34
"To the Virgins to Make Much of Time" (Herrick), 9:239
"To William Wordsworth" (Coleridge), 5:viii; 11:342
Todhunter, Isaac, 7:283
Todorov, Tzvetan, 10:265–66, 402 3; 11:37
"Toilette de Constance, La" (Vigne), 7:45
Tolstoy, Leo, 7:319–29, 616; 8:27, 329, 343, 441, 564; 9:347, 366, 544, 572, 637; 10:41, 78, 209–10, 421, 423; 11:258, 270, 351
Tom Jones (Fielding), 4:246n.8; 5:475; 9:64, 236
Tomashevsky, Boris, 8:336–37
Tommaseo, Niccolò, 8:113–14, 120n.9

Tönnies, Ferdinand, 11:155–56
Tonson, Jacob, 10:94
Tooke, Horne, 5:594–95, 612
Toomer, Jean, 11:374–75
Topicorum Aristoteles Interpretatio (Boethius), 8:515n.4
Topics (Aristotle), 1:203; 10:37
Topics (Boethius). See *De Differentiis Topicis*
Topics (Cicero), 2:421
Topographical Description of the Western Territory of North America, A (Imlay), 11:368
Torch-Bearers, The (Noyes), 9:61
Torquato Tasso (Goethe), 5:89–90
"Torrents of Spring" (Hemingway), 9:41
Totem und Tabu (Freud), 7:xii; 8:60, 68n.4; 10:641; 11:74, 78, 84n.12
Toth, Emily, 11:286
Tourneur, Cyril, 5:693; 8:407, 427
Tournier, Paul, 10:422
Tovey, Donald Francis, 9:x
"Toward a Black Feminist Criticism" (Smith), 10:592, 595, 598
Townshend, Aurelian, 8:413
Toynbee, Arnold, 10:172
Trachiniae (Sophocles), 3:188
"Tradition and the Individual Talent" (Eliot), 8:426; 9:xiii; 11:193n.1
Tragedy (Lucas), 8:191n.1
Tragic Muse, The (James), 9:350, 352
Traité de l'hérédité naturelle (Lucas), 11:87n.26
Trajan, 3:10–11
Travailleurs de la mer, Les (Hugo), 7:472
Travels (Bartram), 5:463
Treasure Island (Stevenson), 7:523
Treatise of the Astrolabe (Chaucer), 3:493; 10:342
Tressell, Robert, 11:337
Trevelyan, George Macaulay, 8:173–75
Trial, The (Kafka), 9:326; 10:157
Trials of Desire (Ferguson), 2:xiii
Trilby (Nodier), 6:45
Trilling, Lionel, 7:xxxii; 8:ix; 10:181, 185, 226, 331n.5, 376, 565; 11:149
Trionfi (Petrarch), 2:136; 4:221
Trissino, Giangiorgio, 2:126, 133, 420; 3:336
Tristan and Isolde (Strassburg), 6:354
Tristan und Isolde (Wagner), 8:16, 230
Tristes Tropiques (Lévi-Strauss), 10:418
Tristia (Ovid), 3:249
Tristram Shandy (Sterne), 7:121; 8:195, 329, 332, 559–82; 9:489; 10:87; 11:87n.25
Triumph of Life, The (Shelley), 8:77, 79, 82, 84–85, 411; 10:520–22, 525–26, 528–29, 534–37
Troades (Euripedes), 1:383
Troades (Seneca), 3:263, 431
Troeltsch, Ernst, 10:79
Troilus and Cressida (Dryden), 10:147
Troilus and Cressida (Shakespeare), 5:87; 6:78; 9:158, 166, 170–71, 177–78, 660, 664–65; 10:172, 410, 491
Troilus and Criseyde (Chaucer), 2:xiv, 298; 355; 3:145, 493; 10:491
Trois Filles de leur mère (Louÿs), 11:107
Trojan Women (Euripides). See *Troades*
Trollope, Anthony, 9:75
Tropisms (Sarraute), 10:417, 424
Trotsky, Leon, 10:552; 11:371
"Troy Town" (Rossetti), 7:468
True Confessions, 10:78
True History (Lucian), 3:650
True Voice of Feeling, The (Read), 9:494
"Tsar Boris" (Tolstoy), 7:290
Tueur sans gages (Ionesco), 10:240
Tullius, Servius, 1:232
Turberville, George, 2:363
Turgenev, Ivan, 7:175, 319, 325, 330; 9:38, 71, 342, 347
Turn of the Screw, The (James), 9:346, 357–58
Turnbull, Colin, 11:129
Turner, Frederick Jackson, 11:375
Turner, J. M. W., 7:xxxvii, xxxix, 449, 670
Turner, Nat, 11:351
Turner, Victor, 10:74
Turner, William, 8:205
Turoldus, 8:376
Tusculan Disputations (Cicero), 2:360; 3:730; 4:260; 5:32
Tuve, Rosamond, 10:72–73, 77
Twain, Mark (Samuel Langhorne Clemens), 9:315; 10:186, 217, 311, 404
Twelfth Night (Shakespeare), 6:79; 9:168, 177, 179
"Twelve Brothers, The" (Grimms), 8:47
Twentieth Century Poetry (ed. Monro), 9:53
"Two April Mornings, The" (Wordsworth), 7:436
Two Cultures, The (Snow), 10:187
"Two Early French Stories" (Pater), 7:xvi
Two Gentlemen of Verona, The (Shakespeare), 9:168, 177
Two Hussars (Tolstoy), 7:319, 327
Two Noble Kinsmen, The, 10:94
"Two or Three Ideas" (Stevens), 7:xiii
"Two Songs, The" (Blake), 7:373-74

Two Sources of Morality and Religion, The (Bergson), 8:150–51
"Two-Days-Old Baby, The" (Blake), 7:359
Tydeus (Theodectes), 1:162
Tylor, E. B., 9:615
Tynan, Kenneth, 10:181, 253
Tynianov, Yurii, 8:338–40, 342, 345
Tynnichus, 1:89
Tyrius, Maximus, 2:402
Tyro (Sophocles), 1:161
Tyrtaeus, 1:273, 473; 3:642, 647, 649

"Über das Schöne" (Bergmann), 7:280
Über die Linie (Junger), 10:521
"Über Sinn und Bedeutung" (Frege), 10:488
"Ulalume" (Poe), 9:31, 467
Ulysses (Joyce), 8:195; 9:41, 78, 184, 326–39; 10:91, 210, 248, 406, 408; 11:110, 153, 380
Ulysses, Fabulous Voyager (Kain), 9:326
Uncle Tom's Cabin (Stowe), 9:440
"Undefeated, The" (Hemingway), 9:39
Under the Net (Murdoch), 10:300
Under Western Eyes (Conrad), 9:75, 344
Understanding Poetry (Brooks and Warren), 10:71
Understanding the New Black Poetry (Henderson), 11:371
"Unexpected Reunion" (Hebel), 8:442
Unger, R., 8:346n.2
Ungern-Sternberg, Alexander, freiherr von, 8:517n.26
Univers imaginaire de Mallarmé, L' (Richard), 11:40, 57, 62n.1
"Unknown Masterpiece, The" (Balzac), 8:297
Untersteiner, Mario, 10:634–36
Untimely Meditations (Nietzsche), 10:476, 481–83
Unto This Last (Ruskin), 7:xxxvi, xl
Updike, John, 10:320
Upton, John, 4:486
Urban, W. M., 9:527
Urizen (Blake), 7:368, 375
Urquhart, Sir Thomas, 8:423
US (Brook), 9:443
Use of Poetry and the Use of Criticism, The (Eliot), 9:102
Use of Riches (Pope). See *Moral Essays*
"Uses of Natural History, The" (Emerson), 10:624
Utopia (More), 2:281, 347

Vadé, Jean-Joseph, 8:366
"Valediction Forbidding Mourning, A" (Donne), 8:406–7; 9:528
Valerius, 5:26
Valerius Maximus, 3:109, 731, 733–35, 737
Valéry, Paul, 8:xi–xii, 145, 417, 419, 432, 441, 451–53, 474–75n.23, 587; 9:33, 35, 300, 426, 430; 10:66, 107, 117, 120; 11:45
Valla, Laurentius, 3:125, 133
Valley of the Dolls (Suzanne), 11:107
Van den Berg, J. H., 7:xxiii, xlvii; 10:616
Van Gogh, Vincent, 10:119; 11:114
Vanity Fair (Thackeray), 7:427, 712; 9:75, 360; 10:515
Vanity of Human Wishes, The (Johnson), 5:626; 8:407; 9:463
Varieties of Religious Experience, The (James), 9:142, 147, 345–46
Variorum Commentary on the Poems of John Milton, A (Woodhouse and Bush), 11:199–217
Varius, P. Licinius, 1:255, 266; 3:425
Varro (M. Terentius Varro), 1:448–49; 2:8, 60, 68, 205–6; 3:110, 186, 341, 411; 8:479–81, 486; 11:266
Vases communicants (Breton), 9:603–4
"Vaudracour and Julia" (Wordsworth), 7:194
Vaughan, Henry, 8:406, 412
Vautel, Clement, 9:594
Vaux, Thomas, Lord, 2:355
Vega Carpio, Lope de, 7:637
Velleius Paterculus, 3:423, 425–26
Vendler, Helen, 11:344
Venice Preserved (Otway), 4:43; 5:650
Venus and Adonis (Shakespeare), 9:37
Vergil (P. Vergilius Maro), 1:266, 297–99, 302–4, 312, 427, 461, 481–91, 521; 2:vii, 18, 20–21, 28–30, 40–42, 47, 72, 76, 97, 110, 113, 129, 132–36, 171, 173, 175–77, 179–80, 192, 255–56, 275–76, 281, 346, 351–52, 360, 363, 388, 390–92, 416–18, 480–81; 3:23, 66, 79–80, 93, 96–97, 109, 114, 139, 147, 153, 169, 174, 187, 201–3, 214, 218, 233, 235, 241–43, 252, 278–79, 296, 308, 312, 314, 324, 326, 335–36, 338–44, 348, 363, 373–74, 383, 393–97, 400–401, 409, 412–15, 425, 430, 432, 447, 452–53, 462–88, 492–96, 502, 553, 558–61, 572, 574, 579, 641–42, 645, 649, 654, 659; 4:21, 31, 52, 54–57, 60, 65, 70, 153–58, 161, 262–63, 272–73, 276–78, 301, 421, 544–45, 576; 5:21, 29, 37, 49, 52–54, 145; 6:200, 239, 246; 7:55, 200, 399n.21, 475, 677–78; 8:157, 309, 388–89n.15, 484, 508–11, 519n.48; 9:250; 10:580–81, 610; 11:76
Vergil Travesty (Scarron), 3:656
Verlaine, Paul, 7:481; 11:43
Véron, Eugène, 7:274, 282

Verse Melodies (Eikhenbaum), 8:335–36, 340
"Verses to the Memory of an Unfortunate Lady" (Pope), 4:557–58
"Verstehen und Auslegung" (Heidegger), 8:386n.10
Verus, Lucius Commodus, 3:11
Verwirrung der Gefühle, Die (Zweig), 8:65
Veselovsky, A. N., 8:322, 326, 329–30, 340
Vian, Boris, 10:240
Viau, Theophile de, 3:338, 346
Vicar of Wakefield, The (Goldsmith), 7:121
Vico, Giambattista, 8:504; 9:viii, 390; 10:43, 624, 640; 11:142, 160
Vicomte de Bragelonne, Le (Dumas), 7:706
Victoria (Queen of England), 11:312
Vida, Marco Girolamo, 3:348; 4:272
Vidal, Peire, 8:313
Vie de Marianne, La (Marivaux), 11:56
Vielé-Griffin, Francis, 9:32
"Vielle Maitresse, Une" (Barbey d'Aurevilly), 7:142
"Vierundzwanzig Stunden aus dem Leben einer Frau" (Zweig), 8:65–67
View of Sir Isaac Newton's Philosophy, A (Pemberton), 10:338
Vigilium Veneris (Bonefonius), 3:80, 85
Vigne, Casimir de la, 7:44
Vigny, Alfred de, 7:485; 9:26
Vilar, Jean, 9:443–44
Village of Stepanchikovo, The (Dostoevsky), 8:342
Villemessant, Henri de, 8:438
Villette (Brontë), 9:79; 11:192, 286
Villiers de l'Isle-Adam, Jean Marie Mathias Philippe Auguste, comte de, 9:35; 10:341, 343
Villon, François, 7:214, 682; 9:123–27
Vindication of the Capacity of the Negro Race, A (Hally), 11:369
Vingt Ans de ma vie littéraire (Daudet), 7:704
Virgil. *See* Vergil
Virgin Martyr, The (Massinger and Dekker), 5:699; 10:94
Vischer, Friedrich Theodor von, 7:279
Vision, A (Yeats), 1:155; 7:xiv; 10:173
"Vision of Christ" (Blake), 7:380
Vision of the Last Judgment (Blake), 7:394n.8
Vita Nuova, La (Dante), 6:199; 8:376, 417, 420, 513–14, 519n.49
Vitet, Ludovic, 7:199
Vitrac, Roger, 8:598, 605
Vitruvius Pollio, 3:187; 8:485–86
Vivante, Leone, 11:345

Voice of the Negro, 11:369
Voiture, Vincent, 3:345, 636
Volpone; or, The Fox (Jonson), 3:309, 442, 447, 666, 677–78; 9:260–61; 10:404
Voltaire (François-Marie Arouet), 4:323; 5:193, 466–67; 6:41, 58, 473–75; 7:60, 276; 8:153; 10:vii, 615; 11:45, 152, 267
Vonnegut, Kurt, 10:313
Vopiscus, Flavius, 3:318
Vorlesungen über die Aesthetik (Hegel), 8:120n.11
Voss, Gerard Jan, 4:194
Voss, Johann Heinrich, 5:310
Vossler, Karl, 8:369
Vries, Hugo de, 8:202

Wagner, Otto, 7:291
Wagner, Richard, 7:580–83, 606, 633; 8:7–10, 16, 22–25, 29, 31n.2, 87, 226, 230–31; 9:35, 668; 10:285
Wahlverwandtschaften, Die (Goethe), 8:383–84n.7
Waiting for Godot (Beckett), 9:449, 480; 10:203, 242, 248
Walden (Thoreau), 10:398
Waldock, A. J. A., 9:92–93, 95–98
Walker, Alice, 10:595; 11:ix, 285, 375
Wallenstein (Schiller), 8:626
Wallenstein (Schiller, tr. Coleridge), 5:633
Wallensteins Lager (Schiller), 8:366
Wallensteins Tod (Schiller), 5:83
Waller, Edmund, 3:291, 293, 314, 413, 421, 473, 489, 496, 688, 720; 4:500, 534–36; 10:610
Waller, Frederick, 10:94
Walpole, Hugh, 9:64
Walsingham, Sir Francis, 3:89
Walton, Izaak, 10:329
Walzel, O., 8:335
Waning of the Middle Ages, The (Huizinga), 11:85n.15
War and Peace (Tolstoy), 10:202
Warburton, William, 4:485, 559; 5:492
Warhol, Andy, 10:431
Warner, William, 2:366; 3:79, 141; 6:66
Warnock, Mary, 10:297
Warren, Austin, 9:582; 10:146, 171, 489
Warren, Robert Penn, 9:583; 10:71, 74, 400
Wartburg, Walther von, 8:382–83n.2
Warton, Joseph, 9:54, 573
Warton, Thomas, 6:84; 11:206
Washington, Booker T., 11:367, 369
Washington, George, 7:709
Washington, Mary Helen, 10:597
Washington Square (James), 9:71, 349, 352

Wasserman, Earl, 6:viii
Waste Land, The (Eliot), 7:xviii; 9:85, 188, 381, 466, 523, 565, 579; 10:91, 210; 11:153–54, 214
Watson, James, 5:335–36
Watson, Thomas, 2:197–98, 201, 363–64
Watson, William, 8:216
Watt, Ian, 11:155, 229
Watt, James, 10:313
Watteau, Antoine, 7:473, 687
Waugh, Evelyn, 9:571
Waverley (Scott), 5:93; 7:73
Way of All Flesh, The (Butler), 11:153
Way of the New World, The (Gayle), 11:376
Way of the World, The (Congreve), 5:664; 7:243–46
Weaver, Harriet, 8:426
Weavers, The (Hauptmann), 8:293, 626
Weber, Carl Maria von, 10:587
Webster, Daniel, 6:414
Webster, Grant, 11:277–79
Webster, John, 5:693; 8:206, 407, 427; 9:638, 671
Weighing of Souls, The (Aeschylus), 1:366
Weil, Simone, 10:301
Weinberg, Bernard, 10:169
Weisstein, Naomi, 11:177
Well-Tempered Critic, The (Frye), 10:390
Wellek, René, 10:169–70, 175, 394, 489–91, 498–99, 543; 11:377
Welles, Orson, 9:666
Wells, H. G., 8:192–93
Wertmüller, Lina, 10:313
West, Benjamin, 6:253, 291n.12
Westermarck, Edvard Alexander, 9:571
"Western Wind" (anon.), 9:467
Weston, Jessie L., 9:565
Wharton, Edith, 9:69, 242, 245, 344, 348
What Is Art? (Tolstoy), 9:544; 10:210
What Is Literature? (Sartre), 10:379
What Maisie Knew (James), 9:354; 10:323n.4
What You Will (Marston), 5:690
Wheatley, Phillis, 11:369, 380, 383, 386
"When I consider how my light is spent" (Milton), 11:203–6
Whetstone, George, 7:458, 460
Whibley, Charles, 8:423
"Whispers of Immortality" (Eliot), 10:99
Whistler, James, 8:5–6, 216
White Devil; or Vittoria Corombona, The (Webster), 5:693–94
White, E. B., 9:582
White, Hayden, 11:143
"White Eagle, The" (Leskov), 8:439
"White Knight's Song, The" (Carroll), 6:viii

"White Mythology" (Derrida), 11:236
"White Ship, The" (Rossetti), 7:468
Whitehead, Alfred North, 9:26–27, 30; 10:163, 165, 234
White-Jacket (Melville), 10:98
Whitman, Walt, 7:xxxii; 8:xii, 248–59; 9:315; 10:89–91, 409, 416, 581–83, 585, 625–26, 628–31
Whitney, Charles, 3:xix–x
Whitney, Geoffrey, 10:579
Whoroscope (Beckett), 10:616
"Why Are Books Expensive in Kiev?" (Leskov), 8:437
"Why the Arts Are Not Progressive" (Hazlitt), 10:228
Wickhoff, Franz, 8:456
Wife of Martin Guerre, The (Lewis), 9:244
Wild Duck, The (Ibsen), 8:32n.5
Wild Huntsman, The (Burger), 5:199–200
Wilde, Oscar, 7:xiii, xxxiii–xxxvi; 8:86, 263; 9:59, 354, 653; 10:164, 199, 316–17, 321, 376–79, 381, 393, 582, 623, 626, 632, 643–44; 11:ix, 153
Wilhelm Meister's Lehrjahre (Goethe), 5:87, 210; 7:441; 8:98; 9:186, 381
Wilhelm Meister's Wanderjahre (Goethe), 8:438; 11:178
Wilhelm Tell (Schiller), 5:91
Wilkins, John, 10:335, 337
"Will as Vision, The" (Pater), 7:xviii
Will to Power, The (Nietzsche). *See Wille zur Macht, Der*
Wille zur Macht, Der (Nietzsche), 7:618; 10:261, 285, 521, 523; 11:235
Willey, Basil, 9:250; 10:335
"William Bond" (Blake) 7:372
Williams, Francis, 11:380
Williams, John A., 11:376
Williams, Raymond, 11:158, 163, 377
Williams, William Carlos, 9:487–88; 10:582
Wilson, Edmund, 9:247; 10:181, 185, 189, 312, 341, 390, 401; 11:277
Wilson, Edward O., 8:x
Wilson, J. Dover, 10:77–78, 174
Wilson, John, 5:545; 10:231
Wilson, Robert, 11:100–101
Wimsatt, W. K., 1:xiv–xv, xvii–xviii; 3:xi; 4:xiv; 10:146–48, 335, 378, 439–40, 503, 543
Winchilsea, Anne Finch, Countess of, 8:182; 11:182–83, 188
Winckelmann, Johann Joachim, 5:21, 380; 6:148; 7:275, 277, 410; 8:264
"Winckelmann" (Pater), 7:xviii–xix
Windham, William, 5:612–13

Wings of the Dove, The (James), 7:531; 9:343, 346, 348, 355–56
Winner Take Nothing (Hemingway), 9:41, 47
Winters, Yvor, 9:69, 71, 523–25, 577–79; 10:312
Winter's Tale, The (Shakespeare), 5:428; 9:493
Winthrop, John, 11:178
Wit and Its Relation to the Unconscious (Freud), 10:464
Witch, The (Middleton), 5:692
Witch of Edmonton, The (Rowley, Dekker, and Ford), 5:693
With Respect to Readers (Slatoff), 10:435
Wither, George, 3:420, 472
Wittgenstein, Ludwig, 8:viii, xi; 10:149, 244–45, 362, 387, 560, 562–63; 11:373
Woe or Wonder (Cunningham), 9:241
Wolf, Kurt H., 8:386n.10
Wolff, Cynthia Griffin, 11:317n.3
Wolff, Michael, 10:443, 445
Wölfflin, Heinrich, 8:235, 320, 346n.2
Wollheim, Richard, 8:ix–x; 10:640
Woman Killed with Kindness, A (Heywood), 5:690–91
Women in Love (Lawrence), 9:76, 78, 592; 10:409; 11:95
Wood, James, 9:573; 10:165
Wood-Thompson, Susan, 10:594
Woodhouse, A. S. P., 11:200, 204
Woodhouse, Richard, 6:266
Woodson, Carter G., 11:367
Woolf, Virginia, 9:246, 248, 344, 535; 10:133–34, 136, 594; 11:389
Woollet, William, 5:136, 143
Wordsworth, William, 2:428n.39; 5:vii, x, xiii–xv, xxi–xxii, 146–49, 409, 411–13, 416–26, 429–33, 436, 439–40, 445–46, 452–63, 507–16, 530–31, 534, 544–62, 566, 568, 619–28, 650; 6:vii–xi, 138, 220, 259, 263–66, 392; 7:xvi, xix, xxxvii–xxxix, xlii, xlvii, 71–72, 181–95, 215–16, 408, 414, 417, 427–37, 446–49, 694, 707, 709; 8:98, 102, 398, 432, 536; 9:26, 29–30, 35, 58, 62n.7, 88, 100–101, 380, 476, 499–502, 512–13, 518–19, 561, 639; 10:155, 166, 228, 231, 233–34, 236n.2, 337–41, 398, 404–6, 499, 506–7, 524, 543–49, 564, 607–8, 612, 614, 616–18; 11:viii, 190
"Wordsworth" (Pater), 7:xxvii
Wordsworth and the Poetry of Sincerity (Perkins), 10:227–28
World and a Clock, The (Cowley), 4:506
World as Will and Representation, The (Schopenhauer), 7:585; 8:276
World Elsewhere, A (Poirier), 10:570

World Tomorrow, The, 11:369
World's Body, The (Ransom), 10:563
World's Great Men of Color, The (Rodgers), 11:369
Worringer, Wilhelm, 8:283
"Wortbildung als stilistisches Mittel, Die" (Spitzer), 8:372
Wotton, Sir Edward, 3:81
Wotton, Sir Henry, 3:87, 536
Wright, Richard, 10:x; 11:351, 369, 371, 388
Writers and Their Critics (Peyre), 10:171
Writing of Fiction, The (Wharton), 9:242
Wuthering Heights (Brontë), 7:470; 9:79; 11:97
Wyatt, Sir Thomas, 2:355, 395; 3:105
Wycherley, William, 3:716–17; 5:664–65, 668; 7:238
Wyclif, John, 3:496

Xenarchus, 1:149
Xenophanes, 1:172, 367; 7:548
Xenophon, 1:213, 219, 279, 327–29, 340, 343–44, 346, 353, 412–13; 2:130, 276, 278, 281, 283, 347; 3:16–17, 181, 187, 434, 624, 729–30; 4:266; 7:210; 9:430

Yalden, Thomas, 4:x
Yale French Studies, 11:360, 362
Yates, Frances, 10:431
Yeats, W. B., 6:vii; 7:xiv, xxxiii, xxxv; 8:88; 9:35–36, 88, 326, 328, 374, 376, 529–30; 10:88, 96–97, 99, 133, 155, 173, 182, 302, 569, 584–85, 612, 617, 624, 643; 11:155, 164
Yellin, Jean Fagan, 11:385
Yellow Wallpaper, The (Gilman), 11:191–93
Young, Edward, 6:241; 7:46; 9:560; 10:609
Young, J. Z., 11:14–16, 18–19, 23, 25
Young, Robert E., 9:246
Young, Wayland, 11:108

Zastrozzi (Shelley), 7:17
Zeno, 1:311
Zenobia, Queen of Palmyra, 3:317–18
Zeuxis, 1:154
Zhirmunsky, V., 8:335–36
Zielinski, Tadeusz, 8:561
Zoilus, 1:307, 332; 3:325
Zola, Emile, 7:520, 525, 704, 720; 8:41, 226, 283, 297; 9:27, 340, 342; 10:179
Zoroaster, 3:147, 149, 157–58
Zosimus, 3:318–19
Zupitza, Julius, 8:387n.10
Zurbarán, Francisco, 8:230
Zweig, Stefan, 8:65

Acknowledgments

RAYMOND WILLIAMS

"The Creative Mind" is taken from *The Long Revolution* by Raymond Williams, © 1961 by Raymond Williams. Reprinted by permission.

JACQUES DERRIDA

"Force and Signification" is taken from *Writing and Difference* by Jacques Derrida, © 1978 by The University of Chicago. Reprinted by permission of The University of Chicago Press and Georges Borchardt, Inc., on behalf of Editions du Seuil.

ANGUS FLETCHER

"Psychoanalytic Analogues: Obsession and Compulsion" is taken from *Allegory: The Theory of a Symbolic Mode* by Angus Fletcher, © 1964 by Cornell University. Reprinted by permission of Cornell University Press.

LEO BERSANI

"Murderous Lovers" and "Persons in Pieces" are taken from *A Future for Astyanax: Character and Desire in Literature* by Leo Bersani, © 1969, 1974, 1975, 1976 by Leo Bersani. Reprinted by permission of Little, Brown & Co.

SUSAN SONTAG

"The Pornographic Imagination" is taken from *Styles of Radical Will* by Susan Sontag, © 1967, 1969 by Susan Sontag. Reprinted by permission of Farrar, Straus & Giroux, Inc.

FREDRIC JAMESON

"Conclusion: The Dialectic of Utopia and Ideology" is taken from *The Political Unconscious: Narrative as a Socially Symbolic Act* by Fredric Jameson, © 1981 by Cornell University Press. Reprinted by permission.

EDWARD W. SAID

"Introduction: Secular Criticism" is taken from *The World, the Text, and the Critic* by Edward W. Said, © 1983 by Edward W. Said. Reprinted by permission of Harvard University Press and Richard Scott Simon Ltd.

ACKNOWLEDGMENTS

SANDRA M. GILBERT & SUSAN GUBAR

"[Infe]ction in the Sentence: The Woman Writer and the Anxiety of Author[ship]," taken from *The Madwoman in the Attic: The Woman Writer and the [Nine]teenth-Century Imagination* by Sandra M. Gilbert and Susan Gubar, © 1979 [by Y]ale University. Reprinted by permission of Yale University Press.

STANLEY E. FISH

"Interpreting the *Variorum*" is taken from *Critical Inquiry*, Spring 1976, © 1976 by The University of Chicago. Reprinted by permission of The University of Chicago Press and the author.

TZVETAN TODOROV

"A Dialogic Criticism?" is taken from *Literature and Its Theorists: A Personal View of Twentieth-Century Criticism* by Tzvetan Todorov, translated by Catherine Porter, © 1984 by Editions du Seuil, © 1987 by Cornell University. Reprinted by permission of Cornell University Press.

FRANK LENTRICCHIA

"Part Five" is taken from *Criticism and Social Change* by Frank Lentricchia, © 1983 by The University of Chicago. Reprinted by permission of The University of Chicago Press and the author.

JULIA KRISTEVA

"Word, Dialogue and Novel" is taken from *The Kristeva Reader*, edited by Toril Moi, © 1986 by Columbia University Press. Reprinted by permission.

ELAINE SHOWALTER

"Women's Time, Women's Space: Writing the History of Feminist Criticism" is taken from *Tulsa Studies in Women's Literature*, Spring–Fall 1984, © 1984 by The University of Tulsa, reprinted in *Feminist Issues in Literary Scholarship*, edited by Shari Benstock. Reprinted by permission of Indiana University Press.

SHOSHANA FELMAN

"Jacques Lacan: Madness and the Risks of Theory (The Uses of Misprision)" is taken from *Writing and Madness* by Shoshana Felman, translated by Martha Noel Evans and the author with the assistance of Brian Massumi, © 1978 by Editions du Seuil, © 1985 by Cornell University. Reprinted by permission of Cornell University Press.

ACKNOWLEDGMENTS

NINA AUERBACH

"Women on Women's Destiny: Maturity as Penance" is taken from *Romantic Imprisonment: Women and Other Glorified Outcasts* by Nina Auerbach, © 1986 by Columbia University Press. First published in *Massachusetts Review*, 1979, © 1979 by The Massachusetts Review, Inc. Reprinted by permission of The Massachusetts Review.

TERRY EAGLETON

"Conclusion: Political Criticism" is taken from *Literary Theory: An Introduction* by Terry Eagleton, © 1983 by Terry Eagleton. Reprinted by permission of the University of Minnesota Press and Basil Blackwell.

LESLIE BRISMAN

"Afterword" is taken from *Milton's Poetry of Choice and Its Romantic Heirs* by Leslie Brisman, © 1973 by Cornell University. Reprinted by permission of Cornell University Press.

ALICE WALKER

"The Black Writer and the Southern Experience" is taken from *In Search of Our Mothers' Gardens: Womanist Prose* by Alice Walker, © 1970, 1983 by Alice Walker. First published in *New South*, Fall 1970. Reprinted by permission of Harcourt Brace Jovanovich, Inc.

BARBARA JOHNSON

"Nothing Fails Like Success" and "Deconstruction, Feminism, and Pedagogy" are taken from *A World of Difference* by Barbara Johnson, © 1987 by The Johns Hopkins University Press. Reprinted by permission. "Nothing Fails Like Success" first published in *SCE Reports*, Fall 1980.

HENRY LOUIS GATES, JR.

"Literary Theory and the Black Tradition" is taken from *Figures in Black: Words, Signs, and the "Racial" Self* by Henry Louis Gates, Jr., © 1987 by Henry Louis Gates, Jr. Reprinted by permission of Oxford University Press, Inc.

PN 86 .A77 1985 vol.11

The Art of the critic